INFORMATION SYSTEMS MANAGEMENT IN PRACTICE

Third Edition

Ralph H. Sprague, Jr.

University of Hawaii

Barbara C. McNurlin

Writer – Information Systems

PRENTICE HALL, Englewood Cliffs, New Jersey 07632

Library of Congress Cataloging–in–Publication Data
Information systems management in practice /Ralph H.
Sprague, Jr., Barbara C. McNurlin. — 3rd ed.
       p.   cm.
    Includes bibliographical references and index.
    ISBN 0-13-465477-3 :
    1. Management information systems.   2. Information resources management.
I. Sprague, Ralph H.   II. McNurlin,.Barbara C.
T58.64.I54   1993   92-37505
658.4'038—dc20   CIP

Editorial/ProductionSupervision: *Kris Ann E. Cappelluti*
Acquisitions Editor: *P. J. Boardman*
Prepress Buyer: *Trudy Pisciotti*
Manufacturing Buyer: *Patrice Fraccio*
Reprint Editor: *Virginia Livsey*
Electronic Page Makeup: *John Jordan*

© 1993 by Barbara C. McNurlin
Published by Prentice-Hall, Inc.
A Simon & Schuster Company
Englewood Cliffs, New Jersey 07632

Printed in the United States of America

10   9   8   7   6   5   4   3   2

ISBN 0-13-465477-3

Prentice-Hall International (UK) Limited, London
Prentice-Hall of Australia Pty. Limited, Sydney
Prentice-Hall Canada Inc., Toronto
Prentice-Hall Hispanoamericana, S.A., Mexico
Prentice-Hall of India Private Limited, New Delhi
Prentice-Hall of Japan, Inc., Tokyo
Simon & Schuster Asia Pte. Ltd., Singapore
Editora Prentice-Hall do Brasil, Ltda., Rio de Janeiro

This book is dedicated to
Dick and Peggy Canning
and Ralph and Virginia Sprague
our parents
for all their inspiration, guidance, and support.

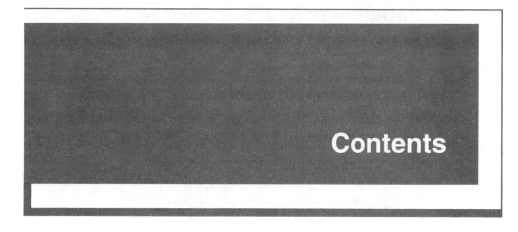

Contents

PART I LEADERSHIP ISSUES

4 **INFORMATION
SYSTEMS PLANNING 105**

PART II MANAGING THE ESSENTIAL TECHNOLOGIES

5 **DISTRIBUTED SYSTEMS:
THE OVERALL ARCHITECTURE 140**

8 MANAGING INFORMATION SYSTEMS OPERATIONS 230

PART III MANAGING SYSTEM DEVELOPMENT

PART IV MANAGING THE NEW UNIVERSE OF COMPUTING

11 THE EXPANDING UNIVERSE OF COMPUTING 333

PART V SUPPORT SYSTEMS

14 GROUP SUPPORT SYSTEMS 404

15 THE GROWING IMPORTANCE OF INTELLIGENT SYSTEMS 436

16 **ELECTRONIC DOCUMENT MANAGEMENT 467**

PART VI INFORMATION SYSTEMS AND PEOPLE

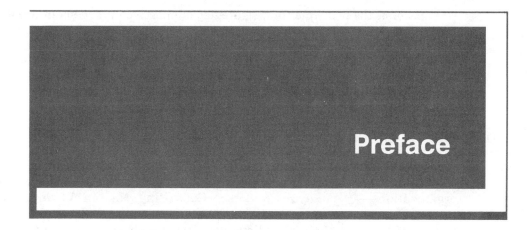

Preface

This book deals with the management of information technology (IT) as it is being practiced in organizations today. Successfully managing IT has become crucial for several reasons:

- Information technology is now a strategic asset that is being used to mold competitive strategies and change organizational processes.
- The situations in which organizations are applying IT have increased in complexity, including more inter-organizational environments.
- The complexity and capabilities of IT are also increasing, at an increasing rate.
- As IT and its uses become more complex, developing strategies and systems to "deliver" the technology has become more difficult.

The net result is a growing need for guidance on the issues, strategies, and tactics for managing the use of IT. To partially satisfy this need, universities and colleges are developing courses that focus on the management of information technology. Textual material for these courses has been sparse for two particularly troublesome reasons.

First, IT is changing so rapidly that textbook authors, technicians, practitioners, researchers, and academics are having a difficult time staying current. For example, in just the past three years, since the second edition of this book was published, the IT field has seen a major revolution in computing architectures (from mainframe-centered to workstation-based) and uses of IT (from outward-looking strategic uses to inward-looking reengineering of business processes). These are just two of the recent upheavals. As a result, courses have had to rely on periodical literature and newspapers.

Second, the principles and strategies of effective management are evolving out of the experiences of practicing managers. Merely collecting reports from the current literature fails to provide the interaction to articulate and codify these principles. Current developments and experiences need interpretation and coalescence to provide the guidance that new and existing managers need to further develop their knowledge and managerial skills.

CONTRIBUTION OF THIS BOOK

We believe this book makes a unique contribution to both of these problems. The primary resource for this book is work we recently performed for several organizations—*I/S Analyzer*, Andersen Consulting, Nielsen Advanced Information Technology Center, Institute for the Future, and Office of the Future. Our writing for these organizations does not merely report current developments and practices, it includes thoughtful interpretation, to provide guidance, principles, and strategies for information systems executives.

Our objective in this book is to capture the material of most current importance to information systems executives—organizing IT around a framework that provides guidance for information systems management. A key element of our writing continues to be company case examples. This book includes over 50 company case examples.

USE OF THIS BOOK BY PRACTICING MANAGERS AND CONSULTANTS

In the management of information technology, this book is useful to several levels of managers.

1. Senior executives who want an overview of the issues and strategies in managing IT, with examples of what other companies are doing
2. Information systems executives who must implement IT as a strategic resource, to help their organizations attain their overall goals and objectives
3. Information systems managers who are responsible for major technical areas, such as system development, technology planning, and operations
4. Managers of functional units who (1) want to better understand the issues and processes of providing IT support for their areas of responsibility, or (2) are now responsible for overseeing the management of IT in their function

We believe that practicing managers of all types will find this book valuable. By focusing on issues and strategies, while explaining technical concepts, this book provides an overview of information systems management for corporate executives and managers. By combining the experiences of successful executives in "the real world," this book provides a unique perspective for all information systems managers.

Consultants to executives and managers will also find this book a useful reference, for staying up-to-date on important current issues in the field.

USE OF THIS BOOK AS A TEXT

Future information systems managers who are graduate or undergraduate students will find that this book presents a view of what "the real world" has in store. As a text, it is intended for students who have had at least one information systems course.

At the graduate level, it serves as a second course, beyond the required MIS course. It is especially well suited for the final course in a graduate curriculum on information systems management. In this course, the book gives students conceptual and practical guidelines for dealing with the management of the modern information systems function.

At the undergraduate level, the book can serve as a text for a course dealing specifically with the management of IT, or in the capstone course that summarizes the practice of information systems for students about to begin their careers. Most undergraduate majors in MIS take entry level positions in the information systems department, but their careers will lead them into management. In the short term, they will work with information systems managers who are facing the problems and using the principles dealt with in this book.

This book is not particularly aimed at students majoring in other areas, although non-information systems majors are taking information systems courses in increasing numbers, to better understand how to deal with systems professionals. The chapters on the strategic use of information systems, the expanding universe of computing, system development, and people issues, will be especially pertinent to them.

At the end of each chapter are three types of questions and exercises to reinforce the material in the text.

- *Review questions* are based directly on the material in the chapter, allowing the reader to assess comprehension of the chapter's key principles, topics, and ideas.
- *Discussion questions* are based on one or two topics in the chapter for which there is a legitimate basis for a difference of opinion. These questions focus discussion on these issues when the book is used in a seminar or classroom setting.
- *Exercises* provide an opportunity for the reader to put some of the concepts and ideas into practice on a small scale. In particular, one exercise in each chapter requires a student, or a team of students, to visit a local company and discover how the ideas in the chapter are being implemented in that company.

THE INSTRUCTOR'S GUIDE

We accompany this third edition with an Instructor's Guide, prepared by Jerome McBride of Marist College in Poughkeepsie, New York. The purposes of the guide are (1) to help instructors prepare a strategy and outline for conducting an advanced systems course using this text, and (2) to provide support materials and techniques to enhance the course.

We believe there are five approaches for using this text. The five course modes are:

- A lecture-based course
- A seminar-based course
- A directed study course
- An independent study course
- An action research course

In the Instructor's Guide, McBride suggests some interesting resources to use in these different course approaches. For example, he explains how he has used a computer-based simulation game to help his students understand the consequences of their actions, as they try to introduce technology innovation into an organization.

The Instructor's Guide includes:

1. Outlines for the five course approaches
2. An overview for each chapter
4. References to Harvard Business School case studies for each chapter
5. Transparency masters for all the figures in the text
6. Suggestions on how to conduct site visit exercises
7. Several sample syllabi
8. An approach to using simulation software
9. Critical questions for each chapter, and how to create them

These critical questions deserve a short explanation. Like the discussion questions in the text, critical questions are designed to stimulate critical thinking and discussion among students. McBride has his students create critical questions for each chapter as part of their homework. In the Instructor's Guide, we present critical questions for each chapter, as well as an explanation of how McBride helps his students create them, thereby stimulating their critical thinking.

The advanced course in IT can be exciting—to teach and to take. We have provided the Instructor's Guide to make this one of those exciting courses.

FORMAT AND CONTENTS

This book is divided into six major parts, each dealing with a major portion of the field of information technology. Chapter One precedes Part I, because it serves as the framework around which the rest of the book is built. it traces the growing importance of information systems management and presents a conceptual model to show the key areas, how they fit together, and the principal issues for executives in each area. It also presents a case example of how these ideas are being implemented in a company.

Part I deals with leadership issues, including the role of information system executives, the strategic uses of the technology, and approaches to systems planning. Part II treats the all-important issues in managing the essential information technologies: distributed systems, telecommunications, information resources, and operations. Part III deals with managing system development; its evolution continues to present management with important, yet risky, challenges. Part IV explores the expanding universe of computing, including the technologies and the needed support from the systems department. Part V deals with support systems, that is, systems aimed mainly at supporting professionals and work groups. And finally, Part VI treats several aspects of information technology's impact on people.

Throughout the book, our objectives have been to keep the material practical, to give examples, and to derive guidance for today's and tomorrow's information systems executives based on the experiences of others. To that end, chapters are sprinkled with company examples. These are not so much case studies that require "solutions" or recommendations; rather, they are case examples that show how companies have put some of the ideas in a chapter into practice.

ACKNOWLEDGMENTS

We wish to acknowledge the contribution of Richard G. Canning. His insight and foresight made this book possible. In the early 1960s, he recognized data processing executives' need for case studies, practical research findings, and thoughtful analysis. Through publishing and editing *EDP Analyzer* (now *I/S Analyzer*) from 1963 until his retirement in 1986, Dick Canning devoted a major portion of his professional career to that purpose. His ideas still permeate this book.

We also wish to thank the organizations that have allowed us to draw on work we performed for them—Andersen Consulting, *I/S Analyzer*, Nielsen Advanced Information Technology Center, Institute for the Future, and Office of the Future.

Finally, we thank Tracia McNurlin, who acted as our secretary. Without her assistance, this third edition would not have been completed so quickly.

Ralph H. Sprague, Jr.
Barbara Canning McNurlin
May, 1993

ONE

The Importance of Information Systems Management

INTRODUCTION

The growth of computer and information technology continues unabated. In fact, the rate of growth is accelerating. Although these technologies affect nearly all aspects of human endeavor, the emphasis of this book is on the use of these technologies to manage and operate enterprises.

First known as business data processing and later as management information systems, the field is now called information systems. The operative word is "systems" because it combines the technologies, people, processes, and organizational mechanisms for the purpose of improving organizational performance.

Management has become the prime user of information technology. Although communication and computer technologies are used in space exploration, weapon systems, medicine, entertainment, and most other aspects of human activity, most information technologies are used to manage organizations.

The purpose of this book is to provide guidance to executives who manage the application of these technologies to improve organizational performance. Information systems management has been the job of technicians, but it is increasingly becoming an important part of the responsibilities of managers and information workers at all levels of the organization.

In this chapter, we first review the recent history of the growth of information systems and their management in organizations. Then we identify several trends that are having a major impact on these technologies and how they are used. Finally, we develop a framework for thinking about how information systems are used and managed in organizations. This framework serves as a road map for the rest of the book.

A LITTLE HISTORY

As we begin to consider the management of information technology in organizations, a little history provides some perspective [1]. Although we could go back to the early 1900s, the relevant history starts in the late 1950s. It was in 1957 that the United States passed from the industrial era to the information era. In that year, the number of employees in the country whose jobs were primarily handling information (information workers) surpassed the number of industrial workers. During the 1970s, information workers exceeded 50 percent of the work force. See Figure 1-1.

In the late 1950s and early 1960s, "information technology" (IT) hardly existed. Only the telephone was widespread, and even it did not reach every desk. In addition, telephone toll rates were high, so long-distance calling was rare. Computers were just beginning to be used in data processing applications, replacing the older electric accounting machines. Even where computers were in use, their impact was comparatively modest. A McKinsey study in the early 1960s [2] found that only nine of the twenty-seven computer instal-

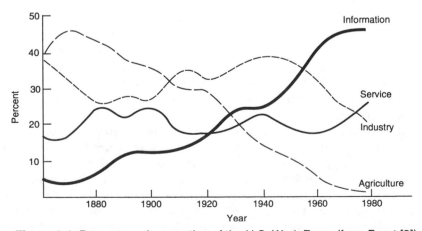

Figure 1-1 Percentage Aggregation of the U.S. Work Force (from Porat [3])

lations analyzed were even covering operating costs, much less providing an adequate return on investment.

Most other information work was done in general offices without much support from technology. Xerographic office copiers existed but were only beginning to catch on. Electric typewriters were commonplace, but the first word processor would not arrive until 1964. Facsimile was used only in specialized applications and would not begin general office use until the 1970s. However, the future of technology support for information workers was extremely bright. Nearly all the foundations of information technology in the 1990s had been invented, and costs were beginning their steady long-term fall.

This change could not come too quickly to satisfy user needs. Information work grew rapidly after 1960. Porat's study on the information sector showed that the total information sector spurted from 17 percent of the economy in 1950 to 58 percent in 1980 [3]. Recent data indicates that the percentage of information workers in the U.S. work force is remaining at about that level [4]. During that same period, the industrial segment plummeted from 65 to 27 percent. These statistics speak of a truly profound change in organizations.

The Classic Infrastructure

As spending on information technology began to grow in the 1960s, better ways to manage it became necessary. Since the various technologies were almost completely independent in their operations, a fragmented approach to information management generally evolved. In this fragmented approach, four major specializations emerged. As shown in Figure 1-2, each had its own products, authority center, and vendors. Furthermore, most offices that used information technology heavily were served primarily by one of the four authority structures.

Business computing, for instance, meant data processing (i.e., records processing) almost exclusively, so computers usually were put under the controller, as electric accounting machines had been before them. In time, of course, data processing became largely independent of the controller in many organizations, for two main reasons. First, the new technology required so many specialists that an independent data processing center emerged. Later, the corporate computer clientele extended beyond accounting, payroll, and billing, further strengthening the center's independence.

Telecommunications received much less attention than its dollar spending should have justified because both telephone and telex services were traditionally supplied by full-service vendors, who relieved user organizations of most administrative burdens. This approach prevented the growth of large staffs, except where internal teletypewriter networks were implemented. The

Figure 1-2 The Classic Infrastructure (from Panko and Sprague)

Product/Service	Typical Corporate Authority	Vendors	Typical Users (Markets)
Data processing management reporting	Director of Data Processing	IBM DEC Honeywell Bull Unisys	Accounting Payroll Reservations Check Processing
Telecommunications PABX Telex Telephones	Telecommunications Administrator	AT&T GTE	Telex room General offices Switchboard
Specialized office products Mailing Equipment Duplicators Microfilm Centralized word processing	Administrative Vice President	Frieden Bell & Howell Kodak 3M	Mailroom Reprographics Records management Word processing center
General office products Typewriters Copiers Convenience word processors	Administrative Vice President	Xerox Savin IBM	Various offices

Reprinted from: Panko, R. R. and Sprague, R. H., Jr., "Toward a New Framework for Office Support," *Proceedings of the ACM Conference on Office Information Systems*, June 1982, Copyright 1982, Association for Computing Machinery, Inc., by permission.

result was low visibility for telecommunications, because most organizations wrongly equated the importance of various information tools with the number of people required to manage them instead of with spending or impact.

Specialized office products for mailrooms, reproduction centers, records management centers, and typing pools were generally purchased by the individual offices using them, although the administrative vice president usually had at least nominal oversight responsibilities. Although spending on these products soon became quite large, their use in out-of-sight operations gave them far less visibility than their dollar spending would justify.

General office products were usually controlled by the administrative vice president. Consisting of small-ticket items such as typewriters, answering machines, facsimile terminals, and convenience copiers, general office products were usually controlled broadly, via the annual budgeting mechanism. This left considerable initiative to individual departments.

When this classic fourfold infrastructure emerged in the 1960s, it made considerable sense. It placed control fairly near users. Furthermore, since the technologies were so diverse, there was no compelling reason to create a unified information management structure.

Pressures for Integration

Although this scattered infrastructure once served a useful purpose, strong pressures toward integrated information management emerged in the late 1970s and continues today for several reasons. First, spending had grown so large that scattered management no longer satisfied basic corporate accountability. Figure 1-3 shows that total spending for technology to support information work of all types was about $120 billion, or $3000 per information worker in 1980 [3]. It has been growing at a rate of about 15 percent annually since then.

Second, technological barriers among various tools rapidly dissolved. Word processors and other intelligent office products became general-purpose computers that could handle many kinds of software. In October 1981, for example, *Office Products News* could count more than 140 products combining word processing and data processing [6].

Figure 1-3 Estimated U.S. Spending on Information Systems: 1980 (from Panko and Sprague)

Category		Spending ($ Billions)
Telephone		$ 36
Information systems support labor[a]		$ 30
Office data processing[b]		$ 27
Text processing		$ 26.8
Reproduction	$ 8.3	
Postal delivery	6	
Paper, not otherwise classified	5	
Word processing	1.5	
Typewriters	1.3	
Electronic mail	1	
Micrographics[c]	0.9	
Calculators	0.6	
Mailroom equipment	0.6	
Pens and mechanical pencils	0.6	
Miscellaneous[d]	1	
Office furniture		$ 2
Total (rounded)		$ 120
Per Information Worker (rounded)[e]		$ 3000

[a]Includes the labor needed to plan, operate, and maintain information systems. Data processing center labor would fall into this category. Does *not* include end user labor.
[b]Includes all data processing done to handle what would normally be considered office functions.
[c]An unknown portion of this micrographics spending really belongs under office data processing.
[d]Includes answering systems, dictation machines, and many other items.
[e]Assumes 38 million office workers.
Reprinted from: Panko, R. R. and Sprague, R. H., Jr., "Toward a New Framework for Office Support," *Proceedings of the ACM Conference on Office Information Systems*, June 1982, Copyright 1982, Association for Computing Machinery, Inc., by permission.

Furthermore, several office technologies that had previously contained no electronic logic were computerized. Many private branch exchanges (PBXS) could handle data communications and protocol conversion. Intelligent copiers served not only as copiers but also as printers and facsimile terminals. Today, it has become difficult to find a significant piece of office equipment that does not contain a microprocessor and cannot be programmed to handle multiple tasks, thus cutting across old authority boundaries in the firm.

In the late 1980s, networks began to eliminate the remaining barriers around traditional bailiwicks. Office products were combined to form "integrated office systems" using local area networks (LANS), whereas traditional information systems began spawning distributed systems. Today, these two network-based approaches are merging.

Clearly, an integrated approach to corporate information services has been needed. Unfortunately, during the thirty years in which information processing was segmented, the different sectors developed very strong traditions and insights that helped each serve its particular clientele. This history still raises serious problems for integration, because each sector tends to see integration as an extension of its traditions and insights to the other "unenlightened" parts of the information processing infrastructure.

THE TECHNOLOGY ENVIRONMENT

The evolving importance of information systems, and the pressure for integration, has been "enabled" by developments in the technologies themselves. Although debates continue on whether technological developments respond to needs, or whether they are the result of technical feasibility, the better uses of technology would not be possible without developments in the capabilities and strengths of the technologies. These changes, summarized subsequently in four areas, constitute a major evolution in the technological environment.

Hardware Trends

In the early 1960s, the main hardware concerns among data processing managers were achieving machine efficiency and tracking new technological developments. Batch processing was predominant, with on-line systems emerging in the late 1960s. As smaller machines came to market, distributing the processing to remote sites became feasible. That prospect was discussed in the early 1970s, although few companies had any distributed systems at that time.

It was not until the mid-1970s that processing power began to move out of the central site—but only very slowly. Often, it was at the insistence of users who bought their own departmental minicomputers and word processors. In the 1980s—mainly because of the advent of personal computers—this trend accelerated far beyond the expectations of most people, especially information systems managers.

Now, in the 1990s, this trend seems to be picking up speed. Desktop and portable workstations are faster and contain more memory than the centralized mainframes of just a few years ago. Reduced instruction set computers (RISC chips) can yield a major increment in speed for routine processing by limiting the variety of instructions built into a chip. A strong trend toward cooperative processing—computers working together in networks—is further distributing processing power out of the data center.

A major trend, then, has been the movement of hardware and processing power out of the control—although perhaps still under the guidance—of the information systems department. This trend is well established and accelerating.

Software Trends

In the 1960s and 1970s, news articles on software and programming generally discussed how to improve the productivity of in-house programmers, who were creating mainly transaction processing systems. Occasionally, the use of outside services was discussed—timesharing services, application packages, and contract programming from independent software houses, for example. The software industry was still underdeveloped, however, so in-house programming remained the concern of information systems managers.

In the 1970s programming issues centered first on modular and structured programming. Then the topic expanded to life-cycle development methodologies and software engineering. One of the aims of the development methodologies was to introduce more rigorous project management techniques. Another goal was to get users more involved in development, at least in the early stages. Eventually, prototyping became a popular way to pursue this goal. The first full report on prototyping appeared in 1981, although the subject had been discussed briefly earlier. Now prototyping is being used by many information systems departments.

For much of the past thirty-five years, programming management issues were targeted at large systems development, with little work on how to build small systems. Most of the effort dealt with how to improve the productivity of full-time, professional programmers. It was only in the late 1970s that programming by other employees was considered. Formerly, users were only involved in requirements definition; programming by end users was not thought practical.

In the middle to late 1970s, two other software trends appeared. One, purchased software became a viable alternative to in-house development for many traditional, well-defined systems. Two, information systems managers began to pay attention to applications other than transaction processing. While management support and decision support systems (DSS) were occasionally discussed, it was not until the late 1970s that these types of applications were taken seriously. Software to support DSS report generation, and database inquiry shifted the initiative from professional programmers to end users.

The 1980s saw efforts to improve the software development process by increasing the discipline for programmers, buying rather than making applications, using more powerful programming and development tools, and encouraging more participation by end users. These paid off, but only incrementally. In the 1990s, many corporations have "hit the maintenance wall." As budgets tighten, they find that the maintenance costs of installed systems are eating up the available resources, leaving nothing for new systems development. As a result, companies are seeking a major shift in the way they build and maintain software. The promising new approach is object-oriented technology. "Object-oriented development" changes the way developers look at data, software, the development process, and even organizational structures. Because it is such a pervasive new set of concepts, we will encounter it in several chapters in the book.

The other major software trend for the 1990s is the push for open systems, driven primarily by software purchasers who are tired of being "locked in" to proprietary software (or hardware) systems. The open systems movement is demanding that different products work together, that is, "interoperate." Vendors have initially been accommodating this demand with hardware and software black boxes that perform the necessary interface conversions, but the cost is lower efficiency.

So the trend in software seems to be demanding revolutionary change rather than just evolutionary improvement. But the installed base of "legacy" systems on which organizations depend for day-to-day existences is tempering the speed and impact of this revolution.

Data Trends

The evolution of a third core technology area—data—has been particularly interesting. In the early 1960s, the discussions centered on file management and organization techniques for files that served individual applications. In the late 1960s, generalized file management systems for managing corporate data files emerged. This more generalized approach led to the concept of corporate databases to serve several applications, followed a few years later by the concept of establishing a data administration function to manage these databases.

In the 1970s, the interest in data turned to technical solutions—database management systems. As work progressed, it became evident that a key element of these products was their data dictionary/directory. The early function of these dictionaries was merely specification and format, but that has expanded significantly. Dictionaries store more than data definitions; they store information about relationships between systems, sources and uses of data, time cycle requirements, and so on.

So, again, for the first twenty years of information processing, discussions on data were about techniques to manage data in a centralized environment. It was not until the advent of fourth generation languages and personal computers (PCs) that there was any interest in letting employees directly access corporate data. Information systems management had at least to be providing access to—and perhaps even distributing—this important resource. The users demanded it.

In addition to distributing data, the major trend in the 1990s will be expanding the focus from data resources to information resources, both internal and external to the firm. Data management has been concerned mainly with internal facts organized in data records. But information resources also include facts from external sources, as well as concepts and ideas in documents from both internal and external sources. These information resources will be represented by a much richer universe of digitized media including voice, video, animation, and photographs. New technologies are becoming available for this purpose, but the challenges will be significant.

Communications Trends

The final core technology is telecommunications. This area has experienced considerable change, and the future promises even more drastic changes. Early use of data communications, in the mid-1960s, dealt with on-line and timesharing systems. In the early 1970s, interest in both public and private (intracompany) data networks blossomed. Telecommunications opened up new uses of information systems. In fact, most people now include both computers and communications in the term *information technology.*

Telecommunications has become an integral component of information systems management. Communications-based information systems link organizations to suppliers and customers. In the early 1980s, there was a groundswell of interest in such interorganizational systems, because they can provide strategic advantage.

Communication technology is a crucial enabler for distributing information technologies and responsibility for their use. This trend, too, is picking up speed in the 1990s. Lans connected to wide area networks (WANS) are leading to computer connectivity among information workers similar to the level of voice connectivity provided by the worldwide telephone system. The growth of this network infrastructure will complete the shift from mainframe-centered to workstation-centric computing that began a decade ago. In the 1990s, we can expect the use of wireless networks to allow people to do their jobs anytime, anyplace.

THE BUSINESS ENVIRONMENT

Just as the technological environment continues to change, so too does the business environment. There are changes in the economic environment that are causing executives to reexamine how their firms compete to be successful, or just survive. There are changes in the labor market that are affecting how companies operate. In this section we explore these two types of changes to better understand the business environment in which information system departments must now operate.

The Changing Marketplace

The changes occurring in the worldwide business scene have been widely discussed in both the public and technical press. The effects of the turbulence can be seen in the large number of corporate restructurings that have occurred since the mid-1980s. Information technology is contributing to such changes. It allows information to move faster, thus increasing the speed at which events occur and the pace at which individuals and organizations can respond to events. Following are the main changes we see occurring in the marketplace.

The Quality Imperative. Competition in international markets is now focused on quality. Originally, quality meant reducing defects in product output. Now, the emphasis is shifting to quality as defined by the customer. This customer satisfaction emphasis has, in turn, focused management's attention on the key business processes in the organization. Information systems will be a primary resource for examining and "reengineering" these key business processes to improve organizational performance.

Concern for the Environment. Ecology, recycling, and the "green" movement came to management attention in the early 1990s around the globe. Companies now tout their recycling efforts, environmental mutual funds have arisen, and "save the planet" concerns are voiced by a growing portion of the populous. The Earth, and all its inhabitants, will be a major issue for executives throughout the 1990s, to reverse the destruction of the past few decades.

Consumer Computing. The 1990s will see an increase in systems that let consumers access organizational computer systems. Bank automated teller machines (ATMs) are an early example of this trend, where customers can check account balances, determine whether certain checks have cleared, and establish automatic bill-paying processes. Companies are developing systems that will allow consumers to purchase products, inquire about the state of an order, and, in general, become a "user" of their internal information systems.

Deregulation. Deregulation of some major industries—airlines, banking, telecommunications, trucking, and others—has made it easier for new companies to enter these industries. In the United States, for example, regional airlines have literally driven major carriers out of some short haul, but lucrative, markets. And the U.S. banking industry has been fighting hard to get Congress to limit the ability of nonbanking firms to enter the banking field. Although it is true that deregulation in the United States is more widespread than elsewhere in the world, this trend is under way in many countries.

Crossing Industry Boundaries. Deregulation has prompted companies to cross industry boundaries, such as retailer Sears Roebuck & Co. getting into banking and major brokerage firms offering banklike services with their cash management accounts (loans, credit cards, etc.). "Home shopping" via television is competing with catalog mail-order businesses. Insurance companies are essentially in the securities business, with their single-payment life insurance policies in which owners can direct the investment of the policy cash values.

Globalization. Large U.S. banks, by trading securities on an around-the-clock, around-the-world basis, are also crossing boundaries. Formerly, companies in the "rich" United States created multinational operations by establishing firms or by buying established firms in other countries. But the huge U.S. trade deficit has given foreign firms access to funds with which to buy U.S. businesses. Foreign banks have bought U.S. banks, foreign owners of newspapers and magazines have bought U.S. newspapers and magazines, and so on.

Multinationalism has become a two-way street. Firmly entrenched companies are suddenly finding powerful competitors from abroad entering their markets. The same is happening in manufacturing—globalization. Parts and sub-assemblies are being manufactured in many countries, and then shipped to other countries for final assembly, to cut overall labor costs.

Shorter Product and Service Development Cycles. Companies do not have as much time to develop new products or services and move them into the marketplace. Once they are in the market, their useful lives tend to be shorter. So time has become of the essence. These are just some of the ways in which the worldwide business environment is changing. They are causing more turbulence in the world.

The Changing Work Environment

The traditional work environment is also changing, so the art of managing people is undergoing significant changes. Here are some of the changes in the traditional work environment that will have a major impact on how people work.

Growth of Business Teams. There is a trend toward "working together." Rather than depend on chains of command and the authority of the boss, many organizations are emphasizing teams to accomplish major tasks and projects. In his landmark article, "The Coming of the New Organization," Peter Drucker [7] uses the analogy of a symphony, where each member of the team has a unique contribution to make to the overall result. Task-oriented teams form and work together long enough to accomplish the task, then disband, perhaps to form another team project. This phenomenon is generating major interest in information systems called groupware, which supports meetings, promotes collaborative work, and enriches communications among team members.

Anytime, Anyplace Information Work. Information workers are increasingly mobile. Communication technology has developed to the point where information work can be done anywhere with a laptop computer, cellular telephone, and a modem. Electronic mail, facsimile, and voice mail systems cross time zones in our global village to allow work anytime, anywhere. People are sporadically working at home rather than commuting daily; they are working in their preferred geographical location, even if it is remote from the main office.

Outsourcing and Strategic Alliances. In the effort to become more productive and more efficient, organizations are examining which work they should perform internally and which can be done by others. George Huber identifies this trend as leading to new organizational forms in the 1990s [8]. Outsourcing may be a simple contract for services or a long-term strategic alliance. Between these two extremes are a variety of relationships that are redefining the way organizations work together.

The Demise of the Hierarchy. Most of us accept our current work style and work environment as givens. "It has always been this way" seems to imply it will always be this way. However, work environments are changing, because the old styles are not functioning well in our faster-paced, global environment.

What is a traditional work environment? Calvin Pava of the Harvard Business School [9] suggests that it is dominated by the hierarchical structure. Employees at the bottom have only enough training and receive only enough feedback information to perform one type of job. Several people performing the same type of work belong to a group, overseen by a supervisor.

The supervisor allocates the work among the subordinates, handles problems that arise, enforces discipline, issues rewards, provides training, and so on. Professionals and staff are also supervised, but generally they are given more responsibility for their methods of work. Managers and executives coordinate the work of their subordinate groups.

This organizational structure is no longer the most appropriate, either in factories or offices. Self-managed groups, which work on assembly lines or insurance forms, provide much of their own management, have lower absenteeism, higher yield productivity, produce higher quality work, and are more motivated than workers in traditional settings.

Pava believes that the more turbulent business environment—represented by the worldwide changes discussed previously—challenges the premises of the hierarchical structure of organizations, because of the problems that this structure has in coping with rapid change. Strict hierarchical control is based on a vertical chain of command where lines of responsibility do not cross, and approval to proceed on major initiatives is granted from above. Such organizations cannot respond quickly to change, says Pava, because their structure requires communication up and down the chain of command, which takes time.

He believes that organizations should question the reasons for their structure rather than take it for granted. They may find that less emphasis on strict hierarchies, and more emphasis on dispersed decision making, may be what is needed in our more rapidly changing world.

A Growing Concern for Human "Capital." In their book, *Re-inventing the Corporation*, John Naisbitt and Patricia Aburdene [10] see three major changes in the way organizations will operate. One, they believe corporations will shift emphasis from financial capital to human capital. Human resources are the true competitive edge of a company, they state; therefore, companies that learn how to treat people as assets will increase their profits. One aspect of this trend is the growing corporate concern for the health and fitness of employees. But concern for people will extend beyond corporate boundaries, to customers as well, say Naisbitt and Aburdene.

With all these changes going on, the question becomes: What should be the mission of an information systems department to best support the firm?

THE MISSION OF INFORMATION SYSTEMS

With the business environment and the information technology environment as a backdrop, it is important to get a clear idea of the overall mission of information systems. In the early days of transaction processing, the systems acted as "paperwork factories"—to get employees paid, customers billed, products shipped, and so on. During that era, the objectives of information systems were defined by productivity measures, such as percentage of up-time for the computer, throughput (number of transactions processed per day), and lines of program code written per week.

Later, during the MIS (Management Information System) era, the focus of information systems shifted to producing reports for "management by exception," or summary reports for all levels of management. This era gave us the classic information system objective to "get the right information to the right person at the right time."

In today's environment, missions and objectives such as these are limited and shortsighted. Even the "right information" objective fails to note whether anything useful results from the delivery of the information. We suggest as an appropriate focus the following mission for information systems in organizations.

> *To improve the performance of people in organizations through the use of information technology.*

The ultimate *objective* is performance improvement—an outcome or result goal instead of a go-through-the-steps process goal. The *focus* is the people who make up the organization. Improving organizational performance is accomplished by the people and groups that the organization comprises.

Finally, the *resource* for this improvement is information technology. There are many other contributors to performance improvement, but this book focuses on resources available from the development and use of information technology: computers, software, machine-readable information, and communication technologies. This mission for the information systems function is still fraught with difficulties, such as how to define and measure performance, but it is not limited or shortsighted.

A SIMPLE MODEL

We propose a simple model to help define a new structure for the information systems function in organizations. Figure 1-4 represents the process of applying information technology to accomplish useful work. On the left in Figure 1-4 is the technology and on the right are the users who will put it to work. The

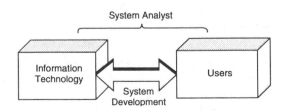

Figure 1-4 A Simple Model of Technology Use

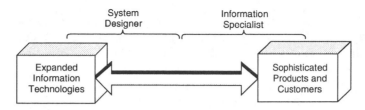

Figure 1-5 Systems Professionals Bridging the Technology Gap

arrow represents the process of developing and implementing systems that apply the technology. In the early days of information systems, this process was conducted almost entirely by a systems analyst.

Figure 1-5 is a simple representation of what has happened during the past thirty years. Technology has become increasingly complex and powerful. At the same time, the uses to which it has been applied have become increasingly sophisticated. Information systems are now viewed as systems "products" in which users have become "customers." The increased distance between the two boxes represents the increasingly complex process of developing and delivering the systems products. It is no longer feasible for one system analyst to understand the fine points of the technology and the nuances of an application. More specialization and skill are required of systems professionals to bridge this wider gap. The Association for Computing Machinery (ACM) curriculum recommendations have recognized this breadth of skills and knowledge by defining one curriculum for systems designers that is primarily technical and another for information specialists that has strong foundations in the applications area.

Systems professionals are not the only ones who can help bridge this gap between the technology and its uses. Technology is gradually becoming sophisticated enough to "reach out" to nontechnical people.

At the same time, users are becoming increasingly knowledgeable and computer literate to deal with computers directly, and even develop their own applications. Figure 1-6 represents this trend. Today, some of the technology is truly user friendly, and a few end user "languages" serve a wide variety of

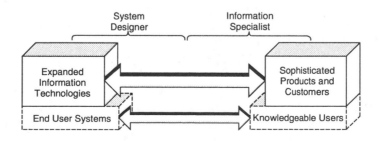

Figure 1-6 End Users Bridging the Technology Gap

applications. Some applications, such as database inquiry, report generation, and spreadsheet manipulation, are regularly developed and used by line managers and professionals. But it will be some time before end users bear the majority of the system development load.

The main point of this discussion is that the technology is getting more complex, the applications are getting more sophisticated, and users are developing some applications. The net result is that the management of the entire process is getting more complex and difficult as it is getting more important to do well.

A BETTER MODEL

Expanding the simple model gives us more guidance into the managerial principles and tasks. We suggest a model that is analogous to the marketing process with three principal elements.

1. A *set of technologies* that represent products developed by a systems department
2. A *set of users* whom we can view as customers for these products
3. A *delivery mechanism* for developing, delivering, and installing these systems that is analogous to marketing activities

Let us look more carefully at each of these elements.

The Technologies

Several forces are contributing to the increased strength and complexity of information technology. One, of course, is the inexorable growth in capacity accompanied by significant reductions in cost and size of raw computers. Another is the merging of previously separate technologies, such as computers, telephones/telecommunications, and office equipment. Still a third is the ability to store and handle voice, image, and graphical data, and to integrate them. Here is a brief list of some rapidly growing technology areas.

- Personal computers
- Distributed systems that link large numbers of multivendor processors
- Wireless telecommunications networks
- Multimedia, integrating voice, image, text, graphics, and more
- Consumer electronics

These technologies can be combined and configured to form systems products that are useful to customers (employees, customers, and consumers). No longer relegated primarily to automating transactions processing, information systems now fill major needs for management reporting, problem solving and analysis, distributed office support, and customer ser-vice. In fact, most activities of information workers are supported in some way by information technology; the same is becoming true of suppliers, cus-tomers, and consumers.

The Users

As information technology takes on this new level of pervasiveness, the old categories of users are no longer appropriate. The users of electronic data processing and management information systems were relatively easy to identify, and the functions of the system were defined to meet a set of their needs. In the future, with most employees depending on integrated informa-tion systems in their daily work, some new taxonomies will be needed.

Panko and Sprague [1, 11] have developed a helpful dichotomy to describe activities of information workers supported by information technolo-gy. It defines procedure-based activities and goal-based or problem-based activities. The value of the dichotomy is that it focuses on the most important characteristics of information workers—their job procedures and goals—rather than on the type of data (e.g., numbers versus text) or the business function (e.g., production versus sales), or even job title (managerial versus professional).

Procedure-based activities consist of large numbers of transactions; each transaction has a relatively low cost or value. Since the activities are well-defined, the principal measure of performance is efficiency (units processed per unit of resource spent). For a procedure-based task, the information worker is told what to accomplish and the steps to accomplish it. Finally, pro-cedure-based activities are based primarily on handling data.

Goal-based activities, conversely, handle fewer transactions, but each one has higher value. These activities, which can be accomplished in several different ways, must therefore be measured in terms of attainment of objec-tives or goals. For a goal-based task, the information worker must under-stand the overall goals, because part of the job is figuring out how to attain the goals. Finally, goal-based activities are based on handling concepts. Figure 1-7 summarizes these two kinds of information activities, giving sev-eral examples from banking.

Some authors use the words "clerical" and "managerial" to refer to these two types of activities. Looking at the attributes, however, it is clear that managers often do procedure-based work, and some clerical workers find goal-based activities a large part of their job responsibilities. Likewise, many of the problems that develop in organizations could be described using a pro-cedure-based approach on a goal-based job.

The most important benefit of this dichotomy is that it reveals how much of a firm's information processing efforts have been devoted to support-ing procedure-based activities. This is understandable, because computers

Figure 1-7 A Dichotomy of Information Work

Procedure-Based	Goal-Based
• High volume of transactions	• Low volume of transactions
• Low cost (value) per transaction	• High value (cost) per transaction
• Well-structured procedures	• Ill-structured procedures
• Output measures defined	• Output measures less defined
• Focus on process	• Focus on problems and goals
• Focus on efficiency	• Focus on effectiveness
• Handling of "data"	• Handling of concepts
• Predominantly clerical workers	• Managers and professionals
• Examples	• Examples
"Back office"	Loan department
Mortgage servicing	Asset/liability management
Payroll processing	Planning department
Check processing	Corporate banking

are process engines that naturally support process-driven activities. As important as they are, it is clear that procedure-based activities are the "wave of the past." The wave of the future is applying information technology to goal-based activities.

Bridging the Gap

In our analogy for this model, the marketing function bridges the gap between technology and users by developing and delivering systems products. Figure 1-8 illustrates the traditional process of delivering separate technologies for different purposes for both procedure-based and goal-based uses. Under the classical infrastructure discussed earlier, this is a fairly straightforward process. For the most part, the authority in charge of a certain type of technology manages that technology, develops products that use it, and delivers them to users. As the technologies become more integrated, however, this delivery process becomes more complicated. Separate authority structures for information systems, office systems, and telephone systems become unworkable.

Most organizations today have recognized this problem and have combined the entire information systems responsibility under one authority. By and large, however, the systems development and delivery function is still the responsibility of the technology managers and still on a product-line basis that comes directly from that technology. That is, transaction processing systems are developed and delivered by one group of systems professionals, office systems by another, and decision support systems by yet another team. See Figure 1-9.

Returning to our market analogy, product-line marketing by producers, such as by a manufacturing sales office, is one popular structure for the mar-

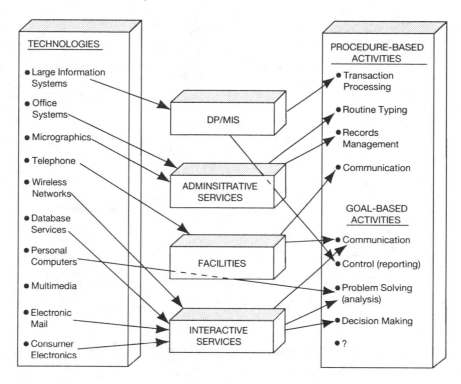

Figure 1-8 Traditional System Delivery Approaches

keting process. When a company is young, the product-line approach is feasible and popular. As an organization matures, however, other marketing approaches become more relevant. A customer segmentation approach, for example, organizes the marketing activities by focusing on segments of customers, defining the full set of customer needs, and then selecting a set of products that together will fill those needs. At this stage of maturity, the marketing organization is usually separated from the production/manufacturing division of the company to facilitate development of marketing expertise. Such a separate marketing group can also exert some pressure and influence on the design of products, drawn from its experience in dealing with customers.

We believe that the information systems function needs to focus more attention on the marketing function for system development and delivery, and consider "marketing channel" approaches such as customer segmentation. Figure 1-10 represents this approach.

Figure 1-10 shows, on the left side, the set of technologies that form the technology infrastructure. These are the technology resources the organization can draw on to build systems to support a variety of activities, both pro-

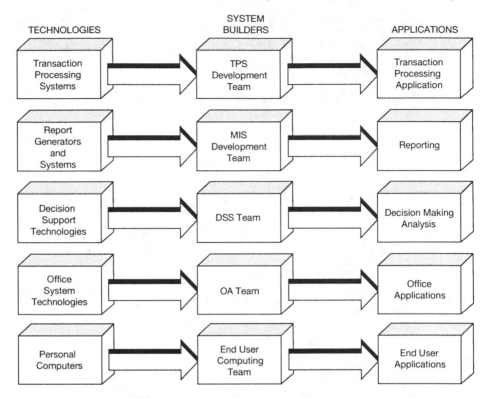

Figure 1-9 The "Product Line" Approach to System Development

cedure-based and goal-based, in the organization. Separate technical categories, such as mainframe, personal computer, office equipment, and telephone, are no longer relevant. Therefore, we show computer hardware and
software, communication networks, and information resources as the three
major categories. We will call these the "essential technologies."

On the right are shown the major applications or uses of technology
using the procedure/goal dichotomy. These categories are not distinct and
separate, of course, but it is helpful to keep in mind the major differences
between these two kinds of activities. These differences lead to different
approaches, and frequently different teams, in the bridging function of systems development and delivery.

Figure 1-10 shows separate teams to deliver services to procedure-
based users and goal-based users. Each team consists of "consultants" or
analysts familiar with the different technologies, so that a full range of
customer needs can be met with a full range of technologies. Efforts by
firms to develop end user computing groups were versions of goal-based
support groups, although their effort was generally not defined that way.
For instance, they often handled training for both types of end user tasks.

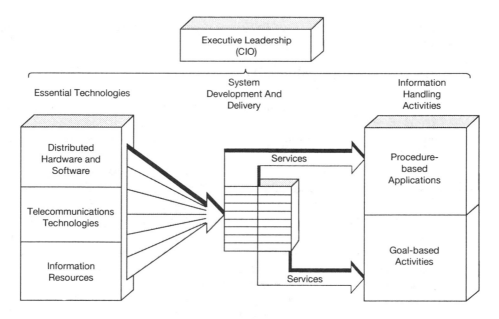

Figure 1-10 A User-Oriented Approach

The procedure-based team was generally represented by the traditional system development group and generally was still an arm of the information systems department.

To summarize this model of information systems function in organizations, there are three major components:

1. The technology, which is increasing in capacity and merging the functionality of several previously separate sets of technologies
2. Information workers in organizations, who will use the technology to support a range of activities to improve performance
3. The system development and delivery function, to bring the technology and its users together

INFORMATION SYSTEMS MANAGEMENT

There is also a fourth component, which may be the most important one of all: overall management of the information systems function. The changes required to develop the necessary organizational structure will not happen without a significant amount of executive leadership. This leadership may come from existing upper-level managers, but it is likely to require a "a chief information officer" (CIO) with a set of executive roles and responsibilities. The CIO must be high enough in an organization to relate to and adopt organizational goals, and assume the responsibility of harnessing the technology to pursue those goals.

The Information Systems Department

Unfortunately, the four-component model of Figure 1-10 does not correspond directly to the structure of most organizations. Generally, the systems department, which is headed by a manager or executive, has responsibility for building and managing the technical infrastructure shown on the left of our model. This infrastructure may be distributed geographically, or functionally, so that equipment, software, and data could reside in many places throughout the organization.

The department head might have the level of responsibilities we described earlier for a CIO. Or the job might be closer to a technical computing systems manager. The community of users might be relatively passive, waiting for the systems professionals to deliver systems, or it might be comprised of knowledgeable, active, creative users who drive the systems development process, depending on the systems department for primarily technical advice and implementation. As a result of these considerations, the nature of the systems function in an organization cannot be directly read from the organization chart. Rather, there are "arenas" of information systems activity that characterize the nature of the function.

1. *Technical arena.* What is the technology infrastructure? Who designs, builds, and manages it?
2. *Application / usage arena.* What is accomplished with the systems and technology? Who takes the initiative in developing and managing them?
3. *Leadership arena.* Who is responsible for developing the vision and doing the planning for "harnessing" information technology to improve the performance of the organization? How is that being done?

Confusion and ambiguity result from dealing with the systems function as if it were a functional department on the organization chart. Recognizing the three preceding arenas, or the four components of our model in Figure 1-10, leads to a fuller understanding of the management of information systems in organizations.

ORGANIZATION OF THIS BOOK

This book is designed to meet the needs of information systems managers—current ones and students who will become managers in the future. The organization of the book corresponds to the major parts of Figure 1-10. Part 1 (Chapters 2 through 4) deals with the strategic issues that will be the responsibility of the top systems executive—the CIO. Chapter 2 deals with the leadership components of the CIO's job; Chapter 3 looks at the strategic role of information systems; and Chapter 4 treats the subject of planning for information systems.

Part 2 (Chapters 5 through 8) deals with managing of the essential information technologies (on the left side in Figure 1-10). Respective chapters discuss creating the distributed systems architecture that is likely to predominate in the 1990s, building and managing the telecommunications systems, managing the corporate information resources, and managing the data centers.

Part 3, which contains two chapters on the system development process, deals primarily with procedure-based systems. Chapter 9 describes the evolution of system development, and the tools and approaches used. Chapter 10 discusses important issues in managing system development.

Part 4, on the evolving computing arena, describes the exploding universe of information technologies—including mobile technologies, electronic mail, and multimedia (Chapter 11). Chapter 12 discusses information systems management's responsibilities for supporting this expanding universe of computing possibilities—many of which will be used for goal-based computing.

Part 5 consists of four chapters describing types of support systems—goal-based systems that support information workers. Included are decision support and executive information systems, group support systems, expert systems, and office systems.

The final two chapters of the book, in Part 6, deal with people issues and information systems. Chapter 17 examines the all-important subject of organizational learning, and Chapter 18 discusses how technology can and should be used to improve the jobs of information workers.

To illustrate how an information systems department has evolved over the years, as the technologies and its users have changed, consider the case of Mead Corporation. Notice how this case example puts several of the ideas discussed in this chapter into a real-life setting.

CASE EXAMPLE: Mead Corporation

Mead Corporation, with headquarters in Dayton, Ohio, is a paper and forest products company with more than one hundred mills, plants, and distribution centers throughout the United States and Canada. Since the mid-1970s, Mead has also been in the information business, with NEXIS®, its news information retrieval service, LEXIS®, its on-line legal research service, and many other on-line services. The company is highly decentralized, with three operating groups—paper, packaging, and paperboard; consumer and distribution; and electronic publishing. Each group has one or more divisions.

Information Systems Organization—1960s and 1970s

In the 1960s, Mead's corporate information systems department provided all divisions with data processing services. By 1967, the department's budget had grown so large that management decided to spin off some of the functions to the divisions. Divisions could establish their own data processing and process engineering groups, if they so desired. Or they could continue to purchase data processing services from the corporate information services department. Many of the divisions did establish their own information systems departments, but all continued to use the corporate data center for their corporate applications.

In the late 1970s, the corporate information services department had six groups, as illustrated in Figure 1-11. The director reported to the vice president of operations services. The six groups under the director were

• Computer operations—responsible for managing the corporate data center

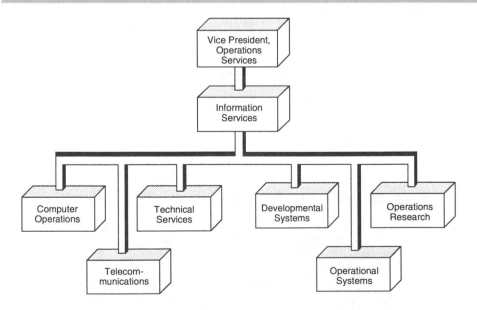

Figure 1-11 Mead Corporation's Pre-1980 Information Services Department (from Mead Corporation)

- Telecommunications—responsible for designing the telecommunications network and establishing standards
- Technical services—responsible for providing and maintaining systems software
- Developmental systems—responsible for traditional system development
- Operational systems—responsible for maintaining systems after they become operational
- Operations research—responsible for performing management science analysis

The 1980s—Focusing on End User Computing

In 1980, management realized that the organizational structure would not serve the needs of the rapidly growing end user computer community. Furthermore, to become an "electronic-based" organization, Mead needed a corporate-wide network. Therefore, the department was reorganized as shown in Figure 1-12 so that the director of corporate information resources reported directly to the company president rather than through the vice president of operations as in the former structure. This change signaled the increased importance of information resources to the company.

The corporate information resources group was responsible for creating hardware, software, and communications standards for the entire corporation; it ran the corporate data center; and it operated the network. All the divisions used the network and corporate data center, and they followed the corporate standards; some operated their own small distributed systems as well, which linked into the corporate network. The three departments within the new group were

- Information resources planning and control—responsible for planning future information systems and technology
- Information services—responsible for most of the traditional information systems functions from the old information services department
- Decision support applications—responsible for "marketing" and supporting end user computing

Information Resources Planning and Control Department

This department grew out of the company's strong planning culture. Decentralization in the 1970s highlighted the need for an information systems planning coordinating body. Although it was small, it had two important roles. First, it took the corporate perspective for information

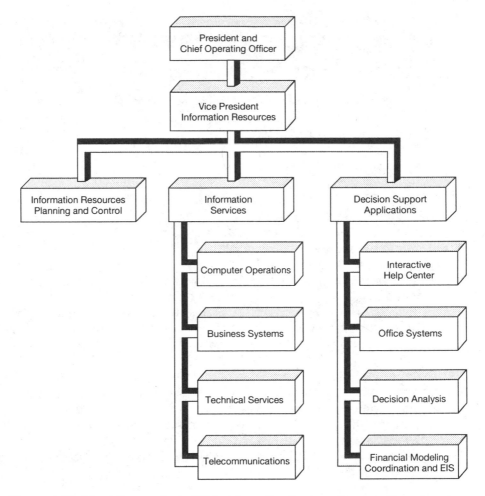

Figure 1-12 Mead Corporation's 1980s Information Systems Services Department
(from Mead Corporation)

systems planning to ensure that Mead's information resources plans
meshed with business plans. Second, it acted as planning coordinator,
helping various groups and divisions coordinate their plans with corporate and information resources plans.

Information Services Department

This department handled computer operations, development of corporate-wide systems, and provided technical services, such as database

administration, system software support, and technical support for end user computing. Finally, it furnished all the telecommunications services to the company.

Most divisions developed their own applications, following the guidelines created by this department. The information systems steering committee—composed of the president and group vice presidents—established a policy that applications should be transportable among the various computing centers and accessible from any Mead terminal. The company's telecommunications network established the guidelines for making this interconnection possible.

Decision Support Applications (DSA) Department

This department provided all end user computing support for the company. It was the marketing arm, selling and training Mead employees on end user computing, while the information services department provided the technical support for the end user systems.

At the time of the 1980 reorganization, DSA had no users, no products, no common applications among its multiple locations, and only five staff members in operations research and two in its office systems support group. By 1985, they were serving fifteen hundred users in some thirty Mead locations with ten staff members. DSA offered fourteen products and eight corporate-wide applications.

The *interactive help center* provided hotline support, introduced end user computing to Mead employees at company meetings, and evaluated new end user computing products.

The *office systems group* supported the dedicated word processing systems and IBM's Professional Office System (PROFS)—which Mead used as the "gateway" to end user computing. This group also acted as consultants to groups contemplating installing an office system. Divisions were free to select any office system, but most followed the recommendations of this group to ensure corporate-wide interconnection.

The *decision analysis group* used operations research tools to develop linear programming models and simulations for users needing such sophisticated analysis tools. It has also built a number of company-wide decision support systems, such as a corporate budgeting model and a graphics software system.

The *financial modeling coordination group* was in charge of Mead's integrated financial system. It also supported executive computing, through IBM PCs used by corporate executives and an executive information system (EIS) accessed through profs. The first version of the system was developed in 1982 as an easy-to-use system to introduce top management to potential managerial uses of computers. Through menus of commands and questions, executives could retrieve monthly summary operating reports, financial statements, forecasting data, and similar information.

Late 1980s Adjustments

The 1980 reorganization separated the more people-oriented activities under DSA from the more technical activities under the information services department. The technology was better managed, and relations with users improved. However, this split in responsibilities caused two problems. One, traditional programmers and system analysts thought that the DSA group received all the new and exciting development work. The second problem was coordinating the two departments. A matrix arrangement evolved to handle both problems, with both information services and DSA people staffing most projects.

The departmental structure implemented in 1980 remained essentially intact throughout the 1980s, with only two major changes. In early 1988, the vice president of information resources began reporting directly to Mead's chairman and chief executive officer (CEO). Second, the DSA group was reorganized, as shown in Figure 1-13.

As users became more sophisticated and less generic, the department created small groups with expertise in specific areas. By the end of the 1980s they were supporting more than five thousand users corporate-wide in three ways—service center help, application development consulting, and local area experts.

The *service center people* continued to introduce new users to technology and provide telephone hotline assistance to experienced users. The *application development consultants* helped users develop more sophisticated applications and guided maintenance of user-written applications, which had become a noticeable problem. They also updated traditional applications to permit end user systems to access the data.

The *local area experts* worked in the functional departments supporting users in their area. They reported directly to their area manager and indirectly to the information resources department. Due to the growing number of user-written applications, they too helped users keep their applications up to date.

So, during the 1980s, Mead found its end user computing focus shifting from introducing new technology to making more effective use of the technology in place. By the end of the decade, they were concentrating on harvesting their investment in IT by using it as a lever to change the way they were doing business.

1990 to Present—Leveraging Their IT Infrastructure

In 1990, the information resources department underwent another reorganization to bring it in line with a new strategy. We first discuss the reorganization, and then present the strategy.

By 1990, management realized that end user systems and large-scale business systems needed to cross-fertilize each other. Users needed one

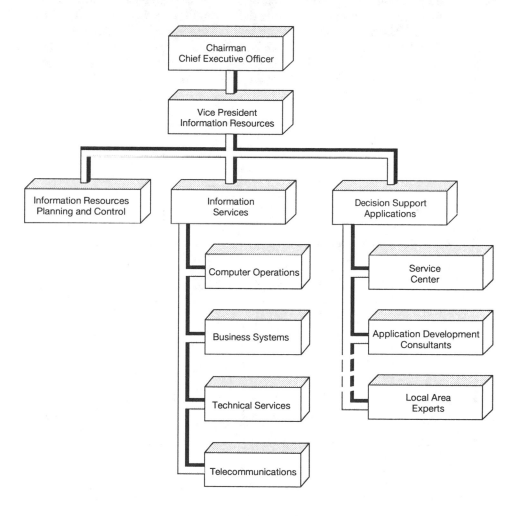

Figure 1-13 Mead Corporation's Late 1980s Corporate Information Resources Group (from Mead Corporation)

place, not two, to go for help; therefore, application development was placed in one group, which was renamed "Information Services," as shown in Figure 1-14.

The emphasis in 1990 was to strengthen the electronic infrastructure of the company. Within this infrastructure, the corporate-wide network had become paramount. Although the network had been created in 1983, its value in connecting Mead to its vendors and customers was not recognized until the late 1980s. Therefore, in 1990, information resources management created a new group—network services—to handle computer operations, technical services, and telecommunications.

The 1990 reorganization also consolidated administrative functions (such as chargeback) into the technology planning and control group.

The 1990 reorganization did not add new functions, but it shifted emphasis from end user computing to building an infrastructure and integrating application development (from small to large systems).

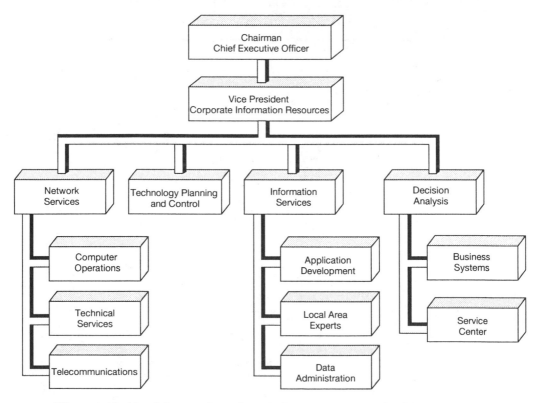

Figure 1-14 Mead Corporation's Current Corporate Information Resources Group
(from Mead Corporation)

Current Strategy

In the early 1980s, Mead installed its first information resources business plan, which emphasized networking and end user computing. By the late 1980s, the objectives had been accomplished. In hindsight, management realized that the 1980 plan had been a technology plan, not a business plan, because its goal had been to get control of IT. Having accomplished this, Mead decided to create a true business plan, one that addressed how to employ its IT resources.

Using the two-by-two matrix shown in Figure 1-15, management realized Mead had only been building systems that fit into the lower-right quadrant—that is, systems that supported the traditional products and business processes internally. Rather than focus on company operations, management decided to shift emphasis in two directions: (1) toward achieving significant structural change in internal company operations and (2) toward using IT to work better with suppliers and customers in traditional areas.

Reengineering the Business. Business reengineering—that is, significantly restructuring the internal operations in a business—has become a major strategic direction for Mead. The company's electronic super highway is playing a key role in this work.

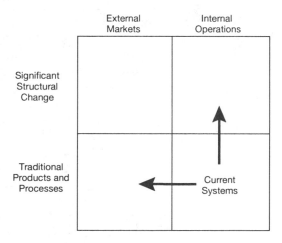

Figure 1-15 Mead Corporation's Strategic Opportunities Framework (from Mead Corporation)

Business processes evolve over time. Mead uses the analogy of cow paths. Cows, in transversing the distance from the barn to pasture, create meandering paths to avoid obstacles and rough terrain. Even after the obstacles have been removed, the cows follow the same meandering paths rather than create new, more direct ones. Often, the information system organization does the same, simply "paving the organization's cow paths" by enhancing the speed of particular business processes but not rethinking those processes. Since information technology removes many time and distance barriers associated with business processes, Mead is now using IT to build super highways rather than simply accelerate existing business processes. This business reengineering is expected to achieve significant structural changes in company operations.

Stressing Customer Satisfaction. The second emphasis is doing business electronically, by extending current business processes and products to suppliers and customers. The motto is: "It is easy to do business with us." Mead will do business using any means a customer wants: (1) through electronic data interchange (EDI) application-to-application transactions across company boundaries, (2) using terminals at customer sites linked to Mead's computers, or (3) over the telephone using voice response.

In essence, Mead is installing various front ends on its existing systems. Its customers are responding, because the new options save them time and improve accuracy.

To improve customer satisfaction further in one division, Mead asked several of larger printers what was most important to them. Their response, "Being able to reach you when we need you, even at 3:00 A.M. or Saturday morning when our presses are having difficulty running your paper." To address this need, Mead lets these customers use the Mead voice mail system, with a *guaranteed 15-minute response time* to every message. The voice mail system has been programmed to outdial the paging system, which sends a signal to the account representative's beeper to call the voice mail system. This use of technology has significantly improved the printers' satisfaction with Mead's service.

The one area Mead is not yet addressing is the upper-left quadrant—creating significant structural change in external markets. Rather than try to hit a "home run" with a grandiose information system, Mead is aiming at the "singles" and "doubles" of using IT to improve customer service.

The basic tactic set forth in 1980 remains in force: to retain central control of the IT infrastructure and distribute responsibility for building and maintaining applications in the business units. Yet, as the uses of information technology have changed, Mead's information resources department has reorganized to focus on those new uses—from end user computing in the 1980s to business reengineering and customer-oriented systems today.

QUESTIONS AND EXERCISES

REVIEW QUESTIONS

1. We define the information era in terms of information work and information workers. How has this sector of the U.S. work force changed during the past one hundred years? What is the current status?

2. What was the nature of information technology in the late 1950s and early 1960s?

3. Summarize the four categories of the classic pattern of information technology.

4. Give two or three characteristics of the technology trends in hardware, software, data, and communications.

5. What are some of the changes occurring in the marketplace?

6. Describe the traditional work environment. According to Naisbitt and Aburdene, what changes are occurring in this traditional environment?

7. What is the mission for information systems recommended by the authors? How does it differ from earlier perceptions of the purpose and objectives of information systems?

8. In the simple model of information technology and its uses (see Figure 1-5), why are the two boxes moving apart? Why are end user systems not joining them completely?

9. Summarize the three components of the marketing model (see Figure 1-9) and show which parts of the information systems process are analogous to each part.

10. List several attributes of procedure-based and goal-based information activities. Which do you think are most important? Why?

11. What is the difference between a product-line approach and a customer-segmentation approach to marketing? How are the two approaches used in developing and delivering information systems?

12. Summarize the main purpose of each of the four groups in Mead's current information resources organization. How do they compare with the parts of the model depicted in Figure 1-10?

DISCUSSION QUESTIONS

1. Do we really need a major change in the way the information systems function is structured? Aren't the necessary changes just minor modifications to accommodate normal growth in computer uses?

2. The procedure-goal dichotomy does not add much beyond the clerical-managerial distinction. Do you agree or disagree? Give reasons for your opinion.

EXERCISES

1. Drawing on current literature, redo Figure 1-2 (the classic infrastructure) to represent better the current situation in information systems.

2. Show how Mead's new organizational structure compares with the model in Figure 1-10 by entering Mead's department/group names and roles on the figure.

3. Contact a company in your community, and prepare a diagram and narrative to describe the organization of its information systems function. Compare it with the models in Figure 1-10, with Mead's 1980 structure, and to Mead's current structure.

REFERENCES

1. PANKO, R. R., and R. H. SPRAGUE, JR., "Toward a New Framework for Office Support," *Proceedings of the ACM Conference on Office Information Systems,* (ACM, New York), 1982.

2. GARRITY, J., and V. L. BARNES, "The Payout in Computers: What Management Has Learned about Planning and Control," in *The Computer Sampler: Management Perspectives on the Computer* (McGraw-Hill, New York), 1968.

3. PORAT, M. U., *The Information Economy* (U.S. Department of Commerce, Office of Telecommunications Policy, Washington, D.C.), 1977.

4. PANKO, R.R., "The Office Workforce: A Structural Analysis," *Office Systems Research Journal,* Spring 1992, pp. 3-20.

5. PANKO, R. R., "Spending on Office Systems: A Provisional Estimate," *Office Technology and People,* July 1982, pp. 177-194. Some data from this paper was published in Panko, R. R., "A Different Perspective on Office Systems," *Administrative Management,* August 1981, pp. 30-32, 75.

6. "Integrated WP/DP Systems," *Office Products News,* October 1981.

7. DRUCKER, P. F. "The Coming of the New Organization," *Harvard Business Review,* January-February 1988.

8. HUBER, G. P. "New Organizational Forms and Emerging Technologies," unpublished working paper, Department of Management, University of Texas at Austin, Austin, Texas, 1992.

9. PAVA, C., "Microelectronics and the Design of Organization," Working Paper No. HBS 82-67, Harvard Business School, Division of Research, April 1982. Also PAVA, C. *Managing New Office Technology: An Organizational Strategy* (Macmillan/Free Press), 1983.

10. NAISBITT, J. and P. ABURDENE, *Re-inventing the Corporation* (Warner Books), 1985.

11. PANKO, R. R., and R. H. SPRAGUE, JR., "Implementing Office Systems Requires a New DP Outlook," *Data Management,* DPMA, November, 1984, pp. 40-42.

TWO

INTRODUCTION

During the past thirty years, the job of information systems executives has been evolving—and the biggest changes seem to be happening right now. It is no longer enough for information systems to support operations; they must play a catalytic role in reshaping and simplifying how organizations work. Systems must not only contribute to the organization's revenues but provide the increasingly crucial infrastructure for "the information age"—providing links within the enterprise as well as to other organizations.

Likewise, the responsibilities of the heads of information systems organizations now go far beyond operating highly efficient "production programming shops." These executives must understand the goals of the enterprise and work in partnership with line peers to use information technology to attain the organization's goals.

We actually see two phenomena occurring. One is the expansion of the top information systems job—the subject of this chapter. The other phenomenon is the shrinking of the traditional portions of the job. The top executive has had a traditional set of responsibilities that have included

- Systems planning
- Data center management and operation
- Management of remote equipment
- Identification of opportunities for new systems
- System analysis and design and construction of new systems.

Several trends are moving those traditional responsibilities out of the systems department into other parts of the organization.

- *Distributed systems.* These systems lead to the migration of equipment to user areas. This equipment is operated under the control of the users, and generally purchased with their funds, sometimes following guidelines (but frequently not specified standards) from the information systems (I/S) department.
- *Ever-more knowledgeable users.* These users take on increased responsibilities. They identify the high-leverage applications and frequently take the initiative in systems analysis and design.
- *Better application packages and better development tools.* These packages and tools result in less need for armies of programmers and analysts to do brute force system development. Head count and budget go down as a result.
- *Outsourcing.* At times the most effective strategy, outsourcing is based on fiscal and managerial considerations for handling data center operations, application maintenance, network management, and PC support. Budget and head counts go down further.

Thus, as shown in Figure 2-1, the top systems executive is seeing the traditional job responsibilities "nibbled away." If this manager is unwilling or unable to take on expanded responsibilities, the job is down-graded or endangered. Fortunately, there are many new challenges that result in expanded responsibilities for growth-oriented managers who aspire to become a CIO. And this is, indeed, happening. For example, in a widely celebrated example, CIO Cathy Hudson outsourced Kodak's data center operations to IBM, telecommunications to Digital Equipment Corporation, and PC support to Businessland. Soon thereafter, she was given an expanded set of responsibilities: serving as the director of process improvement for a major division of Kodak.

Yet, as noted earlier, the top information systems job continues to expand. In 1986, when the first edition was published, the leading information systems executives were talking about their new role as architects of the enterprise-wide information systems infrastructure. There was much talk about the strategic use of information systems.

In 1989, attention had shifted to helping to formulate corporate policy, with an emphasis on creating a vision of the role of information systems in the future. In other words, from 1986 to 1989, the focus of the top information systems job had swung significantly toward addressing business issues.

The challenge facing today's information system executives is using information technology as a catalyst for revamping the way enterprises work. To accomplish this task, information systems executives must have a high enough position to influence the use of IT as a major underpinning of the enterprise of the future. Reflecting this higher level of responsibility, many companies have changed the title of the "vice president of MIS" or "information systems director" to "Chief Information Officer (CIO)."

In this chapter, we discuss the "what" and "how" of the top IT executive's job, looking first at the top job itself by summarizing five major responsibilities, and then exploring several ways the information systems function is evolving in organizations.

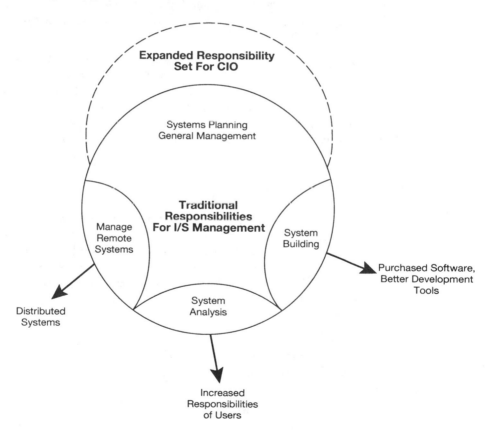

Figure 2-1 Traditional Responsibilities Being "Nibbled Away" from Systems Executives

THE CIO'S RESPONSIBILITIES

To take a leadership role in reshaping the way the enterprise works and competes, we see information systems executives having the following five primary responsibilities:

1. *Understand the business,* particularly of the markets in which the firm sells its products and services
2. *Establish credibility of the systems department,* thereby increasing the confidence of executive management in ideas presented by systems management
3. *Increase the technological maturity of the firm,* making it easier to take advantage of computer and telecommunication applications throughout the firm
4. *Create a vision of the future and sell it,* setting a goal for the use of information technology within the organization and sell that goal to others
5. *Implement an information systems architecture* that will support the vision and the company in the future

Some of these responsibilities are likely to be new to many systems executives. Each organization will have a different situation. Some, for instance, will already have established good credibility with top management. Some will have many years of experience experimenting with new technology, so their firm is relatively mature at using and managing information technology. Most executives will not need to start from scratch in all five areas, but many may find that they must work to move ahead in several of them.

Understand the Business

If information system executives are to play an important role in reshaping a business's operations, they must understand that business. In the past, studying a business generally meant learning how part of it was being run. However, studying internal operations is not enough nowadays. Today, it is also important to understand the environment in which a business operates, because "the rules of the game have changed" in how companies compete with one another. Here are seven approaches CIOs are using to understand the business and its environment.

- Have project teams study the marketplace
- Concentrate on lines of business
- Sponsor weekly briefings
- Attend industry meetings with line executives
- Read industry publications
- Hold informal listening sessions
- Become a "partner" with a line manager

Have Project Teams Study the Marketplace. To learn about the business, broaden the kinds of information that project teams seek in their study of the business, then have them describe their findings to systems management. For example, the project study might begin with a broad overview of the company, gathering the following information about the company and its industry:

- History and framework
- Current industry environment
- Business goals and objectives
- Major practices of competitors
- Pertinent government regulations
- The inputs, outputs, and resources of the firm

Such an overview study can be conducted for a business unit or a product in a few weeks. The study is apt to uncover some surprises, revealing things about the industry and company that even line people might not know. Systems management can be briefed on the findings, thus educating them about the markets in which their firm participates.

Concentrate on Lines of Business. Robert Benson of Washington University in St. Louis, Missouri, and Marilyn Parker of IBM have been studying how to manage information on an enterprise-wide basis [1]. They began their study thinking that they should develop data modeling tools. However, since the mid-1980s, their thinking has broadened significantly.

One of their findings is that to help a company be successful, information systems need to serve individual lines of business rather than a whole company. Planning for an entire enterprise without considering "lines of business" overlooks both competitive and performance matters. A line of business is where business and technology planning can be linked they now believe.

At the Enterprise-wide Information Management (EWIM) conference hosted by the two researchers a few years ago, Benson characterized a line of business as all organizational units that conduct business activities with common customer, product, and market characteristics. For example, certain schools in a university have one line of business—undergraduate education. Other schools have two lines of business—undergraduate and graduate education. The customers, products, and market characteristics for the two are different; thus they are different lines of business.

Information systems can serve lines of business in two ways. One is by supporting current operations, which Benson and Parker call "alignment." The second is by using systems to influence future ways of working, which they call "impact." Benson and Parker suggest asking the following questions about each line of business to decide what each one needs.

1. Are we organized to serve that line of business?
2. Do we have an "account manager" in the systems department who has responsibility for that line of business?
3. Is there someone within that line of business who oversees systems activity and talks the business language?
4. Do we have a sponsor in the line of business?
5. Do we have the attention of their management?
6. Does the line of business offer an opportunity to use systems in new ways?

By becoming familiar with lines of business, systems executives can better help them use systems to support current operations and influence the future, say Benson and Parker.

Sponsor Weekly Briefings. A third way to learn about the business is to sponsor short briefings each week for systems management and staff—presented by line management or staff. We have attended such meetings and found them most informative. They were about one-half hour long, with one speaker describing a part of the business. Managers and staff from different departments were invited to talk to a small group of information systems managers and staff about their business and its marketplace—the products and services they offered versus what the competitors offered, the strengths and weaknesses of the firm and competitors, growth projections, possible changes in the market, and so on.

For example, in the aircraft industry an engineer could give the basics of the commercial aircraft business—sizes of planes, number of people they hold, lengths of flights, expected competition, how the field is changing, five-year and ten-year market projections, and so on. In the financial services industry, a manager could describe various types of customers and how they have changed, products now offered by the firm and competitors, changes in the world financial marketplace, and so on. At such briefings, it is helpful if the presenter provides a written summary of the ideas presented, so attendees can take something away with them. A brief question and answer period is also very useful.

To understand the business, one needs to understand the marketplace. Few employees get exposed to this breadth of knowledge. By sponsoring short presentations by the people closest to a business, systems management can help fix that problem without cutting into working time too greatly.

Attend Industry Meetings with Line Executives. Another way to learn about the business is to accompany a line executive to an industry conference—not a computer conference. We have found that attending a conference is one of the quickest ways to uncover issues currently facing an industry. These conferences contain the jargon used in the industry and the approaches others have used to market products, handle regulations, respond to competition, and so on. Attending with a line executive can be even more enlightening, because he or she can explain what the company is or is not doing in areas discussed by the speakers. Such joint attendance is also likely to foster a new friendship.

Read Industry Publications. One of the best ways to stay abreast of an industry is to read their publications. Getting a well-rounded view of an industry may require reading several publications a month. For example, news publications can provide information on new products, current issues, company changes, and so on. On the other hand, newsletters, reports, and research journals generally provide better analyses of industry trends, discussions of ongoing research, and projections about the future.

One information systems executive we know spreads this job around in his department. Every systems person is responsible for reading certain periodicals and routing interesting articles to others.

Hold Informal Listening Sessions. In his book, *Thriving on Chaos* [2], consultant Tom Peters presents hundreds of suggestions on how managers can learn to not just cope with a chaotic business environment but thrive on it. In numerous places in the book, Peters urges people simply to listen and learn. His ideas are appropriate for information systems management in their dealings with their customers—both internal to the firm and external.

Yogi Berra, the famous baseball player, once said, "You can see a lot by observing." Similarly, Peters urges employees to listen to customers to determine their needs. Since product life cycles are shrinking, companies need to spot new trends earlier. Becoming a listening-intensive organization can help here.

Peters recounts several instances in which people have created informal "meetings" to break down barriers among people who usually do not talk with one another. For instance, one hospital administrator set aside one early morning each week for having coffee and rolls available in her office, with an open invitation for doctors and administrators to drop by and chat. She had some lonely breakfasts at first, she told Peters, but they have evolved into the "real staff meeting" of the week. Another hospital administrator held an informal staff meeting at lunchtime every two weeks at a local pub and invited some doctors. The doctors felt honored to be invited and their attendance helped break down stereotypes on both sides and improve communications.

These get-togethers are held in a setting that is not charged with tension, participation is voluntary, and their purpose is just to chat. They could be used to break down the stereotypes and communication barriers between systems professionals and linemanagers.

Become a "Partner" with a Line Manager. In 1987, the Society for Information Management [3] initiated its Partners in Leadership award. Each year, the award is presented to two organizations, honoring one systems and one business executive in each enterprise who, through their alliance, have achieved significant business results. This award has been well received and is highly sought. It indicates an important transformation that is occurring in the field. Since partnering is important to becoming business oriented, we discuss it in more depth in the second half of this chapter.

Summary. These, then, are seven ways that CIOs and their staff members can learn the businesses of the organization. With this knowledge, CIOs are in a better position to create a vision of using information technology in their firm. It is important that specific steps or mechanisms, such as these, be implemented in the department; otherwise, the job of learning the business will be displaced by day-to-day work.

Establish Systems Department Credibility

The second major responsibility of the CIO is to establish the credibility of the systems organization. Before the systems executive and the systems department can be viewed as an important force in the future of the organization, they must be viewed as successful and reliable today. This suggests that the information systems departments has two missions, says Joseph Izzo, of the management consulting firm of A. T. Kearney [4]. One is to maintain today's systems, and the other is to work on tomorrow's systems.

These two missions have very different goals and therefore need to be managed separately and quite differently. The "today" operation should concentrate on providing service, says Izzo, while the "tomorrow" operations needs to focus on helping the business operate better. The first job of systems management is to get the "today" operation in shape. Until that is done, they will have little credibility with top management, says Izzo.

Managing the "Today" Organization Better. The "today" organization includes computer operations, technical support (including telecommunications network support), and maintaining and enhancing existing applications. Since its main mission is service, the service levels of these various operations need to be measured.

To run the "today" operation, Izzo suggests hiring managers for each of these functions who are like foremen—that is, they are delivery oriented and demand a high level of service from their department. Many systems organizations have a poor response rate, says Izzo, because they do not staff their organization correctly.

He recommends the following staffing levels, based on the workloads he has seen at more than twenty companies. About 80 to 90 percent of requests for system development take less than 160 hours to complete, he says. Most are one- or two-day projects; Izzo calls them *minor requests*. A department needs 25 to 35 percent of its work force to handle these requests, he believes. Another 9 to 15 percent of the requests take up to one work-year to fulfill;

Izzo calls them *intermediate requests*. This workload requires 50 to 65 percent of the department's work force. The remaining 1 to 5 percent take more than one work-year. The *major requests* require 10 to 25 percent of a development work force.

Of these three types of development, Izzo points out that most departments only manage the majors. To manage the full range more professionally, Izzo recommends separating them into these three categories and handling each differently. Complete all minor requests within thirty days, on average, he recommends; don't prioritize them, just do them. To handle the intermediates, establish user committees to determine the merit of the requests. Let the line people prioritize this work by determining which projects get implemented and when. For the majors, follow the elaborate procedures that companies already have in place.

Once the "today" organization is in shape, then systems management has the credibility to propose its new ideas for the future. In Chapter 8, we will further discuss running today's operations.

Increase the Technological Maturity of the Firm

Technologically mature organizations are those in which management is comfortable *managing* the use of IT and employees are comfortable *using* the technology. These organizations are the ones most likely to take advantage of new uses of information technology.

How can information systems management help others in their firm become comfortable with IT? They can provide education—to make others aware of uses of IT as well as their role in either using or managing the technology. Systems departments are getting quite a bit of help in familiarizing people with computers. Computers and information systems are featured in the news media, computers are used in almost all areas of everyday life, and younger employees have literally been "brought up" on computers.

Information systems management also has the job of helping end users adapt to changes caused by IT, and encouraging innovative uses of the technology. In Chapter 17, we discuss some ways that a systems department can increase its firm's technological maturity, and put the company in a better position to use new information technologies for strategic purposes.

Create a Vision of the Future and Sell It

Information system executives are no longer reactive, providing only support. They manage some of the most important tools for influencing the firm's future; therefore, they are becoming more "proactive" by helping to create a vision of the firm's future and its use of information technology, and then selling those ideas to others.

What is a Vision? It is a statement of how someone wants the future to be or believes it will be. It is used to set direction for an organization. One of the most often-cited examples is the compelling statement U.S. President John Kennedy made in 1961: "We will put a man on the moon, and return him safely to earth, by the end of the decade." And it did come to pass. On July 21, 1969, the United States landed a man on the moon. His vision provided a direction for the U.S. space program for a decade.

Cynthia Beath and Blake Ives, of Southern Methodist University [5], present the following visions from chief executives.

- George Davis, chief operating officer at Otis Elevator, wants any sales person in his company to be able to completely order an elevator in a day.
- Robert McDermott, president of USAA—an insurance company for current and retired military officers—wants policy holders to accomplish their objective in a single phone call.
- Mim Eschenbaum, vice president of Rittenhouse Homes, wants customers to be able to get a house designed and built from a retail store.
- Edward Johnson II, president of Fidelity Investments, wants to reprice mutual funds on an hourly, rather than daily, basis.

Why Develop a Vision? The word "vision" is seen everywhere these days, because in turbulent times such as we face today, people are looking for some stability. A vision of a desirable future can provide stability when it sets the direction for an organization. In his book, *The Renewal Factor* [6], Robert Waterman discusses the difference between vision and strategy. Strategies tell how someone is going to get somewhere. It is their plan for the future. Strategies are fine as long as the future is relatively predictable, says Waterman. But we are now in turbulent times. No one can predict some of the most important events that will affect companies, he says, because these events are likely to be random, not linear or rational.

Since IT is important to the success of many firms, visions about their future need to include use of these technologies.

Who Should Create the Vision? A growing number of chief executives are relying on their information system executive to create the corporate vision for using IT, because innovative uses of computers are providing ways to significantly change the way companies do business.

Where can CIOs come up with such inspirations? Listen to all ideas, no matter how crazy they sound, recommends Joel Barker [7].

At a conference hosted by The Dooley Group [8], a management consulting firm, Barker asked the question: What types of people are most likely to find new ways to solve problems? His answer: people who anticipate dramatics shifts that might occur in the future. These types of people are generally outsiders, he says, because they see things in different ways. They have faith in themselves, but they are unpracticed in the field under question. So they bring a fresh viewpoint to problems in that field. They do not know what cannot be done, so they try many new things. These visionaries are generally young people just entering a field or older people who are changing careers, and they love to tinker.

Insiders have an investment in maintaining the status quo, because they understand the way a field operates. Outsiders do not have this investment, so they are more likely to come up with new solutions, says Barker.

Getting a Vision. We found two ways to create visions. One is to explore the present. Think about how it might be improved. For example, study the problems CEOs face today and look for ways to solve those problems. A second approach to creating a vision is to "scout" the future. Look at trends that appear likely to continue as well as changes that might disrupt current trends. The PC disrupted the computer field in the early 1980s. What other disruptions lie ahead? People who uncover such shifts and take advantage of them early can give their firm a competitive edge.

By exploring the present, Peters [2] suggests four approaches. One is to look at prior experiences and ask: What bothers you most about the organization? When people were (or were not) working well with one another, what seemed to be going on? Based on answers to these and similar questions, fix things that are wrong. Second, try participation by involving people inside and outside the firm to uncover their top ten irritants and their ten best experiences. Their ideas might inspire a vision. Third, clarify the vision over time, perhaps by holding a two-to-three day meeting with subordinates to study the data and stories in detail to refine shared views and values. And fourth, remember to listen. Visions are seldom original, he notes. A visionary may be the person who focuses attention on an idea at a point in time, but that visionary is likely to have heard it from someone else.

By scouting the future, the Institute for the Future [9] studies trends for their ten-year forecast. The institute helps organizations plan their long-term futures by discussing near-term and long-term outlooks in numerous areas— such as the U.S. economy, demographics of the United States, U.S. labor force, technology, U.S. government, and international situation. They present the issues that they see arising from the trends. Examples include the advent of wireless communications infrastructures and the use of information technology as an worldwide competitive tool.

Another way to scout the future is to look for discontinuities, or shifts in trends. The people at the Institute for the Future call them "wild cards;" Joel Barker calls them "paradigm shifts." By whatever name, they create major changes in the way people think about the world. The pen-based notebook computer is such a shift, concern for the earth's environment is another, and competing on time is still another.

Barker encourages people to "scout" the future, looking for discontinuities by listening to unusual ideas and new ways to solve existing problems. The more people a company has scouting the future, the better off they are, says Barker, because the future is more likely to be revolutionary than evolutionary. By spotting a revolutionary event early, a company has an advantage over competitors that are not thinking about the future.

At the Dooley Group conference, attendees offered the following ideas on possible shifts that could change the way people think in the next fifteen years

- Decline in the growth of cities
- Holograms to replace travel
- Small is better than big
- Personalized products
- Portable and personal two-way communication
- Small but very powerful batteries
- Manufacturing in outer space
- A power shift from a manufacturing base to a knowledge base
- Deterence of the aging process

Selling a Vision. Once you have a vision about how you think the business should operate in the future, you need to sell that idea to others. Webb Castor [10], an independent consultant whose job has always been selling, irrespective of his job description, has several recommendations for selling an idea.

To sell an idea requires understanding the marketplace, says Castor, emphasizing, what the potential customers *want* rather than what they *should have*. To find out what they want, listen. Listening is actually a potent form of selling. By understanding and fulfilling someone's needs, you help them be successful, says Castor. And by making the buyer successful, the seller becomes successful.

Often, personal relationships are the key to selling an idea successfully, says Castor, because people like to do business with people they know and trust. But if you believe you will not be effective, bring in a spokesperson. And, finally to be a successful salesperson, keep your customers informed, says Castor. If you can do nothing else to ease a bad situation, at least keep the others informed. Customer care is very important in selling—products or ideas.

Implement an Information System Architecture

Although it used to be considered strictly a technical issue, implementing a new information system architecture really means rethinking company operations—how it works, what it does, with whom it works, and so on.

"Don't build an architecture to support old ways of operating" is the admonishment we hear over and over these days.

What kinds of attributes should new systems architectures have? Peter Keen [11], of the International Center for Information Technologies presented his views at a conference cosponsored by the Society for Information Management (SIM) and The Conference Board. His ideas are summarized in SIM Network [3a].

Large organizations—both in industry and government—are reaching the limits of complexity, says Keen. Complex organizational structures are now impeding the missions of organizations. Information technology planning should therefore focus on simplifying organizations to ensure their health. CEOs should look to information technology to help them redesign their organizations.

Organizations can be simplified by increasing direct contact between people, Keen believes. Information technology can help by reducing the need for intermediaries, thereby flattening organizational hierarchies. The technology also can help organize information for easier access. This is particularly needed for document-based information, where complex organizational structures have emerged just to process documents. Management should shift its attention from using IT for competitive purposes to using it to redesign their organizations to operate more simply, says Keen.

Keen is not alone in emphasizing that a systems architecture should be put in place after rethinking how the business will operate in the future. The hot topic in the field these days is "reengineering" the firm, meaning redesigning how it operates—often by making IT a more integral part of operations. Developing a systems architecture has become much more than a technical exercise; it has become a strategic business issue.

Various approaches and methods of developing architectures are presented in several chapters throughout the book. In Part 2, we outline several architectures for distributed computing, telecommunications, and information resources, respectively.

Summary. Of these five areas of responsibility, several may not seem new. Running an efficient operation to develop credibility and planning the systems infrastructure have been part of the top systems job for some time. Most information systems executives have also long assumed an important role in training and education to increase the organization's ability to assimilate IT. However, only recently has it become clear that CIOs must know as much about the business processes and goals as they know about the technology, maybe more. Moreover, the concept of creating an overall vision of the role of IT, and selling it throughout the organization, was quite foreign to many CIOs until recently.

The following case example illustrates how one company developed and used a vision of IT to enhance its business performance.

CASE EXAMPLE: The Boeing Company

The Boeing Company, a major U.S. aerospace company with head-quarters in Seattle, Washington, has three major components.

- Boeing Commercial Airplane Group manufactures the 747, 757, 767, and the forthcoming 777 airplanes.
- Boeing Defense and Space Systems manufactures missile systems, space systems, military airplanes and helicopters, and other military systems.
- Boeing Computer Services supplies information system support to Boeing and government agencies, offers commercial computing services, and does research and application development in new information technologies.

At an annual conference of the Society for Information Management [3] in the mid 1980s, the president of Boeing Computer Services, described two visions—one Boeing had achieved and another they were developing. In 1991, Boeing developed a third vision—one intended to carry them into the year 2010.

Vision 1: The Right Part in the Right Place at the Right Time. In the late 1960s, business was good at Boeing, but the company had a severe parts shortage that was hindering production. If a part was unavailable when needed, a tag—called a "traveler"—was affixed to the aircraft in place of the missing part. At that time, the company had twenty-five hundred to five thousand travelers per month attached to planes under construction.

To correct this situation, they created this vision: *the right part in the right place at the right time*. From 1966 to the mid-1980s, Boeing installed fifteen major information systems as well as dozens of smaller ones to implement this vision. The parts shortage problem used to be greatest when a new aircraft was being introduced. For example, in 1966 when the 737 was "rolled out," the number of travelers jumped to more than eight thousand a month. But by the mid-1970s, parts shortages had been reduced to fewer than one hundred a month. And in the early 1980s, introduction of the 757 and 767 models caused barely noticeable increases in parts shortages.

Information systems helped them solve the parts shortage problem and implemented their vision. In doing so, however, Boeing had created islands of automation; systems had trouble passing information back and forth to one another. Meanwhile the company's marketplaces had changed. So they needed a new vision.

Addressing the Changing Marketplace. In the aerospace and defense markets, ways of doing business had changed by the mid 1980s. There were tighter budgets in the U.S. Department of Defense—one of their major customers—and the U.S. government had shifted up-front development costs to suppliers. Therefore, Boeing experienced pressure to use rapidly changing technologies in their products.

In the commercial aircraft market, deregulation led air carriers to expand hub-and-spoke operations where shorter flights and smaller planes were the norm. Fluctuating fuel prices made fuel economy a major concern in aircraft design. Boeing also faced more intense competition from foreign as well as domestic aircraft companies.

Boeing believed their competitiveness in the commercial airplane market depended on their use of information systems. They saw information systems helping in three ways.

1. *To increase their responsiveness to the market.* Systems would help them "design to cost"—meaning, design planes with the aircraft purchaser's operational costs in mind. Information systems would also help Boeing keep aircraft delivery schedules flexible, so they could deliver products earlier than competitors. They also believed information systems would help them tailor an existing aircraft for a customer without having to redesign it completely.

2. *To help them gain a competitive advantage by making after-sale support more efficient.* With IT, they would be able to create airplane documentation based on original design data. They would be better able to manage- spare parts inventories worldwide. And they would use artificial intelligence in embedded diagnostics systems to do troubleshooting during maintenance.

3. *To help them streamline their design and build process.* The vision was based on this third use of information technology.

Vision 2: An Enhanced Information Stream. Boeing's vision in the mid-1980s was to create an *enhanced information stream,* because building and supporting an aircraft is really an information process. An enhanced information stream means that every step in designing and building aircraft uses, adds to, and enhances a continuing stream of information.

First, a product is defined using a computer-aided design/computer-aided manufacturing (CAD/CAM) system. Then, each succeeding step in the design, build, and support process uses that digital information, adds to it, and enhances it. The various "islands of automation" would feed into one "seamless information pipeline." Even after-sale support information would be based on this enhanced digital description of a product.

This vision required several significant changes in the company. One change was organizational. Boeing had to break down traditional organization barriers. Thirty years of computing had led to islands of automation based on organizational structure. If information was to be used better, it had to cross organizational lines. One way Boeing restructured itself was to establish design/build teams composed of people from engineering and manufacturing as well as other disciplines.

Boeing also streamlined their design and manufacturing processes *before* they automated rather than automate their traditional ways of doing business. Finally, they used computers for as many jobs as possible, such as using computers to track engineering changes.

Vision 3: A Strategic Business Process Architecture. In 1991, Boeing reassessed their position and undertook a long-range study to develop a new vision—for both the company's business processes and information systems in the year 2010. The team found that the Boeing had often put the cart before the horse in that information systems plans had driven business plans. The company had a clear vision for IT but no vision for business processes. The study is therefore defining the world-class production processes that both the commercial airplane group and the defense and space group will need to succeed in 2010, as well as the computing infrastructure to support those processes.

The study began with Boeing defining their existing business process architecture to understood how they conduct business and to compare with how they want to conduct business in 2010. The 2010 "strategic business process architecture" will then provide the basis for their IT architectures, as shown in Figure 2-2. To define this business vision, Boeingis asking the following fundamental question.

- What business processes should we use?
- What information do we need to accomplish these processes?
- How are the processes and information related?
- How is the data managed?
- Which hardware, software, and networks are required?

Once the 2010 business processes are defined, Boeing plans to develop them with the same intensity they use to design and develop a new airplane. This will require addressing how to fundamentally change their old, ingrained "legacy" systems without disturbing company operations. "Owners" of business processes will be established to develop the migration plans, for both the business processes as well as the supporting computing environment.

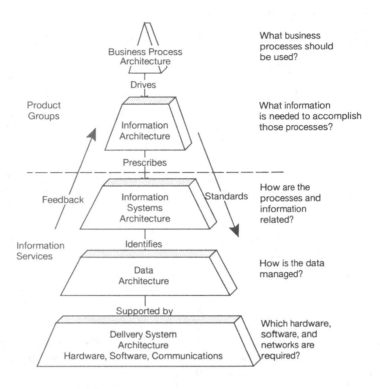

Figure 2-2 The Boeing Information Services 2010 Study (reprinted courtesy of The Boeing Company)

Although Boeing is currently the dominant airplane manufacturer in the world, the company must make changes to maintain that position. Airbus, the European consortium, has grown from 0 to 25 percent market share, and is now aiming for 40 percent. Toyota, the most efficient manufacturer in the world, is also expected to enter the business in the near future. Boeing management believes that instituting change from their current position of strength is the only way they can ensure success in this more competitive future.

THE EVOLVING SYSTEMS FUNCTION

The changing roles and responsibilities of the CIO just discussed are largely the result of the evolution of the systems function. In the second half of this chapter we discuss several dimensions of this evolution, beginning with the escalating benefits derived from IT.

This, in turn, changes the way managers view IT and its role. Recent research shows that there is a wide dispersion of views among top executives on this subject. In this context, we explore the likely changes coming in systems departments.

The Escalating Benefits of Information Systems

The authors of *Strategic Choices* [12]—Kenneth Primozic, Edward Primozic, and Joe Leben—describe the evolution of systems and the escalating benefits they provide organizations. The authors introduce the notion of "waves of innovation," which they define as how IT is used by industry and by enterprise. They identify five waves of innovation, as shown in Figure 2-3. They are

- Wave 1: Reducing cost
- Wave 2: Leveraging investments
- Wave 3: Enhancing products and services
- Wave 4: Enhancing executive decision making
- Wave 5: Reaching the consumer

Wave 1: Reducing cost began in the 1960s when the use of IT focused on increasing the productivity of individuals and business areas. The goal was to achieve clerical and administrative savings.

Wave 2: Leveraging investments, which began in the 1970s, concentrated on making more effective use of corporate assets to increase profitability. Systems were justified on return on investment and increase of cash flow.

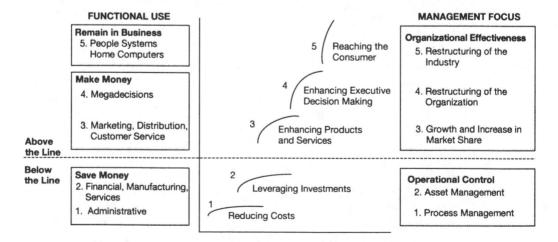

Figure 2-3 Waves of Innovation (from Primozic, *et al* [3])

The authors note that the focus in both of these waves was saving money, not making money—by better managing processing and assets. Systems were developed mainly for administration, finance, and manufacturing.

Wave 3: Enhancing products and services began in the 1980s and was the first time that attention shifted to using IT to produce revenue—by gaining strategic advantage or creating entirely new businesses.

Wave 4: Enhancing executive decision making began later in the 1980s and focused on changing the fundamental structure of the organization as well as creating real-time business management systems.

The authors point out that waves 1 and 2 could be implemented at any time—because of their internal focus—but waves 3 and 4 must be implemented once an industry leader sets a new direction. Companies that do not follow suit cease to remain competitive.

Wave 5: Reaching the consumer is just beginning, say the authors. It uses IT directly with consumers, thus it is leading to new marketing, distribution, and service strategies. In essence, it is changing the rules of competition, which is precisely the focus of leading edge firms—to restructure their industry by focusing on creating new businesses that can yield order-of-magnitude greater growth potential.

In this framework, waves 1 and 2 are "below the line," in that they focus on saving money. Waves 3, 4, and 5 are "above the line," because they concentrate on making money and staying in business. Most organizations are just at the top of wave 2, say Primozic *et al*; they have not yet begun to build information systems that make money—even though the leaders in their industries may have crossed the line quite some time ago.

Once companies do cross the line, top management must be involved, because they must steer the company in the new business environment where systems play an integral part in managing the enterprise. The risks of inappropriately using IT for competitive purposes are too great for them not to play a leading role. So joint planning by top management and systems management must occur, say the authors.

To illustrate how one company has maneuvered through these five waves, consider the example given by the authors: the American Airlines SABRE system.

CASE EXAMPLE: The Sabre System

Primozic *et al* [12] believe that the American Airlines computer reservation system—SABRE—represents a prime example of a system that has progressed through their five waves of innovation.

Waves 1 and 2. The system was built in the mid-1960s to reduce the costs of making airline seat reservations and to leverage the reservation-making assets of the airline. The system moved American from a manual-based reservation operation to a computer-based one.

Wave 3. In the mid-1970s, American offered the system to travel agents, giving them a way to make reservations directly through on-line terminals. American also enhanced the offering by adding functions of importance to travel agents, such as preparing trip itineraries. SABRE was a win-win proposition—the travel agents liked the direct access and American increased barriers to agents switching to other carriers' systems.

Wave 4. In the late 1970s, American expanded their reservation service to hotels and rental cars, through alliances with these suppliers. In so doing, American was transforming themselves and perhaps the entire industry, from an airline company to a travel company. At about the same time, American also added a yield management component to SABRE, which allowed them to reprice seats more dynamically, to maximize revenue.

Wave 5. In the 1980s, American extended their reach to the consumer in two major moves. First, they introduced EAASY SABRE, the computer reservation system that consumers can access directly from their PCs. Second, American introduced their frequent flyer program, AAdvantage, thereby stimulating frequent business flyers to fly American and gain points for free trips. Furthermore, it allied the program with Citibank's credit card and MCI, giving their AAdvantage members free miles by using the credit card and the telephone company.

This example makes it very clear that top management had to be involved as soon as SABRE moved into the money-making wave 3, when they began offering the system to their customers, the travel agents. That was a heart-of-the-business move, and it had to be led by the business executives of the organization, not the information system executives.

CEOs' Attitudes Toward Information Systems

If top management's intimate participation in systems planning is so crucial, how likely are they to be involved? "Not very likely" is the sad answer we surmise from an ongoing study of the attitudes of chief executive officers (CEOs) toward the worthiness of information technology. At a recent meeting of the Chicago Chapter of the Society for Information Management, Diane Wilson [13] of Massachusetts Institute of Technology's (MIT) Sloan School reported on a research study she has been leading that delves into CEO's pre-conceived notions about the benefits of IT. She believes that CIOs, and their staffs, will be better able to work with senior executives if they understand the fundamental assumptions these executives hold about receiving payoffs from it.

The researchers interviewed eighty-four CEOs in ten industries for two hours each, asking them about the competence of their systems department and what they personally expect of IT and from their systems department. An interesting, yet sad, side note is that several of them commented that this was one of the first times they had talked about IT in a relaxed, exploratory fashion.

Most of the CEOs interviewed—52 percent to be exact—are neutral, believing they do not have enough knowledge to direct IT investments. They are difficult to work for, says Wilson, because they do not provide the necessary leadership.

Wilson and her colleagues placed the other 48 percent of the CEOs into four quadrants, depending on whether they took an optimistic or pessimistic view of the benefits of IT, and whether they had high or low confidence in their information system department. We draw on her comments in the following description. (See Figure 2-4.)

Quadrant 1. CEOs in this category have a high degree of confidence in receiving benefits from IT investments, as well as confidence in their systems department's ability to deliver those benefits. Twelve percent of the CEOs interviewed are in this group. The main challenge in managing IT under this type of executive, says Wilson, is that the CEO generally takes a hands-off attitude and delegates the entire job to the CIO.

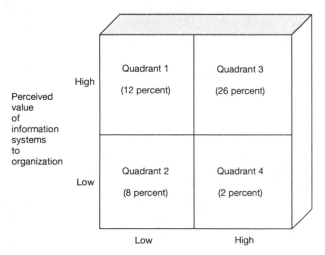

Figure 2-4 CEOs' Attitudes Toward Information Systems (based on Wilson[13])

Quadrant 2. Although still having a positive belief in the benefits of applying IT, CEOs in this category are well aware that implementation problems can destroy that potential. These executives, who were 26 percent of the CEOs interviewed, can tell war stories to back up their beliefs. So they take a hands-on approach to managing IT. They believe they must establish the standard for using information in decision making throughout the firm, they review all important IT decisions, and they step in when problems arise to minimize the risk of IT not delivering on the promised benefits. They generally see their CEO as the technologist and the IT visionary.

Quadrant 3. CEOs counted here are pessimistic about IT, believing that all systems will be delivered over budget. Although they have confidence in their information system department, they manage mainly on cost, to protect the enterprise from the risks. This group constituted 8 percent of Wilson's sample.

Quadrant 4. CEOs in this category, which constituted 2 percent of the interviewees, believe that IT is harmful because it introduces chaos and too much change for people to cope well. Generally these executives have gotten their skepticism from a bad experience, so they have little or no confidence in the systems group. They see their role as keeping a lid on demand for IT and they discourage others from adopting IT.

Wilson is in the midst of completing this research; she has yet to study the CIOs in these firms to see how their management style maps to the CEOs' pre-disposition on it. All the CEOs have been visited a second time, all agreed with the category in which they were placed, and only one had changed categories—from quadrant 2 to believing he did not have enough knowledge to provide leadership. At this mid-point in her study, Wilson believes she will find a correlation between a CEO's view and the limits of what the CEO can hope to accomplish.

Primozic *et al* [12] make a disturbing observation on this same subject. In briefly retracing history, they point out that when computers were initially used to store *data,* companies appropriately had data processing departments. When people began retrieving *information,* not just data, from the systems, the name changed to information systems departments. They see an even more profound shift starting: from storing just words and numbers to storing charts, audio, video, and models. These represent concepts, that is, *knowledge,* and this shift will affect how we use computers. In organizations in which top management does not even yet acknowledge the importance of traditional *data processing,* what will happen to them as we move into the knowledge management era?

Related questions are being asked these days about the information systems department. What is its role? Is it likely to disappear any time soon? We address these issues next.

Where Are Systems Departments Headed?

There has indeed been much talk lately about the demise of the information systems department; therefore, we are presenting two quite different views on the future. One is from a well-known consultant; the other is from a panel of industry academics and CIOs.

One Consultant's View

Chuck Gibson of CSC Index [14] foresees a dramatically revamped job description for information systems departments arising in the next few years. In essence, the departments will perform two very different functions: managing outsourcers and outsourced functions, and ensuring that information services are tied to business needs.

Outsourcing Management. The day-to-day work is likely to be outsourced, says Gibson. That includes data center operations, network operations, PC maintenance, and even application development and maintenance. The goal is to improve return on assets by moving these assets off the financial books while retaining control over their use. Outsourcing is also being used to deal with top executives' frustrations with their information systems department.

To outsource work, however, accountability and control must be increased to the point that management does not lose control. This implies greater reliance on, and greater clarity in, service level agreements than most departments have had in the past.

Outsourcing will also require information systems managers to trade in their operational job for a contracts administration job. Atlthough many systems executives believe that outsourcing will decrease their influence, Gibson believes it will do just the opposite. Their power will increase while their risk will be reduced. They will not be held so accountable for mistakes, yet they will become the influential intermediary between users and outsourcers.

Systems executives face several challenges in moving to outsourcing. One is separating the technology from the applications. Outsourcing vendors will want to use their favorite platforms to attain the economies of scale they require to offer attractive prices. Outsourcing might therefore require replacing products currently in use. Department executives must gracefully migrate employees to these unfamiliar products. Furthermore, they must help systems staff join the outsourcer. This can be a tough move for many systems people, because they will undoubtedly do some new work, they will have far less contact with end users, their benefits package may change, and they will need to adapt to a new work culture. Negotiating equitable new jobs and easing this move are major challenges for systems management.

This future systems department will have a core of contract administrators as well as a small group of technical support people who will provide front-line support to users. Most technical support, however, will come from on-site outsourcing staff.

Strategic Alignment. The other major function to be handled by the information systems department of the future will be aligning information systems and IT investments with business needs. Strategic alignment will be carried out by a small team of ten to twenty highly respected problem solvers, Gibson surmises. If operations have been outsourced, the group will identify new applications and ensure that the outsourced architecture supports these critical applications. This coordination may become especially challenging in building strategic interorganizational systems.

If IT operations have *not* been outsourced, the strategic alignment group will be responsible for migrating the company toward a common architecture. Rather than developing that architecture from scratch, this group of internal consultants will only be able to implement it piecemeal, seizing opportunities to use enterprise standards project by project. The projects will be chosen for criticality, not for highest payback. When an urgent need arises, the team of internal consultants will know how to respond fast and implement a system that moves the organization closer to the desired architecture.

Gibson recently saw this approach in action, and he believes it is the only way information systems executives will be able to guide their organizations in the future. The firm in question wanted a data warehouse to provide data access to all the divisions. The company began by designing the data warehouse and then looking for the highest payback applications. When that approach faltered, they took a new tack: addressing the urgent need of a new division manager to access financial data. In building an executive support system for this manager, the group created a piece of the warehouse. The second piece will contain performance data of sales people, because that is the next most urgent company need. As such needs arise, the group will gradually migrate the company closer to the desired goal.

In the future information systems department, the outsourcing managers will essentially "keep the car running" while the strategic alignment group "changes its tires." This is the only way the department can shed its history of being seen as the anchor that keeps the firm from changing, says Gibson. Information systems executives can no longer simply make business processes more efficient, yet cast them into concrete. They must stay ahead of change and direct the organization.

Five Years from Now. Outsourcing is likely to have serious ramifications in five to ten years, Gibson told us, and the pain will be felt first by the strategic alignment consultants as they receive sudden demands from uninformed management. This will occur if line executives lose their IT competence because IT responsibility has been outsourced. If line managers are not continually required to integrate IT into their current work and new business opportunities, their organization will become less competitive.

Competence in IT must become pervasive in business units and melded into management's thinking, says Gibson, not outsourced onto someone else's shoulders. In three to five years, companies that have outsourced IT and lost this knowledge will begin to "insource" it to recoup their loses. Wise companies will avoid losing IT expertise through selective outsourcing.

A Panel's View

Paul Berger [15] has produced a series of video tapes of roundtable discussions about managing IT. On the first tape, he asked the question: Are information systems departments doomed to extinction?

Most of his CEO and academic panel members believed that the function will not go away, as long as it changes with the times. If a systems department hangs on to old ways—that is, trying to do everything itself—then, yes, it may disappear, the panel agreed. Controlling IT from one place no longer works, and is no longer appropriate, because systems departments no longer have a monopoly on technical knowledge.

The role of the department has changed from being like a craftsman to being like a city planner—with responsibility for creating, running, and enhancing the IT infrastructure. The role is to knit networks, processing, data, and skills together corporate-wide. The infrastructure needs to support both centralized and decentralized modes of work, because companies are moving toward having both coexist at one time. Furthermore, the pendulum will continue to swing between centralization and decentralization, the panelists seemed to agree.

Although the function will not disappear, it is decentralizing, because IT has become more integral to companies. It should not be pigeon-holed into a separate department, as it has been. It must change from a well-defined organizational structure to a more amorphous one, where the work is performed in many places.

To maintain cohesion, the central group needs to set direction and build a matrix of accountability among the business units. This approach will work as long as the leaders get people moving in the same direction. Without central guidance, costs increase because efforts are duplicated.

To help business units manage the use of IT, information systems departments need to share their knowledge and act as the catalyst. Spur others to use the technology, the panelists suggested, by giving them permission to experiment with the technology and providing support when they need it.

The "power" of systems departments in the future will come more from leadership, influence, and capability—and less from control. The measure of success will no longer be numbers of people but contributions to the business, said the panelists.

The panel noted that some companies have "outsourced" portions of their information systems department to other firms. Is this wise? they asked. It can present serious risks, they thought. If management abdicates an integral part of the business, they not only could become dependent on others to process competitive information, but they could lose corporate memory in those areas. The outsourcing decision will become more prevalent in the future, because information systems departments cannot maintain expertise in all areas; therefore, management needs to decide which expertise it wants to keep in-house. We discuss outsourcing further in Chapter 8.

Information systems may be very much like manufacturing, one panelist said. In the 1960s, companies had staff manufacturing groups. Now, manufacturing is decentralized out into the line units; there are no central manufacturing groups. If the systems function is the same, it will become a line, not a staff function.

The panelists arrived at two principles. First, *guidance* has become a larger part of the information systems department's role to help enterprises make better use of IT. Second, *coordination* of the work of others—whether by outside firms or within line organizations—is an increasingly important role.

Building Relationships with Line Departments

If, indeed, the future role of the central systems organization is to do more guiding and coordinating, how are companies making these changes? In the book *Transforming the IS Organization* [11a], Peter Keen presents the following three-point agenda for transforming the systems organization:

1. Redefine roles and skills for the systems organization
2. Manage information technology risk through oversight
3. Build relationships

Redefining Roles and Skills. Keen believes that words such as *innovator, consultant,* and *broker* will become associated with information systems professionals more than words such as developer and maintainer. Keen sees four roles emerging in systems departments. One is development support, which he says is similar to account management. The second role is business support, which he equates to project coordination. But for current systems project leaders to fill this role they need more people management skills. The third role is technical services, where the job holders are technically current. And the fourth role is business services. These people help set priorities for business unit systems planning. Keen notes that there will be more hybrid roles than in the past, which creates more ambiguity in planning careers.

Managing Risks. Information system risk is increasing because projects are becoming more complex, more widespread, and more expensive, says Keen. In addition, information systems personnel are being distributed among the central systems department, division systems departments, and functional systems departments. In such a situation, no one person can be expected to monitor and manage the overall risk, says Keen. Thus, top management must be responsible for oversight of IT plans, with users and information systems managers being responsible for execution of systems.

Building Relationships. Keen believes that managing the information systems function now means dealing with greater ambiguity, which requires forging new kinds of relationships. There is no way that the systems department can make the organizational changes by itself that are required to make full use of IT. The roadblock to competitive advantage generally is not technology, says Keen; it is implementation. Successful implementation requires working closely with line people. Thus, systems departments cannot remain insular, as many of them have. They need to establish better relationships with outside organizations, senior management, and users.

Cooperative external relationships. Due to the dynamic changes in many industries, and the huge investments needed to react to these changes, information systems departments must establish cooperative external relationships, says Keen. In such relationships, both vendor and customer know more about each other's future plans, they work more closely on projects, and they may even undertake some joint ventures. This has not been the traditional mode of working between systems departments and vendors, so some new forms of "partnering" probably need to be developed.

Partnerships between systems and senior management. Since information systems are becoming so important in corporate strategy, the mission and vision of the use of IT need to be voiced by senior management. This job cannot be delegated to systems management. Senior management needs to be aware that it is their role to direct the use of IT.

As an example, Keen cites the case of a large foods company in which the CEO decided that the systems and line executives should work together more closely. The firm began a large education program for systems and senior management. They organized activities, such as workshops, that brought systems and senior management together—so that they would learn to speak the same language and share a common understanding of the strategic importance of IT. The company received immediate benefits from this program, says Keen, and important new information systems were implemented soon afterward.

Partnering between systems professionals and users. Keen believes that companies need to establish structural methods to instill mutual trust and respect among systems professionals and end users, and to focus the motivations of these groups. As an example, he cites a bank that developed a letter of credit product in response to a surprise offering by a foreign competitor. The bank undertook the unusual step (for them) of including marketing people and clients on the development team. The team rapidly prototyped a PC-based product, tested it with selected clients, and fended off the competitive product.

To make this structure work, the bank had to redefine the boundaries between the team's work groups, giving each one access to the others' resources. This meant going against some established practices. The team met the challenge of the competitor, and at the same time, significantly improved relations between the information systems and marketing groups.

Federal-Mogul provides an example of a company that is improving relationships between information systems and line departments, and moving responsibility for managing the use of IT out to the line at the same time.

CASE EXAMPLE: Federal-Mogul

Federal-Mogul makes engine bearings, oil seals, ball bearings, fuel systems, electronics, and other parts for cars, light trucks, and heavy trucks. About one-half their parts are sold to original equipment companies—such as Ford, General Motors, and Chrysler. The other half goes to the "after market," that is, to repair businesses. Most of the effort at the corporate systems department goes toward support of the after-market portion of the business.

Headquarters are in Southfield, Michigan, not far from Detroit. Their mainframe serves forty-three parts service centers in the United States and Canada, but the twenty manufacturing sites use stand-alone Hewlett-Packard systems.

The recent challenge in the information systems department was to change their orientation from cost reduction to customer service. In the middle to late 1980s, cost containment was emphasized, so development groups were centralized to cut costs. Recently, however, new business executives emphasized the need to have the right information technology in place to succeed in the future. Thus, the company is planning a significant increase in IT investments—not only to create new systems but to replace old ones.

As they looked to the future, systems management realized they would have to know as much about each line of business as the people in each business unit. They decided to model their department after an independent sales organization, even though they would not actually be an independent unit. This meant getting systems managers to know each line executive and his team. So, systems management created a new position—account executive.

Account Executives. The departments of sales and marketing, logistics, corporate staff and world trade each have one account executive; manufacturing has two. They each report directly to their respective line executive and indirectly to the CEO. These account executives supervise the members of the systems staff that specialize in building systems for that function. In effect, the line executives have their own systems manager and systems staff. The line executives are also in charge of their own systems budget for that group. Thus, each month, the functional executives see what they are spending on information systems support, and they can reallocate resources as they choose.

Besides managing their functional systems staff, the account executives are also responsible for keeping their function's systems plans coordinated with corporate direction. Decisions on which user requests to implement are frequently based on how well the requested work matches the firm's strategic direction. Systems people formerly filled all user requests and were measured on user satisfaction. That measure was appropriate because their users were the mid-level managers. Now, however, the users are top management, so the focus has shifted to strategic issues.

Although the reporting structure has been decentralized, the physical location of most of the systems staff has not changed. They still reside in the central systems department. The programming staff is resisting physically being moved out into user departments, we were told. They fear they will be stranded among nonsystems professionals and that they will be constantly "bothered" by users to make little changes and fix things. They want to be with other programmers. To date, systems management has not forced them to move but that will come eventually.

All but one of the account executives is also still physically located in the systems department. Interestingly, the one account executive who has moved into his line area really likes being with the end users. Being on-site helps him solve their problems much faster.

Benefits. Federal-Mogul is deriving several benefits from this new organizational structure of the systems groups.

1. Users are accepting systems changes more readily. The users sense the desire of the systems department to be of better service.
2. Line executives more clearly understand their information processing responsibilities. Since they now are in charge of the budget for their own systems work, they are becoming more involved in systems planning.
3. This change has told the rest of the systems organization that a change in culture is occurring. Systems professionals are expected to become more of a "partner" with business unit staff.
4. Systems executives have spurred line management to plan further ahead, because they need longer lead times to put the supporting systems in place.

Challenges. One challenge in this structure is encouraging the account executives to broaden their thinking beyond the function they service. Since the account executives also report indirectly to the information services vice president, they are expected to include company-wide considerations in their own systems planning—which they have been doing. They get together to discuss cross-functional implications of future plans. Other challenges in this new arrangement are career paths and training. Since there are only two levels of systems professionals in each functional area now, there is little career growth in that area, except to move back into corporate systems management or into the line group.

One key to making this approach work is getting the support of the business executives, the vice president told us. He got them to see the need for this closer working relationship, but he had to push it. This will help the systems people better support their business, he told them. Interestingly, one account executive who did seek out the priorities in the business unit found that the priorities of the top executive and the middle managers did not agree. This discrepancy encouraged the group to reexamine their priorities and led to a meeting with the company president, who, in turn, explained his priorities.

Another key to this structure is learning to say "no." Since the operational managers are no longer the top priority users, some of their requests need to be turned down—when they do not align with company strategy. It is not possible to satisfy many masters, they have learned.

The third key to success is having very senior people in these account executive positions. Federal-Mogul has people who have had fifteen to twenty years of systems experience, they understand the business, they have good credibility with the users, and they have bought into the philosophy of the job.

In all, the vice president of information services is optimistic that this step toward "partnering" will pay off in even better use of it resources.

CONCLUSION

The transformation that information systems departments are grappling with these days, says Dick Dooley [8], is learning how to create organizations where IT decision making is shared. The main responsibility for managing the *use* of IT needs to pass to senior line executives, while the management of the IT infrastructure is retained by the systems group. This transformation is reflected in the following sayings attributed to du Pont, says Dooley:

- "We used to do it to them"—meaning the systems group required end users to obey strict rules for getting changes made to systems, submitting job requests, and so on.
- "Next, we did it *for* them"—meaning, the du Pont group moved to take a service orientation.
- "Now, we do it *with* them," which reflects the "partnering" being discussed so widely in the industry.
- "We are moving toward teaching them *how to do it themselves.*"

To achieve this transformation, CIOs must play a leadership role in their enterprise and encourage partnering with the line, at all levels in their organization.

QUESTIONS AND EXERCISES

REVIEW QUESTIONS

1. Briefly summarize each of the five responsibility areas in the leadership role for CIOs.
2. The text suggests seven ways to "learn the business." Summarize these seven ways, briefly.
3. How does Izzo suggest staffing the "today" organization?
4. What is the difference between a vision and a strategy?
5. Describe Boeing's three visions.
6. Describe the five waves of innovation from Primozic *et al.*
7. Briefly describe the five attitudes CEOs take toward IT, according to Wilson's study.
8. What are the two major roles that systems departments are likely to play in the future?, according to Gibson.
9. According to Keen, what three types of relationships do CIOs need to foster?
10. Describe the job of account executive at Federal-Mogul.

DISCUSSION QUESTIONS

1. The definition of a vision is not the responsibility of the CEO. It is the responsibility of the CEO and the other senior executives. Agree or disagree? Why?
2. Do you agree that the "rules of the game have changed" enough to warrant redefinition of the CIO's role? Won't the primary responsibility continue to be managing IT? Aren't there other executives that are better prepared and perhaps better motivated to know the business and its vision?
3. Discuss the disturbing question asked by Primozic *et al.* As we move into the knowledge management age what is going to happen to organizations whose senior executives do not yet appreciate the value of data processing, let alone information or knowledge processing?

EXERCISES

1. There is considerable discussion of the evolving role of the chief information officer. Find at least two articles that make conflicting arguments and summarize the differences.

2. There is also much discussion about partnering between systems and line organizations. Find at least two articles that discuss such partnering and summarize the factors they mention that contribute to successful partnering.

3. Contact the CEO in an organization. What is his or her title? How does he or she perceive the leadership role of the job? How do these characteristics relate to those in the text? How is he or she encouraging partnering with line departments?

REFERENCES

1. For more information about the EwIM work and a set of working papers, contact Dr. Robert Benson, Center for the Study of Information Management, Washington University, Campus Box 1106, One Brookings Drive, St. Louis, MO 63130 or Marilyn Parker, IBM, P.O. Box 12195, Dept. 997, Bldg. 668, Research Triangle Park, NC 27709.

2. PETERS, T. *Thriving on Chaos: Handbook for a Management Revolution* (Alfred A. Knopf, N.Y.), 1987, 561 pages.

3. SOCIEY FOR INFORMATION MANAGEMENT, 401 N. Michigan Ave., Chicago, IL 60601.

    a. KEEN, P. "Technology Creates Simplicity, not Complexity," *SIM Network*, April-June 1987, P. 1-3; part of SIM membership.

4. JOSEPH IZZO, A. T. Kearney, 500 S. Grand, Los Angeles, CA 90071.

5. BEATH, C., and B. IVES, "The Information Technology Champion: Aiding and Abetting, Care and Feeding," *Proceedings of the Twenty-First Annual Hawaii International Conference on System Sciences,* vol. 4, (IEEE Computer Society, Los Angeles, CA). (Vol. 4 has ten papers, case studies, and abstracts from the conference sessions on strategic and competitive information systems.)

6. WATERMAN, R., *The Renewal Factor: How the Best Get and Keep the Competitive Edge* (Bantam Books, New York), 1987, 338 pages.

7. JOEL BARKER, *Discovering the Future: The Business of Paradigms*, Infinity Limited, 831 Windbreak Trail, Lake Elmo, MN 55042. His book, published in 1985, is also available from Infinity Limited.

8. THE DOOLEY GROUP, 1380 Kenilwood Lane, Riverwoods, IL 60015.

9. THE INSTITUTE FOR THE FUTURE, 2740 Sand Hill Road, Menlo Park, CA 94025.

10. WEBB CASTOR, 19 Georgeff Road, Rolling Hills Estates, CA 90274.

11. PETER KEEN, International Center for Information Technologies, 1000 Thomas Jefferson St., N.W., Washington, DC 20007.

   a. Elam, J. J., M. J. Ginzberg, P. G. W. Keen, and R. W. Zmud, *Transforming the IS Organization,* 1988.

12. PRIMOZIC, KENNETH, EDWARD PRIMOZIC, and JOE LEBEN, *Strategic Choices: Supremacy, Survival, or Sayanara* (McGraw-Hill, New York), 1991, 272 pages.

13. DIANE WILSON, Sloan School of Management, MIT, 1 Amherst St. Room E40-146, Cambridge, MA 02139.

14. CHUCK GIBSON, CSC Index, 5 Cambridge Center, Cambridge, MA 02142.

15. PBC MANAGEMENT VIDEO PROGRAMS, headed by Paul Berger, P.O. Box 6813, Lawrenceville, NJ 08648.

THREE

The Strategic Role of Information Systems

INTRODUCTION

As we noted in Chapter 2, top management in many organizations has looked on information systems as necessary for company operations but not having much effect on their main areas of concern—earnings, market share, developing new ventures, and so forth. That view, however, is changing. Information systems can and do influence these competitive measures. Systems are competitive tools.

But not all companies that try to use IT as a competitive tool achieve the desired results. The reason: They are using outmoded processes. The 1980s search for achieving competitive advantage with IT taught an important lesson: merely automating current ways of working yields little. The organization's processes need to be "reengineered" to take advantage of the technology. So besides being a competitive tool, IT can be used strategically as a catalyst for fundamentally revamping archaic ways of doing business—ways that were appropriate for slower, paper-based processes but impede speedier computer-based operations. This use is the major, new, innovative use of computing to appear in the early 1990s.

A third important use of IT is linking organizations. Competitive systems often electronically link a company with its suppliers or customers. Reengineered business processes, for order entry, invoicing, paying, and billing, often use creative approaches to send data between organizations. The 1990s will see an acceleration of the trend toward "strategic alliances" between organizations, as they seek to serve the global marketplace. All these require development of interorganizational systems, to permit regional, national, and global electronic working.

In this chapter we deal with these three strategic uses of computing:

- As competitive tools
- To reengineer business processes
- For interorganizational linkage

AS COMPETITIVE TOOLS

In his now-classic article, "Reengineering Work: Don't Automate, Obliterate," in the July-August 1990 issue of *Harvard Business Review,* Michael Hammer [1] began by stating that the watchwords for the 1990s would be innovation and speed, service, and quality. These would be the keys to success in the 1990s marketplace.

In their quest on these four fronts, we see organizations using computers as competitive tools in two ways. One, to beat the other guys, and two, just to stay alive—that is, to be permitted to stay in the ball game. Those who do not keep up can fall so far behind that they are no longer competitive; they are acquired by the more nimble enterprises.

For a glimpse at these two uses of IT for competitive purposes, we discuss them in reverse order—first to stay in business and then to move ahead—in the important areas of speed, service, innovation, and quality.

To Stay in Business

The basis for competing in more and more industries has become sophisticated computer systems. For airlines, hotels, and rental car companies, a computer reservation system is a must—either their own or someone else's. In the drug and hospital wholesaling industries, those with an automated order entry and distribution system have gobbled up those without these systems. In financial markets, computerized trading and settlement systems are overtaking open outcry systems slowly but surely. In manufacturing, CAD and engineering, and, increasingly, electronic data interchange, are mandatory to compete. And the list goes on. As industry leaders increasingly turn to computerization to address quality, service, innovation, and speed, their competitors must do the same, or find themselves at a disadvantage.

In a few cases, the leaders have such a head start that competitors must form alliances to "get back in the game." Two examples are Galileo and Amadeus, alliances formed by European airlines to build global computer reservation systems. None of the airlines could tackle this job alone, and they feared that American Airlines or United Air Lines would capture the deregulated European market if they did not have comparable systems.

Another example is the collaboration of the three largest Swiss banks, the three regional Swiss stock exchanges, the national settlement house, and wire services in building Swiss Options and Financial Futures Exchange (SOFFEX), the world's first fully computerized options and futures exchange. Part of their motivation was to offer Swiss investors a market for Swiss financial instruments. Another motivation was to remain one of Europe's financial centers—that is, to stay competitive with London, Bonn, and Paris. Amadeus and SOFFEX are described in more detail in Andersen Consulting's *Trends in Information Technology* [2].

A New View of Experience Curves. In Chapter 2 we discussed the book *Strategic Choices* [3], by Kenneth Primozic, Edward Primozic, and Joe Leben, describing their concept of waves of innovation. Another concept from the book is their idea of "experience curves," and the importance of staying abreast or losing. Traditionally, an experience curve states that the cost of using a new technology decreases as the firm gains more experience with it.

Primozic *et al* present a new view of experience curves, which consists of a set of connected curves rather than one continuous learning curve (see Figure 3-1). Each curve represents fundamentally different technologies—in the

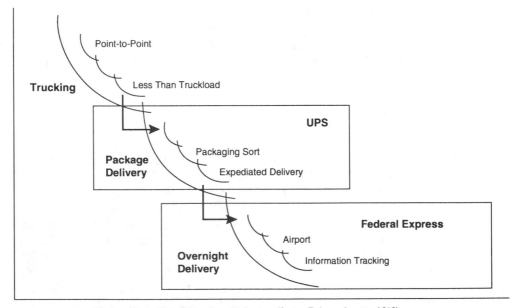

Figure 3-1 The Shipping Industry (from Primozic *et al* [2]).

product and its manufacturing and support processes. Switching from one curve to another requires substantial investments, but that decision must oftentimes be made among competing technologies, none of which is yet the clear winner. A firm that correctly identifies a new market, and the technologies to exploit it, shifts to the new experience curve and is very successful. However, sometimes management has such an emotional attachment to the current experience curve that it fails to see the next one and loses its market share to swifter competitors.

To demonstrate this principle of keeping up or losing out, consider the authors' example of the shipping industry.

CASE EXAMPLE: The Shipping Industry

Primozic *et al* [3] present an intriguing discussion of the shipping industry to illustrate their concept of "experience curves." As shown in Figure 3-1, the trucking industry initially shipped two types of truckloads of goods: full truckloads point to point and less than truckloads (LTL).

A New Industry: Package Delivery. But when United Parcel Service (UPS) based its entire business on LTL shipping, a new industry segment was born: package delivery. As a result of this new experience curve, the shipping industry changed, and UPS actually became much larger than the trucking companies, because UPS served a market with far more customers. The new technology that was key to UPS' success—and thus represented this particular experience curve—was efficient package sorting at distribution centers to maximize use of the trucks.

Another New Industry: Overnight Delivery. UPS, however, did not guarantee a delivery time nor track packages. Federal Express capitalized on these two missing functions, jumped to a new experience curve, and started yet another new industry segment: overnight delivery. Again, they became larger than UPS because they tapped an even larger market. And for UPS and other package carriers to compete, they too had to invest in the technologies to guarantee delivery and track packages. Needless to say, information technology played a crucial role in this experience curve.

Is Another New Segment Emerging? Interestingly, the authors point out that Federal Express may now be creating a newer experience curve: inventory and distribution management services. Due to their distribution network and information systems, they can handle inventory for large corporate clients and guarantee overnight delivery of these inventoried items. On this experience curve, clients can outsource not only their inventory but also distribution to Federal Express. Such clients could include parts suppliers, manufacturers, distributors, and retailers. Handling shipping directly to consumers could be the biggest market of all, surmise the authors, as electronic marketing to the home increases.

To Gain Market Share

"Competing with time," "The customer is king," "Total quality management," and "Innovate or die" have been the rallying cries of various companies, industries, and consultants over the past few years. These are the competitive watchwords of the early 1990s; therefore, not surprisingly, organizations are applying computers to competing in these realms. As an example of a company that is competing on quality, consider Federal Express.

CASE EXAMPLE: Federal Express

Federal Express, with headquarters in Memphis, Tennessee, is the leading overnight package carrier in the world. In fact, they started the industry in 1973. Their 1990 revenues were $7.7 billion, when they handled 1.5 million packages a day, using 430 aircraft, 31,000 delivery vans, and 91,000 employees at some 1,700 locations worldwide.

In October 1990, Federal Express received the Malcolm Baldrige National Quality Award in recognition of its effective management of a corporate-wide quality improvement program. We recently described their quality program in *Uncovering the Information Technology Payoffs* a special report from *I/S Analyzer* [4].

Federal Express's announced corporate goal is:

> We are committed to delivering each shipment entrusted to us on schedule 100 percent of the time. Equally important, we will maintain 100 percent accuracy of all information pertaining to each item we carry. Our objective is to have a 100 percent satisfied customer at the end of each transaction.

To them, this translates into quality.

Corporate-Wide Quality Improvement

Federal Express's quality program began in the early 1980s with quality circles in various areas of the company. In the mid-1980s, the company purchased a training program from ODI [5] to help them develop a corporate-wide program. The quality concepts were tested in two areas—business service centers and vendor accounting. Based on the success of these two pilots, the quality improvement program was rolled out company-wide in 1986. It has five main tenets.

- The program started at the top of the corporation.
- It tracks actual failures rather than percentages of success.
- The measures are from a customer perspective.
- Everyone's compensation is based on quality improvement.
- Solving root causes of failures is the main goal.

The Program Started at the Top of the Corporation. The training was first given to senior management, using the training curriculum developed by ODI.

All the top 340 officers and directors of the company went to a training class between June 1 and July 31. The class, which was led by Federal Express's quality professionals, reviewed the basic quality concepts and the quality measures that would be used. The training stressed the importance of processes in achieving quality customer service and the need to improve those processes continually.

Federal Express then took an unusual approach to training the rest of the company. They required these managers to present this class to their subordinates. This ensured that they not only learned it but that they passed it on. In turn, those subordinates taught their subordinates and so on down through the corporation. This training took place in 1987, 1988, and 1989.

It Tracks Actual Failures Rather Than Percentages of Success. Until 1985, Federal Express measured quality via success rate percentages, in such areas as on-time delivery, correct billing, calls answered on time, resolving customer complaints, and employee satisfaction. When they initiated the pilot projects in 1985, they looked to see what was missing from this form of measurement. They discovered that the small percentage difference between their 98.5 percent success rate and 100 percent zero defect rate was hiding a "hierarchy of horrors"—that is, a large number of lost packages, improper bills, damaged packages, unanswered telephone inquiries, and so forth.

The Measures are from a Customer Perspective. SQI is the sum of daily averages in twelve failure categories. All twelve are from the customer's viewpoint. They are listed below, with their severity weight—a 10-point weight is the most severe, and a 1-point weight is the least severe.

1. Missed pickup—10 points
2. Lost package—10 points
3. Damaged package—10 points
4. Delivery on wrong day—5 points
5. Complaint rehandled—5 points
6. "Overgoods" (package without addressee)—5 points
7. Late delivery on right day—1 point
8. Invoice adjustment requested by customer—1 point
9. Trace (customer request for status of a package)—1 point
10. Telephone call that is abandoned by customer—1 point
11. Missing proof of delivery—1 point
12. Special international SQI indicator—1 point

Each failure is recorded on a daily basis, multiplied by its severity weight, and added to all other failures to arrive at a single worldwide SQI. This number is reported weekly to all employees, and they pay close attention to it, because their compensation is based on it.

Everyone's Compensation is Based on Quality Improvement. SQI gets attention because every manager and professional employee above a certain level is compensated, in part, based on this index. In conjunction with SQI, other quarterly goals are set. If the goals are met, these managers and professionals get a bonus. If they are not met, no one does. Bonuses thus reward teamwork, not individual effort. Every location can see every other location's SQI. So they know where they stand with respect to their peer locations around the world.

The impact of this quality management program can be seen from the fact that the absolute number of SQI points went down 20 percent from 1988 to 1990, even though the number of packages handled rose 42 percent. That is quite an achievement.

Solving Root Causes of Failures Is the Main Goal. The main reason for tracking failures is not to deride employees but to root out the poor processes that cause the failures. To see that this happens, Federal Express has quality action teams (QATs), cross-functional teams responsible for decreasing the number of failures in one of the twelve SQI areas.

One team is the proof-of-delivery team. It is headed by the vice president of systems development, because the information systems division is responsible for seeing that the signature received on delivery of a package is matched with the billing information stored in the Memphis database.

This ten-member team regularly includes people who are either affected by these failures or can make changes to reduce the number. Currently, the team includes two station managers—from Washington, D.C., and Seattle—two people from the customer invoicing department, several engineers who work on the SuperTracker scanning device, and several members of the information systems division. (SuperTracker is a handheld device used to scan the bar code on a package and enter the name, address, time, etc. as the package moves through the system.) See Figure 3-2.

The team meets once a month to investigate that month's largest root cause of proof-of-delivery failures. The ten to fifteen main root causes are noted, and the team decides how to address the most serious one. Within the team are "root cause teams" that look for ways to eliminate their root cause. They have a lot of incentive for "getting out of the spotlight" by reducing the number of failures resulting from their root cause.

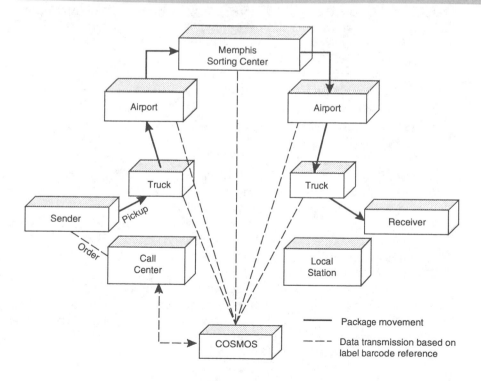

Figure 3-2 COSMOS IIB - Federal Express

For example, if "carrier did not get signature" is their root cause, the team might make sure that the carrier training classes stress the importance of this procedure. Or if they notice that one station had an inordinate amount of proof-of-delivery failures, they might ask the station manager from a more efficient station to visit the other station to help them solve the problem.

Management of the quality program is assisted by forty quality professionals in the firm, but direct control is assigned to both QATs and continuous improvement teams. The latter do not work on specific problems; instead, they continually monitor a process. If it has a sudden change in quality, they find out why. Members of both teams also have bonuses tied to improving quality in their specific areas—even if they do not have complete control over the causes.

It was this type of ingrained quality management that earned Federal Express the Malcolm Baldrige National Quality Award in 1990.

The Role of Information Systems

One indicator of the importance of information systems at Federal Express is that their IT division head was promoted to chief operating officer. Another indication of management's interest in IT is the company's five "critical success factors"—the first of which deals with IT.

- Continuously improve quality
- Improve the value of our services
- Get closer to our customers
- Make an international business profitable
- Produce a strong cash flow

A major contribution of the IT division to the quality program is the COSMOS IIB system, which automatically gathers much of the SQI data. The system is therefore not only the major on-line system for answering customer inquiries about package status, but it is also a major feedback system for the employees. It tells them how well they are doing on improving customer service quality.

The COSMOS IIB System. Soon after the firm was founded in 1973, a company-wide computer system was installed as its operational backbone. That system, which has been continually enhanced, is now called COSMOS IIB (see Figure 3-2). The system runs at the Memphis data center, which houses nine IBM 3090s and handles 14 million transactions a day, or nearly ten transactions per package in the system. The center is linked via 56 kbps (thousand bits per second lines) running IBM's System Network Architecture (SNA), to 75 dispatch centers and 24 call centers, which handle customers' calls requesting package pickup.

Use of COSMOS IIB starts when a Federal Express courier or station employee scans the bar code on an envelope using the company's handheld SuperTracker device when a package is picked up. This initial scan automatically time and date stamps the package. When the courier returns to the delivery truck and places the SuperTracker in its "shoe," this information is transmitted to the Memphis data center. The average elapsed time from scanning to posting in the Memphis database is four minutes.

From this point on, each time the package changes hands—loaded in the truck, loaded on a plane, unloaded at a distribution center, and so forth—the bar code is scanned, thereby updating the package's location. At any time, the sender or receiver of the package can obtain a status report by calling Federal Express. When the package is delivered and signed for, its delivery time and "proof of delivery" are recorded.

This entire operation is supported by COSMOS IIB, and as mentioned, several of the twelve failure measures are taken directly from its data. The IT division plays an important role in the company's quality improvement program by providing timely and accurate data to employees so they see what needs to be improved.

Benefits of the Quality Program

Federal Express is realizing some significant benefits from their zealous pursuit of quality. They have "proven" that quality equals productivity. The day they achieved the lowest SQI—99.7 percent service level—was the day they also achieved the lowest cost per package. They believe they have demonstrated that quality has a bottom-line effect.

Quality also has a cultural effect: There has been a noticeable increase in teamwork and cooperation at the company. One of the reasons Federal Express won the Malcolm Baldrige National Quality Award was that the six Baldrige examiners who visited the company for three days were impressed with how ingrained quality had become in the company.

Quite by accident, these examiners got to see quality-based teamwork in action while visiting the IT operations department. One of the mainframes went down, which automatically caused a "red alert" alarm to go off. People literally ran to their assigned posts and got the system up and running in minutes. This type of teamwork is also happening more often across organizational boundaries.

Gradually, employees are feeling empowered to be responsible for quality, even when it is not in their area. They are more willing to suggest improvements. And they are being rewarded for making these efforts.

Uncovering Strategic Uses of Systems

It bears repeating that IT is only one component in competing successfully. The major lesson of the 1980s was that technology alone does not yield success. Strategy, people, business operations, and technology must all be aligned; moving ahead in one and not the others undermines effective execution.

Even so, it is a useful exercise to look for opportunities to use IT strategically. So we discuss the following two approaches for uncovering strategic uses:

- Analyze competitive forces
- Study "strategic thrusts"

Analyze Competitive Forces

The most widely quoted framework for thinking about the strategic use of IT is the competitive forces model proposed by Michael Porter of the Harvard Business School. The following discussion draws on his book, *Competitive Strategy* [6], as well as on the ideas of Gregory Parsons [7], who was formerly at Harvard and is now at the University of Maine. Porter believes companies must contend with five competitive forces, as shown in Figure 3-3.

One force is the *threat of new entrants* into one's industry. For instance, says Parsons, information technology—in the form of automated teller machines—has substantially eroded the barriers to entry of new "branch banks" in the banking industry. Conversely, in the distribution industry, IT has built new barriers. New entrants are faced with their competitors' automated order entry networks already in place.

A second force is the *bargaining power of customers and buyers.* Buyers seek lower prices and bargain for higher quality, says Porter. From an information systems viewpoint, sophisticated quality control systems are being used by automobile manufacturers to make steel producers more conscious of quality, says Parsons.

A third force is the *bargaining power of suppliers.* For instance, IT is allowing suppliers of funds to financial institutions (depositors, investors) to

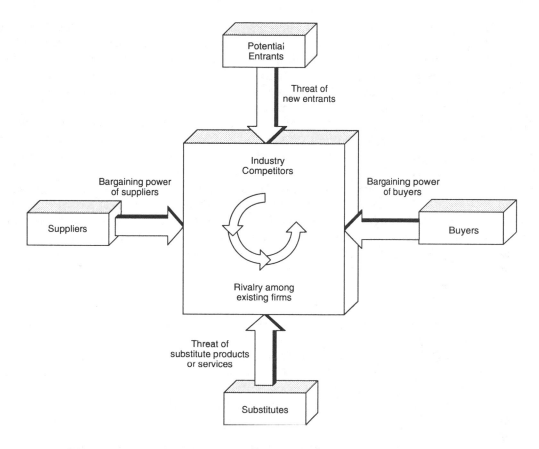

Figure 3-3 Michael Porter's Competitive Analysis Model (from Porter [6])

monitor the economy and move their funds easily, says Parsons; this is increasing their power.

A fourth competitive force, according to Porter, is *substitute products or services.* In the information systems arena, electronic mail can be a substitute for paper mail. And CAD/CAM systems allow competitors to duplicate an innovative product faster.

The fifth force is the intensity of *rivalry among competitors.* The most intense rivalry exists in slow-growth industries with equally balanced firms, where there are high fixed costs, and without significant "switching" costs—which deter buyers from switching from one product to another. Here too, says Parson, information technology is having its impact. Frequent flyer programs linked to credit cards and long-distance telephone companies are changing rivalries significantly. Similar "IT-based" alliances are appearing in other industries as well.

Porter's Strategies. Porter presents three strategies for dealing with these competitive forces. His first is to differentiate products. By making products or services different (that is, better in the eyes of customers), a firm may be able to charge higher prices, perhaps deter customers from moving to competitive products, lower the bargaining power of buyers, and so on. This is probably the most popular of his three strategies.

Porter's second strategy is to become the low-cost producer. He warns that being simply one of the low-cost producers is not enough. Not being the lowest-cost producer causes a company to be stuck in the middle, with no real competitive edge.

His third strategy is to focus on a segment of a product line or a geographical market—finding a niche. Companies that focus on a niche can often serve their target market effectively and efficiently—at times being both the low-cost producer and having a highly differentiated product as well.

Again, this framework has been a popular way to view competitive threats and opportunities.

Study Strategic Thrusts

Extending the work of Porter, Charles Wiseman of Columbia University Business School uses a framework that he calls "the theory of strategic thrusts," described in his book *Strategy and Computers* [8]. Wiseman proposes studying strategic thrusts by purposely searching for opportunities rather than letting ideas appear as they might from around the organization. To understand the steps in his approach, consider the work he did with GTE.

CASE EXAMPLE: GTE

Rackoff, Wiseman, and Ullrich [9] describe a five-step process for uncovering strategic opportunities used at GTE, a large international telecommunications and electronics company. They used this process in their largest—division-their domestic telephone operations division. The division has its own data services unit, GTE Data Services.

In phase 1, as shown in Figure 3-4, the head of information systems planning of the data services unit introduced his president to the idea of using IT to gain competitive advantage. This introduction was accomplished through informal meetings and memos. The purpose of this phase was to get the president's endorsement to proceed.

With the president's approval, a three-day idea-generation meeting was held off-site. It involved middle managers and systems analysts from the data services organization.

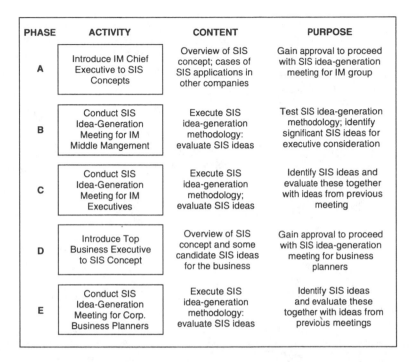

PHASE	ACTIVITY	CONTENT	PURPOSE
A	Introduce IM Chief Executive to SIS Concepts	Overview of SIS concept; cases of SIS applications in other companies	Gain approval to proceed with SIS idea-generation meeting for IM group
B	Conduct SIS Idea-Generation Meeting for IM Middle Mangement	Execute SIS idea-generation methodology: evaluate SIS ideas	Test SIS idea-generation methodology; identify significant SIS ideas for executive consideration
C	Conduct SIS Idea-Generation Meeting for IM Executives	Execute SIS idea-generation methodology; evaluate SIS ideas	Identify SIS ideas and evaluate these together with ideas from previous meeting
D	Introduce Top Business Executive to SIS Concept	Overview of SIS concept and some candidate SIS ideas for the business	Gain approval to proceed with SIS idea-generation meeting for business planners
E	Conduct SIS Idea-Generation Meeting for Corp. Business Planners	Execute SIS idea-generation methodology: evaluate SIS ideas	Identify SIS ideas and evaluate these together with ideas from previous meetings

Figure 3-4 SIS Planning Process (from Rackoff, Wiseman, and Ullrich [9])

The session began with a tutorial on the theory of strategic information systems, presented by Charles Wiseman. This tutorial explained the approach they would be using to uncover and categorize opportunities. His approach begins by identifying the target of the application. Is the system to be aimed at suppliers, customers, or competitors, he asks? Next, determine how IT might be used to pursue a strategic thrust, says Wiseman. He proposes five thrusts, which can be used either offensively (to seek competitive advantage) or defensively (to reduce a competitor's advantage).

One thrust is *differentiation*—distinguishing a product from others. A second is *cost*. For example, a cost thrust might lower a firm's costs or raise costs for competitors. A third thrust is *innovation*—doing something new that may change the way business in the industry is conducted. A fourth is *growth*. Sales growth could come from geographical dispersion, for example. The fifth thrust is *forming alliances*. A company could expand by forming an alliance with another enterprise through acquisition, merger, or such. Companies often choose a combination of thrusts when formulating a strategy, says Wiseman, and IT can play a key role in making a strategy possible.

Following the tutorial, some twenty case examples were discussed and categorized. Then the information management planning staff described GTE's competitive position—its markets, business strategy, products, suppliers, competitors, strengths, and weaknesses.

Next, the group divided into brainstorming teams of five to six members each. The teams were given different areas to explore. One group looked at opportunities relating to suppliers, another studied customers, a couple looked at existing information systems, and others looked for new systems. The groups filled in a short form for each idea.

Following the two-hour brainstorming period, each team presented its ideas to the entire group. Duplicate ideas were eliminated, and others were clarified. Then the ideas were ranked by their degree of competitive advantage, their development cost, their feasibility, and the likelihood that the idea would provide a sustainable competitive advantage. This ranking scheme identified four categories of systems—from "blockbuster" to "not worth further consideration."

In the final phase of the three-day meeting, the most promising ideas were refined. A second meeting was then held with information systems personnel from the local GTE telephone companies. Both meetings uncovered many of the same opportunities, and each reached a consensus on the "blockbuster" ideas.

Next, the data services president—satisfied that the process was producing results—gained approval for a third brainstorming session from the top business executive of the telephone operations division. This third meeting involved marketing and strategic planning managers—those responsible for initiating new strategic directions. This session also produced consensus on opportunities.

The entire process identified some one hundred ideas for uses of IT. Of these, eleven were rated as having high potential, with five believed to be "blockbusters." Funds were allocated to develop these. This planning effort opened the eyes of many managers to the potential of IT, say the authors. The company has subsequently added a strategic IT module to its long-range plan.

TO REENGINEER BUSINESS PROCESSES

Although the emphasis in the 1980s was on using IT for competitive advantage, the thrust in the early 1990s has turned inward, specifically to using IT as a catalyst to "reengineer" outmoded business practices. By "reengineering," we mean fundamentally redesigning how the enterprise works—its procedures, control mechanisms, reporting relationships, decision makers, compensation criteria, and so forth—and generally making IT an integral part of operations. The goal is to rid the firm of ways of working that were appropriate for the paper-based world, and replace them with work modes that leverage the attributes of IT.

We see four main reasons for this shift from an external to an internal focus in applying IT:

1. The pressures of the 1990s are forcing companies to focus on new competitive strategies—quality, cycle time, customer service, and niche markets.
2. There were enough failures in the 1980s in using IT to gain competitive advantage to force management to rethink its strategies for achieving this goal.
3. Companies are being forced to cut operating expenses so significantly that traditional methods no longer work.
4. The cost/performance of computer hardware and telecommunications has dropped so dramatically that IT has become practical for a far wider variety of uses than a few years ago.

These four drivers are forcing management to seriously consider fundamentally changing how their businesses operate.

Where Are We Headed?

To see what changes are likely, we need to see where we are headed. In 1990, in his book, *Shaping the Future*, Peter Keen made the eight prognostications about business in 1993 shown in Figure 3-5. Since he has been an insightful observer in the field for many years, his views are worth serious consideration. We believe that most organizations will not have reached them by the mid-1990s.

1. Every large firm in every industry will have from 25 to 80 percent of its cash flow processed on-line.
2. Electronic data interchange will be the norm.
3. Point-of-sale and electronic payments will be core services.
4. Image technology will be an operational necessity.
5. Work will be distributed, and reorganization will be commonplace.
6. Work will increasingly be location independent.
7. Electronic business partnerships will be standard.
8. Reorganizations will be frequent, not exceptional.

Figure 3-5 Peter Keen's Prognostications for the Mid-1990s (from Keen [10])

Every large firm in every industry will have from 25 to 80 percent of its cash flow processed on-line. Many were above 50 percent in 1990, through computer reservation systems and on-line ordering, distribution, point of sale, and customer service systems. He foresees the future being *the on-line company* where uninterrupted communication links are a business necessity.

EDI will be the norm. Just as customers do not transact business without telephones, some large organizations now require their suppliers to use EDI. It will become as central to global operations as telex and fax, he projects. The economics are too compelling to ignore: error rates cut in half, delays reduced by days, and costs saved from $5 to $50 per document.

Point-of-sale and electronic payments will be core services, just like EDI, airline reservation systems, just-in-time (JIT) inventory systems, and computer-integrated manufacturing. It makes no sense to have JIT and other zero-delay operations without accompanying on-line payment systems. JIT inventory is sure to lead to JIT payment.

Image technology will be an operational necessity, he projects. Documents have become the enemy, because they cause organizational complexity and administrative overhead. Image processing, at long last, applies IT to the true cost-intensive operations: document processing. The 1990s will be the decade of imaging, he believes.

Work will be distributed, and reorganization will be commonplace. Whenever enterprises reorganize, the work and the information is redistributed. Since many corporate changes will occur, the information, communications, and processing must be able to move with the work.

Work will increasingly be location independent. When cash flow is on-line, reasons Keen, work can be brought to people using workstations rather than vice versa. Therefore, IT can lead to new sources of organizational advantage.

Electronic business partnerships will be standard. Every large firm will have extended its IT infrastructure to encompass customers and suppliers, predicts Keen; therefore, alliance partners may be chosen based on the quality of their IT facilities.

Reorganizations will be frequent, not exceptional. Furthermore, the flexibility of a firm's IT platform will significantly affect how quickly it can reorganize. In short, this platform will be the major determinant of its "business degrees of freedom" in the 1990s, says Keen. The infrastructure determines what products can be sold and which markets and locations can be addressed.

Using Information Technology as a Catalyst for Change

Several researchers have discussed ways IT can be used as a catalyst for change. We present just two views here; both from professors at the Harvard Business School.

To "Informate" Rather than Just Automate. In her 1988 book, *In the Age of the Smart Machine* [11], Shoshana Zuboff coined the term "informating," which she defines as using information gathered about automated processes to improve the process or change the work performed.

If managers took advantage of this newly identified use of computing, they probably would restructure their organizations significantly, postulates Zuboff. But in the companies she studied, managerial status quo was too deeply ingrained for the managers to empower their employees to use this process information to make significant changes. To do so would mean that they—the employees—would do some of the work of the managers. What would that leave for the managers to do?

We have just begun to hear about companies that are applying Zuboff's ideas, because of the recent emphasis on business reengineering.

To Structure the Firm in New Ways. To achieve the on-line world mentioned by Keen, and to successfully function in it, some companies have already restructured themselves to take advantage of the new organizational options afforded by IT. At a recent meeting of the institutional members of the Society of Information Management [12], Professor Warren McFarlan noted that IT allows companies to organize the way they choose. In itself, IT does not favor centralization or decentralization; companies can choose either, or perhaps both. To illustrate his point, he described one of his favorite case studies, Otis Elevator, and how it is taking advantage of IT organizationally.

CASE EXAMPLE: Otis Elevator

Otis Elevator, with headquarters in Hartford, Connecticut, is the largest U.S. manufacturer of elevators. Although manufacturing is the heart of its business, the company makes money in after-sales service. Traditionally, the company's 122 branch offices have been the interface with its customers, because mechanics are dispatched from these sites. These offices report to twenty districts, which create monthly summaries of performance. These districts, in turn, are organized into three zones, which produce total performance reports for the Hartford headquarters one month after receiving reports from districts.

Thus, Otis has a bottom-up structure with autonomy at the branches. The problem with this structure is that some of the branches are well run whereas others are not. Some dispatch repairmen within fifteen minutes; others take two to three hours, and require two or three visits to finish a repair. Furthermore, quality-control problems were not visible; they have been hidden in the branches.

Centralizing Customer Service. To rectify this situation, in 1986, all requests for service in the United States. were directed to OtisLine— a centralized dispatch center with a database containing a description of each of the 500,000 installed Otis elevators, along with each one's service record for the past year. When a service request is made, the operator displays that elevator's record on the screen and then uses an expert system to choose a mechanic. Within two seconds, the "brick" (beeper) on that mechanic's belt rings (softly, so as not to disturb his work), the mechanic views the message on a five-line liquid crystal display, and uses the radio phone to find out more about the problem.

As a sidelight, these "bricks" have had an unexpected effect on company camaraderie. The mechanics have a fairly lonely job; therefore, a radio phone was included with the beeper. Thus the mechanics can talk to each other; and talk they do—about the line-up for the upcoming softball game, the bowling league, and so on. These phones have facilitated communications, especially informal communications, which the company has wisely allowed to continue.

Due to this centralized information management, Otis can consolidate information about elevator repairs, identify design problems, and redesign their product line faster. Otis also uses the centralized information to flag mechanics' problems and identify who needs more training on repairing certain types of elevators.

Between 1986 and 1990, Otis was able to decrease elevator service problems by 50 percent, because of their centralized tracking system. And it was information technology that allowed them to organize this way.

Decentralizing Decision Making. The next iteration in Otis's transformation will address the question: Why do we need branches, districts, zones, and a corporate office? Why not consolidate districts and zones? These sites were originally established to maintain control, but with the centralized system, the company can allow the branches to manage their own mechanics, while headquarters maintains centralized control over dispatching. Otis is thus considering moving more decision making down to the branches.

Otis can consider such a reorganization because their control mechanisms have changed—from people to IT. This shift is understandably upsetting company personnel. Therefore, to institute further organizational changes, the chairman must lead, because the process of getting buy-in is large.

As of 1991, Otis was continuing their long-term program of architecture development, so as not to give their competitors a chance to catch up. In addition to focusing on providing better service, they are now concentrating on reducing their cost structure and moving decision making downward in the organization.

Principles for Guiding Business Reengineering

In his ground-breaking 1990 article on reengineering mentioned at the beginning of the chapter [1], Michael Hammer presents seven principles for business reengineering. They are lessons he has learned about how to think about business processes in new ways.

For example, as shown in Figure 3-6, Ford Motor Company significantly revamped their accounts payable department by instituting "invoiceless payments." Rather than pay suppliers when an invoice was received which required matching fourteen data items, they switched to paying when goods were received (which required only matching three data items)—as long as those goods are recorded as on order in the company's database. This radical change reduced head count in the accounts payable department by 75 percent and significantly simplified the payment process.

Hammer notes that to succeed at reengineering, the organization must challenge its old rules and assumptions, such as "customers do not repair equipment," or "invoices are necessary to pay bills," or "local warehouses are needed to provide good customer service." The lessons he has learned are as follows.

Organize Around Outcomes, Not Tasks. Many business processes have become complex because they link specialized tasks and paper files—which only one person at a time can use. Focusing on the desired outcomes helps people consider new ways to get the work done. For instance, one person at a workstation can do the tasks formerly split among ten or twenty who each handled only one piece.

People Who Use the Output Should Perform the Process. Hammer means that the people who need, say, supplies should be able to order them through an on-line purchasing system themselves. Why have intermediaries when none are needed? Once the database of approved vendors is established, people can use it to perform their own ordering.

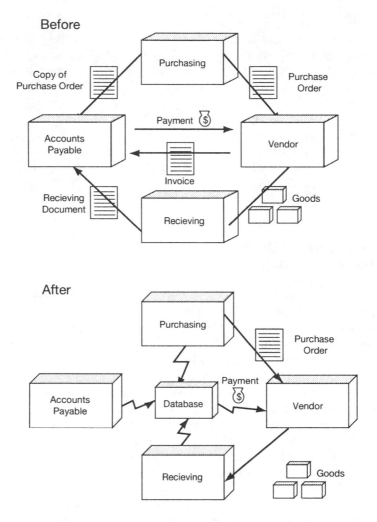

Figure 3-6 Ford's Reengineered Accounts Payable Process (from Hammer [1])

Include Information Processing in the "Real" Work That Produces the Information. This means that those who produce the information should also process it. Again, following this principle eliminates the specialization so prevalent in business—where one group collects data and others process it. As an example, at Ford, the receiving department produces the information about the goods it has received, and it also processes the payment information rather than passing it to the accounts payable department.

Treat Geographically Dispersed Resources As If They Were Centralized. By using networks and common systems, companies can simultaneously get the benefits of centralization (economies of scale) and decentralization (flexibility and responsiveness). For instance, a central purchasing department can negotiate contracts, and local departments can draw on the database for their ordering.

Link Parallel Activities Rather Than Integrate Them. This lesson recommends coordinating similar kinds of work while it is in process rather than after completion. For instance, groups building the various subsystems of a product can use a collective database and workstations to coordinate their work while working in parallel and shortening product development. Or dispersed bank departments can keep track of each other's dealings with common customers in the same way.

Let "Doers" Be Self-Managing. By putting decisions where the work is performed, and by building controls into the process, companies can compress themselves both vertically and horizontally, says Hammer. They no longer need to separate the workers from the managers, because decision aids, such as expert systems, can be given to doers.

Capture Information Once and At Its Source. Since it is no longer difficult to transmit information, departments and functions do not need to collect it themselves; they can share what others have collected.

As his final recommendation, Hammer urges management to think big—take seventy-eight days out of an eighty-day cycle, cut overhead by 75 percent, eliminate 80 percent of the errors, and so forth. These are not unrealistic goals for many companies, he believes.

Lessons about Reengineering

The consultants at Andersen Consulting are noticing that an increasing amount of their work calls for "business integration"—that is, aligning strategy, people, technology, and business processes—to significantly cut costs, reduce non-value-added work, and streamline client organizations. Unless these four elements are synchronized and tackled in concert, they say, the benefits of it will be diluted.

Their largest business integration program to date has been with the U.K. Department of the Social Security (DSS). We will briefly describe the work and then discuss the lessons Andersen Consulting learned about business reengineering.

CASE EXAMPLE: U.K. Department of Social Security

DSS collects national insurance contributions and pays benefits and entitlements. Along with the Employment Service, they have eighty thousand employees in two thousand local offices throughout the United Kingdom. The departments work with 10 million pensioners, 5 million people on income support (to maintain minimum living standard), 2 million unemployed, 285,000 families on family credit (to encourage parents on low incomes to continue to work), and 40 million national insurance contributors.

In 1983, department management decided to replace processing claims on a benefit-by-benefit basis with handling claimants on a "the whole-person" basis. This new program synchronizes the major elements of the department: strategy, people, technology, and processes with three main objectives.

- To make the local offices more efficient and to save money
- To make the national programs more effective and to provide better service
- To give employees more satisfying jobs and better working conditions

This whole-person strategy depends on significant use of IT. An integrated set of systems keeps track of all the government's national insurance and benefits dealings with each person; therefore, a clerk in any local office can immediately get a "snapshot" of each citizen's dealings with DSS and Employment Services. Formerly, benefits were compartmentalized so that this cross-department view could not be attained. The new systems break down these organizational walls.

Andersen Consulting has been the lead consultant for this program, which contains twenty major projects to be implemented over twelve years' time. Equally important as developing the computer applications has been introducing change to the eighty thousand employees, many of who have never used computers; therefore, change management has constituted a major part of the program.

The four main components in the technical infrastructure are a central index, branch office LANs, a country-wide X.25 network that uses Open Systems Interconnect (OSI) protocols, and four main data centers.

To achieve the whole person image, the department created a central index containing the name, address, and national insurance number of 55 million people, along with the benefits they receive. The index will eventually be accessible from forty thousand terminals in the seventeen hundred branches.

A local server in each branch serves forty to fifty terminals on a LAN, linking the server via an X.25 network to one of four data centers. In addition to being communication nodes, these servers also store the screen templates used by the applications. This local storage reduces communication volumes over the X.25 network. That network uses all OSI protocols up to level 4, the network layer. The four data centers house eighty-three mainframes. The applications run on these mainframes rather than on distributed workstations or servers, so that consistency is maintained across the local offices.

Use of IT has significantly increased DSS's organizational flexibility, and in so doing, has opened up new ways to deliver social security. For example, twenty offices in downtown London have been moved to Scotland and Northern England. Telephone calls from the London residents are routed to these distant back offices for the price of a local call. These citizens are now receiving better service over the phone than they formerly received in person, the department now has an ample supply of labor, and office space is much less expensive in these outlying areas. The departments will also be able to draw on the central index as an information resource to better understand and serve specific groups of claimants.

Looking back over the progress to date, Andersen Consulting and DSS have learned the following lessons, among others, about business integration and reengineering business change. For a more complete discussion, see the DSS *Close-Up* [13] published by Andersen Consulting.

Business Integration is a Process, Not a Project. A valuable lesson learned through the DSS work is that business integration is an ongoing program of interrelated projects that are conducted over many years' time. The business vision drives a whole host of programs—for building the technical infrastructure, redesigning operations, introducing change, and so forth. Since such fundamental changes take years, such an endeavor needs a continuing, stable point of reference, perhaps through several changes in management.

People Need Time to Change. One reason such endeavors take so long is that people need time to change. The goal of the team leaders is to institute just the right amount of change, not too much for them to absorb. A vision of a new way of working can be unsettling to many employees. Therefore, give them time, recommends Andersen, time to see the vision will work and time to realize that the changes will be worth the effort.

Recognize the Potential Up Front. On the other hand, most people do not appreciate up front how significantly the business could be changed for the better. Get people to "dream" about how they would like to improve the business, up front, recommends Andersen. And get them thinking about the full effects of the changes early. Thoroughly talk about the options for several years into the future.

Make Job Changes Throughout the Organization. Reengineering work can concentrate mainly on redesigning workers' jobs. Andersen recommends focusing equally on the jobs of middle managers, because they are in danger of either losing their job or doing entirely new kinds of work. Furthermore, project leaders need to manage all the constituencies—clerical workers, line management, upper management, and even customers. Significant change projects impose severe stresses; they need the energies of all those involved, as well as significant managerial guidance to succeed.

Manage the Pace of Change. A major lesson learned at DSS was that managing the people component was as large a task as developing the systems. Therefore, they developed a "change management" strategy to test out the new procedures, redefine jobs, help employees understand the coming changes, and get help in making the transition.

A model office was created to help the civil servants visualize the new work style. A real caseload was handled by some forty volunteers from around the country. They studied the ergonomics of the new work environment, they chose the furniture, and they tested the training programs and prototype software.

New job definitions were written for the supervisors, who would no longer need to spend their time double-checking the calculations of their workers. The new system handled this complexity. To define their new job, a team used job satisfaction models and workshops with local office staff.

Twenty-two offices pilot tested the first version for six months before it was approved for nationwide rollout. From there, ten offices were added each week. These "pilot offices" have continued to play an important role in fostering change, by testing out new work procedures and recommending the best ones to the other offices. Originally, many of the local office managers thought that they could achieve the required productivity increases by just computerizing their procedures. Once they realized this was not the case, they sought guidance on ways to restructure the work.

Regional implementation teams were established to provide hands-on help in managing the transition. The managers of these teams are responsible for the overall schedule for each region—from managing office renovations to scheduling training sessions. They assist local office managers in preparing their change program—deciding who gets trained and when, determining how they will achieve the mandated cost reductions, and figuring out how existing files will be entered into the system.

Training for local office staff is being held at thirty-two area training centers. Every week, some fourteen hundred staff begin the ten-day training course. While they are being trained, rotating conversion staffs handle their office work.

Andersen Consulting and DSS conclude that business integration can succeed if a guiding vision is put in place, if program management is given proper support, if the underlying technical problems are tackled fully and early enough, and if people are given the appropriate help in changing the way they work.

The Role of the Systems Department

The Index Foundation, a research arm of CSC Index, explored the role of information technology in transforming the business in a recent report [14]. They studied several roles for the systems department, all based on the premise that IT is an essential ingredient of redesigned processes.

Be an Influencer. According to the report, systems directors will be influencers; although it is unlikely they will lead the transition. Few systems departments have the power and influence to spearhead the transition. Senior line managers are in a far better position. However, systems directors are likely to make an important contribution in the development of the business vision, by explaining to senior management the kinds of structural changes needed to exploit IT. Furthermore, a systems director may lead the "alignment team," that is, the team that harmonizes IT with the firm's business strategy and structure.

Participate on Multifunctional Teams. Multidisciplinary teams will be the change agents, says the Index Foundation specifically chartered with defining new business processes and the supporting information systems. These teams are appearing both in the systems department and in functional divisions, states the report; they include people from planning, organizational development, human resources, and information systems. With their experience in systems analysis, systems staff are well qualified to participate in the analysis and redesign of processes as well as define the IT requirements to support those processes.

Build More Flexible Applications Faster. Organizations that move to managing processes rather than functions will innovate continually, says the Index Foundation; therefore, they will need application systems that are both quickly built and flexible. Application packages are one way to increase delivery speed, but single-function packages will not suffice. Suites of packages that fit together to cover a wide range of business functions are needed. Such packages do exist. Computer-aided software engineering (CASE) tools, prototyping, and perhaps even object-oriented development techniques are other approaches to increasing development speed, notes the report.

To achieve flexibility, systems need to be designed, built, and maintained from the viewpoint that they will continue to evolve. For example, the research report references one firm that first reduced paper flow by automating its order processing and accounting functions. It then linked order processing with accounting, by providing terminals to distributors. It also increased throughput speed and reduced paper work in its factories by introducing computer-integrated manufacturing. These systems then became the building blocks for a higher-order system that links ordering, processing, and manufacturing. Orders are now downloaded from distributors' terminals directly to shop-floor computers, enabling the company to process orders, manufacture, and ship products within 24 hours. This manufacturer saw their system portfolio as continually evolving; that is the view of a process-oriented firm.

Introduce Process-Supporting Technologies. Existing systems may not be robust enough to support new business processes, especially if they are undocumented and are built on incompatible IT platforms. In a process-driven firm, systems must be integrated and must use process-supporting technologies. Image processing is one such technology, because it allows various departments to link their processes. Electronic data interchange is another such technology, because it opens up the electronic marketplace. Other process-supporting technologies include video conferencing, electronic mail, and groupware (for supporting business teams), observes the Index Foundation.

Be the Custodian of the Firm's Technical Architecture. A technical architecture is the key to systems flexibility and adaptability. This architecture is the set of rules and standards that define how the information systems will work—from data to telecommunications to the display screens. Without it, integrating systems to support a process-based organization is virtually impossible, according to the CSC Index researchers. Furthermore, without central control of that architecture, the firm cannot exercise control across the firm's use of IT. The two major challenges for the systems department in defining the architecture is permitting diverse systems and technologies to co-mingle, and sorting out the competing standards in the open systems arena. There are no risk-free paths these days, reports the Index Foundation, but the system's department's role is crucial in assisting its organization's move from a functional orientation to a process orientation.

FOR INTERORGANIZATIONAL LINKAGE

Several trends are increasing the need for companies to develop links to other organizations. Many of the competitive systems described earlier require the flow of information to suppliers and customers. The reengineering of fundamental business processes often requires changes in the information flows between organizations, as in the case of Ford's accounts payable system. Finally, many companies are forming "strategic alliances" that require coordinated systems in their joint ventures. Thus, the third strategic role of IT is for interorganizational systems.

Characteristics of Interorganizational Systems

We define interorganizational systems (IOS) as those that require at least two parties with different objectives to collaborate on the development and operation of a joint computer-based system. Generally, each party develops and operates its portion of the system, but each portion will not work without the other parts. We see eight characteristics of interorganizational systems that distinguish them from other types of systems.

IOS Require Partners. The main distinguishing characteristic is that it takes at least two parties to create an IOS. Thus the partners in the venture must have a *willingness* to cooperate. This is not always as easy as it sounds, especially if the resulting new business arrangement requires changing the way a company operates or is expensive to implement.

The partners must also have the *ability* to perform the work. For example, the in-house systems in some companies are not able to accept EDI transactions without a substantial programming effort. EDI is the computer-to-computer exchange of standard business transactions including payment/remittance advice, request for quotations, receiving advice, purchase-order change requests, and even corporate trade payments. Some banks' systems are not able to easily process the corporate-to-corporate electronic payments that sometimes accompany EDI transactions.

So the partnership required in interorganizational systems is not only based on readiness but also on willingness and ability.

Standards Play a Key Role. Standards play a major role in permitting many IOS efforts to get off the ground. Companies want to leverage their system development investment as much as possible. If they develop a system to work with one trading partner, they want to reuse portions of that system for other trading partners.

Data and communication standards permit companies to reuse systems they build. If standards are available, companies are willing to build systems that would not be economically feasible for a single use. For internally built systems, the standards can be company policies. For intercompany systems, the standards need to be industry, national, or international standards.

Education Is Important. The education of potential partners is often more of a hurdle than the technology. In the emerging field of EDI, education of potential trading partners is far and away the biggest problem. Although EDI technology is straightforward, many information systems people (and corporate executives) are not familiar with EDI. In a cooperative effort, the more advanced partner often must pull the other partners along through education.

Third Parties Are Often Involved. Coordination of joint systems often entails using a third party—perhaps to educate people, probably to develop and maintain the standards, and often to provide the links between the separate company systems.

As an example, suppose that you decide to send purchase orders to your suppliers electronically. How are you going to do that? Are you going to have your operations people create a schedule for dialing each supplier's computer at a specified time each day to deliver those orders? What happens if one of those computers is down at the time you are to make the call? What procedure will you use to retransmit the order?

Instead of working out all these details, it might be easier to use a third-party service that provides electronic mailboxes to all these suppliers. You make one call a day to deliver the orders, and the service distributes the purchase orders to the proper mailboxes. When benefits come from volume, the greater the number of trading partners, the more complex interconnecting the systems becomes. Third parties reduce this complexity.

The Work Must Be Synchronized. Another distinguishing feature of interorganizational systems is that the various efforts need to be synchronized. For instance, suppose several companies are using a data format standard to exchange invoices electronically. What happens when the standard is updated? How do the companies synchronize their switch to the new version? Synchronization can be achieved by the standards body issuing the updated standard along with a predetermined cut-over date. Then all trading partners know when others will be ready to accept the new version.

There is also the need to synchronize communication schedules, pilot tests, recovery procedures, and the like. Although these are not new problems, the magnitude of the cooperative effort can increase the complexity of the problem, so new solutions may be required.

Work Processes Are Often Reevaluated. IOS appear to nudge companies to reexamine their work procedures. Often, computer systems have been developed to mimic the paper systems they replaced. In IOS, this may be less appropriate. For instance, companies have discovered that sending EDI shipping notices electronically completely eliminates the need to send invoices. Once a shipping notice has been received, and the merchandise has been accepted, the recipient company can issue a payment without an invoice. Obviously, such a change must be acceptable to both trading partners, and both must alter their company procedures.

The element that causes the most changes in company procedures is time. Consciously or unconsciously, most people factor in waiting time when they deal with paper media. For example, the engineers in one company

1. They require "partners."
2. Standards play a key role.
3. Education is important.
4. Third parties are often involved.
5. The work must be synchronized.
6. Work processes are often reevaluated.
7. Technical aspects are not the major issue.
8. Efforts often cannot be secretive.

Figure 3-7 Characteristics of Interorganizational Systems

requested paper purchase orders knowing that they had ten days to make changes before the purchase orders would be sent. When the company moved to electronic purchase orders, that ten-day "information float" time disappeared. This caused havoc in the company, until the employees adjusted to the new time element. So companies need to be careful when they significantly change the timing in a business process.

Technical Aspects Are Not the Major Issue. In interorganizational systems, technical issues are minor compared with the relationship issues. The major challenge is building the new electronic relationships. As mentioned earlier, this often requires reevaluating current practices and educating many levels of employees.

Efforts Often Cannot Be Secretive. Last, but not least, IOS often require more openness than traditional system development, especially when industry standards are being adopted. Companies that want to promote electronic collaboration through industry standards find that they must become involved in the standards work to keep the standards evolving and useful. They also find that they need to demonstrate their commitment to the standards by publicly talking about their work and presenting it to potential partners.

Electronic Data Interchange

EDI is the computer-to-computer exchange of standard business transactions including payment/remittance advice, request for quotations, receiving advice, purchase-order change requests, and even corporate trade payments. EDI is just beginning to include corporate-to-corporate payments. Very few companies, and banks, currently pay their suppliers electronically using the EDI X12 standard. Communication protocols are just beginning to be standardized among industries. Several industries include communication standards in their EDI implementations.

At a forum sponsored by the EDI Association [15], Phyllis Sokol, an EDI consultant, stated that there are three levels of EDI. The most basic EDI level is establishing a *computer-to-computer* link with a trading partner, said Sokol. This level creates a physical link, it causes the least disruption to corporate procedures, and it also produces the least benefits. The second level is *application-to-application* EDI, where each company links one or more of its in-house systems to the EDI interface. At this level, there is no manual intervention between transactions that pass between the various company applications, there is more disruption of current corporate procedures, and the benefits of EDI are much greater, said Sokol. Currently, the greatest interest in EDI exists at this level. The most advanced use of EDI is *changing the way work is performed,* to gain the greatest benefits. One change that some companies are making is to centralize EDI-based functions, such as purchasing, she said.

The applications that have the greatest potential to benefit from EDI have three characteristics, added Sokol.

1. They involve many standard transactions.
2. These transactions require careful and accurate reporting.
3. They make it easier for the customer to purchase goods and services.

As an example of an industry-wide cooperative effort in the field, consider the TradeNet system, which is described in *Trends in Information Technology* [2].

CASE EXAMPLE: TradeNet

In trading, time is money. Given a choice, trading companies will use whichever regional trading city handles their products faster. Singapore is the island nation at the tip of the Malaysian peninsula—at the intersection of the Indian and Pacific Oceans. Trading is their lifeblood. They handle $85 billion in trade annually. To remain world class, the government created TradeNet, an EDI network, to handle all customs transactions in Singapore electronically. It has become a crucial piece of the information communication infrastructure in their nation.

Before TradeNet, obtaining customs approvals for shipments from the various Singaporean agencies took days. Couriers stood in line at the agencies to get paper declarations stamped by hand. With TradeNet, approvals take fifteen minutes and are available twenty-four hours a day. TradeNet acts as a hub between government and industry. The government agencies all agreed on one electronic declaration document for import and export control. This form is filled in by importers and exporters on a personal computer and transmitted to the TradeNet computer, which issues the appropriate approvals if the requirements set forth by the agencies are fulfilled. TradeNet has been extremely successful. It went into operation in January 1989, and by mid 1990 it was handling 64 percent of all trading.

The prime motivation for TradeNet was increasing business efficiency to position Singapore as a global business hub. Trading companies now generally get the customs approvals before their shipments arrive in Singapore, so that they do not need to warehouse their goods. Thus, TradeNet has, in some ways, changed how the shippers operate.

Electronic Markets

Another major type of IOS is electronic markets, said Yannis Bakos [16] of the University of California, Irvine, speaking at a University of California, Los Angeles symposium. He distinguished between information links and electronic markets.

An *information link* is a value-added chain between two organizations, such as between a dealer and a manufacturer, or a supplier and a buyer, said Bakos. Information links are used after the two organizations have established a relationship. EDI fits into this category.

Two important reasons for creating this form of IOS are (1) to increase *by orders of magnitude* the amount of information passing between the two organizations and (2) to decrease response time between the two enterprises. Operating efficiencies can be increased by reducing the costs of coordination between the parties. Reduced inventory may allow the organizations to migrate to JIT operation.

An *electronic market,* on the other hand, is a computerized marketplace with several buyers and several sellers, said Bakos. Generally, someone acts as the market intermediary. Examples of these intermediaries are airline reservation systems and computerized security trading systems.

Goals of electronic markets are (1) to reduce the search costs of buyers, making it easier for buyers to compare offerings; and (2) to create a critical mass—the more organizations connected, the more valuable the system to each participant. This has become the case with fax—the availability of transmission standards and worldwide connections have given fax a competitive edge over electronic mail for communications among organizations.

Electronic markets threaten the monopolistic power of suppliers, because buyers can compare offerings more easily. Therefore, electronic markets promote price competition as well as product differentiation. Competitive advantage for suppliers in an electronic market depends on their bargaining power and their operating efficiency—as compared with their competitors.

Most interorganizational systems are hybrids of these two forms, said Bakos. And for an IOS to make a difference in a marketplace, it must cause order-of-magnitude changes. To demonstrate this principle in action, we describe the electronic cotton marketplace, TELCOT.

CASE EXAMPLE: TELCOT

The Plains Cotton Cooperative Association (PCCA), in Lubbock, Texas, was founded in 1953 to buy cotton from its member growers in Texas and Oklahoma, and resell it to textile mills. By the late 1960s, PCCA was buying more than 90 percent of its members' cotton, because it had assumed the risk of reselling the cotton, say Lindsey, Cheney, Kasper, and Ives [17] in their 1990 second place SIM competition paper.

In other parts of the country, the growers shouldered the risk by selling their cotton in pools and receiving the average price of a type of cotton once it had been sold. This arrangement allowed everyone to compete equally. But most U.S. cotton growers dealt with independent brokers.

By the early 1970s, PCCA was in significant trouble, handling only 20 percent of its members' cotton, because the members could obtain higher prices by dealing directly with independent brokers. To survive, PCCA had to provide better service than these dealers. To do this, PCCA installed a computerized market-making system for cotton: TELCOT. TELCOT acts much like a stock exchange. The venture was risky, because telecommunications-based systems were in their infancy in 1975, especially in rural areas. Furthermore, PCCA's users were computer novices. However, the system was a success, because of the enhanced marketing features it offered.

Previously, growers called gin operators to figure out asking prices for specific lots of cotton. These telephone negotiations were time-consuming and not always fair, because (1) gin operators received commissions for arranging sales; and (2) buyers would call gin operators about their crops without intending to sell, just to compare price quotes. TELCOT eliminated this telephoning by providing an electronic market where the growers could offer their cotton using several options.

- Regular order—offer their cotton for fifteen minutes on the exchange and accept the highest bid about the preset minimum price

- Firm offer—offer their cotton for a firm price
- Loan advance—receive a cash advance based on a government standard price

Since 1975, TELCOT has continued to enhance the marketing features, such as permitting buyers to make counteroffers or describe the cotton they want to buy.

TELCOT has transformed the cotton business in Texas and Oklahoma. More than two hundred cotton gins, forty buyers, and twenty thousand cotton growers use PCs to access PCCA's IBM 3090 mainframe to execute some 115,000 on-line transactions a day. From 1975 to 1990, because of the success of TELCOT, PCCA grew from a $50-million to a $500-million business.

PCCA's Changing Views on Information Technology. Lindsey *et al* make the interesting point that TELCOT demonstrates how top management can significantly change its view of the importance of information technology. The authors describe these changes using the Strategic Grid developed by Warren McFarlan, James McKenney and Philip Pyburn in 1983 [18].

As shown in Figure 3-8, before 1975, information technology played a support role in PCCA, because management did not see either the efficient operation of existing applications nor development of new applications as critical to the cooperative's success. From 1975 to 1977, however, management used IT to turn the cooperative around. Although the

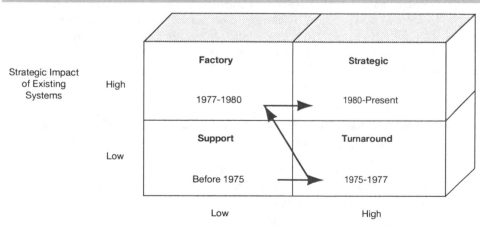

Figure 3-8 The Strategic Grid and PCCA's Movement Over Time (from Lindsey, *et al* [17], reprinted by permission of MISQ.)

existing accounting applications had low priority, PCCA's survival depended on the new TELCOT applications.

In 1977, once TELCOT was a success, IT was seen as a factory; little new development was undertaken, and heavy emphasis was placed on maintaining TELCOT. However, in 1979, several competitors appeared, giving TELCOT stiff competition. Therefore, starting in 1980, PCCA management shifted to seeing IT as strategic—adding an emphasis on new development. For example, in 1990, TELCOT

- Began communicating to gins via FM radio and satellite to overcome landline transmission problems
- Implemented an electronic title exchange, similar to electronic funds transfer, making a warehouse receipt a legal document
- Started using bar codes on cotton bales for EDI, to transfer information between gins, warehouses, and cotton mills

In short, PCCA has continued to innovate, demonstrating that the strategic use of IT is more important than the technology itself, providing ever-increasing flexibility to both cotton buyers and sellers.

CONCLUSION

The message of this chapter is that IT has become a strategic asset; sharp senior executives are using it as such. They see the possibilities of using IT as a catalyst to significantly change how their organizations work, moving processes and jobs from the paper-based world to the electronic world.

The lesson of the chapter is that this endeavor should not be taken lightly. Since it requires people to change, it takes time, constant guidance from the top, and continual "wins" along the way to keep moving forward.

QUESTIONS AND EXERCISES

REVIEW QUESTIONS

1. What two ways are companies and alliances using IT to compete?
2. What are experience curves, according to Primozic *et al*?
3. How is Federal Express using IT to compete on quality?
4. What are Porter's five competitive forces?
5. Briefly describe Wiseman's approach of studying strategic thrusts.
6. What are the four forces causing management to consider seriously reengineering how their business works?

7. List Keen's projections for the mid-1990s.
8. Define "informate."
9. How has Otis Elevator restructured itself?
10. What reengineering principles does Michael Hammer recommend?
11. What lessons did Andersen Consulting and DSS learn about managing business integration endeavors?
12. What will be the systems department's five roles in business reengineering, according to the Index Foundation?
13. What are the characteristics of interorganizational systems?
14. Briefly describe the TradeNet system.
15. What are the two types of interorganizational systems, according to Bakos?
16. Describe TELCOT.

DISCUSSION QUESTIONS

1. Using systems for competitive purposes is no different from traditional systems. Agree or disagree? Discuss.
2. Reengineering business processes is no different from installing systems traditionally. Agree or disagree? Discuss.
3. When companies work in collusion with each other, they may violate antitrust laws. How might such laws impede the development of interorganizational systems?

EXERCISES

1. Find an article or description in a journal or business periodical that describes how a company is using information technology for competitive purposes. Which (if any) of Porter's three strategies is used?
2. Find two articles on reengineering business processes. What principles and lessons do they present that differ from the ones in this chapter? What roles did the information systems department play?
3. Think of an industry, company, or country that could use the approach TradeNet used. How would it give them strategic advantage?
4. Visit the chief information officer of a local firm. What systems have they developed for competitive purposes? Are they reengineering any of their business processes? Do they have any interorganizational systems? If so, explain what they are doing.

REFERENCES

1. HAMMER, MICHAEL, "Reengineering Work: Don't Automate, Obliterate," *Harvard Business Review*, July-August 1990, pp. 104-112.

2. McNURLIN, BARBARA (ED.), *Trends in Information Technology* (Andersen Consulting, Chicago, IL), Fall 1991.

3. PRIMOZIC, KENNETH, EDWARD PRIMOZIC, and JOE LEBEN. *Strategic Choices: Supremacy, Survival, or Sayonara,* (McGraw-Hill, New York), 1991, 272 pages.

4. CARLSON, WALTER and BARBARA MCNURLIN, *Uncovering the Information Technology Payoff, (I/S Analyzer*, Special Report, United Communications Group, Rockville, MD), Fall 1992, 176 pages.

5. ODI, 25 Mall Road, Burlington, MA 02183.

6. PORTER, M.E., *Competitive Strategy* (The Free Press, New York), 1980. Also see *Competitive Advantage*, 1985.

7. PARSONS, G. L., "Information Technology: A New Competitive Weapon," *Sloan Management Review* (Sloan School of Management, Cambridge, MA), Fall 1983, pp. 3-13.

8. WISEMAN, C., *Strategy and Computers* (Dow Jones-Irwin, Homewood, IL), 1985.

9. RACKOFF, N., C. WISEMAN, and W. A. ULRICH, "Information Systems for Competitive Advantage: Implementation of a Planning Process," *MIS Quarterly*, December 1985, pp. 285-294.

10. KEEN, PETER G. W., *Shaping the Future: Business Design Through Information Technology* (Harvard Business School Press, Boston, MA), 1991, 264 pages.

11. ZUBOFF, SHOSANA, *In the Age of the Smart Machine* (Basic Books, New York), 1988, 468 pages.

12. SOCIETY FOR INFORMATION MANAGEMENT, 401 N. Michigan Ave., Chicago, IL 60602.

13. CLOSE-UP: THE U.K. DEPARTMENT OF SOCIAL SECURITY (Andersen Consulting, Chicago, IL), May 1991, 16 pages.

14. THE ROLE OF INFORMATION TECHNOLOGY IN TRANSFORMING THE BUSINESS (Index Foundation, Cambridge, MA), Research Report 79, January 1991, 42 pages.

15. EDI ASSOCIATION, 1101 17th St., N.W., Washington, DC 20036.

16. BAKOS Y. YANNIS, Graduate School of Management, University of California, Irvine.

17. LINDSEY, D., P. CHENEY, G. KASPER, B. IVES, "TELCOT: An Application of Information Technology for Competitive Advantage in the Cotton Industry," *MIS Quarterly,* December 1990, pp. 347-357.

18. McFARLAN, F. W., J. L. McKENNEY, AND P. PYBURN, "The Information Archipelago—Plotting a Course," *Harvard Business Review,* January- February 1983, pp. 145-156.

FOUR

Information Systems Planning

INTRODUCTION

Planning has always been an important task in information systems. The long lead time for hardware delivery, the difficulty of software development, and the preparation needed for training and implementation have all demanded advanced planning. The planning task formerly was primarily technical, focusing mainly on hardware and software. With the advent of strategic systems, planning took on new dimensions and required new linkages with the business planning process. Specifically, managers have had to become aware that uses of computers can have significant effects on their organization's competitive position, and that information systems planning needs to be coupled more closely with the goals of the organization. In fact, information systems planning, or lack of it, can now affect business plans.

What is strategic planning? Strategic planning means planning the future strategy of an organization, that is, the direction the organization wants to go. On the other hand, tactical planning describes how an organization will reach its goals. There are also other kinds of information systems planning, such as project planning to schedule information systems projects or annual budgetary planning. In this chapter, we concentrate on strategic planning—figuring out what an organization wants to do in the future—with particular emphasis on the role that information systems will play.

A Typical Planning Cycle

Over the years, we have heard numerous objections to the need for information systems planning, mainly based on the argument that things change so fast that any plans are soon obsolete—so why bother? But this may well be the Achilles' Heel of information systems. Poor planning leads to plans that performance cannot match. And the broken promises lead to loss of credibility and confidence in the ability of the information systems function to perform. But interest is growing in doing good quality planning.

A fairly typical way for companies to work on future plans is to divide their planning horizon into several time periods, such as

1. The coming year
2. Years two and three
3. Years four and five
4. Year six and beyond

Different planning approaches appear to apply more appropriately to some of these periods than to others.

The Coming Year. Generally, plans for the coming year are well along and have already been sold to management. The projects are already either under way or will soon start. Commitments have been made on resources, time schedules, costs, and benefits. It is almost too late to make significant changes to the plans—at least, without substantial embarrassment. Of course, some projects can be terminated suddenly, as occurs, for instance, when a steering committee sees that a major project is getting into deeper and deeper trouble, and kills it.

In general, there is not much flexibility in initiating major new projects in the next year, or even in reorienting projects already under way. What can be done in this short time might be to install an improved project management system; it may help reduce problems in schedules, costs, and performance for the remainder of the projects. Small pilot projects can also be initiated to explore technologies that appear to be promising for the future.

Years Two and Three. It is probably in years two and three in the future that the largest improvements can be realized from using a better planning methodology. Although plans for projects in this time frame have been reasonably well developed, they are still open to change because final commitments generally have not yet been made. Project management techniques can have a greater impact on the projects scheduled for these years, because the methodologies can be used for the entire projects including the up-front planning.

Years Four and Five. For years four and five, companies may not yet have a clear idea of specific projects that will be undertaken. If they are following a long-term strategy, they know generally what they want to be working on, but projects may not have been delineated.

Suffice it to say that in years four and five in the future, management has quite a bit of flexibility to plan major projects, if the expertise and facilities will be in place to support the projects. This brings up the point of having an information systems "architecture" and "infrastructure." There has been much talk lately about creating data architectures, application architectures, and enterprise network architectures. Often, these consist of policies and guidelines to be followed rather than crystallized designs. But an architecture has to be realistic; it must solve the problem that is addressed.

The term *infrastructure* has also become common. From the information systems viewpoint, infrastructure refers to the facilities that support computing in a firm—generally the hardware, software, networks, and system development capabilities that are in place. But companies are working on another infrastructure as well—their decision-making infrastructure. This identifies who in the company will make which types of decisions regarding IT as well as the type of information technology education they need. Such education is a prerequisite for moving computing decisions out to business units.

Year Six and Beyond. More and more companies are planning six and more years in the future, especially in planning the systems architecture and infrastructure needed to support the businesses they expect to be in. Yet few are paying attention to the staff capabilities they are likely to need six to ten years ahead, nor planning how to develop those capabilities.

Linking Business and Systems Planning

Information systems planning and business planning are gradually being linked with information systems plans supporting corporate plans. But, with the growing emphasis on using computers for competitive advantage, information systems plans may actually lead business strategy. This about-face in the importance of planning computer use has prompted companies to ask how they can link business and systems strategy more effectively. The answer we found was that IT decisions are being pushed out to line management (as we noted in Chapter 3) and to steering committees.

Using Steering Committees. Information systems steering committees generally consist of top executives from various company line organizations—manufacturing, finance, marketing, administration, and so on. Their job is to "steer" major information system investments in the directions that

most benefit the company. Drury [1] performed a study of steering committees to see the impact of alternative structures. After conducting pilot interviews with a few information systems executives, he sent a questionnaire to
such executives in four hundred medium to large size companies.

Drury wanted to find out how five alternative structures of a steering
committee might affect its effectiveness across thirteen advantages cited in
the literature. He studied the following alternatives.

1. Is the chairman from a high or low organizational level?
2. Is there greater or less representation by users than information systems on the
   committee?
3. Are meetings held regularly or irregularly?
4. Are items on the agenda derived from sources outside or inside the information
   systems department?
5. Are decisions of the committee generally imposed or reached by agreement?

Thirteen claimed advantages of steering committees were studied. Four
of those were

1. The steering committee increases the attention of top management to computing.
2. Users become more involved in systems.
3. The systems department is more aware of user needs.
4. There is better long range planning for information systems.

In general, Drury found that steering committees did increase top
management attention, user and systems awareness of each other, and
their involvement in each other's needs. However, the committees appeared
neither to help nor hinder the actual management of the systems function.
Furthermore, the committees did not improve the efficiency of the department, decrease waste in the purchase of equipment, improve the evaluation
of vendor sales presentations, nor improve performance measurements in
the department.

Drury found that the committees scored higher on all thirteen advantages when they held regular meetings, with agenda items drawn from outside the systems department, and with decisions agreed on rather than
imposed. However, the position of the chairman and the committee representation were not so consistent for achieving all the advantages. For instance,
he found that user awareness of information systems was highest when the
committee had a low-level chairman, and more users, and were agreed on
decisions. On the other hand, the evaluation of the systems department was
highest when the committee had a high-level chairman, agenda items were
from outside the department, and decisions were agreed on.

Drury concluded that no single committee structure will achieve all the
advantages cited in the literature. And he believes that the level of the chair-

man and the representation on the committee are more critical determinants of which advantages will be achieved than the literature suggests. So one ingredient in successful strategic information system planning is getting the involvement of business executives, perhaps through steering committees. Another ingredient is a planning methodology.

VARIOUS APPROACHES TO SYSTEMS PLANNING

Due to the importance and the difficulty of systems planning, it is valuable to have a framework or methodology to guide the process. Over the years, several approaches have been proposed to help information systems managers do a better job of planning. The approaches presented here take different views of information systems planning. Some look at the assimilation of IT in organizations, some focus on defining information needs, and others discuss categorizing applications systems. The seven planning approaches and techniques we discuss are

- Stages of growth
- Critical success factors
- Investment strategy analysis
- Scenario approach to planning
- Linkage analysis planning
- Creative problem solving approaches
- Enterprise modeling

Stages of Growth

Richard Nolan and Chuck Gibson published a landmark paper in 1974 entitled "Managing the Four Stages of EDP Growth" [2]. In it they observed that many organizations go through four stages in the introduction and assimilation of new technology. Since that time, Nolan has elaborated on the theory by adding two more stages [3]. Although the bases of the theory have come under some criticism [4], the basic ideas still provide a useful framework for information systems planning. Here is a brief description of the four stages.

Stage One: Early Successes. The first stage is the beginning use of a new technology. Although some stumbling generally occurs, early successes lead to increased interest and experimentation.

Stage Two: Proliferation. Based on the early successes, interest grows rapidly as new products and services based on the technology come to the marketplace.

These are tried out in a variety of applications. This proliferation stage is the learning period for the field, both for uses and for new products and services.

Stage Three: Control of Proliferation. Eventually it becomes apparent that the proliferation must be controlled. Management begins to feel that the costs of using the new technology are too high, and the variety of approaches generates waste. The integration of systems is attempted but proves difficult, and suppliers begin efforts toward standardization.

Stage Four: Mature Use. At this stage, the use of the particular new technology might be considered mature. The stage has been set for introducing still other new technologies, wherein the pattern is repeated. In fact, an organization can be in several stages simultaneously, for different technologies.

Stages of Growth Modified. McFarlan and McKenney [5] discuss a somewhat modified version of the four stages (or "phases," as they prefer). Their four phases are

1. Identification and initial investment
2. Experimentation and learning
3. Management control
4. Widespread technology transfer

This version of the four phases casts the important second phase in a somewhat different light. Nolan and Gibson gave a negative name—proliferation—to this phase, leaving the impression that users are being almost irresponsible by adopting the new technology too rapidly. McFarlan and McKenney point out that this is the stage when experimentation and learning occur; it is a trial-and-error phase. If too much control is exerted too soon, important new uses of the technology can be killed off.

McFarlan and McKenney believe that the value of this "stage theory" approach is that it gives a better understanding of the factors that affect the formulation of information systems strategy; therefore, it will allow managers to do a better planning job. Since the management principles differ from one stage to another, and because different technologies are in different stages at any point in time, the stage model is an important aid to the systems planning process.

Critical Success Factors

John Rockart is the director of the Center for Information Systems Research (CISR) at the Sloan School of Management, at MIT. In 1977, Rockart and his colleagues began developing a method for defining executive information needs. The result of their work is the Critical Success Factors (CSF) method [6]. It focuses on individual managers and their current information needs, be it factual or opinion information. The CSF method can be used to help companies identify information systems they need to develop.

For each executive, critical success factors are the few key areas of the job where things must go right for the organization to flourish. There are usually fewer than ten of these factors that any one executive should monitor. Furthermore, they are very time dependent, so they should be reexamined as often as necessary to keep abreast of the current business climate. These key areas should receive constant attention from executives, yet CISR research found that most managers had not explicitly identified these crucial factors.

Rockart finds that there are four sources for these factors. One source is the industry that the business is in. Each industry has CSFs that are relevant to any company in it. A second source is the *company itself* and its situation within the industry. Actions by a few large, dominant companies in an industry will most likely provide one or more CSFs for small companies in that industry. Furthermore, several companies may have the same CSFs but, at the same time, have different priorities for those factors.

A third source of CSFs is the *environment*, such as consumer trends, the economy, and political factors of the country (or countries) that the company operates in. A prime example used by Rockart is that, before 1973, virtually no chief executive would have listed "energy supply availability" as a CSF. Following the oil embargo, however, many executives began monitoring this factor very closely. The fourth source is *temporal* organizational factors—areas of company activity that normally do not warrant concern but that are currently unacceptable and need attention. A case of far too much or far too little inventory might classify as a CSF for a short time.

One way to use the CSF method is to list the corporate objectives and goals for the year. These are then used to determine which factors are critical for accomplishing the objectives. Then two or three prime measures for each factor are determined. Discovering the measures is the most time-consuming portion of this stage, he says. Some measures use hard, factual data; these are the ones most quickly identified. Others use "softer" measures, such as opinions, perceptions, and hunches; these take more analysis to uncover their appropriate sources.

Investment Strategy Analysis

Another framework to support systems planning is based on somewhat traditional techniques of portfolio planning and investment analysis. David Norton, one of the founders of Nolan, Norton & Co., describes one approach his company uses to help its clients plan their investment strategy for information systems [7]. Norton expects four major types of applications to be in use in the 1990s.

1. Institutional procedures—the processing of internal transactions, as represented by many of today's mainline systems
2. Professional support systems, such as engineering support, managerial decision-making support, and similar activities

3. Physical automation

4. Systems that serve users outside the company, such as customers and suppliers

In addition, there will continue to be expenditures to provide the basic technical infrastructure to permit the development and use of these applications. Network protocols, database standards, and computing platforms are prime examples.

To build a framework for an investment strategy, set up a two-dimensional table, says Norton, with these four types of systems, plus the infrastructure, as the column headings. The rows are the main functional components of the business, such as research and development, manufacturing, marketing, and other service and support functions. Figure 4-1 illustrates this approach.

To demonstrate how the analysis works, Norton uses figures from two aerospace manufacturing firms. In the base year, each spent about 3.5 percent of sales on information systems. For an aerospace manufacturing company, the functional components might be engineering, quality assurance, manufacturing, finance, and administration.

As shown in Figure 4-2, seven years later, Company Alpha was spending 6.0 percent of sales on all information systems, with 2.4 percent of sales for professional support. Company Beta's overall expenditure had dropped to

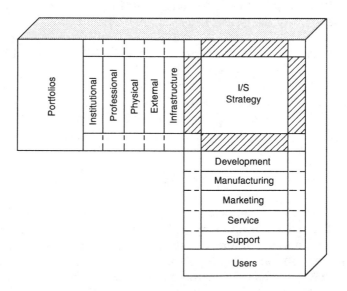

Portfolios: Describe the allocation of information systems resources
for different classes of applications
Users: Describe the allocation of information systems resources
to different classes of users

Figure 4-1 Information Systems Products and Customers (from Norton [7])

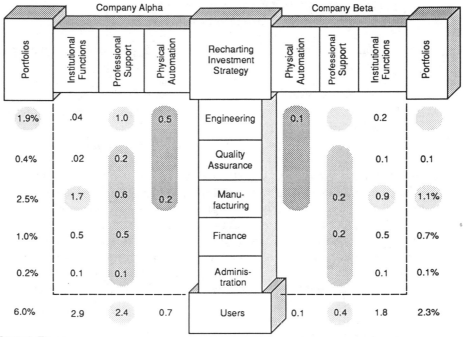

Portfolios	Institutional Functions	Professional Support	Physical Automation	Recharting Investment Strategy	Physical Automation	Professional Support	Institutional Functions	Portfolios
1.9%	.04	1.0	0.5	Engineering	0.1		0.2	
0.4%	.02	0.2		Quality Assurance			0.1	0.1
2.5%	1.7	0.6	0.2	Manu-facturing		0.2	0.9	1.1%
1.0%	0.5	0.5		Finance		0.2	0.5	0.7%
0.2%	0.1	0.1		Adminis-tration			0.1	0.1%
6.0%	2.9	2.4	0.7	Users	0.1	0.4	1.8	2.3%

Strategic Thrusts

1   Alpha is investing heavily in refurbishing its manufacturing systems around integrated database technology

2   Alpha is investing heavily in the productivity of its engineers

3   Alpha is investing generically in the productivity of all professional groups

4   Alpha is investing heavily in CAD/CAM technology to improve the linkage between engineering and manufacturing

Figure 4-2 Patterns of Spending by Portfolio Segment (from Norton [7])

2.3 percent of sales, with only 0.4 percent of sales for professional support. These patterns evolved because Company Alpha had decided that its strategic advantage lay in increasing the productivity of its key resource—its engineers and other professionals. The company gave substantial IT support to the engineers. Company Beta gave much less support to its engineers. (Since neither company spent much for external systems or for building a technical infrastructure, these categories are omitted from the columns in Figure 4-2.)

As Norton points out, Company Alpha believed IT was a strategic tool, so the company encouraged its innovative use in four ways.

1. Renovate existing manufacturing systems around database technology.
2. Invest heavily in increasing the productivity of the engineers.

3. Foster innovation among the professional staff.
4. Invest heavily in CAD/CAM technology.

Company Beta, on the other hand, viewed IT as an overhead item. Its use of IT followed three strategies:

1. Create new systems only when the old ones fail.
2. Let others prove the value of new uses of IT before we start doing things differently.
3. Invest in IT only when it will have a direct bottom-line impact.

Norton points out that there can be substantial differences in the ways that companies in the same industry invest in information systems, as this example illustrates. The strategies of these two companies were not stated explicitly, yet they were clearly evident in conversations with the company executives. Also, such an analysis of current expenditures helps bring out the true "intensity of beliefs" about the use of technology, says Norton. It allows managers to stand back, see where investments are currently being made, and then decide where they *should* be made, to align the IT investments with the business strategy.

The Scenario Approach

Professional planners and executives have often used a scenario approach to planning. The approach is gaining in popularity, supported by computer-based decision support systems, and driven by the key words "what if." In systems planning, the scenario approach provides a way to manage the assumptions required for planning by creating scenarios that combine trends, events, environmental factors, and the relationships among them. The scenarios help identify some problem areas that could arise if some factors change, such as the amount and type of competition or changes in wage rates. Once these scenarios have been generated, managers choose several that *could* happen. Then one "most likely" scenario is selected as the basis for long-range plans.

Scenarios also provide flexibility in plans and a means of escape, should it be necessary. This is the role of the other scenarios that are less likely but still feasible. They identify the leading-edge indicators that management should monitor. In these times of rapid change, about the only thing that is certain is that some of the views of the future will prove to be quite wrong. The selected scenario of the future is used to develop a phased schedule for achieving the desired ends. Projects required to implement the scenario are divided into phases, and the commitment to proceed is given for the next phase of each project over time. The goal is to highlight unexpected changes and require reassessments of the continued feasibility of the scenario.

Another role that scenario creation can play is to protect against errors of judgment by management by flushing out management "mind-sets" (basic assumptions) that are no longer relevant. In this period of major change, many old "rules" based on things that commonly happened in the past may no longer apply.

Some people will reject the idea of ten- or twenty-year future scenarios as being not worth the trouble because no one is able to forecast the future with any consistency. There is some validity in this view. Companies are being acquired and merged. There are changes in the business environment because of foreign competition and government regulations. Changes in technologies are accelerating. However, the type of strategic approach discussed here *expects* things to change, so "midcourse corrections" are part of the scenario process. As scenarios of the future are regenerated at later points in time, they will certainly show new pictures of the future. That is the time for management to assess the changes, to determine if plans must be modified, and to decide if a new approach is needed.

Elements of a Scenario. So many variables come into play when attempting to visualize the future that no "simple theories," based on just a few variables, will be adequate. Following are some of the elements that should be considered in information systems plans.

The business environment. It is not difficult to think of many factors that affect the general business environment, which in turn can affect information systems. These include

- Environment
- Mergers, acquisitions, and alliances
- Regional trading blocks
- National budget deficits
- Shortened product development cycles
- Changes in the strength of different currencies

Then there is the impact of new technology on the business environment. For instance, what will be the impact of the increased use of "digital money" (such as debit cards and other forms of electronic funds transfer) and the increased use of network services, EDI, and other technology-based competitive systems?

Government and society. Possible new government regulations and new social attitudes are other important considerations when developing scenarios. At an International Conference on Information Systems (ICIS), Richard Mason of Southern Methodist University talked about important issues in information systems. He identified some ethical issues that are likely to affect organizations and their information systems department.

One issue is *information accuracy*, said Mason. If significant societal problems emerge because of data errors, government regulations are almost sure to follow. A related issue is *privacy*, said Mason. Any database with information about people runs the risk of invading personal privacy.

A third issue is the potential for inequalities in *access to information*. Being literate is the first step in accessing written information, but accessing information in computer systems needs additional skills. Thus, larger budgets for training and education may be required to help employees become more computer literate.

A fourth issue is *property*, particularly the rights to intellectual property. For instance, it is relatively easy and inexpensive to make copies of computerized files, thus possibly compromising the property rights of the information creators. Perhaps even more threatening are "expert systems" that can capture experts' knowledge and embed it in computer programs. Do those people need to be compensated for this use of their knowledge?

The scenario approach makes it possible to factor in the possibility of government regulations in one or more of these areas as one extrapolates today's trends of computer use into the future.

"People" changes. It would be a mistake, when setting up scenarios of the future, to think that employees in ten years will be like they are today. With today's turbulent conditions, employees may well come to expect that employers will train them in new skill areas, so that they (the employees) do not become job obsolete. At present, many employers seem to treat this as an employee responsibility, but that may change.

Another major people factor in scenario building is the distribution of ages. Currently, relatively fewer young employees are in the work force. The next surge of young workers into the work force will start about 1995.

Then there are changes in the attitudes and expectations of employees. For instance, Florence Skelly, of the firm of Yankelovich, Skelly & White [8], at a conference of the Information Industry Association, discussed how the environment that exists when people are just reaching working age affects their attitudes and expectations for much of their working lives. In the 1950s young people in the United States were influenced by the then-popular attitude of acquiring material things. These people are now in the fifty to fifty-five age bracket and represent much of middle management. During the 1960s and 1970s, affluence was more taken for granted, and the attitudes of young people turned toward fixing society's ills. The people who reached their working age during that period have recently entered the work force. So the current entrants into the work force might have expectations for "curing ills."

Finally, as far as the 1980s are concerned, said Skelly, the attitude has become much more pragmatic. It is recognized that "you cannot be, do, or have everything, so select what it is you desire and lay out your plans for getting it. Win by wit and wisdom. Be competitive." This may well be the attitude of young people entering the work force in the next five to ten years.

Financial Considerations. An important element in scenarios is the financial dimension. For instance, technology costs will be substantial. Companies will require benefits from these sizable IT investments. The main problem is the definition of "benefits" and "return on investment." The benefits that derive from straightforward cost displacements, such as increased productivity or reduced staffing, will be only moderate in the future. The significant benefits will come from using IT to create more "high producers" in companies, gain competitive advantages, or radically change the way technology is used. The real management challenge is perceiving these as benefits to justify the cost of new uses of technologies.

Technology. Technology forecasting is a particularly tenuous activity. Scenarios that make assumptions about not yet developed technology are even more dangerous. There are few experts who, back in the mid-1970s, accurately predicted the explosive growth of the microcomputer technology. In fact, it is likely that, even in 1981, IBM substantially underestimated the sales of its PC when it was first announced.

Creating Scenarios. Scenarios can be developed in various ways, ranging from strictly manual methods to highly automated ones. We will discuss one approach that is used at the University of Southern California, in Los Angeles. Sol Enzer [9] describes how strategies for introducing new information systems might be developed using this scenario approach. This approach uses the INTERAX program for creating scenarios. The use of such automated tools can make it easier to generate new scenarios periodically.

The INTERAX system includes:

- A "deterministic" model of the future, created by the user, and often represented as a spreadsheet model that can be run on a personal computer, if desired

- A "cross-impact" model for injecting probabilistic events into the scenarios, and human analysis and interaction at each "future year" to determine what new policies and actions might be called for

As mentioned, the deterministic model might be a spreadsheet in which the columns are years (or, if more precision is desired, quarters of years), and the rows are the factors under consideration.

For a study of the introduction of new information systems, some of the rows might be estimates of the number of employees in the company, the number who would be using PCs or workstations, the number and size of new information systems that are installed, and so on.

The cross-impact model is a simulation model by which "uncertain" future events can be injected into a scenario. To aid users, the INTERAX system provides data about anticipated future changes in the technology, government regulations, economic trends, and so forth, covering the next two decades. This data was collected from a large Delphi study involving experts from several disciplines.

The basis of the cross-impact model is a matrix about possible major events and trends, and the possible impact of those events and trends. For instance, possible events pertaining to the use of PCs might be: (1) the cost of a PC drops to below $500, with a 0.5 estimated probability of it happening by the year 1997; (2) a PC will become as easy to use as a telephone, with a 0.3 estimated probability of it happening by 1997; and (3) severe employee resistance to using terminals and PCs will develop, with a 0.2 estimated probability of it happening by the year 1997.

The rows of the matrix then specify the cross-impacts. If the cost of a PC *does* drop to below $500, what does this do to the probability of it becoming as easy to use as a telephone, and the probability of severe employee resistance occurring? Let's say the former probability is reduced 50 percent, and the latter is increased 25 percent. For each event, the matrix shows the estimated impact it might have on the occurrence of the other events.

The outputs from the cross-impact model are the inputs to the deterministic model, one period at a time. The cross-impact model then triggers changes in the values in the deterministic model, based on the events, trends, and their interrelationships that have "occurred." The total model thus moves step by step into the future. It says to the user, in effect, "Here we are at the end of 1995. Here is what has happened during the year, according to this scenario. What do you want to change in your strategic options for 2000?" Note that the system is *not* predicting the future. Rather, it is giving some plausible scenarios of what could happen. As an example of a company that uses scenarios in its planning, consider Denny's.

CASE EXAMPLE: Denny's Inc.

Denny's Inc., with headquarters in La Mirada, California, is in the food services industry. The company has five divisions. On the retailing side are Denny's restaurants, Winchell's Donut houses, and El Pollo Loco chicken restaurants—with more than two thousand restaurants and fast food locations throughout the United States and five other countries. Proficient Food Company distributes food products to these retail outlets. And in the area of food manufacturing, Portion-Trol Foods produces some of the food products used by the retail stores.

The vice president for information services believes that information systems directors need to do more than introduce new technology into their companies. They need to *anticipate* what their companies will need in the future.

To put an information systems strategic plan in place, the vice president coordinated meetings with the company and division presidents to find out their views of Denny's future. He found that the company was growth oriented, and that it might grow through acquisitions, mergers, or cooperative ventures. But it was likely to stay in the food services business. With this knowledge in hand, he realized that his department had to ready itself for such growth. So he brought in managers who understood how large companies function.

The company, and its various departments and divisions, uses a five year rolling plan. In planning five years ahead, the department managers go off-site for several days to generate company and systems scenarios. Using business scenarios from the past—and determining how accurate these have been—the managers try to anticipate what the company will look like in five years. They generate several possible scenarios. Some seem very probable, whereas others seem highly unlikely; they try to cover the gamut. Then the group concentrates on the four or five most likely scenarios. For each one, they develop a high-level systems plan.

The information services controller takes these plans and looks for the common elements in each from a systems perspective. Which systems elements are in all the plans? Which are in 80 percent (or 60 percent or 40 percent, etc.) of the plans? Which of the plans require relational databases? Which require networks? Which require voice workstations? And so on. The group then reconvenes to discuss the plans and scenarios and choose one system plan. They attempt to fully support the most likely scenario, cover 70 percent of the needs of the next most likely scenarios, and cover 30 percent of the least likely ones.

Their more near-term plans are refinements of these five-year plans. Plans for the year ahead for each division are presented to the 200 top managers of the company once a year, where each major group describes its plan to the others. This one-day meeting creates a common level of understanding of the changes that each company area is initiating.

Linkage Analysis Planning

Kenneth Primozic, Edward Primozic, and Joe Leben [10] in their book *Strategic Choices* explain their planning methodology, linkage analysis planning. Briefly, it means examining the links that organizations have with one another with the goal of creating a strategy of utilizing electronic channels. Their planning methodology has five basic parts:

1. Understand "waves of innovation"
2. Exploit experience curves
3. Define power relationships
4. Map out your "extended enterprise"
5. Plan your electronic channels

Understand "Waves of Innovation." We discussed these waves in Chapter 2, along with the example of American Airline's SABRE system. Briefly, the authors see the first two waves, which yield low returns on IT investments, as concentrating on saving money. Waves 3 through 5, which have steeper sloping lines signifying greater potential returns on investment, focus on making money. Most companies are at the top of Wave 2, say the authors, because they do not yet build systems that make money.

Exploit Experience Curves. As we noted in Chapter 3, along with the example of the shipping industry, the authors see a set of experience curves rather than one continuous learning curve. Each of their curves represents fundamentally different technologies, both in the product and in the process to make and support it. Switching from one curve to another requires substantial investments, but a firm that correctly identifies a new market, and installs the technologies to exploit it, shifts to the new experience curve and is very successful.

Define Power Relationships. In order to create a strategy for building electronic links among enterprises, Primozic *et al* believe that management must first understand the power relationships that currently exist among these various players. For this analysis, they begin with Michael Porter's model of competitive forces [11], which include competitors, buyers, substitutes, suppliers, and potential entrants. To this model they add: technology, demographics, global competition, government regulations, and "whatever is important in your environment." The goals of this step are to: (1) identify who has the power, and (2) determine what threats and opportunities exist for the company in the future.

The analysis begins by identifying *linkages*, which are relationships the organization has with other entities. Figure 4-4 in the upcoming case example is a good illustration. The links are represented by lines between organizations (shown in boxes). Once identified, management needs to determine who is managing each link. Oftentimes, no one is—which should be of concern. From here, the team picks the most important link and decides how the firm can control that link. The authors believe that winning organizations in the 1990s will be those that control the electronic channels—i.e., the electronic linkages among enterprises.

The discussion of how to gain power within one's world of linkages brings up a host of questions. Two important ones are: How might alliances with other firms—across industries or even with competitors—help us? How do we need to restructure ourselves to seize an opportunity, or ward off a threat?

Map Out Your "Extended Enterprise." These questions lead to the fourth step in their approach to planning—the extended enterprise. An extended enterprise includes all of one's own organization plus those organizations with which one interacts—such as suppliers, buyers, government agencies, and so forth. (See Figure 4-3.)

The purpose of this step is to get management to first recognize the existence of this extended enterprise, and then to begin to manage the relationships that exist in it; because Primozic *et al* believe that successful 1990s managements will focus on the extended enterprise. They see two fundamental principles to managing these relationships:

1. The enterprise's success depends on the relationships among everyone involved, which includes employees, managers, suppliers, alliances, distribution channels, and so forth.

2. Some 70 percent of the final cost of goods and services is in their information content; therefore, managing information as a strategic tool is crucial.

An extended enterprise diagram might deal only with external players, such as the government, stockholders, traditional competitors, the financial community, and so forth. Such a chart includes everyone whose decisions affect the organization or who are affected by its decisions. The analysis then moves on to discussing how the links might change, and who and how each link should be managed. In the extended enterprise, each relationship will prosper only when it is "win-win," say the authors. For example, in return for maintaining a buyer's parts inventory and providing just-in-time delivery, the supplier may be paid electronically upon delivery of goods. Such an arrangement profits both parties.

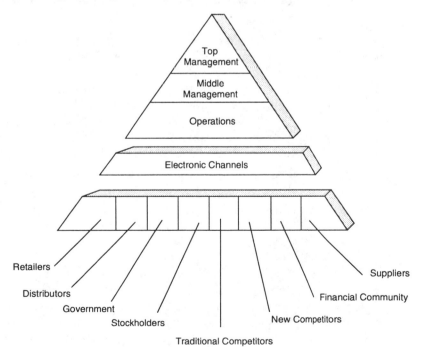

Figure 4-3 The Extended Enterprise (from Primozic *et al* [10])

Competitive advantage will depend increasingly on being able to exploit the collective resources of one's extended enterprise, say Primozic *et al*. Such enterprises often require electronic channels to exchange business transactions, which leads to the fifth step in their planning approach—planning the electronic channels.

Plan Your Electronic Channels. An electronic channel is an electronic link used to create, distribute, and present information and knowledge—as part of a product or service or as an ancillary good. These channels focus on the information component of products, which is mainly in marketing, administration, distribution, and customer service. The authors believe that those who control the electronic channels in the 1990s will be the winners, because they will be able to address new niche markets as they arise. Furthermore, as use of IT leads to a smaller, faster-paced world, organizations with the longest electronic reach into their extended organization will have an advantage.

The authors use linkage analysis charts to help management conceptualize the key issues they face in an extended enterprise, and focus on the factors that are critical to their future success. This methodology has been used by the Electric Power Research Institute, whose story we tell next.

CASE EXAMPLE: Electric Power Research Institute

The Electric Power Research Institute (EPRI), with headquarters in Palo Alto, California, is a large private research firm serving over 700 electric member utilities. Their 350 staff scientists and engineers manage some 1,600 R&D projects at any one time. The projects—which study such subjects as power generation, superconductivity, electronic and magnetic fields, and acid rain—are conducted by over 400 utility, university, commercial, government, and other R&D contractors, on behalf of the members. For an in-depth discussion of EPRI, see Reference [12].

Their Challenge. EPRI's mission is to deliver the information and knowledge from their research projects to the 400,000 employees in the 768 member utilities—to help them be more competitive. In 1983, management realized EPRI had to compress the "information float"—the elapsed time from the availability of research findings to the use of those results in industry.

The institute was suffering from "infosclerosis"—the hardening and clogging of their information arteries. Due to the volume of research findings—8 gigabytes of information in 1991—moving information in and out was extremely difficult. In addition, because of the documentation and publishing the results often were unavailable for up to 24 months, so the reports were not as timely as they could be. Nor were they accessible, because they were published in massive reports. Solving this information delivery challenge was critical to EPRI's survival.

Their Vision. Their vision was to assist their members in exploiting EPRI's product—knowledge—as a strategic business resource, whenever and from wherever they choose. To accomplish this vision, EPRI is building state-of-the-art electronic information and communication services.

Their delivery vehicle is EPRINET, an electronic "channel" that includes

- A natural-language front-end for accessing on-line information
- Expert system-based products that contain the knowledge of their energy experts
- Electronic mail facilities for person-to-person communications
- Video conferencing to foster small-group communication.

Using Linkage Analysis Planning. To focus the EPRINET effort, and to identify the services and products that would offer strategic business advantages to their members, EPRI used the linkage analysis planning methodology in a three-day workshop led by Kenneth Primozic. The workshop began with management stating that (1) EPRI was both an R&D organization and a knowledge provider, and (2) the goal was to leverage knowledge as a strategic asset.

From this starting point, Primozic asked, "Who is linked to EPRI in creating and distributing knowledge?" The participants identified the co-creators as contractors, research firms, universities, the government, and technology. They identified the recipients as the utility industry, universities, research labs, government policies, and knowledge as capital—as shown in Figure 4-4. Each of these represented a link to EPRI, so the group then studied the present and future power relationships in each buyer-seller link. During these discussions, they saw how some

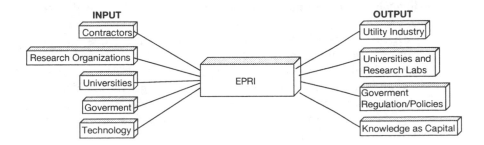

Figure 4-4 EPRI's Linkage Analysis (from Mann *et al* [12])

current customers (such as universities or research labs) could become future competitors and change the power relationship in a link.

Since management's goal was to leverage knowledge, the group listed all the ways this could be achieved. Then they focused on the most important way, which turned out to be treating knowledge as capital. During this analysis, management defined the following critical success factors for giving EPRINET a sustainable competitive advantage:

- Establish the "right" mix of product offerings, a mix that allows people to pick, choose, and combine at the lowest possible cost.
- Keep all customers in mind, which includes utility executives, research engineers, and operations people.
- Use IT—specifically expert systems and natural language—to make the system easy to use and access.
- Create a range of "knowledge packages" targeted to specific audiences.
- Establish a timely, reliable, secure, global distribution channel.

EPRINET was made available in May 1990, and a marketing campaign began soon thereafter. The number of users has climbed steadily since then, with over 1,000 users in 258 utilities, 248 contractors, and every EPRI employee as of early 1991. Frequent users report that the system is indeed broadening the number of people they can stay in contact with and allowing them to uncover EPRI research findings that they would not have found otherwise.

Creative Problem Solving

Creative Problem Solving (CPS) approaches are procedures and techniques designed to solve complete problems in creative ways. Evolving over the past two or three decades, CPS techniques are proving useful to enhance several of the systems planning approaches discussed earlier. We discuss it here because, with modern variations, it is proving to be extremely valuable in leveraging combinations of other techniques. We will illustrate this in the final case example.

A major reason for the increased value of the CPS approach in systems planning and development is the recent work by J. Daniel Couger at the University of Colorado at Colorado Springs. Couger [13] has developed a variant to the CPS model that can facilitate I/S planning. He has also formed the Center for Research on Creativity in Information Systems (CRCI), sponsored by a group of organizations interested in supporting the development of theory and insight on this subject.

CPS has evolved from several analytical approaches. The most widely used framework for problem solving was originated by Herbert Simon [14], who proposed a three stage approach: intelligence, design and choice. *Intelligence* involves recognizing the problem and analyzing problem information to develop a useful problem definition; *design* is the generation of solutions; and *choice* involves the selection and implementation of a solution. The most widely used CPS model, developed by Sidney Parnes [15], contains five phases: fact finding, problem finding, idea finding, solution finding, and acceptance finding.

A unique feature of CPS is its use of divergence-convergence activities in each phase of the problem solving process, representedly a diamond shaped symbol. Each phase begins with a divergent activity (idea generation, where the alternatives are expanded) and concludes with a convergent activity (in which only the most promising ideas are selected for further exploration).

The Couger variant to the CPS model is shown in Figure 4-5. It contains three refinements. One, which he calls "creative opportunity delineation and problem solving," is the addition of an opportunity identification step.

The *second* refinement is his emphasis upon nonlinearity and recursiveness of the model, that is, the steps are not really linear, although the graphical representation implies that one step follows another. Further-

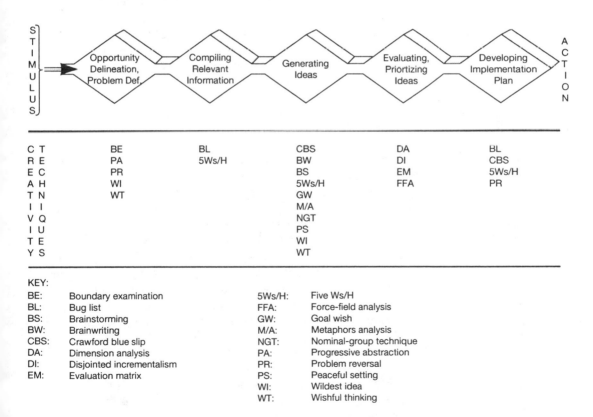

CREATIVITY TECHNIQUES			CBS	DA	BL
	BE	BL	CBS	DA	BL
	PA	5Ws/H	BW	DI	CBS
	PR		BS	EM	5Ws/H
	WI		5Ws/H	FFA	PR
	WT		GW		
			M/A		
			NGT		
			PS		
			WI		
			WT		

KEY:

BE:	Boundary examination		5Ws/H:	Five Ws/H
BL:	Bug list		FFA:	Force-field analysis
BS:	Brainstorming		GW:	Goal wish
BW:	Brainwriting		M/A:	Metaphors analysis
CBS:	Crawford blue slip		NGT:	Nominal-group technique
DA:	Dimension analysis		PA:	Progressive abstraction
DI:	Disjointed incrementalism		PR:	Problem reversal
EM:	Evaluation matrix		PS:	Peaceful setting
			WI:	Wildest idea
			WT:	Wishful thinking

Figure 4-5 Couger Variant of the Creative Problem Solving Model (from Couger [13])

more, the problem solver may need to revisit prior steps (recursion). For instance, it may not be possible to define the problem until the second phase—reviewing all the relevant data—has been performed. Or the idea generation phase may uncover the need for more data before the problem solvers are able to fully attack the problem or opportunity. Or the problem solvers may decide in the evaluation phase that the generated ideas are not an optimal solution, requiring recursion back through phase three, the idea generation phase. There are also situations where not all of the phases are necessary, such as when the problem is clear to everyone, so phase one is unnecessary. On the other hand, the literature is replete with cases where the problem solvers assumed they understood the problem and spent time solving the wrong problem.

Couger's *third* refinement is his identification of various creativity techniques for each problem-solving phase. Normally, creativity techniques are used only in the idea generation phase, but Couger believes they are valuable throughout the process, as follows:

- In phase one, creativity techniques can be used to help generate multiple problem/opportunity definitions.
- In phase two, creativity techniques can be used to identify other salient facts.
- In phase three, creativity techniques can assist in generating a variety of solutions.
- In phase four, creativity techniques can help identify various evaluation approaches.
- In phase five, creativity techniques can be used to identify alternative approaches for assuring a successful implementation.

The brainstorming technique, generally used in phase three, may be the only technique listed that is familiar to most persons in the systems field. Use of other techniques is illustrated in the upcoming UTMC case example.

Couger believes that the CPS model is useful in a variety of I/S systems activities. He has shown in a recent article [16] how it can be incorporated into the system development life cycle to ensure that more creative alternatives are considered at each stage of the life cycle. He believes it is especially effective in I/S planning. At United Technologies Microelectronics Center (UTMC), its use led to an innovative approach of integrating Hoshin planning techniques (HPT) with enterprise modeling (EM) and business process redesign (BPR). The power of CPS for systems planning is illustrated in the UTMC case.

Enterprise Modeling

The UTMC case that follows illustrates some techniques which can be called "enterprise modeling." As described by [17], their story suggests that there is a need for focus at the enterprise level, and that several techniques and approaches may need to be used together.

UTMC's enterprise model development methodology used general planning techniques as its foundation; therefore, it can be applied by any organization. The issues addressed by UTMC's enterprise model are important to virtually all businesses today. Work on the enterprise model has positioned UTMC to address four of these most important issues:

- Reshaping business processes through IT
- Aligning I/S and corporate goals
- Instituting cross-functional systems
- Utilizing data

CASE EXAMPLE: United Technologies Microelectronics Center (UTMC)

United Technologies Microelectronics Center, Inc. (UTMC), headquartered in Colorado Springs, Colorado, is a subsidiary of United Technologies Corporation (UTC). Established in 1980, UTMC helps other UTC divisions integrate custom and semi-custom microelectronics into their military and defense systems. In 1985, UTMC opened a wafer fabrication facility and expanded its charter to marketing semi-custom and military-standard VLSI circuits to high-reliability military and aerospace companies outside of UTC. This significant shift in business focus had a dramatic effect on UTMC's marketing, manufacturing, engineering, and design activities. Today, UTMC also engages in government and customer-funded research and development.

The shifts in business objectives and the associated changes in management information needs strained UTMC's information architecture. In early 1990, senior management decided to operate the business more efficiently by using real-time integrated data. With this goal in mind, management tasked MIS department with developing a computer systems integration strategy and identifying opportunities to reengineer UTMC's business processes. MIS management proposed the development of an enterprise model to achieve these objectives.

While the MIS department investigated different enterprise modeling techniques, UTMC's CEO attended a seminar on the Hoshin Planning technique—a set of Japanese planning tools used to solve general business problems. After the seminar, he was excited about the prospect of creating a UTMC culture that utilized these planning techniques. Acknowledging his interest, MIS management modified and integrated the Hoshin planning techniques into an enterprise model methodology. Creativity techniques were used to design the methodology and incorporated into it.

Rather than taking the data focus inherent in many modeling methodologies, UTMC's methodology used a process focus, which meant that the resulting model would not be biased toward the current systems and databases. Instead, it would represent ideal or target business processes, which would identify opportunities to reengineer current business practices.

UTMC's CEO fully supported the project's goals and methodology because the newly defined methodology not only promised to address his systems and process concerns, but its Hoshin orientation was compatible with his cultural objectives for UTMC.

Enterprise Modeling Methodology

The methodology's focus on target business processes meant that the entire enterprise needed to be subdivided into functional units, which are depicted by the seven levels of business process hierarchy in Figure 4-6.

With the business processes understood, the methodology called for understanding and documenting the target process interrelationships. Next, the implementation viewpoint was linked to the process view by mapping the processes to information systems and then defining the interrelationships between systems via a target system architecture. Finally, UTMC identified and ranked the differences between its current

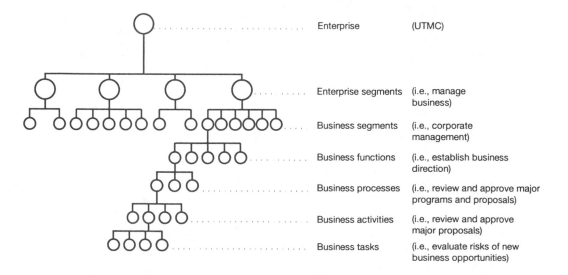

Enterprise	(UTMC)
Enterprise segments	(i.e., manage business)
Business segments	(i.e., corporate management)
Business functions	(i.e., establish business direction)
Business processes	(i.e., review and approve major programs and proposals)
Business activities	(i.e., review and approve major proposals)
Business tasks	(i.e., evaluate risks of new business opportunities)

Figure 4-6 UTMC Business Process Hierarchy

environment and the target model. This final step identified the environmental changes UTMC would need to reengineer the business.

Assembling Business Segment Teams

The reengineering work would be performed by business segment teams. To choose these teams, MIS collaborated with the vice president of operations to prototype the new methodology and functionally decompose the company's overall business activity into major enterprise and business segments. Figure 4-7 depicts the resulting four enterprise segments and 15 business segments.

Senior management organized a team of six to ten employees for each of the 15 business segments. Team members represented a diverse cross-section of the UTMC employees and included all levels of management. Approximately 16 percent of UTMC employees served on the teams.

Constructing the Model

As part of the adapted Hoshin methodology, the MIS department held four separate meetings with each business segment team. At each meeting, MIS management continually stressed that current practices and organizational structure should not influence the model. The MIS group used creativity techniques during each meeting to solicit new ideas.

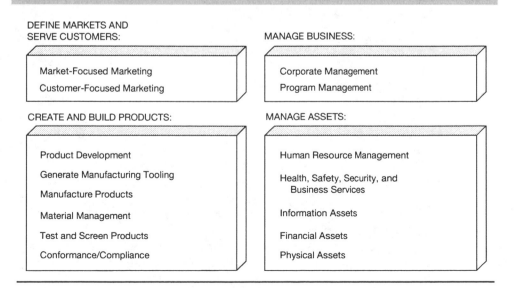

DEFINE MARKETS AND SERVE CUSTOMERS:

- Market-Focused Marketing
- Customer-Focused Marketing

MANAGE BUSINESS:

- Corporate Management
- Program Management

CREATE AND BUILD PRODUCTS:

- Product Development
- Generate Manufacturing Tooling
- Manufacture Products
- Material Management
- Test and Screen Products
- Conformance/Compliance

MANAGE ASSETS:

- Human Resource Management
- Health, Safety, Security, and Business Services
- Information Assets
- Financial Assets
- Physical Assets

Figure 4-7 UTMC Enterprise and Business Segments

The First Meeting—Affinity from Chaos. During the first meeting, each business segment team identified target business activities and grouped them according to their natural relationships to each other. The grouping activity used the Hoshin planning affinity technique to develop an affinity diagram. The Hoshin planning affinity technique is an excellent tool for understanding complex issues, practitioners have found, and it is very effective at helping organizations overcome traditional ways of looking at situations. Both of these qualities were essential in this first step of the modeling process.

To develop an affinity diagram, team members first used the "blue slip creativity technique" to identify all business activities associated with their business segment. Each activity was written on a post-it note that was randomly placed on a large piece of blank paper. Then the participants silently grouped the post-it notes. This process allowed each member to participate equally. Finally, using a consensus approach, participants created business process headings for each group and business function super-headings for combined groups. For example, the affinity diagram for the business segment "corporate management" had the following clusters of activities.

- Establish/implement/support policies
- Business planning
- Manage resources
- Provide leadership
- Establish business direction

The resulting affinity diagrams became the basis for a second meeting with the business segment team.

The Second Meeting—Refining and Organizing. During the second meeting, each team refined the business processes catalogued in the affinity diagram. The Hoshin planning tree diagram was used to organize the processes into a hierarchy. This involved a lively brainstorming session and required the participants to arrange the business activities into a tree diagram for each business function. This "rational" process complemented the "creative" affinity process by identifying missing or misplaced business activities. Next, the MIS group leaders modified each business segment's affinity diagram to reflect the tree diagrams.

Figure 4-8 shows part of the tree diagram for the "establish business direction" function of the "corporate management" business segment.

The Third Meeting—Defining Process Interrelationships. During the third meeting, each business segment team identified the information that flowed between their segment's varied business processes as well as the information that flowed to and from other business segments. The MIS leaders used the creative approach of extension to adapt the Hoshin planning interrelationship digraph to show this data flow.

The Fourth Meeting—Mapping Processes to Systems. During the fourth meeting, each business segment team used the Hoshin planning matrix to map the business processes to the systems that support them. Figure 4-9 shows the matrix for corporate management.

Defining the Target System Architecture

Next, the MIS team resolved disparities between the 15 business segment process interrelationship digraphs, where one group's digraph identified a relationship that another group's did not. Some of these omissions were oversights, but many highlighted existing business process problems. Exploration of these "disconnects" enabled the MIS team to identify opportunities to improve cross-functional awareness, cooperation, and integration.

With the business segment process interrelationship digraphs in agreement, the MIS team was ready to apply the knowledge gained during the 60 business segment team meetings. This resulted in a digraph for the entire organization. To complete the executive overview of the enterprise, the MIS team also developed an enterprise-wide affinity diagram and tree diagrams for each of the four enterprise segments. These diagrams were derived directly from the completed process knowledge base.

The MIS team used the business segments' process-oriented interrelationship digraphs and their process/system matrices to develop interrelationship digraphs for information systems for each business segment. These represented the ideal systems architecture tailored to meet UTMC's business needs. The diagrams showed each system and identified target system interfaces to all other systems. This target system architecture enabled UTMC to evaluate its current system portfolio. And clearly indicated the need for new systems, the need to enhance or restructure existing systems, and the need for new system system interfaces.

Initiating the Change Process

The enterprise model not only served as a "roadmap" for all future systems development, but it also identified many reengineering oppor-

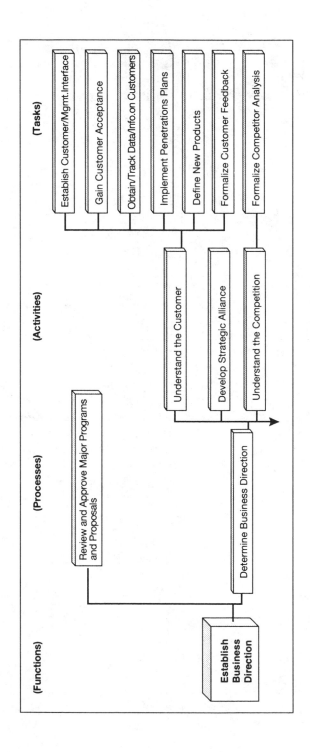

Figure 4-8 Tree Diagram—Corporate Management—Establish Business Directions

	Allocate Resources	Management Process	Performance Mgmt.	Strategic Planning	Operational Plan	Business Model	Define Market	Rev. & Approve Major Programs & Proposals	Identify New Initiatives	Establish Leadership	Make Timely & Effective Decisions	Establish Community Involvement	Ensure Compliance	Develop HR Policies
Business Model	x			x	x	x	x	x						
Objective Tracking System		x		x										
Decision Making Tool		x		x	x	x	x	x	x	x	x			
EIS System		x	x									x		
Hoshin Planning		x					x	x	x	x	x			
Strategic Scheduling System												x		

"X" indicates that the system addresses the business process

Figure 4-9 System/Process Matrix–Corporate Management

tunities. This second result continues to be very important to UTMC's senior management because of their on-going need to reengineer their business in today's competitive marketplace. Each of the 15 business segment teams reconvened to identify and set priorities for the business changes necessary to achieve the target model. The teams ranked each of their recommended changes as a high, medium, or low priority based on the following criteria:

- Company goals that will be met
- Magnitude of problems that will be solved
- Integration advantages
- Logical sequence of changes
- Benefits that will be received

The ranking process identified 25 company-wide high priority changes. Many groups identified the same changes as high priorities, such as the need to improve engineering data collection and analysis.

Next, each business segment team elected a representative to participate in the final company-wide ranking. These representatives presented their team's high priority business changes to the other representative, who then rated each change against the criteria supplied by UTMC's operating committee. The rating criteria included the seven Malcolm Baldrige Award criteria:

- Improve leadership
- Manage and analyze information
- Improve quality planning
- Develop and achieve human potential
- Continuous quality improvement
- Provide quality goods and services
- Know and satisfy customer

Additional criteria critical to UTMC's success included:

- Make effective decisions
- Improve utilization of employees
- Free up time to sell products
- Introduce new products in a timely manner

This rating process produced a list of UTMC's greatest process improvement opportunities. That is, the most important opportunities included:

- Significant changes to UTMC's work in progress and material planning process
- Cost accounting enhancements to support improved management decision making
- A UTMC business model to evaluate the impact of business alternatives on the overall company
- Enhanced costing scheduling and reporting of UTMC programs
- Greater customer focus
- Process changes to efficiently certify material vendors

Enterprise Modeling Results

During the modeling process, UTMC experienced many unexpected positive results. Nearly all the 80 business segment team members initially had difficulty thinking in terms of business processes. They generally thought along organizational lines and focused on historical responsibilities without considering the business purpose for their actions. The model building experience helped them to see relationships between groups that originally were not clear to them. Comments such as, "I always wondered how we did that" and "I never knew you did so much" were frequently made during the meetings.

The enhanced teamwork and understanding generated by the meetings supported UTMC's goal to develop a culture consistent with the Malcolm Baldrige National Quality Award. Identifying all the business processes in the company and encouraging UTMC employees to orient their thoughts toward processes have been important first steps toward this goal.

UTMC's CEO noted that these intangible results alone represented a respectable payback for the effort expended constructing the model. Impressed with the model, he requested that the MIS team that had worked with the 15 business segment teams document their observations. The team produced a list of 15 observations about UTMC's culture and nine general observations about UTMC's culture and nine general observations about UTMC business processes. These observations addressed such areas as:

- Cultural inconsistencies throughout the company due largely to UTMC's short history. By addressing these issues, overall teamork and cross-functional cooperation could be enhanced.
- The difficulty in looking beyond current ways of working to define the"target" enterprise. Company-wide creativity training would improve UTMC's ability to adapt to a changing business environment.
- The difficulty employees experienced in balancing "divergent" activities, such as looking for better ways of doing their jobs, with the "convergent" activities of performing their every-day tasks. Arriving at the proper balance is a continuing management challenge for UTMC.
- The challenges management faces in clearly communicating future process changes and functional responsibilities. The enterprise model interrelationships digraphs should provide a company-wide method for communicating such changes.

Since there was such broad employee involvement in developing the model, management considers the model to be a valuable company resource. They look to the model for insight when they assume new responsibilities or need to understand how another part of the company works.

While the rest of the company was gaining an increased cross-functional appreciation of UTMC, the MIS managers and analysts were gaining a valuable broad perspective of the company. When the MIS team began working with senior management on the corporate management model segment, they were able to demonstrate the knowledge they obtained from developing the other segments of the model. Previously, the senior managers saw a great need for a new UTMC business planning company, but they were unable to envision its structure. Aided by the incomplete model, the MIS team was able to present senior management with a proposal that eventually led to defining a single business planning system to support the company-wide planning process.

Building for the Future

Implementation of the enterprise model at UTMC has dramatically changed the way the company plans for process and system changes. The model has provided a foundation for building long range MIS plans and has facilitated alignment of the MIS department with UTMC's business needs. This focus will allow UTMC to maximize the return on its I/T investment. And the enterprise model's integration blueprint is helping MIS management supply UTMC. managers with concise, timely, and accurate information to support executive management decision making.

The enterprise model has also helped UTMC develop a culture that seemed unattainable just a few years ago. The cross-functional teams that designed the model's business segments improved teamwork, communications, and mutual understanding among UTMC departments. The enterprise model also helped tie together several major UTMC initiatives, including the Malcolm Baldrige Award, Hoshin planning, creativity, and product development's stage gate program.

According to UTMC's vice president of operations, Bob Cutter, "The enterprise modeling activity has assisted in focusing UTMC on a process culture. This will provide the foundation for significant improvements in future years. The improved cross-functional awareness and teamwork achieved during the initial phase of the project have already provided tangible payback. Understanding your own business processes and capability in the first step towards total customer satisfaction."

CONCLUSION

Based on the successes and failures of past information system planning efforts, we see two necessary ingredients to a good strategic planning effort. One is that the plans must look toward the future. This may seem obvious, but in these turbulent times, the future is not likely to be an extrapolation of the past. So a successful planning effort needs to support "peering into the future."

A second necessary ingredient is that information system plans must be linked to business plans. Again this may seem obvious, but, again, unless the planning methodology specifically requires such links, the systems plans may not be relevant because they do not support the corporate strategy. This is not so likely as it was a few years ago; business plans and system plans appear to be drawing closer together in more and more companies.

In this chapter, we have described a number of the most popular approaches to information system planning at the strategic level. No single method is best and no single one is the most widely used in business. In fact, many companies use a combination of these approaches, because they deal with different aspects of planning.

QUESTIONS AND EXERCISES

REVIEW QUESTIONS

1. Give one reason why planning is important.
2. Describe a typical planning cycle.
3. According to Drury, what are the two most important determinants of a successful information systems steering committee?
4. What is the main contribution of the stages of growth theory to information systems planning?
5. What are critical success factors? How do they contribute to the systems planning process?
6. Explain how the investment strategy analysis approach can be used to formulate (or reveal) strategies in the use of information systems.
7. What are the advantages of the scenario approach to planning?
8. The text identifies the following areas that scenarios should include. Give a few considerations in each area that are relevant to systems planning.
   a. Business environment
   b. Government and society
   c. People changes
   d. Financial considerations
   e. Technology
9. Why does Denny's use a scenario approach to planning?
10. Briefly describe the goal of linkage analysis planning and the five steps in it.
11. What was EPRI's challenge and how did they solve it?
12. What is the creative problem solving approach? List Couger's three variants to the classical CPS method. Why is this a valuable approach for information systems planning?
13. Draw a chart showing the steps in the enterprise modeling process used by UTMC. For each step, give the purpose and the name of the chart or diagram that represents the output from that step.

DISCUSSION QUESTIONS

1. Which of the frameworks for systems planning seems most useful to you? Why?
2. If you were in charge of system planning for a small firm, what questions would you ask the company officers to determine which planning approach(es) would be most appropriate?
3. In Chapter 2, we state that strategies are out, visioning is in, because no one can plan in turbulent times. In this chapter we say that planning is crucial. How do you reconcile the two viewpoints?

EXERCISES

1. Survey the current literature on the subject of systems planning. Are there other approaches or frameworks not mentioned in this text? What automated products are available on the market to assist information systems executives in the planning process?

2. Visit the chief information officer of a local organization. What planning process does it use? What is the planning horizon? To what degree do the systems plans and the business plans relate to each other?

3. Create a simple information linkage analysis chart of your current personal relationships. Put yourself in the middle box, and each relationship in its own box around you, with a line from you to each of them. Who has the "power" in each link? How might that power shift in the future? Which is the most important relationship to you? How could you make it more "win-win?"

4. Ask the CIO of a nearby company what electronic channels his or her firm has in place. Ask about the benefits both parties receive in each link.

REFERENCES

1. DRURY, D. H., "An Evaluation of Data Processing Steering Committees." *MIS Quarterly* (MISRC, University of Minnesota, 271 19th Avenue South, Minneapolis, MN 55455), December 1984, pp. 257-265.

2. NOLAN, R. L., and C. F. GIBSON, "Managing the Four Stages of EDP Growth," *Harvard Business Review* (Reprint Service, HBR, Soldiers Field, Boston, MA 02163), January/February 1974, p. 76ff.

3. NOLAN, R. L. "Managing the Crisis in Data Processing," *Harvard Business Review* (address above), March/April 1979.

4. BENBASAT, I., A. S. DEXTER, D. H. DRURY, and R. G. GOLDSTEIN, "A Critique of the Stage Hypothesis: Theory and empirical evidence," *Communications of the ACM*, ACM (Order Department, Box 64145, Baltimore, MD 21264), May 1984, pp. 467-485.

5. McFARLAN, F. W., and J. L. McKENNEY, *Corporate Information Systems,* 211 pages.

6. ROCKART, J. "Chief Executives Define Their Own Data Needs," *Harvard Business Review* (address above), March/April 1979, pp. 81-92.

7. STAGE BY STAGE, Nolan, Norton & Co. (Boston, MA), Vol. 4, No. 4, Winter 1985.

8. YANKELOVICH, SKELLY & WHITE, 575 Madison Ave., New York, NY 10022.

9. ENZER, S., "How to Think Strategically," *New Management* (Box 3007, Costa Mesa, CA 92628), Vol. 2, No. 1, 1984, pp. 53-56.

10. PRIMOZIC, K. I., E. A. PRIMOZIC, and J. LEBEN, *Strategic Choices: Supremacy, Survival, or Sayanara* (McGraw-Hill, NY), 1991, 272 pages.

11. PORTER, M., *Competitive Strategy,* The Free Press (866 Third Ave., New York, N.Y. 10022), 1980. Also see *Competitive Advantage*, 1985.

12. MANN, M. M., R. L. RUDMAN, T. A. JENCKES, and B. C. McNURLIN, "EPRINET: Leveraging Knowledge In the Electric Utility Industry," *MIS Quarterly* (address above), September 1991, pp. 403-421.

13. COUGER, J. D., *Creative Problem Solving (CPS) and Opportunity Finding*, CRCI Working Paper 92-1, University of Colorado, Colorado Springs, January 1992.

14. SIMON, H. A., *The New Science of Management* (Harper and Row, New York), 1960.

15. PARNES, S. J., R. B. NOLLER and A. M. BIONDI, (ED.), *Guide to Creative Action* (Scribner's Sons, New York), 1977.

16. COUGER, J. D., "Ensuring Creative Approaches in Information System Design," *Managerial and Decision Economics,* Vol. 11, 1990, pp. 281-295.

17. SNOW, T., and MELCIOR, T. "Designing a Target Enterprise: Business Modeling at United Technologies Microelectronics Center," presented at the Dooley Group 10th Annual Executive Conference, December, 1991.

FIVE

INTRODUCTION

In Part 2—Chapters 5 through 8—we discuss the essential information technologies, beginning with the overall architecture of future information systems. It has become obvious that this architecture will be *distributed systems*. In fact, the ideal structure that is evolving is an enterprise-wide distributed network of systems that uses products from multiple vendors. This architecture would conceivably allow any device to access information from, or do processing on, any other device.

The architecture of the past has been mainframes performing batch and on-line processing, communicating with "dumb" terminals—those without their own processing capabilities. That architecture is slowly giving way to distributed systems, as companies move applications (or parts of applications) off their mainframes, when economics favor the move.

We believe that the development of distributed systems will be based on three cornerstones.

- Cooperative processing
- Open system interconnection
- Distributed databases

In this chapter, we discuss distributed systems in general, and focus on the first essential technology: cooperative processing. The second essential technology—the telecommunications infrastructure based on open systems interconnection—is discussed in Chapter 6. Chapter 7 will discuss the third crucial technology—distributed databases—as well as other information and data issues. Finally, Chapter 8 looks at data center operations.

What Is a Distributed System?

How often the question is asked, "What is a distributed system?" And how seldom a single answer is satisfactory! The reason is that so many definitions exist. Following are five system structures that have been called *distributed*.

A Hierarchy of Processors. A hierarchy of processors is the most familiar *information system* structure, because it has been the one favored by mainframe vendors. As shown in Figure 5-1, the system has a large, controlling computer at the top of the hierarchy, and PCs or terminals at the lowest level. In between can be one, two, or more levels of processors, with the total workload shared among them. The important characteristic of this structure is that the mainframe, or host computer, is the central, and controlling, component.

It is not always clear just where the data is to be stored in such a system. One view is to store all data at the top. Another is to have the master records at the top but selected subsets at intermediate levels; the master records are then updated periodically and revised records are sent to the intermediate

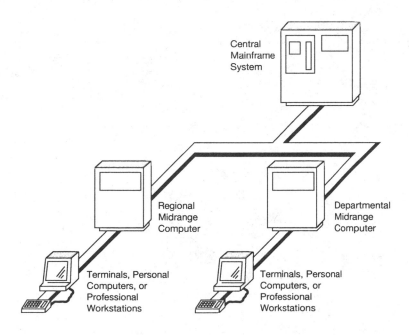

Figure 5-1 A Hierarchy of Processors

files. Still another view is to store master records where they are most used and periodically provide updated records to the top for backup purposes. In any of these views, however, it is assumed that any node on the network can access any data record within the system, as long as it is authorized to do so.

Decentralized Stand-Alone Systems. Decentralized stand-alone systems do not really form a distributed system at all. They are basically a holdover from the 1960s, when departments put in their own departmental computers, with no intention of connecting them to other systems. Hence, they are decentralized, not distributed. As shown in Figure 5-2, this structure has been somewhat modernized to allow a *little data* to *flow* among the stand-alone systems. But this flow is mostly upward to the corporate system. Sometimes, but not often, files from several of these systems can be accessed from a single terminal. The distinguishing feature of this architecture is that it represents the "islands of automation" so familiar in companies today.

LAN-based Systems. Systems based on a LAN have become widely used as the basis for distributed systems. This approach began in the office system arena with LANs providing the links between PCs, print servers, and gateways to other networks. As shown in Figure 5-3, this structure has no hierarchy. Like the telephone network, a LAN-based system allows "peer-to-peer" communications among components—rather than hierarchical communication through a

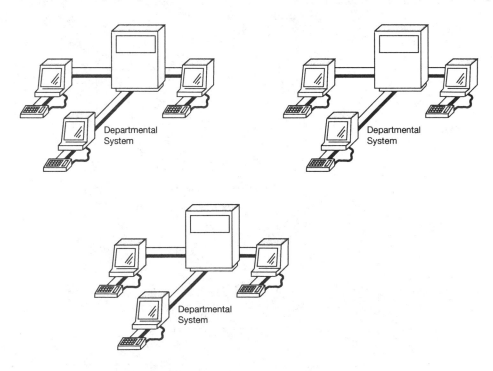

Figure 5-2 Decentralized Standalone Systems

Figure 5-3 A LAN-based System

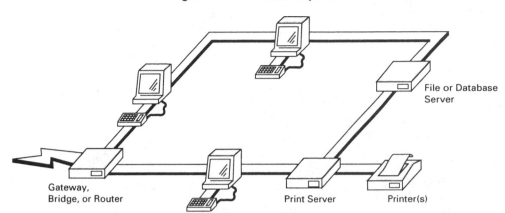

File or Database
Server

Gateway,
Bridge, or Router

Print Server   Printer(s)

central hub. This is the key characteristic of this structure: No computer is more superior than another, as is the case in the hierarchical structure.

LAN-Based Systems that Communicate with Mainframe-Based Systems. LAN-based systems that communicate with mainframe-based systems is another structure for distributed systems. As shown in Figure 5-4, it is essentially a combination of the hierarchy approach (for mainframe-based processing) and the LAN-based system (in offices). This structure is likely to be the "interim" structure for many years to come, as companies link their various automation islands. This structure allows them to retain their IT investments, but it does not take full advantage of advances in the technology nor cause them to rethink their business processes.

Cooperative Systems. Cooperative systems are the newest member of the distributed system family. As shown in Figure 5-5, a cooperative system melds and extends the previous approaches. All the components are linked to each other via interconnected LANs and WANs. In essence it is an internet—a network of networks. The underlying design principles are that all machines are equal, and no machine is the hub of the system. However, it is quite likely that mainframes will be the central database servers and communication servers, because only they will be able to serve tens of thousands of nodes.

A cooperative system is defined as one in which the various components cooperate with each other to perform a task. As an example, to obtain, say, sporting event tickets, an order taker at a workstation accesses a mainframe database over a WAN to see seat availability and reserve the seats. Once the selection is made, the system uses a credit card server, on its own LAN or a nearby one, to process the charge. Finally, the workstation application would request the print server on its own LAN to print the tickets.

Cooperative systems will be the architecture of choice because they allow companies to take advantage of the characteristics of individual machines, while, at the same time, extending the usefulness of their current IT investments.

Figure 5-4 LAN-Based Systems that Communicate with Mainframe-Based Systems

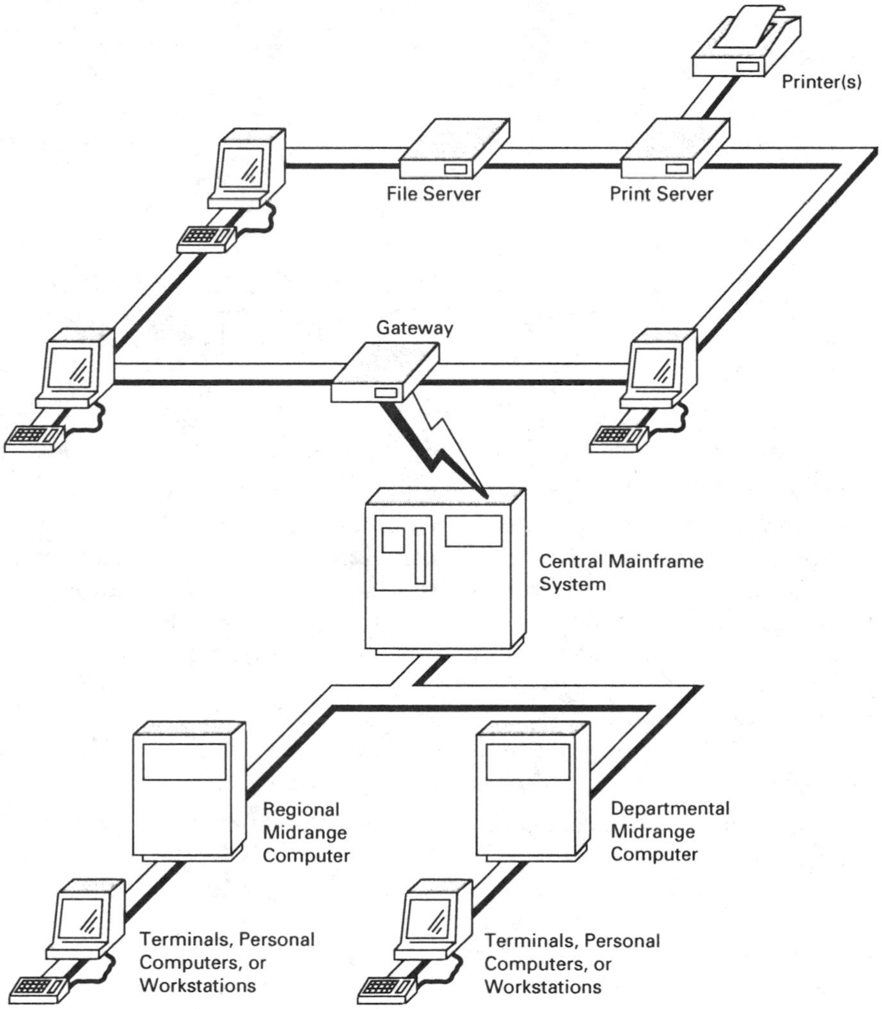

Evolving Toward Cooperative Processing

Distributed systems are indeed evolving. Figure 5-6 demonstrates this evolution, beginning with the data processing era in the upper left consisting of mainframe host computers with terminals attached. Later stages in the evolution have PCs replacing terminals as the primary access device. Other variations of this stage have regional or departmental computers as shown earlier in Figure 5-1.

Meanwhile, PCs also gained popularity as stand-alone personal productivity tools as shown in the upper-right corner of Figure 5-6. As PC users expanded applications (beyond word processing and spreadsheets to communication and database access), PCs became workstations interconnected

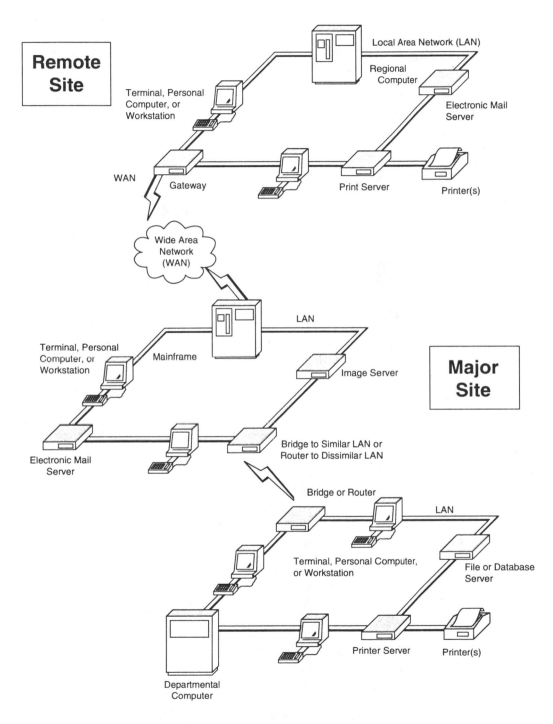

Figure 5-5 Cooperative System

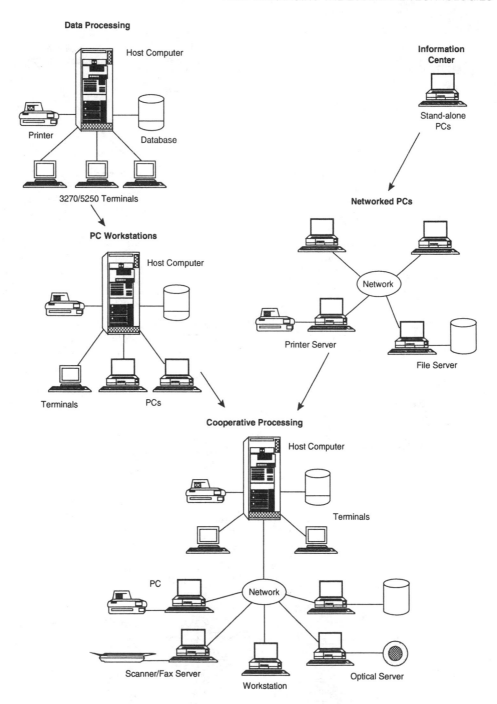

Figure 5.6 Cooperative Processing Evolution
(Reprinted by permission of Metafile Information Systems, Rochestoer, MN)

through a LAN. Cooperative processing is emerging as the convergence of these two evolutionary trends to provide the full range of capability required by information workers in organizations.

Four Attributes of Distributed Systems

The degree to which a system is distributed can be determined by answering four questions.

- Where is the processing done?
- How are the processors and other devices interconnected?
- Where is the information stored?
- What rules or standards are used?

Distributed processing is the ability for more than one interconnected processor to be operating at the same time. This usually means processing an application on more than one computer. The goal in distributed processing is to move the processing as close to the user as possible, or to use those machines that do a part of a job best. The latter is cooperative processing, a subset of distributed processing.

An advanced form of distributed processing permits interoperability, which is the capability for different machines using different operating systems on different networks to work together on tasks. They exchange information in standard ways without requiring changes in command languages or functionality and without physical intervention.

Charlie Bachman [1], a pioneer in the database and distributed system fields, pointed out to us that there are really two forms of interoperability. One is the transparent communication between *systems* using system protocols. In this form, the systems decide when to interoperate. People implementing the International Standards Organization OSI reference model have developed protocols for standard file and job transfers to permit this form of interoperability, says Bachman.

The second form of interoperability is the interactive or two-way flow of messages between *user applications*; it is already supported by OSI. In this form, user applications can be activated by receiving messages. Both kinds of interoperability are important, says Bachman.

Connectivity among processors means that each processor in a distributed system can send data and messages to any other processor through electronic communication linkages. A desirable structure for reliable distributed systems has at least two independent paths between any two nodes to provide automatic alternate routing. Planned redundancy of this type is critical for reliable operation. Such redundancy has not been implemented in most LANs, which is one reason they have been so fragile.

Distributed databases are being defined in at least two ways. One divides a database and distributes its portions throughout a system, without duplicating the data. Any portion is accessible from any node, subject to access authorization. Users do not need to know where a piece of data is located to access it—the system knows where all data is stored.

The second definition sees a distributed database as one that contains distributed duplicate data. The same data is stored at several locations, with one site containing the master file. In this approach, synchronizing data is a *significant* problem. In either approach, common data definitions are important.

Systemwide rules means that an operating discipline for the distributed system has been developed and is enforced at all times. These rules govern communication between nodes, security, data accessibility, program and file transfers, and common operating procedures.

In the 1990s, these systemwide rules are increasingly based on "open systems," which operate on products from many vendors, avoiding the problem of being "locked in" to proprietary systems from one vendor.

The Changing Meaning of "Open Systems"

The key phrase in the distributed system world is "open systems." Unfortunately, the meaning is not very clear, principally because that meaning keeps changing. In the 1980s, open systems referred mainly to telecommunications and meant a company's intention to implement products that followed the OSI reference model as soon as feasible.

In about 1990, the definition expanded to include operating systems. To some, in fact, open systems became synonymous with the UNIX operating system, because it runs on many more platforms than any other operating system. At about that time, UNIX was recognized as *possibly* being appropriate for mainline business computing. Today, that tentativeness has disappeared; UNIX has become a significant contender because the main criteria for choosing an operating system these days is its openness. By this definition, UNIX is the clear winner.

Interestingly, in 1992, the definition of open systems appeared to shift again; this time to the interfaces between applications. Now "open" appears to mean standardized interfaces that allow products to interoperate across multivendor networks. This new definition allows individual products to be innovative yet connectable.

With this new focus of attention has arisen the importance of "application program interfaces" (APIs). APIs define the way to present data to another component of a system—a machine, database, and even an electronic mail system. They make writing distributed systems far easier.

It would not surprise us if the meaning of open systems expands further, because data is not currently included in it. In the early 1990s, the only open data component was structured query language (SQL), the standard intermediary language for accessing databases. In the mid-1990s, we expect a data component of open systems to be defined, one that embraces object-oriented databases.

So the term "open systems" keeps expanding, because it truly is the crux of distributed systems that will allow products—hardware, software, data, and communications—from multiple vendors to work together.

Although some people see the main reason for distributing systems as improving the use of computer resources, that is just a technical reason.

The real organizational impetus behind distributed systems is moving responsibility for computing resources out to the business units that use them. With that in mind, we now briefly address this side of the coin—the business reasons for distributing applications and the responsibilities that go with them.

When to Distribute Computing Responsibilities

Information systems management needs a corporate policy for deciding when the development, operation, and maintenance of an application should be distributed. Individual end users and departments should not be left on their own to make these decisions, especially where connectivity to the enterprise-wide network is important.

Although technical considerations are critical, they should not be the prime force behind a system architecture. Rather the major reason for choosing a particular distributed system architecture hinges on: *Who should make the key management operating decisions?*

Decision-making responsibilities are being pushed down in organizations, with business managers and self-managing work groups being given more autonomy and responsibility for the resources they use. One such resource is IT. People who make the decisions about how their portion of the business operates also should be making the decisions about how they use IT.

Francis Wagner, a business data processing pioneer, once told us that he believes people perform best when they are responsible for their own mistakes. If they have no one to blame but themselves, then the quality of their performance increases. The result is a more effective use of corporate resources.

We therefore see a driving force behind distributed processing being the desire to give more people more control over their work. This autonomy can happen at any of six levels—company, division, site, department, group, or individual.

James Wetherbe, of the University of Minnesota [2], suggests asking the following three *business questions* before distributing information systems functions and the responsibilities that go with them.

Are the Operations Interdependent? When it is important for one operation to know what another is doing, those operations are interdependent; therefore, their planning, software development, machine resources, and operations need to be centralized, says Wetherbe, to keep the operations synchronized. Two industries in which interdependency is important are manufacturing and airlines.

Are the Businesses Really Homogeneous? If the operations do not need to know what each other is doing, then many systems functions can be decentralized, *unless* the operations truly have a lot in common.

For example, in the fast-food business, each franchise has the same information processing needs; they are very homogeneous. But they do not need to know what each other is doing, so they are not interdependent.

Under these circumstances, processing may be distributed, but planning, software development, and hardware selection should be centralized, says Wetherbe.

Deciding whether the information processing in two parts of a business is truly homogeneous is not always obvious, says Wetherbe. For instance, not all department stores are the same. One major retailer found that they needed to create two information systems for handling credit charges—one for their upscale stores and one for their discount stores. The needs of the two types of stores were so different that a single system would not suffice. But, says Wetherbe, their corporate information systems department does control planning. This has given them the ability to seize marketing opportunities quickly when they can reuse systems built by either operation. So, centralized planning is important, whether processing is distributed or not, he says.

Does the Corporate Culture Support Decentralization? Even if the business units do quite different things and do not need to know what each other is doing, corporate culture might dictate that some functions be centralized.

Wetherbe cites the example of a large company with sixty widely diverse business units. Although it might appear logical for this company to distribute all functions, they have chosen to centralize finance, human resources, and systems planning. They want to offer corporate-wide career opportunities, with as little retraining as possible. With the central staff doing systems planning and coordination, the company can more easily move people and reuse systems.

If none of these three criteria—inter-dependency, homogeneity, or corporate culture—forces centralization, Wetherbe suggests letting each business unit direct its own information systems activity, with the central organization coordinating the plans.

Two Guiding Frameworks

Now that we have briefly addressed why to distribute systems, we look at how, via two guiding frameworks—one from an organizational perspective and the other from a technical perspective.

An Organizational Framework. One possible structure is to locate processing power and information storage at six levels in an organization. Starting at the top of the organization, these six levels are

1. Corporate headquarters
2. Regional or country processing centers
3. Site processing centers (plants, warehouses, branch offices)
4. Departmental processors
5. Work group processors
6. Individual workstations

Not all levels need exist in any given organization. For instance, the region or country level is often omitted. Most of these levels are self-explanatory, except perhaps work groups. A work group is a relatively small group of people (perhaps ranging from three to thirty) who do essentially the same work. Any one person in the group can substitute for any other, if necessary. In an accounting department of a medium-sized organization, the entire accounts payable function might be handled by one work group. In a much larger organization, with a much larger accounting department, perhaps only the transportation accounts payable would be handled by one work group. Other groups would handle the other accounting functions.

Note that these six levels tend to fall into two categories as shown in Figure 5-7. *The top three levels* corporate, regional, and site—are the domain of traditional information systems. These are the levels where computers have often resided in the past. *The bottom three levels*—department, work group, and individual—traditionally have *not* had local processing power and information storage. Terminals may have been provided, but they have been tied to processors at one of the top three levels. These bottom three levels are where the bulk of the employees of an organization reside and work.

Typical Organizational Structures. The six-level architecture is based primarily on a conventional hierarchical structure—headquarters, divisions, plants, functional departments, and work groups. For instance, one very typical organizational structure for a manufacturing organization groups the people within a plant into five functional departments: engineering, production, marketing, accounting, and personnel. All the marketing people work within the marketing department, regardless of the products they market. In this type of organizational structure, computing power is needed (1) for the marketing department as a whole, (2) for groups of people within marketing, where each group is concerned with one product or product line, and (3) for the individuals in each of the groups.

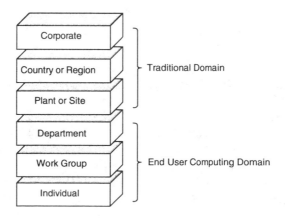

Figure 5-7 A Six-Level Architecture

Figure 5-8 Components of the SUMURU Distributed System Architecture

Processors
    Single-user systems (SU)
    Multiple-user systems (MU)
    Remote utility systems (RU)
Networks
    Local network (LN)
    Remote networks (RN)
Services
    Terminal access
    File Transfer
    Computer mail
Standards
    Operating systems

Other Organizational Structures. There is growing interest in organizational structures that are based on profit centers, projects, products, or customers. The most common instance of this is a *matrix,* where employees have one boss for administrative matters and another for job-related matters. An example is an engineer who reports to an engineering supervisor for raises and such, and to a project executive for the particular product being designed. In a matrix organization, the computing power could be provided for departments, projects, and individuals.

Another structure defines groups of employees in *self-managed work teams* that are product and customer oriented. The idea of manufacturing cells—where all the machines needed to manufacture one type of part are clustered in a cell—is spreading to the service industry. A self-managed work teams contains all the people who serve a particular customer or offer a particular product. These people represent all the necessary functions, legal, marketing, customer service, and so forth. The intent is to give them more autonomy and decision-making power to serve their customers better. By allowing them to manage themselves, it is hoped that they can offer more personalized and faster service.

The six-level architecture appears to be appropriate even for organizational structures such as matrices and self-managed work teams.

A Technical Framework. In 1982, Einar Stefferud, David Farber, and Ralph Dement developed a conceptual framework for distributed systems [3]. It uses the acronym SUMURU, meaning "single user, multiple user, remote utility." Surprisingly, SUMURU is as appropriate today as it was in 1982—perhaps even more so, because distributed systems are now the focus of the computer field.

Their framework is based on the premise that the migration of computer power to end users will be the driving force for network-based information systems. What is needed, the authors say, is a coherent plan to guide this migration. The plan includes four components—processors, networks, services, and standards. Figure 5-8 summarizes the SUMURU components and Figure 5-9, illustrates the architecture.

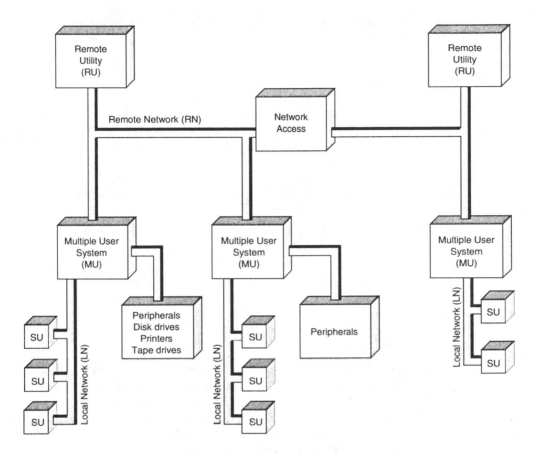

Figure 5-9 The SUMURU Architecture

Processors. The authors see three levels of processors, usually with associated information storage. The name of their architecture, SUMURU, comes from these three levels. *Single-user systems* (SUs) can operate in a stand-alone mode but also will be connected to local networks (LNs). Today, SUs are the "clients" in client/server computing. *Multiple-user systems* (MUs) will serve local groups of users. Today, these are the servers. These MUs will also provide (1) backup facilities for other MUs, (2) heavier duty computation for SUs, (3) program libraries for themselves and SUs, and (4) database management for central files.

Ideally, say the authors, the SUs will be scaled-down versions of the MUs— able to run the same software (to reduce software development and maintenance) but without all the features needed for shared operation on an MU.

Remote utility systems (RU) will provide the heavy duty computing, corporate database management, remote batch processing, and backup for the MUs. For most organizations, RUs are the corporate mainframes as well as commercial value-added network services, such as on-line news wire services and commercial databases.

Networks. The authors see a network architecture consisting of two levels. LNs will provide high-speed information transfer as well as close coupling between several SUs and a local MU. Today these are LANs. The MUs may provide personal files, shared files, and program libraries for the SUs, and they can be the gateway between the LNs and remote networks. *Remote networks* (RNs) provide connections among MUs and connection to both in-house and commercial RUs. The RNs—which today are called metropolitan area networks (MANs) and WANs—generally will have lower transfer speeds than the LNs, but still should have enough bandwidth to provide file transfers within reasonable time limits.

Services. The authors see three main types of services that this network architecture will provide. *Terminal access* is from a terminal tied either to an MU or a SU. The terminal must be able to access any MU, RU or SU, subject only to management constraints (not technical barriers). The SU might well act as a "dumb" terminal in this instance. Users must also have *file transfer* ability to send and receive entire files. To do this, a user must have both read and write privileges at both ends of the transfer. Finally, the system must provide an *electronic mail* service.

Standards. Corporate standards are needed in three areas: operating systems, communication protocols, and database management systems (DBMSs). Corporate standards on operating systems are designed to minimize barriers to transferring and using programs and data. Ideally, the selected operating systems should run on more than one vendor's equipment. UNIX fits this description. Standard communication protocols will be needed for terminal access, file transfers, and computer mail. In the communication area, Transport Carrier Protocol/Internet Protocol (TCP/IP) has become a defacto standard in private industry and government. Formerly, it was just seen as a precursor to OSI. In the database arena, no distributed database management systems have become a standard.

As mentioned, this distributed system framework has stood the test of time; it is still an appropriate design guide for distributed system architects.

It should be clear by this point that distributed information systems have three crucial ingredients: processing, communications, and data—along with the standards or rules that govern them. As noted earlier, we see distributed systems being built on principles in these three arenas:

- Cooperative processing
- Open System Interconnection
- Distributed data

We now turn to the first "cornerstone of distributed systems:" cooperative processing.

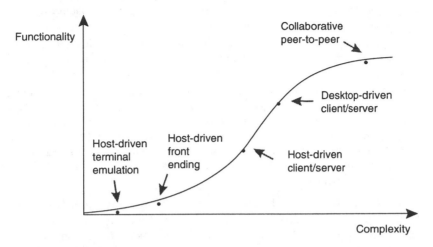

Figure 5-10 The Evolution of Client/Server Computing
(Reprinted by permission of Apple Computer)

COOPERATIVE PROCESSING

Cooperative processing means that processes on two or more geographically dispersed computers cooperate to complete a task. In a primitive way, we have had a form of cooperative processing with this broad definition for several years, in the form of terminals connected to host (usually mainframe) computers.

Five Forms of Cooperative Processing

Lani Spund [4] of Apple Computer identifies several forms that are evolving from this early form. Figure 5-10 shows five types of client/server computing on a functionality/complexity curve.

- With *host-driven terminal emulation*, the desktop computer runs an application that connects to a host as a standard host terminal. In the 1980s the original "dumb" terminals were replaced by PCs that had to operate in "terminal emulation" mode whenever they communicated with the host.

- With *host-driven front ending*, the desktop computer runs a host-based application by providing an interface (usually graphical) that is easier to use than the typical host-based interface. The desktop application intercepts the character streams from the host and interprets them for a more "user friendly" display and interaction. In addition, the desktop application can collect information from the user in this same friendly interface mode, and send it to the host as pseudokeystrokes.

- With a *host-driven client/server*, the desktop runs an application that turns it into a server capable of receiving messages from the host. These messages cause the desktop application to perform specific tasks, such as displaying a menu, window, or dialog box. In addition, the desktop can send information back to the host, at the prompting of the host or a user response. Essentially, the desktop acts as a slave or server to the mainframe.

- With *desktop-driven client/server* structures, the host functions as a transaction processing server. The desktop application submits queries for data or updates to the server. Standard services on the server perform the requested services.

- With *peer-to-peer* structures, processing occurs simultaneously on both the desktop and the host, with control of the application switching between the two. This arrangement combines the desktop-driven and host-driven client/server structures into a single application. In the peer-to-peer model, both the host and the desktop can request services from each other. This permits simultaneous execution of multiple applications on various hardware platforms, each acting as a node in a network.

Note that by the end of this evolutionary sequence, the terms "host" and "desktop" lose their traditional meanings. In fact, even in the two client/server structures, whether host- or desktop-driven, any computer can be the "client" and any can be the "server," depending only on which machine is requesting, and which is filling the request.

To explore cooperative processing, which we believe will be the processingmode of choice in distributed systems, we will discuss:

- Why it is important
- The processing components of a cooperative system
- A case example of a departmental cooperative system

Why Cooperative Processing Is Important

In network-based businesses, cooperative processing in general—and client/server computing specifically—will play an important role, for the following five reasons:

Lower Cost. First, cooperative processing permits lower-cost enterprise-wide computing. By allowing companies to mix and match client and server machines, cooperative processing allows developers not only to use lower-cost machines for new systems but also to link them to existing systems, thereby preserving their organization's investments in those systems. The significant amounts of money saved using microprocessor-based machines are the main driver in moving to cooperative processing. But the significant prior investments are equally strong inducements not to change. The mix-and-match capability of client/server computing permits both to occur and also creates more flexible system architectures, where companies can plug in new technologies as they become feasible.

Focus on the User. Second, cooperative processing makes the end user—via the workstation—the focus of computing. Cooperative processing reverses the role of the mainframe and the workstation, and turns traditional computing on its head. Whereas the hosts—be they mainframes or minicomputers—were previously the focus of attention, now, the desktop workstation is. This brings PCs and their successor—the workstation—into mainstream computing.

The important point is that this shift of focus, which occurred in 1989 to 1990, relates to enterprise-wide computing, not just personal computing. Cooperative systems blend the autonomy of PCs with the systemwide rules and connectivity of traditional information systems. This combination causes a major shift in the way corporate-wide computing is viewed, making the main purpose of computing to put a wide variety of data and processing at people's fingertips.

Work Group Computing. Third, cooperative processing expands the computing universe by aiming at work groups. We discussed the six levels in the organization that must be supported by computer-based systems in Figure 5-7.

The top three levels—corporate, regional, and site—have been served by mainframes. The fourth level—departments—has been served by stand-alone minicomputers. The bottom level—individuals—has been served by PCs and end user computing. But work groups have been neglected. They are now the focus of cooperative processing.

By combining the power and connectivity of technical workstations and mainframes with the price and ease of use of PCs, cooperative processing encourages people to work together, via networks. It is aimed at work group computing to support people who do similar kinds of work. These people need both local and remote processing capabilities, on-demand, which is what cooperative processing is all about.

New Organizational Structures. Fourth, cooperative processing supports new organizational structures via its connectivity. By providing a platform that supports individuals and groups who are geographically dispersed, cooperative processing allows companies to experiment with new ways of working. There is growing interest in organizational structures that are based on profit centers, task forces, products, or customers.

An important new structure puts employees in multifunctional groups that are, say, customer oriented. For instance, a gas company might divide its company into two main groups—residential and industrial customers. Within each could be groups of employees from very different parts of the organization—engineering, distribution, customer service, research and development, and marketing—who now need to work together to serve their target market. The intent is to have one group of employees responsible for handling all the needs of a specific set of customers. When this structure is employed, computing power and telecommunications need to be provided for each work group, as well as the individuals within it.

Organizational Flexibility. Finally, cooperative processing increases organizational flexibility. One of the major drawbacks of traditional computing is that it casts business processes in concrete—that is, in hard-to-change hardware and software. By modularizing systems into client and server portions, new technology and new software components can more easily be added, without affecting the rest of the system. Thus, cooperative processing allows companies to be more responsive to change, because their computer systems are less likely to impede making organizational changes.

For these business reasons, we see cooperative systems as the computing architecture of the 1990s. As an example of how one company has used cooperative processing for a mission-critical system, consider Northwest Airlines.

CASE EXAMPLE: Northwest Airlines

When Northwest Airlines, with headquarters in St. Paul, Minnesota, merged with Republic Airlines in 1986, they doubled their business and became a major national carrier. To compete as a world class carrier, they realized they had to revamp several of their core systems. One of these systems calculates revenue from passengers.

At the time, Northwest sampled a very small percentage of their passenger tickets to estimate revenue. This approach was not yielding accurate passenger or revenue data. To improve accuracy, they needed to audit all their redeemed tickets—something few major airlines do.

The system they built, with the help of Andersen Consulting [5] and their computer-aided software engineering (CASE) product Foundation, uses a cooperative processing architecture and integrates products from eleven vendors and just about as many different technologies—including expert systems, imaging, relational databases, high-resolution workstations, servers, and LANs.

Management's Goals

Management established the following six major goals for the new passenger revenue accounting (PRA) system:

- Enforce their pricing and commission rules, to ensure that their services are properly priced and that travel agencies sell them at the correct fares.
- Calculate earned income for the corporation as well as track and reconcile air transport liability accounting.
- Cope with the volume explosion and the rapid pace of change caused by airline deregulation.
- Unhook volume growth from staff increases, so that the department could handle more work without equivalent increases in staff. The department had grown 700 percent since 1972—to six hundred people. At that projected growth rate, the department would soon need its own building, unless it changed the way it worked.
- Gather, organize, and disseminate marketing information for making decisions on pricing, flight scheduling, and response to competitors' moves.
- Provide the flexibility to audit and report on special deals with travel agents and corporate purchasers.

The Distributed Architecture

Data communications are an integral part of this distributed system, which uses both LANs and a MAN among three buildings. The host IBM 3090 is linked to the backbone Ethernet LAN via an SNA-TCP/IP gateway.

The Ethernet backbone acts as a metropolitan area network, linking numerous Ethernet subnetworks. Ten of the subnetworks connect a Sun application server to about forty diskless Sun workstations, which run UNIX. Northwest has minimized traffic across the backbone by designing the network to keep most client-to-server traffic on each subnet. In addition to the application servers, Northwest also has a FileNet image server for storing images of redeemed ticket coupons. They also have several special servers that perform the ticket auditing each night using expert system technology.

The workstations provide the passenger revenue accounting auditors with windows to the data stored on the various systems—the mainframe that stores the ticket database, external computer reservation systems, the application servers that store tickets with discrepancies, and the image database. The system accommodates large file transfers between these workstations and the mainframe, because part of the processing is done on the IBM host, and part is done on the workstations. For these file transfers, Northwest created a standard way for the COBOL applications (on the mainframe) to talk to the C applications (on the workstations). The workstations also draw on the host applications via 3270-terminal emulation on the Suns.

Image processing is also a key element. Each day, Northwest receives some 50,000 auditor coupons from travel agents and 100,000 lift coupons (redeemed ticket stubs) from passengers. Formerly, Northwest employed twenty to forty people full-time just to retrieve these coupons from their huge storage basement. Now, Northwest scans both types of coupons, creating a photograph-like image and an index for each one. The images are stored on FileNet optical disks in jukeboxes.

The Revenue Accounting Process

Each day, Northwest receives data from three sources: (1) magnetic tapes of ticket sales taken from computer reservation systems and consolidated by regional clearinghouses, (2) "audit coupons" from travel agents, and (3) "lift coupons" redeemed from passengers as they board a plane.

The sales data is stored in a DB2 relational database and processed on the IBM mainframe. If all the information is not provided, the sales data is queued to an auditor, who adds the missing information by viewing the appropriate auditor coupon image that has been scanned into the system. Then, the sales data for performing the nighttime audits is downloaded to Sun servers, and a C program retrieves all the travel agency rules that apply to each of these tickets.

At night, the sales data is run through expert systems, which apply the appropriate rules to recalculate the lowest fare, commission, and taxes. If the recalculation does not match the travel agency's auditor coupon data, the recalculation and corresponding coupon image are made available for review by an auditor.

The next morning, Northwest auditors view the various pieces of data in different windows on their workstations and decide how to handle the discrepancies. Since all the coupon images are available electronically, handling one box of coupons takes two to three hours rather than the former two to three days.

When a passenger's redeemed flight coupon is received by the department, the verified sales data is credited as earned income. Monthly books now close on the seventh of the month—one-half the time previously required. Thus, earned revenue can be recognized 50 percent faster.

Lessons Learned

The people at Northwest learned the following four major lessons about developing complex distributed systems:

1. ***Benchmark and Prototype New Technologies to Verify Vendors' Claims.*** Do not let vendors run the benchmarks by themselves. In image processing, for instance, have the vendors scan most of the kinds of documents in the application, especially if different kinds of paper and different colors of ink are common.

2. ***An Open Architecture Works on Mission-Critical Applications.*** The passenger revenue accounting system had to integrate a variety of technologies. By using an open architecture, Northwest reduced the risk in building such a system. Risk was further controlled by creating an interface to these systems that shielded the developers from the technicalities of the new technologies. Finally, integration was demonstrated early, through a small test project.

3. ***Large Distributed System Projects Need a Vendor Coordinator.*** Due to the complexity of PRA, there was no such thing as a clean design for creating a stable set of specifications for the vendors, so a big challenge was keeping the right people on the Northwest, Andersen, and vendor teams informed of current status. To fill this role, a full-time coordinator made sure that all the various projects stayed in close contact with each other. Otherwise, the end results would not work together.

4. ***Use of CASE Was Mandatory.*** Management believes that Northwest could not have done a project of this size without the tools and

approaches of CASE. For one thing, CASE allowed more developers to work on different components of the system in parallel. And without CASE they could not have supported the team of up to 170 developers. Furthermore, it allowed users to play a larger role in development; even to the point of using the CASE design tool to document user procedures, design reports, and supply the text in the help system. Finally, CASE will allow them to use the data definitions from PRA in future systems, which will substantially shorten development time and improve system quality.

The huge system, which took sixty-five thousand workdays to complete, has become a model for airline revenue accounting systems. Managers from over a dozen airlines around the world have visited Northwest to study it.

Components of Cooperative Systems

Host-terminal systems have processing only in the host, so choosing the host operating system is the underlying processing decision. But cooperative systems have processing all over the place—on mainframes, workstations, servers, and superservers. This dispersion significantly complicates the operating system decision, as well as many other decisions. So before we discuss the hardware components in distributed systems, we need to address the subject of operating systems.

Operating Systems

The big question to many people is which operating systems to use. At the moment, we see MS-DOS with Windows prevailing on client machines, because it has such a large installed base on PCs. OS/2 is more likely to be used on servers to handle mission-critical applications, because it is part of the IBM family—although this projection is less certain because of the slow acceptance of OS/2. And we see UNIX cutting across both client and server.

Two "wild cards" are pen-based computing operating systems and the operating system being developed by the joint IBM-Apple venture for RISC systems. Their popularity, and influence, remains to be seen.

As noted earlier, UNIX is a big winner in the client/server derby. It is designed for networking and powerful workstations, which puts it in line with the precepts of distributed systems. It is open—the key selling point these days—and it is multitasking. Therefore, it will be increasingly used in departmental and distributed applications—on both clients and servers.

The stumbling block has been the number of versions of UNIX; however, the Open Software Foundation, an independent organization is selecting among various vendors' offerings, and has put together a UNIX environment: (1) an operating system, OSF/1, (2) an architecture to tie systems together, distributed computing environment (DCE), and (3) an environment for managing distributed computing, distributed management environment (DME). This development is helping companies standardize on UNIX. One company that has taken a gamble on this new environment is Charles Schwab & Co.

CASE EXAMPLE: Charles Schwab & Co.

Charles Schwab & Co., based in San Francisco, California, is the largest discount brokerage in the United States. To keep pace with its rapidly expanding business, Schwab has decided to scrap its mainframe-centered computing systems and replace them with client/server systems. As described by Elisabeth Horwitt [6], Schwab expects to have 60 percent of its applications on client/server machines by 1996, so that it can more easily cope with the fluctuating transaction volumes caused by the volatile stock market.

Schwab has chosen the Open Software Foundation's protocols, believing that by taking a more open and nonproprietary approach, they can better control computer operating costs. Schwab was one of the first large firms to fully commit to OSF, in mid-1992.

The client/server platform is based on OSF/1 (OSF's operating system); the hardware is a mix from IBM, Digital Equipment Corporation, and Hewlett-Packard. The transaction processing architecture is OSF's DCE, which will tie the applications across multivendor systems. This architecture uses "remote procedure calls."

Barry Nance [7] calls remote procedure calls (RPCs) the tools of choice for building client/server systems. With RPCs, a "call" statement from one application requesting work from another application looks like a standard subroutine call; however, the second application can be located on any type of machine. The fact that the client and server modules execute on different machines is transparent to the application, says Nance. The RPC-generated code creates a communication session between the two computers and then "sends" the request and later "receives" the answer. The generated code manages the entire communication session, taking that burden off the application.

Schwab uses a fiber distributed data interface (FDDI) backbone running at 100 mbps between its three San Francisco buildings. Routers to interconnect the LANs in the three buildings use TCP/IP and Novell protocols. Schwab expects to eventually be able to offer "bandwidth on demand"—with speeds up to T1 (1.544 mbps)—to its remote offices.

The entire open system is to be managed by OSF's DME. One of the most important components of the Schwab system, or any other large distributed system, is the network management component. Unless the company can manage the entire day-to-day network operations from a single (or a few) network management workstation, the system will not be reliable. Schwab has started by using Hewlett-Packard's OpenView network management system and Tivoli System's products; both are providing a migration path to DME, which has not yet been fully defined.

To reduce the risks of adopting these OSF standards before they have been formally defined, Schwab has joined the Open Software Foundation, so that it gains access to some OSF products before they are commercially available, says Horwitt. Schwab is also working with firms outside the brokerage industry that are tying their mainframes to distributed UNIX networks.

In addition to allowing Schwab to more easily expand, the new distributed architecture is permitting the company to reengineer its business. One eighteen-person business team, for example, is analyzing current work processes in various Schwab business, looking for ways to combine them in more logical, efficient ways. It appears that this redesign will involve moving applications closer to the users, such as placing the centrally handled mutual funds business in the branch offices—a move made possible by Schwab's OSF-based distributed architecture.

Mainframes

One of the biggest computing trends is downsizing—that is, moving applications to smaller machines, as Schwab is doing. Another term used is "rightsizing," which means moving applications to the right size machine. The growth of mainframe sales has slowed significantly because of this trend. In fact, there has been quite a bit of talk about mainframes going away. That is not likely to happen, because mainframes will play an important role in cooperative systems.

They are likely to continue as the primary database servers, because their database management systems are highly sophisticated, and reliable *distributed* database technology is not yet available. In addition, they will probably act as the main communication nodes for enterprise-wide nets, because of their huge processing power. By 1995, International Data Corporation (IDC) [8] expects mainframes to operate at 300 to 500 million instructions per second. Finally, they will retain the very large applications for which large numbers of users need real-time data. Customer information systems and high-volume transaction systems come to mind. So although many applications will move off mainframes, these computers will have a role in enterprise networks.

Workstations

Workstations, as noted earlier, are the focal point in cooperative processing, because they initiate the requests for services that are provided across the networks. Workstations are coming in an ever-widening variety.

On the small end are notebook, heldheld, and palmtop systems, which will communicate over wireless networks.

On the high end are workstations with photorealistic color that run three-dimensional visualization software—for simulating complex interactions and designing products, equipment, bridges, and buildings. Such workstations are becoming so powerful that companies no longer need to build some physical models—the simulated model is enough. Furthermore, says Phillip Hester of IBM's Advanced Workstation Division Engineering Center [in 9], product developers will even simulate how people will interact with these products by using virtual reality technology that allows someone to move around in a computer-simulated space and manipulate the objects in that space.

The growing power in all these end user devices will be absorbed by the interface to hide the system's complexity and to make use much more natural. Interfaces will be graphic user interfaces (GUIs), they will increasingly use color, and they will permit people to speak, handprint, draw, and gesture—as well as type and point—to communicate with the system.

Servers

Servers come in various flavors and sizes, because many of them perform specialized functions. We expect to see image servers, electronic mail servers, video servers, voice mail servers, credit card servers, expert system servers, and so forth. Due to this variety, client/server computing will only blossom when server (and workstation) vendors create standard APIs for passing data between these machines. Specialized computer-to-computer interfaces are just too expensive to develop and maintain.

There are two major ways client processes make requests of servers in client/server computing. One method is message-based, in which the client sends a message to the server. The other is call-based, in which the client sends either a RPC to initiate processing on a server or a SQL call to a database server to obtain data from its database. Both forms require processing at both the client and server end, which greatly reduces the amount of communication traffic between the two, as compared with past communication methods. This promise of less network traffic is one of the attractions of client/server computing. Another is that it easily facilitates "snapping in" new clients and servers, if vendors use common APIs.

Superservers

A new class of component is the superserver, which first appeared in 1989 with the introduction of Compaq's SystemPRO. The need for these servers is growing as users move from LANs to enterprise nets, which support hundreds of workstations with each server, perform mission-critical processing at these server nodes, and handle heavy traffic.

PC LAN servers appeared in the mid-1980s. They were high-end PCs that supported tens of users and did little processing. Most servers are still of this genre. Superservers, on the other hand, are specially built, not souped-up PCs. They have multiple processors, lots of memory (from 12 to 16 megabytes), huge amounts of disk space (from 6 gigabytes up), high-speed input/output channels, and fault tolerance via redundant components.

The multiple processing in these servers is done through either symmetric multiprocessing—where any processor can perform any task—or asymmetric multiprocessing—where each processor performs a certain task, such as handle the network operating system or perform database management. These servers run popular network operating systems—such as Novell's NetWare or Banyan's Vines—so that developers can work with familiar interfaces. However, until CASE tools and multiprocessing network operating systems become prevalent, building server-based applications will be too complex for many companies to attempt.

Some people believe that UNIX on RISC machines will be the favored choice for superservers, because UNIX is the only multitasking operating system that runs across many platforms, and because RISC machines are faster than traditional CISC (complex instruction set computing) machines. Most superservers today, however, run on non-RISC Intel chips, such as the 80386 and 80486.

MIGRATING TO DISTRIBUTED SYSTEMS

We conclude this chapter by addressing the subject of migrating to distributed systems—that is, systems that include both distributed processing and distributed data. Robert Murray [10] believes that companies will migrate to these systems in the 1990s following the eight phases shown in Figure 5-11.

Figure 5-11 Eight Phases To Distributed Systems (from Murray [10])

1. Host-based, real-time query and update

2. Host-based, real-time query and update with additional query through file transfers to PCs

3. Host-based, real-time query and update with additional query through file transfers to PCs and batch updating permitted from PC data

4. Real-time query and update from either host or PC

5. Homogeneous cooperative processing without two-phase commit, where like databases run on the same hardware and system software platforms

6. Heterogeneous cooperative processing without two-phase commit, where databases run on a mix of platforms

7. Homogeneous cooperative processing with two-phase commit

8. Heterogeneous cooperative computing with two-phase commit

Phase 1. The first phase is characterized by host-based, real-time query and update. This phase is traditional on-line information system processing, where dumb terminals access host-based applications to view and update data. It is the starting point for just about everyone.

Phase 2. The second phase provides additional query capabilities through file transfers to PCs. Traditional host-based applications treat PCs (using terminal emulation software) and terminals alike—that is, as if they have no local processing capabilities. In this phase, those applications are extended to allow PCs to download portions of a database, for use in their local applications but not to update the host database. This capability first became available in the early 1980s and is widespread today.

Phase 3. The third phase adds batch updating from PC data. This phase reverses the philosophy of phase 2 by making the PC database the master. The host is only for backup and consolidation of data. For a payroll application, for example, time charges would be updated within local PC databases and then batch uploaded to the host, where the payroll is calculated and the checks are printed. In this case, the traditional host application only needs a new input routine to accept these batches, says Murray. In this move toward cooperative processing, the host acts as the backend database server and processor, and the PC acts as the front end, probably with a GUI, to manipulate and update the local data.

The challenges companies encounter in this phase are deciding how to distribute the data (either by distributing a divided database or distributing duplicate data), and maintaining duplicate sets of data editing and validation routines. In addition, the systems department must ensure that all the remote computers are using the same version of software.

Phase 4. The forth phase enables real-time query and update from either host or PC. This phase extends the capabilities of the PCs by allowing them to update the host on-line. The main question developers ask in this phase is whether to simply put a GUI onto the existing application or whether to redesign and redevelop the host application. The former is a band-aid; the latter is a cure. Although users are demanding more integrated data, the needed standards and tools for building cooperative systems may not be available, thus complicating this decision.

Phase 5. The fifth phase introduces homogeneous cooperative processing without two-phase commit, that is, like databases run on the same hardware and system software platforms. This phase adds true distributed databases, across similar or identical platforms. Although several vendors claim to provide this capability, says Murray, they require too much system overhead. He recommends waiting until the state of the art in distributed databases has been proved before converting to such a distributed database, because conversions are very expensive.

Phase 6. The sixth phase moves to heterogeneous cooperative processing without two-phase commit, that is, databases run on a mix of platforms. This phase extends the previous one by permitting distributed databases across mixed platforms. To qualify for this level, says Murray, the application software must not be required to handle security and updates. These functions must be performed by the operating systems, network, and DBMS. In this phase, the network keeps track of all duplicate copies of data and updates them automatically. But these updates will occur only in batch, which can lead to data inconsistencies.

Phase 7. This seventh phase adds the all-important two-phase commit capability (to homogeneous databases), giving a system a true distributed database. As noted earlier, with two-phase commit, all duplicate copies of data are locked and updated before they are unlocked and the transaction is committed—in a two-step process. If any of the updates fail, the entire transaction is backed out. This capability is not expected before mid-decade, says Murray.

Phase 8. This phase extends phase 7 to heterogeneous databases. Companies that position themselves now to move into this environment will dominate, Murray believes.

The technical problems of moving to this new genre of systems cannot be minimized, says Murray. We would add that the systems are orders of magnitude more complex, the needed development tools and interface standards are not available, development methodologies and good practices are not in place, and few developers have the right skills.

CONCLUSION

Distributed systems will dominate the computing development agenda this decade. Strong economic, functional, and technical incentives are behind the move. Yet, the field is in its infancy, with the sudden arrival of client/server computing and the recent acceptance of UNIX in business systems. The 1990s will be the era of distributed systems—systems much different from the ones that characterized the 1980s.

QUESTIONS AND EXERCISES

REVIEW QUESTIONS

1. Give five examples of system structures that can be called distributed.
2. What are the four attributes of a distributed system?
3. List and briefly explain the questions that can be asked in deciding whether to distribute computing responsibilities.
4. Describe the two guiding frameworks for distributed systems.
5. What are the three cornerstones on distributed systems, according to the authors?

6. Define cooperative processing and client/server computing.

7. Define the five forms of cooperative processing.

8. Give the five reasons the authors believe cooperative processing is important.

9. What are the components of Northwest Airlines PRA system?

10. What four lessons did Northwest learn about building cooperative processing systems?

11. What are the five components of distributed systems? What is each one's function?

12. Why is Charles Schwab adopting osf's distributed system environment?

13. What eight phases does Murray believe companies will go through to get to truly distributed systems?

DISCUSSION QUESTION

1. Do you believe the advantages of distributed systems outweigh the disadvantages? Why, or why not?

EXERCISES

1. Find an article in the current literature that describes a distributed system.

   (a) Describe it using the four attributes given at the beginning of this chapter.

   (b) Does it relate to the sumuru architecture? How?

   (c) What benefits are claimed for the system?

2. Identify a company in your local community that is using what it calls a distributed system. How do the system's characteristics compare with those given in this chapter? What problems has the information systems department encountered building the system, and how has it dealt with these problems?

REFERENCES

1. CHARLES BACHMAN, Bachman Information Systems, 8 New England Executive Park East, 6th floor, Burlington, MA 01803.

2. WETHERBE, J. C., "IS: To Centralize or to Decentralize," SIM Network , January 1987.

3. STEFFERUD, E., D. FARBER, and R. DEMENT, "SUMURU: A Network Configuration for the Future," *Mini-Micro Systems*, May 1982, pp. 311-312.

4. SPUND, LANI, VITAL Technical Architecture Guide, Apple Computer, 1992.

5. ANDERSON CONSULTING, 69 W. Washington St., Chicago, IL 60602.

6. HORWITT, E. "Schwab Invests Big in OSF," *Computerworld*, April 20, 1992, pp. 1, 14.

7. NANCE, B. "In Praise of Remote Procedure Calls," *Byte*, March 1991, pp. 338-340.

8. "Information Systems: The Next 10 Years," IDC White Paper, *Computerworld* (suppl.), November 1990.

9. ALEXANDER, MICHAEL, "Looking Ahead to the Next Century," *Computerworld*, March 4, 1991, pp. 18.

10. MURRAY, R., "In Depth: Cooperative Processing Phase-In," *Computerworld*, August 19, 1991, pp. 61-64.

SIX

Building the Telecommunications Highway System

INTRODUCTION

We treat telecommunications in this chapter in the broad sense—the sending of information in any form from one place to another, electronically. In this sense, the telecommunications system is an "electronic highway system" for the flow of information among the corporate office, regional offices, sites, departments, work groups, individuals, and the outside world. Many information systems departments are responsible for designing, building, and maintaining that information highway in the same way that governments are responsible for building and maintaining streets, roads, and freeways.

Once built, the system provides an infrastructure for the flow of information. That flow will be managed not by systems professionals but by users, just as users manage the flow of cars and trucks on the physical highway network. Government agencies provide standards and laws for the flow of highway traffic, enforced by the police and highway patrol. In the same way, the information systems department will develop and enforce the telecommunications standards for information traffic. This analogy could be pursued in more detail, but the point is clear. The telecommunications system has become as important to the movement of information in organizations and society as the highway system is to the movement of people and physical goods.

The world of telecommunications can no longer be divided into the voice, data, and message services. Instead, it must be considered in terms of total available capacity (bandwidth) that will be allocated among these services as well as fax, computer and video conferencing, security, business television, factory automation, and other advanced services. In short, telecommunications management will deal with the *integrated* use of total communications capacity.

THE EVOLVING TELECOMMUNICATIONS SCENE

In this chapter we discuss the issues we believe are important to managing the telecommunications function in large organizations. The chapter has three major parts. This first section describes the telecommunications scene by discussing the status of telecommunications today and then looking at two important trends: broadband technologies and wireless communications. This discussion sets the stage—and defines the jargon—for the second section, which discusses building networks. The final section focuses on standards, specifically open systems interconnection.

The Status of Telecommunications Today

To better understand what is feasible and likely in the the near future, we begin this chapter by describing where things stand today. From there we will discuss new developments, and we finish up with what companies are trying to achieve and how they might accomplish those goals. To begin, then, we see seven "facts of life" relating to telecommunications.

- Organizations have a multitude of networks.
- The reach of networks is expanding organizationally.
- The telecommunications industry is being destabilized.
- Global network services are emerging.
- New technologies are improving bandwidth use.
- The focus of network designers is now interconnecting LANs.
- Electronic mail provides a new communication infrastructure.

Organizations Have a Multitude of Networks. Most organizations have served their telecommunications needs through separate, dedicated networks—a voice telephone network, a data communications network, office system networks, manufacturing site networks, and a video conferencing network, not to mention countless LANs. One aerospace company investigated their in-plant networks at one site. Instead of finding seven networks, as they had expected, they uncovered *nineteen*!

In most cases, each network has its own transmission medium (such as twisted pairs of wires or coaxial cable), because the networks were built at different times. There is little or no sharing of network capacity among applications, because each network was designed to be application specific. When a new need arises, it is generally given its own network. As a result, each department usually has its own networks.

Due to this proliferation, many buildings have little room for more wiring. The ducts and conduits are stuffed. The above-ceiling spaces are full. With so many wires in place, companies face the difficult task of servicing them—and rewiring them, as work sites are moved.

The net result is that these independent networks are "islands of automation." They cannot be monitored from a central site, they cannot share data, and they cannot take advantage of computing resources on other networks. Therefore, today, there is a great deal of interest and energy devoted to connecting these islands and permitting them to interoperate.

The Reach of Networks Is Expanding Organizationally. Alan Kamman of the Nolan, Norton & Co. consulting firm [1] suggests that wealth will be created by organizations that can move information—replacing the movement of physical goods in importance. Companies will use connectivity in increasingly broader ways, he says, seeking competitive advantage. He illustrates his belief by describing three types of existing networks. These demonstrate the ever-broadening scope of networking.

Single-organization networks can span the globe. The Digital Equipment Corporation network, for example, has more than forty-one thousand nodes in twenty-six countries. It allows the firm to operate in an elaborate matrix fashion, while maintaining central guidance.

Industry-specific value-added networks were the fastest-growing types of networks in the 1980s, says Kamman. They link suppliers to one buyer in a specific marketplace. An example is J. C. Penney, whose network not only links its employees but also ties in manufacturers of apparel and fabric, such as J. P. Stevens and du Pont. Penney electronically orders fabric and material and the manufacturers deliver them directly to the apparel manufacturers, in a JIT fashion.

Extended enterprise networks interconnect single-organization networks. They are not limited by industry, and they provide a type of electronic information consortium. The Mitsubishi Group represents an example, says Kamman. The group is comprised of twenty-eight members, ranging from an oil company to a steel manufacturer to a bank. Each member has its own company network, but now these are interconnected. In addition, one hundred other corporations—such as Nikon Camera and Kirin Beer—have financial links and electronic connections to these twenty-eight. No single firm dominates in networks with this arrangement.

Companies that are building such internets are constructing the infrastructure of the future, say Kamman.

The Telecommunications Industry Is Being Destabilized. Victor Schnee of Probe Research [2] sees significant changes occurring in the telecommunications industry. He believes computer vendors and user companies need to anticipate these changes, because they are destabilizing the industry. By that he means, "The rules of the game will change, *dramatically*."

Primarily, the long-held belief that local telephone companies have a "natural monopoly" for providing access to telephone services is eroding. New technologies, such as wireless networks, permit bypassing local access. Furthermore, says Schnee, the restrictions on the seven Regional Bell Operating Companies (created by the 1984 AT&T consent decree) will end within a few years. The decree restricts them from selling information services, manufacturing telecommunications equipment, and providing long-distance services. The process began in 1991 with the lifting of restrictions on offering value-added services. Such actions will open the local access arena to true competition, says Schnee, and will erase the distinctions between local and long distance telecommunications businesses.

Currently, the bottleneck to receiving advanced telecommunications services is the local level, contends Schnee. When this bottleneck is opened to competition, an explosion in services will occur. As telecommunications companies restructure to compete in this new world, they are likely to acquire computer companies, just as AT&T acquired NCR. Since opportunities in the network business are likely to dwarf those in the computer business, he believes that savvy computer companies will, in turn, acquire telecommunications firms. In fact, he believes that a few network-based, integrated it superpowers are likely to emerge as new IT markets form. In short, he expects significant changes in this industry during the 1990s.

Global Network Services Are Emerging. On a broader scale, deregulation of the telecommunication industry is occurring around the globe. Fewer Postal, Telephone, and Telegraph ministries (PTTs) monopolize their country's telecommunications today than ten years ago. In those countries where PTTs do maintain a monopoly in voice communications, deregulation is "sneaking in" through new value-added services, where competition is allowed.

Furthermore, telecommunications companies and PTTS are forming alliances to provide global networking services. For instance, British Telecommunications, France Telecommunications, Deutsche Bundespost, and Nippon Telegraph and Telephone intend to create a global, broadband communication utility. Some large companies are likely to prefer using vendor-managed international data networks rather than build and operate their own private networks, because international networking is extremely complex. Users need the most help globally, because each PTT has its own rules and regulations, desired equipment is not always available, and so forth. Although vendor-managed networks provide one-stop shopping in this complex arena, companies still need to monitor the performance of the "outsourced" networks.

New Technologies Are Improving Bandwidth Use. While telecommunications bandwidths are getting broader, a countervailing trend is squeezing more data through existing links. Due to new technologies, companies are able to do more with less. The two areas where this development is most evident are in LANs and data compression.

An important development in the LAN arena is the introduction of 10Base-T, which allows companies to run Ethernet over inexpensive unshielded twisted pair wire. Until 10Base-T was adopted as a standard in 1990, Ethernet required expensive coax cable. 10Base-T uses a star topology, say Bechtold and Mier [3], where each workstation is individually wired to a hub. Standard Ethernet uses a bus topology, where each workstation is linked to a backbone cable. 10Base-T has made LANs affordable in many situations, it has eased network management of LANs, and it has given a midlife kicker to the ten-year-old Ethernet standard.

The second more-with-less development uses advances in data compression. Speaking at a MacWorld conference, Adriaan Lightenberg of Storm Technology [4] discussed two data compression standards that have become important in the world of multimedia systems. One is Joint Photographic Experts Group (JPEG), the original video compression standard that retains all the information for each image. JPEG compresses files 6:1 for excellent quality images, 15:1 for high quality, and 24:1 for good quality. The second standard, Motion Picture Experts Group (MPEG), is used to compress moving images. It allows 100:1 compression, because it only stores the difference between successive frames. It retains sufficient quality for moving pictures, but not for photographs and slides, where people expect very high quality. Thus, MPEG is important in video conferencing, where the goal is to present the highest-quality picture using the least amount of bandwidth.

The Focus of Network Designers Is Interconnecting LANs. Just as the focus of computing has shifted from data centers to desktops, so too has the focus of networking shifted from WANs to LANs. Increasingly, the job of WANs is to interconnect LANs, because the goal is interoperability among client and server machines. A new participant in this networking hierarchy is MANs. As the name implies, these networks provide high-speed links in a metropolitan-size area. With their arrival, there is potentially a three-tiered hierarchy of networks—LANs connected to MANs connected to WANs. The highest speeds are in the shorter-distance LANs and will continue to be there. Furthermore, the internets that companies build will be hybrid in that they are likely to use both private and public networks.

Electronic Mail Provides a New Communication Infrastructure. The most interesting new platform for distributed systems is, believe it or not, electronic mail. In fact, Nina Burns [5], of Network Marketing Solutions in Menlo Park, California, believes that electronic mail will become the infrastructure for information distribution.

This new development has, of course, spawned a new term: "mail-enabled applications"—a new generation of applications designed specifically for distributed systems that use electronic mail as the communication platform. The applications generate electronic mail messages to users or other applications. One example is a host-based application that monitors critical data for a power plant, such as weather data, megawatt load, maintenance schedules, and so forth. When a change occurs, the application sends an electronic mail message to the appropriate manager, such as a weather alert to the plant manager.

To support this new class of applications, several large software companies have published APIs for electronic mail systems, which they call "interface specifications." Their goal is to get vendors to adopt these specifications for their products. The two main contenders arise from the LAN marketplace. One is Vendor Independent Messaging (VIM) from Lotus Development Corporation, Novell, IBM, Apple Computer, and Borland International. VIM is intended to be a cross-vendor messaging API. The other contender is Messaging Application Programming Interface (MAPI) from Microsoft; it is intended for Windows applications.

The electronic mail API provides the interface between the application and the messaging service. It tells applications how to send messages, access mail directories, and store mail, says Burns. Therefore, software vendors and in-house developers need only write code to one mail system interface. They can therefore write distributed systems without being communications experts. The main benefit of using these APIs is that the electronic mail engine can be changed without requiring the applications to be changed. Also, applications that use the same API can work together, because they use the same message formats, says Burns.

Burns believes that messaging systems will play a large role in future distributed systems because they provide such flexibility, acting as the transport vehicle for all kinds of messages. Mail-enabled applications will permit people to call up the mail system without leaving their application. In fact, it will be as easy to mail a message as it is to save it or print it. The mail system APIs will make it far easier for developers to write applications that send messages.

These then are seven observations about the status of telecommunications today. Now we address two major trends in this arena: the coming era of broadband and the promise of wireless communications.

The Coming Era of Broadband

Broadband telecommunications is where more than one signal travels over a communication medium at one time. The driving force behind the current push for broadband—in LANs, MANs, and WANs—is the increasing use of computers in business. As organizations put more kinds of data on computers, they need greater bandwidth to ship that data around. This drive is accelerating, due to high-performance workstations, distributed systems, and multimedia computing.

Figure 6-1 T-carrier bandwidths in USA and Europe

USA	EUROPE
• T1 = 1.544 mbps (equivalent to 24 voice circuits)	2.048 mbps
• T2 = 6.312 mbps (96 voice circuits)	8.448 mbps
• T3 = 44.736 mbps (672 voice circuits)	34.368 mbps
• T4 = 139.264 mbps (4,032 voice circuits)	139.264 mbps

In this section we discuss the following alphabet soup of technologies that are aimed at filling this drive for broadband:

- Fiber Distributed Data Interface (FDDI)
- Fast-packet technologies—frame relay and cell relay
- Switched Multimegabit Data Services (SMDS)
- Synchronous Optical Network (SONET)

Before beginning, however, we need to explain the terminology used in describing network speeds—specifically T-carriers and DS-carriers. A T1 line is equivalent to a group of twenty-four voice grade lines, which means its capacity is 1.544 mbps. The hierarchy is shown in Figure 6.1. Notice that the U.S. and European standards differ in T1 through T3. Due to these differences, international telecommunications must change speeds at gateways.

T-carriers are used mainly to carry analog voice signals that have been digitized, says William Morgan, of W and J Partnership [5]. With the arrival of true end-to-end digital circuits, the nomenclature has changed to DS. DS-0 is 64 kbps, whereas DS-1 is the digital equivalent of T1, DS-2 to T2, and so on.

Now on to our discussion of the technologies. In the broadband arena, there are three potentially competitive broadband technologies: FDDI, frame relay, and SMDS.

FDDI

FDDI is an international standard for operating a fiber optic cable network at 100 mbps (nearly T4 speed). It uses token passing and maps into the two lowest OSI layers. FDDI has generally been seen as most appropriate for backbone networks that link LANs in a building or between buildings, because it can support up to five hundred workstations up to two kilometers (1.2 miles) apart. An FDDI net consists of two rings sending data in opposite directions. The second ring is usually for backup. Thus, these networks are highly reliable.

In a white paper, the people at Network Peripherals [6] state that FDDI will also be important for interconnecting workstations, in certain circumstances. One such circumstance is work groups that use professional workstations, because they tend to request large file transfers, such as 4 to 5 megabytes. A traditional Ethernet, which operates at 10 mbps, can be over-loaded with four or five of today's workstations (running at 10 to 20 MIPs); tomorrow's more powerful ones will totally swamp these LANs. Handling such large chunks of bursty traffic on a traditional LAN would be like trying to inhale olives through a straw, says Network Peripherals.

A huge-bandwidth LAN will also be essential for workstations that display the results of high-volume calculations, perhaps from a supercomputer. The pipeline between these two machines must move data fast enough to permit a realistic simulation. Such a high-performance graphics workstation needs to receive 2 to 3 millions bytes per second, which is 16 to 24 mbps—almost three times the bandwidth of Ethernet.

Although FDDI was originally developed for use with fiber optics, standards for its use with both shielded and unshielded twisted pair wire were announced in 1991. This advance was possible, explains Rosenblatt [7], because most workstations are located closer than the 2 kilometers in the original standard; such configurations can therefore use FDDI over wire. This advance provides a migration path for today's LANs, by permitting increased bandwidth to workstations without recabling.

FDDI has also been discussed as appropriate for MANs. The city and county governments in Tallahassee, Florida, are using FDDI in this manner, says MaryFran Johnson [8]. When their local telephone company, Centel's Central Telephone Company of Florida, heard that they were planning to install their own FDDI network, it built them a FDDI MAN. These government offices need FDDI to move images and data in a geographical information system among three government buildings—the city hall, the county courthouse, and the city electrical department. A 10-mbps LAN would have been swamped by that volume of data. So rather than install their own network, the governments are outsourcing their network to Centel.

From all we have heard, FDDI promises to be a very important technology, at least in the LAN backbone arena, if not for direct connection to workstations and in MANs.

Fast Packet Technologies

The term "fast packet switching," as defined by the people at Vertical Systems Group [in 9], is a communication architecture that supports both voice and data at T1 speeds and above. It switches at least 50,000 packets a second and has no error detection. The term currently refers to two emerging packet switching technologies: frame relay and cell relay.

Frame relay uses variable-length packets and is slated to replace the workhorse of today's data networks, X.25. It is the fast-packet technology for bursty communications, such as the traffic that occurs between terminal and host or between LANs. Like X.25, it ships data in variable-length packets but envelopes the data in a frame that contains destination information. Unlike X.25, it performs error checking and correction only at the originating and receiving nodes rather than at each node along the path. This significantly decreases overhead and increases throughput speed. So while x.25 operates at 56 kbps, frame relay operates at the T1 speed of 1.544 mbps, and higher. x.25 has robust error checking because it was designed years ago for the more error-prone unshielded wiring. Frame relay, on the other hand, rids itself of this overhead by taking advantage of today's more reliable digital circuits.

In addition, frame relay provides bandwidth on demand because it creates virtual circuits. That is, it does not require a dedicated connection, the way a voice telephone call does. It is therefore appropriate for transmitting images, still-frame video, and bulk files in private networks, where the infrastructure can be built to support it.

Frame relay can be relatively simple to implement, because it is based on the x.25 architecture. It may not require new equipment, only new software in the switches. There appears to be a question, however, of whether frame relay is feasible internationally, because the error rates on transoceanic cables may be too high to support it. Even so, frame relay is being considered in that arena. In short, frame relay is an important technology for interconnecting LANs, perhaps around the world.

Cell relay is faster than frame relay—ranging from T1 (1.544 mbps) on fiber to over DS-4 (155 mbps)—because it transmits fixed-length packets, which require less processing, says the Vertical Systems Group. It is the underlying technology for SMDS, which we discuss next—a service offered initially by local carriers.

The fixed-length packets in cell relay technology are suitable for voice and video, because these transmissions must have fixed intervals between packets to produce natural-sounding speech. Frame relay, with its variable-length packets, is not appropriate. This explains why public carriers are pushing SMDS—they have traditionally focused on voice—and why frame relay is moving more quickly in private data networks.

Cell relay is also being touted as the transmission medium for multimedia communications; hence, it is receiving much attention these days. The CCITT's standard for cell relay is called Asynchronous Transfer Mode (ATM). Most discussions about transmitting multimedia center around ATM, rather than Integrated Services Digital Network (ISDN), because ATM can handle so much more traffic. It is slated to start at T1 (1.544 mbps) whereas basic rate ISDN has two 64-kbps channels.

SMDS

SMDS (switched multimegabit data services) is a switched service for MANs that uses cell relay technology, explains Dawn Bushaus [10]. It was developed by Bell Communications Research (Bellcore), the research consortium of the Regional Bell Operating Companies formed when AT&T was deregulated in 1984. SMDS is used at speeds between T1 (1.544 mbps) and

DS-3 (45 mbps); service offerings over the public switched network are starting with the T1 speed. The service is being offered by local telephone companies and promoted for linking LANs within metropolitan areas; it is tariffed in the United States by the FCC.

As Elisabeth Horwitt [11] explains, the service is packet *switched*, which means that unlike traditional packet networks, the fiber optic links are shared among several transmissions at one time. Therefore, customers that need this huge amount of bandwidth on an irregular basis can get it, because they share the cost. Traditional point-to-point networks, which were the only ones that formerly provided this much bandwidth, were only economical if used continually.

Furthermore, says Bushaus, because SMDS uses the public switched network, users will have public addresses for receiving high volumes of data from anyone. Another advantage of SMDS is that the network remains under the control of the public carriers, so they are responsible for its management. As with the other broadband technologies, plans for SMDS have broadened. Long distance carriers are now looking into offering it between MANs, which will provide nationwide service within the United States.

One pending use of SMDS at Stanford University, says Horwitt, will be transferring medical images (such as computed axial tomographic (CAT) scans) and earth resources mapping images among buildings on the campus.

There is currently much discussion about which of these high-speed offerings—FDDI, frame relay, cell relay, or SMDS—will be used in which services. Bushaus points out that SMDS and FDDI are likely to be more complementary than competitive, with SMDS used to interconnect FDDI LANs. A more likely competitor to SMDS is frame relay. But because it currently only operates at up to T1 speeds, many of the regional Bell operating companies see it as just a stepping stone to the faster SMDS, which goes from T1 to DS-4 speeds. If this acronym soup sounds a bit confusing, it is.

SONET

The transport network for broadband services will be SONET, says Dawn Bushaus [12]. It is a set of international standards for transmission over fiber-based networks at speeds of 51.84 mbps (above T3) to a whopping 13 gigabytes per second. It is being promoted by Bellcore. Although a few years off, one of the promises of SONET is that it will allow networks to use equipment from different vendors due to its "midspan meet." The midspan meet will consist of an information model and message sets for making translations between equipment. It will be used first by companies that currently have multiple T3 networks in place.

The important point is that broadband communications will play a big role in future distributed systems, and all these technologies are vying for their part in that scenario.

The Promise of Wireless Communications

Wireless communications are already with us, in the form of cellular carphones, portable telephones, very small aperture terminals (VSATs), pagers, building-to-building microwave links, and infrared networks. With people becoming increasingly mobile—in their work and their personal lives—wireless communication options will grow in three areas: wireless LANs, wide-area personal communication services, and wireless WANs. We discuss the first two in this chapter, and the third in Chapter 11.

Wireless LANs

Wireless LANs, which are currently more expensive than wired LANs, have the advantage in certain settings, says Peter Clegg in *LAN Times* [13]. These settings include hazardous environments, historic buildings where wiring ducts are full, for disaster recovery, and in temporary installations. Furthermore, there are many instances in which temporary communications are needed, says Clegg, such as for audits, special projects, seasonal businesses, and so forth. Even in permanent locations, about one-half of the respondents to a *LAN Times* survey said that they relocate nodes on their LANs about six times a year. Wireless LANs are much easier to reconfigure than their wired counterparts.

Wireless LAN Technologies. Robert Rosenbaum [14], of Windata, a wireless information network company, expands on Clegg's discussion with a good description of the technologies used in the emerging wireless LAN marketplace. He notes that wireless LANs use either light (in the form of infrared) or radio (in the form of narrowband or spread spectrum) technologies to transmit signals.

Infrared light LANs transmit at frequencies just below red light—the lowest frequency in the light spectrum visible to humans. Like other forms of light, infrared light cannot penetrate solids, such as walls, ceilings, dust, and rain. Therefore, all the transmitters and receivers must be in line of sight with each other or be reflected off a surface. But infrared has the advantage that it has a wide bandwidth (say, for FDDI, which transmits at 100 mbps). No government bodies control light frequencies; therefore, it can be used unlicensed anywhere.

Narrowband radio frequency (RF) LANs transmit on a center frequency, which can cause "ghosts" (to use television terminology) that pollute the signal, as signals are deflected off objects. Use of smart antennae can overcome this problem, but RF transmitters must be licensed, because governments regulate the use of radio signals.

Spread spectrum LANs use RF bands that have already been allocated to wireless nets in the United States by the Federal Communications Commission. So that transmissions do not interfere with one another on the same frequency, the signal is "spread" by transmitting a "chip pattern" rather than the actual bits. Each network has its own "chipping code," so that each receiver only accepts signals that it can decode. Spread spectrum technology provides highly reliable communications in RF-noisy environments, such as factory floors.

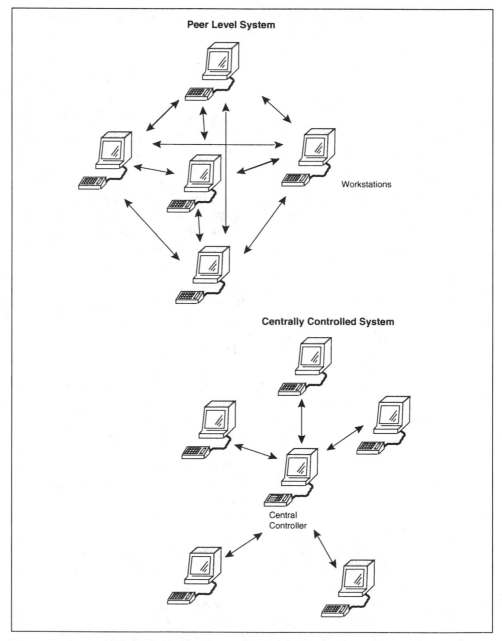

Figure 6.2 Wireless LAN Configurations

Wireless LAN Topologies. Regardless of the technology used, wireless LANs have two basic topologies, says Rosenbaum. *Peer-level systems* allow each unit to communicate with every other unit. This is the lowest cost alternative, because no master control units are needed. But this topology generally breaks down as traffic grows, because more and more collisions occur, unless a token ring protocol is used. Furthermore, when nearby units and faraway units transmit simultaneously, the bandwidth is not used efficiently. Peer level systems also make security and diagnosis more difficult.

The second topology is wireless LANs with central controllers. In these systems, a central controller is linked to a wired LAN, and communicates with user units that connect with, say, eight workstations. The control unit handles all communications (to near and far workstations) and has centralized network management and access control (see Figure 6-2).

Wireless LAN technology is new, and its use is likely to grow as prices drop.

Personal Communication Services

The vision of the future is person-to-person rather than station-to-station communications. That is, each person will have his or her own personal telephone number, associated with a lightweight telephone that he or she carries around. As Sam Ginn, CEO of Pacific Telesis Group (one of the regional Bell Operating Companies) [15] discusses, the benefit will be that people can communicate anywhere.

Personal communication services (PCS) will spring up around these networks, permitting people to not only transmit telephone conversations but also computer-based information, voice mail, electronic messages, call screening, and other personal services.

PCSs will unlock levels of freedom we do not now know, says Ginn, and they will become important in special events, such as political conventions and sporting events, as well as for emergencies, such as those caused by natural disasters. But before these systems become a reality, complex technological and public policy questions need to be addressed.

The most fundamental issue, says Ginn, is the overcrowded RF spectrum. In the U.S., the government uses about one-half the radio spectrum for marine navigation, air traffic control, military communications, and space exploration. Television, AM/FM radio, and civil services (such as police and fire) use a large part of the nongovernment spectrum. The remaining bands are taken up by taxi dispatchers and ham radio operators.

Where are PCSs going to get their bandwidth? he asks. At the moment, that is an unresolved question—in the United States as well as in other countries. Some believe the bandwidths allocated to existing cellular systems will suffice. But no one knows how much bandwidth PCSs will need. In addition, if countries assign different frequencies, cross-country communications will be difficult. Furthermore, if the frequencies assigned have trouble penetrating buildings, then costs will be higher, because vendors will need to build more powerful systems. Frequency allocation is a complex issue that deserves careful consideration before countries act, says Ginn. These are not national issues, they are international issues.

Since PCSs hold the promise of tremendous personal freedom and control over one's own communications, Ginn recommends five actions that need to be taken.

1. Continue to develop an understanding of the technologies and how people might use them.
2. Policy makers need to make the best use of the available spectrum.
3. Telecommunications companies need to stay aware of international developments.
4. Telecommunications companies need to focus on ways to use the existing telecommunications infrastructure.
5. Telecommunications companies need to understand what customers want. Market demand is a good guide to the proper use of the scarce spectrum.

The regional Bell Operating Companies, such as Pacific Telesis, are not the only companies interested in offering PCSs, because these could be used to bypass their local connections. Cable television companies, which already have fiber links to homes, might want to carry these signals, perhaps in combination with cellular links. The arena is now in turmoil, as vendors decide how they want to address this market of the late 1990s.

Now that we have unleashed this barrage of telecommunications acronyms, we turn to a more comprehendible topic: building telecommunications systems.

BUILDING THE NETWORKS OF THE FUTURE: INTERNETS

We believe there are three main guidelines for companies in creating their networks.

- Create an overall architecture.
- Stress connectivity.
- Use standards.

In this section we discuss these three areas.

Creating an Overall Architecture

First of all, what do we mean by an architecture? A network architecture is not a diagram or a set of diagrams. Rather, it is a set of company policies and rules that, when followed, are expected to lead to the network environment that is desired. International standards—specifically the gradually developing OSI standards—have become important in architecture planning.

What do we *not* mean by an architecture? An overall network architecture, as presented here, does not imply one telecommunications network for all uses. Nor does it imply or require that the offerings of only one vendor be used, in an attempt to achieve connectivity. It also does not imply the need to standardize on one type of technology for providing local connectivity. Nor is the architecture one design for a multilevel network of computers, that all units of an organization must use. In short, an overall network architecture is not one utopian solution for all network problems. It is a set of policies, principles, and guidelines that will lead to more widespread connectivity.

Factors to Consider

Some of the factors that will influence an organization's overall architecture are the following.

The Desired Levels of Computing. At what levels—ranging from corporate headquarters to individual office employees—is it desired to provide computing power and data storage? As we noted in Chapter 5, we see computing power needed at six levels: (1) corporate, (2) region, country, or division, (3) site, (4) department, (5) work group, and (6) individual.

Level 2—region, country, division—is where there can be substantial differences from company to company. For a global corporation, this level might reside at a complete company that has been bought by the firm. At the other extreme, this level might not even exist for a medium-sized, very centralized company with one main location.

Company Organization. The company's policies on centralization versus decentralization of management and operations play a key role in the overall architecture.

Current Computing Environment. This factor includes the existing computers, which usually come from different manufacturers (IBM, Digital, Bull, and so on). Few organizations these days have hardware from only one manufacturer, operating systems from only one vendor, DBMSs from only one company, and telecommunications services from only one carrier. Each additional variable increases connectivity problems.

Company Policies on the Use of Standards. How important does the company consider the use of information system standards? The more that standards can be employed, the cleaner the overall architecture can be made. In the absence of standards, tailored solutions must be used for each communication interface.

How Will It Serve the Business? Peter Keen addresses telecommunications planning and architectures in his book, *Competing in Time* [16]. His theme is that telecommunications planning must follow from business planning. He cites many examples of how companies have successfully used telecommunications to improve their competitive positions. To add flavor, he also includes some examples of failures—and draws some "do and don't" conclusions for increasing the chances of success.

He sees the 1990s as the decade of integrated technologies, all under the general management of the information systems function. These technologies include computers (from micros to supercomputers), telecommunications, laser memories (such as compact disks), artificial intelligence and expert systems, CAD and CAM, voice mail, electronic mail, various forms of conferencing (video, audio, computer), and others.

The driving force will have to be managers who see how these technologies can best be used to serve the business. However, overall management of the use of these technologies must be coupled with crucial technical skills. A range of technologists will be required, and it will be no simple matter to obtain those skills.

In short, says Keen, planning for the use of telecommunications in the 1990s should begin with the business needs, and where the business wants to go, not with the technology. Further, this planning has three main steps, says Keen:

- *Vision*. What is happening in our industry? Where do we want to go?
- *Policies*. The bridge between a vision and the architecture of systems to support the vision.
- Architecture. The high level design of the systems and infrastructure to accomplish the vision—that is, the systems, people, and procedures.

The role of the overall architecture, then, is to recognize these diverse factors and then specify the desired computing environment for the future as well as the policies to bring it about.

Emphasizing Connectivity

The key challenge in network design these days is connectivity, said Howard Frank, of Network Management [17] in a speech at a TCA conference. Consider the characteristics of a "typical" large user company in the United States, he said. Such a company has more than five thousand voice and five thousand data service devices, more than five hundred locations (and is opening and closing locations on a weekly basis), two major data centers, and more than one thousand leased circuits. It obtains long-distance communication services from multiple suppliers, local services from several regional Bell Operating Companies and independent telephone companies, and has multiple special data networks.

The goal today is not a single, coherent network but rather finding a means to interface many dissimilar networks, he said. With this in mind, he offered the following advice:

- Build systems that are coherent at the interfaces. Let the users think they have one network.
- Be realistic about time frames. Every big advance in the past *twenty* years was not predicted; they were only understood after they were in existence.
- Remember that progress takes longer than advertisers would have you believe. Practically nothing can be started today that will have strategic significance for at least five years, often ten. Mission-critical information systems and their supporting networks take that long to develop and install.

No major new networks are now being built by users, said Frank. Instead, existing networks are being augmented. There are many changes being made including interconnecting networks. The network management project has turned into a network management process.

Therefore, today: (1) there are hundreds of telecommunications vendors in the marketplace, (2) there are no integrated systems yet, (3) there are no universal standards yet, and (4) vendors are just recognizing the *problems*, not creating the solutions yet. The challenge for telecommunications management is to support the business objectives of the company rather than concentrate on making life easier for telecommunications managers.

The Push for Connectivity

More and more organizations are seeing the need to tie together their islands of automation, seeking what the worldwide telephone system already provides: the ability for any telephone user to be connected with any other user. Connectivity means allowing users to communicate up, down, across, and out of an organization.

This push is not new. Many organizations have been working at it—and making progress—for years. Whenever companies have had multiple brands of computers, sooner or later, most have sought to provide a means for those computers to communicate. Often they have replaced applications-oriented networks with generalized networks. Many companies have also standardized on a few vendors to permit easier connectivity.

There are two main elements of connectivity—technical connectivity and procedural connectivity. Technical connectivity means that it is technically possible to interconnect two units so that they can communicate. Procedural connectivity means that procedures are in place to permit and facilitate communication.

Technical Connectivity. There are two underlying concepts in technical connectivity: internets and interoperability.

Internets play an important role in achieving technical connectivity, but not all networks and internets will provide equal connectivity. Einar Stefferud [18] foresees the highest speed networks reserved for tightly coupled work groups that he calls "collegial working groups." These are the engineering design teams, product development groups, customer service teams, and other work groups whose ability to share information and ideas quickly and easily is critical to their work. The network services made available among members of such groups must have high reliability and fast response, says Stefferud. He believes that a major challenge in the 1990s will be providing work group support that takes advantage of the capabilities of computers and networks.

The network connections *between* different work groups will not need to bear the same amounts or kinds of traffic, but they will need to be interconnected. He cites the situation at a research center. Their network that connects work groups and laboratories has a maximum speed of 10 mbps, while the gateway to the outside world runs at only 9600 bps. Currently, this speed discrepancy is not a problem, since most of the traffic at the center is internal. However, when the need arises to routinely access outside databases and to form tightly coupled work groups that extend beyond company boundaries, the center plans to increase their gateway speeds.

So networks and internets will be needed to provide technical connectivity especially within and among work groups.

Interoperability. The concept that best describes the promise of linking client machines to server machines via an internet is "interoperability." It means the capability for different machines, using different operating systems, on different networks to work together on tasks—exchanging information in standard ways without any changes in the command language or in functionality and without physical intervention.

According to William Darden of Northrop Corporation, a truly interoperable network would allow IBM mainframes running MVS to interoperate with servers running UNIX and OS/2 and with PCs and workstations running other operating systems. Interoperability is a responsibility of processors, not networks, says Darden.

Interoperability is at the heart of cooperative processing. Achieving true interoperability could have a large impact on the utilization of corporate IT resources, because it can harness the vast amount of unused computing cycles on desktops. Although this level of interoperability is not currently feasible, the vision is clear and vendors are pursuing it vigorously.

Procedural Connectivity. In most organizations, technical connectivity has been the center of attention. Not much time and effort have been expended on procedural connectivity—where procedures and policies allow or disallow connectivity. However, some researchers are addressing the question. For instance, Malone ET AL at MIT's Center for Information Systems Research [19], propose several policies that could be applied to filter electronic mail. One method is to charge the senders of unsolicited electronic mail in proportion to the value of the recipients' time. Another type of filtering allows each person to set up his or her own filter list. "If a message comes from A, display it immediately. If a message comes from B, I will read it with the rest of my mail. If a message comes from C, refer it on to D." And so on.

The goal of computer connectivity, both technical and procedural, is similar to that of the telephone system. Technically, it should be possible for any computer to communicate with any other computer. But access among them should be subject to procedural constraints.

The Connectivity Components of Networks

In Chapter 5 we discussed the processing components of distributed systems—operating systems, mainframes, workstations, servers, and superservers. In this section we look at the telecommunications components by discussing the various kinds of devices being used to achieve connectivity. As networks have grown and become more complex, so have the products they use. Peter Stephenson [20] presents the best description of the three main connectivity components—bridges, routers, and gateways—because he relates them to the seven OSI layers.

Bridges, says Stephenson, interconnect networks that use different physical media, such as linking twisted pair to coaxial cable. They work at layer one (the physical layer) of OSI. They also work on layer two (the data link layer) because they can link network segments that use different low-level protocols, such as Ethernet and Token Ring. Bridges can even pass data through intermediary networks that do not understand the data. So they are important in mixed-protocol environments. Bridges are intelligent, and they do a lot of processing. They learn addresses, examine packets, forward packets, and direct traffic to its designation—because they know the ultimate destination of the packets.

Routers determine the most efficient route between networks. They operate at level three (the network layer) of OSI, and they are speedy, because they only direct traffic to the next router. They do not worry about the networks' various media or access protocols, as bridges do. And unlike bridges, they also do not examine every packet, only the ones addressed to them. Routers are generally used between networks that use the same high-level protocol, such as TCP/IP; therefore, they may not be usable in networks that have "just grown" and use multiple protocols.

A hybrid of a bridge and router is called a "brouter." By combining the functions of both, brouters can be the best (although expensive) solution in complex, heterogeneous networks. When brouters look at a packet, they decide whether it is routable, and if so, they route it. If not, they bridge it.

Gateways operate on the top three levels of the OSI model—the session, presentation, and application layers. They are the most sophisticated means of connecting networks, and they are used for linking networks with different high-level protocols, such as connecting TCP/IP to SNA. Since these protocols have nothing in common, the gateway must translate all the data that passes between the two. Gateways are used to connect networks to hosts, says Stephenson, and to link LANs to a long-haul network, such as an X.25 packet switched public data network.

Smart hubs, new connectivity devices, are intelligent wiring centers used to interconnect devices on one or more LANs. On the high end are multiprotocol hubs that handle a variety of bridging, routing, and gateway functions. These capabilities allow them to interconnect unlike LANs. Hubs are also increasingly performing network management functions, sometimes on a building-wide basis. Thus, they help network managers manage their growing LAN population.

The people at Northeast Consulting [in 21] believe that as companies move away from proprietary networks, such as SNA, to multivendor internets, "internet nodal processors" will become the interconnectivity cores of these networks. They see today's multiprotocol smart hubs as the forerunners of those nodal processors.

Their analysis brings up an important point: In the world of internets, there need to be intelligent nodes that manage the network by feeding operational data to network managers, and by providing the bridging, routing, and gateway services to achieve interconnectivity. This is a new type of computer—one that is likely to be the workhorse of the large internets of the 1990s.

OPEN SYSTEMS INTERCONNECTION (OSI)

Most of the complications in networking are caused by incompatibilities, and incompatibilities can be reduced by using standards. Standards should be the foundation of the overall architecture, because they offer the greatest long-term benefits. Tailored solutions should be reserved for filling gaps where standards are not yet available. Fortunately, network standards—including de facto standards—are coming into being at a fairly fast pace these days.

Open Versus Closed Networks

A *closed network* is one that is offered by one supplier and to which only the products of that supplier can be attached. Mainframe and minicomputer manufacturers used this approach for years to "lock in" their customers. An *open network*, on the other hand, is based on national or international standards so that the products of many manufacturers can be attached to it.

The International Standards Organization (ISO), CCITT, and other standards bodies have adopted a seven-level OSI Reference Model for guiding the development of international standards for networks of computers. It is called a "reference model" because it only recommends the functions to be performed in each of seven layers; it does not specify detailed standards for each layer. Those are left up to the standards bodies in the adopting countries.

IBM's Systems Network Architecture (SNA) began as a closed network. But because many suppliers have either adopted SNA or provide interfaces to it, SNA has moved out of the "closed" category into a more open one.

Closed networks have traditionally been adopted for the top three computing levels—corporate, regional, and site—where minis and mainframes are used. Open networks have been favored by suppliers serving the lower three computing levels—departments, work groups, and individuals. But with the prospect of distributed systems becoming a reality, OSI's seven-layer model is seen as a comprehensive network architecture for all levels.

The OSI Model

The OSI model is a layered architecture in which "messages" sent from one party to another go through several layers of control. The following is a four-level analogy of one executive mailing a letter to another executive. It shows the flow of "data" and control information through the layers.

- At layer 4, the business executive writes a letter and gives it to a secretary.
- At layer 3, the secretary puts the letter into an envelope, addresses the envelope, puts the return address on the envelope, stamps it, and then mails it.
- At layer 2, the mail carrier takes the letter to the post office sorting office, where all mail for the same postal district is put into one bag with the destination postal office name on it. Mail of different types—Express Mail, first-class mail, third-class mail—have their own bags.
- At layer 1, the postal service delivers the mail bag to the destination sorting office.
- At layer 2, the sorting office checks that the bag has been delivered to the right office. Then the letters are sorted by area and passed on to the individual carriers, who deliver them.
- At layer 3, the recipient's secretary rejects any mail delivered to the wrong address, opens the letter, and passes it on to the recipient, saying, "Here's a letter from. . . ."
- At layer 4, the recipient takes the letter and reads it.

Notice that control information—the address and type of delivery—is on the envelope or mailbag. This control information determines the services to be provided by the next lower layer, and it contains addressing information for the corresponding layer on the receiving end. It defines the interfaces between the layers as well as the dialog within a layer.

When a layer receives a "message" from the next higher layer, it performs the requested services and then "wraps" that message in its own layer of control information for use by the corresponding layer at the receiving end. It then passes this "bundle" to the layer directly below it. On the receiving end, a layer receiving a bundle from a lower layer unwraps the outermost layer of control information, interprets that information, and acts on it. Then it discards that layer of wrapping and passes the bundle to the next higher layer.

In a similar way, the OSI Reference Model describes the standard control procedures to be applied at each of its seven layers. In Figure 6-3, Smalheiser and Florence [22] give a good description of the main function of each of the seven layers of OSI.

Migrating to OSI

Despite the rosy picture that OSI connectivity promises, many questions remain about the fate of proprietary network systems that are not OSI compatible—but which will still be useful in the 1990s. Users of many proprietary systems face the dilemma of staying with their present systems or converting to the OSI protocols.

- Layer 1, *the physical layer*, is responsible for the physical connection of devices to a network.
- Layer 2, *the data link layer*, mainly does error correction. It makes sure that no data is lost or garbled.
- Layer 3, *the network layer*, routes transmissions to their destination.
- Layer 4, *the transport layer*, ensures the integrity of each message—resequencing portions, if necessary, and handling flow control.
- Layer 5, *the session layer*, controls the dialog for each application. It acts as a moderator, seeing that the messages are sent as directed and allowing interruptions, if necessary.
- Layer 6, *the presentation layer*, translates data to and from the language and format used at layer 7.
- Layer 7, *the application layer*, is the applications themselves.

Figure 6-3 The Seven Layers of OSI (from Smalheiser and Florence [22])

It is not only the proprietary network users who have to worry about migrating to OSI. Many organizations have adopted TCP/IP. Although TCP/IP is an open network system, only the two lowest layers use the OSI model, so the TCP/IP community also faces problems migrating to OSI. Major TCP/IP users are working on this transition.

Those organizations that use a proprietary system should not feel that they must throw away their present system in favor of OSI, says Einar Stefferud, a networking consultant [18]. Vendors eventually will make the transition, he says, or provide some kind of gateway interconnection.

Frederic Withington, formerly with the consulting firm of Arthur D. Little, believes, for example, that IBM's SNA will give way to OSI. The major limitation will be the cost of conversion. But even that cost will be overcome by the efficiencies and effectiveness gained by using OSI. By the mid 1990s, Withington foresees the mix consisting of 25 percent using OSI, 30 percent using SNA, and 45 percent using older protocols.

As with the large corporate networks, Withington believes LANs will not make the switch to OSI as long as they perform their intended functions. If there is no need to provide a wider range of connectivity to other systems and networks, then there will be little incentive to migrate LANs to OSI. But when full interconnection becomes important, even at the local level, OSI will dominate, Withington believes.

Stefferud takes a different view. He believes some vendors are favoring gateways to OSI. This is both good and bad news, says Stefferud. Gateways allow connectivity between the two networking systems—but for a price. When a gateway is used, some functionality must be sacrificed—speed, compatibility, or some other consideration. As long as the functionality is adequate for the job, then there is no problem with a gateway, says Stefferud. Once the capacity of the gateway is exceeded, however, something must be done to remedy the situation.

Some vendors have aggressively supported OSI. For example, in the late

1970s, Digital decided to support OSI. In 1985 they issued a statement of direction and they have been an OSI advocate ever since. NCR and Bull are also both strong advocates of OSI. In fact, because of NCR's success in this area, they were acquired by AT&T in 1991.

Thus, help for migrating to OSI is coming from many directions. Progress will be made fastest by groups involved in open systems, says Stefferud. It also appears that vendors who see OSI compliance as a strategic move for their companies are speeding up their migration efforts as well. As an example of a company that is vigorously pursuing OSI, consider Northrop Research and Technology Center.

CASE EXAMPLE: Northrop Research and Technology Center

Northrop Corporation, with headquarters in Los Angeles, California, is a diversified aerospace company. Their work spans the fields of advanced aircraft and electronics. Northrop Research and Technology Center (NRTC) researches new technologies for its corporate parent, from computer science and applied optics to microelectronics.

One of NRTC's major efforts has been to link its diverse working groups and laboratories using a high-speed network. These groups use a wide range of systems and technologies. In addition, they want their networking scheme to interface with their clients' networks. This internetworking would allow different computers on different networks to communicate with each other on a peer-to-peer basis. The people at NRTC see these "networks of networks" as the dominant corporate computing environment in the 1990s.

The problem confronting NTRC is twofold. First, they want to implement a network that conforms to existing standards and also leaves room to accommodate future international networking standards. Second, Northrop's primary client—the U.S. Department of Defense—has immediate need for internet capabilities.

The people at NRTC feel strongly that internets in the 1990s will use the OSI model. NRTC believes that they need experience using this internet architecture, to prepare for the future. Rose and Cass describe some of the NRTC work and experiences an internetworking [23].

NRTC's Approach

The answer to NTRC's network dilemma—planning for the future while accommodating the present—was to take a two-step process. Their first step was to choose an existing nonproprietary internet protocol. Their second step is to migrate from that protocol to the OSI standards, as they become available.

For the interim, NRTC has settled on TCP/IP. This packet-switching, inter-netting protocol is based on the work done in ARPANET. ARPANET is the pioneer of large-scale packet switching internets developed under the auspices of the U.S. Defense Department's Advanced Research Projects Agency (DARPA).

TCP/IP is a vendor-independent protocol that allows equipment on a large variety of networks to talk back and forth to each other. The TCP portion provides the flow control of OSI layer 4. The IP provides the rout-ing services of layer 3. TCP/IP uses OSI layers 1 and 2 for physical and data link services. NRTC chose TCP/IP for two reasons. First, it provides internet standards that work today. Second, it is the protocol used by Northrop's largest client, the U.S. Department of Defense.

The hardware side of NTRC's network is an Ethernet running at 10 mbps. The effective transfer rate on the Ethernet ranges from 100 kbps to 1.2 mbps, depending on the capabilities of the communicating machines and the overhead expended on protocol conversion. NRTC also has an external "gateway" with two leased lines running at 9600 bps to the nearby Information Sciences Institute. This gateway allows the NTRC network to access outside networks, such as the Defense Data Network. Currently, most NTRC data communications are in-house, and they find that their current network transfer rates suffice. For communicating with outside groups, they will increase the speed of the gateway above the 9600 bps rate that they now use.

The TCP/IP network that spans the NRTC complex of buildings connects some fifty separate "nodes," with equipment from fifteen different vendors. Distances between computers are up to one-quarter of a mile. The "nodes" include Digital minicomputers, IBM PCs, specialized electronics design sta-tions, parallel processors, laser printers, LISP machines, RISC workstations, and other widely different systems—all talking over the same network.

The beauty of the TCP/IP system at NRTC is what does not happen—exten-sive network maintenance is unheard of. Maintaining the network requires no more than one to two hours a week. Each laboratory or working group has a system administrator, who works with the central systems group. The central group only needs to do custom programming or intervene when a product does not perform to its own specifications. For the most part, the TCP/IP system works with little assistance from the operators.

Not only is there little troubleshooting required for the network, there is also little work needed to connect a new host. Installation of new nodes does not disrupt network operations. All fifty hosts are con-nected using off-the-shelf products—from either a computer vendor or a third party company. Using off-the-shelf hardware greatly eases their network maintenance burden. The people at NRTC let the vendors inte-grate and support the network connections. Thus, the NTRC staff is free to do its research, instead of maintaining its network resources.

The Future at NRTC

For future development, one group is working on keeping NTRC in a position to exploit the OSI recommended standards as they become implemented. One major concern has been that the TCP/IP system does not provide a good environment for developing applications based on the OSI model. Therefore, they have developed a nonproprietary product called "ISO Development Environment" for writing applications that will run on OSI-based networks. It uses the TCP/IP protocols for OSI layers 3 and 4, and it uses OSI draft standards at the higher levels. This development environment yields two advantages. First, they can begin to develop OSI applications using a "mature and stable" TCP/IP internet environment. Second, their development environment provides a good platform for migrating from TCP/IP-based networks to OSI-based networks.

By embracing TCP/IP as an interim solution—while focusing on OSI as their ultimate goal—NRTC is attempting to gain the best of both worlds: Internetting today, with OSI compatibility tomorrow.

SUMMARY

The overall telecommunications highway system has become clear, but its specifics are not. It will be global internets, consisting of private and public links with varying bandwidths, some of which permit bandwidth on demand. These internets will be composed of equipment from many vendors and will therefore use a variety of protocols. Although OSI is the promised one-for-all telecommunications standard, this future does not appear to be imminent. Therefore, the best guidelines to follow in building internets is to base them around an architecture, stress connectivity, and use standards.

QUESTIONS AND EXERCISES

REVIEW QUESTIONS

1. Explain how a telecommunications system is analogous to a highway system.
2. What are the seven "facts of life" in the telecommunications industry, according to the authors?
3. What are broadband telecommunications?
4. What are T-carriers? Explain their hierarchy. How do they differ from DS-carriers?
5. What is FDDI and where is it likely to be used?
6. Describe the two types of fast packet switching technologies and how they differ.
7. What is SMDS? Who will be offering this service?
8. What is SONET? Why is it important?

9. Where are wireless LANs likely to be the best alternative? Describe the two kinds of technologies that these LANs use.
10. What are personal communication networks? Why is there a potential market for them?
11. What are the three main guidelines for building networks?
12. What is an architecture? What is it not?
13. Why is connectivity the key challenge of network design, according to Howard Frank?
14. Describe the two kinds of connectivity.
15. Define interoperability.
16.· Describe the jobs of the four connectivity components of networks—bridges, routers, gateways, and smart hubs.
17. Briefly describe OSI's seven layers.
18. How are companies likely to migrate to OSI?

DISCUSSION QUESTIONS

1. The chapter implies that a company should stay at the forefront of telecommunications technology lest it fall seriously behind. On the other hand, it might be better to let others go first, and then learn from their mistakes. Which of these approaches is better? Why?
2. What telecommunications services really need to be available at a workstation? Which ones should be available at a work group site, such as a conference room?
3. The telecommunications marketplace is changing so rapidly, with new developments appearing every year. Yet investments in network equipment are large and need to be amortized over many years. How would you approach acquiring the needed links in this dynamic environment? Give the reasoning behind your answer.

EXERCISES

1. Read five articles on telecommunications. What other developments not discussed in this chapter do they see as important and why? Present a short briefing on these to the class.
2. Contact the information systems manager at a company in your community. What is their telecommunications architecture? What telecommunications standards are they using? What are their plans for the future?

REFERENCES

1. KAMMAN, A., "Global Networks," *Stage by Stage*, (Nolan, Norton & Co., Lexington, MA), vol 9, no. 6, 1990, pp. 1-6.

2. SCHNEE, V., "What You Don't See Can Hurt You," *Computerworld*, April 8, 1991, p. 25.

3. BECHTOLD, B., and E. MIER, "White Paper: Happy Birthday to a Standard that Works," *Communications Week*, October 14, 1991, pp. WP3- WP35.

4. ADRIAAN LIGHTENBERG, Storm Technology, 220 California Ave., Suite 101, Palo Alto, CA 94306.

5. WILLIAM MORGAN, W and J PARTNERSHIP, 17211 Quail Court, Morgan Hill, CA 95037.

6. "FDDI For Workgroup Computing," (Network Peripherals, San Jose, CA), October 1990, 10 pages.

7. ROSENBLATT, A, "Data Communications," *IEEE Spectrum*, January 1991, pp. 48-51. This article is part of "Technology 1991," a series of articles on important technological developments, pp. 30-82.

8. JOHNSON, M., "An Offer They Couldn't Refuse," *Computerworld*, April 15, 1991, p. 56.

9. WEXLER, J., "Frame Relay Showing Its Stuff," *Computerworld*, November 12, 1990, pp. 67-76.

10. BUSHAUS, D., "The Evolution of SMDS," *Communications Week*, January 14, 1991, pp. 26.

11. HORWITT, E., "Stanford Explores 45M Bit/Sec Net Standard," *Computerworld*, October 15, 1990, p. 78.

12. BUSHAUS, D. "Where is SONET?" *Communications Week*, March 18, 1991, pp. 33-36.

13. CLEGG, P., "LAN Times Lab Tests Wireless LANs," *LAN Times* ,July 8, 1991, p. 79.

14. ROSENBAUM, R., "The Technology Behind Wireless LANs," *LAN Times*, July 8, 1991, pp. 84-87.

15. GINN, S., "Personal Communication Services: Expanding the Freedom to Communicate," *IEEE Communications Magazine*, February 1991, pp. 30-39.

16. KEEN, P., *Competing in Time: Using Tele-Communications for Competitive Advantage*, (Ballinger Publishing Co., Cambridge, MA), 1986, 235 pages.

17. HOWARD FRANK, Network Management, Inc., 11242 Waples Mill Road, Fairfax, VA 22030.

18. EINAR STEFFEREUD, Network Management Associates, 17301 Drey Lane, Huntington Beach, CA 92647.

19. MALONE, T. W., S. A. BROBST, K. R. GRANT, and M. D. COHEN, *Toward Intelligent Message Routing Systems*, Center for Information System Research (MIT , Cambridge, MA), August 1985.

20. STEPHENSON, P., "Mixing and Matching LANs," *Byte*, March 1991, pp. 157-164.

21. GIRISHANKAR, S. "Are Nodal Processors the Future?" *Communications Week*, September 23, 1991, pp. 19-21.

22. SMALHEISER, K., and D. FLORENCE, "An OSI Tutorial," *Business Week*, McGraw-Hill, Inc. (1221 Avenue of the Americas, New York, N.Y. 10020), June 1, 1987, pp. 131-36.

23. ROSE, M.T. and D.W. CASS, "OSI Transport Services on Top of the TCP," *Computer Networks and ISDN Systems*, (Elsevier Science New York), vol. 12, no. 3, 1986, pp. 159-173.

SEVEN

Managing Information Resources

INTRODUCTION

The internal and external information resources available to organizations are increasing by leaps and bounds. Lower cost storage, increased processing speeds, and higher capacity communications are making internal data available in larger quantities than ever before. New digital handling of voice, video, and image data is increasing the variety of information formats and content as well. At the same time, external data, both hard facts and "soft" intelligence information, are increasingly available from public databases and environmental scanning services.

In the midst of this growing richness of information resources, many companies are still struggling just to get internal alphanumeric data under control. The so-called database era has brought many benefits and advantages including separation of data and programs, reduction in data redundancy, and easier access to data for problem solving and decision making. It is apparent, however, from conversations with systems executives, that much progress is still to be made in organizing and handling information resources.

In this chapter we explore the managerial strategies and tactics for handling information as a corporate resource. The first section identifies some problems in managing data as a resource. The second surveys the evolution of database management systems. The third section focuses on upcoming need to handle distributed data. The final section explores the various types of information that companies need to manage as they treat information as an organizational resource.

GETTING CORPORATE DATA INTO SHAPE

Attempts to get corporate data under control began with the use of software called database management systems (DMBS) in the late 1960s and early 1970s. These software products have increased greatly in functionality and power since that time. A "database administrator" function soon evolved to manage DBMS and their use. In the 1970s, the broader role of "data administration" evolved to manage the entire data resources of the organization. In this section we first identify the nature of the problem that has led to the need for managing data. Then we explore the status of data management by looking at projects in twenty firms.

The Problem: Inconsistent Data Definitions

In a nutshell, the problem has been incompatible data definitions from application to application, department to department, site to site, and division to division. How has this happened? John Zachman [1] blames expediency. To get application systems up and running quickly, system designers have sought the necessary data either from the cheapest source or a politically expedient source, says Zachman. Generally, this has meant using data from existing files and adding other new data. In effect, data has been "dribbled" from application to application. The result has been data showing up in different files, with different names for the same data, the same name for different data items, and the same data in different files with different update cycles.

The use of such data may be acceptable for routine information processing, but it is far from acceptable for management uses, says Zachman. Management cannot get consistent views across the enterprise under such conditions. Also, changes in data and programs are difficult to make, because a change can affect files anywhere in the organization. Furthermore, such inconsistency makes it difficult to vary tracking and reporting of the organization's products, markets, control structure, and so on to meet changing business conditions.

If a major role of the information systems department is *managing data*—instead of getting applications running as quickly as possible—then quite a different scenario would occur. All the types of data in which the organization is interested would first be identified. Then the single source of each data type would be identified, along with the business function that creates that data. Finally, a transaction system would be built to collect and store that data, after which all authorized users and applications would have access to it.

This data-driven approach does not result in one huge database to serve the whole organization, but it does require administrative control over the data, as well as designing the database(s) to support end users from the outset. So, recommends Zachman, start out by describing the data the enterprise needs. Then select the approach for providing the data that gives a good balance between short-term, application-oriented goals and long-term, data-oriented goals.

The Role of Data Administration

The use of DBMS improved the problems of inconsistent and redundant data in many organizations. It is clear, however, that merely installing a DBMS is not sufficient to manage information as a corporate resource. Therefore, two additional thrusts have moved organizations in this direction: broader definition of the data administration role and effective use of data dictionaries.

Database administration concentrates on administering databases and the software that manages them. Data administration is broader. One of its main purposes is determining what data is being used outside of the organizational unit that creates it. Whenever data crosses organizational boundaries, its definition and format need to be standardized, under the data administration function.

The "data dictionary" is, and will increasingly become, the main tool by which data administrators control standard data definitions. All definitions are entered into the dictionary, and data administrators monitor all new definitions and all requests for changes in definitions, to make sure that corporate policy is being followed. We consider the functions of a data dictionary in more detail after discussing four main functions of data administrators.

Four Main Functions

To bring order to the data mess that exists, data administration has four main functions:

- Clean up data definitions
- Control shared data
- Manage distributed data
- Maintain data quality

Clean Up the Data Definitions. Data administration needs to have the responsibility and authority to ensure data and information compatibility throughout an organization by getting rid of undesired definition redundancies and inconsistencies. For instance, two or more names should not exist for the same data item, nor should the same name be used for two or more different data items. In most companies, sorting out existing data synonyms and then reconciling them is a monumental job.

In this role, data administrators design the standard data definitions, the data dictionary, and the databases to reconcile conflicting user needs. They also design the data integrity system to flag suspected data and guard against inaccurate, invalid, or missing data. Finally, they need to train users on the meanings and proper use of data. Unless users are trained in the use of the data definitions, the clean data will not stay that way for long.

Control Shared Data. While data used solely by one organizational unit might be considered "local" and under the control of that unit, data used by two or more units should be considered shared data. The data administration function must control the definitions, and some of the processing, of all shared data.

There seems to be a controversy in this area. One side says that essentially all the data in the organization should be under the control of data administration. Just because some data is currently not being used across organizational boundaries is no reason to suppose that it will not be in the future, when access will be much easier. The other view is that each organizational unit can do whatever it wishes with its data; only data that must flow to other units needs to be standardized. It is impractical to try to standardize everything, and it would impose unreasonable rigidities, say these people. Data administrators have to confront this issue and decide how broadly or narrowly to define "shared" data.

The data administration function must also analyze the impact of proposed changes to programs that use shared data. All programs that would require changes need to be identified before approving the change. A data dictionary is a tremendous help here, because it provides one place to look for all uses of the data. Finally, approval to proceed with the change might be held up until all affected programs have been changed to keep those applications from aborting. Changes also require informing users of changes in meanings of data, if this occurs. Otherwise, users may base decisions on incorrect assumptions about the data they are using.

Manage Distributed Data. Shared data, as defined here, crosses organizational boundaries. Distributed data, on the other hand, is geographically dispersed. It too may cross hierarchical levels of the organization. Managing data in a distributed dimension, with probably several levels of detail, presents some significant challenges to data administrators, especially in this era of cooperative processing and portable computing. We discuss some of the options and cautions for distributing data later in this chapter.

Maintain Data Quality. Cleaning up data definitions, and the other important functions of data administration, can become useless unless policies and procedures are developed to maintain data quality. A dominant guideline has been to decentralize or distribute this function—put the owners of the data in charge of edited and verifying data accuracy and quality. But this requires resolving the question of who owns the data.

The Importance of Data Dictionaries

In the previous section, we referred to a data dictionary as the primary tool to manage data definitions. Data dictionaries are systems and procedures—either manual or automated—for storing and handling an organization's data definitions. A data dictionary does not, in itself, generally produce data for an organization. Instead, its purpose is to eliminate errors of understanding, ambiguities, and difficulties in interpreting data.

Ideally, a data dictionary should be considered at least as soon as a database management system is considered. An ideal sequence is to (1) set up the data administration function, (2) develop data standards, (3) purchase and install a DBMS, and (4) install a data dictionary as the first database application. This is particularly appropriate if the DBMS has a data dictionary function as one of its capabilities. If, on the other hand, the organization obtained its DBMS previously and has several applications in production using it, then the successful installation and use of a dictionary will require more time and effort.

The worst situation, and probably the most prevalent, has been bringing in a data dictionary after the database management system has been in use for a number of years. Early DBMS often functioned mainly as an access method rather than as a true DBMS, so many database applications were run with little integration among them. There is little or no documentation of data definitions, so they were redundant and inconsistent. This is the huge clean-up mess many large organizations face if they wish to use a data dictionary effectively. Fortunately, the dictionaries now on the market are often designed to help companies deal with this situation.

Managing the Data Resource

Although data administration functions have been in place for many years, there has been long-standing debate about the effectiveness of corporate-wide data management efforts. To address this issue, we turn to the most insightful study performed to date on data management practices. We present this study as a case example of what is actually happening in practice.

CASE EXAMPLE: MIT Center for Information Systems Research (CISR) Study

Dale Goodhue of the University of Minnesota, along with Judith Quillard and John Rockart of MIT's CISR [2], were the researchers in this study. Their goal was to answer the question: "How are firms managing their data?" They interviewed 230 people in forward-thinking systems departments in twenty *Fortune 500* firms, and they studied thirty-one successful data management projects to uncover the success factors behind those projects. The researchers explored the policies, processes, controls, standards, and tools used on these data management projects, and investigated the motivational techniques used, the results achieved, and the major data management problems and issues that arose.

One major finding was that none of the projects achieved the goal that has long been touted in the literature: building a master data architecture that identifies strategic opportunities and guides all new system development.

The other major finding was that no single approach dominated data management. Firms took diverse approaches with respect to four areas:

- Business objectives
- Organizational scope
- Planning method
- "Product," that is, the deliverable produced

Within each of these four areas, however, there were dominant approaches that characterized success. But before we describe those findings, we look at traditional approaches to give a perspective for the results.

A Short History

Goodhue, Quillard, and Rockart point out that there have traditionally been three approaches to managing data corporate-wide: a technical approach, an organizational approach, and a business approach.

- *Approaches with a technical focus* include database management systems, data dictionaries, and data entity-relationship modeling.
- *Approaches with a focus on organizational responsibilities* include establishing database administration and data administration groups, and formulating administrative policies and procedures for ownership, access, and security of data.
- *Approaches that take a top-down, business planning approach* include planning processes—such as James Martin's [3] information engineering and Robert Holland's [4] strategic systems planning—which link business objectives to acquiring and using data.

The technical and organizational approaches have proved to be inadequate, note Goodhue, Quillard, and Rockart. For example, Coulson [5] points out that data dictionaries (representing one technical approach) have not solved data management problems. And Kahn [6] demonstrates that most data administration groups (representing one organizational approach) have not succeeded in correcting critical data management problems. For instance, data administrators have failed to provide sufficient management support, says Tillman [7].

The third approach has received great attention because its goal is to support the business rather than install new tools or create new organizational units. However, the goals of these planning approaches have often required major commitments of resources and have often not been easy to accomplish.

Study Findings

As noted earlier, the thirty-one projects differed in four categories: business objectives, organizational scope, planning process, and delivered "products." Here is a brief review of those differences.

Business Objectives. The researchers found that the most successful data management projects aimed at solving a clear, specific business problem or exploiting an opportunity. Generally, a line manager needed to respond to a change. Often, the systems department initiated the efforts by educating line managers of the possibilities.

The most dominant objective (in sixteen of the the thirty-one projects) was *improved information for managers*—senior managers, middle managers, and key staff. This need often arose when managers needed to analyze changing market trends or more closely monitor profitability, noted the researchers. These managers wanted better access to data and higher data quality.

The business objective in six of the projects was *better coordination of operational activities*. This required better communication among functions, which implied the ability to easily share data.

Three projects aimed to increase *organizational flexibility*, to allow corporate restructuring or refocusing. Increased flexibility depends on more than effective data management, note Goodhue, Quillard, and Rockart. But restrictive data structures can hamper flexibility by not allowing employees to easily take new views of data. For example, for an insurance company to offer a "flexible benefits" program, it must be able to access its policy data in new ways—ways that were never envisioned by the original system designers and are often not permissible without significant reprogramming.

Improved effectiveness of the systems function was the business objective in six cases, so that higher quality systems could be developed faster. These efforts were expected to lead to higher short-term IT costs—due to the data management work—but lower application development and maintenance costs in the future.

Organizational Scope. The projects used one of three scopes: thirteen were functional, eight were divisional, and ten were corporate.

Planning Approaches. The firms in the study took four planning approaches. Seven of the thirty-one firms used *no planning process* at all. Five others used a *strategic data planning* approach, which is a rigorous, top-down approach to understanding and modeling data. The goal is an architecture of major subject area databases along with a plan for their implementation. The underlying assumption of top-down data modeling is that firms cannot plan effectively without a clear understanding of the business and the data it uses. However, attempts to model business and data have not yielded such an architecture. The clearest benefit in one firm was better understanding of its data by those involved in the planning process, note the researchers. In two other firms, data modeling led to an architectural basis for future data management efforts, but no IT plan.

In fifteen of the thirty-one projects, the firms *targeted a particular function or business area*. These limits made the projects effective and feasible.

Four of the firms limited scope by taking the *80/20 approach*—going for 80 percent of the benefits from products with 20 percent of the work of global planning. This approach is the middle ground between the "quick hit" view of the targeted approach and the massive investment of time and effort in the strategic data planning approach.

"Products." The researchers uncovered five data management "products" in the thirty-one projects.

The most prevalent "product," occurring in eleven of the thirty-one projects, was *information databases*—subject area databases for staff analysis and line management. These databases are "secondary" in that they are periodically refreshed by drawing data from transaction databases or other primary sources. The researchers point out that these databases are important products because they can be created by writing "bridges" to obtain data from existing systems, without requiring the operational systems to be rewritten.

In seven of the thirty-one projects, the deliverable was *subject databases* for operational systems. These databases were organized around an important business area, such as customers and products, rather than around a function, such as order processing or production scheduling.

Two projects resulted in *common systems*—systems developed by a central organization for use by numerous organizational units—with accompanying databases. Although common systems are not new, they have rarely been developed for data management purposes, say Goodhue, Quillard, and Rockart. But developing common systems requires surfacing and resolving differences in data definitions in the various systems to be replaced. Data in common systems can also be used as a foundation for future data management efforts.

Rather than new databases, the "product" in four cases was providing managers with *better access to current databases*. These enhanced services were generally provided by staff members in an information center by locating the need data and training the users on how to use a fourth generation language to access the data. These services are obviously the most helpful when operational data is high quality.

Five of the firms focused on developing *architectural foundations for the future* by building a corporate-wide data model. Two firms developed corporate-wide data definitions as the sole product of that project.

Major Patterns

A major purpose of the study was to determine if there was a predominant pattern for a successful data management project. The answer was no, but three major patterns did arise, as shown in Figure 7-1.

The *most striking pattern* (solid arrows) was followed in six firms. These sought to improve managerial information in a functional area by targeting specific business opportunities and by building information databases to support those opportunities. Two other firms that followed almost the same path took a corporate or divisional scope. The need for management information is a strong impetus for data management projects because executives need consolidated information across the board—financial, operational, quality, and customers. These needs can often be addressed through an information database.

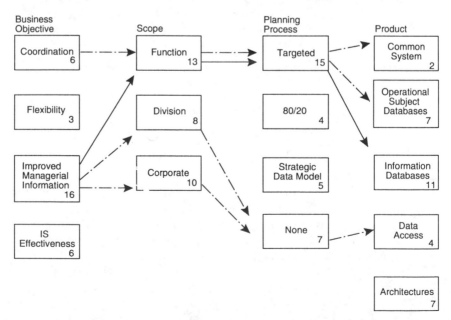

Figure 7-1 Framework for Data Management (from Goodhue, Quillard and Rockart [2])

The *second prominent pattern* (dashed arrows) was used by four firms. These companies, which sought better coordination of operations in a functional area, chose key business opportunities and built databases to address their operational needs.

The *third pattern* (dotted arrows) was used in four other firms. These companies sought to improve management information—either corporate or divisional—by implementing data access services; these firms used no explicit data planning processes. This option is important because it places data where it is valuable: in the hands of end users at minimal cost. It can even be used in companies with many common systems, extensive data definition, and coding standards.

Two of these three major patterns (and eleven of the thirty-one cases) reflect the importance of limiting scope to a function and carefully targeting the planning work. It also points out the significance of allowing functional managers to use data management efforts to assist them in their areas of responsibility.

The number of occurrences of three of the components in Figure 7-1 are "high action areas" that should be carefully considered by all data management staff. One is the need for better managerial information, which motivated sixteen of the thirty-one efforts. The second is addressing a targeted need without a formal planning process, which was used in fifteen of the projects. And the third is information databases, which were developed in eleven of the thirty-one efforts.

Conclusions

Goodhue, Quillard, and Rockart draw seven conclusions from this extensive study. Briefly, they are as follows.

One, business benefits can result from improving data management. For example, a chemical company reduced spare parts inventory by 20 percent by using a common system. An energy company can now consolidate financial reports in four days with four people rather than the former two weeks with six people. And a computer company can now answer a wide range of ad hoc questions—such as the actual effect of a price change—that previously could not be answered at all.

Two, lack of data standardization is a major managerial problem. Since most computerized data meet specific application needs, the data cannot be shared across applications. This problem was recognized when managers were unable to combine data from different functions. Without standard data definitions, the data could not be combined.

Three, total standardization is not the goal. Due to the hard-to-resolve differences in how data is defined and sorted, company-wide standardization is impractical. To succeed at a reasonable cost, data standards should therefore be developed only where it makes business sense—in obvious high payback areas.

Four, the 80/20 approach is becoming increasingly important. The study showed that high-impact areas can be quickly spotted and targeted without a laborious strategic data planning effort. These targets can then lead to the next targets for action. The researchers believe this approach to planning will increase.

Five, information databases will be the dominant product, because they are less expensive and more quickly implemented than rewriting existing applications. Furthermore, they are likely to be a significant piece of a de facto architecture for future development work, speculate the researchers.

Six, resources must be balanced between long and short term. To address data problems, firms need to allocate resources to developing a long-term data standard, as well as to improving access to current data.

And seven, difficult organizational issues must be addressed. Data management often surface tough issues for corporate management. Three important issues are (1) executives' concern for short-term results, (2) countering the centralization caused by data management, and (3) the effect of data management on the information systems department's culture and line management responsibilities. Unless such issues are addressed, the data management efforts will not succeed.

THE EVOLUTION OF DATABASE MANAGEMENT SYSTEMS

One of the most active areas of software development has been database management systems. Two major principles of this development are the concept of three levels of data management and several alternative "models" for organizing data.

The Three-Level Database Model

One of the easiest to understand discussions of database technology is by James Bradley [8]. He describes the work of the Standards, Planning and Requirements Committee of the American National Standards Institute (ANSI/SPARC) in the mid-1970s. The main concept that came out of the work of this committee was the *three-level database*. Most of today's major DBMS have adopted this three-level concept. The following discussion is taken from Bradley, Martin [9], and Atre [10]. It begins with the level that the application programmer sees.

Level 1 is called the external, conceptual, or local level. As Figure 7-2 illustrates, this level contains the various "user views" of the corporate data used by application programs—each has its own view. At this level, there is no concern for how the data will be physically stored or what data is used by other applications.

Level 2 is called the logical or "enterprise data" level. It encompasses all an organization's relevant data, under the control of the data administrators. Data and relationships are represented at this level by one or more DBMS. This level contains the same data as level 3, but with the implementation data removed.

Level 3 is called the physical or storage level. It specifies the way the data is physically stored. A data record consists of its data fields plus some implementation data, generally pointers and flag fields. The end user, of course, need not be concerned with these pointers and flags; they are for use by the DBMS only.

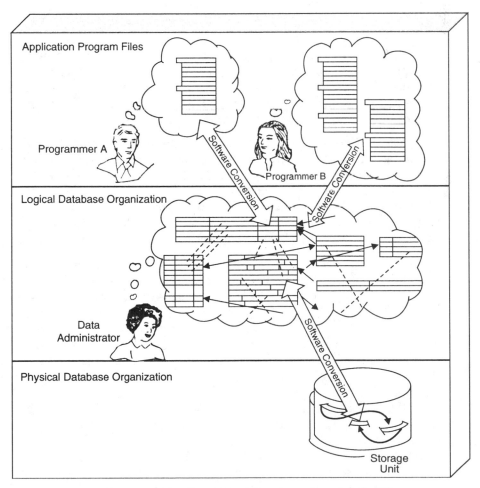

Figure 7-2 The Three-Level Database (from Martin [9])

The advantages of this three-level model are important to the design of a DBMS. The logical data can be separated from the physical storage method, so that different physical devices can be used without changing the application programs. The logical data relationships can also vary for different programs that use the data, without requiring data redundancy. In addition, applications can use a subset of the database and organize it, again without redundancy, in the best manner for the application.

Three Traditional Data Models

The second major concept in database management is alternative ways to define relationships among data and the DBMS. These so-called data models are methods by which data are structured to represent the real world and the way that data are accessed. There are several data models in use today, but three have been the most widely used since the 1970s—hierarchical, network, and relational.

The hierarchical model structures data so that each element is subordinate to another in a strict hierarchical manner, like the boxes in an organization chart. This model uses the terminology "parent" and "child" to represent these relationships. This approach, where a data item can have only one parent, is represented by IBM's IMS database management system.

The network model allows each data item to have more than one parent. Assembly parts lists illustrate this structure, where the same part can be used in more than one assembly. This approach is represented by the CODASYL-type database management systems, such as Computer Associates' IDMS. In both the hierarchical and network models, the data relationships are stated explicitly, generally by pointers stored with the data. These pointers provide the means by which the user's program accesses the desired data records.

The relational database management system was proposed in 1970 by Edgar F. Codd of IBM [11]. It is the most recent of the three traditional models. Perhaps more than any other approach to database management, his work has triggered a debate on which data model is conceptually "best." In the relational model, the relationships among data items are not expressly stated by pointers. Instead, it is up to the DBMS to find the related items, based on the values of specified data fields. Thus, all employees of a certain department are found by searching for the department number in each employee record.

Relational databases store data in tables. Each row of the table, called a "tuple," represents an individual entity (person, part, account). Each column represents an attribute of the entities. Eight relational operations can be performed on this data, as shown in Figure 7-3.

Relational systems are not as efficient as hierarchical or networked database systems, where the navigational maps through the data are prede-

Figure 7-3 Relational Operations

- SELECT chooses particular columns.

- PROJECT chooses particular rows.

- JOIN concatenates rows from two or more tables, matching column values.

- PRODUCT concatenates rows from two or more tables but does not match column values.

- INTERSECTION selects rows whose value(s) exist in both tables.

- DIFFERENCE selects rows whose value(s) exist in one table but not in the other.

- UNION merges two tables that have similar data, eliminating duplicates.

- DIVISION also merges two tables, but with more complicated selection capabilities. For a simple example, suppose there is a table that contains all the products you buy and a table that contains all your suppliers and the products they sell. Relational division can be used to find all suppliers that can supply all the products you buy.

---

fined. But because they allow people to create relationships among data on the fly, relational systems are much more flexible. Hence, they have become the database technology of choice in today's systems.

The relational model has caught the attention of the industry because computer scientists see it as a good "theory" of data structure, while users find its tabular representation comfortable and familiar. Database management systems based on the relational model were first used primarily to handle end user queries; they are now widely used in high-volume transaction systems with huge files.

Much of the current interest in relational systems comes from their capability to enable on-the-spot concatenation of data from several sources. This is precisely the capability end users want, because they do not know the format of many of their ad hoc queries ahead of time. This capability also increases the flexibility of large mainline systems.

Next-Generation Database Management Systems

Next-generation database systems, according to a special issue of *Communications of the* ACM [12], are object-oriented or extended relational DBMS. As Cattell [12a] of Sun Microsystems notes, these DBMS are designed to widen the use of databases to new kinds of applications—CASE, CAD, medical applications, office automation, and knowledge representation for artificial intelligence.

These systems will draw on *data management* techniques from the past, but they will include two other major concepts as well. One is *object management*—the management of complex kinds of data, such as multimedia and procedures. The other concept is *knowledge management*—the management of many complex rules for reasoning and maintaining integrity constraints between data. Together, these three techniques—data, object, and knowledge management—describe the underpinnings of the next-generation database management systems.

The new data models in these DBMS, which have already been built and tested in research labs, have two important architectural features, says Cattell. First, they are designed for high performance on objects. And second, they are closely integrated with programming languages. Some even combine the programming language and data manipulation language. Yet all these systems retain traditional DBMS features including end user tools, high-level query languages, concurrency control, recovery, and the ability to handle huge amounts of data efficiently.

For data modeling, these systems combine the best features of relational DBMS and object-oriented programming languages, says Cattell. In fact, there are two main categories of next-generation DBMS, depending on their heritage: programming language or database system. One family, such as ObjectStore and Gemstone, are extensions of object-oriented programming languages, which add database capabilities. The other family, represented by Starburst and Postgres, extend relational DBMS with object-oriented language capabilities.

Object-Oriented Database Systems. As we noted in Chapter 1, there is growing use of object oriented technologies in several areas of information systems. One of those areas is database management. The newest data model is object oriented. The object-oriented approach expands the view of data by storing and managing "objects," each of which consists of

1. A piece of data

2. "Methods"—procedures that can perform work on that data

3. Attributes describing the data

4. Relationships between this object and others

Objects are important because they can be any type of data—a traditional name or address, an entire spreadsheet, a clip of video, a voice annotation, a photograph, a segment of music, and so on. A collection of objects is called an objectbase, although such terms as object database, or object-oriented database are used by some vendors to signify the relationship between objectbases and database management.

Although these new database models may not replace the traditional three (hierarchical, network, and relational), they will *significantly* expand the kinds of data stored in databases.

Stonebraker and Kemnitz [12b] provide an example of an application that requires object management, as well as data management and knowledge management. It is a newspaper application that needs to store text and graphics, and be integrated with subscription and classified ad data. In this application, the customer billing requires traditional data management, while storage of text, pictures, and the newspaper's banner require object management. Finally, it needs the rules that control the newspapers layout. One rule might be: Ads for competing department stores cannot be on facing pages.

Stonebraker and Kemnitz believe that *most* data management problems in the 1990s will inherently requires all three dimensions: data, object, and rule (or knowledge) management. Their product, Postgres, is designed to fill these needs.

A Look to the Future. Silberschatz, Stonebraker, and Ullman [12c] report on a workshop held by the National Service Foundation in 1990 to identify the forces that will drive future database technology and the corresponding research needed to meet these needs. The workshop participants drew three main conclusions:

1. Twenty-first century technologies will require radically new database technologies.
2. Next generation database applications will look very different from today's applications. They will involve much more data, multimedia support, complex objects, rules processing and archival storage.
3. Cooperation among organizational units will require heterogeneous distributed databases.

In short, the next database challenges are twofold: building next-generation database management systems and developing heterogeneous distributed database systems.

Future Database Applications. Silberschatz, Stonebraker and Ullman give five examples of future database applications that cannot be handled with today's database products or technologies.

- NASA estimates that it needs to store 10^{16} bytes of satellite images from just a few years worth of space exploration in the 1990s. How can it store and search such a massive database, which is enough to fill ten thousand optical disk jukeboxes?
- CAD data for a skyscraper must maintain and integrate information from the viewpoints of hundreds of subcontractors. For example, when an electrician drills a hole in a beam to run an electrical wire, the system should, ideally, recalculate the stresses on the beam to ensure that its load-bearing capabilities have not been compromised.
- The U.S. National Institute of Health and the U.S. Department of Energy have a joint project for constructing the DNA sequence of the human genome, which is several billion elements long. Matching patients' medical problems to differences in genetic makeup is a staggering problem requiring new data representation and search technologies.

- Large department stores record every product code scanning action of every cashier in every store. Corporate buyers explore this data using ad hoc queries to uncover buying patterns. Such "data mining" is sure to grow, not only in retailing, but in medicine, science, and many other fields.
- Databases of insurance policies are going multimedia—storing photographs of damaged property, handwritten claim forms, audio transcripts of appraisals, images of insured objects, and even video walk-throughs of houses. Such image data is so large that these databases will be enormous. This application also pushes the limits of available technology.

Research Areas. To permit these kinds of next-generation databases, research is needed in many areas including the following. Databases will need to store new kinds of data, such as protein structures, program standards, and images. Databases will also need to be able to "chunk" large objects into manageable pieces for applications to process. Future databases will further need to permit rules processing. For example, a design database should notify the designer when one of his system designs is affected by a modification made by another designer. These systems could encompass elaborate sets of triggers to track important actions. Separate rule-based systems, common today, probably are not efficient enough to handle these large complex situations.

We also need new data models, say Silberschatz, Stonebraker, and Ullman, to handle spatial data, time, and uncertainty. Finding the closest neighbor to a data element in three-dimenional space requires new multidimensional access methods. Exploring the state of a database at a point in time, or retrieving the time listing of a data value, will be functions requested by engineers, retailers, and physicists. Unfortunately, time is not supported in today's commercial databases.

Some databases will also need the ability to attach probability to data, such as the probability that an object in a satellite photo is a specific phenomenon.

Just as there is essentially one worldwide telephone system and one worldwide computer network, some believe we will eventually have a single worldwide file system. To achieve this requires collaboration among nations, which is actually happening in some areas—in physical sciences, the human genome is one example.

Defense contractors want a single project database that spans all subcontractors and all portions of a project. An auto company wants to give its suppliers access to new car designs, under certain circumstances. Both of these needs require intercompany databases. Future database systems will accommodate distributed heterogeneous databases. The challenge is making these databases behave as though they are part of a single database. This is interoperability—the main challenge of distributed systems, as we noted in Chapter 5.

Yet another challenge for future DBMS is providing easy-to-use, uniform browsing tools that work across the heterogeneous databases. These query systems must be able to explain to a user where an inconsistency occurred, or where a database was missing; otherwise, these systems cannot be trusted to perform complete searches.

Silberschatz, Stonebraker, and Ullman suggest that "mediators" will be built to coordinate users' requests with heterogeneous databases. These special programs would know how to handle very specific kinds of queries, so they will be able to detect and report missing data and inconsistencies.

Finally, security is a major failing in today's DBMS, and distributed, heterogeneous databases will exacerbate the problem. Companies may want to permit access to some portions of their databases while restricting other parts. This will require reliably authenticating inquirers. Unless security and integrity are strictly enforced, users will not be able to trust the systems.

To date, the database industry has shown remarkable success in transforming scientific ideas into products, say Silberschatz, Stonebraker, and Ullman. Further advanced research is need to tackle these challenges just noted.

THE COMING CHALLENGE: DISTRIBUTING DATA

As Cattell noted, the second main challenge facing the data management field—besides developing next-generation DBMS—is distributing data. In Chapter 5, we noted the trend toward distributed processing. In this section, we define distributed databases, note some major technical issues, and then explore alternatives to "true" distributed databases.

The situation in the early 1990s in distributed databases appears to be similar to that of on-line systems thirty years ago. A few organizations are pioneering the use and encountering the problems. Others are thinking about the promised benefits of distributed databases, which include

- Saving money by offloading database processing to less expensive machines
- Lowering telecommunications costs by placing databases closer to users
- Decreasing dependence on a single computer manufacturer with various interoperating DBMS
- Moving control of data closer to data owners
- Increasing the scope of DBMS to manage more kinds of data, and then linking them at the workstation
- Permitting the storage and coordination of various kinds of multimedia data

However, the technology is not yet in place for companies to reap these benefits. Although it is much better understood than just a few years ago, the field is in its infancy.

"True" Distributed Databases

Popular discussion and development of distributed databases has taken place only in the past few years; they are no longer only in the research realm. In this section, we will describe some of the current, leading ideas on what constitutes a "true" distributed database.

Guiding Principles. Chris Date [13], of Codd and Date Consulting Group, formulated twelve rules for a distributed database. These have become the definition of a distributed database. They are listed in Figure 7-4.

---

1. ***Local autonomy.*** Local data is owned and managed locally, with local accountability and security. No site depends on another for successful functioning.

2. ***No reliance on a central site.*** All sites are equal, and none relies on a master site for processing or communications.

3. ***Continuous operation.*** Installations at one site do not affect operations at another. There should never be a need for a planned shutdown. Adding or deleting installations should not affect existing programs or activities. Likewise, portions of databases should be able to be created and destroyed without stopping any component.

4. ***Location independence*** (transparency). Users do not have to know where data is physically stored. They act as if all data is stored locally.

5. ***Fragmentation independence*** (transparency). Relations between data elements can be fragmented for physical storage, but users are able to act as if data was not fragmented.

6. ***Replication independence.*** Relations and fragments can be represented at the physical level by multiple, distinct, stored copies or replicas at distinct sites, transparent to the user.

7. ***Distributed query processing.*** Local computer and input/output activity occurs at multiple sites, with data communications between the sites. Both local and global optimization of query processing are supported. That is, the system finds the cheapest way to answer a query that involves accessing several databases.

8. ***Distributed transaction management.*** Single transactions are able to execute code at multiple sites, causing updates at multiple sites.

9. ***Hardware independence.*** Distributed database systems are able to run on different kinds of hardware with all machines participating as equal partners where appropriate.

10. ***Operating system independence.*** Distributed database systems are able to run under different operating systems.

11. ***Network independence.*** Distributed database systems are able to work with different communications networks.

12. ***Database independence.*** Distributed database systems are able to be built of different kinds of databases, provided they have the same interfaces.

Figure 7-4 Twelve Rules For Distributed Databases (From C. J. Date [13])

Figure 7-5 Seven Kinds of Transparency (from Stonebraker [14])

1. *Location transparency.* A user can submit a query that accesses distributed objects without having to know where the objects are.

2. *Performance transparency.* A distributed query optimizer finds the best plan for executing a distributed command, which means that a query can be submitted from any node in a distributed database and it will run with comparable performance.

3. *Copy transparency.* The system supports the optional existence of multiple copies of database objects.

4. *Transaction transparency.* A user can run a transaction that updates data at a number of sites. It behaves exactly like a local one, with the ultimate effect being that it either commits or aborts; no intermediate states are possible.

5. *Fragment transparency.* The distributed dbms allows a user to cut up a relation into multiple pieces and place them at multiple sites according to certain distribution criteria.

6. *Schema change transparency.* Users who add or delete a database object from a distributed database only need make the change once to the distributed dictionary. They do not need to change the catalogs at all sites that participate in the distributed database.

7. *Local DBMS transparency.* The distributed database system is able to provide its services without regard for the local DBMSs that are actually managing local data.

Transparency

These 12 rules, in essence, describe a transparent system, which means that a distributed database looks exactly like a nondistributed one to a user. Although we do not want to belabor the jargon used in this emerging field, we do need to introduce one more set of definitions. This set explains the various types of transparency. These seven kinds of transparency were formulated by Michael Stonebraker of the University of California, Berkeley [14], another leading thinker in this field. They are presented in Figure 7-5.

These two sets of definitions, from Date and Stonebraker, have become the operating principles for the distributed database field. Although not stated in so many words in these two sets of operating principles, distributed databases depend on the underlying databases being relational databases.

Technical Issues in Distributing Data

Among the myriad technical challenges facing designers of distributed systems, three stand out when distributing data. Until these are resolved, distributed data will not be practical for mainline business applications. The three are

- Choosing a standard data access language
- Synchronizing distributed databases
- Optimizing queries

Standard Data Access Language

The one current standard in the distributed database field is SQL. It was developed by IBM in the mid-1970s, and although it was not accepted as a means of accessing hierarchical and network databases, it has become the standard language for accessing relational and distributed databases. Although vendors tend to implement their own versions of SQL, the two main versions are ANSI SQL and IBM SQL.

SQL is not a full-application development language nor an end user query tool. Rather, it is an English-like language for manipulating data and performing queries against relational tables. It has three components.

1. A *data definition language* for creating relational tables, creating indexes to data, and defining fields of data
2. A *data manipulation language* for entering information into a database and accessing and formatting the data
3. A *data control language* for handling security functions

Use of SQL provides several benefits. It can be embedded in procedural languages, such as C or COBOL, and it can be incorporated in packages that run on PCs and workstations, such as spreadsheets. As an intermediary between applications and databases, it insulates applications from changes in physical and logical database structures. Furthermore, it provides the foundation for standard communications among heterogeneous databases. The SQL Access Group, a consortium of mainly vendors, is defining application programming interfaces (APIs) for databases, so that a heterogeneous database system can be built without creating individual DBMS-to-DBMS gateways.

Synchronizing Distributed Databases

Maintaining the integrity of data—that is, assuring that like data remain the same even when distributed—is one of the most serious technical challenges in operating distributed databases. It requires that databases containing the same data remain synchronized and be changed in tandem. The method that is currently used to ensure data integrity is "two-phase commit." In two-phase commit, none of the affected databases is committed to an update until all have performed the update.

The example in Figure 7-6 illustrates the steps involved in a two-phase commit. It uses two financial data centers, one in the Southern California and another in Northern California. A transaction to transfer $10,000 from a Northern California account to a Southern California account would follow the nine steps. Notice that the Northern California host controls the entire transaction. If both computers cannot commit, or verify the transaction, the update is backed out. For example, if there were a breakdown in communications, although both databases must be updated, neither system would be aware of that fact; therefore, the updates would be backed out.

The goal is to implement the two-phase commit procedures at databases, not in application programs, so that programmers do not need to develop them. This capability is gradually being added by DBMS vendors.

Optimizing Queries

Another of the big technical challenges in distributed databases is determining the fastest and most efficient steps to handle a query. For example, suppose a query from a PC requires a "join" between a 250,000-record table on a remote node and a 1,000-record table on the PC. It would be most efficient to move the PC's table to the remote node, because it has so many fewer elements. This is query optimization, and it requires the query optimizer to know the sizes of the databases, the capabilities of the machines, the speeds of the networks, and the workloads on the machines. Routines for optimizing queries are just now appearing in DBMS products.

True distributed database management products are just now emerging on the market; however they will not be in widespread use for some time. In the meantime, companies will choose alternatives.

1. The Northern host receives the request for transfer from the Southern host.

2. The Northern host checks that its account is available for update and locks it.

3. The Northern host checks that the Southern account is available for update and either locks it or instructs the Southern host to issue a lock.

4. The Northern host debits its account for $10,000.

5. The Northern host transmits a credit transaction for $10,000 to the Southern host.

6. The Southern host credits its account for $10,000.

7. The Southern host notifies the Northern host that its update was successful.

8. The Northern host finalizes and logs the transaction.

9. The Northern host releases its lock and instructs the Southern host to release its account.

Figure 7-6 An Example of Two-Phase Commit

Alternatives to "True" Distributed Databases

It is quite likely that many databases do not have to be fully distributed; less dramatic alternatives may suffice quite well. Following are five alternatives:

- Downloaded data files
- Copies of data stored at nodes
- Not fully synchronized databases
- Client/server databases
- Federated databases

Downloaded Data Files

Sending data from mainframes and minis to PCs is very common. In fact, it is the most popular method for distributing data. In some cases, report files are distributed in place of printed reports. When delivered in this manner, the report formats can be changed to meet local needs. And, of course, users see the data much earlier than when the printed reports are physically distributed.

End users can also request downloads of selected files. After processing, these may or may not be returned to the host to update its files. Companies that do not allow uploading data to production files from PCs fear that the integrity of the data will be compromised. Many do not even allow direct downloading of data from production files to PCs. Instead, data is extracted from the production files and put in "extract" files or information databases (to use the CISR terminology), from which it is downloaded.

Copies of Data Stored at Nodes

A second approach to distributing data is to locate working copies of data at nodes. These data files are accessible to remote users for query and sometimes to post updates and changes. This so-called memo posting provides fast answers to queries and helps process customer activity during the workday. The master files reside at one or more data centers, and the "official" updating of the files is done at these centers, usually at night. Then, during early morning hours, only the new and changed records are downloaded to the nodes, for use during that workday.

Not Fully Synchronized Databases

Einar Stefferud [15] points out that it may not always be necessary to have distributed databases that are synchronized at every point in time—as long as the errors can always be caught quickly and fixed easily. This is the case with the distributed name service on networks. This service stores the names and addresses of files on the network. Each service node has one authoritative copy and one secondary copy of these names and addresses.

The secondary copy is kept in cache (fast memory) and is responsible for refreshing itself from the primary copy. But it does not worry about synchronization, because if it gives out a wrong address, the requesting message quickly discovers the error and returns and asks the primary copy for the correct address. Where this alternative is possible, it is a simple and robust solution, says Stefferud.

Client/Server Databases

George Schussel [16], who hosts several database conferences, believes there are significant differences between true distributed databases and client/server databases. He says the difference is in the concept of "location transparency." In a true distributed database, each node has a copy of the DBMS and the dictionary; therefore, the application need not know the location of the data because the node can determine the access strategy. In client/server systems, on the other hand, only a few nodes run the DBMS, so the applications must know where the data is located. Therefore, they do not support location transparency. Nevertheless, they are very appropriate for higher-performance transaction processing. These systems include SQLBASE from Gupta Technologies, SQL Server from Sybase, Oracle, RDB from Digital, Ingres, and Informix.

Federated Databases

At a recent workshop of the future of DBMS [mentioned in 17], the researchers stated that companies are likely to have "federated databases" rather than distributed databases. This means that existing databases will retain their autonomy, their data will continue to be defined independently, and the local DBMS will essentially take care of itself, while retaining rules for others to access its data.

We have seen this approach work when incompatible databases—such as those that contain text, alphanumeric, and image—are needed in a single application. These databases are left intact on their own machine, and their data is pulled together at the workstation. The application software on the workstation calls on the various databases, and displays data from each one in a different window, in whatever format it has been programmed to use. For handling multidimensional data, this is the approach we expect companies to take. A good example of this approach is the Northwest Airlines System, discussed in Chapter 5.

TOWARD MANAGING INFORMATION

Information systems executives have been preoccupied with implementing databases because they address computerized data. And although data administration has broadened their perspective to managing data as a corporate resource, most organizations do not have their databases fully under control. Merging information technologies, and the increasing availability of external data, are forcing attention to managing information resources in a still broader context. This context calls for managing information—including documents, unstructured text, voice messages, diagrams, pictures, and statistical tables—as a valuable corporate asset.

In the early days of management information systems, many people felt that it was impossible to make progress in serving managers' information needs until the transaction processing systems were fully operational and up to date. In reality, transaction processing systems did make the development of management information systems easier. But most organizations developed the two separately. In a similar way, it is tempting today to say that existing databases must be completely under control before trying to manage the new forms of information. Just as before, however, information systems executives will not have the luxury of doing only one thing at a time. Information management must begin now, even if data management is not yet under control.

Four Types of Information

To characterize the full scope of information management, and to explore some of its ramifications, it is helpful to consider four types of information. First, there are two types of information generated and managed internally in the organization.

1. Information based on data records such as those found in databases
2. Document-based information such as reports, opinions, memos, and estimates

The first type of internal information pertains primarily to entities, such as individual employees, customers, parts, or transactions. Well-structured data records are used to hold a set of attributes that describe each entity. The second category of information pertains primarily to *concepts*—ideas, thoughts, and opinions. Less structured documents or messages, with a wide variety of information forms, are used to describe these.

The same two types of information are also generated externally to the organization. There is external record based information, such as government data on economic and financial conditions, stock price quotations, and airline schedules. There is also external document based information, such as reports, newsletters, and economic forecasts. Figure 7-7 shows these four types of information in a simple matrix, along with the information management activity that has characterized each in the past.

Internal record based information has been the focus of attention of information systems because that is the type of information computer-based application systems generate and manage easily. External record based information has become more popular recently in the form of public databases; end users themselves have generally handled the procurement

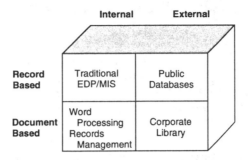

Figure 7-7 Four Types of Information

of this data, often using outside database services. Generally, information systems executives have paid little attention to document based information, either internal or external, as a corporate resource. Those areas have been the responsibility of either the administrative vice president or the corporate library. Let us look at attempts to manage information as a corporate resource using these four categories to structure the discussion.

Internal Record-Based Information

Thus far, this chapter has dealt primarily with the internal record based cell of the matrix in Figure 7-7. As we have seen, the three-level database is the conceptual model for organizing internal record based data. Database management software manages the data using data models that defines the relationships among entities and attributes of the data. The three dominant data models are the hierarchical, network, and relational model, with object-oriented data management promising to play a strong role in the future.

The CISR report showed how companies have been organizing data management projects to reap the benefits of databases. Furthermore, techniques are evolving for managing distributed data. Notice that nearly all these techniques and approaches deal primarily with internal record based data. They need to be expanded and enhanced as we move toward managing the information resources represented in the other three cells. That is where object-oriented techniques will play a large role, because they apply data management techniques to other forms of data.

Internal Document-Based Information

The management of internal document based information has resided in most companies with the vice president of administration. Areas of responsibility have been records management (document records, not data records) and word processing. But, as word processing systems have become more multifunctional and more like other departmental data processing systems, their supervision has shifted. In many cases, they are now overseen by someone in the information systems department. Records management is still generally overseen by the administration department.

Document management was identified as one of the crucial issues facing CIOs in the 1990s [18]. CIOs must look to managing a new set of technologies for handling *documents*—both electronic versions of paper documents and new multimedia documents—for a variety of applications. For our purposes, a document is a semiformal "package" of information with some organizational impact that is filed, transmitted, and consequently maintained. Traditional database management of alphanumeric records deals with facts that are driven by an entity (such as an account number) and their attributes. In documents, a fact is replaced with a concept, an entity with an idea, and attributes with information that illuminates the idea.

Electronic document management includes a variety of technologies, such as document and image processing, text retrieval, hypertext and hypermedia, EDI, and desktop publishing. In addition, electronic document management includes the technologies that have been used for years in traditional records management areas—micrographics (film and fiche), computer output microfilm (COM), and automated records center applications. The documents handled by this enlarged set of technologies might be letters, blueprints, sales notes, voice mail messages, images, or multimedia documents. Increasingly, they will include documents from external sources such as news items, government or industry reports, and even incoming correspondence.

Data management and document management together encompass the total information resource of the firm. The information systems manager should plan to unify these two resources. However, this unification involves understanding the true importance of document management. For example, studies show that 95 percent of the information in most organizations required to conduct business is in document form; only 5 percent is in computerized files and records. Despite more than 40 years of progress in computerizing information processes, many organizations still have a huge, crucial amount of "paperwork" required to do business. Despite fifteen to twenty years of developing management information systems, decision support systems, and executive information systems with data, we have just begun to include the valuable information contained in documents, particularly those from external sources.

External Record-Based Information

It has generally been users, not the information systems department, that has managed the acquisition of information from external databases. Strategic planning departments, financial planners, and other user departments have sought out services that provide this type of information. Yet, with the increasingly turbulent business environment, companies will want to coordinate their use of such external services, as well as combine internal and external information to better understand industry trends. As an example of an external source of record based information, consider the PIMS service and how TRW uses it.

CASE EXAMPLE: Profit Impact of Market Strategy (PIMS)

The PIMS service is an example of a source of external numeric data. PIMS is a computer-based service offered by the Strategic Planning Institute (SPI) of Cambridge, Massachusetts [19]. This database service has data on the actual experiences of a large number of diverse business units, where a "business unit" is defined as an organization that sells a distinct set of products or services, serves a specific set of customers, and competes with a well-defined set of competitors.

The methodology originated at the General Electric (GE) Company in the early 1960s, when GE was looking for "laws of the marketplace." GE turned the project over to the Harvard Business School in the 1970s for further refinement, and soon thirty-five other corporations were participating. The service is now being offered by SPI, an autonomous nonprofit institute, and has about 200 participating corporations ranging in size from $10 million to $80 billion in annual sales. The database has data on the experiences (both good and bad) of some 2500 business units. An example will help explain what PIMS is and how it is used.

Most queries ask: "If we change an *action* variable, such as our price relative to competitors, what is the probable impact on a *result* variable, such as profit, cash flow, or market share?" The inquirer might be investigating the impact of three possible price increases—say, 5, 7, and 10 percent. Another type of query asks: "We want to improve a result variable; what actions are available to do this, and how do they compare?"

As queries are entered, PIMS searches its database for look-alike business units. For all business units that had essentially the same values as the inquirer's business unit, and had actually used the value of the specified action variable (say, a 5 percent price increase), the result variables are obtained and averaged. If three possible price increases are being investigated (5, 7, 10 percent), then three different sets of business units are retrieved—those that made a 5 percent price increase, those that made a 7 percent increase, and so on. The result variables are then averaged for these three sets of look-alike business units. Clearly, the larger the experience database, the more look-alike business units are likely to be found. So PIMS provides a way of analyzing the effects of alternative strategic decisions, based on actual experiences of other companies.

Use of PIMS at TRW. TRW, Inc. is a diversified, decentralized operating company with three main operating sectors—automotive, industrial/energy, and aerospace/commercial electronics. The three sectors have eighteen groups, which in turn are divided into eighty-eight divisions, and the divisions are made up of 140 business units. Corporate headquarters is in Cleveland, Ohio.

Robert A. Saslaw, director of planning for TRW, described his company's use of computers for strategic planning at a conference. Some 65 of TRW's 140 business units participate in PIMS on a voluntary basis, and data about these units is stored in the PIMS database.

TRW has had a finely honed budgeting system for many years, said Saslaw, but PIMS has allowed the company to think well beyond just trying to meet budget in its planning process. One of the biggest benefits of PIMS, said Saslaw, occurs when managers or executives fill out the PIMS questionnaire. They find that they learn a lot about their business from this exercise.

The managers of the participating business units think strategically, because PIMS directs their attention to planning parameters. When it is used, PIMS replaces the "this year versus last year" measurement syndrome, because it reveals that a business unit might be doing better than last year but still be losing market share. PIMS is used for competitive analysis, for a quick verification of five-year strategic plans, for acquisition and investment analysis, for portfolio analysis, for competitive strengths and weaknesses analysis, and other similar purposes.

External Document-Based Information

Information systems executives have probably considered external document based information as the least manageable form of information. It has been the responsibility of corporate librarians in most companies. Yet, as the amount of such external information grows, and as more and more of it becomes computerized, it will become increasingly important for inclusion in information systems executives' jurisdiction.

Of growing interest is environmental scanning—searching the world of external information in areas relevant to an organization. Environmental scanning services have been available for many years. They review publications, clip out pertinent articles or create abstracts of these articles, and then pass them along to the client. A newer development is the delivery of this information to a company's internal computer, perhaps even a PC, where it can be searched, browsed, and interpreted by managers.

It is not surprising that there is an extremely rapid growth of computer-based document and reference services. Jane Fedorowicz [20] describes this growth and the technology advances that have enabled it. She cites a study by Information Market Indicators, Inc. that shows U.S. businesses increased their on-line database expenditures by 117 percent in three years [21 and 22]. Companies are retrieving more and more information from text databases, such as Dow Jones News Retrieval, CompuServe, Dialog Information Service, and Mead Data Central. For individuals, Prodigy has brought inexpensive, easy database access to the PC.

	Typical Corporate Authority	Information Sources	Technologies Used
Internal record-based information	Information systems department	Transaction processing Organizational units	DBMS Data dictionaries Enterprise data analysis techniques
Internal document-based information	Administrative vice president Word processing center Records management	Corporate memos, letters reports, forms	Word processing Micrographics Reprographics Text retrieval products
External record-based information	End users Corporate planning Financial analysis Marketing	Public databases	Time-sharing services Public networks Analysis packages
External document-based information	Corporate library	Public literature News services Catalogs and indexes Subscriptions Purchased reports	Bibliographic services Environmental scanning Public networks

Figure 7-8 The Scope of Information Management

The increased reliance on external market indicators and improved sources of information have dramatically boosted the demand for on-line text database services. Telecom estimates that demand for its services is growing at 25 percent per year or more. One source estimates that there are more than 7,000 on-line databases available worldwide [23]. Another survey identified 5,043 on-line databases, compared with only 1,000 in 1982 [24].

Typically, users of these systems are trained librarians who provide a service within their company, or PC users who access general purpose databases. Most of the time, the results of the search are hard copy reports of bibliographic, financial, or other stored information. Some decision support and executive information system products, such as Pilot's EIS or Metaphor/IBM's Data Interpretation System, provide links to external databases and display the results of prespecified searches on the screen.

In summary, information systems executives need to take a broader view of information management if they plan to manage it as a corporate resource. As a way of representing the breadth of this topic, Figure 7-8 lists the four categories of information and shows the typical corporate authority, sources of information, and examples of technologies used in managing each.

Emphasis on Information Management

The job of guiding computerization of these various types of data is the responsibility of information systems departments. In some cases, converting paper documents from the outside world into electronic form as soon as they arrive at the company may be appropriate—in the mail room or in a specific department. From there, routing is fully electronic.

Integration of the various types of data introduces issues of storing and handling image and graphic data, as well as text and numbers. In desktop publishing systems, the various kinds of data are stored together. The same may be desired in office systems. Millikin [25] points out that the Wang image system allows users to integrate data processing and office applications, by, for example, adding images to database records.

But integrated storage is not always necessary. Robert Castle, of FileNet [26], described at an OIS conference how he has seen companies add imaging systems to mainframe databases. The two types of databases are rarely stored on the same machine, he said, but the index for an image can be added to a database record. This complicates the indexing process, but it permits the master database to present users with images as part of its records. With this approach companies can choose to simply install links between various systems.

Until the mid-1980s, most information systems executives we have talked with preferred not to deal with the image systems installed in their companies. Those document management systems generally used microform and were mainly of concern to records management people. But as links between record based systems and document based systems have been needed, information systems executives are becoming involved.

SUMMARY

This chapter explores the evolution of managing information as a corporate resource. It starts with the data administration approach to getting inconsistent, redundant, inaccessible computer data into shape. Then it discusses the main tool—database management systems—used in this effort. The challenge of distributed data management, as part of the trend toward distributed systems, is now being faced. Finally, the move toward information management, in the broadest context, recognizes four types of information and focuses on how to manage them all.

Organizations are realizing the importance of their data, so interest in information is growing on several fronts—coordinating internal and external records and documents, defining enterprise data, giving users better access to data, and even distributing data.

QUESTIONS AND EXERCISES

REVIEW QUESTIONS

1. What is the main problem in managing data?
2. What are the four roles of data administrators?
3. What are the major approaches that companies are taking with data administration, according to the CISR report?
4. Identify the four components of the CISR framework, and the options within each.
5. What are the main "patterns" in this framework that companies exhibited in their data management projects?
6. Define the three-level database concept. What are its advantages?
7. What are three traditional database "models"?
8. What is the next-generation DBMS?
9. Give one example of an application that will require these new DBMS?
10. According to Stonebraker and Kemnitz, what three things must the new DBMS manage?
11. What are the twelve guiding principles and seven kinds of transparency that describe "true" distributed databases?
12. What are three tough technical challenges in creating distributed database systems?
13. What are five alternatives to true distributed databases?
14. What are the four kinds of information that define the scope of "information management"? Describe each briefly.

DISCUSSION QUESTIONS

1. In this chapter the assertion is made that information systems departments should concentrate on managing data and information rather than getting systems up and running quickly. Discuss the pros and cons of this argument.

2. Some data administrators believe that only data that crosses organizational boundaries should be under their control, to ensure consistent data definitions. Other believe that all data should be under their control, because in the future someone else may want to share that data. With which view do you agree? Why? What are the data administration implications of your view?

3. Why do you think companies will want to distribute databases, given the technical challenges they face?

EXERCISES

1. Find several articles on one of the four kinds of information presented in Figure 7-7. What new ideas on the (1) corporate authority, (2) technologies used, and (3) information sources did you gain from these articles? What evidence did you find of a merging (or a diverging) of the management of these different types of information?

2. Experiment with a database management package on a micro. Describe its capabilities using as an example a small application that you develop.

3. Visit a local company with a data administration function. Talk to the data administrator and find out the following:

   (a) What the department sees its role to be in the company

   (b) What types of data problems the group is trying to solve

   (c) What kinds of data the department controls and does not control

   (d) Which database management systems are used for which types of applications

   (e) Which data dictionary is used and why

4. Visit a local company and talk to either the corporate librarian or the manager of records management. Find out the following:

   (a) What computer and communication technologies are used to store, catalog, and retrieve documents, literature, and citations

   (b) What kinds of information sources are used

   (c) What various kinds of searching capabilities are available

   (d) What kinds of information technology are used to disseminate information

REFERENCES

1. ZACHMAN, J., Zachman International, 2222 Foothill Blvd., Suite 337, La Canada, CA.

2. GOODHUE, D., J. QUILLARD, J. ROCKART, "Managing the Data Resource: A Contingency Perspective," *MIS Quarterly*, September 1988, pp. 373-391.

3. MARTIN, J., *Strategic Data-Planning Methodologies*, (Prentice-Hall, Englewood Cliffs, NJ), 1982.

4. HOLLAND, R. H. "Tools for Information Resource Management," presented at the GUIDE Conference, New Orleans, LA, November 9, 1983.

5. COULSON, C. J., "People Just Aren't Using Data Dictionaries," *Computerworld*, August 16, 1982, pp. 15-22.

6. KAHN, B. K., "Some Realities of Data Administration," *Communications of the ACM*, October 1983, pp. 794-799.

7. TILMAN, G. D., "Why Data Administration Fails," *Computerworld*, September 7, 1987, pp. 73-76.

8. BRADLEY, J., "The Elusive Relation," *Computerworld*, March 8, 1982, pp. 1-16. (This material was based largely on the author's book *File and Data Base Techniques*, (Holt, Rinehart & Winston, New York), 1982.

9. MARTIN, J., *Principles of Data-Base Management*, (Prentice-Hall, Englewood Cliffs, NJ), 1976.

10. ATRE, S., *Data Base: Structured Techniques for Design, Performance, and Management*, (John Wiley, New York), 1980.

11. CODD, E. F., "Relational Database: A Practical Foundation for Productivity," *Communications of the ACM*, February 1982, pp. 109-117.

12. "Next-Generation Database Systems," *Communications of the ACM*, October 1991, pp. 31-131.

    a. CATTELL, R. G. G., guest editor, pp. 31-33.

    b. STONEBRAKER, M. and G. KEMNITZ, "The Postgres Multi-Generation Database Management System," pp. 78-92.

    c. SILBERSCHATZ, A., M. STONEBRAKER, and J. ULLMAN (Eds.), "Database Systems: Achievements and Opportunities," pp. 110-120.

13. DATE, C. J., *An Introduction to Database Systems* vols. 1 and 2, 4th ed., (Addison-Wesley, Reading, MA), 1987.

14. STONEBRAKER, M. (Ed.), *Readings in Database Systems*, (Morgan Kauffman Publishers, San Mateo, CA), 1986.

15. EINAR STEFFERUD, Network Management Associates, 17301 Drey Lane, Huntington Beach, CA 92647.

16. SCHUSSEL, G., "In Depth: Distributed DBMS Decisions," *Computerworld*, May 6, 1991, pp. 81-83.

17. EDELSTEIN, H., "Database World Targets Next-Generation Problems," *Software Magazine*, May 1991, pp. 79-86.

18. "Critical Issues in Information Systems Management, 1991-1995," *I/S Analyzer*, January 1991, pp. 9-10.

19. PIMS, The Strategic Planning Institute, 955 Massachusetts Ave., Cambridge, MA 02139.

20. FEDOROWICZ, J., "A Technology Infrastructure for Document-Based Decision Support Systems" in R. Sprague, and H. Watson (Eds.), *Decision Support Systems: Putting Theory Into Practice*, 3rd ed., (Prentice-Hall, Englewood Cliffs, NJ), 1993.

21. JENKINS, A., "Firms Work To Control On-line Database Charges," *PC Week*, March 11, 1986, pp. 41-42.

22. JENKINS, A., "On-line Databases," *PC Week*, March 11, 1986, pp. 83-84+.

23. REED, N., "On-Line Databases: Can They Help Your Business?" *Australian Accountant*, September 1989, pp. 70-72.

24. NICHOLLS, P.T., "A Survey of Commercially Available CD-ROM Database Titles," *CD-ROM Professional*, March 1991, pp. 23-28.

25. MILLIKIN, M.D., "Wang Tries a New Approach: Integrated Image Management," *Patricia Seybold's Office Systems Report*, May 1987, pp. 1-14.

26. FILENET CORPORATION, 3530 Hyland Ave., Costa Mesa, CA 92626.

EIGHT

Managing Information Systems Operations

INTRODUCTION

A discussion of managing the essential information technologies is not complete without describing operational issues facing information system executives. Since the late 1980s, because of corporate restructurings, the recession, and the changing economics of computer hardware and software, the subject of computer operations has received a lot of attention. Operations are important because, if the systems department is not professionally run, systems executives lose credibility. Then they either end up fighting fires instead of setting policy, or they find themselves out of a job, or they see their operations outsourced.

We begin this chapter by presenting one former information system executive's views on the breadth of the operations job and how it needs to be managed. Then we discuss four major operational issues.

- Improving data center operations
- Outsourcing information systems functions
- Managing today's complex networks
- Providing disaster recovery for distributed systems

WHAT ARE OPERATIONS?

In a lecture at the University of California at Los Angeles (UCLA), William Congleton described the important operational issues he faced in the information systems department he ran.

Why Talk about Operations?

Keeping the shop running is getting increasingly difficult, he said. The reasons become apparent at budget time. His total annual information systems department budget had the following split:

- Thirty-three percent was spent on systems and programming—of which 70 percent went to maintenance and 30 percent went to new development.
- Ten percent was spent on department administration and training.
- Fifty-seven percent went to operations.

So operations are important because they involve more money than any other part of the department.

At his company, operations included computer hardware at sixty-four locations including twelve seaports, twelve parts warehouses, and twelve sales offices. Hardware included computers, disk drives, tape drives, printers, and terminals. Operations also included communication lines and equipment, and software, such as operating systems, compilers, and networking software. In addition, the budget included data center personnel, such as systems consulting for programmers, operators who scheduled and ran production jobs, mounted tapes, delivered reports, and monitored the machines and network. And operations included disaster recovery planning and security.

"Putting all these things together sometimes gave me more excitement than I could stand," quipped Congleton, "plus they were more expensive than I wanted. Therefore, achieving a 10 percent reduction in operations had a far greater effect that a 10 percent reduction in any other area. That is why operations are important."

Solving Operational Problems

Operational problems are obvious to the entire corporation—reports are late, terminals have slow response times or are down, and data is wrong. What can be done to improve operations? There are three strategies, said Congleton. One is to buy more equipment. As equipment costs drop, this solution might appear most cost-effective until you run out of room for the equipment. The second approach is to fight fires and rearrange priorities continuously—getting people to solve the problem at hand. This solution really only moves the problem of poor management from one hot spot to another. The third solution is to document and measure what you are doing continually, to find out the *real* problems, not just the apparent ones. Then set standards.

This is the solution Congleton preferred. It is needed no matter who runs operations—the in-house staff or an outsourcer.

Operational Measures

Operational measures are both external and internal. *External measures* are what the customer sees: system up-time (or down-time), response time, turnaround time, and program failures. These directly relate to customer satisfaction. *Internal measures* are of interest to systems people: computer usage as a percentage of capacity, availability of mainline systems, disk storage used, job queue length, number of jobs run, number of jobs rerun because of problems, age of applications, and number of unresolved problems.

Problems reported by the external measures can generally be explained by deviations in the internal measures. To help uncover the problems related to equipment capacity, quality of applications, or improper use of systems by users, numerous venders sell monitoring software and devices. Other measurement systems log performance of the various kinds of computer and telecommunication equipment, said Congleton. Tape and disk management systems allocate space in the most efficient ways. Schedulers, which have been available for the past 20 years, schedule jobs on computers. And library management systems keep track of versions and backups of files and programs. So there are plenty of tools to help information systems departments measure how efficiently their data center equipment is being used.

The Importance of Good Management

Tools are useless, however, unless information systems management has created a corporate culture that recognizes and values good operations, said Congleton. It is difficult to find good computer operations managers, because the absence of prestige (and sometimes pay) does not attract individuals with the proper combination of skills and training. This is unfortunate, said Congleton, because in a good environment, an operations job can be very rewarding—both financially and professionally.

The skills required of a computer center manager are similar to those needed in a factory or oil refinery. The factory manager must schedule work to meet promised delivery dates, monitor performance as work flows through the key pieces of equipment, and respond quickly to production breakdowns. In a well-run factory, the manager can usually recover from one or two individual problems. In a poorly run factory, there are so many little problems that the manager does not know where to start to fix the problems. The same is true in a computer center where the "factory equipment" is the disk drives, computers, input/output channels, communications lines, and the like.

The vice president of information systems must take an active interest

1. Hardware costs continue to drop. If this decrease lulls management into not taking an aggressive interest in this area, poor operations and inefficient programs will waste computer resources faster than falling hardware costs can compensate.

2. Lights-out computer rooms or unattended operations will be the norm. Companies are replacing computer operators and other data center personnel with software and hardware, so that the centers can run without people.

3. The increasing use of PCs and workstations is spreading operational problems to LANs.

4. The number of automated tools to run computers and networks is increasing. But as systems become more powerful, they also become more complex.

5. Expert system technology is being used to automate computer operations.

FIGURE 8-1 Trends in Operations (from Bill Congleton)

in good operations, and strike a proper balance between developers and operators. In most cases, only the vice president can effectively influence the developers to take the time and effort to design and program good operational characteristics into their applications. A poorly designed or written computer program can create operational problems that make even a good operations manager look bad. However, if the operations manager is managing well, he or she can identify problem programs and ask that they be rewritten to improve performance.

In conclusion, the chief information officer needs to be concerned about operations, said Congleton, but should emphasize putting the proper operations environment in place. The key to managing operations is the same as in any management job, he concluded: Set standards and then manage to those standards by finding an outstanding operations manager (see Figure 8-1).

IMPROVING DATA CENTER OPERATIONS

Companies are taking two internal approaches and one external approach to improving data center operations. First, they are increasing efficiency. We discuss that subject by looking at the results of a study that compared efficient and not-so-efficient centers. Second, they are automating data centers, so they run in unattended mode. And third, as the external approach, they are outsourcing operations.

Running Efficient Data Centers

At a conference, Christopher Disher of Nolan, Norton & Co. (NNC) [1] described a study conducted by NNC to find out why some data centers were more efficient than others.

Disher pointed out that companies spend 50 to 60 percent of their computing expenditures on data center operations, but few companies have known how to reduce these expenses—except to outsource them. In their study, NNC collected data from 160 data centers on expenditures, number of staff, staff mix, and machine resources. Not surprisingly, they found larger data centers achieved economies of scale. But they also discovered wide variations in expenditures among similar-sized centers—some centers were spending millions of dollars more a year to achieve the same results as other centers.

NNC found no correlation between expenditures and the industry in which a firm operated. However, NNC did find that the following four characteristics of application quality correlated to data center efficiency:

1. *Functional quality of the applications*, measured by how well they meet user needs
2. *Technical quality of the applications*, measured by how easy they are to maintain and how efficiently they run
3. *Application age*
4. *Portfolio coverage,* measured by how much of the work of the business that can be automated has been automated.

The least efficient centers—meaning, those that spent more money than similar centers doing the same amount of work-had older applications; their average system age was 8.7 years as compared with 4.2 years for the most efficient centers. The technical quality of their applications was poorer, and they did not support as much of the business—24 percent of the business as compared with 40 percent in the more efficient centers.

The most efficient centers had younger and higher-quality applications. This was not by accident; many of these information systems departments had purposely redesigned, rewritten, or replaced many of their old applications—to run more efficiently and to use fewer machine room staff. Thus, they had reduced the number of print deliveries, tape mounts, and other manual operations in their machine rooms.

The NNC study found the efficient and inefficient centers also had a different mix of staff. The inefficient centers had more employees, some 50 percent of whom were "hands-on people"—tape mounters, console operators, print distributors, and so on. The efficient centers had fewer data center employees, and some 65 percent of these people were "knowledge workers"—technical service, management, planning, and operations support people.

Application quality turned out to be the main factor that distinguished efficient centers from inefficient data centers, said Disher. Applications written ten years ago are likely to be more expensive to operate than most people realize, he concluded.

One of the companies that has worked with NNC to improve its data center's efficiency is Mutual of Omaha.

CASE EXAMPLE: Mutual of Omaha

Mutual of Omaha is an insurance company with headquarters in Omaha, Nebraska. About 75 percent of its business is in health and accident insurance, but it also handles mutual funds and provide property, casualty, and life insurance. Mutual of Omaha was interested in the data center work done by NNC and asked them to help improve data center operations. David Pepple described these experiences at a conference.

About 30 percent of the systems staff works in operations, said Pepple, and about 50 percent of the systems budget is spent on operations—hardware planning, technical support, the computer service center, and voice and data communications. The company has one data center with seven processors: three for production work, two for development and testing, and two for end user computing. They also have minicomputers, micros, terminals, and handheld computers throughout the company.

The goal at Mutual of Omaha was to provide data center services at the least cost. Their main question concerned future direction: Should they decentralize the center or not? The NNC study postulated that they would gain economies of scale by remaining with one data center. They wanted to know if that would be true.

In comparison with the NNC database, Mutual of Omaha found that their application portfolio was quite old: the average application was a high-volume, batch application about eleven years old. They had the average number of people in their data center compared with other centers their size, but they spent much less money than others. Although this apparent efficiency looked good on the surface, they discovered two reasons for the lower expenditures.

First, for the past ten years they had kept technology costs low because of careful planning. That was good. Second, they had a larger percentage of hands-on people in their center than other centers, and these people have lower salary levels. That was not so good. They did not have the mix of people that NNC said reflected an efficient data center operation.

After some study, Mutual of Omaha believed they could reduce data center staff by 30 percent with a resulting cost reduction of 25 percent.

But to reduce staff, they would need to change data center operations significantly. They would need to reduce the amount of hands-on work by moving files from their 60,000 tapes to disk and by reducing the amount of printing done at the center.

As the applications are recoded or replaced to reduce tape storage and printing operations, the job mix in the data center will change. As a result, they will have more knowledge workers and fewer direct operations people. They will need to retrain people, create new operations career paths, and hire new types of operations people.

By updating their old applications, Pepple believes they will obtain the economies of scale that others in the NNC study have achieved; thus they have decided to remain with one data center.

Toward Unattended Computer Centers

The hope of fully automating mainframe data centers is fairly recent. Here are the basic ideas behind it.

Howard Miller [3] defines a data center, in the broadest sense, as a computer processing center—without regard to computer size or computer vendor. He defines unattended operations as the totally automated operation of all data center functions; it is a dark-room environment in which computers run without human intervention.

Unattended operations, he believes, require the elimination of such traditional and seemingly essential functions as console monitoring, data entry, input/output control, and manual media distribution. Automation also should eliminate the work of data center librarians, production coordinators, and help desk consultants.

Unattended operations can only be achieved, says Miller, through special features of hardware, operating system software, physical security software, environmental monitoring systems, process control facilities, application software, and manual functions. Many of these features are currently available; they include the following (see Figure 8-2):

- Computers that operate in an unattended mode
- Software that manages computer processing in unattended mode
- Physical and data security software that features interactive problem notification and resolution functions
- Environmental monitoring systems that have interactive data center monitoring, problem reporting, and problem resolution
- Process control facilities that permit processing both batch and on-line work in unattended mode
- Application software written for operating in an unattended mode
- Manual functions that either are eliminated or automated

FIGURE 8-2 Steps to Implementing Unattended Operations (from Miller [3])

1. Define the areas of human intervention and divide them into two categories: (1) procedures that are easy to eliminate, and (2) those that are difficult to eliminate. Further divide the difficult procedures into those that can be resolved with installed software and those that require new software.

2. Define the instructions that could be added to application software to eliminate the procedures identified in Step One.

3. Agree on a method for incorporating the new instructions into new applications and into all changes made to existing applications.

4. Isolate the instructions that are easy to implement, organize them into projects, and do them.

5. When unattended operation appears easy to achieve, organize a project to do it.

Magnetic tape is a major obstacle to unattended operations, says Miller. Cartridge tapes handled by robotic arms have become a viable alternative. Furthermore, each person who handles data reduces its reliability and increases its cost. Therefore, Miller believes the data entry task belongs to point-of-collection devices, such as electronic cash registers, ATMs, data collection devices, and on-line source data entry. Printing, he says, should also be discouraged. Applications should be designed to provide data on-line. A good guide for reducing printing is to limit its use to exception reports of ten pages or fewer.

Miller believes some of the benefits of unattended operation are

- Improved quality of data center service
- Increased flexibility in data centers
- Higher productivity in operations
- Improved quality of life for data center employees

He believes organizations are beginning to see these benefits and are moving toward unattended data centers. The direction of computer technology is to permit data centers to operate as utilities, with little or no human intervention.

How Close Are Fully Unattended Operations?

Rosemary LaChance [4] has been pushing for unattended data center operations for more than eight years. Her business card carries the slogan, "It's better with the lights out." She and her partner, Arnold Farber, were running a data center at a bank in 1984 when they saw the need to automate operations. We talked to LaChance about progress being made in moving to unattended computer center operations.

The question no longer is "Do we need to automate our data centers?" said LaChance. The question has become: How soon? Outsourcing is forcing systems management to study how well their centers are being run. Even executive management has turned some attention to data center operations, because they now realize that computing is the heartbeat of their company. It is not a technical luxury, so it must operate effectively and efficiently. If the in-house staff cannot do it, they are willing to hand the responsibility over to an outsourcer.

Information systems departments can underbid outsourcers, LaChance told us, if they are doing a good job. Outsourcing is fine for the short term to allow the in-house staff to move to a new computing platform. Some applications, such as payroll, are also appropriate for outsourcing. But for the long term, LaChance believes companies will be better off automating their computer operations rather than outsourcing them.

Computer operators are going the way of telephone operators: being available for complex work but not for handling routine day-to-day work. The operators in today's lights-out data centers work behind the scenes installing new software releases, fixing breaks, installing new equipment, and planning how to keep the center running. These centers look like the DASD (direct dccess storage device), or —no people. Today's operators can work a normal 8:00 a.m. to 5:00 p.m. workday, leaving the center to operate unattended at night and on weekends.

Companies that have moved to unattended operations have found ways to prevent computer programs from nighttime "abending"—encountering an "abend" (abnormal end). They have programmed their computers to fix themselves, restart automatically from remote instructions, and even automatically transmit backups to remote mass stores or cartridge tape drives. The systems alert the fire department, not a remote operator, when a fire alarm goes off. PCs rather than operators are used to monitor operations, because PCs can respond faster and more consistently and accurately. On-line reports have replaced printouts. And tape drives have been replaced with tape cartridges run by robotic arms. These systems can assure on-line access to historical data within three to four minutes, so not as much data needs to be kept on disk drives.

But automation is not necessarily cheaper, LaChance told us. Saving money cannot be the driving force. Improving quality of service is the true benefit.

Unattended operation is not only changing the work of operators, it is changing the job of data center management. These managers no longer need to be technical managers. They need to be business managers, says LaChance, because their job is providing good service. They need to understand the business needs and fulfill them. And they need to be planners rather than reactors. One leading-edge firm recently promoted a line manager to data center manager, because they understand this new need.

Companies that are moving the fastest toward unattended operations are those that are fighting for survival, are facing outsourcing, or have executives who allow creativity in the data center. Running a data center without automation is like trying to solve today's problems with yesterday's tools, says LaChance. Lights-out data centers are possible today; a few firms have done it.

A Product Wish List

In a Gartner Group report [5a], Schulman divided the market for unattended operations products into two sectors. The first market is companies that require "industrial strength" products for two reasons: either (1) their systems are large and complex, or (2) they recognize the strategic importance of managing operations more efficiently and effectively. "Industrial strength" products provide companies with a way to manage their operations in a more integrated fashion.

The second type of product is for companies that only want to handle message management. They are seeking immediate relief from operator console overload.

To have a "true" industrial strength product, The Gartner Group says, the following four components are necessary:

An Automated Operator. This system monitors messages from the operating system, subsystems, and applications. It initiates actions by matching elements of message text to if . . . then rules. The actions an automated operator might take include suppressing messages, rerouting them, replying to them, or initiating a series of preprogrammed commands. An automated operator also can initiate messages and then examine the results.

One goal of using an automated operator is to manage the data center by preventing or predicting events, rather than reacting to them after they have happened. Thus, an automated operator also must be capable of calling for help—either by sending messages to an on-site computer operator through a terminal or by beeping an off-site person.

An Enhanced Console Facility. This system is a companion to an automated operator. Although an automated operator monitors messages, an enhanced console facility can consolidate complex or frequently used commands, such as start up a system, shut one down, or reconfigure a system. In addition, an enhanced console can give end users a means for submitting jobs, manipulating them, and inquiring about their status or their output—from an on-line terminal.

An Operations Automation Language. This language is used to write commands and procedures to automate data center policies and procedures. When well implemented, it allows both systems programmers and operators to create procedures for automating operations.

A Timed Events Automation Facility. Automating timed events is the final element in the Gartner Group's list of essential features. This capability is needed, they say, because precise execution of events at prescribed times or intervals is essential to the operations job.

CASE EXAMPLE: US West

US WEST, with headquarters in Denver, Colorado, is one of the regional telephone companies created following the break-up of AT&T. The corporate information services department is responsible for providing information services to all of US WEST's subsidiaries—including US WEST Communications, which provides local telephone service to fourteen western states.

US WEST operates ten data centers in seven western states. Consolidating these centers as much as possible is a mission of the information services department. Initially, they are maximizing efficiency at each center, then they will reduce the number of centers and manage the remaining ones with as few people as possible. Systems managers believe data centers can be managed better and more efficiently through software rather than people.

In the mid-1980s, two systems programmers were given six months to study data center operations and create a long-range strategy for improving efficiency and, where possible, automating operations. At the time, no software tools for automating data center console operations were on the market, so the programmers worked with the basic IBM software used at US WEST. This two-man team concentrated on the operations of the main US WEST Communications data centers in Bellevue, Washington; Seattle, Washington; and Portland, Oregon.

Since that time, the two-man team has grown to a department of seven people. Each of the staff members specializes in a different aspect of system automation—systems programming, systems operation products involving the local systems department, and database and administrative control. In addition, other teams have been established at the other US WEST data centers, and a manager is assigned to coordinate the efforts of all the teams.

The First Step: Message Management. The team first analyzed system message traffic. The messages studied were those displayed on the control consoles in the Bellevue computer center. These messages appeared on operators' console screens at the rate of 10 to 15 per minute.

Few of the messages were critical, but all had to be read by the operators. Most were status report messages. One might tell an operator to initialize a new tape, to which the operator would need to give a go—ahead response. Another might tell the operator that all tape drives are in use. A normal operator response would be "wait." An alternative response could be to reroute to other available drives.

The two-man team categorized the messages into two groups—those that always required the same response and those that could have a variety of responses. They found that one-half of the messages always needed the same response. To relieve the operators from looking at these messages, the staff wrote a program to trigger the appropriate responses without human intervention.

Their next step in better managing system messages was to add some decision-making capabilities to take care of the messages that had several responses. All possible courses of action to all probable messages were encoded in "command lists"—lists of what normally would be complex commands. The system can then trigger the appropriate response when a message occurs. The automation team has created some one hundred of these commands, and they are adding more on a regular basis. This is an ongoing task because the workloads at the data centers are constantly changing. This arrangement still requires an operator to issue a command, but the group intends to automate this procedure in the future.

More than 80 percent of the messages that previously flashed on the operations console screens are no longer seen by the operators. This automation resulted in an immediate productivity payback. One operator can easily handle a set of consoles that formerly required several operators. And that operator can be more efficient. With fewer messages to review, the operators can concentrate on those messages that do appear. The routine messages are being handled by the system.

We visited the control center in Bellevue. It was staffed by one person and its atmosphere was one of relaxed efficiency. Before the automation project was started, there was much more tension and chaos in the center, we were told.

On some weekends and national holidays, US WEST Communications runs either the Portland or Bellevue data center unattended. Personnel at the other center become responsible for monitoring and controlling the systems in the "dark" center.

More Recent Work. US WEST Communication's more recent efforts have involved PCs. The automation group is consolidating message traffic from multiple systems into one PC. They also are displaying more of the traffic data in graphical form to help the operators more quickly and easily understand the messages.

They have been using Netview, IBM's network management system as a network management tool—to link remote systems at the other data centers that are working toward unattended operations. They are beginning to use Netview as an automation tool, to control those remote processors.

Benefits of Their Work. The people at US WEST Communications told us they have increased productivity at their data centers and improved system availability without increasing data center staffs. They have achieved some unattended operations on weekends and national holidays, and they have consolidated most of the functions of their Seattle center with those in Bellevue. Only one computer system remains in Seattle. They are currently investigating having all the data centers operate in an unattended mode by being monitored and controlled from a single location.

Recommendations to Others. Although there were no software tools available for automating data center console operations when US WEST Communications embarked on its project in the mid-1980s, there are many products today. For a company just getting started in unattended operations, the automation staff suggests considering these tools. They recommend looking first at how operations are currently being handled and then deciding which operations should be automated.

The automation team also recommends involving as many of the people who will be affected by the project as possible. They encountered some fear of change as they implemented their automation steps. But those fears disappeared as soon as the operations staff realized that automation would increase the quality and amount of work they could perform.

The automation project staff also found the ideas of the operators and others were essential to the success of the project, because these people were the operations experts. In all, about two dozen people at the Bellevue and Portland data centers made important contributions to the unattended operations project. In the future, the staff plans to ask for help from the people at the other centers as their centers are automated.

At US WEST Communications, the goals of the automation project have been shared and understood—to provide better service to users and manage the data centers better with fewer people. Throughout the installation, we saw people wearing buttons proclaiming, "Availability is Job #1." We also saw signs promoting a contest, with rewards going to those who contribute to system availability through their efforts or ideas. We were told it is a very lively competition.

OUTSOURCING INFORMATION SYSTEMS FUNCTIONS

The new phenomenon that appeared in the information systems field in the late 1980s was outsourcing, which means turning over a firm's computer operations, network operations, or perhaps other information systems functions to a vendor for a specified time—generally, at least for three years. Outsourcing has become an option that most CIOs need to consider to satisfy their management that their operation is being run efficiently and effectively.

At a recent meeting of the Chicago Chapter of the Society for Information Management, Mel Bergstein of TSC [6] talked about outsourcing. His main message was that outsourcing is not a fad. It is another step in the evolution of the information systems field. He believes both system integration and outsourcing will be central to managing information systems in the 1990s.

The Driving Forces Behind Outsourcing

Outsourcing descended on information systems departments as a follow-on to the merger and acquisition activities in the 1980s, said Bergstein. In the 1960s, only 10 percent of the U.S. economy had global competition. In the 1970s, that rose to 70 percent. In response, companies had to *focus on core businesses* in the 1980s, which led to the huge amount of merger and acquisition activity. This activity was also driven by a new market for corporate control. High-yield bonds allowed a few people to buy a company, leveraging it with debt. Companies were "priced" based on their *shareholder value,* that is, their discounted cash flow.

These two drivers—focus and value—led companies to restructure. These two forces are continuing to work in the 1990s, with companies focusing on core businesses and asking themselves, "Where do we really add value?" As examples, some apparel companies no longer cut, sew, manufacturer, or distribute goods, said Bergstein, because they see their core businesses as design and marketing. Likewise, some publishers no longer manufacture books. They manage and finance projects—and outsource everything else.

So outsourcing is part of the drive for focus and value, and it is not solely an information systems issue, said Bergstein; it is a business issue. Since top management must stress value, they must consider outsourcing in all their nonstrategic functions.

The Expanding Scope of Vendor Options

Outsourcers perform the same activities for a company that its information systems department performs in-house. But, over time, the amount of work done by outsiders has increased, said Bergstein, as the following expansion in vendor-customer relationships illustrates.

One traditional relationship that information systems departments have had with vendors is to *buy their professional services,* such as planning (or consulting), building or maintaining applications, building or maintaining networks, and training. Another relationship is to *buy a product,* which may or may not include training. A third relationship is to *buy transactions*, such as payroll checks from a service bureau or credit reports from a credit-rating service. This third type of relationship is good for buyers because

Activities	Relationships				
	Professional Services	Product	Transactions	Systems Integration	Outsourcing
• Planning/consulting	(X)				
• Building/maintaining applications	(X)				
• Building/maintaining networks	(X)				
• Training users/clients	(X)	X	X	X	X
• Operating platforms					
• Performing administrative functions					
• Building/using product					

Figure 8-3 Customer-Vendor Relationships (from Mel Bergstein, TSC [6])

their costs become variable, and hence more controllable. It is also good for the sellers, because in taking the risks, they can have higher margins.

A fourth way to acquire information systems services is to *use a systems integrator*, who generally handles the entire package—the planning, development, maintenance, and training—for major systems projects. Finally, the most bundled approach is *outsourcing*, where the outsourcer contracts to handle all or most of certain information system activities. The main difference between the latter two options is that system integration is project based, whereas outsourcing is time based.

This five-option continuum, shown in Figure 8-3, demonstrates how the IT field is moving, said Bergstein. As you move from the professional services category (on the left) to outsourcing (on the right)—that is, from the more traditional services to the newer ones—four changes occur in the vendor-customer relationship.

1. Information systems management loses an increasing amount of control, because more of the activities are turned over to outsiders.
2. The vendors take more risk as they offer options on the right.
3. The economics improve—that is, the margins improve—as vendors offer services on the right.
4. The importance of choosing the right vendor becomes more important to the right, because there is more at risk in using an outside source.

Contractual Choices in Outsourcing

Outsourcing contracts come in many flavors, said Bergstein. The vendor may operate the network or data center as a utility, or do all application maintenance, or handle administrative functions, or manage the reengineering of business processes. Similarly, the contracts can vary by the amount of sharing between the two parties: where the work will be performed—on the customer or vendor site—and whose applications will be used—again, the customer's or the vendor's. Finally, the structure of the deal can be a contract, a joint venture, or even a purchase.

Bergstein briefly described a few examples. He said that Kodak's agreement with IBM is for IBM to operate Kodak's data center as a utility, at Kodak's site, with Kodak's applications, on a contract basis. In contrast, the deal between General Motors (GM) and Electronic Data Systems (EDS) is for EDS to reengineer some of GM's business processes as well as operate their systems on a utility basis and perform application development at GM's sites. The contract was a purchase—GM bought EDS.

Recommendations to Management

Outsourcing is like a marriage, said Bergstein, so the decision is not trivial. The decision to outsource data center operations, PC support, application development, network management, help desks, application maintenance, or other systems activities should hinge on the answers to four questions, he believes.

- *Which information system activities are strategic to our company's business?* Those that are not are candidates for outsourcing.
- *Will outsourcing save us at least 15 percent?* If not, outsourcing is not a good choice. Outsourcers believe they can do the work for less, by taking advantage of economies of scale, enforcing standards, and using better price/performance equipment.
- *Does our firm have access to the needed technology and expertise?* If not, outsourcing may be the answer to acquiring these resources.
- *Does outsourcing increase our firm's flexibility?* Outsourcing shifts capital budgets to operating expenses, which can give a firm more financial flexibility. Furthermore, outsourcing may free up personnel to work on new systems, while the outsourcer maintains the existing ones. Also, it can increase the firm's flexibility for acquiring new technologies sooner.

But there are four activities that management should not outsource, warns Bergstein. These are their strategy, the architecture of the system (including the network), the decisions about when to introduce information systems into the organization, and management of the vendor. Although management can outsource the development and operation of information technologies, it should never outsource its policy role. And when the systems department is well managed, and where IT is a core competency, outsourcing should not be an option.

Outsourcing is an important question facing today's information system executives. Another equally challenging issue is how to manage today's complex networks.

MANAGING TODAY'S COMPLEX NETWORKS

Network management—generally thought of as the day-to-day management of network operations—will become one of the crucial jobs of the systems department in the 1990s, whether it is handled by the in–house staff, outsourced to a vendor, or performed by a telecommunications carrier. Networks have played a role in systems ever since terminals were connected to mainframes. But the links in these single-vendor, terminal-to-host systems are relatively simple, and have been managed by the mainframe's communication front end processor. With the appearance of multivendor distributed systems, managing the internetwork is orders of magnitude more complex. Since processing is performed around the internet and not just in one place, when the network is down, the "system" is down. In a growing number of firms, the network is increasingly becoming the system. Keeping it up and running is therefore akin to keeping the data center operational.

The Scope of Network Management

The Index Foundation issued a report to its members on network management [7] that noted the definition of network management is generally taken for granted yet rarely defined. Definitions that do exist vary. Iso has defined network management as the facilities to control, coordinate, and monitor the resources that allow communications in an OSI environment. The five-part OSI management framework contains management of faults, accounting, performance, security, and configuration and naming.

The Index Foundation, however, believes this ISO definition is too narrow; therefore, they define network management as "The set of activities required to plan, install, monitor, and maintain all network components in order to achieve specified service levels reliably, at an acceptable, and agreed, cost." So the Index definition extends the ISO definition by including planning and user support as well as change management. Their definition has the following five activities:

- *Fault handling.* Identifying, diagnosing, and repairing faults that occur to network components or finding alternate service.
- *Performance monitoring.* Tracking usage to identify the need for additional capacity; regularly analyzing performance of networks, services, and suppliers; and measuring service levels to users.
- *Change management.* Installing and controlling additions, moves, and changes of users, hardware, software, and circuits, as well as controlling the network configuration and maintaining the network inventory.

- *Tactical planning.* Ensuring that the networks can accommodate future growth or new services in the near future.
- *Cost control.* Monitoring operating costs and reconciling invoices.

In addition, the network management group shares responsibility with other groups in the systems department to bill users for services, provide end user support via help desks and training, negotiate contracts, and provide network security, says the Index Foundation report.

Now that we have provided a brief definition of network management, we turn our attention to trends in network management.

Trends in Network Management

We gleaned the following five trends from our research on network management:

- Network management standards are emerging.
- Integrated network management is becoming a major goal.
- Management of distributed applications is coming.
- Automation of network operations will increase.
- Outsourcing of network management will increase.

Network Management Standards Are Emerging. The network management world appears to be converging toward one, two, or three network management standards—one de facto, one formalized, and one enhancement. Just as TCP/IP has become the de facto internet protocol standard, as people wait for the OSI reference model to be turned into products, the same is happening in network management. Simple Network Management Protocol (SNMP) was designed in 1988 to manage TCP/IP networks. SNMP was originally thought to be the interim network management protocol until the OSI network management protocol Common Management Information Protocol (CMIP) becomes available. However, like TCP/IP, SNMP became the de facto network management standard, not just on an interim basis.

But, in June 1992, an enhancement to SNMP appeared, called Simple Network Protocol (SNP), which threw a monkey wrench into the network management arena. As Horwitt notes [8], SNP fills some of the major gaps in SNMP, such as sharing information between network management workstations, collecting data in bulk instead of one piece at a time, and providing greater security mechanisms. The newcomer shows great promise, yet it is not apparent which of the three will dominate.

All three rely on two important components: agents and a management information base (MIB). Agents are pieces of software that reside on network devices and send usage statistics and alarms to the network management system. SNMP, CMIP, and SNP define the kinds of data and the format of the data gathered by these agents, so that the network management system can receive consistent management information across components supplied by multiple

Figure 8-4 Differences Between Two Network Management Standards:
SNMP and CMIP (from Taylor [9])

1. SNMP polls devices, asking for each one's status, while CMIP uses reporting, which means that devices report their status only when it has changed. Therefore, SNMP uses more overhead, because it is communicating with devices more often.

2. SNMP asks for very specific information with each request, while cmip wants to know all about the status. Thus, each has its efficient and inefficient uses.

3. CMIP has more features; but not everyone sees those features as useful. For example, CMIP can move a table of 10,000 information items better than SNMP. (Not everyone agrees that this speed discepancy exists.)

4. SNMP is smaller, faster, and less expensive; CMIP requires more processing power and more memory.

5. SNMP only requires simple communications protocols on OSI Layers 1 and 2, such as Ethernet and token ring; while CMIP requires a reliable transport layer (Layer 4), such as TCP/IP. This difference makes CMIP better at retrieving large amounts of data but harder to use in uncovering faults.

6. CMIP is an international standard controlled by ISO and vendors can test their products against conformance tests from the Corporation for Open Systems (COS). SNMP is not an international standard, so some users may be required to use CMIP.

7. SNMP has many more products available—routers, Ethernet hubs, fiber devices and Ethernet devices.

vendors. The MIB is the central database that defines and stores the kinds of data to be collected by the network components, such as their operational status, their location on the network, performance statistics, and so forth.

Although the three are quite similar, they do differ, notes Sharon Fisher [9]; see Figure 8-4 for a comparison of SNMP and CMIP. Proponents from all three camps believe the standards could coexist, with SNMP focusing primarily on communications with a network manager, while SNP and CMIP focus on communications between management systems.

Integrated Network Management Is Becoming a Major Goal. The term integration has several meanings in the world of network management. One obvious meaning is being able to manage entire internets, even when they include LANs, WANs, and maybe even MANs.

Another meaning of integration is the ability of network management products from different vendors to work together and appear as a single system to the network manager. An ultimate goal of a network management system is to allow a network manager sitting at a workstation to see what is happening on any of the corporate networks—in one window. That is not yet possible for complex internets of LANs and WANs. Today, if various parts of networks can be monitored from one workstation, it is done via different windows—one for each vendor's gear.

One of the roadblocks to this form of integration has been that each network management vendor has designed its software to be the "manager of managers," so integration is supposed to be achieved by all other vendors' products sending them the network alerts. In essence, there have been too many "bosses" and not enough "workers." For a truly integrated multivendor network management *system*, the vendors must allow their products to be workers to others' products.

A third, and more sophisticated, meaning of integration combines network management with system management. It means being able to correlate network alarms and traffic flow with database and computer use, says Elisabeth Horwitt [10], because poor network performance could be from the network, a computer, or the network operation system.

A fourth form of integration is between voice and data networks. And a fifth form adds management of distributed applications to other management duties, as we discuss next.

Management of Distributed Applications Is Coming. A new view of network management is cropping up, allowing network managers to also manage distributed client/server applications. Lotus, for example, is embedding network management software in its work group product Notes, so that servers running Notes can send SNMP management information to an SNMP network management system. A network manager can use these statistics and alarms to monitor how well Notes is performing across an internet, see whether any of the Notes servers are running out of disk space, and so forth, says Stanley Gibson [11]. We believe this will be a growing trend as large distributed computing systems are built. In fact, network management is likely to become a large percentage of the development work in these systems.

Automation of Network Operations Will Increase. Steve Miller, network manager of AutoSource, a retailer in Indianapolis, Indiana [cited in 12], believes that network management software should be proactive. Today, this is not true. The tools listen to the network's wire conditions and sends an alarm when a threshold has been exceeded. Miller would much prefer these triggers to identify the problem, launch the fix, and then notify him of the solution. The system should try to find him through fax, electronic mail, or paging only if the network cannot be automatically fixed. This would be a more proactive and automated system.

Tom Henderson [12] points out that Miller's desire is one reason for including network management functions in network operating systems—so that the operating system can initiate the fixes. There has been much discussion in the communication industry press lately about the best location for network management software. Inclusion in the network operating system provides the highest vantage point for viewing the entire network. But this option is not always the most efficient or does not provide as many features as other options, some people argue.

The other major option is to include the software in the intelligent network nodes, such as the hubs, concentrators, routers, bridges, and packet forwarders. There has been much action and progress in this second alternative. But because of the complexity of networks, the only way they to reduce downtime is to automate as many of the functions as possible.

Outsourcing of Network Management Will Increase. Due to the crucial role of networks in today's businesses and the increasing complexity of these networks, we believe that more and more companies will outsource network management functions. We expect them not only to outsource day-to-day oversight of network operations but also to outsource ownership of the communication nodes and some of the links. This appears especially true of multicountry and intercontinental networks, which are so complex to build and operate. Finding telecommunications talent in many countries is a difficult task in itself, a task that might best be left to an international telecommunications provider.

These then are five trends we see in the network management world. Now we wrap up our discussion of network management by presenting some advise on building network management systems.

Guidelines for Building a Network Management System

The people at the Index Foundation [7] provide the following guidelines for building a network management system.

Choose a Strategy. Since an integrated network management solution is not yet available, companies can choose between three strategies to implement such systems.

One option is to take a single-supplier approach, by restricting network components and network management tools to one vendor. Many companies have taken this approach by sticking with their mainframe vendor. However, there are three drawbacks from choosing this option, says the Index Foundation report. One, no vendor can possibly supply all the needed components. Two, it is not a viable option for most companies because they already have multivendor networks. And three, one vendor's offerings may not fit the user organization as well as products from other vendors.

Due to these drawbacks, some companies have opted to build their own customized integrated network management system. Since it is an expensive route, this option has been chosen mainly by very large organizations, such as major financial institutions, the airlines, and computer manufacturers. They generally buy network management tools and then write custom software to process and analyze the data supplied by those tools.

Due to the limitations of the first option, and the huge expense of the second, most companies take the third alternative: mix and match. They use a variety of incompatible network management tools, each of which does only a part of the job and requires its own network center workstation. Since the tools cannot be coordinated, these companies are significantly benefiting from SNMP.

Select Network Components Based on Network Management Capabilities. A key criterion for choosing network components, notes the Index Foundation, should be their ability to supply network management information. Some network managers even go so far as to suggest that they will buy future network management tools first, and then select the networking components that those tools can manage.

Most companies are taking a hierarchical approach to network management, with data gathering and control performed closest to the network components. These tools filter what they receive and only pass the relevant information to the central network management system, which handles planning, design, billing, and management reporting. It appears that many network component vendors are taking this piece of advice to heart and including SNMP in their products.

Expect Expert Systems to Play An Important Role. Expert systems will be important in future network management systems in at least three areas, says the Index Foundation. One is to assist with fault analysis, used either at the network help desk or by the first-level technical support staff. But, for the next few years, these systems are likely to be restricted to handling only one vendor's equipment. A second use is in providing more intelligence for automated network control functions. This will further the move to more automated network management systems. And the third use is for assisting with network design.

Justify Investments in Business Terms. Network managers generally have trouble justifying network management expenditures because the benefits are difficult to explain, except in technical terms. To identify the business case for such tools, use one of the following approaches, the Index Foundation suggests. One, estimate the cost of down-time. Or two, present a risk-based business case for applications that are time critical. When systems that require continuous operation go down, not only does the company lose current business but also loses future business as well. But if a system does not require continuous operation, use a cost-based justification. Estimate the additional costs that the company could accrue during downtimes. Whichever approach is taken, use business benefits rather than technical benefits, they advise.

And speaking of down-time, another major challenge for information systems management is recovering from disasters, natural or man-made. We discuss that subject next.

DISASTER RECOVERY FOR DISTRIBUTED SYSTEMS

Although information systems are just one part of a company operation, they have become a crucial part. Thus, disaster recovery for information systems has become important, even though the subject has been discussed for a long time.

Disaster recovery practitioners we talked with were unanimous in their views that (1) contingency planning needs to be an integral part of doing business and (2) commitment of resources to disaster recovery process must be based on an assessment by top management of cost versus risk.

Companies essentially have two options for disaster recovery: use internal or external resources.

Using Internal Resources

Organizations that rely on internal resources for disaster recovery generally see this planning as a normal part of system planning and development. They cost-justify backup processing and telecommunications based on company needs during foreseeable emergencies. We found companies using the following four approaches to backing up their computer systems, data, and communication links with company resources:

- Multiple data centers
- Distributed processing
- Backup telecommunications facilities
- LANs

Multiple Data Centers

Organizations with large data processing budgets often have multiple computer centers. These centers can provide at least some backup for critical applications in emergencies.

For backing up data, companies create protected disk storage facilities-sometimes called "DASD farms." These farms, or data warehouses, are regularly refreshed with current operating data to speed recovery at an alternative data center. They are normally company owned, unattended sites, and remote from the primary data centers. They house disk controllers and disk drives that can be accessed either on-line or in batch mode.

Some organizations that do not have multiple data centers provide alternative communications among company sites through backup telecommunications equipment and communication lines to outside disaster recovery centers and service bureaus.

Distributed Processing

Other organizations are using distributed processing to deal with disaster recovery. They perform critical processing locally rather than centrally. This distribution of processing permits operations to continue uninterrupted for several days when a disaster hits a data center. Companies that use this approach standardize hardware and applications at remote locations, so that each local processing site can back up another one.

Distributed processing solutions to disaster recovery can be quite costly when data redundancy between the central and remote sites is required. Therefore, this alternative is most commonly used for applications that must continue to operate, such as order entry and financial transaction systems. But until distributed database technology becomes available, files cannot be distributed cost effectively.

Backup Telecommunications Facilities

Companies appear to be handling telecommunications backup in two ways: (1) by building duplicate communications facilities, and (2) by using alternative technologies that they redeploy in case of an emergency.

Depository Trust Company (DTC) of New York City is a cooperative owned by financial industry clients. It serves as a clearinghouse for the settlement of securities trades, and it provides services to the banking and brokerage industry. The company uses Sungard Disaster Recovery Services [13] facilities for processing backup.

DTC operates a large telecommunications network, linking its users at remote sites to its data center in New York City through leased and dial-up lines. DTC is expanding its network with a complete duplicate backup communication center at an alternate location in New York City. This center includes duplicate lines, telecommunication switches, modems, and multiplexors that can be quickly linked to disaster recovery facilities at Sungard to keep the remote sites on-line if the corporate computer center becomes inoperable.

Other companies turned to alternative communication technology when their communication links fail, such as when the infamous Hinsdale fire destroyed the Hinsdale Illinois Bell Telephone Company central office switching station. The station handled 118,000 long-distance lines, 30,000 data lines, and 35,000 local voice lines, reported Jeff Bozman [14]. It served as a hub for some thirty local exchanges in northeastern Illinois. The fire disrupted telephone service to the area for up to four weeks. Local companies used at least two alternative technologies to handle their telecommunications needs in this emergency.

Crockett [15] reported that MONY Financial Services in Syracuse, New York, switched a satellite link from its smaller San Juan, Puerto Rico, office to its large Hinsdale office by installing a very small aperture terminal (VSAT) dish on the roof. It was used to communicate via satellite to a communication hub in New York City, and from there via land lines to Syracuse. The San

Juan office then instituted its own communication backup plan—using terrestrial lines to communicate to Syracuse.

Zurich Insurance Company, in Schaumburg, Illinois, used a different alternative, reported Crockett. They established a line-of-site microwave link between their headquarters office and an AT&T switching office located about two miles away. Several companies turned to microwave to bypass the Hinsdale center. Crockett reports that thirty-eight temporary microwave links were established either by AT&T or MCI in the Chicago area.

One way to avoid being dependent on one telephone company switching office is to have communication links to two local switching centers. This option appeared unnecessary and too expensive for many companies, until the Hinsdale fire. More recent outages, especially in New York City, have made most top executives aware of the danger of depending on one common carrier.

Local Area Networks

LANs will increasingly be used to provide backup as they carry more of a company's traffic. Servers on one LAN can be used to back up servers for other networks. As with mainframe DASD farms, data servers used for such backup need to be "refreshed" on a regular basis to keep their data up to date. This is accomplished by linking the networks through shared cabling. Network master control programs permit designating alternative devices when primary ones fail.

Using External Resources

In many cases, a cost-versus-risk analysis may not justify committing permanent resources to contingencies; therefore, companies use the services of a disaster recovery firm. These services include:

- Integrated disaster recovery services
- Specialized disaster recovery services
- On-line and off-line data storage facilities
- Service bureaus, consortia, and informal cooperative arrangements

Integrated Disaster Recovery Services

In North America, major suppliers of disaster recovery services offer multiple recovery sites interconnected by high-speed telecommunications lines. Services at these locations include fully operational processing facilities that are available on less than twenty-four hours' notice. These suppliers often have environmentally suitable storage facilities for housing special equipment for their clients.

A Gartner Group study [5c] estimates that subscription fees for fully operational facilities typically run from $1,500 to $15,000 a month. Using a backup center costs from $4,000 to $10,000 a day. In addition, a fee is often charged each time a disaster is declared; it can run as high as $25,000. Mobile facilities—where a mobile trailer containing computer equipment can be moved to a client site—are available at costs similar to fully operational facilities. And empty warehouse space is priced from $500 to $1,000 a month, Gartner reports.

Recognizing the importance of telecommunications links, major disaster recovery suppliers have expanded their offerings to include smaller sites that contain specialized telecommunications equipment. These sites allow users to maintain telecommunications services when disaster recovery facilities are in use. They house control equipment and software needed to support communication lines connecting recovery sites with client sites.

Specialized Disaster Recovery Services

Some suppliers of backup services can accommodate mainframe clients who also need to back up midrange machines. In addition, a growing number of backup services are designed solely for midrange systems. Some will even deliver a trailer with compatible hardware and software to a client location.

Telecommunications backup has become an important consideration in many companies. In the United States, some of the Regional Bell Operating Companies offer a type of recovery service—a network reconfiguration service. For example, Pacific Bell offers a service that allows users to reconfigure individual channels within T-1 lines. Users can reroute circuits using either PCs or terminals that are linked directly to Pacific Bell network computers. Thus, telecommunications people at user sites can reroute their circuits around lines with communication problems.

Other specialized telecommunications backup services are beginning to appear. For example, Hughes Network Systems, in Germantown, Maryland [16], helped a company that had forty-nine of its pharmacies affected by the Hinsdale telephone switching station fire. Within 72 hours, Hughes installed a temporary network of VSATs at twelve sites. The thirty-seven remaining sites had small satellite dishes installed within two weeks. Other firms offer data communications backup programs, where they will store specific data communications equipment for a customer and deliver that equipment by air to the customer's recovery site when needed.

On-Line and Off-Line Data Storage

Alternative locations for storage of tapes and other records have long been a part of disaster planning. Services generally consist of fire-resistant vaults with suitable temperature and humidity controls.

Several suppliers offer "electronic vaulting" for organizations that need to have current data off-site at the time a disaster occurs. These suppliers use two methods to obtain current data from their clients. One method uses computer-to-computer transmission of data on a scheduled basis. The other method uses dedicated equipment to capture and store data at a remote location as it is created on the client's computer. This latter method assures uninterrupted access to data from an operationally ready disaster recovery facility selected by the client.

Service Bureaus, Consortia, and Agreements

Service bureaus can offer limited but economical emergency processing support. Their primary business is serving the normal operating needs of their clients, but they can be used for backup purposes. However, unless special capacity provisions have been made to assure priority for disaster recovery, they cannot handle large emergency workloads for several weeks of backup use.

Consortia with other user organizations are another backup option, but they have had limited success. They are most effective when a third party administers the arrangements. And each member needs to be sure that its hardware and software remain fully compatible.

Moberg [17] describes how four firms in Minneapolis, Minnesota, formed an alliance to provide voice communication backup for each other and to share the lease of a spare PBX. They each use the same type of PBX, they are in the same industry, and they have agreed to provide remote communication facilities to each other in case of emergency. The agreement was drawn up by a consultant, and a local telecommunications company performs backup installation when needed. After testing the arrangement twice, these four companies found that they can establish communications for three hundred telephone lines in about eight hours.

SUMMARY

Disaster recovery needs have not always shaped the architecture of computer systems, so the cost of reconfiguring these systems to provide the needed redundancy and backup can be prohibitive. In these cases, external backup alternatives may be a more cost effective form of "insurance." But companies planning major network and system enhancements today appear to be including disaster recovery as an integral part of their system design. For example, they are connecting their external recovery sites into their corporate networks. We anticipate companies will use both internal and external resources rather than relying on just one or the other.

To illustrate the use of disaster recovery facilities, consider the case of Household International.

CASE EXAMPLE: Household International

Household International, with headquarters in Prospect Heights, Illinois, is a major provider of consumer lending, banking, insurance, and commercial financial services in the United States. The company also provides similar services in the United Kingdom, Canada, and Australia through subsidiaries.

The core of its consumer finance business is serviced by some seven hundred consumer lending branches and sixty bank branches throughout the United States. Household is also a large credit card issuer in the United States and operates a major credit card service center in Salinas, California. Household's major data center is in its corporate offices. The center is linked to the branch network via leased lines, with regional connections to more than ten thousand remote devices and terminals.

Typical of large financial services institutions, Household justified its disaster recovery planning based on legal and regulatory requirements and the need to maintain uninterrupted customer service. The centralized design of its data network simplified recovery planning but made the headquarters data center critical to recovery.

The company established a full-time staff to prepare, maintain, and "exercise" (test out) disaster recovery plans. After exploring several alternatives, including adding reserve processing capacity to their network, Household decided to rely on Comdisco Disaster Recovery Services [18]. Comdisco is a major supplier of alternative site data processing services in North America.

Services provided by Comdisco include use of facilities at one or more of their several recovery centers throughout North America, and "hot site" equipment and software to provide immediate operational support on request. In addition, Comdisco provides technical assistance in disaster planning, testing, and the use of recovery centers. Household viewed the monthly cost of these services as their most economical recovery alternative.

After six months, all critical banking applications had been tested at the alternative site, and contingency procedures had been developed for the bank branches. Household had also begun developing contingency plans for the consumer lending operation and testing application programs at the alternative site. In addition, they had begun developing business recovery priorities and operating procedures for end users.

In the midst of this effort, nature intervened. At 9:00 A.M. on a Friday, after meeting with key personnel, Household declared a disaster. More than nine inches of rain had fallen on the Chicago area in twelve hours. Widespread flooding had closed major highways, leaving thousands of homes and businesses without power or telephone service. A retention pond at corporate headquarters had overflowed, causing an overnight runoff into the basement of the headquarters building where the data center was located. By 10:30 A.M. the water had risen to thirty-one inches—nine inches above the twenty-two-inch false floor—and it rose further before the disaster ended.

With telephone lines down in the area and the company PBX out of service, the recovery coordinator relied on plans made early in the year. Computer operations were transferred to the Comdisco alternative site in Wood Dale, Illinois, which was twenty miles away. Fortunately, he made his call to Comdisco early; other clients who called later were relocated to sites as far away as New Jersey-some eight hundred miles (thirteen hundred kilometers) away. Since five Chicago area businesses declared disasters, Comdisco's hot site resources in Illinois were quickly saturated.

At the backup site, work began on restoring vital bank and check processing systems. Critical processing for most bank branches resumed within twenty-four hours. Teller systems at bank branches used local computers, so they operated without interruption. However, on-line information on the current status of customer accounts was not available until the following Monday.

After pumping out the flooded data center, the data processing staff found extensive damage to disk drive motors and circuit boards below the high water mark. However, they were able to restore the communication control units quickly. They were then able to use these units as the links for all communications between the backup-site computers and the remote terminals installed in the branches. Illinois Bell—the local telephone company—used a central switch to establish a link between the disaster recovery alternative site and the Household home office.

By the third day, all the important work that had been moved to key Household locations was up and running, and communication links among these locations were working. Communication links to all offices were available by the sixth day.

A few days after the disaster, more than 220 analysts and programmers were assigned to work at the alternative site on a twenty-four-hour schedule. The disaster recovery coordinator arranged for special food service, dressing facilities, and rest areas at the alternative site. And workstations were created using rented furniture and equipment.

Special meetings were held with senior management to establish recovery priorities for the consumer lending operation. Daily meetings, chaired by the executive vice president of information systems, were attended by nearly all managers and vendors affected by the disaster—some forty to fifty people in all. These meetings became the day-to-day means for reporting status, handling special problems, and developing recovery schedules. The meetings turned out to be the best means for communicating quickly and making decisions using the existing organization. The meetings lasted several hours each day and covered a wide range of topics. Thus, no special organizational structure was used for managing the disaster; however, the disaster recovery manager played a key role in coordinating the recovery.

The company left the backup site on the fifteenth day. Eighteen days after the disaster, normal operations had been fully restored.

Lessons Learned

They told us they learned six lessons from this disaster, which they offer as recommendation to others.

1. Consider the risks of a natural disaster in selecting a data center location. Areas with high exposure to flooding, heavy rainfall, fire hazards, or earthquakes will be more costly to protect against these risks.

2. Create a plan to return to the primary site after the disaster. This plan is just as important as a plan to move to an alternative site.

3. Do not expect damaged equipment, disks, and tapes to always be replaced in kind or restored to original condition. Therefore, make plans for new configurations, and regularly monitor sources of equipment and supplies to assure early delivery of replacements.

4. Test hot-site resources under *full workload conditions* to ensure that sufficient computer capacity is available to meet high-priority needs.

5. Plan for alternative telecommunications routing for multiple-site operations during a disaster. Houschold's original telecommunications disaster recovery plan called for key sites around the country to handle the headquarters' processing load in case of a home office disaster. But the quick recovery of the communication control units at the headquarters data center allowed Household to use an alternative plan: to rely mainly on processing at the nearby disaster recovery site. Thus, for sixteen days they operated with both the headquarters center and the disaster recovery center. The other key Household centers handled mainly their normal work, but their computers were available if needed.

6. Maintain critical data at the alternative site or at another nearby location for fast system recovery.

Household has used its experience to refine and complete the plans it started before the rain storm. In addition, Comdisco services have been extended to other subsidiaries under a corporate-wide contract. In retrospect, key participants believe that the early restoration of the headquarters' computer center, the existence of computer and telecommunications backup procedures, staff members who were familiar with the backup plans, and use of normal management channels were all important in their rapid recovery.

CONCLUSION

Interestingly, the subject of managing computer operations has received a large amount of attention since the late 1980s, because business factors have led managers to reappraise all their operations, even systems. We believe that outsourcing will be a hot topic for many years to come, because there are so many opinions on its effect on a company's ability to remain flexible and retain IT competence within the firm. The move to true distributed systems also presents more challenging operational issues, as companies decide where to place their processing and data. Clearly, operations is one of the essential technologies that needs to be managed, and in this chapter we have touched on some of its aspects.

QUESTIONS AND EXERCISES

REVIEW QUESTIONS

1. What does the operations budget at Congleton's company include?
2. What are three solutions to operations problems, according to Congleton?
3. What are six trends in data center operations, according to Congleton?
4. How much of their information systems budget do companies normally spend on operations, according to a Nolan Norton study?
5. Companies that run efficient data centers also have applications with what four characteristics, according to Disher?
6. What is Mutual of Omaha doing to make its data center more efficient?
7. What are five steps toward automating data center operations, according to Miller?
8. How close are fully unattended operations, according to LaChance?
9. What are the components of an "industrial strength" automation product?
10. What are the driving forces of outsourcing, according to Bergstein?
11. What are the five customer-vendor relationships?
12. What four questions should management ask when investigating outsourcing?
13. What are five components of network management, according to the Index Foundation?
14. What are five trends in network management?
15. What four pieces of advice does the Index Foundation give about building network management systems?
16. What internal disaster recovery alternatives are used by companies?
17. What external disaster recovery services are available to companies?
18. What six lessons did Household International learn from its disaster?

DISCUSSION QUESTIONS

1. Outsourcing offloads a burdensome technical responsibility and allows management to focus on its core business. Outsourcing strips a company of an important core competence—its know-how. Which statement do you agree with and why?

2. Distributed systems will eventually mitigate the need for companies to contract for outside disaster recovery services, because companies will have multiple sites to do their own internal backup. Do you agree or disagree? Why?

EXERCISES

1. Read several articles on unattended computer operations. How are operators reacting to their job being taken over by computers? What work are they now doing? How do they like their new job?

2. Read a few articles about outsourcing. What did you learn about outsourcing that is not mentioned in this chapter? Relay them to the class.

3. Read a few articles about network management. What new ideas did you learn that are not presented in this chapter? Present them to the class.

4. Visit a company in your local community. Learn about their disaster recovery plans. Which threats are they aimed at? Which threats are not dealt with?

REFERENCES

1. "Transforming the Data Center in an Information Utility," a session presented at the 1987 AFIPS National Computer Conference.

2. CHRISTOPER DISHER, Nolan, Norton and Co., 150 N. Michigan Ave., Chicago, IL 60601.

3. MILLER, H. W., "Planning for Unattended Data Center Operation," *Mainframe Journal*, January-February 1988, p. 10.

4. FARBER/LaCHANCE INC., P.O. Box 26611, Richmond, VA 23261.

5. THE GARTNER GROUP, 56 Top Gallant Road, Stamford, CT 06904.

   a. SCHULMAN, J., "Industrial-Strength ASO Product Features: Part I and II," "ISV ASO Products: Part I and II," and, "OPS/MVS: The ASO Pacesetter," *Software Management Strategies* Service, April 8, 1988.

   b. WEIL, J., "Disaster Recovery Alternatives," a one-page document from their *Industry Service Report*, No. SPA-150-530.1.

   c. Marlin, S., "Costs of Recovery Planning," a one-page document from their *IBM Large Computer Market Key Issues Report*, No. SPA- 823-544.1.

6. MEL BERGSTEIN, TSC, 205 N. Michigan Ave., Chicago, IL 60601.

7. *Network Management*, Index Foundation, Research Report No. 65, August 1988, 58 pages.

8. HORWITT, E. "Change in Air on Network Management," *Computerworld*, June 29, 1992, p. 16.

9. FISHER, S., "Dueling Protocols," *Byte*, March 1991, pp. 183-190.

10. HORWITT, E., "Distributed Management Tools Coming," *Computerworld*, November 25, 1991, pp. 1, 92.

11. GIBSON, S., "Lotus Notes to Get SNMP Support," *Communications Week*, March 16, 1992, pp. 1, 59.

12. HENDERSON, T., "A Tub Full of Network Management Software," *LAN Times*, April 6, 1992, pp. 26

13. SUNGUARD RECOVERY SERVICES, 1285 Drummers Lane, Wayne, PA 19087.

14. BOZMAN, J. "Illinois Phone Effort Puts Data Links Last," *Computerworld*, May 23, 1988, p. 101.

15. CROCKETT, B., "Users Turned to Satellite, Microwave Links After Fire," *Network World*, June 27, 1988, pp. 31-32.

16. HUGHES NETWORK SYSTEMS, 11717 Exploration Lane, Germantown, MD 20874.

17. MOBERG, K., "MAP: A Plan for Disaster Recovery," *TE&M*, May 15, 1988, pp. 113-114.

18. COMDISCO DISASTER RECOVERY SERVICES, 6400 Shafer Court, Rosemont, IL 60018.

NINE

The Evolving System Development Spectrum

INTRODUCTION

One of the toughest jobs in information systems management is developing new systems. It seems to be an area in which Murphy's Law—if anything can go wrong, it will—reigns supreme. As a result, there has been a significant amount of work since the 1960s devoted to strengthening the tools and methodologies for system development.

Despite the complexity of system development, the information systems field has made significant progress in improving the process of building systems. The traditional approach, with variations, of course, appears in many textbooks and professional books. Two of the first books to describe a life-cycle approach for developing systems were published in 1956 and 1957; they were written by Richard Canning [1].

During the 1970s, a relatively well-defined process, called the "system development life cycle," emerged. This life cycle improved the development process significantly. However, continued backlogs, cost overruns, and performance shortfalls underscored the difficulty and complexity of the system development process.

The 1980s saw progress in more friendly languages and automation of portions of development, such as code generation. Yet, maintenance contin-

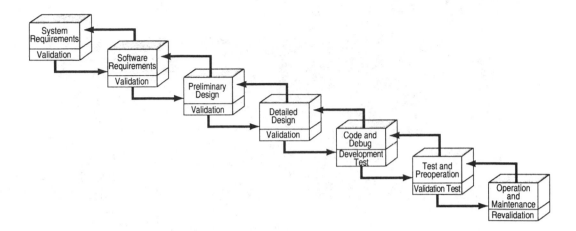

Figure 9-1 The "Waterfall" Software Life Cycle (from Boehm [3])

ued to eat up 70 to 80 percent of the system development resources in most companies. The 1990s, at long last, hold out the promise of significantly increasing developer productivity and reducing maintenance through further automation and dramatically different development approaches. Yet, most developers are reluctant to believe such claims, because they have heard of too many "silver bullets" in the past that did not live up to expectations.

In this chapter we review the spectrum of system development choices that has arisen over the past thirty years. This spectrum includes the gamut of programming languages, methodologies, and development tools. The chapter concludes with a look into the near future.

THE 1950s THROUGH THE 1970s

The history of system development has actually occurred over more than forty years. An excellent book, edited by Couger, Colter, and Knapp [2], shows how techniques and processes evolved from precomputer approaches through fourth and fifth generation approaches.

The famous "waterfall" diagram in Figure 9-1, from Barry Boehm [3], illustrates the "classic" system development life cycle popularly used in the 1970s. Norman Enger [4] expands on this classical approach in Figure 9-2 by describing the life cycle phases in somewhat different terms, and illustrating the activities and resulting documents for his phases.

The traditional approach has been generally characterized by

- Hand coding in a third generation language (such as COBOL)
- A "structured programming" development methodology
- An automated project management system
- A database management system

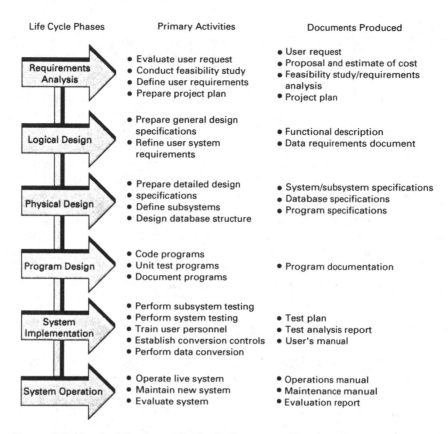

Life Cycle Phases	Primary Activities	Documents Produced
Requirements Analysis	• Evaluate user request • Conduct feasibility study • Define user requirements • Prepare project plan	• User request • Proposal and estimate of cost • Feasibility study/requirements analysis • Project plan
Logical Design	• Prepare general design specifications • Refine user system requirements	• Functional description • Data requirements document
Physical Design	• Prepare detailed design • specifications • Define subsystems • Design database structure	• System/subsystem specifications • Database specifications • Program specifications
Program Design	• Code programs • Unit test programs • Document programs	• Program documentation
System Implementation	• Perform subsystem testing • Perform system testing • Train user personnel • Establish conversion controls • Perform data conversion	• Test plan • Test analysis report • User's manual
System Operation	• Operate live system • Maintain new system • Evaluate system	• Operations manual • Maintenance manual • Evaluation report

Figure 9-2 Classical Systems Life Cycle Phases and Products (from Enger [4])

- A mix of on-line and batch applications in the same system
- Development of mostly mainframe applications
- Programming by professional programmers only
- Various automated (but not well-integrated) software tools
- A well-defined sign-off process for system delivery
- User participation mainly in requirements definition and installation phases

Goals of Traditional Structured Development

The methodologies that companies adopted as their standard approach through the 1970s were meant to handle the complexities of system design and development. Their use has had three goals.

More Discipline. By establishing standards for processes and documentation, the traditional system development life cycle attempted to eliminate personal variations. At first it seemed to threaten programmers' creativity, but the discipline increased productivity and the developers' ability to deal with complexity. Complexity was handled using successive decomposition of system components, coupled with preferred practices for conducting analysis, design, and construction. The result was a more disciplined system development process.

Higher Reliability and Fewer Errors. The methodologies recognized that mistakes of both omission and commission were likely at all stages of system building. One of the main tools for coping with this tendency has been inspections, performed at every development stage and at every level of system decomposition. The goal has been to catch errors as early as possible. The methodologies also recognized that iteration would be required to redo parts of the system as mistakes are uncovered.

More Efficient Use of Resources. The project management approaches usually included in the methodologies contributed to cost savings, increased productivity, and better allocation of human resources. By imposing a time and cost control system, the classic approach decreased (but did not eliminate) the tendency for system development efforts to incur cost and time overruns.

Emphasis on the Early Phases

In the late 1970s, developers began concentrating on the early phases of development because the longer an error persists, the more costly it is to correct. Boehm [3] notes that if correcting an error in the requirements stage costs $1, the cost will be $5 to correct the error if not caught until the design stage, $10 to correct in the programming stage, and a whopping $100 if is not found and corrected until the operational stage. For this reason, system developers want to catch serious errors in the requirements and design stages.

This emphasis on doing the early phases right was evident in two system development approaches that emerged in the 1970s. One was data-driven development, where emphasis was placed on defining a program's data first, because it is more stable, and then defining the processes to manipulate that data. Several data-driven methodologies appeared in the late 1970s.

The second approach was group design sessions, to more quickly solidify requirements and design of a new system. The approaches, the most common of which was Joint Application Design (JAD), forced developers and users to specify an entire application in just a few days' time, down to detailing the screen layouts, by participating in day-long design sessions. JAD and the other group design techniques followed specific steps to ensure that the design process was completed in those few days and accomplished its goal. These sessions significantly accelerated design because they brought together all the decision makers at one time and one place.

THE EARLY 1980s

In the early 1980s, two major developments occurred in the way some applications were built. One was the availability of fourth generation languages (4GLs). Previously, developers only had third generation languages, such as COBOL and PL/1. The other development was an alternative to the traditional system development life cycle—where system requirements were fully defined before design and construction began. The alternative was software prototyping—also called iterative development—made possible by the advent of the 4GLs.

Fourth Generation Languages

Fourth generation languages are really more than computer languages; they are programming environments. The major components or characteristics of 4GLs are listed in Figure 9-3.

The heart of a 4GL is its DBMS for storing formatted data records as well as unformatted text, graphics, voice, and perhaps even video. Almost as important is the data dictionary, which stores the *definitions* of the various

Figure 9-3 Features and Functions of Fourth Generation Languages

- Database Management system
- Data dictionary
- Nonprocedural language
- Interactive query facilities
- Report generator
- Selection and sorting
- Screen formatter
- Word processor and text editor
- Graphics
- Data analysis and modeling tools
- Library of macros
- Programming interface
- Reusable code
- Software development library
- Backup and recovery
- Security and privacy safeguards
- Links to other DBMS

kinds of data. The language that the programmers and users use is nonprocedural, which means that the commands can occur in any order rather than
the sequence required by the computer. The commands can be used interactively to retrieve ad hoc information from files or a database or to print a
report. This facility is provided by a report generator. The screen painter
allows the user or programmer to design a screen by simply typing in the various data input field names and the locations where they are to appear, or by
choosing graphics off of a menu. Some 4GLs include statistical packages for
calculating time series, averages, standard deviations, correlation coeffi-
cients, and so on.

Suggestions on Using a Fourth Generation Language. Mary Rich
[5], an independent contractor who has worked with 4GLs since the mid-
1970s, has some suggestions on their use. Applications especially suitable for
4GLs are those subject to rapid changes, or where the need for ad hoc reporting is high, as in personnel or budgeting systems. She also recommends that
4GL programmers spend time doing system analysis work before they begin
coding. It is true that 4GLs, when coupled with a prototyping methodology, do
not require the same exhaustive systems analysis as the classic approach
with handcoding in COBOL. However, inexperienced 4GL programmers can get
themselves into problems if they forego analysis, thinking that prototyping
makes this unnecessary. Prototyping does allow developers to experiment
with different ways of doing things, such as changing the database structure.

However, because 4GLs permit easily creating and manipulating data,
their improper use can lead to a proliferation of "little databases." This is a
management problem, says Rich, not a technical one. Systems management
should establish and enforce policies for database maintenance by the end
users. Users will think twice about creating little databases if this policy is
enforced. Another potential problem is "private programs." If a user wants to
turn a program over to the information systems department to maintain,
Rich recommends that management require a minimum level of
documentation—a user guide, plus comments in the program that describe
the overall flow and the complex algorithms.

Due to their ease of use, fourth generation languages led to a new programming practice in the early 1980s—prototyping.

Software Prototyping

According to *Webster's Twentieth-Century Dictionary*, the term "prototype" has three possible meanings: (1) It is an original or model after which
anything is formed, (2) it is the first thing or being of its kind, and (3) it is a
pattern, an exemplar, or an archetype.

David Naumann and A. Milton Jenkins [6] believe the second definition
best fits the prototypes used in data processing because such prototypes are a
first attempt at a design that generally is later extended and enhanced.
Franz Edelman, a pioneer in the use of software prototyping, described the

process of software prototyping as "a quick and inexpensive process of developing and testing a trial balloon."

A software prototype is a *live, working system*; it is not just an idea on paper. Therefore it can be evaluated by the designer or the eventual end users through its use in an operational mode. It performs actual work; it does not just simulate that work. *It may become the actual production system*, or it may be replaced by a conventionally coded production system. Its purpose is *to test out assumptions* about users' requirements, or about the design of the application or perhaps even about the logic of a program.

A prototype is a software system that *is created quickly*—often within hours, days, or weeks-rather than months or years. With only conventional programming languages, such as COBOL, it was much too expensive to create both a prototype and a production version. So only production systems were developed. With 4GLs, people can get prototypes up and running quickly. The prototype *is relatively inexpensive to build,* because the language creates much of the code.

Prototyping *is an iterative process*. It begins with a simple prototype that performs only a few of the basic functions. Through use of the prototype, system designers or end users discover new requirements and refinements to incorporate in each succeeding version. Each version performs more of the desired functions and in an increasingly efficient manner.

To demonstrate a dramatic use of a 4GL and prototyping, we describe work at Santa Fe Railroad in the early 1980s. Their use of a 4GL was, *and still is,* unique because it took the opposite approach of just about everyone else. Most companies used 4GLs for management reports and end-user applications—that is, as a sidelight for their operational systems. Santa Fe, on the other hand, used the 4GL for their operational system, and left the management reporting in COBOL. The reasons for their unusual decision are made clear in the following case example.

CASE EXAMPLE: Santa Fe Railroad

The Atchison, Topeka, and Santa Fe Railway Company, with headquarters in Topeka, Kansas, had twelve thousand miles of railroad track, running from Chicago, Illinois, to California. They had two thousand locomotives, fifty-two thousand freight cars, and nine thousand truck trailers.

In the early 1980s, many of their trains were reaching their destinations without the accompanying paperwork. This was against Interstate Commerce Commission rules, so the railroad began receiving heavy fines for this missing paperwork. The railroad had to write a new waybill system in a hurry, but the systems department could not do the job using the traditional development methods. And no other railroad's application systems were appropriate for Santa Fe, because much of their business was in "piggybacking"—loading two truck trailers on a flat car and shipping them to their destination. Then Santa Fe heard about Mapper, a fourth generation language from Unisys. Since it appeared to be the only alternative, a freight scheduler and several clerical supervisors were taught Mapper and given the assignment of automating the paperwork for the huge Corwith piggybacking yard in Chicago.

In adopting Mapper, Santa Fe Railway made three significant programming decisions.

- Create an operational system in a 4GL using prototyping.
- Teach operational railroad employees to program rather than teach programmers to understand the intricacies of railroad operations.
- Create generic databases that would remain stable and be used throughout the company.

The group started by creating the generic databases, with standard data definitions, formats, and functions. The basic waybill system for the Corwith yard was created in several months' time, followed by a yard inventory system, and then a full-blown trailer-on-flat-car system. The complete operations expediter system (OX), which consisted of these three interrelated systems, was put into operation in eighteen months. The system handled the day-to-day railroad operations and sent subsets of data to the IMS PLUS corporate database-for corporate marketing, accounting, and operating summary purposes. Later, as the system expanded—with the addition of more switching yards— new databases were created for each yard. Each database used the same generic data definitions, formats, and functions. The Mapper database grew large but was composed of many small databases, identical for each yard. Mapper could handle this structure; in all it processed 1.7 million transactions daily.

With the adoption of Mapper, Santa Fe divided its data processing systems into two parts: the operational system and the corporate database. The operational system was converted to Mapper, whereas the corporate database was kept in COBOL because the railroad had a large investment in IBM programs that they did not want to replace. Interestingly, the two parts had quite different characteristics. The traditional IBM shop, which maintained the corporate database, had 116 application programmers, forty-four systems support people, and eighty people in operations. The Unisys center, which ran the railroad operations using Mapper, had only thirty-five application programmers, eleven systems support people, and thirty-two people in operations.

Although the two shops performed an equivalent amount of work, the Unisys shop was more cost-effective. Only one-third as many people were needed to run the Unisys operation—78 versus 240. He attributed the difference to their use of Mapper. Mapper required less support, he contended, but, at the same time, it did require about twice as much hardware. In total, the overall data processing costs for Mapper applications were one-half those of COBOL applications.

Santa Fe also noted that the Mapper programmers were four to eight times more productive than the COBOL programmers in new system development. The Mapper portion required one-half as many people, who created their system in one-half to one-fourth the time. Furthermore, system problems were handled either by the run designers in one day or by the operational people themselves on the spot. The system was controlled by the operational staff, so there were essentially no complaints to the information systems department about its functioning.

In retrospect, the vice president of information systems believed that a 4GL can have a *significant* impact on a company but only if it was used to automate daily operations-not merely as a tool for generating reports. The operational world was the most volatile part of the railroad, so that was where Santa Fe wanted the fastest and most versatile programming.

A Controversy: Evolution or Revolution?

In the 1980s, there was much debate about the effects of 4GLs and prototyping on programming. The debate really revolved around the question of how to make significant progress in system development. Which was better, people argued, an evolutionary approach or a revolutionary one? That debate continues today.

The Evolutionary Viewpoint. Some contended in the early 1980s that 4GLs and prototyping really only affected a small portion of the development effort—mainly coding—and thus provided only marginal benefits. The largest productivity problems came from errors introduced during system analysis and design, and by the paperwork associated with large projects. Therefore, the evolutionists argued, the new techniques should be merged into the traditional life cycle methodology. Meaningful productivity increases would come from improving the proven conventional techniques, such as structured programming.

These critics further point out that prototyping with a 4GL was largely a manual process, so the quality of the result varied with the individuals involved. Furthermore, 4GLs might not make efficient use of the computer, or might not handle large databases. There also might be difficulties in interfacing such a system with applications that had been developed in other languages. Since these 4GLs did not encourage structured programming, the design of the system might not be well structured or well planned. Thus, almost constant changing might be necessary. So, said these critics, prototyping via a 4GL was not the answer to faster system development.

The proponents of the "conventional approach" further believed that fine-tuning the development process—through automation and reuse of code and other development products—was the real key to big gains in programmer productivity.

The Revolutionary Viewpoint. The other point of view said that 4GLs definitely did increase programmer productivity *but only when* applied to programming in a new way—not just used as another language. These tools allowed people to work differently, not just faster—and that was the key to using them successfully. These 4GL proponents argued that traditional programmers were having a difficult time adapting to the rapid, iterative programming allowed by 4GL—where the application framework was the primary concern and details were ignored until later. The traditional programming "mind-set"—that is, the concern for fully specifying a system beforehand, programming this static set of requirements, and concern about code detail and exactness—was actually a disadvantage, not an advantage, to using 4GLs, they said.

Thus, these proponents preferred to train people knowledgeable in a business area rather than programmers in how to use a 4GL. These proponents saw the need for a *revolution* in programming.

Which point of view was right? Perhaps surprisingly: both. And the debate continues. The evolutionists are moving to CASE to automate structured programming principles, whereas the revolutionists are adopting object-oriented development. In addition, the two have merged somewhat. Prototyping has indeed become an important development stage in many client/server development projects, because it allows the developers to prove the new concepts on a small scale and thereby reduce the technical risk for the entire project.

THE LATE 1980s

System development in the late 1980s evolved further. In particular, the two developments just mentioned—CASE and object-oriented development—widened the spectrum.

Computer-Aided Software Engineering

The structured programming and analysis techniques of the 1970s brought some discipline to the process of developing large and complex software applications. Yet those methodologies required tedious attention to detail and lots of paperwork. CASE aimed at automating development of large applications in conjunction with these structured techniques.

Definitions. At a CASE Symposium, sponsored by Digital Consulting, Inc. [7], Carma McClure [8], a CASE pioneer, defined CASE as any automated tool that assists in the creation, maintenance, or management of software systems. In general, a CASE environment includes

- An information repository
- Front-end tools for planning through design
- Back-end tools for generating code
- A development workstation

Often not included—*but implied and necessary*—are a software development methodology and a project management methodology.

An information repository forms the heart of a CASE system and is its most important element, said McClure. It stores and organizes all information needed to create, modify, and develop a software system. This information includes, for example, data structures, processing logic, business rules, source code, and project management data. Ideally, this information repository should also link to the active data dictionary used during execution so that changes in one are reflected in the other.

Front-end tools are used in the phases that lead up to coding. One of the key requirements for these tools is good graphics for drawing diagrams of program structures, data entities and their relationships to each other, data flows, screen layouts, and so on. Rather than store pictorial representations, front-end tools generally store the meaning of items depicted in the diagrams. This allows a change made in one diagram to be reflected automatically in related diagrams. Another important aspect of front-end design tools is automatic design analysis, for checking the consistency and completeness of a design, often in accordance with a specific design technique.

Back-end tools generally mean code generators, for automatically generating source code. A few CASE tools use a 4GL. Successful front-end CASE tools are likely to provide interfaces to not just one but several code generators.

The final component of a CASE system is a *development workstation*. Currently, most are based on the IBM PS/2 or UNIX. A workstation with its own processing and storage is mandatory because of the graphical manipulations needed in CASE-developed systems. Also, prices have now dropped to the point where dedicated development workstations are easier to justify.

The use of CASE has promised numerous benefits: increased programmer productivity, higher-quality systems, easier maintenance, better communication among developers, and coordination of extremely complex jobs that could not even be attempted manually. One of the most intriguing CASE products and approaches we encountered is the "Timebox," which is a technique that uses CASE to guarantee delivery of a system within 120 days. Even more intriguing, the technique was developed by a user company—Du Pont—and then turned into a product that they market. Here is that story.

CASE EXAMPLE: Du Pont Cable Management Services

Du Pont Cable Management Services was formed in the late 1980s to manage the telephone and data wiring in Du Pont's office buildings in Wilmington, Delaware. AT&T had owned and managed the wiring for Du Pont's voice networks, but in 1984, responsibility passed to Du Pont's corporate telecommunications group. At Du Pont's Wilmington headquarters campus, cabling is complex and wiring changes are continual. The average telephone is moved one and one-half times a year. Much of the telephone moving cost is labor to find the correct cables and circuit paths.

When the cable management services group was formed, the manager realized he needed a system to maintain an inventory of every wire, telephone, modem, workstation, wiring closet connection, and other piece of telephone equipment. Technicians could then quickly locate the appropriate equipment and make the change. Although several cable management software packages were available, none could handle the scale nor workload required by Du Pont. The only option was a custom-built system.

The company needed a flexible system because the company's telecommunications facilities were expanding—from voice to data and video. So the system would need to handle new kinds of equipment. Furthermore, because the need for cable management services was new and not unique to Du Pont, the manager believed he could sell cable management services to other large companies. Therefore, the system needed to be tailorable.

Since the manager did not want to hire programmers, he decided to use Du Pont Information Engineering Associates [9], another Du Pont business service unit.

Du Pont Information Engineering Associates *(IEA)* began selling system development services to others in the late 1980s. It was spawned in the mid-1980s by some Du Pont system developers who were using CASE. These developers used Application Factory, a code generator for DEC VAX systems marketed by Cortex Corporation, in Waltham, Massachusetts [10]. These developers believed they could significantly speed up development if they combined the code generator with software prototyping and project management. The resulting methodology, which is used by IEA, is called RIPP—rapid iterative production prototyping.

Using RIPP, a development project can take as few as 120 days to complete; it has four phases.

- *Phase 1: Go-ahead.* Day 1 is the go-ahead day. IEA accepts the project and the customer agrees to participate heavily in the development.
- *Phase 2: System definition.* Days 2 through 30 are spent defining the components of the system and its acceptance criteria. At the end of this phase,

IEA presents the customer with a system definition and a fixed price for creating the application.

- *Phase 3: The Timebox.* The following 90 days are called a "Timebox," during which the IEA/customer team creates design specifications, proto- types the system, and then refines the prototype and its specifications. The final prototype becomes the production system.

- *Phase 4: Installation.* On day 120, the system is installed. The customer has three months to verify that the system does what it is supposed to do. If it doesn't, IEA will refund their money and remove the system.

Cable Management's Use of IEA. Cable management group contracted with IEA to develop the cable tracking system. After spending the first 30 days defining the scope of the project, IEA estimated that the system would require two Timeboxes to complete—about 210 days.

During the first Timebox, IEA developed those portions that the cable management group could concisely define. During these 90 days, one cable management engineer worked full-time on the project, another worked part-time, and IEA had a project leader and two developers. The system they developed included display screens, the relational database, basic system processes, and reports. At the end of the 90 days, IEA delivered a basic functional system, which Du Pont began using. The second Timebox added features uncovered during this use. Both parties agreed this phase was ambiguous, which might affect the 90-day limitation. So they extended the project to 110 days. By that time, the development team had entered Du Pont's complete wiring inventory, enhanced the basic system, and delivered a production version.

In all, the system took about nine months to develop. The department manager realized that was fast, but he did not realize how fast until he talked to other telecommunications executives who told him their firms had spent between two and three years developing cable management systems.

The cable management group is very pleased with their system. It was initially used only to manage voice wiring, but has since been extended to handle data communications wiring. They also sell cable management services to other companies.

Lessons Learned about CASE

From conferences and articles on the subject, we gleaned the following seven lessons for introducing CASE and reaping the most benefits from its use.

Quality Improvements Precede Productivity Increases. One conference featured several speakers from companies that had recently begun using CASE. All of the speakers said they did not receive immediate productivity gains, because of the significant amount of relearning involved in using the tools. However, the quality of their CASE-developed systems was much higher than they had expected. They all seemed pleasantly surprised at this benefit.

CASE-developed systems have fewer analysis and design errors, and system testing takes much less time. Maintenance of these systems is dropping dramatically, because changes can be made to designs rather than to code, and the system checks on the effects of changes. And development productivity is expected to increase eventually, as developers become more accustomed to using the new tools.

Implementing CASE Means Big Changes. CASE tools significantly change the way companies develop systems; therefore, introducing CASE means managing change in the systems department. The speakers encountered more resistance from division systems management than they anticipated, and a lot more training has been needed than they planned.

One company chose a CASE product and then conducted a six-month pilot. Development productivity did increase—the system was estimated to take fifty-two man months; it actually took thirty-seven. The developers in that division became enthusiastic about using CASE. However, the operating units that had not participated in the project did not share that enthusiasm. Management has had to push them constantly to use the new technology by offering free CASE software, continually discussing CASE in the company newsletter, and even performing internal audits. Use of CASE does not spread of its own volition, this company learned.

Ronald Norman of San Diego State University studied one unsuccessful introduction of CASE [11] and discovered that the major cause of the failure was mixed messages from systems management. Management did not say what would happen to developers who *did not use* the system. Since the developers saw no repercussions from sticking with their old approaches, that is what they did. Therefore, Norman recommends that management adopt one of the following three approaches and stick with it. Either (1) stress training and benefits, (2) influence groups to accept the CASE system and change their attitude, or (3) coerce them by making its use mandatory. Each approach will work, but the staff is less likely to change if management jumps between the three and sends out mixed messages, says Norman.

Settle on a Development Methodology First. Every speaker at the conferences pointed out that the foundation for CASE tools is the system development methodology. If developers are not strictly following one methodology, automated tools will not help much. So all the user companies had to first get their developers to adhere to one approach. Once this happened, there was little problem getting the automated tools accepted, one speaker said.

View CASE as a Strategic Technology. Many of the speakers introduced CASE for competitive reasons. Some said they could build complex mission-critical systems only by using an automated approach. Others saw no other way to cut development time by 50 percent—which was what they believed they needed to stay competitive. Others said they needed to change systems quickly. Still others saw CASE as eventually solving their huge development backlog and maintenance problems because development components can be so heavily reused.

Treat CASE as a Development Project Itself. Since the introduction of CASE is a major undertaking, it should be treated like any other major system project. Vaughan Merlyn, of the Ernst & Young Center for Information Technology and Strategy [12], suggested starting with a group design session, treating the system department as the users to find out what they want. Let the system development managers design the application development architecture they want in, say, five years. Then review where the company is today, he suggested. These discussions will raise the important issues and get the participants to "buy into" the mission, which paves the way for selling CASE to others.

Create a Technical Support Group. With CASE, developers no longer use dumb terminals for development; they use PCs and workstations connected to LANs. They also use new, unfamiliar, and complex development tools and access a development repository. All this adds up to a complex development environment—an environment that needs technical specialists to support it. The CASE support team generally consists of LAN technicians who keep the machines up and running; methodology and tools specialists who create the standards, train the developers, and act as technical consultants to the projects; and database experts who maintain the development repository.

Interestingly, once a company has created such a support staff of very technical people, their knowledge can be leveraged across a large number of projects of less knowledgeable developers. The CASE environment permits employing less technical programmers than traditional projects because the CASE tools handle the technical aspects; the programmers concentrate on the business functions in the system.

Do Not Wait for the Perfect Tools. Several industry observers noted that many companies cannot decide which CASE tools to buy, so they wait. The advice of all the speakers was: "Get on with it." Pick a tool or an approach and try it out. Since CASE products will evolve, the optimal tool probably is not available yet. But the foundation—the development methodology—can be laid. The longer companies wait, the further they fall behind, several speakers said.

There is no question that companies began joining the CASE bandwagon in the late 1980s, especially when they had huge, complex systems that defied traditional management methods. Today, it has become common knowledge that CASE is mandatory for developing the devilishly complex client/server systems. This will continue to be the case through the 1990s for companies that opt for the evolutionary approach represented by the CASE technology.

The revolutionary approach represented by object-oriented technology received much publicity in the late 1980s because it promised an even greater potential for companies to reduce significantly the massive maintenance burden they currently carry.

Object-Oriented Development

The revolution in business system development that occurred in the late 1980s was object-oriented development. Object-oriented programming languages had been used in computer science research labs since the 1960s. Then object-oriented development languages and tools moved into PC system development where they became the mainstay, especially for developing graphical user interfaces. By the late 1980s, object orientation was beginning to be noticed for business system development. That trickle became a tidal wave when client/server systems appeared in the early 1990s, as developers attempted to simplify the extreme complexity of client/server systems by reusing objects. In the early 1990s, object-oriented system analysis and design techniques began to appear, to be used in conjunction with the object-oriented languages, such as C++ and Smalltalk.

Object-oriented development differs from traditional development in several ways. These are listed in Figure 9-4.

What Is an Object? Brad Cox [13], one of the pioneers in the field, points out that object-oriented programming is not so much a coding technique as a code packaging technique. It packages functions with data so that the two can be reused. These reusable components are called "classes." At run time, each class can produce instances called "objects." Objects hold all the code and data in an object-oriented system, says Cox.

- Object-oriented development creates a new type of system: a model of the business. When an object-oriented system runs, it simulates that business. This is conceptually different from the traditional view of separate data and processes.

- Developers and users communicate with one another using business terms— such as accounts, customers, statements, and so forth—rather than using technical terms.

- Object orientation does not separate code and data as in conventional systems; both are bundled together in objects.

- The data is active, not passive, in that the data (in objects) knows how to perform work on itself. In traditional programs, the program is active and the data is passive.

- The inherent characteristics of object-oriented languages practically mandate reusing existing components, unlike conventional development where reuse is optional.

- New development is just like maintenance; both reuse existing components to create new functions.

Figure 9-4 The Ways Object-Oriented Development Differs from Traditional Development

Figure 9-5 An Object

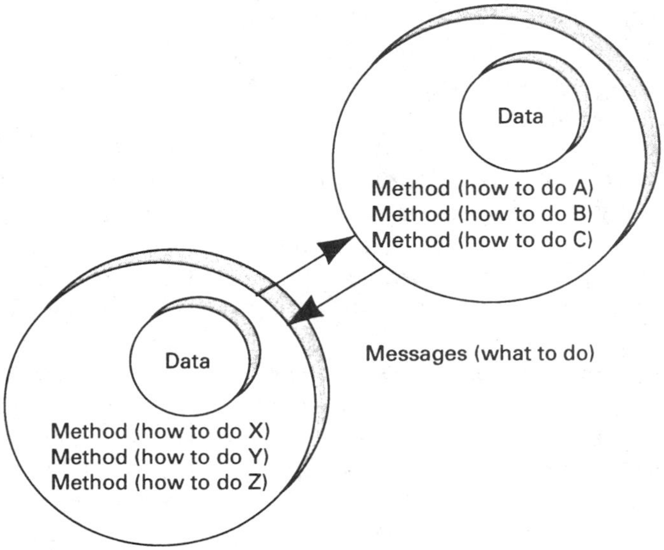

Objects. As shown in Figure 9-5, each object is some private data and a set of operations (called "methods") that can access that data. An object performs one of its operations when it receives a message. The object responds by first choosing the operation that implements the message request, then executing this operation, and finally returning the results to the requestor. An object's data is private; it cannot be manipulated by other objects.

Combining data and procedures in an object—*encapsulation*—is the foundation of object orientation. It restricts the effects of changes by placing a wall of code around each piece of data. All accesses to the data are through messages that only specify what should be done—the object chooses how its operations are performed. A change in one part of the system need not affect the rest of the system but can be dealt with inside the part directly affected. Thus, encapsulation helps produce software that is far more tolerant of change. Furthermore, object-oriented systems separate the "what to do" in the messages from the "how to do it" in the methods, as shown in Figure 9-5. This separation is one of the keys to permitting reuse.

Classes. Objects are organized into classes and instances. The concepts of class and instance will be familiar, says Cox. "Betsy is a cow" is just a short way of saying "Betsy is an *instance* of the *class* cow." Betsy is a cow, but Betsy is also Betsy, the individual. She is like other cows in most ways; yet different in the ways that set her apart from the herd. Classes are arranged in hierarchies shaped like trees, says Cox. Specific classes, such as Holstein, are at the branches; intermediate classes, such as cow or mammal, are at the trunk; and generic classes, like vertebrate or animal, are near the root. Such hierarchies allow a wealth of information to be derived about any given instance. By knowing that Betsy is a cow, one can immediately conclude that she eats grass, is warm blooded, feeds her young on milk, and so on. This class hierarchy, a simple technique for organizing facts used in object-oriented programming, permits inheritance.

Allowing classes of objects to inherit characteristics from other classes of objects—*inheritance*—is an innovative aspect of object-oriented systems not provided by conventional languages. Inheritance allows automatically broadcasting traits, attributes, and code. Programmers do not start each module with a blank page but instead reuse classes already in the library, modifying them by describing how the new class differs from the one in the library.

Inheritance permits defining new software in the same way we introduce a concept to a newcomer—by comparing it with something that is already familiar. Inheritance links concepts into a related whole, so that as a higher-level concept changes, the change is automatically applied throughout. It provides enormous simplification because it reduces the number of things that must be specified and remembered.

The appeal of these ideas is the possibility that the software industry might obtain some of the benefits that the silicon chip brought to the hardware industry: namely, the ability of a supplier to deliver a tightly encapsulated unit of functionality to be specialized for its intended function, yet independent of any particular application.

Object-oriented development is most important in three types of applications.

- Graphical applications. Inheritance provides consistent behavior among objects, which is important in providing easy-to-remember user interfaces.
- Multimedia applications. No other database management technique can handle a variety of data, such as voice, data, images, text.
- Complex systems. Objects manage complexity better by reducing the dependencies among functions.

Object-oriented development is the reigning standard in the PC and workstation world because it significantly eases development of the graphical user interfaces. Developers just point and click at generic items— menus, dialog boxes, radio buttons, and other components of graphical displays—and then rearrange them to create a screen. This form of programming is becoming known as "visual programming."

Although object-oriented development promises significant benefits, there are also costs, especially at the outset. Initial object-oriented projects can frustrate project managers and users, because the developers spend much time defining and redefining classes and class hierarchies. The initial projects also require more effort than if done conventionally. But thereafter, projects can take less effort, if the classes are reused.

Object-oriented development is primarily entering the business world by way of client/server systems, but it has occasionally been used in mainframe development. One pioneer was Brooklyn Union Gas, which contracted with Andersen Consulting to build the utility's mainline customer information system using object-oriented techniques. For more on this use, see *CLOSE-UP: Brooklyn Union Gas* and *Trends in Information Technology,* both from Andersen Consulting [14].

CASE EXAMPLE: Brooklyn Union Gas

Brooklyn Union Gas provides natural gas for some 1.1 million customers in the New York City area. In 1986, their thirteen-year-old crucial customer information system had become so inflexible that it was inhibiting the company from adding new kinds of marketing-driven services, and from meeting new regulatory requirements. The straw that broke the system's back was a mandate to generate plain-language, graphical customer bills. The system could not be extended to print those bills. In short, this heart-of-the-business system was preventing the utility from responding to change.

Management Issues Behind the New System. Management considered various approaches to updating the system. Replacing individual functional components was deemed too prohibitively expensive and risky; therefore, the company had to replace the system entirely. In directing their information system division to proceed, management made it clear that the utility should never be placed in that untenable situation again, where it would have to replace the entire mainline system all at once. The new system had to allow piecemeal upgrades.

After weighing the alternatives, systems management chose object-oriented development, believing this state-of-the-art technology would provide the most stable, yet flexible, base for gracefully absorbing significant technical and business changes over the next 20 years. This stability and flexibility would come from the use of objects, which are based on data and are therefore inherently more stable than processes. The utility would always have customers, meters, and bills, even though the processes surrounding these items might change. Furthermore, the objects would be discrete pieces that could be changed without affecting each other.

The new system was to perform 70 to 80 percent of the same functions as the former customer information system. To cost-justify the investment, Brooklyn Union treated it as an asset—one that could be depreciated just as they depreciate their four thousand miles of pipe. On average over the 1980s, the utility replaced twelve miles of pipe each year at an annual cost of $18 million. In the same way, the new system will require regular "parts replacements" to accommodate the technological changes expected through the year 2010.

The project was truly pioneering. No other organization in the world had created a mainframe-based object-oriented system of this size—10,000 program modules, 400 on-line programs, 118 batch programs, 150 on-line dialogues, and 1,000 business functions. The system was to handle 10 messages a second during peak hours, and generate 40,000 bills, 80,000 credit activities, and 250 reports each night. The system, which was used by 80 percent of Brooklyn Union's employees, had to work. To reduce the risk of the undertaking, the utility froze many of the other variables. They stayed with their familiar language, PL/1, extending it with object-oriented concepts. They also stayed with the mainframe platform because of its stability and its well-understood performance characteristics. Eventually, the utility intends to move the system to a workstation environment.

Building the New Customer Information System. The project began in 1986 and culminated in January 1990; it was a joint effort between the Brooklyn Union and Andersen Consulting. The project began with development of a data model, which was important to their successful use of object-oriented development because the objects would be based on these defined data elements—customer, billing account, meter, and so forth. In 1986, systems management spent three full months exploring object orientation including creating a sample program to demonstrate the technology. Developers were gradually introduced to the new concepts by initially concentrating on using functional decomposition to define "function managers"—programs that coordinate the work of objects. Then the developers moved on to defining objects to perform those functions.

To package the objects to achieve long life, the system is divided into three layers, as shown in Figure 9-6. The user interface layer connects the system to the outside world. This layer is most subject to change, because as new technologies arrive—such as workstations and handheld devices—they will be added via this layer. In fact, these new technologies will be able to draw on the same code in the other two layers. The second layer is the function layer, which defines business functions, such as "apply a payment." The 10 to 20 business steps performed in each function are coordinated by the "function manager." Once invoked, a function manager delegates its work to objects by sending them messages in the proper sequence. The third layer is the object layer, which contains both business function objects and data objects.

Benefits of the New System. Brooklyn Union is receiving a number of benefits from its pioneering use of object orientation in the mainframe world. The new system is smaller, even though it handles more functions. The old system had 1.5 million lines of code; the new one is 40 percent smaller with 900,000, because the batch and on-line programs use the same code, eliminating redundancy. The system is also easier to maintain. Since going into production, several enhancements have been made, with a dramatic reduction in the amount of new code that has had to be rewritten. One example involved developing a new on-line dialogue to correct service-order discrepancies. The change required two thousand new lines of code, but, in reality, the function draws on forty thousand lines of code—a twenty-to-one gain over traditional maintenance. Maintenance is also easier because it is just like new development; both reuse objects to create new functions. The result is that creating a new function in the system now takes no longer than resolving the business problem—a significant advance for the utility.

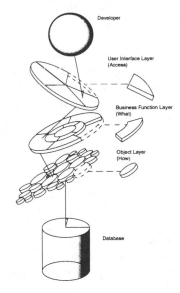

Figure 9-6 The Three Layers of
Brooklyn Union Gas' Object-Oriented System
(from Anderson Consulting [13])

Figure 9-6 The Three Layers of Brooklyn Union Gas' Object-Oriented System
(from Andersen Consulting [14])

THE EARLY 1990s

The beginning of the 1990s saw broader use of both CASE and object-oriented techniques. As happened with 4GLs and prototyping, the best parts of each are likely to meld to form new system development approaches in the late 1990s. Here is a brief recap of the main points of the system development history presented in this chapter, to give a prelude to the future.

The system development field achieved discipline through structured development in the 1960s and 1970s. In the late 1970s, the field turned toward ease of use, with the advent of 4GLs and prototyping. These two approaches made development of smaller systems cost-justifiable. In the 1980s, CASE and object-oriented techniques aimed to simplify development, both of huge corporate systems as well as small personal systems. In the 1990s, we believe system development is turning yet another page in its history—flexible systems. Of course this is not really a new goal, but it is made more achievable by the progress to date.

The Drive for Flexibility

Information system flexibility means different things to different people. Here are several viewpoints on flexibility.

The business view of system flexibility is being able to adapt information systems in concert with corporate changes. Information systems have cast specific ways of doing business in concrete, not allowing a company to change its operating procedures or move into new lines of business as quickly as management would like. These inflexible mainline systems are a liability to an organization's ability to compete. Thus, we see system *adaptability* to the changing business environment as the most important definition of system flexibility.

The user view of flexibility means both intuitive and tailorable user interfaces. Users want applications that have an intuitive "look and feel," where the correct way to perform an action is obvious. Currently, intuitiveness is being achieved through the use of consistent commands and screen layouts. The WIMP interface—meaning, windows, icons, mouse, and pull-down menus—has become the most popular graphical interface. As the power of workstations increases, voice and handwriting interfaces may make computer applications even easier to use. Users also want to be able to tailor their interface to suit themselves—adapting it to their work style and reducing the number of commands or procedures they need to remember.

From the information systems department view, flexibility means several things. One is *portability*—being able to move applications among machines or operating systems. UNIX has become an important operating system in business computing because it provides portability among workstations, minis, and mainframes. Flexibility also means *maintainability*. A new attitude began emerging in the late 1980s toward maintenance. The previous view had seen existing systems as sunk costs—their investment could not be recovered. The new view sees existing systems as valuable assets that can be reengineered to preserve their knowledge of how the firm operates and to incorporate new ways of working.

Although CASE and object-oriented development increase flexibility, perhaps even more innovation is needed. That is the subject we discuss next.

Building Open Applications

We recently learned of an approach to system development aimed at building flexible systems. It is also revolutionary in that it is truly a paradigm shift from traditional methods. The product, HOLO, draws together object orientation and expert system technology into a unique model to achieve independence between data, logic, and processes. HOLO was developed by Miles Burke [15] over the past twenty years and appeared on the market in the early 1980s.

Burke's goal was to create a system design methodology for developing "open applications," which he defines as applications that are platform independent, easily changed, and fully integrated with (not just linked to) other applications. HOLO can generate COBOL programs to run under mainframe relational and nonrelational DBMS, or UNIX programs for a client/server environment.

Burke has three even more unbelievable goals.

1. Reduce the size and complexity of large systems *by orders of magnitude.*
2. *Dramatically* speed up development.
3. Reuse data and logic *across all applications* in an organization.

Interestingly, HOLO seems to be accomplishing all three. As just one example, the basic elements in one HOLO application type can indeed be reused across the following wide range of applications: production scheduling, order entry, employee benefits management, and credit card processing, to name a few.

Burke sees applications as having three parts: information, functions, and processes. Information is captured in *theme databases*. Functions, that is, the logic of the system, are captured in *focused logic units*, which address an object at a time. And processes, that is, the business policies that direct the system's processing, are captured in *business factors* in expert system rules. All three components are encompassed in the HOLO model.

Since HOLO contains new concepts, it has its own vocabulary. We will describe the following four major components of HOLO, defining a few of the terms along the way:

- Model-driven architecture
- Theme databases
- Object-oriented structure
- Rules-driven processing

Figure 9-7 The HOLO Model

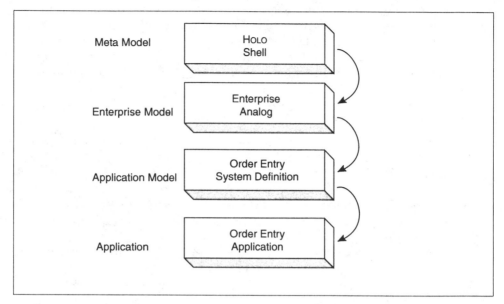

Model-Driven Architecture

HOLO is implemented as a model, and the applications built with HOLO are driven by that model. The generic elements in HOLO are housed in the HOLO model and are used to satisfy the specific data, logic, and processes of a business via an application. Creating a new application involves creating an instance of a generic theme based on the users' requirements. The resulting model (application) is independent of the company and its organizational structure; therefore, it can be restructured as quickly as the decision rules describing the company's procedures can be restated.

HOLO is actually a hierarchy of models arranged in four layers, as shown in Figure 9-7.

- Enterprise model
- Application model
- Application instance

Meta Model. This top layer holds all the generic rules about the HOLO method and enforces those rules so that an enterprise model and its resulting applications are consistent and act consistently.

Enterprise Model. HOLO generates application programs from this second layer so that the only manual activity in building a HOLO-based application is design. Maintenance, too, only involves design. There is no manual coding in HOLO. Furthermore, there is no need to translate information between development stages as in traditional development. All use the same modeling technique. The enterprise model itself has four levels, as shown in Figure 9-8.

FIGURE 9-8 The Enterprise Model

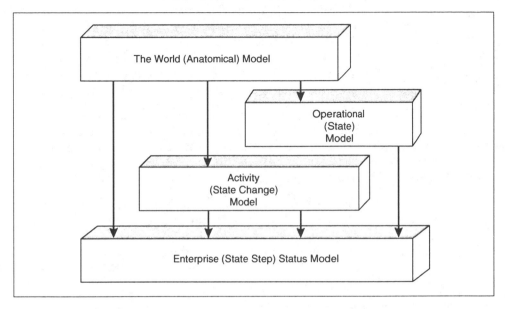

The top level of the four-level enterprise model is the world (or anatomical) model. It contains the anatomy of the business in four realms—people, places, things, and activities. "Because you are in business, you have these four things," says Burke, "and associated with these four realms are a set of generic themes." Each theme has a specific purpose and a specific set of attributes. For example, the demand theme has a consumer, bill payer, supplier—three roles that a person can play—along with data about what is in demand, quantity, required date required, and so forth. Places, things, and activities have their own set of attributes and behaviors. So when an element is defined in one of the four realms, the HOLO enterprise model knows all its potential characteristics. This depth makes each element definition very rich in meaning.

The second level of the enterprise model, called the operational (or state) model, is derived from the first level. This operational model describes how the various elements interact within the business. "Because you do business, you do these things," says Burke, "such as order entry, payroll, accounts receivable, inventory management, and so forth. HOLO represents these business transactions by separating information, functions, and processes, as we discuss shortly.

This second layer uses the basic objects of the business identified in the anatomical model to capture the operational data of the business in the form of operational records, called state themes.

Together, these top two layers of the enterprise model can be viewed as a prebuilt map of the entire business world. As impossible as this sounds,

HOLO is able to incorporate most business activities into a small set of elements, because it works at such a generic level. Therefore, at this level, HOLO can describe any system—or even all the activities in any company—using the four realms and the state themes. In fact, nothing in an enterprise needs to be outside the system. New functions can be added without requiring a new or different system. They become integrated into the existing system, precluding the traditional need for interfaces between applications.

The third level in the enterprise model is the activity (or state change) model, which captures changes in the specific instances of the state themes. For instance, as a piece of work goes through a sequence of processing steps, its "state" changes with each step; these changes are recorded in this state change level of the enterprise model.

The fourth level is the enterprise status model, which is one view of a situation at a point in time. A profit and loss statement is such a status model, as is a list of outstanding orders. These views are obtained by drawing data from the three higher layers in the enterprise model.

So the entire enterprise model defines the business in a form that can be used to define the application.

Application Models. This third level of HOLO is created from the enterprise model. An application model is an instance of the enterprise model and describes the specifics of the application.

Application. Finally, the fourth model in HOLO is the application itself. It is created by executing the application model through the Orchestrator, which orchestrates application execution.

Theme Databases

One of the most intriguing concepts in HOLO is themes, of which there are several types. The four realms in the anatomical model are called themes. The person theme is *associate,* which is a person who can play any number of roles, such as supplier, customer, employee, bill payer, and so on. The place theme is called *location,* the thing theme is called *item,* and the event theme is called *activity.*

The operation state level contains state themes. One is *demand,* which Burke defines as "someone wants something." A second is *asset* which is a valued item, and a third is *inventory,* which is a count of items in locations. Burke has defined seven state themes. These themes are so generic that they span systems that appear to be very different, but, in actuality, are not. For instance, demand-type systems include human resources processing, order entry, shop floor scheduling, complaint handling, purchasing, and credit card processing. In each one, somebody wants something.

Each theme contains an *estate*—its basic behaviors. Therefore, if a system is defined as a demand-type system, HOLO developers know that certain behaviors must be defined, such as, who wants something (demand identification), what is wanted (demand item), how much (quantity), when (dates), who will use it (demand consumer), who will supply it (supplier), price, and so forth.

The HOLO model contains the design template for each theme within its enterprise model; so systems can be built quickly by just defining the specifics of the company in a theme database, defining the application logic in focused logic units, and specifying the rules of the business in business factors. The HOLO Orchestrator draws on these elements to yield a functioning application.

Object-Oriented Structure

HOLO implements the enterprise model using object-oriented principles. Each element in the model is implemented as an object, with one type of data and one *focused logic unit*. As its name connotes, a focused logic unit contains the logic to process one type of data. These units are like the methods that surround data in object-oriented systems. A demand-type object might be a purchase order, customer order, or maintenance order. Each of these objects is responsible for managing *all* the uses of it. Therefore, there is only one place where its use can be initiated, and one place where its changes need to be made.

Rules-Driven Processing

All decisions in an application program exist because of a business policy, elective options, or resource contraint. These decisions are called business factors in HOLO. The decisions are formally managed objects. Logic in an application consists of processing sequence control and business factors. Processing sequence in HOLO is controlled by the Orchestrator using business factors and process definitions. This separation is a key reason why HOLO-based systems can be easily restructured. Only the business factors need to be changed; the logic stays the same. The result is simpler and more flexible systems.

The business factors in a system are initially written by the development team. But once the system is in production, the users can perform most of the system maintenance, which involves just reconfiguring the rules or adding new ones.

HOLO Yields Flexible Systems

Another way to look at the HOLO architecture is in terms of the famous three-level architecture created in the 1960s, and, to date, applied only to data; see Chapter 7. In this architecture, the conceptual level (the middle level) is the most generic, enterprise level. The logical level is a portion of the enterprise level, such as one application's view. And the physical level is the implementation of an application view. The importance of this structure is the middle level, which acts as a buffer between the other two. Either of them can change without affecting the other.

HOLO parallels this three-level structure in its data. The conceptual level is the theme databases. The logical views are the data fields displayed on the screen in applications. And the physical level is the data definition language used to implement those data elements. This separation of *data* is not unique to HOLO; many modeling approaches separate data this way.

However, other system development approaches do not separate *logic* in this manner; HOLO does. At the conceptual level are the focused logic units, which contain the logic for an attribute (a field), independent of specific applications. There is one focused logic unit for each kind of object. The logical process level is handled by the Orchestrator, which relies on business factors and current states to sequence the execution of the generic logic units. This distinction is missing in all the other development approaches we have seen. Finally, the physical level is the code matched to information objects.

HOLO achieves flexibility by separating the "what to do" (processing sequence) from the "how to do it" (function logic). The benefit is that large systems can have much simpler structures, and maintenance involves only changing the business rules, not the function logic. For example, if the company decides to give certain customers discounts during a special promotion, the system only needs one generic function to perform the new calculation and a new business rule to specify which customers are eligible for the promotion. The result is an elegant, simple structure, with the most generic information and logic at the top of the model and the most company specific at the bottom.

One of the drawbacks of information engineering projects has been that they never seem to finish. Companies can define data forever. With HOLO, this does not happen, because the templates are finite and very specific. Therefore, developers know the boundaries of a project and the amount of work to be done before they start. This attribute turns large projects into smaller ones, and even integrates different applications as a by-product, just by extending existing models to include new functions. HOLO applies an engineering discipline to system development by providing standard, generic pieces for applications, along with a way to assemble them. Not only can radical changes be made faster, but complex systems can be built that other approaches cannot accomplish, as several HOLO users have demonstrated. Finally, systems can be structured in any manner, with the pieces located anywhere and integrated without relying on programmed interfaces.

HOLO appears to us to demonstrate a major step forward in building more flexible systems—toward simplifying systems, shortening development time, and reducing maintenance. To illustrate how HOLO is being used, consider Owens-Corning Fiberglass.

CASE EXAMPLE: Owens-Corning Fiberglas

Owens-Corning Fiberglas (OCF), with headquarters in Toledo, Ohio, is the world's leading manufacturer of fiber glass materials and a major producer of polyester resins. The products are manufactured in two basic forms: textile filaments that are combined into strands, yarns, and mats to reinforce plastic, rubber, and paper products; and wool-like materials for thermal and acoustical insulation.

OCF has two main divisions. The Industrial Materials Group (IMG) manufactures yarns, resins, and reinforcements used as substitutes for steel, wood, and aluminum. The Construction Products Group (CPG) manufactures insulation and roofing for residences, commercial construction, home repair, and commercial renovation.

Each group has its own I/S staff. IMG has twenty-two people who develop applications, provide end user support, and manage contractors and systems integrators. Systems management encourages use of third parties and software packages, which keeps staff count low. The CPG systems department, with forty people, has a similar scope as the IMG group.

The corporate I/S department has two major groups.

- Corporate systems development, with forty people, is responsible for systems development and maintenance of systems for finance, purchasing, human resources, legal and safety and environment.
- Information technology, with sixty people, manages and operates corporate-wide computing and telecommunications services.

Rethinking System Development

In 1987, the directors of the three systems departments, together with the director of the corporate information technology group, chartered a "CASE" team to identify ways to improve application development significantly. After analyzing the existing portfolio, the team realized that the kinds of applications and databases produced by the traditional development process had to change. The team therefore created a "principles-based application and data architecture," where one of the key principles was reuse. Reuse was to be the lever for significantly improving development and supporting the corporation's objectives of quality, teamwork, and responsiveness.

With this understanding, the team refocused its CASE evaluation away from tools and toward a methodology that could create application and data components that would be massively reusable.

During the ensuing search, OCF evaluated HOLO, but it was bundled with a mainframe toolset and produced IMS database designs—technologies OCF did not want to employ. The team therefore acquired an integrated CASE toolset. Two years later, the CASE tool had paid for itself by increasing productivity by 15 to 25 percent. It had reduced the technical aspects of design and programming, it provided good team communication features, and it was self-documenting. But it did not produce the kinds of design differences needed to achieve the 300 to 500 percent improvement in system development that OCF wanted. So the company reassessed the marketplace.

Again, HOLO appeared to be the best choice. This time, Miles Burke was amenable to porting the HOLO generator to an open systems format, so OCF urged him to work with Hewlett-Packard. That joint effort came to fruition in May 1992 with the delivery of a UNIX-based HOLO toolset and generator.

In the meantime, IMG management had spent a year creating a strategic master plan. What began as simply an assessment of the information systems grew into a study of how the entire division needed to reengineer itself. One finding of this study was the need for a common IT infrastructure. At the time, the manufacturing plants had different systems. Two crucial pieces of the infrastructure were group-wide customer and product databases.

But the more challenging issue facing IMG's I/S department was meeting top management's mandates to improve system quality while operating with *a level budget for the foreseeable future.* Systems management knew these demands could not be met using the current development approach, because it required "leaving a soldier behind" to maintain each system. This army of maintainers was eating up the department's budget. That traditional path would lead to their becoming a maintenance-only department by 1995. Even purchased packages had this drawback. Systems management could see only one way to thrive with a continually flat budget: aim for near-zero maintenance.

Introducing HOLO

OCF likes HOLO because it has the attributes originally identified by the CASE task force. It emphasizes reuse and separates process, logic, and data. It promises to reduce development costs and improve quality concurrently. Most important, HOLO promises to reduce maintenance significantly by allowing users to rework existing decision rules to change a system. OCF expects maintenance to become one-tenth its former size on HOLO-based applications. HOLO will also allow OCF to build common core applications that can be easily tailored to suit local needs, without destroying the underlying commonality. This flexibility will be a competitive advantage, they believe.

Originally, OCF considered implementing HOLO company-wide. IMG was amenable to this plan because the division desperately needed to redeploy many of the core systems in the new master plan. CPG, on the other hand, had just rewritten their major systems, so a new methodology would not immediately benefit them. Therefore, OCF decided to pilot-test HOLO in IMG, with help from the corporate I/S department. Corporate I/S management wanted to foster company-wide adoption as well as establish corporate-wide data standards. This incremental approach is giving management time to become comfortable with HOLO's viability before deciding whether to make it the company's standard development methodology.

OCF reduced the risk of using the unconventional HOLO approach by starting with two pilot projects. At their conclusion is a go/no-go decision point. They further reduced risk by initially generating familiar COBOL, by working side by side with Miles Burke employees on the pilots, and by instituting check points at various stages in the contract.

The Pilot Projects

The first pilot project created a database front-end to feed two existing, crucial databases: customer (of which IMG has two thousand) and product (of which there are eight thousand). The goal was to achieve commonality across manufacturing sites yet maintain the flexibility to accommodate differences among the plants. The pilot involved creating databases as well as writing functional logic and business rules.

To develop the customer database front-end, OCF staff, along with four Miles Burke employees, built two HOLO anatomical databases: associate (which describes people in the customer role) and location (which describes where those customers are located). When combined, these two databases contain all the fields in the IMG customer database. The product configuration management system was then built using those two databases plus a third—item (which describes the products).

The second project reengineered a business process—transportation—which handles the shipping of customer orders via third-party trucking companies. Due to complex rates, arranging the transportation and paying the carriers has been complicated and riddled with paperwork and inefficiencies. Therefore, OCF decided to simplify the process by contracting with just a few carriers and negotiating fewer rates. The trucking companies are notified of pending shipments and have agreed to accept or reject the offered loads in forty-eight hours. They are then paid on delivery rather than after submitting an invoice.

To build the transportation system, IMG used the three new anatomical databases and added one theme—deliverable (which, in this CASE, describes the shipping activity).

Using HOLO

Populating HOLO databases follows the same requirements analysis steps as traditional development. But rather than enter data elements into a data flow diagram or entity-relationship diagrams, they are placed into the appropriate parts of the HOLO anatomy and theme database model.

The corporate systems group placed a data modeler, analyst, manager, and developer on the pilot project. They interviewed users on data requirements and then mapped those requirements into the HOLO model using the Maxthink outlining package. This textual model then was used to populate a relational database. User transactions were built by designing the screens using the data elements from the appropriate databases. The function logic and business rules were created using the workbench tools from Miles Burke.

OCF found that creating the customer and product applications took roughly the same amount of time as using traditional methods. The transportation project, on the other hand, was able to reuse many of the components, so effort was about 25 percent less. Initial planning for future projects indicates that this reuse benefit will approach 50 percent as more components become available for reuse.

OCF has further discovered that use of HOLO does not impact interfacing the new applications to existing ones. Since interfaces represent more than 50 percent of the development effort (and significant maintenance), OCF is sequencing the HOLO projects to minimize interfaces.

A chief benefit of HOLO has been that the developers did not start with a blank sheet of paper. In fact, they did not even start with just a template, because the HOLO shell contains predefined and coded meanings, attributes, and relationships. Much of the development work is already done; therefore, OCF estimates that their developers will eventually do only 65 percent of the work required in traditional development. The HOLO work also proceeds much faster. To date, most of the milestones have been accomplished ahead of schedule. The more components OCF builds in HOLO, the more can be reused, and the less new work is needed. The real benefit, however, is that HOLO systems require practically no maintenance.

Planning for the Future

While one group worked on the pilots, another designed OCF's target distributed computing environment. It uses the OSF open systems standards and a relational DBMS running on the H-P UNIX platform. Manufacturing sites will continue to use their H-P 3000 and 9000 mini-computers connected via LANs.

In the pilot projects, OCF implemented HOLO on an OS/2 server to verify the concept, and then ported the applications to a UNIX server. Microsoft Windows is the interface providing access to the UNIX applications and databases services. By year end 1992, OCF was scheduled to implement a distributed, on-line transaction processing capability, allowing the HOLO applications and databases to be dispersed across OCF's worldwide network—a significant achievement in a short time.

CONCLUSION

The traditional approach to system development from the 1960s evolved to give the process more discipline, control, and efficiency. It was valuable in moving programming and system analysis from pure free-form "art" to a better defined "craft." Problems remained, however, with long development times, difficult user involvement, and lack of flexibility in the resulting systems.

In the late 1970s, data-driven development and group design sessions stressed improving the early phases in development to catch problems early. Then, in the early 1980s, 4GLs and software prototyping permitted more rapid development, and even experimental development, and were thus seen as revolutionary techniques to conventional developers.

In the late 1980s, two more important trends influenced system development—CASE and object-oriented development. The first one represented the evolutionary viewpoint of automating the tried-and-true structured development techniques. The second one was revolutionary, yet built on traditional system design tenets, such as hiding information from others to localize the effect of system changes.

A promising technique for the 1990s, HOLO, is merging several past principles to permit developing highly portable, flexible systems. Perhaps it represents a major new tack for system development.

QUESTIONS AND EXERCISES

REVIEW QUESTIONS

1. What are the goals of the traditional system development life cycle approach?
2. Refer to the list of features and functions of 4GLS in Figure 9-3 Briefly explain each.
3. What are the problems of "little databases" and "personal programs"? How do 4GLS help or hinder in dealing with these problems?
4. What are the main characteristics of the prototyping approach?
5. Describe the main points of Santa Fe Railroad's use of Mapper.
6. What is the programming controversy that continues today?
7. Define the components of a CASE system.
8. What is unique about Du Pont Cable Management Service's use of CASE?
9. What are seven lessons learned about CASE?
10. How does object-oriented development differ from traditional development?
11. Describe an "object."
12. Why did Brooklyn Union Gas choose object-oriented development?
13. Describe three views of system flexibility.
14. What are the four main components of HOLO?
15. Describe the main points of Owens-Corning Fiberglas' use of HOLO?

DISCUSSION QUESTION

1. Some say companies will make the greatest strides be taking the evolutionary approach to system development—automating traditional approaches. Others say the revolutionary approach is best—using entire new approaches. Which side do you take, and why?

EXERCISES

1. Find a detailed description of a CASE toolset. Possible sources include a reference service, vendor literature or brochures, and articles in publications. What features does it have? How do the features fit into the four components listed in the chapter?
2. Visit a company in your community that has an information systems department with at least five professionals. Prepare a short CASE description to summarize the company's current approach to developing systems. Does it have one standard approach or a combination of several? Is the standard approach close to the structured approach? Develop a flowchart or diagram to depict the standard approach.

3. Find four articles on object-oriented systems. What are the benefits listed for those systems?

4. Present a scenario of what you think system development will be like in leading-edge firms in five years. What will change? What will not change?

REFERENCES

1. CANNING, R. G., *Electronic Data Processing for Business and Industry*; and Installing Electronic Data Processing Systems, (John Wiley & Sons, New York), 1956 and 1957.

2. COUGER, J. D., M. A. COLTER, and R. W. KNAPP, *Advanced System Development/Feasibility* Techniques (John Wiley & Sons, New York), 1982.

3. BOEHM, B., *Software Engineering Economics* (Prentice-Hall, Englewood Cliffs, NJ), 1981.

4. ENGER, N. L., "Classical and Structured Systems Life Cycle Phases and Documentation," in *System Analysis and Design: A Foundation for the 1980s*, edited by Cotterman, W. M., J. D. Couger, N. L. Enger, and F. Harold (Elsevier North Holland, New York, NY), 1981, pp. 1-24.

5. RICH, M., PFS Inc., 731 Bayonne St., El Segundo, CA 90245.

6. NAUMANN, J. D., and A. M. JENKINS, "Prototyping: The New Paradigm for Systems Development," *MIS Quarterly*, September 1982, pp. 29-44.

7. DIGITAL CONSULTING, Inc., 6 Windsor St., Andover, MA 01810.

8. CARMA MCCLURE, Extended Intelligence, Inc., 25 E. Washington Blvd., Chicago, IL 60602.

9. DU PONT INFORMATION ENGINEERING ASSOCIATES, Nemours Building, 9th Floor, Wilmington, DE 19898.

10. CORTEX CORPORATION, 138 Technology Dr., Waltham, MA 02154.

11. NORMAN, R. J., G. F. CORBITT, M. C. Butler, and D. D. McElroy, "CASE Technology Transfer: A CASE Study of Unsuccessful Change," *Journal of Systems Management*, May 1989, pp. 33-37.

12. VAUGHAN MERLYN, Ernst & Young Center for Information Technology and Strategy, One Walnut St., Boston, MA 02108.

13. COX, B., *Object Oriented Programming: An Evolutionary Approach* (Addison Wesley Publishers, Reading, MA) ,1987.

14. *CLOSE-UP: BROOKLYN UNION GAS* and *TRENDS IN INFORMATION TECHNOLOGY* (Andersen Consulting, Chicago, IL), 1991.

15. MILES BURKE AND ASSOCIATES, 7631 E. Greenway Rd., Suite 4, Scottsdale, AZ 85260.

TEN

Management Issues in System Development

INTRODUCTION

System development has been, and continues to be, one of the largest information systems jobs in organizations, whether it is performed by the centralized systems department, an outsourcing vendor, or within a functional unit. As the spectrum of tools, development methodologies, languages, and staff has broadened, so too have the kinds of applications developed. This broadening of application types raises two measurement questions—measuring programmer productivity and estimating the benefits of systems. In addition, the more applications a company uses, the greater the need for building high-quality systems and improving "legacy" systems—the ten-to twenty-year-old systems. These and other system development issues confront information system executives daily. In this chapter we address the following four system development management questions:

1. How can programmer productivity be measured?
2. How can the benefits of systems be measured?
3. How can higher-quality systems be developed?
4. How can legacy systems be improved?

HOW CAN PROGRAMMER PRODUCTIVITY BE MEASURED?

Proving that programmer productivity has increased is difficult without before-and-after measurements. Since most organizations are busy creating and maintaining systems, they rarely measure their efforts effectively, although this has changed over the past few years. Lines of code have been the traditional (poor) measure. Some companies do not even measure lines of code; instead, they compare elapsed time or resource usage to demonstrate improved productivity. But with the current variety of languages and computing platforms, even that comparison does not work well. The foremost measurement approach today is function point analysis because it does allow comparisons among vastly different system development projects.

Function Point Analysis

Function point analysis was conceived by Allan Albrecht of IBM [1] in the mid-1970s and is based on a users' view of a system.

Function point analysis looks at five types of functions.

- *External inputs* are such things as input transactions from keyboards and other applications and locations that add or change data or control information in logical files.
- *External outputs* are paper reports, screen displays, control information, and transactions sent to other applications and locations.
- *External inquiries* are queries against a logical file that do not add, change, or delete data in any logical files.
- *Logical internal files* are data stored for an application.
- *External interface files* are data stored by another application but used by the application under study.

Albrecht classifies each function by its *level of complexity*—simple, average, or complex. Each function is then multiplied by its classification weight. Albrecht has determined the weights by "debate and trial." For example, an input of low complexity is multiplied by 3, an average one by 4, and a highly complex one by 6. Adding up all the weighted functions yields a total number of "unadjusted function points" for an application.

To "adjust" the function point total for uncounted functions, Albrecht uses fourteen characteristics of applications that can have a ± 35 percent impact on the complexity of the application as a whole (not the individual functions). If a characteristic is not present, or has no influence, Albrecht gives it a 0 value. If it has average influence on the application, it gets a value of 3. A strong influence throughout an application deserves a 5 rating—meaning that the application will be more complex and therefore more difficult to create.

Albrecht's fourteen application characteristics, in the form of questions, are listed in Figure 10-1.

Adding up the ratings assigned to these fourteen characteristics leads to the final adjusted total of function points. Once this total has been estimated, it can be used to estimate system size in terms of lines of code; or to determine development time, based on past studies of function point analysis by language; or to judge productivity improvements, based on past projects.

Using Conventional Languages. In a study of twenty-four projects that used either COBOL, PL/1, or DMS (IBM's data management system), Albrecht [1a] found that productivity per function point varied considerably, and that one function point was roughly equivalent to 120 lines of COBOL code. On these projects, productivity ranged from a low of two function points per work-month for two large COBOL projects to a high of fifty-two function points created in a month for a small DMS project. He believes the variations were due to the characteristics of the projects.

Figure 10-1 Application Characteristics for Function Point Analysis (from Albrecht) [1]

1. Does the application use data communications?
2. Are data or functions distributed?
3. Are there specific performance objectives that need to be met?
4. Will the application run on a heavily-used configuration, so that there are special design considerations needed?
5. Is the transaction rate of the application high?
6. Will there be online data entry?
7. Will the application be designed for end user efficiency?
8. Will there be online updating?
9. Is complex processing involved?
10. Is the application intended to be usable in other applications?
11. Are ease of conversion and installation important?
12. Is ease of operation important?
13. Will the application be used at multiple sites?
14. Is it being specifically designed to facilitate change?

Albrecht found that the amount of work-effort could be fairly accurately predicted, based on function points. As the number of function points increased, the amount of time to complete one function point increased by a predictable amount. Thus, complex systems took more time to design and develop per function point than did simpler systems.

Using Unisys's LINC. An important attribute of this measurement technique is that it can be used to compare projects that use different languages. Professor E. E. Rudolph did just that, by studying the differences between using a third and a fourth generation language [2]. Rudolph notes that medium-to large-size programs range from five hundred to (say) two thousand function points. Determining the number of function points in this size system takes from two to four hours, using either design documentation or source code.

In his study, Rudolph evaluated thirteen applications in six New Zealand organizations. Two of the applications were written in COBOL, the rest were written in LINC, a 4GL from Unisys. LINC generates COBOL source code, which made Rudolph's study even more interesting. He found that, on the average, fourteen lines of LINC code would generate one function point. Relating his work to the work of Albrecht and others, he further found that a COBOL programmer generally writes 114 lines of code to generate one function point (close to Albrecht's figure of 120 lines). PL/1 requires 62 lines of code.

The LINC projects averaged one work-hour to create each function point. In contrast, the average COBOL applications took about twenty hours per function point. That was surprising but not as surprising as how these figures changed as the projects grew larger. With LINC, productivity remained at about one function point per hour, no matter what the size of the project—one hundred function points up to two thousand functions points. But in COBOL or PL/1, the work-hours per function point increased as the size of the project grew (as Albrecht had pointed out). Large projects with, say, two thousand function points were averaging fifty hours per function point. The lowest figure Rudolph has ever seen for COBOL programming is ten hours of effort to create one function point.

Therefore, Rudolph believes that the "wild" claims made about 4GLs are not wild after all, even for typical data processing projects. The studies he has referenced include measurements of the entire development cycle, not just the coding portion.

HOW CAN SYSTEM BENEFITS BE MEASURED?

Cost-justification of information systems is on the minds of many executives these days, because expenditures have been increasing, salaries are higher, and results often have fallen quite short of promises. In a *Fortune* magazine article in the mid-1980s entitled "The Puny Payoffs from Office Computers" [3], Bowen noted that the business investment of hundreds of billions of dollars in office systems had not produced any discernible improvement in "white-collar" productivity. This perception persists today.

Bowen believed that office systems had boosted productivity, but simultaneously other factors were worked to decrease it. These factors included government-imposed paperwork, increased complexity of tax codes, more complex products, and so on. Investments in IT also might have been on applications with low payoffs, noted Bowen. Or companies might not have always made the best use of the technology because they did not change the way they worked when installing a new system. This allowed the existing poor work habits to persist, thereby reducing the beneficial impacts of the system. As noted in Chapter 3, this final argument has proved to be a real culprit in stealing productivity gains from new uses of IT.

However, another culprit is incorrect metrics. Companies have often measured the wrong things. There can be a marked difference between measuring efficiency (doing something right) and measuring effectiveness (doing the right thing). The largest payoffs from it lie in improving effectiveness, but most measurement techniques have focused on measuring increased efficiency. Thus, the real benefits have gone unmeasured.

Office systems and desktop systems are not the only systems that cause measurement problems. Decision support systems—which include executive information systems, management support systems, and expert systems—intend to change such "unmeasurable" actions as improved decisions, better identification of opportunities, more thorough analysis, and enhanced communication among people. Strategic systems, which aim to improve a firm's competitive edge or protect its market share, also elude measurement. It makes no sense to determine their return on investment (ROI) in terms of hours saved, because their intent is the totally different goal of increasing revenue. Finally, infrastructure investments, on which future applications of all kinds will be built, cannot be justified on ROI, because they have none. Only the subsequent applications will show a return on investment.

In their research for the special report *Uncovering the Information Technology Payoffs* [4], Walter Carlson and Barbara McNurlin uncovered the following four suggestions, as well as numerous others, on how to deal with these measurement dilemmas:

- Distinguish between the different roles of systems.
- Measure what is important to management.
- Use "anchor measures."
- Assess investments across organizational levels.

Distinguish between the Different Roles of Systems

Paul Berger [5], a management consultant, believes that companies can measure the value of IT investments by using many of the management measures now in place. Some of his ideas are found in *Measuring Business Value of Information Technologies* [6]. Information systems can play three roles in a company, Berger told Carlson and McNurlin. They can *help other departments do their job better.* Berger calls these "support systems." Their goal is to increase organizational efficiency.

Second, information systems can carry *out a business strategy.* Examples are CAD systems that customers and suppliers can use together to design custom products. Another example is electronic data interchange (EDI) where computers of suppliers or customers communicate directly with a firm's computers. ATMs are another example. These strategic systems are measured differently from support systems because they are used directly by customers, suppliers, and clients, says Berger; support systems are not.

Third, systems can be sold as *a product or service or as the basis for a product or service.* For example, offering a cash management account that combines a checking account, a cash management account, and an investment account would not be possible without the underlying information system. Another example is testing or design software that a company sells to another firm, says Berger.

Measuring the benefits of these three kinds of systems differs.

Measuring Organizational Performance. Organizational performance has to do with meeting deadlines and milestones, operating within budget, and doing quality work. Performance measures *efficiency* of operations, says Berger.

Several years ago, Berger worked on developing a large human resources system with decision support capabilities, and then tracking its benefits. To measure the value of the system, the development team compared the productivity of people who used it with the productivity of people who did not. Data was collected on the cost of operating the system and the total costs of running the human resources departments.

Operating costs did not rise as fast in the human resources departments where the system was used, the team found. In the base year, two departments had costs of $82 per work unit. "Cost of a work unit" was the annual cost to process one employee—including hiring, salary administration, benefits, counseling, overhead loading, and so on. At the end of that year, the system was installed in one of the departments. In the second year, the unit cost in the department using the system rose to $87; the cost in the nonusing department rose to $103. By the fifth year, the using department had a cost of $103 per work unit, whereas the nonusing department's cost was $128 per work unit. Following the fifth year, all human resources departments used the system, so no further comparisons could be made. But during those five years, the unit costs in the departments using the system rose about 25 percent; the nonusing department's costs rose more than 56 percent.

Measuring Business Value. Measuring business unit *performance* deals with internal operational goals, whereas measuring business *value* deals with marketplace goals. Systems that are part of a business plan can be measured on their contribution to the success or failure of that plan. But, for systems to be measured on their business value, they must have a *direct* impact on the company's relationships with its customers, clients, or suppliers, says Berger.

The system cited previously was measured on departmental performance. It could not be measured on business value, because its effect on the corporate bottom line was indirect. No direct link to increased revenue could be identified. This distinction is important in measuring the value of IT investments.

In another firm, several information systems were developed to help their direct-marketing people analyze their customer base—both current and potential customers. The goal was to improve the quality of their customer base so that sales per customer would increase, while, at the same time, sales and promotion costs would decrease.

After implementing the systems, advertising and customer service costs decreased. The company also experienced higher customer retention and lower direct sales costs compared with industry standards. Since they were able to equate the particular information system expenditures to marketing, they could identify a direct correlation between system costs and sales revenue. They could measure business value. The information systems affected their sales directly through marketing decisions the system supported, so the value of the investment could be stated in business terms.

Measuring a Product or Service. An information system can be offered as a product or service, or it can contribute to a product or service that is intended to produce revenue. In these cases, its value is measured as any other business venture–by its performance in the market. The measures are typical business profitability measures, such as return on investment, return on assets, and return on equity.

Measure What Is Important to Management

Charles Gold, at the Ernst & Young Center for Information Technology and Strategy [7], recommends measuring what management thinks is important. Information systems support can only be linked to corporate effectiveness by finding all the indicators they use, besides the traditional financial ones. Relating proposed benefits to these indicators can make it easier to "sell" a system, at both the individual and aggregate level.

Try to assess benefits in terms such as customer relations, employee morale, and "cycle time"—meaning, how long it takes to accomplish a complete assignment, he suggests. Each is a measure that goes beyond monetary terms, but that few executives deny are vital to a company's success. He gave Carlson and McNurlin two examples.

A power company kept a log of how many complaint letters its customers sent to the Public Utilities Commission each month, as a measure of customer satisfaction. This commission regulates the utility companies within its state.

The power company installed a computer system for its customer service representatives, giving them on-line access to the information they needed to answer customers' questions. When the system was in operation, the number of complaint letters decreased; when the system was down, the number of letters increased. So, one aspect of the effectiveness of this system was measurable in terms of public opinion.

A second possible measure is "cycle time." Faster cycle time can mean much more than saving hours. It can mean higher-quality products, beating competitors to a market, winning a bid, and so on. The benefit may have nothing to do with saving money. Rather, it may focus on *making* money.

So, says Gold, concentrating only on cost and monetary measures may be short-sighted. Other measures can be even more important to management.

Use "Anchor Measures"

To quantify benefits of it, Peter Keen [8], director of the International Center for Information Technology, suggests using "anchor measures." An anchor measure is an operational indicator of performance that can be used over time to assess the impact of IT.

These measures depend on management objectives. For instance, if management is aiming to cut costs, appropriate anchor measures might be the annual cost of serving a customer, or cost per transaction, writes Keen. On the other hand, if management seeks revenue or market, appropriate anchor measures would be revenue per customer. For measuring the value of EDI, the measure might be document costs per shipment or average delivery time. Although it may not be possible to translate these into financial figures, they are valuable measures of performance, even when they are not precise.

Keen presents the eye-opening example of how appropriate anchor measures can demonstrate benefits that financial figures ignore. In one company, for example, the traditional matrix of return on assests-to-profits showed that IT had been a drain on the firm over a three-year period. Investments in IT had ballooned the asset base from $2.1 billion to $3.3 billion, ROA had decreased, and IT costs had increased 80 percent. These numbers made the investments look like a disaster. However, using more appropriate anchor measures—sales per employee and revenue per employee—showed that IT may have saved the company. Staff was cut by 200 percent and profits per employee were up 300 percent. But these measures are more appropriate only if management believed that (1) unit costs could be reduced without sacrificing customer service and quality, (2) technology could substitute for people in some areas and avoid costs, and (3) it could help generate more revenue without increasing staff costs proportionately. Firms that believe these tenets shift from depending on variable-cost labor to fixed-cost technology.

Assess Investments Across Organizational Levels

Kathleen Curley, of Northeastern University, and John Henderson, of Boston University [9], recommend measuring benefits at several organizational levels. They have developed the Value Assessment Framework for assessing the value of an IT investment across corporate levels, and applied this framework at one large company.

The Value Assessment Framework

Since the potential benefits of IT investments differ at various organizational levels, Curley and Henderson believe companies need a systematic way to separate these benefits, by organizational level. They see three organizational levels, or *sources of value*, in particular, that benefit the

- Individual
- Division
- Corporation

With the current emphasis on business reengineering and redesigning business processes, Curley and Henderson also see the *impact focus* of an IT investment extending beyond business performance measures to encompass three dimensions.

- Economic performance payoffs—market measures of performance
- Organizational processes impacts—measures of process change
- Technology impacts—impacts on key functionality

Combining the two views forms a 3 x 3 matrix for systematically assessing the impact of a potential IT investment in nine areas. Curley and Henderson applied this framework at a large chemical conglomerate to assess a corporate-wide human resources information system (HRIS). The study uncovered benefits that otherwise would not have been noticed.

CASE EXAMPLE: A Large Chemical Conglomerate

This company, which wishes to remain anonymous, has headquarters in New York City and is one of the largest companies in the world, according to *Business Week* magazine. It is a pharmaceutical and consumer products conglomerate with relatively independent divisions, several formed by a major merger in the late 1980s.

Before the merger, the company undertook steps to leverage its corporate power while retaining the decentralized division-level decision making. One of these steps was to build a corporate-wide HRIS to replace fourteen existing divisional payroll and human resource information systems.

The goal was to create a central corporate repository of employee information and a single definition for "an employee." Some divisions included part-time employees in their head count, others did not. So the company did not have an accurate employee count. Furthermore, any new system would have to allow divisional autonomy in hiring practices and paycheck distribution. That is, it would need to allow paying manufacturing employees weekly and other employees semi-monthly.

The system was implemented across the company before the merger. Then, owing to the system's open design, the new divisions were added effortlessly, while maintaining a single view of the employee.

In the fall of 1991, Curley and Henderson conducted a postimplementation review of the HRIS using their Value Assessment Framework. Twelve employees were interviewed for about one hour each—the HRIS project director, MIS manager, corporate and division human resources (HR) managers, and corporate and division MIS management. The results were presented to the participants in late fall, and the framework was refined for future IT investment evaluations.

Benefits of the HRIS System

The value of the HRIS identified by the interviewees is illustrated in Figure 10-2.

Economic Performance Payoffs. For the individual HR counselors, the HRIS reduced costs—in responding to employees' questions about retirement planning, medical coverage, and training eligibility.

At the division level, the decision support features in the system also reduced costs, by permitting quicker and less costly compliance with government regulations. The divisions' payroll processing costs and costs of hiring, placing, and retaining employees also dropped.

At the corporate level, the benefits have been numerous. The firm has been able to leverage its size in negotiating prices for employee benefits. Without the HRIS, the company would not have been able to offer a new corporate-wide flexible benefits program; the cost would have been too high had each division negotiated on its own. Management believes that being able to provide such cost-effective employee benefits is a competitive advantage in attracting the most qualified people. Furthermore, the company is now able to emphasize the corporate culture across the divisions. This is likely to lead to employees identifying with the company as a whole, which, in turn, will ease interdivision transfers and sharing employees.

Figure 10-2 Sources of Value Assessments for Human Resources Information System

ECONOMIC PERFORMANCE PAYOFFS

Individual HR Counsellor: Lower cost to serve employees

Divisional HR Functions: Reduced cost of regulatory compliance and lower cost to acquire and retain employees

Corporate HR Department: Lower overall cost of providing employee benefits

ORGANIZATIONAL PROCESSES IMPACTS

Individual HR Counsellor: Ability to easily access employee profiles and higher responsiveness to employee requests

Divisional HR Functions: Redesigned processes and increased managerial scope

Corporate HR Department: Flexibility to restructure the HR function, preserve needed skills, and ability to leverage HR activities company-wide

TECHNOLOGY IMPACTS

Individual HR Counsellor: On-line entry of applications eliminates kcypunching

Divisional HR Functions: Greater accuracy, faster response rate, and higher system uptime

Corporate HR Department: Standards for data and processes, and ability to integrate data across systems.

Impacts on Organizational Processes. The system affected specific activities and job functions of the HR counselors. For instance, employees can access the system directly to obtain information on benefits, retirement dates, their next formal review, and so forth—without going through an HR counselor. Most employees still turn to an HR counselor when they have a question. But as the system becomes more embedded in the company's day-to-day operations, management expects employees to turn first to the system rather than a counselor. When this occurs, the counselors will be able to spend more of their time analyzing new initiatives, such as flexible benefits, elder care programs, and so forth.

At the HR function level, the system has completely eliminated a costly medical claims verification process. The database is so accurate and complete that medical claims are now sent directly to the insurer via computer tape. The system has also changed how HR managers have managed corporate restructuring and assessed the firm's work force needs.

At the corporate level, the system allowed the company to restructure while preserving the needed skills. It has also changed how the HR function itself is managed, from the individual HR counselors to the corporate level.

Technology Impacts. The system has affected the specific tasks and responsibilities of the individual HR counselors. For instance, it has completely replaced keying data from handwritten forms with on-line entry of job applications. Accuracy has improved to the point that hiring and payment cycles have accelerated.

At the division level, HR managers can directly access compensation rates and review dates on-line rather than requesting reports from the MIS department.

And at the corporate level, the HRIS eliminated fourteen payroll systems, replacing them with standard definitions and the corporate-wide data that have allowed the company to leverage their human resources across the divisions.

In all, the benefits of the HRIS go beyond automation to improving the HR management process, corporate performance, and the jobs of the HR specialists. The value assessment framework gave management a way to see these multilevel benefits and process redesigns. It also helped the company develop performance benchmarks for the technology, the organizational processes, and the economic impact that they are using to exploit the system more fully.

HOW CAN HIGHER-QUALITY SYSTEMS BE DEVELOPED?

One of the most serious issues in software development arises after the system is installed. The maintenance-upgrade phase of the life cycle typically requires at least as much cost and effort as is expended to develop a system in the first place. In other words, when the system is installed, the job is less than half done! Over the years, it has become clear that maintainability can be significantly improved by building in quality.

Traditionally, over time, systems have experienced "hardening of the arteries," making them less able to accept changes without crashing, and therefore dangerous to the healthy functioning of the organization. Software maintenance becomes a necessary evil in these systems, which are the majority of the systems in existence. In this situation, the maintenance practice is to fix the bugs, add the user-requested enhancements, improve the slow performance, and just keep the application running under a new operating system. Such maintenance causes the quality of the original system's design to deteriorate over time.

Figure 10-3 The Attributes of a Quality System

- It meets users' needs.
- It withstands the test of time, continually meeting the users' needs. That is, it changes gracefully as the users' needs change.
- It contains no bugs. It only does the work it was designed to do, and it does that work properly.
- Its inherent structure stays intact over time, so it remains maintainable.
- It is simple for the users to understand.
- It simplies the user's life; that is, it was designed with the users in mind.
- It is easy to use.

A quality system has several attributes, as shown in Figure 10-3.

What can companies do to build such systems? Following are five tactics we have uncovered:

- Manage the data.
- Focus on the "right" work.
- Experiment with promising new ideas.
- Reuse the work of others.
- Develop a maintenance strategy.

Manage the Data

Data is finally being recognized as a valuable company asset. John Zachman [10], a pioneer in the field of data management, believes that improving data consistency is imperative to the future well-being of organizations. As managers begin to rely more and more on computerized data, they must be able to obtain consistent views of the enterprise. The spread of desktop systems is hastening management's use of such data.

One traditional approach for obtaining data for a new application is to use data from an existing application. Data is "dribbled" from one application to another. This practice leads to different names for the same data, the same name for different data items, and the same data in different files but with different update cycles. Under these circumstances, getting a consistent view of the organization is difficult, if not impossible.

It is also difficult to make changes to data that is scattered among different applications, says Zachman. Even more difficult is maintaining an application that receives dribbled data from other systems and dribbles some of its own data on to other systems. These practices make it difficult to change an organization's infrastructure—its products, markets, organizational structure, and so on—because changing the supporting information systems is expensive. If information systems management sees one of its major functions as managing data, then improving data consistency will improve system quality.

Focus on the "Right" Work

One way to improve quality when building a system in-house is to devote systems staff time to the tougher modules and less time to the easier ones. Unfortunately, that is not usually what happens, said Denis Meredith, at a Los Angeles Chapter meeting of the Association for Computing Machinery. Meredith [11] is an independent consultant in Torrance, California, who specializes in software testing and risk assessment.

Generally, project managers assign the easiest modules first, said Meredith, to get them out of the way. But that is the wrong strategy for developing quality software, because, as a general rule, *modules that are written first are tested the most*. To develop quality software, the first modules written and tested should be the most difficult and the most risky.

How can project managers estimate riskiness when only the design specifications exist? Meredith suggests rating each module on two kinds of risk—failure impact and fault likelihood.

- *Failure impact* is the cost or damage that could occur from a failure. Estimates are based on such things as frequency of use and the value of the results to end users.
- *Fault likelihood* estimates the chances that a system fault will occur. System fault can mean several things: failure to run to completion, failure to comply with government regulations, economic loss through improper payment or billing, inappropriate business decisions based on incorrect or improperly presented information, or loss of data. Estimates of fault likelihood risk are based on such things as module complexity and the technologies to be used.

Meredith suggests that project managers evaluate module risk using a one-page questionnaire [12], then rank the modules based on their scores for these two risks, and finally assign project resources to modules based on their riskiness. The seventeen questions on the questionnaire can be completed in five to fifteen minutes for each module. "It has to be brief, easy to fill in, and useful," says Meredith, "or people will not use it." As an example, one question is: "Kind of module: inquiry, report writer, data extract, algorithmic data manipulation, file or database access, edit, or conversion." Each of these seven possibilities has an associated score—the more complex the type of module, the higher the score. That score is multiplied by a weight for failure impact or likelihood of fault. These weights were estimated by the project manager based on the question's contribution to risk.

The scores for the two types of risk are added separately for each module, and each module is ranked on the two scales. Obviously, the most risky modules have a high score for both failure impact and likelihood of fault; these modules should be developed and tested first, says Meredith. The next most risky are those with a high impact score and low likelihood score. The third most risky have a high likelihood score but a low impact score. The least risky modules score low on both—these modules should be developed and tested last.

The project managers who used this technique at one company told Meredith that it helped them focus their attention on the aspects that were likely to cause problems. So it was doing its job. But Meredith warns that the numbers are only estimates; they should only be used to judge the approximate relative risk of modules. The difference between two modules with scores of 60 and 70 means little. But the difference between modules with scores of 50 and 90 probably indicates significant risk difference between the two. In addition, the actual numbers may not be important, says Meredith. In one case, two project managers evaluated the same project and arrived at quite different numerical totals, but their overall ranking of the modules was the same.

System development strategy should focus on quality, says Meredith. One way to do that is to direct attention to risky modules so that project teams concentrate on the "right" work.

Experiment with New Ideas

Unfortunately, quality has not been an inherent characteristic of past information systems. Some people blame poor maintenance practices, but the problem really starts with a system's underlying design. As is increasingly being heard in total quality management programs, "Quality must be built in, not tested in." As we noted earlier, one aspect of quality is flexibility, which means being able to absorb change without losing the inherent rigorous design of the system. That capability requires a development approach specifically designed to facilitate change.

In 1989 we encountered a system development methodology that does just that. In fact, its creator, Peter Ligezinski, says that it accommodates change so well that it leads to zero maintenance. We believe the field advances only by experimenting with new approaches, and we also believe that built-in system quality will require completely new design approaches. Therefore, we present this unusual approach and the success of one firm, Wiscope, that has used it. We encourage all companies to experiment with promising new ideas, as Wiscope has done.

Zero Maintenance Systems

Peter Ligezinski [13], of SI Associates, in Vienna, Austria, believes that developing flexible systems is the challenge of the 1990s for information systems departments, because business managers will want to introduce changes "on the fly," and do so faster than their competitors. Ligezinski has developed an intriguing system development approach to support the evolution of "zero maintenance systems," which means that users can change and enhance programs without the help of a programmer. This is possible because the programs are controlled by user-entered "control data." A line manager can therefore enter new values for control data so the system will process, say, a new variation of a service, for a limited time only or from now on. Following is a brief description of his approach and a discussion of one system he created that has needed no maintenance since 1982.

To make computer application software adaptable, Ligezinski introduces the idea of "destabilizing factors." These are business changes that influence the internal processing of the supporting software—that is, the software must be "restabilized" (reprogrammed) to bring it in line with the new business environment. Examples of destabilizing factors are

- A new variation of a product
- Handling a new currency
- Changes in regulations
- New business conditions
- An increase in transaction volumes
- Special arrangements with individual clients

Ligezinski takes destabilizing factors into account when he designs systems by creating a special file that can be revised when these business changes occur.

Ligezinski's programs use two kinds of data files. One type contains "real" data—that is, descriptions of data used in the organization. This is the typical type of data file or database. The other type of data file contains control data; it can be changed by end users. Values in control data files determine the processing order of the programs. (Notice the similarity to HOLO discussed in Chapter 9.) To create a control data file, users look at how the company operates as well as how that operation might change. Control data files describe processing rules, when to apply those rules, and where to look for the appropriate data and calculations. They refer to data in the real data files as well as to programs.

Ligezinski's applications use two kinds of computer programs. One type he calls "skeleton programs." These are programs that perform elementary functions on data. They will not vary, no matter how the business environment changes. Thus, they can be put into a library of reusable templates that can be copied and easily changed to handle a specific database. (This feature, too, is somewhat similar to HOLO.) These programs are used for data entry, validation, simple reports, and so on. They can be used in any configuration; they form the software building blocks for a business.

The second type are dynamic programs; their processing sequence depends on the control data. The various subroutines and procedures in dynamic programs are linked by a set of instructions that Ligezinski calls "the interconnect layer." Instructions in this layer control the sequence of processing. At various checkpoints within or between subroutines, an interconnect instruction checks the current value of the appropriate piece of control data. Depending on that value, the interconnect instruction invokes the next processing step.

Ligezinski introduces new systems in two stages. First, the stable processing of the real data is implemented. Users see this phase as automating their files. This stage is relatively easy, he notes. The second phase introduces the dynamic programs. This phase is iterative and often takes quite a bit of time to complete. As users better understand the types of business changes that might lead to software changes, the control files are enhanced. Unfortunately, to be truly maintenance free, the control files must be complete; they cannot be partially done. This is why this phase often takes quite some time, he says. Once the dynamic programs appear to be able to handle any kind of change in the transactions, the entire system and its maintenance are turned over to the users.

Once an application is complete, variations of the system can be created easily, says Ligezinski. New users only need to enter their own values into the control data files. No custom programming is needed. Ligezinski has moved letters of credit and promissory notes management applications to other sites without reprogramming. Here is an example of one system that has actually had no programmer maintenance since 1982.

CASE EXAMPLE: Wiscope

Wiscope is a commodity trader in Lausanne, Switzerland. It handles precious metals, sugar, oil and petroleum, currencies, and various other commodities through commodity exchanges in New York, London, and Chicago. In 1979 it bought a Data General computer to handle commodities trading. Since there were no appropriate software packages available, they hired Ligezinski to write a futures trading system.

Development took six work-years; it was completed in 1981. The system contains some 250 programs—about 300,000 lines of COBOL code—of which some 200 are the nonchanging skeleton programs. About 75 percent of the effort went into designing and programming the fifty dynamic processing programs, says Ligezinski. The system handles all the futures trading functions for the firm including trading contracts, invoicing, telex preparation, management of client data, and so on.

During the design of the system, Wiscope identified six types of destabilizing factors in the futures trading business that might cause changes in the software.

1. The terms and conditions of trading contracts might change, both for individual contracts and in general.
2. Market conditions and rules governing the markets might change.
3. New markets might emerge, or Wiscope might decide to trade other commodities.
4. New units of measure might be used—pounds, metric tons, and so on.

5. New or additional currencies might be used in some trades.
6. The general philosophy of futures trading might change.

The system was able to accommodate all but the last destabilizing factor—a change in operating philosophy—by allowing Wiscope employees to enter changes concerning markets, currencies, units, and terms and conditions.

Since the system was put into production in 1981, it has required only one minor change by Ligezinski, in 1982—to include another company name on the printouts. Other than that, all business changes are entered into the system by the office staff; Wiscope has no programmers. When management decides to trade in a new commodity, for example, they choose the exchanges they will use, lot sizes, trading rules, currencies, and so on. The staff enters these choices into the system. Adding a new commodity is as easy as adding a new customer to a file, they told us. And these kinds of changes are made continually. Wiscope has not yet encountered a business change that could not be handled by the system.

Reuse the Work of Others

As noted in Chapter 9, the current promising new development technologies—CASE and object-oriented development—have one important attribute in common: reuse. Both are making a significant contribution to developers being able to build upon the work of others. There used to be a joke in the computer field that said that while professionals in other fields stand on the shoulders of their predecessors to make progress, system developers stand on the feet of their predecessors. That is no longer true. The computer field has at long last finally found ways to create "standard parts" that can be reused time and again to build new systems.

Software packages have long been one way to reuse others' work, but their shortcoming has been that they are generic, not tailored. Hence, they do not exactly meet one's needs. Most current packages are "table driven" so that users can tailor the package to their needs by choosing the appropriate parameters in the tables. When further extensions are needed, however, unless the system has an accompanying CASE or object-oriented toolset, modifications must often be done manually.

As an example of the type of progress that is being made, we present the work of a utility that acquired a new type of software called "designware." In essence, it is the template for a mainline system including the data model, the system design, and generic user interface screens. Since this type of product was originally developed using CASE, it can be tailored using the same CASE tool. We believe this new type of software offering—which fits somewhere between packaged software and custom coding—will become increasingly prevalent.

CASE EXAMPLE: KPL Gas Service

KPL Gas Service in Topeka, Kansas, is the fifth largest combination electric and natural gas utility in the United States, with 1.3 million customers in Kansas, Missouri, and Oklahoma. When Kansas Power and Light acquired Gas Service Company in 1983, the name KPL Gas Service was adopted. Although the utility is large, it no longer has a monopoly on supplying fuel or electricity. After deregulation forced utilities to operate in a newly competitive environment, KPL began to reassess how it should provide its services. The conclusion: Take a more customer-oriented approach. This required a new customer information system (CIS).

Although the utility needed a custom-built system, they only had the budget for a package. After spending four months evaluating packages used by other utilities, the project team found a better alternative: Customer/1 from Andersen Consulting [14]. This CASE-based "designware" product would allow them to reuse the work of other utilities. The product has many years of development in the data model alone, and because it is delivered in design form based on the Foundation CASE toolset from Andersen Consulting, it is easy to modify.

Customer/1 provides a modifiable blueprint for a utility to build its own customized customer information system. Just as an architect can modify the blueprint of an existing house to build a new one that is "just like that one, except . . . ," so too could KPL Gas Service use Customer/1 as its blueprint. Customer/1 has three parts.

- A data model for a utility CIS
- A customized methodology, based on Foundation, but tailored to CIS development
- A project storehouse, which is an electronic warehouse of design specifications developed by other Customer/1 customers.

Building the New System. After acquiring Customer/1, teams—of systems staff, consultants from Andersen Consulting, and users from district operations and accounting—spent ten months designing the new system. Initially, ten two-person teams—a systems person and a user responsible for a major system function—studied Customer/1 and presented their findings to the other teams. This up-front, in-depth investigation turned out to be crucial to the project's success, because the team members then knew what to use and when to use it. Understanding the data model was particularly important in designing the system's screens and reports. The Customer/1 design guides were then loaded into Foundation's design tool, which served as the project's central repository. These guides were modified to meet the utility's requirements. In some cases, functions were completely redesigned; in others, they were barely touched. But the base data model was never modified, because any changes to it would lead to unnecessary redesign work and corrupt Customer/1's design.

Customer/1 gave the development team a significant head start. Preliminary design took a total of 3,775 work days. Had the team started from scratch, high-level design would have taken almost twice as long. Eight full-time users on the team—formerly senior office managers for eight of the major system functions—played a large role in system design. They were responsible for using the design tool to design all the screens in the system. The detailed designs created from the high-level designs were then translated into programs using Foundation's program generator.

Use of Customer/1 led to a high-quality system, because it provided the developers with a firm base for designing the new system. KPL Gas Service was able to design on top of the quality already present in Customer/1, rather than start from scratch. Many of the functions required minimal changes; therefore, designers could focus on adding new functions. Furthermore, use of Foundation is extending that quality, because it allowed them to make modifications by following the standards and the methodology. And those changes maintain the inherent consistency of Customer/1. In addition, the central repository put documentation at developers' fingertips, so that development items did not need to be duplicated. The items were defined once and referenced from then on, which greatly reduced design inconsistencies. Finally, the program generator enforced standards, providing consistency between programs and making the system higher quality and more maintainable.

Building on the designs of other utilities, KPL Gas Service built a state-of-the-art system in record time—three and one-half years, versus five and one-half years, which is the industry average for this size utility. In addition, it has created the platform for the future. Management plans to use the system as the platform for developing two other mission-critical systems in the 1990s: a workflow management system and a geographical information system

Develop a Maintenance Strategy

Ken Orr [15], a well-known system development consultant, likens application systems to the telephone system. He believes that information systems departments could benefit from taking the view that telephone companies take toward maintaining their telephone service. Telephone companies try to maintain their systems without interrupting service, and they attempt to make the service appear consistent to users by not changing operating procedures. In essence, they try to insulate telephone users from internal system changes.

Orr believes this is a goal for information systems as well and that a good software maintenance program would do just that. It would include

- Continual repair to fix errors
- Continual enhancement to make user-requested changes
- Continual revisions to upgrade systems technologically while protecting user views of each system

Orr asserts that organizations should follow the lead of software companies that manage the entire life cycle of their products. His premise is that maintenance can be managed because most maintenance is redesign, and redesign can be managed using the proper tools. Changes should not be simply added on but should be designed into programs and systems, says Orr. By using the structure chart of a program to determine how to incorporate the change into the design, the program's design will retain its robustness and hence its quality. This requires using a design methodology during maintenance, which many companies do not do.

To manage the maintenance process, Orr suggests using change reports for four levels of change. The problem is first identified in a change *report,* and it is given as high a *change* priority as practical. When a correction is made, a system update is distributed, if necessary. This is the lowest level of change to a system. Then, at regular intervals, a group of updates is combined and released as a *system temporary update*. The documentation as well as the code is updated for this second level of change.

On a longer time frame, a series of system temporary updates are combined into a *system release*. At this time, the changes are retested, documentation is updated, and the changes are integrated. At the most significant fourth level, a *new version* of the system is created. Versions represent major changes to systems, such as major new functions, a restructured database, a new platform, and so on.

As more and more end users begin using computers directly, "backbone" systems will become increasingly important, says Orr, because they will feed the other smaller (perhaps user-developed) systems. Maintaining the quality of these mainline systems, so that they are adaptable, will become increasingly important. He feels that a managed maintenance strategy is necessary to accomplish these ends.

In summary, these are five strategies for improving system quality.

1. Improve the data used in the system by managing it.
2. Concentrate on the hardest modules first, so they are the most fully tested.
3. Keep up with new technology by experimenting with new ideas.
4. Build on the work of others.
5. Manage the entire life cycle of a system rather than leave it to chance.

These are things that can be done to improve new systems. But what about existing applications?

HOW CAN LEGACY SYSTEMS BE IMPROVED?

Most information systems executives feel trapped by the past. They have hundreds or even thousands of old legacy programs and data files that they would love to replace. But with a backlog of perhaps two or more years' worth of new work already in the queue, they see no way of replacing these legacy systems.

Until recently, there have been few choices for dealing creatively with legacy systems. In general, companies could replace an old system with a package or totally rewrite it in a procedural language, such as COBOL. Now there are several other alternatives, made possible by the new tools, new programming languages, and new development techniques.

In this section, we present six tactics for dealing with legacy systems. The first two—rewrite and replace—involve the most drastic change, and probably the greatest resource commitment. The remaining four represent a range of options from minimal refurbishing to substantial rejuvenation.

Rewrite Legacy Systems

In some cases, a legacy system may be too far gone to rescue. If the code is convoluted and patched, if the technology is antiquated, and if the design is poor, it may be necessary to start from scratch. The thought of rewriting a large system in a traditional procedural language is often discouraging, because of the large amount of resources it will take. However, iterative development offers some promise.

Iterative development merges prototyping and traditional development. Prototyping is done as a first step, following problem analysis, to better define system requirements, user interfaces, and difficult modules. Once these portions of the system have been created and tested by the user, the traditional development cycle is used to build the production version. In other cases, the prototype becomes the production system.

An option many companies are choosing is to "downsize" such applications, that is, rewrite them for a smaller platform, such as a midrange machine or a network server. One advantage of this approach is that operational costs are less, as are machine costs. Development costs may also be less, and the systems may be more flexible, if developed with new tools.

Replace Them with Purchased Packages

One reason for choosing a package is to move an old application to a new operating environment—for instance, from a centralized environment to a distributed one. An organization might want to distribute an application's workload among a host computer, some midrange systems, and many PCs and workstations. There are an increasing number of commercial packages that provide links among the computers in such a hierarchy. These packages not only support communication between the three types of machines but they also permit downloading and uploading files.

Another reason to consider replacing an old system with a commercial package is that these products are becoming more versatile. Many offer selectable features that allow purchasers to tailor the package to their work style. The options can be turned on or off using control files, so no programming is necessary. Even end users can specify some of the operating instructions.

An interesting twist comes in packages that are written using an application generator. The generator comes with each of the packages, so it can be used by a programming staff to tailor or extend the package. The generator makes these packages even more versatile. Such "tailorable" packages negate the traditional reason for rejecting packages: "nobody does it the way we do."

Refurbish Legacy Systems

If the old system is maintainable and causing no major problems, it may be worthwhile to add some extensions. Potential extensions would supply input in a new manner, or make new uses of the output, or allow the programs to deal more comprehensively with data.

These extensions—to a COBOL batch system, for instance—can be made using a fourth-generation language, says Mary Rich [16], an independent consultant who has used numerous 4GLs since the mid-1970s. The following are ways to extend a legacy using a 4GL, she says.

Refurbish the Input Process. A front end can be added by using the 4GL's DBMS to create a database that combines fields from the old files with new fields. Once built, all input data flows into the new database. The beauty of this approach is that validation routines can be easily added to check the input data. In addition, the database can use the most appropriate file structure; it need not match the file structure in the original system. A program is then written in the 4GL allowing users to enter data into this new database interactively.

Revise the Data Manipulation Process. Once the new "external" database has been created, data from it and the original system can be merged and manipulated. Writing data manipulation routines for selecting, sorting, comparing, and combining data is far easier using a 4GL than it is using a procedural language. When dealing with poorly designed old files, manipulations can become very complex, so a language that simplifies the programming is important.

As an example, consider the case of one system Rich worked on—a project reporting system. The original system tracked project budgets by project period and account number, but it tracked actual costs by week and major job order number. Due to these differences, users could get meaningful budget-versus-actual reports only by having the system perform numerous complex conversions. Since it was a batch system, by the time the users got the reports of invalid entries, and then turned in the changes to data entry, they were already into the next accounting period. They were never able to reconcile budget-versus-actual data. Figure 10-4 shows the original system and the enhancements.

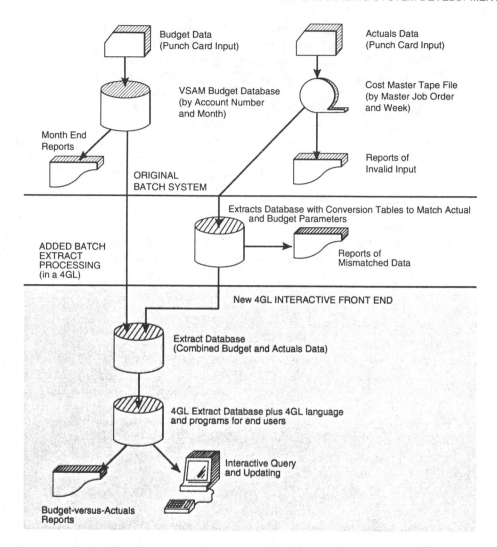

Figure 10-4 A Refurbished Project Reporting System

To improve this process, an extract database was created containing tables to convert actual data to the budget data format. Now actual data can be extracted from the original system and run through these tables to produce reports of mismatches, significantly improving turnaround time.

Extend the Query Capabilities. An interactive query capability can be added by creating a new query database that gathers data from both the old and new portions of the system. However, the query capabilities are likely to be limited. For one thing, the data in the old system probably cannot be updated interactively, but data in the new ones can. Hence, queries will not always retrieve the most recent data. For many users, any on-line query capability is far superior to batch reporting. However, the more powerful querying capabilities will require more data massaging to get the data in shape for the end user database.

Consider again the project reporting system, said Rich. Since the system matches data from old files, new files, and tables, end users cannot create their own queries against data stored in these three ways. Two options are possible. Once users are happy with a report, a standard routine can be created for them to use on their own, print the report, or display it on a PC. Or another database can be created for direct interrogation.

Enhance the Output Process. To enhance the use of data stored in legacy systems, write a procedure to dump the data into a 4GL database, suggests Rich. Then merge that data with new data not stored in the old system to generate new reports, on paper or for on-line access.

Once users get more useful and more flexible reporting, they will not go back to reports generated from the original system. As an example, the original batch project tracking system became unable to create half the programmed reports because of bugs in the programs. It was decided that it would be faster and easier to rewrite the procedures to generate those twenty-five reports in the 4GL rather than search for the bugs in the old system. So that is what was done—and the old reports are no longer generated.

Thus old systems can be refurbished by adding front-end interfaces for users, data manipulation capabilities, on-line query capabilities, and report generation—all based on the database management and programming capabilities of 4GLs.

Restructure Legacy Systems

If an application program is basically doing its job, it may not need much change in function, input/output, or data handling. Yet it may run inefficiently, or be "fragile" or unmaintainable. In these cases, the system can be *restructured*. Numerous vendors offer software products to aid in this process. The most popular ones use automated tools to turn running "spaghetti code" into more structured code. The process involves the following seven steps.

1. Evaluate the amount of structure in the current system—number of layers of nesting, degree of complexity, and so forth. Use the tools to present a trace of the program's control logic. Subjectively evaluating the code is also necessary to determine whether restructuring is warranted at all or if more extensive change is required; this can only be performed by people.
2. Compile the program to be sure it is in working order. A code restructuring tool will not make a nonoperative program run.
3. Clean up and restructure the code using structured programming concepts by running the program through a structuring engine. This automated process does not change the logic of the program; it simply replaces poor coding conventions with structured coding conventions, such as reducing the number of GOTOS, removing dead code and alter statements, highlighting looping conditions, and grouping and standardizing input/output statements. It uncovers the structure hidden inside the convoluted code.

4. Reformat the listing, making it easier to understand, by using a formatting package.

5. Ensure that the old and new versions produce the same output by using a file-to-file comparator.

6. Minimize overhead introduced by restructuring by using an object code optimizer package. After optimization, restructured programs generally require between 5 percent less and 10 percent more run time than the unstructured versions.

7. "Rationalize" the data by giving all uses of the same data one data name. This step is optional.

These seven steps can be used to restructure a functional system or to get it in shape to be reengineered.

Reengineer Legacy Systems

A step beyond restructuring is reengineering, which means extracting the data elements from an existing file and the business logic from an existing program, and moving them to new platforms. This use of the term reengineering should not be confused with the term "business reengineering," which was used in Chapter 3. This term, "system or application reengineering," is much narrower and refers only to software. The other term refers to redesigning business processes. Like code restructuring, reengineering requires automated tools, because the process is too complex to be cost-justifiably done manually. Database reengineering tools began appearing on the market in the late 1980s.

Charles Bachman [17], a pioneer in the database field, introduced the first widely accepted set of database reengineering tools. He believes that the major problem in the computer field has been the way applications have been developed and maintained. Rather than consider existing systems as liabilities that have to be maintained—and thus take resources away from developing new and exciting applications—management needs to see existing systems as assets from which to move forward.

If developers can "reverse engineer" a system—that is, extract the underlying business logic—then they can "forward engineer" that business logic to a new system platform, such as a new database management system. With this approach, existing systems become assets. Developers can extract the intelligence in them rather than start over from scratch as they do today.

Bachman sees a new system development life cycle emerging, using CASE products to help automate reverse engineering. It encompasses all four basic development activities—maintenance, enhancement, new development, and migration. This life cycle is circular rather than linear, as shown in Figure 10-5.

- *Reverse engineering.* Existing programs, along with their file and database descriptions, are converted from their implementation level descriptions— records, databases, code, and so on—into their equivalent design level components—entities, attributes, processes, messages, and so on.

- *Forward engineering.* This goes in the opposite direction—from requirements-level components to operational systems. Design items created by reverse engineering are used to create new applications via forward engineering.

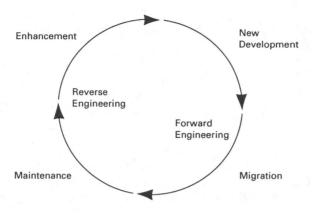

Figure 10-5 The Reengineering System Development Life Cycle (from Bachman [18])

The cycle continues because as new applications go into operation, they become candidates for reverse engineering whenever they need to be changed. Neither people nor automated tools can use this new life cycle by themselves, says Bachman, but together, it becomes feasible.

GTE Directories is one company that is using the Bachman reengineering tools.

CASE EXAMPLE: GTE Directories

GTE Directories is a leading telephone directory publishing company with headquarters in Dallas, Texas. They produce, market, and distribute more than fifteen hundred different telephone directories in some fourteen countries. Since the breakup of AT&T in 1984, GTE Directories has experienced increased competition. To accelerate their response to changing markets, GTE Directories began automating their telephone directory publishing business.

The directory publishing system has four main databases; they use the IDMS/R relational database management system from Computer Associates, in Islandia, New York [18]. The largest database supports all the administrative functions for creating and selling Yellow Page advertising—from sales to photo composition. The second database is used by representatives who sell Yellow Page advertising for non-GTE directories. The third database handles billing. And the fourth database provides order entry for independent telephone companies, for whom GTE produces telephone books.

The databases were originally designed application by application. The result has been that the records contain data elements that have no business relationship to each other, making them very difficult to reuse, enhance, and change. The data administration group acquired the reverse engineering tools from Bachman Information Systems to help them maintain and improve these databases.

Using Bachman Tools. To reverse engineer an IDMS database at GTE Directories, a designer uses the Bachman/Database Administrator for IDMS to display the existing IDMS database definitions on a graphical workstation. The design is reversed engineered into the Bachman/Data Analyst, where the designer makes changes by manipulating the graphical icons. The Data Analyst helps designers draw complete and consistent entity-relationship diagrams because it has the intelligence to identify inconsistencies and incomplete structures.

Once the new database design has been created, the designer forward engineers the database design back to Bachman/Database Administrator and runs the physical implementation design rules. This product makes recommendations to improve the design. When the design is satisfactory, the Database Administrator is used to generate IDMS database statements automatically.

Here are two examples of projects where GTE Directories is using the Bachman tools for database maintenance.

The Blueprint Project

Since the largest database was not properly designed, the data administration group is using the Bachman toolset to create a "blueprint" of what the database should look like. They have reverse engineered the existing IDMS database from its physical to its data model from which they have created a new, properly designed data model using entity-relationship modeling techniques. By experimenting with this model, they have created a design that is more adaptable to change. It is their blueprint for the future, and it is being used to guide maintenance work. As the database administrators maintain the database, they make changes to bring it closer into line with this blueprint. Eventually, they expect to get to this desired database structure.

Without the Bachman tools, they would not have even attempted this project, because they could not have done the "what if" modeling necessary to create the blueprint.

A Reuse Project

The database administrators are reusing some of the data elements in the largest database for a new production scheduling system. The company has been scheduling production of their fifteen directories among their three printing plants using a fifteen-year-old system. Some scheduling data was in the system, some was in the new administrative system.

GTE Directories created a new scheduling system, drawing some scheduling-related data from the administrative database. Again, they used Bachman tools to create the design models for the new scheduling databases. From these models, they use a Bachman tool to generate the necessary database statements. With the new system, sales people will no longer need to interrogate both the fifteen-year-old publishing system and the administrative system—which have different sets of data—to see directory publishing schedules.

Since maintenance is the bulk of the work of the database administration group, the Bachman tools have become invaluable in helping them redesign old databases, design new databases using portions of existing ones, and create their blueprint for the future.

Rejuvenate Legacy Systems

Rejuvenating an old system is a step beyond reengineering, because it adds enough new functions to a reengineered system to make it more valuable to the firm. The system rejuvenation process has four phases, each building on the previous one.

As an example of system rejuvenation, consider the case of ITT Diversified Credit Corporation. They not only cleaned up an old system but also gave it increased strategic value to the firm.

CASE EXAMPLE: ITT Diversified Credit Corporation

ITT Diversified Credit Corporation (DCC), with headquarters in St. Louis, Missouri, is part of ITT Financial Corporation. It was founded in the early 1970s to provide inventory financing (or "floor planning") for retail dealers. Floor planning is a complex system that involves financing and maintaining dealer inventories as well as handling their accounts receivable, accounts payables, and other such activities.

Shortly after DCC was founded and company growth accelerated, the need for an automated floor planning system became evident. So a contract was given to a programming firm to develop a COBOL system quickly. Due to the urgency, the system was not well designed, and the business grew so rapidly that there was no chance to fix the system properly. Six years later, all maintenance was stopped because the 150,000 lines of COBOL code were a real mess. The situation was so bad that the company had to charter a private plane to fly them from the data center to an airport for overnight express mail delivery. Even so, in some cases, the data was a week old.

Phase 1: Recognize a System's Potential. All these factors put DCC at a competitive disadvantage. So, the company initiated efforts to either fix up or replace the floor-planning system. They called in Peat Marwick Main who recommended first cleaning up the existing system using code restructuring tools and then building from there.

Phase 2: Clean Up the System. DCC used the Peat Marwick Main restructuring service to transform the poorly structured COBOL code into more structured, maintainable code in eleven weeks' time. At this point, a very difficult to maintain system had been transformed into a maintainable one.

Phases 3: Make the System More Efficient. The code restructuring service had pulled together all data reads and writes into one section of each program. This allowed DCC to take two important next steps—converting the application to a new operating environment and a new file structure. Additional manual tuning and enhancements were also performed, which greatly reduced system processing times.

Phase 4: Give the System a Strategic Role. In parallel with phase 3, DCC addressed the question, "How can we provide even more timely information to our twenty branch offices, to improve our competitive position in the marketplace?" Two options were considered. Create a mainframe-based on-line system or install a distributed system using midrange computers at the branch offices. DCC chose the distributed system approach, for two main reasons. One, it would substantially reduce communications costs. Two, it more closely fitted DCC's decentralized management approach, making the branch offices more responsible for their own destinies.

The midrange systems were installed in three phases. The first phase moved data entry and some validation out to the branch midrange computers. Transactions were sent to the mainframe to update the master files and generate reports. The second phase moved a copy of the master file to each branch, to improve input validation and permit on-site ad hoc queries. The third phase turned the branch files into the master files, thus converting the data center's files into backup status. This step cut communication costs substantially and moved reporting out to the branches. Electronic mail and integrated word and data processing also commenced at that time.

The managers of DCC are pleased that they were able to move from a large, almost unmaintainable batch system to a state-of-the-art distributed system. They give credit to Peat Marwick for recommending the course of action and for providing project leadership and staffing. They also give credit to the code restructuring service, because it allowed them to develop clean, maintainable code from their old system without missing a single production schedule.

CONCLUSION

As the variety of computer applications has broadened and as companies have become more dependent on IT, the management issues surrounding application development have proliferated. The age-old question of measuring programmer productivity is still around. The relatively new question of measuring the benefits of it is being asked more often, even in the business press. Meanwhile, systems management is grappling with how to create higher-quality, more flexible systems—both for new applications and for upgraded legacy systems. In all, system development continues to be a challenging job, because the health of the organization depends on robust systems, and because they have become the heart of corporate operations.

QUESTIONS AND EXERCISES

REVIEW QUESTIONS

1. List Albrecht's five types of functions used in function point analysis; include examples for each.
2. What did Rudolph find when he compared programmer productivity of different languages?
3. What are the three roles of information systems, according to Berger?
4. What is an anchor measure?
5. List the three individual performance benefits achieved by the large chemical conglomerate.

6. Why does managing data improve system quality?

7. According to Meredith, what is the "right" work?

8. How does Ligezinski achieve zero maintenance?

9. What benefits did KPL Gas Service receive from using Customer/1?

10. List the six ways to improve legacy systems.

11. Identify the four ways to use a 4GL to refurbish an old system.

12. List the steps in restructuring a system.

13. Why did GTE Directories turn to reengineering?

14. List the steps DCC took to rejuvenate its system.

DISCUSSION QUESTIONS

1. The strategy of minimum maintenance until a system must be completely redone is still best for challenging and developing the programmer/analyst staff. The few people that like nitty-gritty maintenance activities can take care of the programs that need it, while most of the development staff can be challenged by the creativity of new development. The six options just make quasi-maintenance programmers out of almost everyone. Do you agree or disagree?

2. The trend toward more and more purchased software portends trouble for the professional system analyst and programmer. Application programmers and system analysts may soon become nothing more than evaluators of packaged software. Do you agree or disagree?

EXERCISES

1. Pick out seven of Albrecht's characteristics of applications. Discuss several ways each can influence application complexity.

2. Make a table showing the advantages and disadvantages of each of the six options for improving legacy systems. Derive from the table a list of characteristics of a legacy system that can serve as a management guideline for deciding which of the options is best in a given situation.

3. Find a company in your community that has more than ten years' experience using computer systems. For that company, develop a descriptive case study, showing how it deals with its legacy systems. Include the following: (a) an inventory of major applications, and (b) the company's strategies for maintenance and modernization. Indicate how the company decides which applications to upgrade and which approaches to use.

4. Identify several listings or directories of available software for purchase. Summarize the nature of the products in the listings by showing the categories and the approximate number of packages available in each category.

REFERENCES

1. ALLAN ALBRECHT has two papers describing function point analysis:

   "Measuring Application Development Productivity," *Proceedings of the Application Development Symposium,* Monterey, California, October 1979. Order from SHARE (401 N. Michigan Ave, Chicago, IL 60611).

   Albrecht, A., and J. Gaffney, Jr., "Software Function, Source Lines of Code, and Development Effort Prediction: A Software Science Validation," *IEEE Transactions on Software Engineering*, November 1983, pp. 639-648.

2. RUDOLPH, E., "Productivity in Computer Application Development," Unisys Corporation, LINC Corporate Program Management, Room 4F17, One Burroughs Place, Detroit, MI 48232.

3. BOWEN, W., "The Puny Payoff from Office Computers," *Fortune*, May 26, 1986.

4. CARLSON, W. M., and B. C. McNurlin, *"Uncovering the Information Technology Payoffs,"* a special report published by *I/S Analyzer,* Fall 1992.

5. PAUL BERGER, Paul Berger Consulting, Inc., and PBC Management Video, P.O. Box 6813, Lawrenceville, NJ 08648.

6. *Measuring Business Value Of Information Technologies* (International Center for Information Technology, Washington, DC), 1988.

7. CHARLES GOLD, Ernst & Young Center for Information Technology and Strategy, One Walnut St., Boston, MA 02108.

8. KEEN, PETER G.W., *Shaping the Future: Business Design through Information Technology* (Harvard Business School Press, Boston, MA), 1991, 264 pp.

9. CURLEY, K., and J. HENDERSON, "Assessing the Value of a Corporate-wide Human Resource Information System: A Case Study," Special Issue, *Journal of Management Systems*, 1992.

10. JOHN ZACHMAN, Zachman International, 2222 Foothill Blvd., Suite 337, La Canada, CA.

11. DENIS MEREDITH, 2042 Kathy Way, Torrance, CA 90501.

12. MEREDITH, D. "A Risk-Driven Approach to Program Development Strategy," *Proceedings of Pacific Northwest Software Quality Conference,* Lawrence & Craig, (Portland, OR) 1986.

13. PETER LIGEZINSKI, SI ASSOCIATES, Loewengass 26/16, A-1050, Vienna, Austria.

14. ANDERSEN CONSULTING, 69 W. Washington, Room 1534, Chicago, IL 60602.

15. KEN ORR and Associates, 1725 Gage Blvd., Topeka, KS 66604.

16. MARY RICH is at 731 Bayonne St., El Segundo, CA 90245.

17. CHARLES BACHMAN, Bachman Information Systems, 48 New England Executive Park East, 6th Floor, Burlington, MA 01803.

18. COMPUTER ASSOCIATES, One Computer Associates Plaza, Islandia, NY 11788.

ELEVEN

The Expanding Universe of Computing

INTRODUCTION

The world of computing seems to be growing by the minute, with more kinds of computers, new telecommunication options, and many new, potential uses announced monthly. In this chapter, we take a snapshot in time (the early 1990s) and sort through the diversity of computing offerings from the point of view of the individual end user, either as an employee, a supplier or customer, or as a consumer. Computing will be a growing part of many aspects of our lives in the 1990s. In the next chapter, we discuss the issues that information systems management faces in supporting this vastly expanded universe of computer users.

From the end users' point of view, it appears that three areas will play dominate roles in their view of computing. These three are

- The world of mobile computing: portable computers and wireless networks
- The expanding role of electronic mail
- The coming user interface: multimedia

This chapter is devoted to exploring these three technical aspects of computing.

333

THE WORLD OF MOBILE COMPUTING

There is no doubt that people are becoming increasingly mobile, not only in where they live and work, but in how they live and work. Therefore, portability has become one of the strongest selling points in today's market, from travel-size cosmetics to pocket-size video games and CD players.

There are two driving forces behind mobile computing: the incredible shrinking computer and wireless WANs. We discuss both in this section.

The Incredible, Shrinking Computer

Dick Tracy, here we come. The real world is driving toward the comic book world at blinding speed and providing more truly personal computing power than comic book artists dreamed possible. In the early 1990s, a whole slew of new kinds of computers stuffed massive power into smaller and smaller packages. We are now in the age of the incredibly shrinking computer.

First there were desktop computers. Then there were "luggables" which felt like bowling balls. Next came true portables—seven-pound PCs that fit inside a briefcase. More recently, pen-based clipboard computers appeared, some with keyboards some without. And now, we have palmtop computers—miniature PCs and electronic organizers that generally fit in one hand. And last, and most intriguing, are personal digital assistants—handy little electronic gizmos that you carry in your pocket to perform any number of tasks. Since the desktop and portable computers are familiar to just about all of us, in this section we will discuss the other new kinds of computers—pen computers, palmtops, and personal digital assistants.

Pen Computers

According to Portia Isaacson, president of the computer market tracking firm The Dream Machine, the preeminent electronic trend in the 1990s is mobile working. Contributing to that trend are what she calls the first truly personal computers: pen computers. Writing in *Mobile Office* magazine [1], Isaacson notes that pen computers are just like notebook computers except that they have a digitizer in place of, or in addition to, a keyboard; therefore, information can be entered by writing on the screen. Pen computers might also have character recognition software for deciphering the hand printing to do database searches, calculations, and so forth. These compute-anywhere, fax-anywhere, take-anywhere machines are a new class of personal technology, says Isaacson.

Ric Manning [2], writing in the same issue of *Mobile Office*, notes that experts see four categories of pen software.

- Forms software with menus and check-off boxes, which turn pen computers into electronic clipboards

- Personal information managers, such as word processing and other desktop applications, which are being customized for the pen environment
- Digital ink programs, which capture, store, and transmit hand-printed notes and drawings
- Portable books, which can be stored on memory cards the size of credit cards, make catalogs, price lists, and other printed material both portable and changeable

The first pen-based software to arrive was the forms packages, as a way to automate data collection. For example, claims adjusters can enter the damage to a car by pointing at a small diagram of car sections and using menus to describe the damage, notes Manning. The computer can then calculate the repair costs on the spot.

Pen computers will have built-in modems as standard equipment, and will work with wireless networks. In fact, with a pen computer equipped with a pager, a person can receive a screen image of a fax, mark it up using "electronic ink" software, and then fax it back, says Manning.

Isaacson sees a spectrum of pen-based computers appearing. Specifically, she sees four main categories—special purpose, tablet, convertible, and omnitablet. *Special-purpose* pen computers, such as GRiD's GRiD Pad, have unique operating systems and development environments for creating customized applications. For example, TraveLite from DFM has compressed storage and digital voice annotation and prompting, which make it appropriate for maintenance departments wanting to access manuals and drawings by touch look-up. Generally, these systems are not powerful enough to run the major pen computing operating systems, PenPoint from Go Technologies and Windows for Pen Computing (Pen Windows) from Microsoft.

Tablet pen computers, look like a clipboard, with a screen where the pad of paper would be. They are meant to operate without a keyboard, so the accompanying stylus is used to draw, write, or point to objects displayed on the screen. These systems can run the major pen operating systems, and Isaacson expects them to compete with keyboard and notebook computers in personal productivity applications, especially in specialized fleet applications.

Convertible and *omnitablet* pen computers support both keyboard and pen input, so they are appropriate for people who want to run keyboard-based software, such as their existing software. Isaacson distinguishes the two types by stating that omnitablets are meant to be a user's only computer; therefore, it must have a large, bright screen, have comparable power to a desktop computer, include a full-size keyboard, and connect to desktop peripherals via a docking mechanism.

Isaacson sees pen computers becoming "companions for people," and the center of computing, acting as either a communicating computer or a computing communicator. Pen computers will dock into desktop base stations to recharge their battery, backup files, and upload and route faxes, data, and voice mail, says Isaacson. They will shrink in size to be wallet or paperback size, and will use the powerful Intel 486 chip. And people will think of them as pint-sized fax tablets or fax phones, with screens that can be shared remotely. The barriers to this future, she says, is the supply of flat panel displays and the weight of batteries that can support color. In all, pen computers are the advent of truly personal computers.

Palmtops

The palmtop computer is exemplified by the Sharp Wizard, first introduced in 1988. The Wizard was originally intended to be a hand-held electronic organizer small enough to fit inside a coat pocket; however, it is being continually enhanced to be much more. The graphical user interface can display up to thirty lines of fifty-three characters each, as well as simple graphics. Incorporated in the screen is a touch panel, which displays available options, depending on the application in use. Touching an icon on the screen with the pen stylus or a finger activates that function. The keyboard, which is 75 percent the size of a standard keyboard, is meant for touch typing.

The Wizard includes the personal productivity applications shown in Figure 11-1.

The memory of this device has increased steadily; it had 256K bytes of memory in late 1992. These devices also have a slot for memory cards (for backup) and program cards that include software for performing such functions as handling personal finances, managing portfolios, graphing investments, checking spelling, referencing a dictionary, and so forth.

- Calendar (with daily, weekly, and monthly views)
- Scheduler (with time line)
- Alarm
- To do list (with project management capabilities to set deadlines, etc.)
- Telephone directories
- Business card directory
- Word processor (to write memos)
- Outliner (for meeting notes and price lists)
- Scrapbook (for entering and saving hand-written letters or graphics)
- Calculator (with paperless printer)
- Home and world clocks
- Programming and database language

Figure 11-1 Personal Productivity Applications in Sharp's Wizard

Since the Wizard and other organizers were meant to be adjuncts to desktop computers, a computer link port permits exchanging data between the two, either by cable or wireless transmission. When coupled with a modem, the Wizard's communication software can follow a script to dial a remote computer and log in. Once it has accessed the remote computer, the device's built-in software can emulate a computer terminal to receive electronic mail, transmit a spreadsheet, and send a fax, obtain a stock quote, and so forth.

At a recent Consumer Electronic Show, the Sharp exhibit represented the Wizard as eventually becoming one's personal, portable link to networks, peripherals, software cards, and computers. Sharp foresees palmtop devices being used to access electronic mail, on-line information database services, and corporate databases, whereas their software cards will be used to inform, assist, entertain, and translate. For busy, traveling executives and professionals, the palmtop organizer comes closer and closer to being their portable office as each new enhancement appears on the market.

Another class of devices in the palmtop family is specialized computers, such as Sony's Data Discman. The size of a paperback book, the Data Discman can play three-inch CD-ROMs (compact disk, read only memory), each of which can hold 100,000 pages of text. It is the world's first handheld electronic book player, says Donald Trivette [3]. It has a small screen that can display text and simple graphics, plus a keyboard. And although people might not use it to read novels, they will use it to reference catalogs, parts lists, encyclopedias, and other reference works.

Personal Digital Assistants

The newest, and most unique, portables to hit the marketplace are personal digital assistants (PDAs). They represent the beginning of consumer computing. First exemplified by Apple's Newton, these specialized palm-size computers are meant to be intelligent assistants, able to store and recall names and addresses, fax notes, and even recognize hand-printed letters, pen strokes, and simple shapes. The 7 1/2- by 3 1/3-inch Newton is a pen-based computer with a speaker for digitized sound output. The stylus can be used to write on the screen or tap one of the six command icons at the bottom of the screen.

The uniqueness of these machines is represented by their "intelligence." Rather than simply performing tasks requested by the user, these devices will be able to perform series of commands and anticipate actions before they are requested. For example, a PDA can format a note into a business letter, supplying the full name and address, salutation, and formatting—perhaps even dial the telephone number to fax it. In short, these little systems will apply their tremendous power to the user interface, making them handy, carry-around digital assistants.

Liza Weiman and Tom Moran [4] illustrate Newton's intelligence through the following examples. Write Gina Smith's name and address in the address book. The system translates your hand printing into characters as you do. Then write "call Gina" in the notebook portion of Newton, circle it, and tap once. All the Gina's in your address book appear at the bottom of the screen in a window, along with their telephone numbers. If your Newton contains a modem, once you highlight the correct Gina and tap the telephone icon, the system dials your phone. Or if you write "lunch with Gina, Monday," Newton knows that lunch is generally an hour-long meeting at noon, so it schedules your lunch for the coming Monday.

So PDAs are meant to be adept at performing certain tasks quickly and easily. They are likely to come in numerous flavors, some for handling hand printing, maybe even handwriting, and some for performing speech recognition. They will also probably be equipped with card slots for storage or other programs.

Weiman and Moran note that Newton has three main components: one for recognizing stylus strokes, one for organizing information, and one for communicating. The first Newton actually has several recognizers, each optimized a certain character set—perhaps a character recognizer, graphics recognizer, and a pen command recognizer. All recognizers will examine each stroke written on the screen and each passes its guess to a controller that decides which is the best guess. The pen command recognizer, for example, allows the user to erase a line by using an erasing motion, insert a word in a sentence by using a caret, add certain information to a file by circling it, or start a new page by drawing a line across the bottom of the screen.

Owen Lindholm, Steve Apiki, and Michael Nadeau [5] point out that the hand-printing recognizer knows that words written in a line go together, and that several written lines form a paragraph. It also knows about size and spatial relationships between characters, so it can differentiate between large and small print. The graphics recognizer cannot only transform hand-drawn symbols into nicely formed ones, it realizes that certain lines are meant to be parallel or touching, even if not drawn perfectly.

The information organizer will also be intelligent, in that it can relate new information to existing data. The data is stored as separate objects with values and tags. Values are the information in the object, and a tag identifies the type of information. Newton links related objects, and any type of form—say, address book, calendar, or business letter form—can retrieve every type of information separately or linked.

Implications for Systems Management

What does this expanding world of small, portable computers mean to information systems executives? As we see it, there are several implications.

First, computer use is likely to take another great leap forward, as it did with PCs. With the explosion of types of portable computers, more employees are likely to find one that fits their needs. Therefore, computing will become a major tool in more employees' lives sooner than many experts probably expected. Information systems executives can take advantage of this more versatile computing environment in ways not envisioned before. Thus, we suggest forming teams to study ways to take advantage of these small, flexible systems. The more pilot projects initiated, the more technology transfer is likely to occur.

Second, this mobile revolution should not go unguided. Systems management needs to be out in front in the mobile technology revolution, not ignore or disregard it as many did with the PC. Otherwise, they will end up playing catch-up. We believe it is folly to view these little computers simply as personal productivity tools, with no relevance to corporate computing. Rather, they should be seen as new windows to organizational computing—windows that are sure to spur new forms of computing that can be shared if fostered in the right environment. Information systems managers should play a large role in creating that environment.

Third, portables may begin to record corporate memory. Portables are not just smaller PCs, although they can be used that way. They have characteristics not generally associated with PCs. For instance, their portability makes them actually feel personal, convenient, and informal. They can be used on the spur of the moment, for a quick task, something people rarely do with a PC. Therefore, they lend themselves to people entering or retrieving small pieces of data and information. For example, if entering information is quick and easy, and provides a benefit to the user—such as easy retrieval later or information to pass to someone else—corporations will finally have a way to tap into the corporate knowledge that is going unrecorded.

And fourth, this new genre of computers may need some new corporate guidelines. If these devices are to play a role in creating the "corporate memory," some issues need to be resolved. Privacy is one. The reason many people prefer to tell others sensitive information, rather than record it, is to maintain some control over its dissemination. Once recorded—say, as a digitized voice note or electronic mail message—however, its privacy is essentially lost, because it can be so easily rerouted via distribution lists to many people.

Corporations need policies about which information should not be recorded in networked databases. Searching electronic information is far easier than paper files, so the deterrent of effort is significantly reduced. Encryption may become an important weapon in safeguarding sensitive electronic information, perhaps used in ways that allow the sender to limit distribution.

It appears to us that mobile computing presents some challenges to corporate systems management—challenges that business executives and end users might raise but cannot resolve on their own. They need leadership.

To illustrate how corporate computing and small computers mesh, consider how Kraft Foodservice is using notebook computers, its first foray into the world of mobile computing.

CASE EXAMPLE: Kraft Foodservice

Kraft Foodservice, with headquarters in Deerfield, Illinois, provides fresh and frozen food products to restaurants, hospitals, schools, and other institutions. In the early 1990s, the company equipped 750 of its sales representatives with GRiD notebook computers, reports Michael Roney [6], to improve ordering and delivery of Kraft products. The system covers eight markets and will eventually encompass 2,500 laptops and forty-five markets across the United States.

Each night, these sales reps turn on their notebook computers and leave them running. While they sleep, the computer, which has been enhanced with a 20-megabyte removable hard drive and a 2,400-bps internal modem, downloads inventory data, sales information, software upgrades, and order status. In the morning, the rep runs the "Good Morning" program, which describes the downloaded items as well as the status of the orders placed the previous day.

The software, which was written by the information systems department, provides data on product availability, delivery information, pricing, account status, and purchasing history, says Roney.

One of the major goals of the system was to help the sales reps surmount one of the most frustrating aspects of the business: receiving accurate, up-to-date inventory information for their customers. Those customers want to know exactly how much of their order will be delivered the following day. Using the laptop, the representatives can access the catalog of eight thousand Kraft items whose status has been updated the night before. Based on this daily update, they can confirm customer orders on the spot, and ensure an accurate order and prompt delivery.

One of the main challenges in implementing the system is synchronizing training with the technology. Due to the rapid changes in the mobile technology field, Kraft is continually upgrading both the software and hardware in the system. To keep the sales reps apprised of the new features of their systems, Kraft has installed a twenty-four-hour, toll-free hotline to field questions.

Wireless Wide Area Communication Services

Wireless communication is in its infancy, especially in the data communication area. We discussed wireless LANs in Chapter 6. Here we look at wireless WANs, the crucial telecommunication component of mobile computing.

David Hayden, of Computer Systems Analysis, presents a concise overview of the the wireless WAN arena in *Mobile Office* magazine [7]. There are three choices, he says, cellular data communications, one-way electronic mail, and two-way mobile data communications.

Cellular Data Communications. The most common form of wireless communications is the cellular telephone. In addition to serving voice calls, these networks can also handle data. In fact, they are the least expensive and most accessible means of wireless data communications, but they also are the most problematic.

People can easily attach their portable computer to their cellular phone using a customized communication package. However, the networks are noisy, they have relatively slow transmission speeds, the signals fade in and out, and data can be lost when the call is handed off from one cell to another. These problems have been tolerated for voice calls, but they may be too disruptive for data communication, which requires continuous, error-free transmission. Vendors are tackling these problems, says Hayden. For example, today's cellular systems, which are analog, are soon to be supplemented by digital cellular systems. Digital cellular is static free, has no fading, and provides full privacy.

One-Way Wireless Systems. A one-way wireless system is essentially a "souped up" paging system that allows people to link their palmtop or notebook computer to a paging receiver and receive electronic mail. This mail can be text messages, changes to the calendar, spreadsheet updates, as well as news, weather, and stock reports. Jeff Ubois [8] notes that paging systems are far more versatile than beepers. They are being transformed from a simple local service to a complex global messaging network.

Four types of paging services are offered, says Ubois. *Tone-only,* which is the most basic and cheapest service, sends a tone to the beeper unit telling the user to call a prearranged telephone number. This service is most effective when coupled with voice mail, because it can alert users of new messages. The second option, *numerical display,* has been the most popular, because it can display a message up to twenty digits. *Voice paging,* the third option, sends the beeper a voice message six to eight minutes in length. This service is expensive and has not been very popular. But it could stage a comeback with new voice compression techniques, says Ubois. The fourth option, *alphanumeric paging,* delivers full text messages, which allows the user to decide what action to take on the spot. Most nationwide services are moving into this fourth option, says Ubois, and it may become popular now that software to send these messages is becoming available. Typing in messages on touch-tone phones is too time consuming for most people.

Paging is increasingly being integrated with other messaging technologies, says Ubois, as a way to alert people of newly arrived voice mail, faxes, or electronic mail. The pager/voice mail connection is currently the most widely used with all major voice mail services offering paging.

Palmtops will be used with pagers. For example, says Hayden, a Motorola NewsStream receiver can be attached to a Hewlett-Packard 95 palmtop computer via a special cradle to receive mail. Motorola's EMBARC paging service, which is available in 70 U.S. cities and costs from $50 to $80 a month and 75 cents a message, is often used as a store-and-forward network to deliver messages in off-peak hours. SkyTel, on the other hand, is often used to receive messages in minutes, at a higher cost. SkyTel also offers the Safari Wireless Mailbox, a joint venture with AT&T, which couples an alphanumeric pager with AT&T Mail and AT&T's Safari notebook computer.

So the high-end pager of the future, says Ubois, will have a computer and communicating device for receiving wireless electronic mail or information monitoring alerts, such as messages from an alerting service that the price of a specific stock has fallen below a certain threshold. Ubois expects paging systems to be used for information gathering and monitoring as well as messaging.

Two-Way Mobile Data Communications. The newest wireless WAN option is packet-switched communication networks, says Hayden. These networks, which use packet radio technology, require special radio modems for communication. The two first mobile data networks available in the United States were Mobitex from RAM Mobile Data, and Ardis from IBM and Motorola. Both networks provide nationwide coverage among specific U.S. cities. Cost ranges from $80 to $150 a month plus 25 cents to 80 cents per one thousand-character message, says Hayden.

The radio modems can be internal or external to the palmtop, pen based, and portable computers. Some specially designed computers—called "wireless PCs" or "portable communicating PCs"—contain both a radio modem for data transmission and a traditional cellular modem for fax transmission.

These packet radio networks, which are in their infancy, transmit data faster than cellular networks. They do not involve handing off transmissions as does cellular, and they include encoding for security and error correction for reliability.

Hayden believes that wireless networks will be used by corporations to support both mobile employees and consumers. For example, the Hoboken, New Jersey, fire department links its fire fighters to fire stations via a wireless network, to transmit important information, such as the location and pressure of fire hydrants, possible chemical hazards in the area, and the location of children and handicapped residents in buildings.

These three wireless technologies, along with future satellite networks, will vastly expand data communication options, says Hayden.

THE NEW ROLE OF ELECTRONIC MAIL

Although electronic mail has been around since the first computer conferencing systems in the 1970s, it is only now becoming an important element in corporate computing. In fact, we see it becoming one of the major components of the "information technology infrastructure" that companies must put in place. In a white paper, IDC [9] claims that electronic mail is the new corporate backbone for providing a host of enhanced communications services—ones that will alter how organizations conduct their business, both internally and externally.

Uses of Electronic Mail

Specifically, electronic mail systems are becoming the platform for

- Integrating voice mail, fax, and person-to-person messaging systems
- Supporting workflow and workgroup applications
- People-to-application communications
- Continual communications between mobile employees and their home office
- Permitting "mail-enabled applications" via messaging APIS
- Intercompany transmissions via EDI

Until recently, electronic mail networks were seen simply as the means to distribute text messages among users. Now, however, electronic mail is seen as the communication vehicle by which people and computer applications interact with each other. This significant broadening of the role of electronic mail is the basis for the renewed, and newly heightened, interest in electronic mail. It is no longer just a people-to-people communication vehicle; it is becoming a people-to-application and application-to-application vehicle as well.

IDC notes that voice mail and facsimile transmissions are now piggybacking on electronic mail networks. So the networks are providing the foundation for integrating the three kinds of mail. In addition, workflow software, which routes electronic work, as well as scheduling and electronic conferencing will also draw on electronic mail systems, says IDC. Specifically, they will use two important electronic mail standards: the OSI X.400 transport standard and the X.500 directory standard. These standards provide the means for connecting disparate mail systems and for addressing messages across mail systems. So as workgroup applications become available, electronic mail systems are likely to be their communication infrastructure.

Furthermore, there is the recent development called "mail-enabled applications," which refers to the emergence of APIS for electronic mail systems. These will allow applications to interact with each other far more easily by using popular electronic mail systems as the go-between. The APIS provide standard interfaces between applications and mail systems.

Finally, electronic data interchange among companies is also likely to adhere to electronic mail standards.

In short, IDC sees electronic mail providing the impetus for reengineering work processes to take advantage of the electronic routing and widespread messaging not feasible in the past.

Types of Electronic Mail Systems

In the 1980s, electronic mail was a primary feature of centralized office automation systems, such as Digital's All-in-1 and IBM's PROFS. These systems allowed internal electronic communications but no links to the outside world. People wishing to communicate externally used computer bulletin boards, computer conferencing systems, and public network services, such as CompuServe. Both types of systems served mainly person-to-person messaging.

Today, LAN-based electronic mail systems are growing the fastest. IDC reports that the number of LAN-based electronic mailboxes doubled between late 1980 to late 1990, and doubled again from late 1990 to late 1991. By 1995 they expect the number of mailboxes to increase one hundred-fold over 1990. This growth comes not only from more person-to-person messaging but from automated routing of work among workstations, with electronic mail as the transport medium.

Electronic mail systems in the future are likely to use a client/server structure, says IDC. User functions, such as the interface, will be performed on the workstations. The behind-the-scenes communication functions—managing and synchronizing directories, filtering and storing messages, and routing transmissions—will be performed on servers. The directory services are likely to be quite elaborate, storing profiles of each user's preferred word processor and spreadsheet, for example, so that messages can be automatically translated for the recipient.

THE IMPORTANCE OF MULTIMEDIA

Information delivery is becoming an important responsibility of information systems departments, to present information in the most natural ways. Multimedia will play a major role as a front-end to a growing number of systems, and it will be the technology of choice for public access systems.

What is multimedia? Several definitions are floating around the field. The one we like best comes from Christine Hughes, publisher of the *Media Letter* newsletter [10]. She defines multimedia as the combination of time-based media—such as voice, animation, and video—and space-based media—such as text, graphics, and images.

Others believe that multimedia means full-motion video. This appears to be the original definition, but now the definition is broadening. Most real-life business uses of multimedia do not employ full-motion video, because it is so expensive. Many multimedia applications can be just as effective using sequences of still photographs in place of motion video.

In the long run, as the computing world becomes multimedia, perhaps Nick Arnett's definition will have the most meaning. Arnett is editor of *Multimedia Computing and Presentations* newsletter [11]. He says that multimedia computing is not about combining media, it is about choosing the right medium for the message.

A humorous, but realistic, definition is that multimedia means making more than two trips to the car to unload the equipment.

Current Status and Future Direction

Multimedia is *the* new computing platform, because it gets to the heart of computing in the 1990s: presenting electronic data and information in their most usable form. To assess the status and direction of multimedia, we attended three conferences—MacWorld [12], Microsoft's Multimedia and CD-ROM conference [13], and the Multimedia Expo [14].

In 1990-91, multimedia became *the* buzzword for selling products for microcomputers. The number of multimedia products—such as video capture boards, multimedia authoring tools, CD-ROM products, audio and music production and editing packages, and multimedia clip art—ballooned. IBM's PS/2 became a multimedia platform, joining the Macintosh and the Amiga.

Until that time, the multimedia folks had been in a world of their own, creating corporate presentations, movies, television, graphics art, and corporate training. Although not yet part of mainstream computing, multimedia is evolving into an important branch. People used to wonder how all that power in workstations was going to be used. The answer has become clear—to make the interface far more natural and intuitive. These enhanced interfaces, in turn, will cause people to want more kinds of information in electronic form.

Like the PC revolution—which caught many systems departments unaware—multimedia could have the same sort of impact. Although no single application is driving it forward, multimedia is advancing on several different fronts. Systems departments ought to take these developments seriously, and provide guidance in all the traditional areas—databases, hardware, software, and communications—because electronic sharing of multimedia data significantly affects all four. Companies will be electronically moving multimedia (i.e., huge files) in the future; it would be wise to begin preparing for that future now.

Multimedia Tools

At the MacWorld conference, Jim Waldron of Burns, Connacher, and Waldron Design Associates [15] described a basic multimedia system on the Macintosh as consisting of

- A Macintosh with 8 megabytes of memory
- Eighty (to 300) megabytes of storage
- A 13-inch color monitor

- Macromind's MacRecorder or MediaTracks [16] for capturing sound and voice via the Mac (Macs have built-in sound playback capabilities)
- Adobe PhotoShop [17] for retouching scanned photos, blending multiple images into mosaics, and painting original artwork, in color or black and white
- Adobe Illustrator [17] for creating drawings
- Either Hypercard or Macromind's Director [16] authoring software for assembling the various multimedia pieces and then retrieving them during playback

This basic system—which does not handle video—costs about $7,500 in the United States. An additional piece of gear might be a scanner. To add video capabilities requires at least another $5,000—for a videodisk player, a video capture card, an audio board for CD-quality sound, and a video camera. Many of the speakers at the conference had built micro-based systems costing more than $25,000, by adding more sophisticated video production and editing, sound production and editing, three-dimensional modeling software, larger screens, and on and on.

The underlying technology for running multimedia applications is hypermedia, says a recent Index Foundation report [18], providing the means to navigate through databases as well as to weave files of different kinds of data together to generate multimedia applications. To distinguish between multimedia and hypermedia, we see multimedia referring to the media, whereas hypermedia refers to how the various elements in an application are linked. Hypermedia is an extension of hypertext, where chunks of text are linked via pointers, allowing a person to read by jumping from link to link, rather than linearly.

Developing a Multimedia Application

Developers generally create a multimedia piece using an authoring tool, such as Director, to synchronize sound clips, graphics elements, and still images along a timeline, which Director calls a "score." The fill-in-the-blank score has separate timelines for specifying tempo, color palette, transitions between elements, and graphics, image, sound, and video elements. For adding animation, Director provides more than fifty special transition effects, each selectable by clicking on a menu item. It also has selectable options for animating graphics and words—such as bringing words on-screen from any position off-screen, fading in, and so forth—at any speed and following any path the developer wishes.

Using such a tool, a developer can specify a photograph or single frame of video as the background, and overlay it with a voice or music while animated graphics and words appear. These various elements can be retrieved from hard disk (internal or external), videotape, videodisk, or CD-ROM.

Currently, most multimedia pieces can only be played back on the platform with which they were developed; however, vendors are beginning to offer cross-platform products, to say, allow developing a piece on a Mac for presentation on an IBM PS/2.

Developing multimedia applications is more like making a movie than writing a software program. In fact, most multimedia developers use television, film, and publishing terminology; multimedia is bringing about the convergence of the publishing, broadcasting, and computer fields.

Two Future Multimedia Interfaces

Multimedia is not a "flash in the pan;" it will change how people interact with computers—not just by presenting data in more natural forms but by permitting new concepts for interacting with computers. To demonstrate such new concepts, there are two possible future user interfaces that incorporate multimedia: agents and rooms.

Agents

Alan Kay, now an Apple Fellow, was one of the developers of the predecessors of today's graphical user interfaces. In recent speeches, conversations, and articles, he talks about "agents" becoming a major interface of the future. An agent is an electronic entity that performs tasks, either on its own or at the request of a person or a computer. Agents are often characterized as talking heads on screens; you talk to them, and they talk to you. That scenario is a bit futuristic, but it epitomizes how people and agents might work together—in a natural, conversational manner.

Rather than manipulate icons, people will manage agents, says Kay. People will have agents that sort their electronic mail and search out items of interest to them from databases and news wires. They may have agents who keep their calendar or format their memos.

When network computing finally arrives, says Kay, the complexity of keeping abreast of all the information available on the networks, and all the people communicating over the networks, will be mind boggling. People can only handle so many icons on a screen; therefore, this form of user interface becomes totally inadequate in the network environment. People will need agents to act on their behalf, scanning the electronic links for the information they need and filtering the deluge of information they will receive. For more of Kay's ideas on interfaces, see [19].

Agent-based computing is arriving. One humanlike interface product on the market is InterFACE, from Bright Star Technology [20]. InterFACE is used to to create a talking face on a screen—either a photograph or a drawing of any kind of face—and then animate the face to be synchronized with speech. Since InterFACE allows 120 facial positions, these heads appear to be talking quite realistically. InterFACE will work with either prerecorded speech, which sounds realistic, or digitally created speech, which does not yet sound very good. Of course, this product presents only one potential visual front-end for agents; a "real" agent behind it would do the work.

Rooms

The researchers at Xerox PARC, a leading U.S. research lab, talk about their work in an issue of *Benchmark* [21], the quarterly Xerox magazine. They believe user interfaces in the 1990s will help people visualize information via three-dimensional, animated "rooms" of information. Their "Rooms" research project is based on the idea that people often use time, location, color, or size to find items in their office. The rooms in this futuristic Xerox interface draw on these notions by having items floating in space, with shadows and other visual cues to help people use their perceptual abilities.

The researchers have created several kinds of rooms; each holds information in a different way. For example, their "cam room" organizes the top 600 nodes of the Xerox organization chart, and fits it onto one screen. Formerly, this organization chart required eighty pages. The tiered structure contains carousels of names, with reporting relationships shown as translucent cones. Click on a name, and the entire structure rotates to bring that name to the forefront. The animation allows the user to see the relationships continually as a new name is brought to the fore. Underneath each name—in a hidden layer that can be seen by clicking on a name—is the biography and photograph of the job holder.

Another room contains a "time wall," where all the information is organized on a timeline. Click on a month, and the wall visually slides by you, bringing the selected month front and center—yet still connected to the other months. This month can be stretched to spread out its files, which appear as though they are floating in space along a timeline.

The goal of the Rooms project is to augment the human intellect, say the researchers, by (1) allowing people to deal with large amounts of interrelated information through visualization, and (2) giving people ways to manipulate the information or structures quickly and easily. These capabilities will allow people to work on larger intellectual problems, they believe. Users of business applications are the intended audience of this PARC research. Eventually, these researchers would like to make the barriers between the paper world and the electronic world disappear altogether.

To demonstrate one use of multimedia for visualizing different forms of data, consider a product that American Airlines offers travel agents; it is called SABREvision.

CASE EXAMPLE: SABREvision

American Airlines, with headquarters in Fort Worth, Texas, is the largest airline in the western world. They have 2,300 flights a day and transport 966 million people a year among 184 destinations worldwide.

The SABRE Information Network, a division of American, recently introduced to travel agents a multimedia adjunct to their text-only SABRE computer reservation system. The new system, called SABREvision, presents hotel information via text, color photographs, and maps—displayed on a PC.

In 1987, American installed their first PCs in travel agencies. Some 50% of the eighty-seven thousand SABRE terminals in more than eighteen thousand agencies are now PCs on LANs. SABREvision takes advantage of this installed base.

The purposes of SABREvision are to improve travel agent productivity and profitability while increasing the number of hotel bookings made through SABRE. Before SABREvision, agents relied mainly on hotel and travel books, because on-line information was insufficient or difficult to find. By teaming up with Reed Travel Group, Reed's electronic Jaguar Hotel Directory can now be used in conjunction with SABRE. The directory contains textual information on 50,000 hotels, with more than 6,600 electronic "pages" with color images and a worldwide mapping system, all stored on one CD-ROM disk. The CD-ROM drive is connected to the file server on each agency's 4-megabit Novell token ring LAN.

An agent can use SABREvision in different ways. One way is to enter a city name and create a list of 'qualifiers' from more than one hundred provided by the system. For example, a client may want a nonsmoking room in a downtown hotel that provides room service, has a pool and exercise room, offers fax service, and costs less than $125 a night. From these qualifiers, the system builds a list of hotels that meet the criteria. Current rates and availability—obtained from SABRE—are integrated with the local CD-ROM data displayed on the agent's screen. Hotels with images on the system are shown in boldface.

Agents can also call up a map of the area, with the locations of major landmarks and the boldfaced hotels noted. The maps have several levels of magnification, and agents can move north, south, east, and west from the on-screen map. Maps, as well as text, can also be printed for clients.

By selecting a hotel listed in boldface, the agent can see color photographs of various aspects of the hotel—a meeting room, a restaurant, a room, the hotel exterior, and an aerial view—along with information about the hotel. Agents can tailor the system by highlighting hotels that their agency prefers and adding comments about individual hotels—to document their experiences or experiences of clients.

Since SABRE and SABREvision are integrated, agents can book a hotel room without leaving SABREvision.

Developing SABREvision. The system, which was developed by North Communications [22], uses three major databases—the map database, the CD-ROM database, and the SABRE host database. The map database is included on the CD that Reed updates each quarter and ships to American, who then distributes the disks to the subscribing agencies.

To integrate CD-ROM into SABREvision, they looked to Online Computer Systems [23], a supplier of CD-ROM hardware, software, and mastering services. Online's OPTI-NET networking software and OPTI-WARE database management system were chosen because they could meet the needed performance criteria. And Online was willing to tailor their retrieval software to fit into the tight memory constraints of the IBM PS/2 model 30s used by some of the travel agencies.

CD-ROMs need special database access software, because their access speeds are so much slower than hard disks. These special DBMS take as many shortcuts as possible to speed up access time. In addition, integrating CD-ROM into an existing PC environment requires tailoring the CD-ROM products; currently, they cannot be just bought off-the-shelf as add-ons.

Aside from the database access software, the major programming task was creating the user interface. Since they were dealing with such a wide range of DOS-based PCs, none of the products for developing windowing interfaces was appropriate—for example, the IBM PS/2 model 30 cannot run Microsoft Windows. Therefore, the interfaces were created from scratch, in C. The programming did not differ significantly from other C programming, except where the programs interacted with the graphics card. These portions needed to talk directly to the device driver. Had the developers been able to use, say, a windows painting product, the interfaces would have been considerably easier to create.

Testing the friendliness of the user interface as well as the speed of the database searches was done in American's usability lab. The system was tested three times—after each of two prototypes and for the final product. One at a time, specially selected agents spent several hours in the lab performing specific tasks. As they used SABREvision, their actions were videotaped, their thinking-out-loud comments were tape recorded, and analysts watching from another room noted areas that needed revision.

The people at SABREvision found that adding multimedia to an existing base of PCs was significantly harder than developing for one platform, or starting from scratch. They recommend that others try to control the hardware and operating system of the application; otherwise, the constraints of older and less powerful machines can significantly add to development costs.

DOUGLAS ENGELBART'S IDEAS

We end this chapter by looking both backward and forward at the same time, by describing ones man's ideas about a good user interface. Several of the most popular features on workstations these days originated at one source: a research team at Stanford Research Institute headed by Douglas Engelbart [24]. Between 1957 and 1977, Engelbart's team conceived and implemented a computer system for knowledge workers called NLS that used a mouse for cursor control, detachable keyboards, split-screen displays, and more. Believe it or not, all of his ideas have still not been widely implemented, so we present them here as a target for the future.

Engelbart believes that the main role of computers is to augment peoples' intellectual work; therefore, an electronic workplace should be relatively easy to learn but not simple-minded. He prefers a powerful system, even though it increases the learning difficulty, because it has the greatest potential for leveraging the effectiveness of knowledge workers. Following are six technical capabilities he believes such systems should have

1. An open-ended vocabulary
2. Fast, concurrent control
3. Writing and structuring
4. Naming and addressing
5. Remote jumps and manipulations
6. Views, filters, and windows

Open-Ended Vocabulary. The system should allow users to receive customizable services, such as the commands they use, the amount of feedback they receive from the system each time a command is issued, the subsystems automatically available at log-on, the time zone the user wants to work in, the number of versions of documents to be kept, and the types of peripherals to be used. The system can achieve this flexibility with a user interface module to define these attributes for each user. Users can modify these attributes, even creating a new command by defining it in terms of other commands. The interface module can act as a translator for all applications, no matter where the applications programs are located.

Fast, Concurrent Control. When people think, they use "little windows in their minds," says Engelbart, and they jump effortlessly from one subject to another, and from one view to another. Information in a computer should be manipulated similarly, he says, and with less than one-fourth-second response time. To permit fast, concurrent manipulation, in the mid-1960s Engelbart designed two devices, the mouse and the chording keyset. The mouse needs no description; it is familiar to most readers by now. The keyset has five parallel keys (somewhat like a piano) that can be used individually or in combinations (chords) to select codes representing letters of the alphabet. It is used with one hand, for command designation and short entries, while the other hand manipulates the mouse, for cursor control and selection. Experienced users can work as fast as they can think, because they can be moving the cursor while they are defining the operation they want to perform next.

Writing and Structuring. Engelbart believes that electronic tools can loosen some of the limitations imposed by paper and pencil, assisting writers in doing their jobs better. His hierarchical file structure has allowed intermixing all types of communications—text, data, graphics, voice, and image. Users can define relationships between items in many ways, such as organizing a document hierarchically and then displaying only section headings to get an overview, or printing only the first two lines of each bibliographic citation, and so on. Users can store items at different levels and quickly move up and down among the levels.

Naming and Addressing. Users should also be able to assign a name or address to any electronic item so that it can be uniquely identified in other documents, messages, and so on. In his system, Engelbart allowed names and addresses to be assigned to single words, lines, paragraphs, sections, graphs, documents, or collections of documents—anything a user chose. A permanent library of addressed items—from one-line messages to book-size documents—was available for retrieval at any time.

Remote Jumps and Manipulations. Once items can be addressed, users should also be able to jump directly to an address, pull an addressed item onto the screen, print a series of addressed items, and so on. Where this is possible, users can easily move through huge amounts of on-line documents by just pointing to 'links' embedded in the text.

Views, Filters, and Windows. Users should be able to select how they format and view information. For instance, they may want to place two or more items side by side to compare them; to facilitate this, Engelbart's project used split screens. In addition, users should be able to retrieve information based on text strings, or look at all items that were recently changed by a specific person. Views and filters are short programs or query commands that allow users to display or print only the information they want. With these capabilities, users can create and store elaborate processes for manipulating documents, filing electronic mail, printing documents, and so on.

Engelbart's conceptual framework for systems includes not only "the tool system" just described but also "the human system"—the methods of work, skills, knowledge, language, training, roles, and organization. The real challenge facing organizations, he believes, is to give balanced support to the co-evolution of both, in a guided manner, so that knowledge work can be truly augmented.

CONCLUSION

In the first two editions of this book, which appeared in 1986 and 1989, much of the excitement in computing related to PCs and end user computing. As far as we can tell, that excitement continues, unabated, but in the now expanded universe of mobile computing and reaching out to consumers. As computers shrink and communications become untethered from wires and strands of glass, the opportunities to serve new audiences grow. That has been the subject of this chapter: the exciting new technologies that are expanding the computing horizons. The question then becomes putting those technologies to good use. That is the question we address in the next chapter, by discussing how information systems management can support the use of these new technologies.

QUESTIONS AND EXERCISES

QUESTIONS

1. What has been the progression of the incredible shrinking computer?
2. What four kinds of software will be available on pen computers, according to Manning?
3. According to Isaacson, what will pen computers become?
4. Describe a palmtop computer.
5. What future role does Sharp see for its Wizard?
6. What is a personal digital assistant? What makes it unique from the other portables?
7. What are four implications of these small computers for information systems management?
8. Why is Kraft Foodservice using portable computers?
9. What are the three types of wireless wide area communication services?
10. What are six potential uses of electronic mail networks?
11. What is multimedia?
12. Describe a typical Mac-based multimedia computer.
13. What are agents? What will they do?
14. Describe Xerox PARC's Rooms interface.
15. What is SABREvision? Why is it an improvement for travel agents?
16. What were the two main programming tasks in creating SABREvision?
17. According toe Douglas Engelbart, what six technical capabilities should every system for knowledge workers provide?

DISCUSSION QUESTIONS

1. The very small portable computers should be no concern to information systems executives except for exchanging messages. Systems executives should concentrate on the large applications, and ignore these small devices. Agree or disagree? Why?

2. Multimedia is not going to take off as everyone expects because the technology is too complex. Agree or disagree? Why?

EXERCISES

1. Talk to two people who use a laptop, tablet, or palmtop computer. What do they like about it? What would they change? How can it be improved? Share their ideas with the class.
2. Read two articles about electronic mail or wireless communication services. What new information did you learn that is not in the text? Share that with the class.
3. Visit a local information systems department and find out how they are using portable computers, electronic mail, wireless communication services, and multimedia. Summarize your visit for the class.

REFERENCES

1. ISAACSON, P., "The Pen's Past, Present and Future" and "A Pen Computer for All Reasons," *Mobile Office,* March 1992, pp. 33-40 and 57-72.

2. MANNING, R., "Stylish Application for Stylus Computing," *Mobile Office,* March 1992, pp. 45-54

3. TRIVETTE, D., "Power Reading: The Data Discman," *Mobile Office,* February 1992, pp. 34-42.

4. WEIMAN, L., and T. MORAN, "Newton: A Step Toward the Future," *MacWorld,* August 1992, pp. 129-131.

5. LINDERHOLM, O., W. APIKI, and M. NADEAU, "The PC Gets More Personal," *Byte,* July 1992, pp. 128-138.

6. RONEY, M., "Special Report: Corporate Computing," *Mobile Office,* December 1991, pp. 35-42

7. HAYDEN, D., "The New Age of Wireless," *Mobile Office,* May 1992, pp. 34-44.

8. UBOIS, J., "Paging: The Whole Story," *Mobile Office,* November 1991, pp. 36-40.

9. "ELECTRONIC MAIL: THE NEW CORPORATE BACKBONE," IDC White Paper inserted into *Computerworld,* June 22, 1992.

10. HUGHES, C., The Myriad Group, P.O. Box 142075, Coral Gables, FL 33114.

11. ARNETT, N., Multimedia Computing Corporation, 3501 Ryder St., Santa Clara, CA 95051.

12. MACWORLD EXPO, P.O. Box 4010, Dedham, MA 02026.

13. MICROSOFT MULTIMEDIA AND CD-ROM CONFERENCE AND EXPOSITION, Cahners Exposition Group, 999 Summer St., Stamford, CT 06905.

14. MULTIMEDIA EXPO, American Expositions, 110 Greene St., Suite 703, New York, NY 10012.

15. WALDRON J., Burns, Connacher, and Waldron Design Associates, 59 W. 19th St., Suite 4A, New York, NY 10011.

16. ADOBE SYSTEMS, 1585 Charleston Road, P.O. Box 7900, Mountain View, CA 94039.

17. MACROMIND, 410 Townsend, Suite 408, San Francisco, CA 94107.

18. "EMERGING TECHNOLOGIES: ANNUAL REPORT FOR MANAGERS," Index Foundation, Research Report No. 73, February 1990, pp. 33-46.

19. KAY, A., "User Interface: A Personal View," in *The Art of Human-Computer Interface Design,* edited by Brenda Laurel, (Addison-Wesley, Reading, MA), 1990.

20. BRIGHT STAR TECHNOLOGY, 1450 114th Ave. SE, Suite 200, Bellevue, WA 98004.

21. "ROOMS WITH A VIEW," *Benchmark*, Summer 1990, pp. 10–12.

22. NORTH COMMUNICATIONS, 3030 Pennsylvania Ave., Santa Monica, CA 90404.

23. ONLINE COMPUTER SYSTEMS, 20251 Century Blvd., Germantown, MD 20874.

TWELVE

Supporting the Expanding Universe of Computing

INTRODUCTION

In the 1970s and 1980s, the use of computers by individuals was called "end user computing" (EUC). "End users" were almost exclusively using computers in their role as employees. Information systems departments established end user computing support groups, often called information centers, to support the use of PCs as well as fourth generation languages on mainframes. The history of Mead Corporation's information resources department, presented in Chapter 1, is typical of this evolution—from developing applications in the 1970s, to encouraging end users to access computers directly on their own in the 1980s, to integrating end user computing into enterprise-wide computing in the 1990s.

In the 1990s, there is no widely accepted term for the use of computers by individuals, because today this use is no longer just a small category of computing. It is the future of computing. Computing does not emanate from a data center as it formerly did; it is everywhere.

We see the universe of users of corporate computing also expanding. As shown in Figure 12-1, the users of corporate information services through the 1970s and mid-1980s were mainly employees, at their work site. Then, in the mid-1980s, organizations opened up access to their computer systems to some supplier and customer organizations. In the late 1980s, with the advent of portable computers, information systems departments began to support their mobile employees, giving them direct access to corporate computers wherever they were located. Today, in the 1990s, we see this universe of users expanding further still to consumers. Serving them is the next frontier for corporate information system departments.

In this chapter we address the question of how information systems management can respond to this expanding universe of users, and the expanding universe of information technologies. We begin with a brief history lesson on how companies have supported traditional end user computing, and the changes needed to support the new environment.

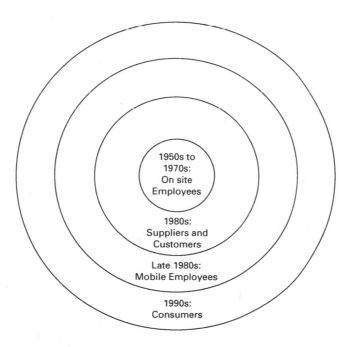

Figure 12-1 The Expanding Universe of Users of Corporate Computing Services

SUPPORTING TRADITIONAL END USER COMPUTING

End user computing has evolved to the point that it is no longer seen as a separate entity from mainline computing. The two evolved together, essentially during the ten years of the 1980s. Separate end user computing groups still exist, but they no longer attract the attention of top information systems management. They are just one of many parts of an information systems department. However, their approaches to managing end user computing can now be applied to implementing cooperative processing systems, field force automation, and consumer computing.

Traditional end user computing was introducing people to computers. In the 1980s, this job was handled by information centers—the primary end user computing support organization. The following history and update is drawn from "Information Centres in the 1990s," a paper by Janet Cohen of the Index Foundation [1] to which Barbara McNurlin contributed research and ideas.

Yesterday's Response: Information Centers

If you had asked information systems executives to define an information center in 1980, you would probably have gotten few knowledgeable answers. The same question in 1985 would have been answered by a description of the functions their information centers performed. In that short time, the information center idea became an industry, with installations spreading like wildfire. During that time, the IBM PC was introduced (in August 1981), so most people knew little or nothing about personal computers. They were novices with simple computing questions.

Information centers were yesterday's response to the need to bring end user computing into firms, mainly via personal computers. The watchword of information centers was "support"—support and train every interested employee on every type of product. The centers focused on conducting training classes, staffing help desks, and doing trouble-shooting consulting. Their main goal was to help employees become self-sufficient in using computers and creating their own applications.

Information centers emerged as separate groups within information systems departments, generally located away from the systems department—usually out among functional departments. They did not grow very large, no matter what the size of the firm. In one case, thirty-five staff members were serving ten thousand employees. The staff members became experts in specific products—spreadsheet, word processing, and database— and specialized in either mainframe or personal computer products. To bring some control to the rapidly proliferating number of PCs, information center managers initiated hardware and software standards. As noted earlier, the goal of this initial response to end user computing was to speed up the integration of information technology into firms.

Top management believed that once employees were given PCs and a few hours of training, they would become self-sufficient. Therefore, after the first few years of dramatic growth, information centers were not given more resources. In fact, top management expected them to go away, believing they were no longer needed. An often-quoted article was in the November 1987 issue of *Datamation* [2], which described how Quaker Oats disbanded its information center because its purpose had been fulfilled.

Interestingly, the lack of funding gave rise to a problem that few information system executives knew about: "the PC guru," people who became so enamored with a PC product or application that they promote its use wherever they could. They became the bane of information centers, because they often promoted nonstandard products. The cost of undoing problems caused by PC gurus may have been high, but it was only seen by information center managers. Many line and systems managers thought these gurus were doing the firm a favor, by devoting some of their time to helping others with computing. This would be true, *if* they were following company policies and standards.

Yesterday's information center performed its job in helping employees learn about computing, but that is not today's environment. So the information center solution, as originally conceived, is no longer the answer in most large firms, but the lessons are still valuable.

Today's Environment and Response

Today's end user computing environment differs markedly from the 1981 to 1985 environment. Everyone who could be called a "power user"— that is, someone who takes the initiative to learn how to use computer applications in their work—now has a computer. And employees who use PCs generally know quite a bit about the computer products they use. Therefore, when they run into a problem, their requests and questions are complex, difficult, and time-consuming to answer. Furthermore, end user computing has evolved into a demand-pull environment, where users may want new products faster than the support staff can supply them.

The business environment is also quite different today. Information technology is now seen as being important for competitive purposes. It is not just to improve efficiency; it allows people to do jobs in different ways.

The result of these trends is that yesterday's solution does not fit today's environment. To continue to exist, support groups need to refocus their efforts. At an Information Center conference, sponsored by Weingarten Publications [3], Naomi Karten, a well-known EUC consultant [4], described the changes she believes support groups must make in the 1990s. Essentially, she sees a shift from promoting end user computing (in the 1980s) to supporting business needs (in the 1990s).

For example, support groups need to switch from only reacting to user requests to dedicating a percentage of their effort to finding unfilled business needs; otherwise, the maintenance jobs will eat away all the time set aside for this strategic work. One way to approach this work is to do targeted marketing, perhaps creating short videos for specific audiences explaining where specific products might be of most use to them.

Likewise, these groups need to shift from supporting individuals to supporting departments to better ensure that the *right* business problems are being served by computing. Similarly, they need to move from supporting all needs to supporting high-payoff needs, so they will be seen as contributing to the firm. Note that the shift in supporting end user computing is really no different than the shift being made in systems departments as a whole—aligning computing efforts with business goals.

The support staff at Dylex, a retailer with headquarters in Toronto, Canada, presents a good example of accomplishing these two aims. The information center manager uses a "swat team" approach to both act quickly and coordinate the work of others, especially on projects that could be of strategic importance to the firm. For example, he assembled a cross-functional swat team to help a regional manager who felt his salespeople could benefit from having laptop computers. The team that investigated the possibilities included a corporate telecommunications specialist, a system analyst from the appropriate division's information systems department, a representative of the regional manager, and an information center staff member.

To illustrate how one information center has made the shift to the new environment, consider the work of the information center at the County of Los Angeles, California, described in the Index Foundation report.

CASE EXAMPLE: The County of Los Angeles, California

The County of Los Angeles, California, with 8.5 million residents, would be the seventeenth largest country in the world if it were a country. Los Angeles County employs eighty thousand people in some forty departments—law enforcement, health services, libraries, parks and recreation, and so on. Each department has its own information systems group, and most have three or so end user computing staff members.

The central information center (CIC) is part of an internal services department that provides all kinds of services to county departments. Thus, the CIC is a profit center. The manager of the center believes that EUC support must cover four areas.

- *Day-to-day support.* Help desks, troubleshooting, and training—that is, all the support work that will not go away

- *Implementation*. Work that takes less than a day or two to complete, such as installing new hardware and software for PCs and LANs
- *Strategic areas*. Uncovering applications that change the way the organization does business
- *Awareness*. Keeping others up-to-date on trends and new developments in computing

To accomplish the huge amount of potential work in these four areas, the goal of the CIC is to offload responsibility for the traditional EUC work—day-to-day support and implementation—to local EUC coordinators and groups, while keeping the other work—in the strategic and awareness areas—in the central EUC group. Specifically, the central group is leveraging its knowledge and expertise in four areas: EUC franchising, education and awareness, technology review center, and alternative delivery systems.

EUC Franchising. The purpose of EUC franchising products and services is to strengthen the local EUC groups and make them self-supporting. Franchised products include EUC support plans, EUC handbook, how-to booklets, rotating clinics, and a toll-free help desk.

- EUC *support plan* includes policies, a marketing plan, and management guidelines for running an EUC support group. A local EUC group contracts with the central EUC group to assist in drawing up this plan.
- EUC *handbook* is sold to local groups to give to their constituents. It explains services available from the local as well as central group, and it answers questions most frequently asked by county employees.
- *How-to booklets* are created by the central group for local groups. The first booklet, which was on desktop publishing, explained terms, described software and hardware configurations, and showed some sample page layouts. The second booklet was on LANs.
- *Rotating clinics* are intended to pass on the central's staff's expertise to local support groups. The central staff members visit a local group for a day or two to train new staff, consult on new training classes, help them prepare new marketing materials, and so on.
- A *toll-free central help desk* was established by the central group for users in Los Angeles County who are spread over an 11,300-square-mile area. But rather than staff the desk themselves, the central group uses an outside firm that provides this type of service.

Education and Awareness. The CIC is developing five education and awareness products.

Technology conferences. These are full-day conferences with both vendor booths and seminars. The seminars have different tracks for different audiences—such as managerial and technical. The conferences are free to all Los Angeles County employees. One on document imaging drew five hundred attendees, another on desktop publishing had six hundred attendees, and one on local area networks drew five hundred county employees. At each one, attendees learn about the subject, see demonstrations, and find out where to go for further help. Information center management hopes these conferences will help reduce the number of "unauthorized gurus" who promote non-standard products in these areas.

Newsletters. Newsletters are an extremely good way to disseminate information. The EUC group uses desktop publishing technology to publish a two-color, four-page monthly newsletter.

Directory of applications. To reduce the reinvention of duplicate software applications, the central information center has created a listing of EUC applications developed within Los Angeles County departments.

Product announcements. Each month, the central EUC group sends out fifteen to twenty announcements of new products, which they have investigated and tested.

User group meetings. The central group encourages and coordinates the formation of user groups among county employees to encourage idea exchange and awareness of what is possible with computing.

Technology Review Center. CIC has established a permanent site displaying various hardware and software, intended to help improve information technology buying decisions within the county. One room in the center is a desktop publishing demonstration room. Another room contains equipment that employees can use for an hourly fee. The center also provides some professional services, such as desktop design and production services to help employees who are designing and producing documents. The center also has media training rooms.

Alternative Service Delivery Systems. One of the most strategic services of the group is an alternative service delivery system. Rather than wait for county employees to think of new ways to use information technology, the group has built a prototype touch-screen kiosk that contains a microcomputer and printer. They are selling this kiosk to the various county departments as a new way for them to deliver information to their constituents. For example, these kiosks could show diagrams of buildings to help people locate an office, or they could explain the procedures for, say, obtaining a birth certificate, perhaps in various languages. The kiosk is the EUC group's first alternative delivery service project. They hope it encourages county employees to think of new ways to use information technology to provide information to the public. In the future, they plan to suggest other public access systems and even let the public perform transactions with the county in new ways.

At the County of Los Angeles, the central EUC group is concentrating on the strategic and awareness levels of end user computing. They are acting more as coordinators, and pushing the day-to-day support and implementation work out to the local EUC groups. That is, they are leveraging the expertise of their central EUC staff.

SERVING THE NEW END USERS

To us, the new end users are mobile employees and consumers. Although serving them will involve new technologies—such as mobile technologies, electronic mail, and multimedia—some of the underlying goals of end-user computing still apply. Following are discussions of both new computing audiences, along with examples of how two companies are serving them.

The New Frontier: Field Force Automation

The growth of mobile information technologies has thrown open the possibilities of who can use computers and when. Increasingly, the answer is anyone from anywhere at anytime. Companies are taking advantage of portable computers and wireless networks to unleash their field employees from offices. Field force automation is in full swing, because traveling employees can maintain the all-important link to their office from wherever they are located—in their car, a customer's office, an airport, a hotel room, or at home.

To illustrate how one company is taking advantage of mobile computing to decentralize its business, consider Nissan Motor Corporation/USA.

CASE EXAMPLE: Nissan Motor Corporation/USA

Nissan Motor Corporation/USA, with headquarters in Carson, California, is decentralizing operations and broadening decision making in its field force by drawing on notebook technology and cellular communications.

As Michael Roney [5] notes, for automobile manufacturers to address niche markets successfully, they must stay in much closer communication with their dealers. It no longer suffices for regional offices to allocate cars to dealers without fully understanding the dealers' current demands and preferences. The way to really understand a market is to live in it, not ask about it from afar.

To achieve this up-close understanding, Nissan decided to move its district managers out of regional offices into the communities they serve. The concept was pilot tested in the Dallas region, where the district managers were equipped with AT&T Safari notebook computers with internal 2,400-bps modems, Motorola cellular telephones, and DFI Handyscan handheld scanners.

Along with a new location and a computer system, the district managers received broader responsibilities in such areas as dealer profitability, sales results, warranty status, and customer satisfaction, reports Roney. Formerly, these responsibilities were handled by different people. By consolidating them, the district managers have more complete relationships with their dealers.

But to achieve closer coordination in the other direction—with the region and headquarters—required giving the district managers a way to manage information in more timely, concise, and convenient ways. The new system addresses this need. It allows the district managers to access regional and corporate data to help dealers better forecast monthly sales, more accurately report expenses, and receive better allocations of cars.

Nissan chose the 386-based AT&T Safari computer running Windows because it provided a hardware upgrade path, an easy-to-use interface, an almost-full-size keyboard, and a three-hour battery life. The company is also considering upgrading to 9,600-bps fax modem and adding AT&T's paging system, so that the district managers can receive electronic mail through the beeper and store it on their notebook.

The driving goal behind Nissan's field force automation work is moving decision making as close as possible to the point of customer contact. The new system moves them to the dealer showroom, and allows their district managers to stay in continual close contact with the dealers in those showrooms.

The Next Frontier: Reaching Out to Consumers

Some information systems departments have been directly serving consumers for several years. Some obvious examples are ATMs, voice response systems for checking on the status of a bank account, and self-serve airline reservation systems. But these services have been quite limited. We expect systems departments in the 1990s to expand their reach to consumers significantly. Of course voice response systems will play a major role, but so might home computers.

Convenience is a driving force in the 1990s. Consumers want convenience to ease the numerous demands on their time. Information technology supplies convenience, not only by making corporate information available around the clock, but by making it available from many more locations. Information technology also enables fast response to consumer questions. Again, this increases the convenience of doing business with these organizations. By supporting convenience, information technology can give organizations an advantage over their competitors.

As an example of a corporation using its information technology resources—and peoples' comfort with the telephone—to directly serve consumers, consider Huntington Bankshares' alliance with AT&T.

CASE EXAMPLE: Huntington Bankshares

Huntington Bankshares Inc., with headquarters in Columbus, Ohio, is a $13 billion regional bank holding company with 271 banking offices in seven states. Its mortgage, trust, investment banking, and automobile finance subsidiaries operate fifty-one offices in sixteen states.

In 1991, The Huntington began development of a new in-home banking, bill payment, and information service. It is the first organization to offer services based on the new AT&T Smart Phone.

The New Service. The AT&T Smart Phone is a telephone, a modem, and a display, all in one; AT&T bills it as the next-generation telephone. The phone has a handset along with a 4-inch by 6-inch liquid crystal touch screen display. There are no actual buttons on the phone; all interaction is done via pictures of the buttons on the screen. The screen changes depending on its current use. For example, the standard screen shows a keypad plus additional telephone buttons, such as speaker, redial, and program. The display also has a volume bar and numerous user-created buttons, such as family, friends, emergency, repairs, and so forth. Pressing one of these buttons brings up a second-level menu with a list of the appropriate names and phone numbers.

The telephone is versatile, allowing the customer to choose either the standard typewriter keyboard or an alphabetical keyboard for text entry. It includes standard telephone features as well as enhanced telephone functions, such as caller ID. Caller ID displays the caller's telephone number as the telephone rings, or displays the caller's name if it is stored in the phone's memory.

The Huntington's customers can use this phone for banking, bill paying, and other transactions. By dialing a special, bank-provided phone number, the Smart Phone is connected to the bank's computer system.

After entering a personal identification code and a secret password, the phone displays a list of buttons, such as banking, bill payment, shopping, travel, and so on. Pressing the "bill payment" button, for instance, displays the customer's personal bill paying screen, which displays the list of organizations the customer has previously paid through the phone, such as the gas company, cable TV, department stores, and the like. To pay a bill, the customer touches the appropriate button and enters the amount to be paid. Or a new payee can be added.

The Huntington is providing access to other services as well, such as shopping by catalog, making travel arrangements, and ordering gifts and flowers. Under development are still more services, such as local restaurant menus, entertainment listings, stock quotes, and local weather and traffic reports.

The system has also been designed to provide service on behalf of other financial institutions, thereby allowing The Huntington to provide Smart Phone services to its customers as well as to those of other banks across the United States. Thus, The Huntington can become a service provider to other financial institutions.

The Behind-the-Scenes System. Huntington designed its system to work with the special AT&T telephone. The system, called SmarTel, includes software and hardware for accessing the bank's mainframe, presenting information to the caller's telephone screen, and providing access to third-party information providers.

As shown in Figure 12-2, the entire system contains four components: the AT&T Smart Phones, the public switched telephone network, the SmarTel network service (which acts as the hub of the service), and service providers' host computers.

So The Huntington is using its access to its customers, as well as customers' familiarity with touch-tone telephones, to become an information provider—not only of its own banking services but of services from other providers. Since this is a telephone-based service, the customer has the option of interacting with the service provider either by computer, by touching the appropriate button on the phone, or by voice.

GUIDING THE EXPANSION OF ELECTRONIC MAIL

For the growth in electronic mail predicted in Chapter 11 actually to occur, and for electronic mail to become an intrinsic component of a firm's electronic infrastructure, information systems management must pave the way on several fronts. Following are suggestions for guiding and supporting this recently recognized component of the corporate infrastructure.

Create the Infrastructure

By infrastructure, we do not necessarily mean only the telecommunication links. We also mean choosing standards, fostering integrated messaging, and creating a management structure to oversee electronic mail.

Choose Standards. Standards are crucial because they allow messages to be transmitted between disparate mail systems. These standards include transmission standards, addressing standards, and application interface standards. The information systems department needs to direct the selection and use of these standards.

Two standards that will be essential are the x.400 transport standard and the x.500 directory standard for wans. There is no doubt that these will form the basis for worldwide electronic messaging. Other potential standards are not so obvious, but it would be well to choose one or two of the electronic mail APIS for LAN-based applications.

Foster Integrated Messaging. Another part of the infrastructure job is integrating the various forms of messaging, because users say they want such integration. For example, IDC [6] reported that the following percentage of respondents to its messaging survey of one hundred *Fortune 500* companies wanted integration of messaging media:

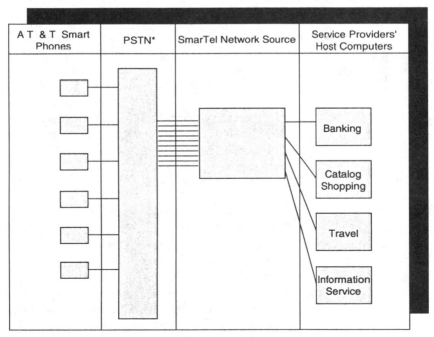

* Public Switched Telephone Network

Figure 12-2 The SmarTel System

- A "universal mailbox" accessible from anywhere (65 percent)
- Integration of graphics/images in electronic mail (58 percent)
- Integration of fax graphics in electronic mail (54 percent)
- Notification of fax receipt in electronic mail (58 percent)
- Notification of voice mail receipt in electronic mail system (54 percent)
- Retrieval of messages in any format from electronic mail system (62 percent)

So integration, among various types of mail systems as well as from within applications, is an important aspect of more fully using electronic mail's potential.

Jeff Ubois [7] points out that new services are emerging to serve this need. Paging and cellular companies offer voice mail and electronic mail, alerting customers when new messages arrive. Electronic mail systems are being used to send faxes and alphanumeric paging messages. And voice mail systems can read electronic mail messages in a synthesized voice.

Fax mail, a new type of service, allows callers to retrieve faxes from a mailbox via any standard fax machine. Like voice mail systems, these mail-boxes can be controlled using a touch-tone telephone. VoxLink, for example, offers a single mailbox for voice, fax, and electronic mail. All three kinds of mail can be stored and forwarded, and electronic mail can be converted to fax or synthesized voice. Ubois expects fax mail to explode as have voice mail and facsimile, because it transforms facsimile from a passive into an interactive medium that can be retrieved on demand.

Create a Management Structure. Finally, the infrastructure really needs to include a management structure, says the Index Foundation [8], specifically in two areas: mail system development and mail system administration. The development role, which is often mistakenly left to local initiative, ensures that the infrastructure is exploited to provide value-added services. The administrative role, which many organizations do not recognize early enough, optimizes the provision of those services. Both roles will have corporate and local components.

Increase Awareness of Potential Uses and Benefits

The Index Foundation, in their report entitled "The Future of Electronic Mail" [8], points out that electronic mail has the potential to become a universal transport mechanism, both within and between organizations. Yet most business people see these systems as trivial. The biggest obstacle to realizing their potential, therefore, is people's image of electronic mail, surmises Index. The greatest need is to increase awareness of potential uses and benefits.

Electronic mail can improve communications between people, but it can also accelerate a production process performed by dispersed team members. For example, the European Space Agency has an electronic mail network with 15,000 external mailboxes. Contractors use these mailboxes to deliver engineering design documents to the agency.

It can also be a convenient mechanism for distributing files (rather than using conventional data communications systems), especially where it is the only common communication medium between all locations. Electronic mail can also automate forms handling for time recording, expense handling, training registration, office supplies, and job openings. Index reports that one large aircraft company has reduced approval time for some documents by 70 percent using electronic mail.

Finally, the Index Foundation believes that by the mid-1990s, electronic mail will be a fundamental component of electronic marketplaces, allowing organizations to trade electronically and undertake cooperative ventures. Today, electronic mail only supports EDI tangentially, providing a way to transmit unstructured messages that currently cannot be handled within EDI's formatted message structure. But emerging public electronic mail services will increasingly support for EDI, says Index, accommodating this diversity as well as providing wider coverage, greater operating efficiency, wider choices, and better security and reliability.

Build Some Mail-Enabled Applications

A "mail-enabled application" is one that uses the messaging handling facilities of an electronic mail system to handle its communication functions. So the application is built on top of the mail system. Message passing between applications is not new; it has been used in airline reservation systems and electronic funds transfer systems for years, notes the Index Foundation report.

Client/server computing, and the desire to link applications that run on disparate machines, has created a newly–heightened interest in "message-based systems." When two applications can interface to the same electronic mail system, they can exchange information via messages. This capability tremendously increases the number of applications that can share data. Until recently, these interfaces had to be specially written, but in the early 1990s, Microsoft, Lotus, and others created APIs for their electronic mail systems. Their goal, of course, is to become the de facto standard for mail-enabled applications.

The Index Foundation believes that the first main types of mail-enabled applications will be for information consolidation and information filtering. An example of information consolidation is a contract engineering firm that needs to consolidate time sheets each month and allocate time to each of the projects. This process can be accelerated if the time sheets are electronic mail forms that are directly usable by the computer applications.

An example of information filtering is a news wire service that continually searches on-line wire services and databases for information desired by its customers. If those customers have specified a set of key words describing the topics of interest to them, matches can be automatically sent to their electronic mailbox.

Index also expects mail-enabled applications to provide workflow support. One example is MailMan, a software product from Reach Software Corporation that acts as a front-end to electronic mail systems. It can be used to route information, track the information, integrate it with other data, and even reformat it to suit the user's machine or preferences—all without having to rewrite the various applications.

Index points out that the first mail-enabled applications are likely to operate on LANs; in time they will operate on x.400 mail networks, or networks that support the x.400 API. Furthermore, groupware—applications that support communication and interaction among members of a group—is an ideal use of electronic mail systems. All these areas are possibilities for experimenting with mail-enabled system development.

ENCOURAGING USE OF MULTIMEDIA

The driving force behind multimedia computing is to make the use of computers more natural by broadening the ways computers and people communicate with one another. We see multimedia important in two areas

- To help people cope with a more complex environment
- To create a more knowledgeable staff

Multimedia will become increasingly important because it is a vastly better—that is, more understandable and more usable—way to present electronic information.

To Cope With Complexity

The business world is becoming more complex. Companies are analyzing more product characteristics in order to target their goods and services to more finely defined consumer groups. Businesses are speeding up their business processes. To become more dynamic, they are keeping track of more variables in a more timely manner. Firms are offering better and faster customer service by keeping more records at their representatives' fingertips. And firms are attracting employees by offering more flexible, and more complex, employment terms.

Two uses of multimedia are emerging to help people deal with such complexity. One helps people grasp complex information and concepts more easily. This is the area of interactive multimedia presentations. The second helps people cope with large amounts of data; this is data visualization.

Interactive Multimedia Systems. Multimedia "slide" presentations that run from a computer have been around since at least 1988. We saw our first Mac-run presentations at conferences in 1989. They were impressive. This idea is being translated into front-ends for some systems.

One example is a kiosk for helping employees choose among options in flexible benefits plans. The system can be stand-alone or linked to a corporate personnel system. Flexible benefits plans are complex when they offer many options. Since few human resources employees know the details of all the options, some companies are turning to multimedia systems to help their employees select the options that best fit their life style. These systems contain video clips of experts explaining the options in such areas as dental insurance, child care, health insurance, vacation time, and so forth. The various segments in the system are controlled by an expert system, which answers an employee's question by showing the appropriate segment.

The people at Meritz [9] have built several such kiosks for clients. They note that the systems generally sell themselves, because management recognizes the problem of communicating complex options in an understandable fashion. These clients receive the benefit of video-taped experts, the flexibility of an interactive system, the assurance of providing consistent information, and the cost-effectiveness of reuse.

Data Visualization Systems. The possibility of seeing the unseeable through computer simulations is opening up to more and more potential users, as the price of workstations drops. Thomas DeFanti and Daniel Sandin established the Electronic Visualization Laboratory at the University of Illinois in Chicago in the late 1970s [10]. They, and their staff and students, have been concentrating on visualization in scientific computing, which is the interactive use of computer graphics animation to study scientific problems. At its best, it combines the number-crunching power of the computer with the pattern recognition capabilities of people interactively.

In the early 1990s, the staff members turned their attention to the financial services industry. They held a week-long workshop where seven financial experts each worked with a graduate student to see how interactive graphics could help them visualize financial data.

One of the two-person teams worked on the traveling salesman problem—that is, finding the shortest route through several points scattered over a geographic area. The team found that by letting a person first create a rough path among the many points, and then giving that approximation to the computer to refine, that the problem got solved very fast—in a few seconds elapsed time. People are good at seeing large gaps among points and avoiding them. Had the computer been given this problem to do on its own, it would have taken hours, if not days, to solve. This example illustrates the power of a person and a computer working interactively on a problem using graphical data. This is one of the key principles of decision support systems, to be discussed in the next chapter.

Another team wanted to see if they could predict interest rate changes for the upcoming six months by matching the current partial patterns with past completed patterns. Once the user selected a section of the trend line, the computer searched the remaining data for a similar pattern and highlighted the best matches it found. Then the financial analysts studied those to find the best match.

Such visualization work in the business realm is very new, but DeFanti, Sandin, and their staff believe that some of the lessons they are learning about scientific visualization can be applied to business problems as well.

At a MacWorld conference, we saw an interesting demonstration along these same lines. The product, MacSpin, from Abacus Concepts [11], allows statistical data to be plotted in a simulated three-dimensional space on a Macintosh. The demonstration plotted automobile data, where each point represented one make of car in one year, with three variables: miles per gallon, weight, and price. The plot could be rotated to show the clusters of points from different angles. Groups of points could also be highlighted to compare American, Japanese, and European cars. For example, the points could even be animated to show changes in miles per gallon over time. The differences between car makes, and trends in their characteristics, became very clear once shown in these various ways.

Those professionals who need to study reams of data to uncover patterns will find data visualization a boon to their work. They include market researchers studying buying trends, corporate executives determining locations for new plants and offices, and analysts studying trends in products.

For a More Knowledgeable Staff

The great promise of multimedia is the training marketplace. Companies are in dire need of better and more cost-effective ways to train and educate their people. Multimedia addresses this tremendous problem.

On-Demand Training. The main trend in this area is JIT training, sometimes called on-demand training—where employees can access training whenever they need it via their workstation. Systems with embedded training are being called "performance systems," because they contribute to increasing employee job performance. Multimedia, perhaps in conjunction with an expert system, will be used in the on-the-spot training portion of more and more applications, we believe.

There are a growing number of examples of multimedia training being embedded in applications. One example is an automobile diagnostic system, to help mechanics diagnose and repair today's increasingly electronics-laden cars. It contains an expert system that suggests tests the mechanic can run to isolate the problem. The context-sensitive help assists the mechanic in performing these tests, via graphics, schematics, and printed instructions. The system also helps the mechanic fix the problem.

Training Via Simulation. In other cases, training is standalone, not embedded in an application. Using multimedia, simulation becomes feasible. The major difference from the past is that this computer-based training (CBT) is not meant to be an adjunct to traditional stand-up classroom instruction; it is meant to replace it. As an example of multimedia CBT, consider what the people at Codex have done.

CASE EXAMPLE: A Training Course from Codex

Codex, in Mansfield, Massachusetts, is an information networking company. They have an educational arm that provides CBT to their own people as well as to customers. Their courses can be obtained through Codex Express [12].

In 1988, Codex decided to experiment with multimedia training by creating a "Basics of Digital Voice Technology" course. Since they knew little about multimedia for the Macintosh, they worked closely with Apple Computer and the multimedia consulting firm of Butler, Ralia and Company [13]. The four-hour course demonstrated that using simulation to teach technical material cut training time in half, and the "students" had a lot of fun using it. The three developers at Codex gained so much experience building that multimedia CBT course that they embarked on creating a second course, "Basics of ISDN (Integrated Services Digital Network)," without outside help.

This four-hour course is taken at a Macintosh or a PC, generally equipped with two megabytes of memory and an external hard drive. The first screen presents "your office." It shows a line drawing of the office of the communications manager of "Heart International"—a fictitious global publishing company that has an advertising agency, lumber mill, lumber supply store, paper mill, printer, and direct mail house. Your task, as this manager, is to recommend to your boss which ISDN applications Heart should investigate, in some detail and with your reasons.

To begin the course, you can click on any item in your office—your inbox, telephone, diskette file, electronic mail, and so forth. It is recommended that you start with the memo from your boss, which explains your assignment. The final memo that you send to your boss—to complete the course—is a fill-in-the-blank form describing the ISDN applications you recommend. To gather the information to write this memo, you can talk to a colleague over lunch, visit a trade show, ask your mentor for guidance on where to find certain information, view a library of "videos," and attend a seminar—in whichever order you choose—all simulated by the system.

The Macintosh version contains 850 Hypercard cards and includes animation; when you click on the diskette file it opens. When you talk to someone, you see a digitized image of that person talking. Codex created their own lip-sync program to make the mouths of these photographed people appear to speak as their voice is played.

The course also contains humor; when you call on your communication analysts, they march across your screen, saying, "Hey, boss," and then provide you with information. And it contains still pictures; the video library is actually a sequence of Hypercard-based graphics animated with different kinds of fade-ins and outs.

The people who have taken the digital voice technology and ISDN say the difference between these courses and traditional CBT is like night and day. CBT seems like electronic page turning, they say; multimedia training feels as if you are having an experience where you are in control of what you do.

Codex management says CBT is cost-effective, because training time is shorter (by at least one-half), it can be given when it is needed (reducing retraining), and it does not involve traveling to a training site. However, development is more costly than classroom training, because of the up-front design costs. The four-hour ISDN course took one work-year of effort, including the outside graphic art help, and the instructional design and programming done in-house.

The Codex development manager's recommendations for companies embarking on writing multimedia training are three-fold:

1. Use a knowledgeable consulting firm the first time to learn the tricks of the trade.
2. Use an authoring language the first time to obtain guidance.
3. Invest in quality graphics artists and designers.

People have high expectations of computers and multimedia—from their experiences with PCs and television. If you do not live up to these expectations, your credibility will be hurt.

Recommendations to Management

Based on our research, here are four recommendations for information systems management regarding multimedia.

Start Working on an Infrastructure. In her newsletter, *Media Letter*, Christine Hughes [14] continually stresses the importance of keeping multimedia in mind when developing the corporate networking infrastructure. Once people start to work with multimedia files, they will surely want to transmit them. Corporate networks need to be designed to expand as such uses grow. The problem is the size of multimedia files—they are orders of magnitude larger than text and data files. Although a page of text requires 2K bytes, one second of sound requires 22K bytes, and a full screen, 8-bit color photograph (with potentially 256 colors) requires 300K bytes, and a 24-bit color image (with up to 16 million colors) requires 1 megabyte. Video, which requires refreshing at least 15 times a second, compounds the size of files even more. Multimedia impacts memory size, local storage, server storage, transmission bandwidth, and processing capabilities.

Be Aware of the Multitude of Standards. As the saying goes, "Standards must be wonderful. Look how many there are." In the multimedia field, the number of standards is truly bewildering, because each form of media has its own collection—none of which will cover all the media. Here is a brief discussion in two areas only—video and compound documents.

Video Compression Standards. As noted in Chapter 6, JPEG is the original video compression standard. It retains all the information for each image, yet compresses files by 6:1 for excellent quality images, 15:1 for high quality, or 24:1 for good quality. Meanwhile, MPEG, which is for compressing moving images, allows 100:1 compression, because it only stores the difference between successive frames. It retains sufficient quality for moving pictures, but not enough for photographs and slides.

Digital video, which is just arriving, has three competing standards

- CD-ROM/XA, which handles video, but restricts it to a portion of the screen,
- CD-I, which uses a special purpose disk player and is aimed at the home market
- Digital video interactive (DVI), which attacks the compression problem most aggressively, but requires large amounts of processing power and a special chip to reconstruct the images

Compound document standards. In the document world, ISO (the international standards body) published Office Document Architecture (ODA) and Interchange Format (ODIF) for moving compound documents between dissimilar document processing systems. A compound document is defined by them as being composed of text, raster graphics (such as facsimile), and geometric graphics (such as computer graphics).

ODA has been pioneered in Europe, say Dawson and Nielsen [15], although North American and Pacific Rim countries have contributed. For instance, it is part of the U.S. Government Open Systems Interconnection Profile (GOSIP).

ODA has three parts—one for representing compound documents, one for exchanging these representations among machines, and a model for processing compound documents. ODA describes documents from two perspectives. One is its layout structure—that is, its presentation, such as groups of pages with a similar "look." The other is the document's logical structure—paragraphs, figures, captions, footnotes, main body, and so forth.

These two brief discussions barely touch on the complexity and diversity of the standards in multimedia. There are also emerging standards evolving for color, audio, and graphics. This is a very dynamic and confusing area.

Start Small, But Look to Future Uses. Companies are getting started by using one authoring tool to create either a simple on-line training session or by putting together a multimedia presentation. Then these techniques can be used to embed training in applications or create front-ends or adjunct systems to corporate applications—wherever text and numbers are not appropriate or sufficient.

One MacWorld speaker noted that her firm had received a quote of $20,000 to produce a multimedia presentation. Instead, her group did it in-house for $2000. Their second one cost $1000, and their third cost only $250, because they had become familiar with the tools, and they were able to reuse some of the multimedia elements.

Speakers gave nebulous costjustifications for using multimedia; most said that multimedia was the only way to present the kinds of information they needed to handle. The costs are usually too high to justify. One speaker did recommend that one way to keep video costs down is to first use a Sony Camcorder to film prototypes of the video portions, before hiring a video crew. Create a mock-up of the entire application first, to see if video is necessary, and if so, where.

In her book, *Making CBT Happen* [16], Gloria Gery says that CBT development costs vary depending on four kinds of variables—human, technical, courseware, and other. She gives three ballpark estimates of development time, based on a detailed discussion of the components of these four variables. On the low end, CBT development can take from 85 to 150 hours of development per hour of CBT. The mid range is 150 to 300 hours. The high end is from 300 hours up.

Assist Developers in Acquiring New Skills. As is obvious by this point, multimedia developers need not only programming skills but also video production skills—even if they are going to be using still frames rather than full-motion video. The production aspects of multimedia are significant, because given their familiarity with television, people will tolerate nothing lower than television-quality productions. Poorly produced multimedia front-ends will, perhaps, be unusable.

As an Index Foundation report on emerging technologies [17] notes, development of hypermedia systems generally requires a multidisciplinary team from the business area, graphics designers, programmers, and people with audio, film, or video expertise. Since such experts are not likely to be found in a systems department, teams building multimedia systems often use outside multimedia production houses to help them with those aspects of the system.

Although multimedia has been used mainly to spice up presentations and training, we believe these roles will grow into major components of many information systems. Multimedia will be used in the front-end, to allow people to use computers more naturally and in a more entertaining manner. It will also appear in the embedded training portions of applications, providing on-demand help.

The move to offload work from intermediaries—such as order entry and customer service people—to machines will not cease. Multimedia will extend this trend to the general public, allowing them to both enter and retrieve information from all sorts of systems. Information delivery will become a major theme in systems departments in the 1990s. It will require drawing on the techniques used in broadcasting and publishing as well as computing. Multimedia has a large role in this intersecting arena.

SUMMARY

Support for end users in the 1980s centered around creating information centers and staffing them with people who liked to help people, rather than write computer programs. But that approach was feasible when fourth generation languages and PCs were new to people. Now, not only has the universe of technologies expanded but so has the universe of users.

In the 1990s, information systems departments will be expected to put in place infrastructures that include support for new computer users, telecommunications options that support all employees (even those who are constantly on the move), and interfaces that can be easily used by consumers. Information systems executives who do not explore all these options do so at their own peril, and the peril of their company's competitive advantage.

QUESTIONS AND EXERCISES

QUESTIONS

1. How is the universe of end users expanding?

2. What was an information center? What was its job in the 1980s?

3. How is today's environment different from the early 1980s?

4. How did Dylex support high-payoff needs?

5. Describe the four main services of Los Angeles County's central information center, and the components of each.

6. What is field force automation?

7. Why is Nissan giving its district managers portable PCs?

8. What is a driving force behind using information technology to serve consumers?

9. How is The Huntington National Bank serving consumers using information technology?

10. What three pieces of infrastructure need to be created to support electronic mail?

11. What is a mail-enabled application?

12. What are two uses of multimedia that help people deal with complexity? Give an example of each.

13. What are on-demand training and training by simulation?

14. What are four recommendations to management for supporting multimedia?

DISCUSSION QUESTIONS

1. End user computing is dead or long live end user computing. Agree or disagree? Back up your opinion.

2. People need offices for the comraderie and to feel part of a company. Unleashing people from company offices will take away this important aspect of their work life. Agree or disagree? Why?

3. Yes, consumers may want convenience, but they also want the human touch. By putting information technology between employees and customers, organizations run the risk of alienating consumers rather than serving them better. Agree or disagree? Why?

EXERCISES

1. Visit a local company and find out how the systems department is now handling end user computing. How has this changed from five years ago? What are their biggest concerns with supporting computing today?
2. Read four articles about electronic mail. What new information did you gain that is not in Chapter 11 and 12? Share this with the class.
3. Read several articles about multimedia. What new information did you gain that is not in Chapter 11 and 12? Share these new insights with the class.

REFERENCES

1. COHEN, J. "Information Centres in the 1990s," Index Foundation, February 1990.
2. BRZEZINSKI, R. "When It's Time to Tear Down the Info Center," *Datamation*, November 1, 1987, pp. 72–82.
3. WEINGARTEN PUBLICATIONS, 38 Chauncy St., Boston, MA 02111.
4. NAOMI KARTEN, Karten Associates, 40 Woodland Parkway, Randolph, MA 02368.
5. RONEY, M. "Special Report: Corporate Computing," *Mobile Office* magazine, December 1991, pp. 35-42
6. "ELECTRONIC MAIL: THE NEW CORPORATE BACKBONE," IDC White Paper inserted into *Computerworld*, June 22, 1992.
7. UBOIS, J. "Fax Mail," *Mobile Office*, June 1992, pp. 138-142
8. "THE FUTURE OF ELECTRONIC MAIL," The Index Foundation, Research Report #82, July 1991.
9. MERITZ, 1385 N. Highway Dr., Fenton, MO 63099.
10. THE ELECTRONIC VISUALIZATION LABORATORY, University of Illinois at Chicago, P.O. Box 4348, M/C 154, Chicago, IL 60680. For DeFanti's original, groundbreaking discussion, see "Visualization in Scientific Computing," a special issue of *Computer Graphics*, from ACM's Special Interest Group on Computer Graphics (ACM, 1515 Broadway, New York, NY 10036), published in July 1987.
11. ABACUS CONCEPTS, 1984 Bonita Ave., Berkeley, CA 94704.
12. CODEX EXPRESS, 20 Cabot Blvd., Mansfield, MA 02048.
13. BUTLER, RALIA AND COMPANY, 298A Highland Ave., Somerville, MA 02144.
14. CHRISTINE HUGHES, The Myriad Group, P.O. Box 142075, Coral Gables, FL 33114.

15. DAWSON, F., AND F. NIELSEN, "ODA and Document Interchange," *UNIX Review*, March 1990, pp. 50–56.

16. GERY, G., *Making CBT Happen,* (Weingarten Publications, Boston, MA), 1991.

17. "EMERGING TECHNOLOGIES: ANNUAL REPORT FOR MANAGERS," Index Foundation Research Report, No. 73, February 1990, pp. 33–46.

THIRTEEN

Decision Support Systems and Executive Information Systems

INTRODUCTION

This is the first chapter in Part 5—a set of four chapters devoted to "support systems." In Chapter 1 we distinguished between procedure-based and goal-based information-handling activities. We noted that the information systems and technologies to improve performance of these two kinds of activities were fundamentally different. The previous two chapters dealt with the technical and managerial environment within which people will be using technology to assist in goal-based activities. The four chapters of this part deal with four sets of applications and systems that have evolved to deal with goal-based activities. These are *systems* that *support* people in performing the information-handling activities to ascertain goals, pursue objectives, and solve problems.

Although the data processing era was developing procedure-based systems for transaction processing and structured reporting via mainframe computers, a few researchers were working on computers that could be used by individuals to solve problems and pursue business objectives. It remained for the "DSS movement" in the early 1980s to develop the philosophies, concepts, and system development strategies that eventually resulted in the phenomenal growth of support systems for goal-based system activities.

These systems evolved under a variety of labels. In this chapter, we discuss decision support systems (DSS), which have taken on a narrow connotation, and executive information systems (EIS), which are aimed primarily at top managers. In the other three chapters in this part, we will discuss

- Group systems, which support the communication and interaction with people as they work in teams or groups (Chapter 14)
- Expert systems, which support decision making in situations that can be structured according to sets of complex rules (Chapter 15)
- Electronic document management, emerging as the key ingredient in office systems, which support the conduct of basic business processes (Chapter 16)

DSS BACKGROUND

DSS is a term to describe systems that support, not replace, managers in their decision-making activities. Decision modeling, decision theory, and decision analysis—developed for many years by the fields of management science and operations research—attempt to make models from which the "best" decision can be derived, usually by computation. DSS give the decision maker access to data and models, but the intelligence, intuition, and judgment of the decision maker are an integral part of the system. Both the term and the systems themselves caught on, and generalized packages for building DSS appeared. Initially such packages were developed for use on mainframes. But the arrival of the personal computer—and particularly the IBM PC—really gave impetus to their use.

Briefly, DSS provide decision support. They help users come to a decision; they do not automatically make the decision. In addition, they are used for decisions that are only partly structured (hence only partly computable). In each case, some amount of human judgment is needed. Sprague and Carlson [1] give a definition that captures the key aspects of DSS. They define DSS as

- Computer-based systems
- That help decision makers
- Confront ill-structured problems
- Through direct interaction
- With data and analysis models

The last two items have become the basis of the technology for DSS, which Sprague and Carlson call the dialog, data, and modeling (DDM) paradigm. In this conceptualization, there is the *dialog* between the user and the system, the *data* that supports the system, and the models that provide the analysis capabilities. Although the components differ somewhat from application to application, they always exist in some form. Sprague and Carlson make the point that a good DSS should have balance among the three capabilities. It should be *easy to use* to support the interaction with nontechnical users, it should have access to a *wide variety of data*, and it should provide

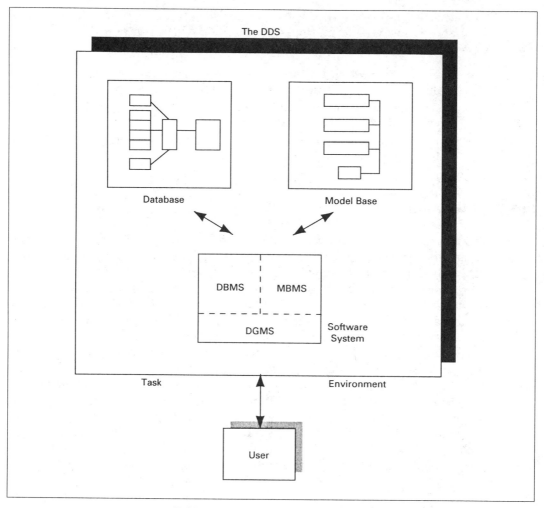

FIGURE 13-1 Components of a DSS

analysis and modeling in numerous ways. Many systems claim to be DSS when they are strong in only one area and weak in the others.

Figure 13-1 shows the relationships between the three components of the DDM model. The software system in the middle of the figure consists of the DBMS, the model-base management system (MBMS), and the dialog generation and management system (DGMS).

New technology continues to affect the dialog, data, and model components. For example, icon-based, touch screen systems provide new options for directing the system. Relational database technology, and more recently object-oriented databases, are influencing how data is stored, updated, and retrieved. Drawing from artificial intelligence advances, there is the potential for representing and using models in new ways.

THE CURRENT STATUS OF DSS

It seems that new topics in information systems are introduced with grandiose promise, only to fall back to a limited and somewhat mundane role. The academics and visionaries develop a theoretical definition; the practitioners understand only pragmatic solutions. If the idea survives the overpromise and underdelivery backlash, it can usually make a valuable contribution to the field.

Management information systems originally promised to be the "electronic nervous system" for organizations; they actually became well-structured reporting systems. Office automation promised the paperless office; it actually became, first, word processing and, later, PCs. In a similar way, the promise of DSS is contained in the preceding definition from Sprague and Carlson. For a while, however, DSS to most practitioners meant a computer-based financial planning system. Fortunately, the promise of DSS is still understood, and interest is still growing. Here are a few examples of DSS.

Typical Examples

The size and complexity of DSS range from simple ad hoc analyses that might be called end user computing tasks to large complex systems that have many of the attributes of a major application in the system portfolio. We will call these "quick-hit DSS" and "institutional DSS," respectively.

Institutional DSS

"Institutional" DSS are generally systems built by professionals, often decision support groups. These systems are intended for organizational support on a continuing basis, and they are generally written using a decision support language. In the past, most have run on mainframes, but an increasing number is being designed to run on micros. The following two examples illustrate institutional DSS.

For Marketing Analysis. Ore-Ida Foods, Inc., is the frozen food division of H. J. Heinz and has a 50 percent share of the retail frozen potato market.

Marketing DSS must support three main tasks in the decision-making process. The first is data retrieval, which helps managers find answers to the question: What has happened? The second is market analysis, which addresses the question: Why did it happen? The third is modeling, which helps managers get answers to: What will happen if . . . ?

For data retrieval, a large amount of internal and external market data is available at Ore-Ida. Much of the latter, such as economic indexes and forecasts, is purchased. However, the company makes very limited use of simple data retrieval. Only about fifteen to thirty pages of predefined reports are prepared each sales period.

Market analysis is the bulk (some 70 percent) of Ore-Ida's use of DSS—for analyzing "Why did such and such happen?" Data from several sources is combined, and relationships are sought. The analysis addresses such questions as: What was the relationship between our prices and our share of the market, for this brand in these markets?

Modeling, for projection purposes, offers the greatest potential value to marketing management. The company has found that, for successful use, line managers must take over the ownership of the models and be responsible for keeping them up to date. The models must also be frequently updated, as market conditions change and new relationships are perceived.

For Sales Forecasting. Sara Lee, in Deerfield, Illinois, uses a DSS for sales forecasting. Formerly, when all sales forecasts came from the sales force, the forecasts were too optimistic so inventories became excessive. When time-series analysis of historical data was used to give sales estimates, the analyses did not handle the impact of sales promotions well. So, the company began using multiple regression models to inject "explanatory variables" into the analyses. An explanatory variable is an additional variable, such as a sales promotion program or the consumer price index of food, that helps explain the performance of the main variable being forecasted. With some two hundred stock-keeping units (such as flavors of a given product), it was difficult to keep these models up to date with all the product promotion plans and other such activities.

More recently, a policy decision that all products within a product line would have the same promotion plans cut the number of models from two hundred to thirty-six. The Kitchens of Sara Lee uses the ADDATA sales forecasting system from Temple, Barker & Sloane, Inc., of Lexington, Massachusetts. This method uses a bottom-up approach, performing time-series analysis of historical data at the SKU level. The trend line or pattern is then projected into the future to forecast the SKU sales for the next several periods. These SKU forecasts are then combined to forecast product sales, which in turn are summed to get product line sales and so on. The percentage that each SKU's sales represents to total product sales is developed.

Then a top-down approach is used. A multiple regression is used to analyze past total product sales data including one or more explanatory variables. The sales pattern is used to forecast total sales for the product. At this point, management reviews the model's total sales forecast and can override the model's figures to give the "final" forecast figures. These final total sales are then distributed back to the individual SKUs by way of the percentages that were developed. Forecast errors in the order of 15 to 20 percent at the SKU level generally are reduced to 1 to 2 percent at the product level. Also, errors in weekly forecasts generally smooth out by the end of the forecast period.

Forecasts are prepared twice a month and transmitted to the company's mainframe for entry into the production planning process. This sales forecasting method has reduced inventories, while at the same time increased the service level (sufficient stock in inventory to meet the demand) to greater than the industry average of 97 percent.

As these two examples illustrate, institutional DSS tend to be fairly well defined, they are based on predefined data sources (heavily internal, perhaps with some external data), and they use well-established models in a prescheduled way. Variations and flexible testing of alternative what-if situations are available, but seldom done during interaction with the ultimate decision maker.

"Quick Hit" DSS

Although there is no commonly used name, the term "quick hit" DSS means a system that is quite limited in scope, is developed and put into use quickly, and helps a manager come to a decision—a decision that the manager might have to make on a recurring basis or one that is strictly one time only. The term "ad hoc" has also been used to distinguish from institutional DSS, although some quick hit systems become used regularly.

A quick hit DSS can be useful for (1) getting managers started in using DSS, (2) providing decision support for certain types of management decisions on either an ad hoc or a recurring basis, (3) providing a basis for deciding whether or not to build a full DSS, and (4) supporting decision situations where the executives cannot wait for a full DSS to be built. A quick hit DSS can be every bit as useful for small companies as for large ones. Three typical types of quick hit DSS include

- Reporting DSS
- Short analysis programs
- Those built with a DSS generator

Reporting DSS. These quick hit DSS are used to select, summarize, and list data from existing data files to meet managers' specific information needs. Other than summarizing the data, a few arithmetic operations may be performed. If computer graphics are used, however, then trends, variances, and so on can be shown. It is likely that reporting DSS is, and will continue to be, the most widely used form of computerized decision support. In fact, reporting DSS were the forerunners to executive information systems, which emphasize reporting with fast response, flexibility, and high-quality presentation. EIS are discussed later in this chapter.

Short Analysis Programs. These programs analyze data as well as print or display the data; they can be surprisingly powerful. Managers can write these short programs themselves, and they generally use only a small amount of data, which may be entered manually.

A major services company with offices throughout the United States and Europe provides a good example. The vice chairman of the board was considering a new employee benefit program: an employee stock ownership plan (ESOP). He wanted a study made to determine the possible impact of the ESOP on the company, to answer such questions as: How many shares of company stock will be needed in ten, twenty, and thirty years to support the ESOP? What level of growth will be needed to meet these stock requirements?

He described what he wanted—the assumptions that should be used, and the rules that should be followed for issuing ESOP stock—to the manager of the information services department. The information systems manager himself then wrote a program of about forty lines that performed the calculations that the vice chairman wanted and then printed out the results. These results showed the impact of the ESOP over a period of thirty years, and those results contained some surprises.

The vice chairman presented the results to the executive committee and, partially based on this information, the ESOP was adopted. Some of the other executives became excited about the results of this analysis and asked if the computer program could be used to project their individual employee stock holdings for ten, twenty, and thirty years. This was done, and it aroused even more attention. At this point, it was decided to implement the system in a more formal fashion. The company treasurer became so interested that he took "ownership" of the system and gradually expanded it to cover the planning, monitoring, and control of the various employee benefit programs.

This example shows that simple programs of one hundred lines of code are indeed practical and can be used to support real-life decisions. In this case, a forty-line program was adequate for the initial evaluation of the ESOP. Eventually, of course, the programs for this system became much larger, but the forty-line program started everything. This example also illustrates the concept of iterative development (a form of prototyping), which is a key concept of DSS.

Decision Support System Generators. These products provide a third approach to developing quick, high-payoff DSS. Vendors sell products that are more than specific DSS packages or general DSS languages. These products include languages, interfaces, and other facilities that aid in setting up specific DSS. Sprague and Carlson point out that a DSS generator can be useful for building several specific DSS within a class of decision support applications.

The Role of Computer Graphics

For almost two decades, supporters of computer graphics systems have been urging their use for business management purposes. The military pioneered the use of computer graphics in command and control. Computer graphics systems have also been put to effective use in such areas as CAD and CAM, real-time simulation, animation, and video games. At long last, computer graphics systems for business management are becoming the norm. Graphics are especially important for business problem solving and decision making because they help managers "visualize" data, relationships, and summaries. They are also important in goal-based information activities because they provide good representations of "concepts" with which managers must deal.

Types of Graphics

A wide variety of graphics forms are in use today. All can be generated by computer, many by microcomputers.

- *Text* plays a critical role in graphics—for listing points that the speaker is discussing, for showing subject titles, for identifying components and values of a chart, and so on. Text must be easily readable.
- *Time series charts* are perhaps the most widely used form of graphics, showing the value of one or more variables versus time. The value scale can be linear or logarithmic.
- *Bar and pie charts* can be used to show total values (by the size of the bar or pie), as well as component values, such as breakdowns of, say, "sources of money received" and "where the money was spent."
- *Scatter diagrams* show the (imperfect) relationship between two variables, such as the number of air travelers that fly on Mondays, on Tuesdays, and so on.
- *Maps* can be two- or three-dimensional. Two-dimensional maps are useful for showing spatial relationships, for example, the locations of customers and the locations of a company's customer service facilities. Three-dimensional maps show surface contours with a three-dimensional effect. With black-and-white rendition, they can show the relationship among three variables; with color, four or even more variables can be related. These "maps" are not limited to geographical information but can show relationships among any three variables, such as the number of employees by age and by years of service with the company.
- *Layouts* of rooms, buildings, or shopping centers convey much information in relatively simple diagrams.
- *Hierarchy charts*, such as organization charts and module charts, are widely used.
- *Sequence charts*, such as flowcharts, show the necessary sequence of events and which activities can be done in parallel.
- *Motion graphics*, such as animation, motion pictures, and television, have an exciting future when, through the use of computers, they are used in combination with the graphics techniques listed previously.

In addition to these traditional graphic forms, new developments are continually increasing the value and capability of computer-generated graphics. Silicon Graphics, Inc., has based their entire product line on powerful graphical capabilities for "data visualization," usually in scientific areas. They are now moving to explore the competitive advantage of data visualization in business areas. The Xerox project that developed the "Rooms" interface, described in Chapter 11, has been expanded into the "information visualizer" project [2] to explore new ways to use graphics and animation to visualize and understand complex information. Apple Computer's development of "QuickTime" makes possible the use of videoclips as part of reports and electronic documents.

In summary, computer-based graphics hold high promise for increasing the effectiveness of decision making and problem solving, because they provide a way to visualize data relationships. The few objections seem to be fading as technology gets stronger and people get better at using graphics as a tool. As an example of a decision support system where graphics played an important role, consider the experience of Marine Terminals Corporation.

CASE EXAMPLE: Marine Terminals Corporation

Marine Terminals Corporation operates marine terminals and provides stevedoring services at California and Alaska ports. Headquarters is in San Francisco, California, and the firm has a second major office in Long Beach. Marine Terminals used a DSS on a proposed project for building a new supply base terminal for the offshore oil industry near Santa Barbara, California.

The project made use of a PC to perform decision support analysis. By testing alternative ways to structure and finance the terminal management and investors were better able to decide whether or not to go ahead with the project. Most of the decision support models were created by the vice president of marketing. He developed a financial projection model to show the financial effects of using different financing methods (borrowing, sale of stock, and so on) and following different operating policies.

One important aspect was the financial effects of different configurations of the terminal. A given number of ships could be loaded or unloaded using one number of berths and working only during daylight hours, or using a smaller number of berths and working around the clock, with consequent higher labor costs. Because each berth costs about $2 million, this analysis was important to both management and potential investors.

The vice president made color slides of the numerous analyses, including net present value of fixed costs, income, operating costs, net income after taxes, and investment tax credits.

Since the proposed terminal was to be built at a very scenic part of the California coast, the effect on the environment was carefully studied. Different approaches for minimizing the visual and environmental impacts of the terminal were considered. The model showed the firm the financial implications of these approaches. The results of these analyses were also displayed by the computer color graphics form. These graphics could be shown to small groups, such as a management meeting, directly on the computer display. Changes could be suggested and entered, with the display changing immediately. For larger audiences, such as for a conference presentation, color slides were created directly from the graphics file.

The terminal project was approved, and the terminal was built. The vice president gives a lot of credit to this "corporate DSS on a micro," where graphics played an important part in the decision making and implementation.

Spreadsheets for Decision Support

Spreadsheets have taken a permanent place in the list of tools for decision support activities. Two major reasons are that

1. They are based on a popular and familiar way to view data (a table), and the relationships between data take the form of a report.
2. They are extremely easy to use.

In terms of the data, dialog, and modeling features cited earlier by Sprague and Carlson, spreadsheets are extremely strong in dialog support. They allow users to make corrections, additions, and deletions quickly and easily as well as perform numerous what-if analyses by changing some values and seeing the results.

As a matter of fact, there are now literally thousands of templates for spreadsheet packages to help users with their decisions. Templates are prepared spreadsheet models into which users need only enter data; all the relationships and calculating formulas are in place. One catalog for a leading spreadsheet package lists templates for financial planning (loan amortization, depreciation, lease versus buy, discounted cash flows and net present value, break-even analysis), real estate investments (financing alternatives, cash flows, impact on taxes, payoff), business record keeping and accounting, budgeting, statistics, general ledger accounting, and more.

There are some limitations to spreadsheets, of course, but their popularity has ensured their continual development. Perhaps 20 to 30 percent of the users will become dissatisfied with spreadsheets for decision support and will want more powerful packages. But *many* users will not graduate from spreadsheets, because of their ease of use, particularly for smaller problems.

Distributed DSS

PC-based DSS applications will continue to grow in strength and complexity, and so will the large institutional mainframe-based DSS. These trends have been in progress for several years, and we see them continuing. They are merging, however, as part of the overall trend toward distributed systems, which we described in Chapter 5. The technical implementation will change, as the architecture shifts from a host-based structure to client/server structures on LANs. But the result will be the same—more powerful DSS with the benefits of PC-based and mainframe-based systems. The primary vendors of DSS software are enabling this development in their regular product upgrades.

Intelligent DSS

Decision support system products are incorporating artificial intelligence tools and techniques. The self-contained, stand alone products in artificial intelligence proved to be like the stand alone statistical and management science models of a decade ago—they have become embedded in a "delivery system" that facilitates their use. DSS are providing the system for assimilating expert systems, knowledge representation, natural language query, voice and pattern recognition, and so on. The result is "intelligent DSS" that "suggest," "learn," and "understand" unstructured tasks and problems. David King [3], director of artificial intelligence for Comshare, a major DSS vendor, lists software agents, expert support systems, and concept-based retrieval as emerging AI technologies that are becoming part of DSS. Due to this significant trend, we deal with it in more detail in Chapter 15.

Summary

DSS have taken their place in the portfolio of applications and tools to support problem solving, decision making, and other goal-based information activities. The DSS label was first used to describe a large general class of applications, and the "DSS movement" of academics and developers defined the concepts, principles, and products to implement the systems. As the field grew, specialized views of DSS emerged: for groups, executives, and office work. The DSS label now refers mostly to systems for analysis of complex situations, having absorbed most of the work of management science and operations research in business organizations. In later chapters we discuss other types of support systems. In the remainder of this chapter we devote our attention to DSS for executives—EIS.

EXECUTIVE INFORMATION SYSTEMS

EIS—and a somewhat more general variant called "executive support systems" (ESS)—appear to be experiencing renewed interest, after a few years of quiet progress. Originally, some authors argued that CEOs would not use computers directly and quoted CEOs who agreed with them. But the tone of such claims does not seem as confident now, because of the experiences of the past several years. In this section we discuss the nature of EIS, the critical factors that determine whether an EIS will be successful or not, what it should do, and what the future might hold.

Executives Do Use Computers!

Lou Wallis [4] reports on three executives from major U.S. corporations who sponsored the development of an EIS and now "wonder how their companies ever did without it." Strong positive testimonials come from Paul A. Allaire, president of Xerox, William D. Smithburg, chairman and CEO of the Quaker Oats Company, and Finn M. W. Caspersen, chairman and CEO of Beneficial Corporation. Each has been using an ESS for some time for the following, notes Wallis:

1. Company performance data—sales, production, earnings, budgets, and forecasts
2. Internal communications—personal correspondence, reports, and meetings
3. Environmental scanning—for news on government regulations, competition, financial and economics developments, and scientific subjects

With this set of functions, these systems qualify for the broader term of ESS. The label EIS is generally used to refer only to the set of functions recorded in point 1. In fact, using the DDM paradigm described earlier, EIS can be viewed as a DSS that (1) provides access to (mostly) summary performance data, (2) using graphics to display and visualize the data in a very easy to use fashion (frequently with a touch screen interface), and (3) with a minimum of analysis for modeling beyond the capability to "drill down" in summary data to examine components. ESS add functions to support the other major responsibilities and activities of top executives—communications and environmental scanning/alerting.

The experience at Xerox is a good example of the successful development and use of ESS. Paul Allaire became the executive sponsor of Xerox's ESS project while he was corporate chief of staff. Although he thought that an ESS would be valuable to executives, he insisted that it earn its usefulness, not that it be "crammed down their throat." In fact, the system began small and evolved to the point where even skeptical users became avid supporters.

A key to success, says Wallis, is that Allaire did not just throw money at a vague sense of problems or grandiose dreams. Improving communication and the planning processes were clear objectives from the start. For example, Allaire describes the problem of getting the briefing information to executives in preparation for regular executive meetings. Due to the time required to prepare the materials, and mailing delays to Xerox international offices, many executives ended up reading a hundred pages or more the night before the meetings without access to related information or time for discussions with staff. Now it is all on ESS. The result is that the executives rarely have a meeting in which they do not have enough information or preparation to make the necessary decisions.

The other job that got executives involved in using the ESS was strategic planning. The ESS helped make this crucial work more efficient and resulted in better plans, especially across divisions. Instead of each division preparing plans that were simply combined, the ESS allowed the executives to explore interrelationships between plans and activities at several divisions. So the ESS is playing an important role at Xerox, and the executives do indeed use computers.

Stories such as this one are appearing frequently in the public and trade press. The implication is that computers are finally being used by executives to help them perform their management jobs better. The underlying message is that the use of computers for executive support is just a matter of using popular software packages and that the only reason more executives are not using computers is their timidity.

We do not think the situation is that simple. Successful support of executive work with computers is fraught with subtle pitfalls and problems. Consider the following case study of a failure.

Doing it Wrong

Watson [5] describes the experience of a (hypothetical) company and their well-intentioned effort to develop and install an EIS. The I/S director at Genericorp had heard of successful EIS experiences, such as Lockheed of Georgia (the case example later in this chapter). He thought such a system would be valuable to his company, so he arranged for a presentation by a DSS vendor; it was very well received by the executive team. After some discussion, they decided to purchase the product from the vendor and develop an EIS. The allocated budget was $250,000.

They assembled a qualified team of I/S professionals, who interviewed executives concerning their information needs (whenever the executives could find the time), and developed an initial version of the system consisting of fifty screens to be used by five executives. The response from these executives was quite good, and in some cases enthusiastic. Several of them seemed proud finally to be able to use a computer, says Watson.

With the system delivered, the development team turned it over to a maintenance team and moved on to other new projects. The maintenance team was to add new screens and new users—in short, to evolve the system. Nine months later, very little had happened, apparently because other systems maintenance projects had been more urgent. About this time, there was a downturn in revenue that generated cost-cutting pressures on nonessential systems; the EIS was discontinued.

What went wrong? Watson identifies five problem areas that serve as a guide to the "hidden pitfalls" that should be avoided in developing a successful EIS.

1. *Lack of executive support.* Although this has been listed as a potential problem area in system development for years, there are special reasons why it is crucial for EIS. Executives must provide the funding, but they are also the principal users so they need to supply the necessary continuity.

2. *Undefined system objectives.* The technology, the convenience, and the power of EIS are impressive, maybe even seductive. But the underlying objectives and business values of an EIS must be carefully thought through.

3. *Poorly defined information requirements.* Once the objectives of the system are defined, the required information can be identified. This process is complicated because EIS typically need nontraditional information sources—judgments, opinions, external text-based documents—in additional to traditional financial and operating data.

4. *Inadequate support staff.* The support staff must have technical competence, of course, but perhaps more important is the understanding of the business and the ability to relate to the varied responsibilities and work patterns of executives. A permanent team must manage the evolution of the system.

5. *Poorly planned evolution.* Highly competent systems professionals using the wrong development process will fail with EIS. EIS are not developed, delivered, and then maintained. They need to evolve over time under the leadership of a team that includes the executive sponsor, the operating sponsor, executive users, the EIS support staff manager, and I/S technical staff.

Although EIS development is difficult, many organizations are reporting that it is worth the effort. Avoiding the pitfalls identified by Watson improves the probability of a successful EIS.

CSFs for EIS

Quite a bit of research on executive, managerial, and office use of computers has been done at the Center for Information System Research, in the Sloan School of Management at MIT [6]. As reported by David DeLong and John Rockart [6a], in a survey of forty-five randomly selected *Fortune 500* companies, thirty had at least one (usually several) executives with terminals on their desks.

The authors then made in-depth studies of the thirty companies and found a variety of experiences, to the point where they could select eight "critical success factors" for what they call an ESS. The top three are (1) a committed and informed executive sponsor, (2) an operating sponsor, and (3) a clear link between the ESS and the business objectives.

A Committed and Informed Executive Sponsor. The desire for an ESS must come from top management, say the authors. Such a system is hardly ever used by executives if initiated solely by the information systems department. One executive must be the sponsor, and must put in the time and energy to see that the system is "right." The sponsor's expectations must be realistic about what the ESS can and cannot do. Furthermore, the sponsor should understand the basics of the implementation process itself—what human and financial resources will be needed, what the organizational impact of the new system is likely to be, and where resistance may appear.

An Operating Sponsor. The development of an ESS is often delegated to a trusted senior executive, say the authors, someone who can communicate both with the other executives and the development staff. This operating sponsor, who needs to be the primary and most enthusiastic user, is the most critical in shaping, refining, and extending the system's capabilities.

A Clear Link to Business Objectives. Often an executive wants an ESS on such short notice that the step of defining the system's business objectives is overlooked, report the authors. The developers assume that the executive is too impatient for this process to be done properly. As identified by Watson earlier, however, this is one of the major pitfalls in EIS development. Business value objectives must be the primary driver.

The full list of critical success factors identified by DeLong and Rockart is

1. A committed and informed executive sponsor
2. An operating sponsor
3. A clear link to business objectives
4. The use of appropriate resources from the information systems function
5. The use of appropriate technology

6. Recognizing the existence of data problems (inconsistencies, etc.) and managing the solution of those problems

7. Managing organizational resistance

8. Managing the spread and evolution of the system

In summary, it is clear that executive use of computers is not a straightforward matter. It involves much more than putting a PC on an executive's desk and providing a few popular software packages—because those software packages usually do not address the needs of the executives.

ACHIEVING SUCCESSFUL EIS

There are many questions to be answered when considering an EIS. Some of the answers are specific to the organization—who it will serve, where and when it will be developed—so it would serve no purpose to discuss them. However, the other questions—why, what, and how—can have more general answers.

Why Install an EIS?

There is a range of possible motivations, on the part of the project's executive sponsor, for installing an EIS.

Attack a Critical Business Need. EIS can be viewed as an aid to dealing with important needs that involve the future health of the organization. In this situation, almost everyone in the organization can clearly see the reason for developing an EIS.

A Strong Personal Desire by the Executive. The executive sponsoring the project may want to get information faster than he or she is now getting it, or have quicker access to a broader range of information, or have the ability to select and display only desired information and to probe for supporting detail, or to see information presented in graphical form. A related motivation occurs within divisions, where corporate management is using an EIS and divisional management feels at a disadvantage without one.

"The Thing to Do." An EIS, in this instance, is seen as something that modern management must have to be current in management practices. The rationale given is that the EIS will increase executive performance and reduce time wasted looking for information.

These motivations are listed in the sequence of strongest to weakest, as far as probable project success is concerned. A strong motivation, such as meeting a critical business need, is more likely to assure top management interest in, and support of, the project. At the other extreme, a weak motivation can lead to poor executive sponsorship of the project, which can result in trouble. Thus, motivation for the EIS is fundamental to its success, because it helps determine the degree of commitment by the senior executives.

What Should It Do?

What the EIS should do is second only to motivation, in our opinion, as a critical success factor. It determines the extent to which executives will actually make hands-on use of the system.

We will present two viewpoints on what an EIS should do, each of which makes valid points. Perhaps these two viewpoints are more complementary than conflicting, but they are not synonymous. It is important that all the people associated with the project have the same understanding of just what the new system is expected to do—how it will provide executive support. These two viewpoints illustrate the types of points that should be settled at the outset of the project.

A Status Access System. At its heart, an EIS should filter, extract, and compress a broad range of up-to-date internal and external information. It should call attention to variances from plan, and also monitor and highlight the critical success factors of the individual executive user.

This view sees an EIS as a structured reporting system for executive management—providing an executive with the data and information of his or her choice, and in the desired form. It is primarily a "status access" system, for monitoring what is going on in the company and in the outside world. With this information at hand, the executive can then work to resolve any problems that he or she has uncovered.

EIS can start small and quickly with this data-and-information approach, but still accomplish something useful. For example, EIS developers asked the company president of one large insurance company what were the ten things he would look at first after returning from vacation. He gave them this list. Two weeks later, they gave him an EIS terminal with those ten items listed on the main menu, as the first iteration of the EIS. The president was delighted, and was soon asking for more!

This data-and-information approach is based on information with which executives are already familiar. Executives already get, or would like to get, most of the information that the EIS provides—but the EIS provides it faster, in more convenient form, pulling things together that previously had to be viewed separately and using graphics to aid comprehension.

Human Communications Support. Much of the work that executives (and other office workers) perform is based on person-to-person communications. The steps in getting results via such communications are the following:

1. Make request and receive promises for action
2. Discuss and negotiate, to clarify an assignment and the responsibility for results
3. Follow up on progress toward, and barriers in the way of, obtaining the desired results
4. Redirect the assignment when necessary and renew commitments, or acknowledge failure of the assignment
5. Receive (or deliver) results
6. Acknowledge completion of the assignment

This viewpoint sees an EIS in terms of the human communications support that it provides. Data and information can help managers discover what is missing, but human communications are needed to bring the missing work into being. The manager makes up his or her mind about some future action and then calls on a "network of help." This network consists of personal relationships with peers, subordinates, clients, customers, suppliers, and others. The manager makes requests, gives instructions, and asks questions to selected members of this network, to get people going on the desired action. The manager acts through communications, and a critical role for many EIS is to support these communications.

Which Is More Important? Both of these viewpoints are valid, and they appear to be more complementary than conflicting. But the question remains: When initiating an EIS project, should it aim at performing mainly data and information handling, or the communications that are needed for action? Some systems on the market accommodate both. Obviously, the choice will depend on the needs of an organization and its executives, but the choice should be consciously made. Ambiguity—or, even worse, vacillation—in what the system should do almost surely will lead to eventual lack of acceptance.

What Data Sources?

Generally the EIS should *not* try to give executives direct access to production data files, even through friendly front-end software. There is just too much detailed knowledge needed to access, interpret, and use such data. Instead, desired information should be extracted from the production databases, formatted, and put into the EIS database. In fact, data and information from many sources should be put into the EIS database. External information and predictive data generally are not found in production databases and will have to be supplied from other sources. The information should be organized in hierarchical fashion, so that highlights are in the top layer. The most important data must be the easiest to find. When a user wants to see supporting detail, it should be available.

Many production data files carry mostly current information, with little historical detail. To spot trends, however, the EIS database needs to carry relevant historical data, such as time series data. Further, the user needs to be able to track the external environment and to spot significant deviations from assumptions.

In general, the information on which EIS would draw includes all four of the sources we identified in Chapter 7—data records and documents from both internal and external sources. Perhaps the fastest-growing information sources, with the development of text retrieval software and high-speed communication lines, is the external document-based information. EIS that tap this information source will give executives greatly enhanced ability to assess environmental and competitive conditions.

To summarize our discussion of EIS, consider how an EIS was developed and has evolved at Lockheed-Georgia over the past several years.

CASE EXAMPLE: Lockheed-Georgia

Lockheed-Georgia, a subsidiary of Lockheed Corporation, has its headquarters in Marietta, Georgia, where it employs some nineteen thousand people in the production of C-5B and Hercules transport aircraft and other programs. Lockheed-Georgia was one of the earliest users of computers for manufacturing and accounting functions—and they are one of the early users of executive information systems.

As described by Houdeshel and Watson [7], the initial interest was expressed by Robert Ormsby in 1975, when he was president of Lockheed-Georgia. The existing information systems had not been designed to provide information for management needs, Ormsby thought. The result was that managers found it difficult to locate desired information. Also, the printed reports often were not sufficiently current, and data inconsistencies (for reasons such as timing differences) led to management misunderstandings.

The Initial Project

In late 1978, work began on the management information and decision support system (MIDS), with Ormsby as the executive sponsor and key initial user. A project team of five was formed, with a manager (who reported to the vice president of finance), two people from finance, and two from information services.

The project got under way with the team's study of the information requirements of Ormsby and his staff. The project team gathered this information, say the authors, by interviewing these executives—and their secretaries—to find out what information they actually received. The executives' use of existing reports was also studied.

Then the team searched for the best sources of the desired information. They wanted adequate detail behind the information presented to the executives to support any probing. The team also wanted to avoid information that had been distorted by the perspective of the organizational units where the data originated.

Design Criteria

Several design criteria played an important role in the eventual success of the project, Houdeshel and Watson report. One important design principle was to make training largely unnecessary, by making the system simple to use. This goal was accomplished by providing a hierarchy of menus; training of a new user is done in one fifteen-minute training session without the need for written instructions.

Another design criterion was that information be organized in a top-down fashion, with a summary paragraph at the beginning, followed by supporting graphs, tables, and text. Explanatory comments would be provided as necessary—to indicate, for instance, that an apparent variance from schedule had almost been corrected.

Other design criteria included fast response times, only a few terminal keystrokes needed to call up any display screen, and features to help executives locate desired information. Further, each user was to have a MIDS terminal (based on a PC) on his or her desk. Color graphics capabilities would help in the presentation of graphic data.

There were no commercial systems of this type on the market at the time, so Lockheed-Georgia developed MIDS in-house. The initial version was working in just six months time. Ormsby was the key user, and when the system was first installed, he could access thirty-one screens of information. The initial MIDS programs and data were on a PC.

How MIDS Has Evolved

Eight years later, in 1986, the MIDS system consisted of more than seven hundred displays, with a user population of thirty top executives and forty operating managers. As the number of users increased, the system was moved to DEC minicomputers and then to an IBM 3081, the authors report. To minimize the use of hard copy, the system did not support printers attached to the PCs. The only printers were in the MIDS office.

A "double" security system was installed to control access to the information. Each user was given a password. In addition, access by a user can be limited to only certain terminals. For example, an executive might be able to access certain sensitive information from the terminal in his office but not from a terminal in a conference room.

The MIDS staff grew from the original five people to a staff of nine—the manager, six information analysts, and two computer analysts. Each information analyst was responsible for maintaining about 100 of the displays—and about 170 displays were updated daily, to meet changing conditions! It has been essential, said the company, that the information analysts understand the information for which they are responsible. Most of these analysts have worked in, or have been trained in, the functional areas they serve, and they are encouraged to take additional appropriate courses.

The Benefits

Lockheed-Georgia feels that MIDS has improved information flow for the executive users, report Houdelshel and Watson. The system provides more timely, accurate, and relevant information, based on the needs of the individual executives. The system highlights problem areas and items requiring management attention and includes pertinent comments along with these highlights.

MIDS has also improved management communications because it operates within the IBM PROFS electronic mail system. Also, two or more executives are able to view the same information simultaneously on their screens, while talking on the telephone. This feature helps avoid disagreements that arise from inconsistent information.

User acceptance has been good. The number of users has grown from one to more than seventy, and the frequency of use (number of screens viewed per user per day) has also grown. Middle managers began asking for a version of MIDS. MIDS II (described below) promises to make that feasible.

During the design phase, no attempt was made to cost-justify the system formally; instead, the project was approached as research and development. Authorization to continue enhancing the system depended at each stage on the usefulness of the previous stage.

Although justification by cost displacement was not a criterion, there have been some cost savings, primarily associated with the reduction in printed reports. In fact, some of the printed reports that MIDS executives no longer receive are ones that were prepared manually (the information is now in MIDS) and ones prepared on other systems (summaries of which are now in MIDS).

Houdeshel and Watson point out several factors that contributed to the success of MIDS. Foremost was a committed senior executive sponsor—President Robert Ormsby. Then came careful design of system and information requirements, along with a team approach to design. The evolutionary development approach was crucial, because no one could (or can) visualize at the outset what the eventual system will be like. Hardware and software were also selected carefully. Now the success of MIDS and advances in technology have led to the next major phase in the evolution—MIDS II. Watson recently described this upgrade.

MIDS II: The Ongoing Story

In 1990, after twelve years of successful MIDS operations, it became necessary to update the hardware technology. This change was required because the Intelligent Systems Company graphics computers that were used by the MIDS support staff to design and update the screens were no longer in production, and replacement parts had become difficult to find. The MIDS staff faced the real possibility of not being able to maintain the system because of lack of hardware. Therefore, the company undertook a comprehensive review of the hardware *and* software options available for MIDS.

They decided it was more economical to purchase commercial EIS software than to develop another system in-house, so several commercial products were evaluated; Comshare's Commander EIS was chosen. It offers many capabilities that facilitate the development and maintenance of an EIS including

- Support for multiple user interfaces
- On-line, context-dependent help screens
- Command files
- Multiple methods for locating information
- Access to external databases (e.g., Dow Jones News Retrieval)
- Interfaces to other software (e.g., PROFS, Lotus 1-2-3)
- Integrated decision support (e.g., System W, IFPS)
- Screen design templates
- Application shells
- Data extraction from existing organizational databases
- Graphical, tabular, and textual information on the same screen
- Integration of data from different sources
- Security for data, screens, and systems
- Support for rapid prototyping
- Support for multiple computing platforms
- Support for hard copy output (e.g., paper, overhead transparencies, 35mm slides)

Two important changes to the Comshare software were requested, however, before a contract was signed. The changes retained capabilities that were in MIDS but not in Commander EIS. The changes needed to be made to the basic Comshare product and not to just a special version for Lockheed to ensure compatibility with later releases of Commander.

The two changes permitted users to operate the system through a keyboard (in addition to a mouse or touch screen) and provided for monitoring the use of the system. Lockheed executives had enjoyed the MIDS system advantage of going from any screen to any other screen without retracing a path or returning to a predetermined point. This capability was retained by allowing executives to enter the number of the desired screen. Monitoring of system usage had always been performed by the MIDS system management, and it had become invaluable in keeping the MIDS system up to date. With these changes, Commander EIS became the development environment for MIDS II.

Even though commercial EIS software was selected for MIDS II, the original screen designs were retained. In fact, when Lockheed asked vendors to prepare demonstration prototypes, they requested screens that looked like those currently in use. Considerable thought and experimentation had gone into screen design over the years, Lockheed's executives were familiar with them, and MIDS II was to continue the look and feel of the original system.

In addition to new software, hardware improvements were made to take advantage of state-of-the-art technology and to position MIDS II in Lockheed's long-range computing plans. The Comshare software helped make this possible through its ability to run on a mixed platform of IBM PS/2S and Apple Macintoshes. A Novell LAN was installed to improve the system's response time and reliability.

MIDS II was developed and rolled out to users in 1992 and is expected to provide a variety of benefits over the original system: faster response time, easier navigation (through "drill down" to more detailed information), better links to other resources (internal and external databases), reduced maintenance costs (automatic update of some screens), shared EIS techniques with other Commander EIS users, and a state-of-the-art technology platform that permits future improvements and growth within information systems long-range plans. The original MIDS system has served Lockheed very well since 1978, and MIDS II is designed to carry this tradition into the future.

CONCLUSION

The concept and technology of DSS have received much attention during the past decade. The theoretical ideal of university researchers became primarily financial planning systems at first. But DSS technology and its application are continuing to grow in strength and value. The current status can be characterized by a predominance of institutional systems, increasing instances of personal DSS, and a growing interest in group DSS. Two other developments include the increased use of computer graphics and the popularity of spreadsheets. We see continued growth of PC-based DSS, distributed DSS that link PCs to mainframes, growing use of group DSS, and the addition of expert systems.

Of these trends, we considered EIS in some detail. Potentially, executive information systems that are within today's state-of-the-art can

1. Provide status information on how things are going both within and outside of the organization
2. Help executives communicate with others to identify and define needed actions
3. Help make those needed actions happen

However, EIS cannot be imposed on executives; they must individually be receptive to it. Furthermore, an EIS must present information in a manner desired by each individual executive, although some standards can be employed on designing the screen displays—the use of colors, size and placement of text, and so on.

Success of an EIS depends, we think, on having a strong motivation for installing it in the first place, a committed and informed senior executive sponsor, an appropriate operating sponsor and project organization, a definition of what the EIS is expected to do (and not do) at the outset, and being easy to use, even for infrequent users.

QUESTIONS AND EXERCISES

REVIEW QUESTIONS

1. According to Sprague and Carlson, what is the definition of a decision support system?
2. What is the DDM paradigm for DSS suggested by Sprague and Carlson? How is it useful?
3. What is an institutional DSS? Give an example.
4. What is a quick hit DSS? When is it useful? Define three types.
5. What are DSS generators?
6. When are graphics useful in decision making?
7. Why are spreadsheets valuable for decision support?
8. What are the major trends in DSS?
9. What are "distributed DSS"? Why is this an important development?
10. What are "intelligent DSS"?
11. What are the three main kinds of support derived from EIS by Xerox, Quaker Oats, and Beneficial Life? Use this list to distinguish between EIS and ESS.
12. What are the two main benefits Xerox derived from the ESS?
13. What are the pitfalls in ESS development identified by Watson?
14. What are the three major CSFS for successful EIS, identified by DeLong and Rockart?
15. What is a strong reason for installing EIS? A weak reason?
16. Give two opinions on the main role of EIS.
17. What were the design criteria that have contributed to the success of MIDS at Lockheed-Georgia?

DISCUSSION QUESTIONS

1. Graphics are crucial to DSS and EIS. Without good graphics, such a system is doomed. Do you agree or disagree?
2. From the case examples and discussions in the chapter, which of the attributes of a DSS or EIS do you think are most important? Why?

EXERCISES

1. If you have ever used a spreadsheet package, describe one of your uses and what decisions the package helped you make.
2. Find one or more current articles on DSS or EIS. What characteristics or attributes are described? How do they compare with the ones in the text?
3. Visit a local company and talk to a user or a developer of decision support systems. What types of DSS are being used or developed? What tools are being used? Briefly describe one or two applications.

REFERENCES

1. SPRAGUE, R. H. Jr., and E. D. CARLSON, *Building Effective Decision Support Systems* (Prentice Hall, Englewood Cliffs, NJ), 1982.

2. CARD, S. G. ROBERTON, and J. MACKinlay, "The Information Visualizer: An Information Workspace," Xerox Palo Alto Research Center, Palo Alto, CA.

3. KING, D., "Intelligence Support Systems: Art, Implementation, and Agents," in *DSS: Putting Theory Into Practice,* 3rd ed., edited by Ralph Sprague and Hugh Watson (Prentice Hall, Englewood Cliffs, NJ), 1993.

4. WALLIS, L., "Power Computing at the Top," *Across the Board,* January-February 1989.

5. WATSON, H., "Avoiding Hidden EIS Pitfalls," *Computerworld,* June 25, 1990.

6. Reports of the Center for Information Systems Research, Sloan School, Massachusetts Institute of Technology, E40-193, 77 Massachusetts Avenue, Cambridge, MA 02139.

   a. DELONG, D. W. and J. F. Rockart, "Identifying Attributes of Successful Executive Support System Implementation," CISR WP 132, January 1986.

   b. BULLEN, C. V., and J. L. BENNETT, "Office Workstation Use by Administrative Managers and Professionals," CISR WP 102, April 1983.

   c. ROCKART, J. F., and D. W. DeLong, "Executive Support Systems and the Nature of Executive Work," CISR WP 135, April 1986.

7. HOUDELSHEL, G., and H. J. WATSON, "The Management Information and Decision Support (MIDS) System at Lockheed-Georgia," *MIS Quarterly,* March 1987.

FOURTEEN

Group Support Systems

INTRODUCTION

This is the second chapter of Part 5 of the book—on systems to support the information-handling activities of people in organizations. In this chapter, we focus on the systems and technologies that support communication and interaction among people as they work in groups. As we will see, there are several forces driving the development and the increasing importance of this kind of support system.

In this chapter, as in all the chapters in this "support systems" part of the book, we primarily emphasize goal-based, systems to support process-independent, less well structured information handling activities. Since there are so many ways people work together, we will define nine types of groups. For all of them, we focus on supporting goal-based activities.

We can identify two generic classes of goal-based activities performed by people in groups. One is *communication* and *interaction* among group members. Communication is the transmission of information from one person to another (or to several others); interaction is repetitive (usually back and forth) communication over time. The other major activity is *decision making or problem solving*, where members of a group reach a decision or form a consensus. It could be argued that communication is a necessary part of group decision making, so it is encompassed by the latter function. It seems, however, that communication is a valuable function in its own right to aid in coordinating activities in an organization, whether or not a decision or consensus is reached.

Much of the current activity in group support systems has originated from one or the other of these two major functions. Office systems, and in particular electronic mail, are oriented toward supporting people-to-people communication. Current interest in "computer supported cooperative work" [1] is also emphasizing technology to aid communication, such as enhanced computer conferencing and systems to assist two or more people work on the same project. On the other hand, group DSS work, evolving from the DSS community, which may include technology to support communication, focuses on reaching a conclusion, decision, or consensus.

Defined across this broad range, the group support system field is a large and rapidly growing one. We therefore consider the kinds of systems and technologies that fit the general description including the variety of names and labels used. A simple two-by-two matrix provides a good classification scheme for the rest of the chapter. In the first section, we identify the reasons why this has become such an important subject for information systems managers. After a general discussion of groups and their activities, we identify the major kinds of systems that provide support for these activities. A couple of case studies illustrate how companies are using two of the popular types of systems. These lead to a set of lessons or guidelines for the development and use of group support systems. We close the chapter with some observations on potential future developments in the use of IT to support groups.

WHAT ARE GROUP SYSTEMS?

Robert Johansen leads a series of projects on "groupware" at the Institute for the Future [2]. It is typical of emerging technologies, says Johansen, that terminology and naming are problems. In his recent book, *Leading Business Teams* [3], he lists the following terms as those being used to refer to this type of system.

- Computer-supported cooperative work (CSCW)
- Work group computing
- Collaborative computing
- Cooperative computing
- Interpersonal computing
- Coordination technology
- Decision conferencing
- Computer conferencing
- Computer-supported groups (CSG)
- Group decision support systems (GDSS)
- Computer-assisted communication (CAC)
- Augmented knowledge workshops
- Interfunctional coordination
- Flexible interactive technologies for multiperson tasks
- Data interpretation systems (DIS)

- Shared systems
- Cotechnologies
- Group support systems (GSS)

One of the early frameworks for classifying and organizing the field, presented by DeSanctis and Gallupe of the University of Minnesota [4], is a matrix showing the intersection of the *proximity* of group members (together or dispersed) with the *duration* of their interaction (limited or on going). Figure 14-1 depicts this matrix, along with examples of a technology that has been used to support group activities in each cell. Note that this matrix is relevant for both communication and decision making. For example, decision making has been the intent of decision rooms, whereas LANs are usually perceived mainly as communication support tools.

Later in this chapter, we will use a variation on this matrix to describe the technologies that are emerging for group support. But first we present the experiences of one company in support meetings with information technology.

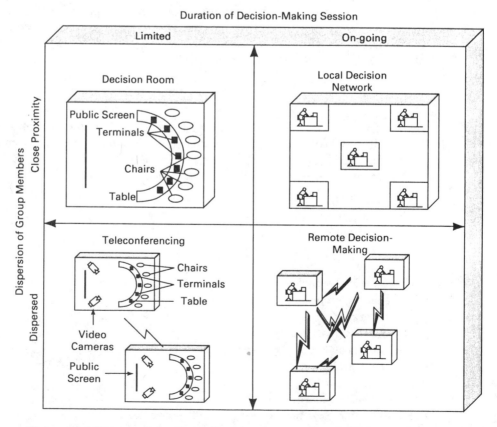

Figure 14-1 Framework for Group Decision Support (from DeSantis and Gallupe [4])

Burr-Brown Corporation, with headquarters in Tucson, Arizona, manufactures and sells electronics parts to other electronic manufacturers. It has about fifteen hundred employees and $180 million in annual sales.

When the University of Arizona, also in Tucson [5], created a decision room in their MIS department, the CEO of Burr-Brown decided to use it for their three-day annual strategic planning meeting. He was so pleased with the results that the firm used it again the following year for the same purpose.

The Decision Room

The room has twenty-four IBM PS/2s, arranged in a semi-circle on two tiers. Up to forty-eight people can use the room, two persons per workstation. A PS/2 in an adjacent control room is the file server, and at the front of the room is a facilitator's control station, as well as a rear projection screen, for video, slides, and movies, and a white board. The room uses an IBM token ring network with Novell network software.

The University of Arizona has developed some twenty decision room software tools; they also sell this software to others. More than one hundred groups have used it. The Electronic Brainstorming System is the most popular; it is used by more than 70 percent of the groups. Like most of the tools, it allows participants to key in ideas on a specific question simultaneously and anonymously. After an idea is entered and sent to the file server, the participant can see the ideas entered by others.

After the brainstorming portion of a meeting, many groups use the Issue Analyzer to organize the ideas. There is also a voting tool to rank ideas and a topic commenter to attach comments to ideas already in the system. Finally, the groups can use the policy formation software to study alternatives. So most group "discussions" using these tools are done via keyboards rather than by talking. Some other tools do encourage face-to-face discussions.

Burr-Brown's Use of the Room

Burr Brown's annual strategic planning meetings had always been held off-site, with some nine to ten executives attending. When they used the decision room, thirty-one executives attended. The MIS department at the university provided a meeting facilitator to help plan the meeting and then facilitate it. During the meeting, the facilitator explained each tool before it was to be used. He also kept participants on track, and was the neutral leader of the meeting, so that

Burr-Brown's CEO could attend as a participant. In addition, an assistant facilitator and three assistants were present. They helped the participants use the hardware and software, make copies of the documents generated by the system, and so on.

Before the meeting, several planning meetings were held to settle on the meeting agenda. Each of the eleven divisions was asked to prepare a document to describe its one-year action plan and rolling five-year plan—including objectives and projected budgets. Participants received these plans before the meeting.

The agenda for the three-day meeting was

- Day 1: Long-term strategy planning
- Day 2: Short-range action planning
- Day 3: Wrap-up in both areas

The meeting began with the group using the workstations to generate ideas about expected corporate performance in the coming years. They then organized these ideas to create the framework for discussing each division's plans.

For the next day and one-half, they entered comments on the five-year strategic plans and one-year action plans of each division, one division at a time.

They also spent some time brainstorming on ways to accomplish the year's objectives and then ranked the ideas. The group settled on specific actions they would take on the top seven issues.

On the last afternoon, they divided into four groups to discuss important topics face-to-face. The planning meeting ended with the four groups presenting their recommendations.

Executive Reactions

After the three-day session, the participants were asked to summarize their reactions to the room. They reported the following.

It Increased Involvement. One senior vice president commented that the decision room allowed them to do in three days what would have taken months. The CEO noted that the past sessions could not be larger than ten people to be manageable; in those sessions, only two or three people really spoke up. With the decision room, thirty-one people were able to attend without hampering deliberations, and the group's comments were much more open than in the past, he noted.

During one of the one-hour electronic brainstorming sessions, 404 comments were made. There were two people at some workstations, with the fewest number of comments from any of the twenty-four and highest being twenty-seven; seven workstations contributed more than twenty. So contributions were relatively evenly distributed across the group.

The group had mixed reactions about the efficiency of the system. In a postsession questionnaire that twenty-six participants answered, eleven stated that it was more efficient than past meetings, nine said it was not, and six were neutral. However, most agreed that the facilitator was important in helping them use the room.

The Planning Process Was More Effective. Several executives mentioned two aspects of the session that enhanced its effectiveness. The main one was anonymity. Due to anonymity, more people asked more questions and made more suggestions than they did in the former meeting methods—where all discussion was done verbally, which identified the contributor.

Second, the planning process itself was extremely educational, said the CEO. "People walked in with narrow perceptions of the company and walked out with a CEO's perception. This is the view that is sought in strategic planning but is usually not achieved," he commented three months after the session. This type of education had not happened at previous planning sessions.

One Year Later. One year later, twenty-five executives participated in a two-day session. About sixteen of them had attended the year before. This year, the intent of the meeting was different. It was to critique plans, so that their impact on others and the support they needed from others were more explicit.

After the CEO described the firm's objectives and the economic climate, the planning session began with the group critiquing the previous year's results, company-wide. The two-day session ended with each business unit manager commenting on the ideas he had received about his unit and how those ideas might affect his unit's action plan.

From the previous year's session, they learned that brainstorming is effective if the groups are structured properly. A large group can consider a few issues, such as corporate objectives, and present their ideas on those topics. But a large group cannot "converse," because there are too many ideas to consider.

For "dialogs," Burr-Brown found it is best to form several small groups, with each group addressing a few issues. One person puts in a statement, another person comments on it, then someone else comments, and so on. In the second year, they conducted small-group dialogs and found them effective.

The company also learned that the room is not a substitute for a planning process. It is excellent for generating many ideas in a short time. But because there is less face-to-face interaction, people are less likely to make commitments and agree on courses of action than in a face-to-face setting. So Burr-Brown does not use the room to reach consensus; they use it to critique plans rather than create them.

The communications manager recommends that others who are planning to use such a room tell the participants about the room beforehand. Just send them a memo that describes the room and include a photograph, he suggested. Also, explain to participants how their comments will be used, he told us, because the use probably will affect how they answer questions.

In all, Burr-Brown participants were pleased with the candor and objectivity the decision room elicited. They believe that its use has enhanced their annual planning meetings.

WHY ARE GROUP SYSTEMS IMPORTANT?

Why should information system executives be interested in supporting groups? In our research, we uncovered opinions in three areas.

- Teams may be the basis for future organizations.
- Coordination theory may guide organizational design.
- Group computing is a new frontier in computing.

Teams: The Basis of Future Organizations?

In the *Harvard Business Review (HBR)*, Peter Drucker wrote an article—"The Coming of the New Organization"—that became the most reprinted HBR article in its first year [6]. Apparently it struck a responsive chord. In it, Drucker states that he believes organizations will become information based, and that they will be organized not like today's manufacturing organizations but more like a symphony orchestra, a hospital, or a university. That is, the organization will be composed mainly of specialists who direct their own performance through feedback from others—colleagues, customers, and headquarters.

This move is being driven by three factors, says Drucker. One, knowledge workers are becoming the dominant portion of labor, and they resist the command-and-control form of organization. Two, all companies—even the largest ones—need to find ways to be more innovative and entrepreneurial. And three, information technology is forcing a shift. Once companies use information technology to handle information—not data—their decision processes, management structure, and work patterns change.

For example, spreadsheets allow people to perform capital investment analysis in a few hours. The calculations are so complex that before this technology was available, these investment analyses generally had to be based on opinion.

With computing, the calculations become manageable and, more important, the assumptions underlying the calculations can be given weights. In so doing, the investment analysis changes from being a budget question to being a policy question, says Drucker, because the assumptions supporting the business strategy can more easily be discussed.

Information technology also changes organizational structure when a firm shifts its focus from processing data to producing information, he says. Turning data into information requires knowledge, and knowledge is specialized. The information-based organization will need far more specialists than middle managers who relay information.

Thus, organizations will be flatter, with fewer headquarters staff and many specialists out in operating units. Even departments will have different functions, says Drucker. They will set standards, provide training, and assign specialists. The work will be done mainly in task-focused teams, where specialists from the various functions work together as a team for the duration of a project.

Team-based organizations will work like hospitals or orchestras, says Drucker. Hospitals have specialty units, each with its own knowledge, training, and language. Most are headed by a working specialist—not a full-time manager—and that specialist reports to the top of the hospital; there is little middle management. Work in the units is done by ad hoc teams, assembled to meet a patient's condition and diagnosis. Symphony orchestras are similar. They have one conductor, many high-grade specialists, and other support people.

Drucker believes we are at the beginning of the third evolution in the structure of organizations. The first, which took place around 1900, separated business ownership from management. The second, in the 1920s, created the command-and-control corporation. The third, happening now, is the organization of knowledge specialists.

Coordination Theory

Thomas Malone, of MIT [7], believes that lessons learned about how large groups coordinate their work can be applied to coordinating large groups of computing resources, or even hybrid groups that include both people and computers.

Malone believes that a multidisciplinary study of coordination theories will advance the computer field. For example, using ideas from economic theory, Malone and others at MIT are studying how to allocate processing resources in a distributed computing environment using prices and competitive bidding. They have found that in networks of workstations, where the machines "contract" to process a task, several configurations are possible. These are analogous to human organizations, he says.

For example, the machines could coordinate their own work, as in a decentralized market. Or some machines could be brokers, as in a centralized market. Or these broker machines could be specialized—printer brokers, high-speed processing brokers, and such—as in a functional hierarchy. Or each processor might have its own peripherals, as in a product hierarchy.

These various forms of coordination all have associated costs. Yet, says Malone, it is likely that it can be used to reduce these costs in human organizations. Look at what has happened as technology has been used to reduce transportation costs, says Malone: (1) people substituted train travel for horse-drawn carriage travel, which (2) increased the amount of traveling people did, because travel was cheaper and more convenient, which, in turn, (3) allowed people to move to suburbs and use shopping malls. These represent first, second, and third-order effects of cheap, convenient transportation.

The use of IT to reduce costs of coordination could have similar effects: (1) IT will replace some forms of human coordination, such as middle management, which (2) may increase the overall amount of coordination—which could change the type of work in coordination jobs or even increase the number of such jobs—which (3) may encourage a shift toward more coordination-intensive organizational structures, such as highly networked, decentralized organizations. Uncovering desirable coordination structures and the effects they may have on organizations are two of the goals of Malone's coordination work.

Group Computing as New Frontier

Robert Johansen of the Institute for the Future, mentioned earlier, defines groupware as electronic tools that support teams of collaborators. He believes groupware represents a fundamental change in the way people think about using computers. The things they need to work together are different from the things they need to work alone. So groupware is different from past software.

There is definitely a need for groupware, says Johansen, because most people spend 60 to 80 percent of their time working with others. Yet, from informal polls he has taken, people seem to feel they are most productive when they are working alone. Thus, they are not happy about how they work with others. This shows there is a need for systems that support groups.

The most successful and likely-to-be-accepted forms of groupware build on existing systems, says Johansen, because the groupware idea is difficult to sell. The first examples of groupware are what he calls "horseless carriages." They help groups do what they are used to doing, without really taking advantage of the technology. One example is the "copy board"—a large whiteboard that can be electronically scanned and printed on paper. Another example is a projector that projects a PC display image onto a large screen.

In the future, groupware that takes full advantage of technology will be just another part of corporate information systems. Such products most likely will be built on existing "platforms"—electronic mail systems, LANs, departmental systems, and public network services, such as the telephone. Thus, Johansen's advice for getting into group support is to build on what you have.

These three areas—the emergence of teams, the need to manage computer-based "conversations" among people and machines, and interest in supporting group processes—appear to be major issues in creating new organizational structures. That is why we see group computing being important.

Characteristics of Groups

Before addressing technology support for groups, let us recognize that there are differences among groups. Some of the characteristics that differentiate groups are the following.

Group Membership. Groups CAM be open, or they can be closed, where membership is restricted. Actually, there is a "gray scale" between open and closed, indicating the degree of difficulty to gain membership.

Group Interaction. The group can be loosely coupled, where the activity of each member is relatively independent of the other members. Sales people who have their own sales territories often fall in this category. Or the group can be tightly coupled, such as a project team where the work of each member is tied closely to the work of the other members. As in the case of gaining group membership, there is a range of group couplings, from loose to tight.

Hierarchy of Groups. A group can be just one part of a "chain of command." Large computer conferences, for instance, are often planned and conducted by a hierarchy of committees. At the top is an ongoing committee that sets the general plans for years in advance and selects the site and the top people for putting on each conference. The top committee for a conference then oversees the work of the various detail committees—program, exhibits, local arrangements, and so on. In addition, each of the detail committees may have subcommittees working on specific portions of their responsibility.

We cite these characteristics to indicate that providing computer-based services for group activities is not a straightforward matter. There are so many possible variations that services are not covering the full spectrum, at least at first. Initial offerings of computer-based group support services are serving intracompany groups rather than groups extending beyond company boundaries. Also, initial offerings are emphasizing support for communication among group members, although they will quickly move beyond that function.

Types of Groups

To further expand our understanding of group support systems, consider the types of intracompany groups for which support will be needed.

Authority Groups. These are groups involving formal authority, such as boss and subordinates, team leader and team members, and so on. Membership is closed, and coupling is tight. Hierarchy often occurs among authority groups.

"Dotted Line" Management Relationships. These are groups where the group leader might provide technical guidance to the group members but do not have hiring, promotion, and firing authority over the members. Again, membership is closed, and interaction is reasonably tight. A nonauthority level of leader-subordinate hierarchy exists.

Clerical Processing Groups. There are at least two general categories of these groups. One is intradepartmental, where the group members are all doing essentially the same work, often under the same boss. The accounts payable section of an accounting department is this type of group. Membership is closed, and interaction can range from tight to loose coupling. It is tight if a person does only part of the job, and then passes the work on to his or her neighboring coworker. It is loose if each person does the complete job, as far as the accounts payable unit is concerned. Numerous LANs and departmental computers have been installed for such groups. There can be a limited hierarchy in these groups, such as "senior" clerical people handling only certain types of processing.

The other category is interdepartmental, where work is passed from department to department. As an example, the entire procurement function involves purchasing, receiving, receiving inspection, accounts payable, and cash disbursement groups, thus forming a super group. Work is passed from one group to the next one in the chain. Membership is closed, and coupling is tight. Hierarchy tends not to be present.

Peer Groups. These are groups where the activities of each member are largely independent of the activities of the other members. One example is a group of executives that regularly exchanges ideas and opinions. Another is a group of secretaries that works for different bosses but calls on each other for help, suggestions, and so on. Still another example is a sales presentation being made to a group of prospects, where each prospect will make his or her own buying decision. Membership can range from relatively open to closed, and the interaction tends to be loosely coupled. Hierarchy usually is not much in evidence.

Project Teams and Task Groups. These groups often involve members who are working full-time in a group with a goal to be accomplished by a specific time. Projects generally are longer in duration than the "tasks" of task groups. These groups can be classified as closed membership and tightly coupled, although sometimes members are at different geographical locations. A hierarchy of project teams or task groups can exist.

Committees. Committee membership generally does not require full-time work by the members. Membership may not be quite as closed as a project team, and interaction might not be as tightly coupled as among committee members. As indicated earlier, a hierarchy of committees can exist.

Information Exchange "Networks." Most people have a list of people they call for advice and information. When a problem arises, a person tends to call a few of these friends and acquaintances, asking for leads to information for solving the problem. Membership tends to be closed, although new names are added, and some old ones are dropped over time. Interaction is loosely coupled, and a hierarchy is not very likely.

In addition to these intracompany groups, there are others that cross organizational boundaries. Computerized group services may not be provided for such groups, at the outset, but we think they will be forthcoming. Two such group types are the following.

Business Relationship Groups. These are relationships with customers, groups of customers, suppliers, and so on. Membership often is closed, in the sense that a new customer or supplier may have to "earn" real acceptance. Interaction is loosely coupled. A hierarchy is not too likely, but favored customers and suppliers can have dominating influences.

Social "Networks." These are groups of people who socialize on an enjoyment basis. Information is exchanged and frequently good work-related ideas are generated in such exchanges. Membership can be quite closed, and interaction is loosely coupled. Here, too, a hierarchy is not too likely.

This wide variety of groups and characteristics suggest that the spectrum of required support systems will be quite broad. In the next section, we look at the systems that are evolving, and then focus on two of the most popular.

TYPES OF GROUP SUPPORT SYSTEMS

Johansen and his team at (IFTF) [3] have identified three main technology "building blocks" for groupware: the telephone, the computer, and the conference room. A significant amount for group work has come from merely bringing these three building blocks together. Conference calls with speaker phones connect groups for voice communication. Computers in a conference room yield high-quality presentations, real-time voting systems, and electronic brainstorming. Computers and phones offer computer conferencing, electronic mail, and remote access to large sets of data and information. The need for group support is strong enough and the benefits are promising enough, that an entire industry is emerging to develop specific applications for group support.

The Groupware Matrix

The IFTF group has extended the DeSanctis-Gallupe matrix shown at the beginning of the chapter to serve as a framework for the emerging portfolio of group support systems [8]. See its version in Figure 14-2.

One dimension of the matrix deals with time, the other with location. The two values on each dimension, same or different, designate whether the members of the group were communicating and interacting over time or distance. The resulting four cells help classify the systems that are evolving to support groups. The "same time, same place" cell in the upper right, for example, includes the electronic meeting support system used by Burr-Brown. The "different time, different place" cell in the lower right incorporates the communication-oriented sys-

Figure 14-2 Groupware Options

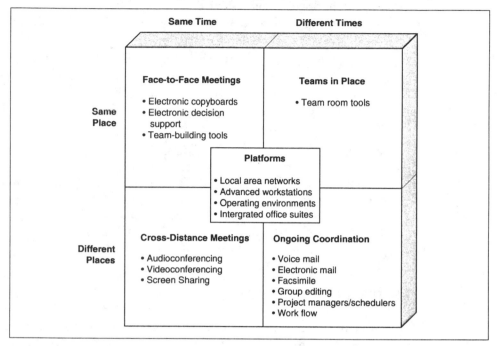

tems such as electronic mail, computer conferencing, and group editing. Most development of group systems has occurred in these two cells, yet there has been little integration among systems in these two cells, or with the other two. It is becoming clear to researchers and developers that true group support systems must aim for support "anytime, anyplace," group working, especially as we approach the emerging new computer environment discussed in Chapters 11 and 12.

Nevertheless, most of the current systems reside mostly in one of the two dominant cells. For this reason, we will discuss each of them more fully, and present a case example to illustrate the use of the technologies and benefits that have emerged. But first, a short description of the technology infrastructure.

The Technology Infrastructure

The center of the IFTF matrix in Figure 14-2 contains the following four "platforms." These constitute the technology infrastructure to support the development and use of group support systems.

Local Area Networks. As we discussed in Chapter 6, LANs are becoming the dominant communication infrastructure. They allow relatively high-speed data transfer among workstations, and they set the stage for continued development of the client/server and cooperative processing architectures that are becoming so popular. Also, most of the systems in the "different time, different place" cell of the time/place matrix are written to run on LANs.

Advanced Workstations. Most current group support systems run on IBM-compatible PCs or Apple Macintosh workstations. In the future, however, more powerful workstations and high-end PCs will be needed to handle the display, storage, and transfer of multimedia documents. Other capabilities that will be required of the workstation include multitasking, a powerful graphical user interface, client/server networking, and access to external document collections.

Operating Environments. This refers to the collection of software layers that define the environment within which the user gets things done on the computer. It includes the functions that have been performed by the operating systems, plus an ever-increasing set of "middleware" that used to be part of the application, plus the "look and feel" of the user interface. Examples of operating environments include DOS, UNIX, OS/2, Mac operating system, and HP's NewWave. Groupware applications, especially those that operate in several cells of the time/place matrix, will depend heavily on the functions of the operating environment.

Integrated Office Suites. The final (potential) piece of the technical infrastructure for group support systems is an integrated office suite. These have been around for several years in the form of DEC's All-in-1, Wang's Office, IBM's PROFS, and HP Desk. A new ingredient in the equation is UNIX. With the growing popularity and relative "openness" of UNIX, the stage is set for a new spate of integrated group support products based on UNIX. In fact, this piece of the infrastructure could act as the integrator for products in all cells of the time/place matrix.

This, then, forms the technical infrastructure within which GSS products will be developed. Unfortunately, companies do not have the luxury of developing the infrastructure first and then developing the GSS applications; they will need to develop simultaneously. Yet there are some dominant products available, and their value is exceptional. Consider the two main application areas of meeting support and communication support.

Meeting Support

As discussed earlier, most people are members of numerous groups—and most groups tend to hold meetings. The frequency of meetings is a function of a group's geographical dispersion, its need for interaction, and the ease of getting together. Group members, all of whom work in the same building, for instance, can generally meet easily—unless they are constantly traveling. This group might meet often, so the problem of "too many meetings" can arise. At the other extreme are groups whose members work hundreds or thousands of miles apart. Such groups meet less frequently, and their meeting time tends to be limited.

The international recruiting firm, Robert Half International, with headquarters in New York City, released the results of a study they commissioned not long ago. The study found that the average executive in U.S. companies spent more than eight hundred hours per year in meetings. Not only is this a large portion of total work hours (on the order of 30 percent), but, even worse, the executives reported that they considered about 240 of those hours to have been wasted in useless meetings.

Problems with Meetings. From the many meetings of various types that we have attended, numerous shortcomings have been evident, starting with the meeting planning and preparation. Often there is no agenda, or only a superficial one. No problems are clearly spelled out in advance, and no specific action items proposed for addressing the problems. If actions (or motions) are proposed, seldom are alternative actions described that have been considered. If documentation about the issues has been provided before the meeting, too often, some members choose not to study the material but rather expect to be "briefed" on it at the meeting. The chairman may even do little or no follow-up between meetings to see if the group's members are carrying out their assignments.

Some meetings are doomed from the start. Key people are late in arriving or do not attend at all. Or some necessary information may not arrive in time for the meeting. Or some group members may forget to fulfill their assignments for the meeting.

Then the meeting chairman may do a poor job of managing the meeting time. Discussion may be allowed to wander from the subject. Time may be spent on briefing attendees or on routine matters—reviewing and correcting minutes of prior meetings, getting committee progress reports, and so on. Such meetings tend to run over their allotted time, with important items receiving poor consideration.

Often, too, a few people dominate the discussion; not infrequently, these people are very repetitious, saying the same things over and over. Conversely, some people do not speak up and contribute their ideas.

Finally, many meetings are wasteful from a cost standpoint. A meeting involving even a few managers and professionals costs hundreds of dollars per hour in salaries alone; large meetings can easily cost thousands of dollars per hour. If travel is required, costs are even higher. Add to this the fact that the participants are unavailable for other activities while tied up in the meetings.

Information Technology Can Help. The goals of group support systems for improving meetings are to (1) eliminate some meetings, (2) encourage better planning and better preparation for those meetings that must be held, (3) improve the effectiveness as they are held.

Eliminate some meetings. The most likely candidates for elimination, it seems to us, are the meetings that do not call for a group decision or group action—they are just for group updating. Progress report meetings are an example, particularly if progress (actual progress versus planned progress) can be reported frequently by means of computerized information systems. Meetings where key people cannot attend, or where needed information is not yet available, can be canceled at the last moment. Electronic and voice mail systems allow the word to be spread rapidly. In short, some of the work done in meetings can be shifted from the "same time, same place" cell to the "different time, different place" cell in the time/place matrix.

Better preparation for meetings. Consider the idea of a "meeting support system" that helps impose a discipline on planning for a meeting. The system might request the meeting organizer not only to enter the time, place, and list of invitees for the meeting, but also the problem(s) to be addressed and the specific action items proposed for solving those problems. Further, the system might request a brief description of alternative actions that have been considered. Finally, supporting documentation could be distributed by the information system or, if too lengthy, at least a summary might be distributed. Action items can be carried forward to other meetings, until they are resolved.

Computer conferencing also can play a significant role in improving preparation for meetings. A computer conferencing system is actually a form of enhanced electronic mail. Participants can log on to a conference (of which they are members) at their convenience, read all entries made by others since they last logged on, and make their contributions. All submissions are saved for the life of the conference; they are not deleted as in electronic mail systems.

In the planning stage of a meeting, such a system can be used for obtaining reactions to the proposed agenda, and then for distributing the agenda and documentation. The first round of reactions to the proposed actions can be entered in the conferencing system, allowing all group members to submit ideas. These actions might even be debated, and other alternatives raised, before the meeting even occurs.

Further, routine matters might well be taken care of before the meeting, such as review and approval of minutes, receiving committee progress reports, voting on routine action items, and so on. Group members can give attention to these matters at their convenience, and valuable meeting time will be saved.

The chairman can use the conferencing system to follow up on the activities of group members to see if they are fulfilling their assignments. Finally, electronic mail and computer conferencing systems can provide a written record of premeeting and postmeeting communications.

There are other ways in which IT can help groups prepare for meetings. Group members can share work files and the use of databases. "Intelligence" files can be established to record all contacts with customers, for example. Personal interest profiles can be created to distribute information to the people who need it. Directories and bulletin boards can be established to help people locate sources of needed information. Systems can be set up whereby scattered group members can simultaneously view the same text or graphics files on their PCs.

Improve the effectiveness and efficiency of meetings. One of the major benefits of meeting support systems is improved meeting efficiency and effectiveness. Meetings are more effective when the ideas generated by the group are more creative and their commitment to the groups activities is great. They are more effective when this happens more quickly.

One of the most popular meeting support systems is GroupSystems, developed at the University of Arizona and marketed by the Ventana Corporation in Tucson, Arizona [9]. GroupSystems has been adopted and marketed by IBM under the name TeamFocus. It consists of a set of tools to support a variety of functions and activities of groups during meetings. Paul Gray and Jay Nunamaker provide a list of the tools in GroupSystems and their functions in several categories; see Figure 14-3 [10].

Tool	Function
Idea Generation	
Brainstorming	Anonymous entry of new ideas
Topic commenter	A set of electronic index cards for simultaneous entry of information on multiple topics
Group outliner	Organization of ideas according to a structured outline form
Idea Organization	
Idea organizer	Organization of comments from idea generation
Issue analyzer	Identification and consolidation of comments from idea generation into issues
Group writer	Joint authoring of a document by meeting participants
Prioritizing	
Vote selection	Choice of voting method (e.g., yes/no, multiple choice, ranking), voting, and vote result presentation
Alternative evaluation	Rating of alternatives according to multiple criteria
Questionnaire	Electronic questionnaire form
Group matrix	Ratings on a two-dimensional matrix
Policy Development	
Policy formation	Structured support for reaching consensus on policy statements
Stakeholder ID	Stakeholder identification and surfacing technique of Mason and Mitroff
Session Planning	
Session manager	Pre-session planning, in-session management, and post session organization of results
Organizational Memory	
Enterprise analyzer	Structuring and analysis of group information in a semantic net
Graphical browser	"Zoom-in" and "zoom-out" on nodes of enterprise analyzer
Group dictionary	Development and storage of formal definition of terms being used by group
Brief case	Immediate read-only access to any stored text file; calculator, notepad, and calendar

Figure 14-3 GroupSystems' Tools Developed at the University of Arizona

In talking with the participants of several electronically supported meetings, we have uncovered the following three dominant advantages and benefits:

- *Anonymity.* The system generally permits anonymous entry of ideas, comments, and suggestions during a meeting. This feature draws out the timid, neutralizes the overly dominant, and eliminates much of the political inhibitions that cause people to hold back in meetings.
- *Parallel processing.* The system allows everyone to contribute simultaneously. In a normal one hour meeting of ten people, each person on the average gets six minutes of "air time." With a meeting support system, it is possible for every one to contribute and interact full-time during the hour.
- *Real-time capture of information.* The results of the meeting are captured as the meeting progresses. It is not unusual for participants to receive a full printout of the meeting results as they leave the meeting. Better yet, in some systems, the files from the meeting are available from the participants' desktop computer through a LAN.

Meeting support systems have been used long enough to generate convincing data on their effectiveness and efficiency. Consider a recent study done at Boeing Corporation.

CASE EXAMPLE: Boeing Aircraft

Brad Post presented the results of a Boeing study [11] of a meeting-support system. The purpose of this study was to answer questions such as

- What are the measurable benefits of using such a technology?
- How does the technology improve work quality?
- What is the return on investment?
- Does the technology enhance or detract from current business team practices?

In short, Boeing needed to know if a solid business case could be made for meeting support systems—including cost, benefits, and qualitative considerations valued by the company.

The system used was TeamFocus from IBM, a version of the GroupSystems developed by the University of Arizona. Boeing used the system over a period of a year and gathered data on sixty-four TeamFocus sessions. The nature and purpose of the meetings varied as follows:

- Planning: 25 percent
- Management strategy setting: 3 percent
- Consensus building: 11 percent
- Survey: 22 percent
- Requirements definition: 28 percent
- Preferred process: 11 percent

Session Activity

- 64 Sessions
- 654 Participants–mean of 10.2 per session
- Mean session length of 4.7 hours
- Mean prepartion time (hour)
  - Customer–7.8
  - PSO–8.9
  - Total–16.7
- Mean post session time–4.5 hours
- Current booking leading time–29 days

Savings to Company

- $432,260 Total labor dollars saved
- $6,754 Mean labor dollars saved per session
- $1,446 Mean labor dollars saved per session hour
- 11,678 Total labor hours saved (71 percent)
- 1,773 Total days of flow time saved (91 percent)

Figure 14-4 Study Data Summary

In the aggregate, the time used in this wide range of team meetings was cut by more than 90 percent, reported Post, that is, the meetings took one-tenth the time that similar work had taken in the past. Post described one project in which a group of engineers, designers, and manufacturing managers used the system to conduct a series of meetings to design a complex control system. Managers said such a job would generally take about a year; using the system, it was completed during fifteen meetings over the course of thirty-five days. Figure 14-4 shows the aggregate data.

The meetings' efficiency was further strengthened by participants' ratings of meeting effectiveness. All 654 participants filled out a questionnaire on the value and success of the sessions. Figure 14-5 shows that their responses were quite positive and in some cases enthusiastic.

These results were strong enough to prove to Post and his managers that it is clearly possible to make a strong business case for meeting-support software.

Nunamaker reports that although there are few studies of this depth and detail, these results are not unusual or unique. Many of the surveys conducted by the University of Arizona on the extensive use of their rooms during a five-year period have yielded similar results.

Communication Support

The other dominant cell in the time/place matrix is the "different time, different place" cell. Activities in this category have been supported by systems for some time under the categories of office automation; recent advances

Question	Mean	Std Dev
Improved channel of communications	3.82	0.49
Helped set clear objectives	3.63	0.52
Provided insightful information	3.90	0.46
Produced more complete decision making	3.69	0.56
Showed higher quality or more valuable session results	3.91	0.51
Improved teamwork and morale	3.62	0.54
Increased commitment to results of session	3.54	0.61
Enable greater efficiency and ROI	4.02	0.46

Scaling: 1–no benifits to 5–great benefits   Participants 654

	Mean	Std Dev
Session well suited to group's objectives	4.04	0.49
Comfortable using the GDSS tools	4.14	0.39
Personal responsibility for group's decisions	3.70	0.55
Other meeting would not have produced same ideas	3.52	0.52
Results achieved in much less time	4.04	0.51
Willing to participate in another TeamFocus session	4.37	0.46
My group could use TeamFocus on a regular basis	3.55	0.56
Comfortable using the keyboard	4.06	0.40
Facilitator beneficial to session	4.24	0.45

Figure 14-5 Participant Questionnaire Responses

in electronic mail, fax, and computer conferencing have made this a very active area of development.

One product that has grown rapidly is NOTES by Lotus of 1-2-3 fame. NOTES is taking its place as the dominant product in this cell of the matrix, just as GroupSystems is the dominant product for meeting support. In fact, a recent *Fortune* article [12] that describes groupware as the productivity payoff from PCs, features GroupSystems and NOTES as the two primary products. Johansen of IFTF says that NOTES is a "bellwether groupware product." Sheldon Laube of Price Waterhouse, the first corporate NOTES customer, thinks that NOTES will perform the same role that 1-2-3 played with spreadsheets. He thinks it is a revolutionary piece of software that will change the way people think about computing. People who had not used computers would do so just to get NOTES. In fact, before NOTES was installed, only four of the members of Price Waterhouse's fifteen member executive committee used PCs. Now they all do.

NOTES can be viewed as a combination of document creator and indexer, database generator and manager, and messaging system. In other words, it is an electronic mail and computer conferencing system that handles documents that can be built and modified with a word processor. Users can put unstructured text documents into databases, with fields that can be searched and indexed, says Schlak [13]. These documents can be shared, modified, and searched by several people as they work on projects. One of the key components that is making NOTES so popular is this focus on handling full documents (rather than just messages) in electronic form. We will discuss other advances in electronic documents and their management in Chapter 16.

GUIDELINES FOR GROUP SUPPORT

With a field as important and as fast moving as this, studies and research on what works and what does not work is very important. We found some interesting studies on supporting work groups with information technology. In this section, we present the findings of some one dozen researchers. Based on their work, we offer the following guidelines for supporting work groups with information technology:

1. Build on electronic mail
2. Support frequent communication
3. Expect changes in group work
4. Accommodate psychological factors
5. Be sure the system fits the culture

Build on Electronic Mail

One of the most logical, and common, platforms for providing tools for work groups is electronic mail. Here is the experience of one organization that illustrates the value of electronic mail for group support, and a report on some research on extending or enhancing electronic mail.

At a Services Firm

Lynne Markus [14], of Claremont Graduate School, studied the use of an electronic mail system at a services firm with headquarters in Los Angeles, California. The firm employs some 7,500 people, 825 of whom are managers—from first level supervisors through corporate officers. Markus wanted to know how managers and executives would use electronic mail.

She studied a regional vice president in charge of three districts and four hundred employees. He is located at headquarters, two of his districts are in the central United States (two time zones east of him), and one district is in the Eastern time zone (three hours ahead of him). He supervises the executive director of each region, and he is the liaison between his districts and the corporate departments—such as pricing, processing, and customer and supplier relations.

He uses electronic mail extensively, leaving his computer on whenever he is in the office, so that he can hear the beep that signals the arrival of a new message. He told Markus that the mail system is his primary communication tool. He believes he could not handle his volume of work without the system.

On the day Markus visited him, he handled 110 electronic mail messages—44 he composed himself, and 66 he received from others. Only 4 of the received messages were via electronic distribution lists, and only 3 others were replacements for paper. The remaining 59 were sent directly to him.

Markus saw that the availability of the "forward" command, in particular, supported the regional vice president in his work in groups. Of the 66 messages he received, 34 were "mosaic messages"—that is, they contained from 1 to 6 additional messages attached to them.

A mosaic message is created by using the "forward" command rather than the "reply" command when composing a response. The intent of the forward command is to transfer a message to a party other than the original sender or receiver. It is used to append one message to the bottom of another. In fact, messages can be forwarded repeatedly, thus building up a transcript of the discussion of a problem or issue, as the mosaic messages are passed from person to person around the organization.

Markus witnessed the regional vice president using the forward command several times the day she visited. In one case, as the intermediary between headquarters people and a regional manager, he coordinated the resolution of a payment question, using electronic mail only. Within eleven minutes, communications between line and staff traversed two thousand miles and four levels of management to resolve this urgent issue. The firm was able to rush payment to the irate supplier that day.

In another case, during a five-hour period, a headquarters vice president, the regional vice president, and one of his executive directors held a sometimes two-way, sometimes three-way, electronic mail conversation about a state law in one of the districts. At the end of the mail conversation, the executive director forwarded the entire mosaic message to one of her subordinates for follow-up. In both of these cases, temporary groups "met" over the electronic mail system, compiled a trail of comments and discussion, reached a decision, and then disbanded.

Markus found the executives at the company preferred to use electronic mail to explain complex or ambiguous issues. They felt such issues were more clearly and quickly explained in writing than in speech. In addition, the mail system provided a record that could be forwarded to others, if appropriate.

Enhanced Electronic Mail

Malone, Grant, Lai, Rao, and Rosenblitt [15] discuss research being conducted at MIT's Center for Information Systems Research on improved group support through enhanced information sharing. Group communications can be improved through by using "templates" and "filtering rules" for electronic mail messages, say the researchers. They are developing such a system, with the initial design based on the results of a study of how more than fifty individuals handle their paper and electronic mail. The initial version of the system is in use at MIT.

Message Templates. Message templates are structured formats for messages; default values can be provided for some of the fields. Templates make it easier for senders to create messages and for recipients to categorize and handle their messages. Groups can define their own message types and message templates to serve their own needs. Further, no one is forced to use the templates by continuing to send and receive electronic mail as usual.

Typical electronic mail systems already make use of templates of a sort. Structured message header information includes To, From, and Subject entries, before the sender can begin entering the text of the message. Date and time are automatically entered by the electronic mail system. Templates developed by the authors go further. For example, the template for messages that announce meetings have the additional fields of time of meeting, place of meeting, sponsor, and topic to be covered.

For most of the fields specified by the template, the system can show the user (on request) the default value of the field, an explanation of the purpose of the field, and a list of alternative values. Groups enter this information when the templates are first defined. As an example, some meetings are held regularly, at the same place and time of day—say, each Tuesday afternoon at 3:00 P.M. in the project office. To send an announcement, the sender need only fill in the date of the next meeting and have it sent to the specified distribution list.

A project team can define its own message types and templates, and subproject teams can have their own meeting notice templates, progress report templates, bug report templates, or whatever. The overall project might have its meeting notice templates, as well as templates for messages dealing with the project's product performance requirements, and other comparable information. It helps if all templates of the same general type—say, meeting notice templates—have the same root template in a template hierarchy, and each subproject has its own additional fields and default values.

Filtering Rules. Electronic mail is such an inexpensive form of communications, and so easy for sending copies of messages to long distribution lists, that recipients can get much mail that is of little or no value to them. How can an electronic mail system help users separate the important (to them) messages from those of lesser importance?

Malone *et al* propose the use of templates to meet this need. One or more of the fields in the template (To, From, Subject, etc.) are used for the IF part of a filter rule. The user fills in the THEN part, describing what is to be done. For example, a user's rule might be: If the FROM field = (boss's name), then display immediately.

Each user can develop several filtering rules, and can add to or change them at any time. Rules can cause some messages to be deleted out of hand, others to be put in a low priority message file, still others to be referred to other people, and so forth.

All of these ideas address the need to make electronic communications among members of groups more effective—to get relevant information to the recipients with less wasted time for both senders and recipients.

Support Frequent Communication

When people are not located near each other, information technology can be used to support cheap, frequent, spontaneous communication, because informal and unplanned interaction is crucial for good teamwork.

An experiment conducted at Xerox Palo Alto Research Center (PARC) supports this viewpoint. When PARC created an audio-video link between two Xerox research sites that are four hundred miles apart, they found that 70 percent of the uses of that link were casual, drop-in style conversations that lasted less than five minutes. The researchers surmise that those communications would not have occurred without the video link. These results suggest that companies should pay more attention to using it to support informal communication, in addition to formal meetings.

Video conferencing has been used this way at two other companies. At Boeing, the engineers building the 757 jetliner, who had tight schedules to meet, needed frequent and informal communication among three sites thirty miles apart— the air field, an engineering site, and a manufacturing facility. They did not have time to travel among the sites, so they rigged up a two-way television system with cameras and television screens at each site. They found that this video conferencing arrangement was, and still is, the only way they can meet tight schedules.

J. C. Penney also uses video conferencing, not to replace existing meetings but to include junior people in video discussions, because these employees do not have the travel budgets to travel between Penney's headquarters sites in New York City and Dallas, Texas. Penney also uses their video conferencing links to broadcast fashion shows from their Dallas studio to their senior buyers around the United States. Before the conferencing links, these buyers relied on merchandising specialists at their previous New York headquarters to select the merchandise their stores would sell. Now, the local buyers make their own selections, tailoring their merchandise to their store's customers.

We believe that as video technology becomes more affordable, we will see a switch from large, formal video conferencing rooms to smaller rooms that can accommodate working sessions of three to four people. Unplanned encounters where people exchange little bits of information are important. Information technology should be used to support this kind of group work also.

Expect Changes in Group Work

At a large Southern California utility, a task force of volunteers—one-half retired and one-half still employed at the utility—agreed to work together for a year to develop a set of recommendations about preretirement planning for employees about to retire. One group was to use computers and electronic mail; the other group was not. The two groups were similar in size and characteristics of the participants. Several differences in the work of the groups evolved because of the difference in technology support. Tora Bikson and J. D. Eveland [16] report on the results.

The Group Structures Differed. Initially, both groups subdivided themselves into six committees. Each committee was to work on one issue, such as finances, health, family and social adjustment, and so on.

The conventional group spent quite a bit of time organizing themselves—balancing the size and makeup of the committees, considering the interests of the members, and so on. Each member joined one committee. The electronic group, on the other hand, spent little time organizing themselves. Each member selected the committees he wanted to join; each of them joined two or more committees.

These committee structures lasted for the entire year. However, during the year, the electronic group also formed six procedure-based committees to coordinate the work between the issue-based committees. So the electronic group formed a matrix organization of committees; the conventional group did not.

Leadership Differed in Two Ways. The degree of centralization differed between the groups. Centralization is the extent to which communications are concentrated among a few group members. The conventional group was the most centralized; they relied the most on a few individuals to carry out the work. The electronic group became the least centralized; their participation was more evenly spread among the group members.

Leadership stability also differed. The conventional group experienced greater stability in leadership roles—the same people tended to play key roles throughout the project. Meanwhile, leadership shifted over time among members of the electronic group—both among the retired and the employed members.

Perceptions of Effectiveness Were About the Same. The groups were asked several times during the project how effective they felt they were. The electronic group was more positive about their effectiveness, although both groups rated their effectiveness high.

Interestingly, the retirees in the electronic group and the employees in the conventional group gave higher marks to the medium—electronic or not—that they were using. The employees felt conventional communications were all they needed; the retirees said the mail system helped them communicate even though they were geographically dispersed.

The employees in the electronic group and the retirees in the conventional group gave lower marks; the retirees even noted that they were at a disadvantage, because they could not easily communicate with each other because they were so geographically dispersed.

The Final Reports Differed. Perhaps most intriguing is the difference in the reports that the two groups produced. The conventional group's report was fifteen pages long and contained mainly anecdotal advice about preparing for retirement that the group had gathered from conversations.

The electronic group's report was seventy-five pages long and was composed mainly of tables describing the results of an opinion survey they had designed and analyzed on-line. They had mailed a thirty-three-question survey to 1,325 retired and working people. Some 441 surveys were returned and analyzed.

It is clear that the work tools significantly affected how these groups approached their task—how they structured themselves, what they chose to do, how they handled leadership, and what their end product contained.

Accommodate Psychological Factors

Marilyn Mantei, of the University of Toronto [17], conducted a study during the design of the Capture Lab at the Center for Machine Intelligence at Electronic Data Systems, in Ann Arbor, Michigan. The goal of the study was to create a conference room that would include computer support but would not impede meeting behavior or hinder verbal conversation. Here are some of the things she learned.

Room Design Creates New Meeting Behaviors. Although the design team wanted to encourage discussion, they also wanted the focus of the new room to be a large screen at the front of the room. Thus, they arranged eight chairs that could swivel and roll around an oval table. No seat was directly in front of the large screen. Each seat had a workstation embedded in the table. When seated, all participants faced their workstation and the front screen.

Mantei studied four groups that regularly met together. She saw the workstations in the room used in three quite different ways.

In *interactive meetings*, everyone used their keyboard when they wished to contribute. This style of meeting was rare, said Mantei. It occurred mainly when everyone was equally comfortable with the software and typed at the same speed.

Rotating scribe meetings were the most common. In this setting, attendees allowed one person at a time to enter everyone's comments onto the front screen. An attendee maintained control of the front screen until another person asked, or was asked, to take over. These meetings had the greatest verbal exchange, said Mantei. Group members rarely appeared bored in these meetings, and typing mistakes were found to be humorous.

In *designated scribe meetings*, only one person used a keyboard during the entire meeting. Generally these were planning meetings where a manager brought a secretary or staff person to take notes. Mantei noticed that attendees often fidgeted in their seats, got up to get coffee, or played with the mouse at their workstation at these meetings—an indication that their attention dropped. In some cases, these meetings turned into rotating scribe meetings, when members became frustrated with the scribe's work or preferred to type rather than talk.

In all the meetings, few people would talk while someone was typing. When they did, they lost their train of thought.

Mantei believes that the most effective workstation-based meetings will shift back and forth between focusing on the front screen for verbal interaction and focusing on the workstations for individual contribution. However, this structure does not appear to happen naturally, she noted; it needs to be learned.

Meeting Dynamics Interact with Room Design. Mantei noticed that in meetings of peers, the group sat around the table. However, when a person of higher position was in the room, the attendees repositioned their chairs. They focused only on the front screen, with the participants in the front of the room moving their chairs back from the screen to see it better. Thus, those participants could not use their workstations; they relied on others to enter their ideas into the system. The power structure in these meetings was very evident, said Mantei; in some cases, management explicitly directed participants to stop typing at times.

Power structure also affected where people sat in the room. Normally, the "power seat" in a conference room is the seat furthest from the door and closest to the blackboard, she said. However, in this room, that particular seat was in shadow because of the back-lit screen. Therefore, the power seat became the seat at the back of the table that gave the best simultaneous view of the screen and the other attendees.

Managers instinctively moved to this seat after very few uses of the Capture Lab, said Mantei. One manager became so uncomfortable in another seat that he left the room and returned with a chair, which he put next to the power seat. Another manager always eased out any person sitting in that seat, by "borrowing" the keyboard from that workstation, until the other person also gave up the monitor.

Mantei concluded by saying that her observations cannot be generalized beyond the four groups she studied nor beyond the company culture she observed. However, she believes that introducing a computer into a social environment—such as a meeting—is likely to have unexpected and dramatic effects on participants' meeting behavior, as they attempt to reestablish their roles in the meeting.

Be Sure the System Fits the Culture

The largest obstacle to installing and using a groupware product successfully is corporate culture. If the two conflict, either the product will fall into disuse or employees will be forced to work as the product requires. Wanda Orlikowski, associate professor at MIT, has discovered two main determinants of success in the use of groupware. One is culture; the other is peoples' perception of a product.

When the unwritten rules of behavior, the reward structure, and tenets of getting ahead in the firm (its culture), do not support cooperation, the effective use of groupware is diluted, she says. Furthermore, when the perception of a product's usefulness vary among different groups of people (such as managers, users, and technologists), then the technologists might not implement systems that users view as useful.

Orlikowski studied the use of a groupware product in a large firm where the corporate culture is "up or out"—perform to expectations or leave. In this highly competitive environment, employees quickly realize that they are promoted based on their individual worth. Their goal is to stand out personally, so they see information as power. Cooperation and sharing, although perhaps verbally promoted, are not seen as true success factors. Therefore, the groupware product has found limited use in the firm, because it conflicts with the individualistic, competitive culture.

Unfortunately, said Orlikowski, neither the technologists nor the senior executives noticed this mismatch when they made the investment decision. The I/S executives who promoted the product honestly saw it as a revolutionary way to move expertise around the firm. Furthermore, because the product is easy to use, they also presumed employees would have no trouble visualizing numerous uses for it.

On study, however, Orlikowski discovered that the users had a completely different view of the product. They saw it as only an incremental improvement, like a "database in the sky." Although it might help them communicate better and work at home more, it would not help eliminate faxes or telephone calls. In fact, they only saw a few uses for it. In addition, they had great concern for the confidentiality, security, and quality of sensitive information—concerns apparently not shared by the I/S executives. The users wanted to personally control the information that they shared. Putting it into the system would dilute their personal control, so there was quite a bit of fear about putting important information into the system.

Furthermore, the employees were not given time to use the product. They were expected to bill 100 percent of their time, and spend their own time entering information into the system and perusing its contents. So the informal messages they received—using the system did not support career advancement—conflicted with the formal "use it" messages broadcast throughout the firm.

Interestingly, the employees who have become the greatest fans of the product, and use it extensively, are the information systems staff. They are not on the up-or-out career track. They share information extensively, so the product matches their culture.

Orlikowski's study not only points out the importance of culture but also of understanding the various viewpoints in implementing groupware, or any new information technology. She believes that three viewpoints—manager, user, and system designer—are significantly different; therefore, they define success very differently. For example, although managers might define success as "the system supports business strategy," systems professionals would define success as "the system meets the specifications." Users would take an entirely different view, saying success is when "the system helps me with my job."

Unless these various viewpoints are surfaced and explored, use of a technology can fail miserably, with everyone blaming the product rather than the true culprits: the corporate culture or the various groups' conflicting perceptions.

Groupware alone will not create sharing in a competitive culture, as Orlikowski's preliminary findings show. The culture must reward teamwork and sharing over individual contributions—a difficult cultural change to make. This is the main message of groupware—it requires the appropriate culture to be effectively used. When that match exists, the benefits can be dramatic.

THE FUTURE

Robert Johansen [18] of IFTF is perhaps best qualified to look into the future of group support systems. In the style of his organization's popular *Ten Year Forecast,* he sees several "sure things," "probables," and "wild cards" in the future of this type of system. The "sure things" are mostly characteristics of the business environment that will maintain the driving forces for group support. They include

- The growing importance of business teams
- The growing international nature of business
- The need for organizations to make long-term commitments to employees whenever possible
- The continued development of telecommunications and computer infrastructures
- The continued increase in the complexity of almost everything—the business environment, business organizations, business group processes, and technology

Within this environment, Johansen sees several likely developments in groupware by 1994-95. These are summarized in Figure 14-6.

	Same Time	**Different Times**
Same Place	• Low-tech computer aids for conference rooms are commonplace. • High-tech, high-touch computer-assisted rooms are finally practical and used, though on a limited scale.	• Team rooms are commonplace, with electronic aids. • Shift work groupware (e.g, international traders, factories) are commonplace.
Different Places	• Greatly increased use of conference calls. • Conference calls with PC graphics and images are commonplace. • Video conferencing continues gradual growth, with some use of computer aids.	• Electronic mail and voice mail have evolved to include group features. • "Total quality" groupware is commonplace. • Text filtering and "information refineries" are commonplace in a few sectors.

Figure 14-6 Probable Future Groupware Developments Circa 1994

In the "same time, same place" cell, systems to support these activities will become more widely used, but many organizations will cling to the the "low-tech" meetings they find comfortable. The real growth may await the development of "high touch" as well as high-tech systems that better accommodate human factors.

Johansen sees systems for "different time, different place" evolving from the considerable infrastructure that is already in place. Electronic mail and voice mail are products that just automate what has been done in the past. Given their popularity, however, they will evolve to add functions in support of group interaction in newer ways. Two other probable developments are the emergence of specialized systems to support quality management processes and a major increase in the ability to handle text and document collections.

Johansen's "wild cards" are developments with a rather low probability. But if they do happen, they will have a major impact on the use of groupware. This list includes

- *Interoperability.* Dissimilar systems that can interact easily would make use of groupware on a large scale easier.
- *Radio LANs.* Their development would truly support communication among people "anytime, any place."
- *Free-form speech recognition.* Easy, reliable, and comfortable speech entry to computers would expand the use of group-support systems radically.
- *User interface.* We are ready for the next breakthrough in interfaces, similar to the decade-old jump from command languages to icon-based systems of the Macintosh and Windows. These current interfaces are quite cumbersome for groupware, because they are based on the metaphor of a single user's desktop rather than a group's work space.
- *A jump in market demand.* Since people's meeting and communication patterns are nearly second nature, systems that radically change these patterns have been accepted only slowly. A wild card happening of some sort might disrupt this gradual growth, resulting in a sharp increase in the demand for groupware. A popular book or a breakthrough product (the groupware equivalent of spreadsheet programs) are possibilities.

Our conclusion is that this area of system development and use is poised for dramatic change in the near future. The needs are strong, the benefits are impressive, and the technology is developing by leaps and bounds. We believe that it will all come together soon, resulting in a major change in the way people work together in organizations.

QUESTIONS AND EXERCISES

REVIEW QUESTIONS

1. What are the two main functions that group support systems can perform? What are examples of technologies used for each?
2. List some of the names being used to refer to systems that support group work.

3. What were some reactions of Burr-Brown's executives to the use of the electronic meeting support system?

4. What are three reasons for the importance of group support systems?

5. Name several types of groups and describe each briefly.

6. Describe the four cells of the time/place matrix, and give an example of a technology used in each.

7. What are the four "platforms" or infrastructures for group support systems described by Johansen of IFTF?

8. What are some ways to use group support systems to improve meetings?

9. What are three advantages or benefits from meeting support systems, such as GroupSystems from the University of Arizona?

10. Identify and briefly summarize the five guidelines for group support systems described in this chapter.

11. Johansen describes his view of the future of group support systems with "sure things," "probables," and "wild cards." Identify and briefly describe two items in each category.

DISCUSSION QUESTIONS

1. Support for communication and coordination is quite different from support for group decision making. The technologies should be different. Do you agree or disagree? Explain your reasoning.

2. Filters are not a good idea on electronic mail systems because they will inhibit communication. Do you agree or disagree? Explain your reasons.

EXERCISES

1. Find an article that describes a group support system of some kind. What is its major purpose? What technology is used?

2. Conduct a survey of products available in the marketplace for group support (by using a directory of software or contacting several vendors). What kind of support do the systems provide? How do they compare with the systems described in this chapter?

3. Visit a local company that is using technology to support group work. Map their activities into the time/place matrix. What infrastructures have they developed?

REFERENCES

1. COMPUTER SUPPORTED COOPERATIVE WORK is a series of annual conferences sponsored by ACM (1515 Broadway, New York, NY 10036).

2. INSTITUTE FOR THE FUTURE, 2744 Sand Hill Road, Menlo Park, CA 94025.

3. JOHANSEN, R. ET AL, *Leading Business Teams* (Addison-Wesley Publishing Co., Reading, MA), , 1991.

4. DeSANCTIS, G., and B. Gallupe, "Group Decision Support Systems: A New Frontier," *Data Base*, Winter 1985.

5. DEPARTMENT OF MANAGEMENT INFORMATION SYSTEMS, College of Business and Public Administration, University of Arizona, Tucson.

6. DRUCKER, P. F., "The Coming of the New Organization," *Harvard Business Review*, January-February 1988, pp. 45–53.

7. MALONE, T., and K. CRANSTON, "Toward an Interdisciplinary Theory of Coordination," CCS No. 120, Center for Coordination Science, MIT Sloan School of Industrial Management, April 1991.

8. INSTITUTE FOR THE FUTURE, *Groupware Resources Guide,* 1992.

9. VENTANA CORPORATION, 1430 E. Fort Powell Road, Tucson, AZ 85719.

10. GRAY, P., and NUNAMAKER, J., "Group Decision Support Systems," in Sprague, R. and H. Watson (Eds.) *Decision Support Systems: Putting Theory Into Practice*, 3rd ed., (Prentice Hall, Englewood Cliffs, NJ), 1993.

11. POST, B., "Building the Case for Group Support Technology," *Proceedings of 25th Annual Hawaii International Conference on Systems Sciences*, IEEE Computer Society Press, January 1992.

12. KIRKPATRICK, D., "Here Comes the Payoff from PCs," *Fortune*, March 23, 1992, pp. 93–102.

13. SCHLAK, M., "I/S Puts NOTES to the Test," *Datamation*, August 1, 1991.

14. MARKUS, M. L., "Electronic Mail as the Medium of Managerial Choice," working paper, MIS Research Program, Anderson Graduate School of Management, UCLA, November 1988.

15. MALONE, T. W., GRANT, K. R., LAI, K. Y., RAO, R., and ROSENBLITT, D. A., "The Information Lens: An Intelligent System for Information Sharing and Coordination," in *Technological Support for Work Group Collaboration*, edited by M. H. Olson, (Erlbaum, Hillsdale, NJ), 1989.

16. EVELAND, J. D., and T. BIKSON, "Work Group Structures and Computer Support: A Field Experiment," *Proceedings of Conference on Computer Supported Cooperative Work*, ACM, 1988, pp. 324–343.

17. MANTEI, M., "Capturing the Capture Lab Concepts: A Case Study in the Design of Computer Supporting Meeting Environments," *Proceedings of CSCW*, ACM, 1988, pp. 257–270.

18. JOHANSEN, R., "Groupware: Future Directions and Wild Cards," *Journal of Organizational Computing*, Vol. 2, No. 1, 1991.

FIFTEEN

The Growing Importance of Intelligent Systems

INTRODUCTION

"Intelligent systems" is the new term being used for real-world uses of artificial intelligence. AI is a group of technologies that attempt to emulate certain aspects of human behavior, such as reasoning and communicating, or they mimic our senses, says Harvey Newquist [1], a well-known consultant and columnist in the field. AI technologies include expert systems, neural networks, fuzzy logic, machine translation, speech recognition, and natural language.

AI has been a promising technology for many years. In the early 1990s, that promise finally began to unfold, but quietly. In particular, expert system technology, also called knowledge-based systems, was seen as a mainstream computing option by many large companies that used it along with other technologies, such as imaging and conventional information systems.

In this chapter we concentrate on expert systems, because they are the most prolific application of intelligent systems. The automobile industry uses expert systems to troubleshoot robots and check cars for noise and vibration. Communications firms use them to diagnose switching circuits. The financial services industry uses them to choose financial planning and tax planning alternatives. Manufacturers use them to plan raw material usage, evaluate designs, control and monitor automated materiel-handling equipment, and identify and track equipment failures at customer sites. Corporate education and training departments even use expert systems as tutors. The list goes on and on.

WHAT IS AN EXPERT SYSTEM?

An expert system is a type of analysis or problem-solving model, almost always implemented on a computer, that deals with a problem the way an "expert" does. The solution process involves consulting a base of knowledge or expertise to reason out an answer based on characteristics of the problem.

Clyde Holsapple and Andrew Whinston [2] define an expert system as "A computer-based system composed of a user interface, an inference engine, and stored expertise—that is, a rule set, a knowledge base, or an entire knowledge system. Its purpose is to offer advice or solutions for problems in a particular area. The advice is comparable to that which would be offered by a human expert in that problem area." An expert system should be able to solve a problem, explain to some extent how it solved that problem, and provide a reliable means of solving similar problems.

Expert systems are not new. The first was the Logic Theorist, developed in 1956 by Allen Newell and Herbert Simon, of Carnegie-Mellon University, together with J. C. Shaw of the Rand Corporation. Another early expert system was DENDRAL, a program that interprets data produced by a mass spectrometer to determine molecular structures; it dates back to the mid-1960s. However, the means for creating expert systems changed with the introduction of artificial intelligence languages such as LISP and Prolog, as well as other new artificial intelligence software development tools. These tools brought expert systems out of the research laboratories and universities and into businesses. The field changed again with the introduction of PC-based development tools, called shells, that used conventional languages, such as C. Today, a wide spectrum of expert system building tools are available, for use by novice end users to experienced knowledge engineers in a systems department.

One of the most famous early expert systems is XCON–expert configurer—which was developed in 1980 for Digital Equipment Corporation by John McDermott of Carnegie-Mellon University. XCON is still used to configure Digital's VAX computer systems. It determines the best physical locations for the components and ensures that all necessary parts are supplied and that all the components are properly connected. XCON consistently ensures correctness and completeness much better than human technicians, and it saves Digital more than $18 million per year.

Components of Expert Systems

There are three components in an expert system.

1. A user interface
2. An inference engine
3. A knowledge base

The *user interface* is the interface between the expert system and the outside world. That outside world could be another computer application or a person. If the system is being used directly by a user, the user interface contains the means by which the user states the problem and interacts with the system. Traditionally, the user interface has been a simple menu, or ordinary word processing, database, or spreadsheet screens on a workstation. But some new systems are using multimedia, as we discuss later in the case of Tulare County. When the expert system is interacting with another application, the interface is the program that presents the facts to the expert system. For example, the Northwest Airlines system described in Chapter 5 contains a program that gathers the data about each airline ticket from the ticket database and presents those facts to the expert systems.

The *inference engine* is that portion of the software that contains the reasoning methods used to search the knowledge base and solve the problem. The expert system generally asks questions of the user to get the information it needs. Then the inference engine, using the knowledge base, searches for the sought-after knowledge and returns a decision or recommendation to the user. Unlike conventional systems, expert systems can deal with uncertainty. Users can enter "Don't know" to questions in some systems, or answer "Yes (0.7)"—meaning "The answer probably is Yes, but I'm only 70 percent certain." In these cases, the system produces several possible answers, ranking the most likely one highest.

A *knowledge base* contains facts and data relevant to a specific application. The inference engine uses this information to reason out the problem. Here are some ways knowledge can be represented in a knowledge base.

Knowledge Representation

Knowledge is being represented in expert systems in an ever-widening spectrum. In this section we discuss that spectrum, beginning with the most familiar representation—rules—and concluding with two very new options—case-based reasoning and fuzzy logic. As these new options appear, the definition of an expert system can likewise expand.

Rules

The most common way to represent knowledge in expert systems is through rules. The rules, also called heuristics, are obtained from experts;

therefore, they can draw upon experience, common sense, ways of doing business, and even rules and regulations. Rules generally present this knowledge in the form of if . . . then . . . statements. The number of rules determines the complexity of the system. Small systems have perhaps fifty to one hundred rules; large systems have several thousand rules. Rules are most appropriate when knowledge can be generalized into specific statements. When this is not possible, the following alternatives may be more appropriate.

Semantic Networks

Semantic networks represent knowledge in nodes. Semantics is the study of meaning, and seeks to define what objects and symbols stand for. In the case of an expert system semantic network, the nodes may contain physical or conceptual objects or symbols, and descriptors for those entities. Two nodes are linked by an arc whose name denotes the meaning of the relationship it represents.

Frames

Frames put knowledge into containers that have slots with information, values, rules, and procedural code that can redirect the query until the correct answers or solutions are found. Frames are fairly similar to objects in object-oriented systems, because the slots can contain code. Frames can be used to represent a salesperson's annual performance because they can hold his or her name and the products sold, along with quarterly sales, quotas, gross margins, and so on. Even if most knowledge is represented in the frames, rules are still needed to perform the inferencing.

Blackboard

The blackboard approach connects complementary expert systems to share information in a common data structure called a blackboard. A "manager" controls the various systems and helps the combined systems arrive at a solution. For example, a blackboard expert system could conceivably be used to solve the problem of sudden surges in automobiles. One expert system could analyze the fuel system, whereas another analyzes the automatic transmission, another the brakes, and another the pedal controls. Using them in concert, the "manager" could see how several elements in combination cause the surges.

Case-Based Reasoning

Case-based reasoning (CBR) is a recently popular form of knowledge representation in expert systems, arriving on the market in 1991. These systems draw inferences by comparing a current problem (or case) with hundreds or thousands of similar past cases. Case-based reasoning is best used when the situation involves too many nuances and variations to be generalized into rules.

Evan Schwartz and James Treece [3] provide an excellent example of a CBR system—the Apache III system used by the intensive care unit at St. Joseph Mercy Hospital in Ypsilanti, Michigan. When Sharon, thirty-five years old, entered the hospital with a potentially fatal respiratory disease, the physicians and nurses in intensive care entered her vital statistics and medical history into a workstation running Apache III. The system drew on the records of 17,448 previous intensive-care patients to predict whether Sharon would live or die. Its first prediction was that she had a 15 percent chance of dying.

As the statistics were entered daily, the system compared her progress to the base of previous cases. Two weeks later, the prediction soared to 90 percent, alerting the physicians and nurses to take corrective action. Then, literally overnight, her chance of dying dropped to 60 percent, and twelve days later to 40 percent. She did recover.

The intensive care unit's director credits the system with catching the improvement four days before his staff would have seen it. So the system is helping the unit respond faster and control costs better.

Esther Dyson [4] points out that CBR permits reusing knowledge, because it allows retrieving all kinds of information associated with cases in a case base, such as instructions, diagrams, active links to hypertext documents, multimedia sequences, and even an automatic phone dialer that calls a help desk. CBRs can present a single recommendation or a set of possibilities, says Dyson, and there are innumerable uses, including

- Answering questions at a help desk
- Matching job requisitions to job candidates
- Selecting form letters to reply to incoming letters
- Finding legal precedents
- Identifying code modules for reuse

A CBR system contains a case base that has been indexed for one of three kinds of retrieval, says Dyson. *Hierarchical* retrieval uses a hierarchy to search for related cases; this approach is the most efficient, but it requires indexing the cases. *Template matching* uses the input case as a straight query against the database to find matches; it uses traditional database indexing techniques. The *nearest neighbor* approach uses common text retrieval techniques to scan the text and calculate the relative closeness of the new case to those in the case base; this technique takes the most processing time.

Dyson believes CBR is likely to become just another retrieval technique used in mainstream applications, just as rule-based expert systems have become reasoning modules in traditional applications.

Fuzzy Logic

Fuzzy logic is an AI technology that allows computers to precisely handle concepts and fuzzy notions, such as tall, warm, cool, good, near, far, and so forth. It therefore allows computer systems to more closely work the way people talk and think. Fuzzy logic was created in 1965 using set theory by Lotfi Zadeh at the University of California Berkeley. It represents yet another way to represent knowledge or information.

Traditional programs require a specific definition for a characteristic, such as 68°F is hot, and 67°F is cold. Such sharp boundaries cause abrupt changes in the output of conventional control systems, notes Kevin Self [5]. Fuzzy logic, on the other hand, allows characteristics to be classified by their "degree of membership in a class," which softens the traditional hard delineations. Fuzzy logic permits precisely dealing with imprecision.

Larry Armstrong [6] explains fuzzy logic by describing how a heater's thermostat works. If the thermostat is set at 68°F, the heater would generally kick on at 66°F and kick off at 70°F if it were controlled by a traditional program that controls an on-off switch on the heater fan. Therefore, the room alternates between too cool and too warm. Fuzzy logic, however, can keep the room at a more constant temperature, because it performs more complex calculations. Each temperature setting is a member of two classes from a set of four—cold, cool, warm, or hot. The 68° setting, for example, might have a 50 percent membership in the cool class and a 15 percent membership in the warm class. Simple if . . . then rules in the system translate these membership percentages into heater fan speed. For instance, a fan speed setting of 50 percent medium and 15 percent low might correspond 44-rpm fan speed. When the temperature changes, the system recalculates the fan speed to maintain the desired 68°F.

Fuzzy logic simplifies complexity; therefore, it is very useful for controlling very complex systems or situations that cannot be easily represented by if . . . then rules. Furthermore, fuzzy logic can be combined with an expert system to handle previously unsolvable problems. The fuzzy logic portion processes the large number of variables into a small number of membership sets that can then be very quickly handled by a small expert system.

Fuzzy logic is being widely used in Japan in consumer products—auto focus cameras, elevators, washing machines, subway trains, and so forth—because it allows smoother operation of machines and appliances. It is being investigated in North America and Europe. Fuzzy logic can also be used to control networks, processing plants, and other operational information systems; therefore, we see it eventually playing a role in systems built by systems departments.

Earl Cox and Martin Goetz [7] believe that fuzzy logic will become important in information retrieval, because it allows people to think in general terms, such as "Find all companies whose revenue is growing rapidly and whose profit-to-earnings is very low." In such a search, the system not only responds with the citations but also indicates where they sit in the fuzzy set—near the defined goal of "growing rapidly" or above or below it. Cox and Goetz also believe fuzzy logic will be used to enable experts to state their expert system rules less precisely. For example, a doctor could have a rule, "If the patient is very old, do not recommend strenuous exercises." They also believe fuzzy logic will reduce software maintenance by reducing the number of rules needed in applications and by separating the variables used by the rules.

By allowing computers to work more like people, fuzzy logic opens up a new range of computer applications and permits existing applications to be able to handle imprecision and changing situations.

Neural Networks

Neural networks are another type of intelligent system. Although they are not expert systems, they are another way of representing knowledge; therefore, we discuss them here.

Neural networks are organized like the human brain. The brain is a network of neurons—nerve cells—which fire a signal when they are simulated by smell, sound, sight, and so forth. As Brian O'Reilly [8] explains, scientists believe that our brains learn by strengthening or weakening these signals, gradually creating patterns. A neural network contains links (called synapses) and nodes that also fire signals between each other. Neural networks are more "intelligent" than the other forms of knowledge representation discussed because they can learn.

O'Reilly presents a good description of how a neural network learns by describing how a simple one might evaluate credit applications. As shown in Figure 15-1, the first layer of this neural net has six "neurons" that represent the criteria for distinguishing good credit risks from bad credit risks. The six criteria are high salary, medium salary, owns a home, less than three years on the current job, prior bankruptcy, and has a dog. (The dog probably does not have an effect, but who knows.) Each of the six is connected to the two neurons in the second layer: profitable customer and deadbeat.

To train the system to distinguish between these two, the network is fed an example: an applicant with a high salary who owns a house and has a dog. Each of these three neurons sends a signal of equal strength to both the profitable and deadbeat neurons, because it has not been trained. The network is trained by telling the two second-level neurons the outcome of this previous loan: It was paid back. So the profitable neuron sends a signal back to the three saying, in effect, "You are right, send a stronger signal next time." The deadbeat neuron, on the other hand, replies with, "You are wrong, send a weaker signal next time." The network is then given many more examples so that it learns the predictors of profitable customers and deadbeats, readjusting its signal strengths with each new case.

Once the network is trained, the high-salary neuron might send a signal worth ten points to the profitable neuron, whereas the homeowner neu-

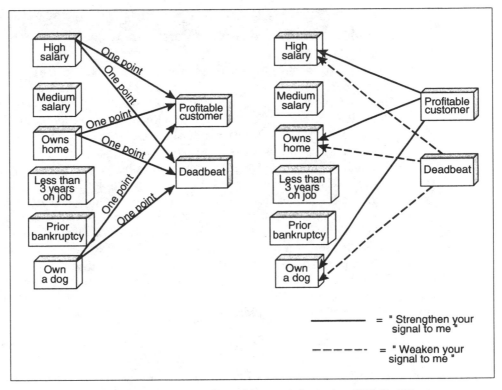

Figure 15-1 Training a Neural Network (based on O'Reilly [8])

ron might send only two points. And the less-than-three-years-on-the-job neuron may send two points to the deadbeat neuron and a minus two points to the profitable one. Since owning a dog is irrelevant, it will send zero points to both. New applications will be evaluated based on these learned patterns.

Neural networks have been used by an automaker to detect defective motors, by oil drillers to describe the progress of underground rock cracking based on sensor data, by a manufacturer to track manufacturing variations to determine the optimum manufacturing conditions, and by computer manufacturers to recognize hand printing. As with expert systems, the extravagant claims made about neural networks in the late 1980s have faded away, and their true uses are gradually being uncovered. Also like expert systems, we suspect they will be used to complement other reasoning techniques.

Now that we have explained the basics of expert systems and various ways to represent knowledge, we present an example of a rule-based expert system with a multimedia front-end, built intentionally for use by the general public. This is a very new use of expert system technology.

CASE EXAMPLE: Tulare County, California

Tulare County, with 300,000 residents, is located in central California. As an agricultural county, Tulare has many people on government assistance. As described in *I/S Analyzer* [9], from 25 to 31 percent of Tulare's residents (some 90,000) are on welfare and another 10 percent are unemployed. About 40 percent of the residents are Hispanic and more than 7,000 are immigrants from Southeast Asia.

The eligibility workers in the Department of Public Social Service qualify residents to receive government aid, but the department has had a tough time retaining these workers because their job is tedious and not highly paid. They must memorize a stack of state and federal welfare regulations six and one-half feet tall; and that stack grows at the rate of one page a day.

Many social service agencies around the world have given their workers computer-based tools to ease their workload. Tulare decided to go further: to build a system that residents can use on their own. Many people believed this could not be done, considering the low educational level of these people and the language translations problems inherent in working with Hispanic and Asian residents. But the system is in and its success has exceeded all expectations.

The system, called "The Tulare Touch," allows welfare applicants to conduct their own interview to qualify themselves to receive funds from the Aid to Families with Dependent Children and food stamp programs. The applicant uses a touch screen (no keyboard) as the system presents the information in one of six languages—English, Spanish, or one of four Southeast Asian languages. A host or hostess, speaking in one of the languages, appears in videos and as the behind-the-scenes voice. This guide introduces them to the system, asks them questions, and presents them with the possible options.

The real driver of The Tulare Touch is an expert system, which runs on the department's IBM 9000 series mainframe. It not only selects the next question and sequence of visuals to show, but it also calculates the applicant's benefits at the end of the interview. The system has a total of 1049 questions; however, because of the expert system, no applicant ever needs to answer all of them.

The system shortens the interview process by handling the thousands of complex rules and regulations better than the eligibility workers. It is also reducing errors and catching more fraud, because it applies the rules more consistently. And department management has found that many applicants prefer dealing with a computer rather than a person, because they believe they get fairer treatment. Economically, this $3 million system is also a hit; it is saving the county $20 million a year, $15 million of which is through reductions in erroneous overpayments—even though their 3 percent error rate is below the national average.

Using the System. When applicants enter one of the six county social services offices, they first talk to a receptionist eligibility worker who determines the reason for their visit and then enters their name into the system. The system checks the mainframe database for other information on the applicant and then initiates a transaction record. If the resident is first-time applicant, or returning for his six-month recertification, the receptionist directs him to a booth with the system that speaks his language. The receptionist also transfers the applicant's records to that system.

The applicant is then interviewed by the system. Animated graphics, combined with the host's "voice over," make the multiple choice questions easy to answer. For example, when the host says "January," the word January flashes on the screen. In some cases, the multiple choices are created on the fly, such as listing family members. Even applicants who cannot read any language can use the system successfully, because it is so visual and combines audio and visual cues.

At the end of the interview, the system prints out a completed application form, which an eligibility worker then reviews with the applicant—to verify the facts, look at any pertinent employment documents, and explain the results. Therefore, rather than filling in forms, the eligibility workers now concentrate on applicants' needs. Their interviews are now of higher quality.

Developing The Tulare Touch. The main problem Tulare encountered in developing the expert system was its design—figuring out the order of the questions to ask the applicants. They used decision trees to diagram the logic, which has made maintenance easy, we were told, even with the continual stream of new regulations. Whenever a change is made, the system indicates which other rules are affected.

The major challenge in designing the multimedia front-end was deciding how to avoid having to recut the laser disk master often, yet keep the system up to date. The mastering process costs $2,000; copies cost $15. To keep remastering down to twice a year, the system only uses video clips of the host or hostess for the introduction and the generic instructions, such as help. Only his or her voice is used everywhere else. Most of the voice portions are stored in analog form on the laser disk; however, new voice and text portions are stored digitally on hard disk, until a new master is cut.

Due to the uniqueness of the system, Tulare is being visited by government agencies from around the world.

Degrees of Expertise

The degree of expertise in an expert system can be characterized by the kind of assistance it might provide a person. It might function as

1. An assistant
2. A colleague
3. A true expert

Although many popular discussions of expert systems view them in terms of the third, or most expert, level, many expert systems are of the assistant or colleague levels.

In the least expert of these, an expert system is viewed as an *assistant* to help do routine analysis and point out those portions of the work where the expertise of the human is required. Dipmeter Advisor developed by Schlumberger Ltd. falls into this category. It reads charts produced by instruments that have been lowered into an oil well that is being drilled. Reading such charts, looking for a small amount of significant data, is a tedious job for humans. The expert system reads the charts and indicates those portions where the human experts should concentrate their attention.

A second level of expertness is that of a *colleague*. With an expert system of this type, the user "talks over" the problem with the system until a "joint decision" is reached. In this type of use, the user may employ the WHY and HOW features to understand the system's train of logic. When the system seems to be going down the wrong track, the user puts in more information to get it back on track. The resultant decision is thus a joint effort.

The third level of expertise is the *true expert* where the user accepts the system's advice without question. This means the expert system performs as well as the top 10 to 20 percent of the experts in the field. Psychologists posit that it takes approximately ten years to acquire 50,000 discrete pieces of expert information, and that an expert possesses between 50,000 to 100,000 different pieces of expert information. So, such a system may employ the expertise of more than one person in a particular field.

Types of Expert Systems

The types of expert systems are broadening. Initially, when the only feasible development approach was to use an artificial intelligence language on a specially designed machine, knowledge engineers developed mainly large systems. But now, smaller systems are easier to cost-justify, because they can be built with PC-based tools and the C language. And as the Tulare County example just demonstrated, these systems can be used in conjunction with other information technologies. In short, a spectrum of types of expert systems now exist, some built by end users on PCs, others built by developers as a piece of departmental or corporate system, and others still purchased as packages. Here are three types of expert systems.

Intelligent Job Aids. Paul Harmon [10] notes that the introduction of PC shells split the market into large systems and small ones. The small systems help users analyze small, but difficult, problems and do not rely on using artificial intelligence languages; therefore, they can be developed by end users. Harmon calls these intelligent job aids. Job aids in general have always helped people by reducing what they need to memorize, and have also helped companies by allowing less trained people to perform the work. Today's intelligent job aids allow the computer to perform more complex tasks, without making the user interface equally complex. These job aid systems also allow experienced users to pass their knowledge on to others.

Expert Support Systems. Luconi, Malone, and Scott Morton [11] discuss expert support systems, which are systems that work primarily as interactive aids to experts. Experts rely on these systems because of their reasoning skills as well as for the knowledge programmed into them. It is the human, however, who provides the overall problem-solving direction as well as knowledge not incorporated in the system.

Expert support systems solve a wider class of problems than expert systems, say the authors, because they do not require all the relevant knowledge to be in the system. Therefore, they can handle real-life situations where constraints on, say, people, parts, and machines change continually. These systems require a good user interface, so that the experts can both control and inspect the system's problem-solving process.

Embedded and Linked Expert Systems. Expert system technology has come to be most heavily used embedded in, or attached to, conventional systems. In some cases, the expert system provides the intelligent link between various systems, determining when each should be executed. In other cases, it collects the information, which is then used by other programs. One example is intelligent business forms, where the expert system assists people in filling out the form. This use ensures more accurate and complete information, and it most frequently appears where the needed information is based on voluminous and complex regulations and rules. Intelligent forms can also be "active documents" in that they may contain enough intelligence to route themselves along the appropriate business process path. Intelligent file folders integrate image processing and expert system technology to collect the images they need automatically—and then notify the knowledge worker when the collection of documents is complete.

Embedded knowledge-based systems can also gather information from other automated systems and provide intelligent search capabilities. Or they can translate output into a more understandable form. For example, a system might translate the figures on an income statement and balance sheet into a textual report that explains what the numbers mean. In so doing, it could also highlight the problem areas. Embedding expert systems in conventional systems is becoming a common way to handle complex data gathering or decision-making tasks.

As noted earlier, companies are most likely to use expert systems linked to other technologies. One example is combining an expert system with a natural language front-end that allows people to speak or type in their native language. Since the Tulare System required all input to be in English, it did not use this combination. Intelligent systems in the future are likely to combine several AI technologies.

Choosing Appropriate Applications

When is expert system technology most appropriate? We answer that question with the following suggested criteria for locating situations where the technology can have the greatest usefulness.

Locate experts under pressure. Find a subject area where the few experts are under severe job pressure. They may be doing a lot of traveling, receiving urgent phone calls at night or on weekends, and so on. Such experts generally will welcome a system that removes some of this pressure.

Look for complex jobs. Find a job that has become sufficiently complex that the people are having a difficult time doing it accurately. Examples might be job shop production scheduling, dispatching, or equipment configuration checking. Northwest Airlines in Chapter 5 and Tulare County and Merced County in this chapter are prime examples of fulfilling this need.

Handle important but infrequent decisions. Another possibility is to find a decision area that is very important but not performed frequently enough for people to develop (and retain) expertise. Examples are how to repair complex machines that rarely break down or what to consider when shopping for a home mortgage.

Consider life safety areas. Where life safety is important, and decisions must be made in a hurry, expert systems may help the people who are responsible to make faster, better decisions. Network and systems management systems, as examples, are gradually incorporating expert systems.

Focus on the decisions of another organization. An expert system that has captured the decisions of some other organization—such as a government regulatory agency—is not only useful but likely to be accepted by the employees.

Selecting areas such as these for building expert systems should not only improve operational efficiency and effectiveness, but also reduce employee resistance and promote acceptance of the systems.

USES OF EXPERT SYSTEMS

Although expert systems are playing an increasing role in company operations, we will concentrate on three specific uses: to assist knowledge workers for competitive purposes, to deal directly with customers, and to augment conventional systems.

To Assist Knowledge Workers

To get a sense of how the expert system field is advancing, we attended the Fourth Artificial Intelligence Satellite Symposium, hosted by Texas Instruments [12]. The focus of the symposium was how expert systems are being used by knowledge workers. Harry Tennant of Texas Instruments (TI), the host of the symposium, proposed that knowledge workers will benefit from expert systems by using them

- To create information
- To manage information
- To keep technically current
- To contribute to their creativity
- To increase their motivation

To Create Information. Creating involves getting an answer to a question, said Tennant. Expert systems can help. An interesting system described at the symposium is a purchase-approval system. The company developing the system has contracts with the U.S. government, but individual requests to purchase items under those contracts must be approved individually. The company is developing an expert system to make these approval decisions automatically. Once fully developed, they will ask the government to authorize this system as the firm's official purchasing approval agent. If the government agrees, the expert system—not a government employee—will approve such purchases. The government, of course, would audit the decisions.

To Manage Information. Managing information involves looking for questions, problems, or anomalies, or locating information that may be needed in the future, said Tennant. A new development in this area is "agents"—computer programs that work on their own to perform a task they know how to do. Agents often are expert systems with some reasoning capability. One point of view sees future computing as just collections of agents, each performing its own work, he said.

As an example, one hotel has created a system that surveys future reservations each night, comparing them to expected reservation patterns. In some cases, management wants to know about discrepancies. In other cases, the executives have defined the actions they want the expert system to take when specific conditions arise. The system prints out its findings and actions taken for hotel management to use the following morning.

For the next five years, said Alan Kay, a fellow at Apple Computer, end users will "manipulate things" in computer systems. However, in ten years time, they will no longer directly manipulate things via computer. They will begin to "manage" these things—such as agents. These agents will have so much intelligence and autonomy, said Kay, that people will need to manage what they do, because some agents may become too eager in their work. The agents will help people better manage information.

To Keep Technically Current. Expert systems help people gain knowledge or remember things, said Tennant. They are particularly good at what people do poorly: remembering details. The TI symposium showed expert systems that help people fill out complex requisition forms, ask the right questions of audit and tax clients, handle an emergency situation in a power plant, and repair robots that rarely break down (and are therefore difficult to remember how to fix). All the systems helped people stay technically current, without having to remember the details.

To Contribute to Knowledge Worker Creativity. Creativity means relating remote bits of information, said Tennant; the further apart the bits, the more creativity is needed to relate them. Inductive learning systems— where the systems learn from examples—are most helpful when people do not know everything about a process, said Tennant; the system helps them gain new knowledge from the data.

One of the most fascinating expert systems described at the symposium was a diagnostic system for a tubing process. Although that manufacturing process was fairly well understood, because of years of experience, some unexplainable fluctuations in tubing quality continued to appear sporadically. The engineers created an inductive learning system to uncover the cause of the anomalies. They fed it data from actual tubing processing, and it generated the rules represented by the data.

Unexpectedly, the system uncovered a relationship the engineers had not seen. It found a new rule—temperature fluctuations of the lubricants had to be controlled around the *original* lubricant temperature, not around the temperature of the machine. Such insights are dramatic, but they are not yet common, said Tennant.

To Increase the Motivation of Knowledge Workers. Knowledge-based systems can eliminate frustrations and allow people to do the work they want to do, said Tennant. For example, one hotel has given its registration clerks management's daily goals to use when registering guests. Rather than just "following the rules," the clerks use these their discretion when assigning rooms and rates to attain these goals. The clerks like the system because it helps them deal with guests more equally and consistently.

During the symposium, several people stated that improving the processes that knowledge workers use or the products they produce is of strategic importance to companies. Thus, these people are using expert systems to help knowledge workers at important decision points.

A case in point is the system built at Merced County, California, to help its eligibility workers evaluate welfare applications. This work is described in two publications by Andersen Consulting, *Close-Up: Human Services Agency, Merced County, California* and *Trends in Information Technology* [13].

CASE EXAMPLE: Merced County, California

Merced County, California, has some 178,000 residents to whom the country government provides traditional public services. The Human Services Agency determines residents' eligibility for welfare and other government programs. Due to the variety to programs that need to be administered, each eligibility worker previously dealt with nearly 750 different forms and was responsible for distributing some $2 million a year in benefits to recipients. Due to the importance of accuracy, these clerks spent 75 percent of their time checking and rechecking eligibility criteria after completing an interview with an applicant. The jobs were complex and not well paying; therefore, turnover was 35 percent a year. Furthermore, the agency's case load was rising 15 percent a year, which was straining their budgets and resources.

To rectify the situation, agency management decided to entirely revamp the way services were delivered based on attaining three objectives.

- *Focus on families* by having each eligibility worker manage households eligible for multiple programs rather than only serving individuals.

- *Make a computer system responsible* for applying regulations, making accurate calculations, determining benefits, and managing tickler files. This would free the eligibility workers to concentrate on the applicants' needs.

- *Significantly reduce administrative costs* with an eye toward decreasing staff size without sacrificing service.

With the help of Andersen Consulting, the agency built a system that standardizes the all-important interviewing process. It guides the eligibility worker through the interview process by presenting each question to ask the applicant, with the exact wording to use. Based on the applicant's answer selected from the multiple-choice options presented on the screen, the system decides what further questions to ask. Therefore, each interview is tailored to the applicant's specific situation.

The heart of this system is a 4,500-rule expert system, which resides on each of two hundred Hewlett-Packard workstations. All the code was written in ADS, a product of Aion Corporation [14]. This expert system not only guides the interview but also performs all the calculations and determines who in the household is eligible for programs and what benefits the applicant is qualified to receive. During the interview there are no longer any paper forms, system codes, regulation books, or calculators.

The system operates in a cooperative processing environment with 70 percent of the on-line activity handled by the workstations. The remaining processing is handled by a departmental server and a central host.

The system was meant to do more than simply automate the agency's existing manual operations; it was intended to improve them. Therefore, management involved many staff members in the project. During design, the project team uncovered hundreds of agency policies and procedures that required changing if the organization was to be streamlined. To involve the supervisors in initiating change, a two-day working conference was held. Teams of supervisors and managers tackled groups of procedures and policies, rewriting 85 percent of them in those two days. One team alone rewrote seventy policies. Agency management also enlisted the help of professionals in the community who work with the same disadvantaged people during system design.

The system was successfully installed, and the agency is receiving numerous benefits. Clients are receiving better, faster, and more consistent services. The quality of work life in the agency has improved, because the system interprets the detailed eligibility rules and performs the complex calculations; therefore turnover has dropped. And regulatory changes are incorporated faster. Finally, follow-up work and reminders are not forgotten, because they are performed by the system. All these benefits allow the eligibility workers to handle more applicants and handle them in a more humane manner.

For Competitive Purposes

Many of the speakers at a Texas Instruments Symposium pointed out that knowledge-based systems have strategic significance to companies. Unfortunately, few executives realize this, the speakers noted. Expert systems can help people make better and more consistent decisions. They can disseminate knowledge and expertise—not just data—to employees, customers, suppliers, and others. And these systems can handle complex tasks, making them cost-effective. GM Delco developed an expert system that became a competitive tool. Here is that story.

CASE EXAMPLE: GM Delco Products

GM Delco Products designs and manufactures electrical components used in General Motors cars, such as custom direct-current motors used in windshield wipers, door locks, power seats, and such.

Designing a custom motor is time-consuming, even with a CAD/CAM system. Just one component of these motors—a brush—can take two to four weeks to design. A full motor can take one year.

Delco Products has only three experts in the area of brush design, so they decided to create an expert system to help engineers design brushes. The expert system, which run on Delco's DEC VAX computer, contains 270 rules and fifty-five external functions that allow it to interface with the company's CAD/CAM system. The system can be accessed by design engineers throughout the world via telecommunications.

To design a custom motor using the system, an automobile engineer describes the constraints of a motor to a design engineer. The design engineer uses this information to answer some fifteen questions posed by the expert system. With this data, the motor expert system creates a production-level drawing of the brush on the CAD/CAM system; the only things missing are a part number and an authorization signature.

Once the expert system was built, it was tested by comparing its designs with those actually used in General Motors cars over the past thirty years. When the testers encountered a discrepancy, they refined the expert system.

The system has competitive importance because it has speeded up the brush design process to the point that motor design engineers now can create several designs—a luxury they did not previously have. By experimenting with brush designs, the engineers can substantially increase the life expectancy of a motor—a benefit Delco had not foreseen. Thus, with this expert system they not only design components faster, but they can also design products of higher quality. Both speed in responding to change and increased product quality are important competitive factors.

To Augment Conventional Systems

Expert systems have been quietly slipping into business systems as a complement to traditional processing. Tim Mikkelsen [15] sees three ways of combining expert systems with conventional systems.

1. The expert system is the main controlling program.
2. The expert system is embedded within an existing application.
3. A conventional language is used to do symbolic, rather than numeric, processing.

The first approach is where *the expert system is the main controlling program*. In this approach, when the expert system needs information, it calls the appropriate program or subroutine, which may be written in another language. This approach can be taken with existing expert system tools, says Mikkelsen, because many of them provide facilities for calling other programs, or accessing databases or spreadsheets.

The second approach is to *embed an expert system within an existing application*, says Mikkelsen. In this case, expert system modules and conventionally coded modules can call each other; neither one is necessarily the controlling module. This approach can be taken only when the development environment allows developers to create programs in the appropriate languages, says Mikkelsen. Hewlett-Packard, for example, has been working on such an integrated environment to allow programmers to write applications in a combination of five languages in the UNIX environment—C, Pascal, Fortran, LISP, and Prolog.

Harry Reinstein, of Aion Corporation [14], believes companies will benefit most from expert systems by using them to enhance current applications. He also believes expert systems are easier to maintain than conventional systems, because changes are made to descriptions, constraints, and rules that are easier to understand than conventional code. Also, maintenance utilities available with most expert system shells are powerful. By combining these two ideas—enhancing current applications and easing maintenance—he suggests writing the most volatile portions of systems as expert system modules.

Mikkelsen's third approach to integrating conventional and expert systems is to *use conventional languages to do symbolic processing*. Expert system applications can be written in any language, but the effort is much harder in conventional languages. To overcome this hurdle, Mikkelsen recommends prototyping the expert system portion of an application with expert system tools—to test the concept and explore the possibilities.

Expert system development is gradually becoming just another form of programming—a new approach to dealing with previously unprogrammable applications. Expert systems are just one component of a computer application—a component that may or may not be hidden from the user.

As an example of a company that combined a conventional system and an expert system, consider Northern Telecom.

CASE EXAMPLE: Northern Telecom

Northern Telecom is a telecommunications company with headquarters in Mississauga, Ontario, Canada. They manufacture private branch exchanges, telephone systems of all sizes, satellite repeaters, electronic switching systems, and other telecommunications equipment. We talked to the manager of CAM systems in the information systems department in Santa Clara, California. He told us of a project that combines an expert system with a traditional information system.

The Application. The company's product administration system contains information on all products that Northern Telecom manufactures including how they are designed and manufactured. It runs on IBM computers at the firm's twenty-two manufacturing plants and uses a distributed relational database accessed using SQL. The twenty-two sites save the daily changes and update the master database at night. Then, the master database sends revised records to all twenty-two sites.

The systems department wanted to enhance the system by adding procedures for processing engineering changes to reduce the engineering changes approval cycle—from several weeks down to days or even hours. At the time, all but one of the plants used paper-based engineering change procedures. Of course, moving from paper to electronic form speeds things up. But the system could also reduce the amount of information needed by people in an approval chain, if it only asked questions relevant to that particular type of change. This capability would reduce the time a change request spends at each step.

The twenty-two manufacturing plants also used different procedures; therefore, the developers could not create one common procedure that all the plants would use. They therefore decided to create a system that lets each plant manager create customized engineering change procedures for that plant.

Choosing an Approach. After reviewing the specifications for the new system, an outside programming firm concluded that it was an expert system application, for the following reasons:

- It needed to include knowledge about when to authorize or not authorize a proposed engineering change, so it needed a database of decision rules.

- The engineering change process is complex; links between authorization steps can be quite involved, especially when exceptions or new requirements occur. Thus, Northern Telecom needed a modular system to reduce the complexity.

- The engineering change process was not well understood. People had a difficult time explaining when they would not approve an engineering change. Therefore, the firm needed a system that could be updated easily as new change procedures were uncovered.

- The system needed to be maintained by end users; only a system with an English-like user interface would permit user maintenance.

After studying several expert system development products, the company chose ADS from Aion Corporation [14]. Using ADS, expert systems can be developed and run on either an IBM mainframe or a PC. These expert systems can call conventional applications or be embedded within them, and they can access SQL relational databases. These capabilities were just what Northern Telecom needed.

To test the concept, two programmers spent two months building a fully functional prototype. It contained 113 screens, ten menus, and accessed the engineering database. Coding was surprisingly fast, we were told. ADS appeared to increase programming productivity by 30 to 50 percent over a conventional language. The objectives of the prototype were to learn about ADS, to test the feasibility of the application, and to see whether an expert system could be embedded in the existing system. After the prototype was used on a test basis for one month, the team received approval to create the production system using ADS.

Programming the Application. The developers used ADS to create *menus* for initiating change requests, processing changes, inquiring about change status, and so on. The system first leads the user through the appropriate dialog to uncover what is needed. If a change is to be initiated, the system assembles a customized "script" of the steps needed to obtain approval of the change—based on the questions initially answered by the user. The system routes the request to each person specified in the script, and even helps each person reach a decision.

The developers also defined *decision rules* for the various authorization steps. Once the system is given the pertinent facts by an engineer, designer, or purchasing agent, it uses these rules to recommend a decision.

The team also created *escape hatches*, so that users can leave the expert system if it has no built-in procedure for handling a step. A main concern of the programmers was that users would revert to their old, paper-based procedures whenever they encountered something lacking in the system. The escape hatches are meant to help users handle such situations.

The programmers also used ADS to write *interfaces* between the expert system, the relational database, and existing Pascal, C, and Fortran routines. Creating these links was easy, we were told, and they allowed the programmers to use whichever language was best for a particular task. For example, they often chose to create reports using one of the conventional languages.

The team also created a *set of tools* to help plant managers build scripts defining engineering change procedures used at their site. Each script describes who is to handle each step under each circumstance, how exceptions are to be processed, and so on.

Due to the complexity of the application, the programmers believed it would take at least two years of use before all the decision rules used at the various plants had been uncovered and encoded in the system. To make the system useful during that time, they were able to add rules on-line without interrupting the production system.

In all, Northern Telecom was very pleased with their use of expert system technology; they believe the application would not have been practical using conventional programming technologies.

MANAGING EXPERT SYSTEM DEVELOPMENT

As we noted earlier, expert systems can range from a few rules to thousands of rules. These systems are being developed by end users, information systems professionals, and third-party developers. Based on our research, we offer the following three guidelines for managing the development of expert systems:

- Quantify the development effort
- Take a balanced approach
- Draw on end-user computing lessons

Quantify the Development Effort

Mark Meyer and Kathleen Curley [16], both of Northeastern University in Boston, recently developed a four-part framework for categorizing expert systems. They then studied fifty expert systems being used in production to determine whether particular approaches were used to develop the four kinds of systems.

Meyer and Curley classify expert systems on two dimensions: knowledge complexity and technical complexity. Knowledge complexity relates to the depth and specialization of the knowledge of the experts as well as the scope of the processing and level of expertise required in the application. Technical complexity relates to the depth and scope of the development effort, the user environment, and other technical considerations. Combining these two dimensions yields the matrix showing in Figure 15-2.

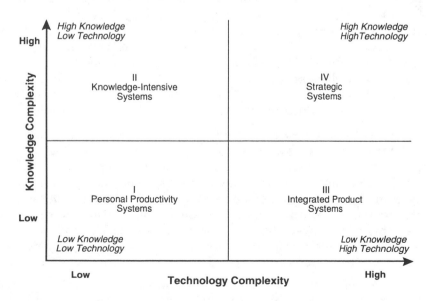

Figure 15-2 An Expert System Framework (from Meyer and Curley [16])

Quadrant I: Low Knowledge, Low Technology. These personal productivity systems contain the least knowledge and technical complexity. They are often developed by end users and generally work on stand-alone PCs or without significant database or communication links. An example of this type of expert system, write Meyer and Curley, is a systems called TAX that is used by a European airline to monitor the travel of employees stationed abroad longer than one year. The company pays the country taxes during this time, if required. The purpose of the system is to help these employees plan elective business and personal travel to reduce the company's tax liability. TAX has a small knowledge domain. It runs on one PC. And it was developed in three months time using a PC expert system shell. Development cost was $15,000.

Quadrant II: High Knowledge, Low Technology. The knowledge-intensive systems include expert systems with "deep" knowledge, that is, requiring elaborate reasoning in a highly specialized field. These systems may also span several domains; however, they are technically fairly simple and operate on a single hardware platform with small databases. One example given by Meyer and Curley is the Coal Advisor, developed by an American engineering service company to assist coal buyers make purchasing decisions. The system takes into consideration more than one hundred characteristics of coal and includes multiple domains in depth, yet it runs on a stand-alone PC with a graphical user interface. It took three years and $2 million to build.

Quadrant III: Low Knowledge, High Technology. These integrated product systems have fairly simple knowledge bases but significant technical attributes, so they require formal project management and testing, similar to major systems projects. One such system is Extel, developed in Europe by a computer firm and a telephone company. It assists customers in selecting the best telephone service, based on their calling patterns. The knowledge base is straightforward; however, implementation is not because the system is dispersed throughout hundreds of branch offices and requires accessing central databases. This system took three years to develop, and costs between $1 and $2 million.

Quadrant IV: High Knowledge, High Technology. These strategic systems require large-scale knowledge engineering (that is, creating rules from expertise) and complex technology, such as integration with other systems. An example is a life underwriting system that operates on both a PC and a mainframe. It combines medical, actuarial, and underwriting knowledge to screen and rate insurance applications. It also requires working with client mainframe systems and external databases. The different data models in these various systems significantly complicated development. The system took more than three years to build for a cost of more than $5 million.

Development Lessons Learned. Meyer and Curley uncovered several development lessons from categorizing fifty systems using this framework.

Although the final systems had different overall development times, building a prototype of the system—which was always done—took about six months for all but the very complex systems in quadrant 4. The complexity of the system design for these systems lengthened the prototyping stage.

The systems were mainly user driven—68 percent of the fifty systems were conceived by the users, and only 14 percent originated with a systems person. The remainder were inspired by customers, consultants, and vendors. Likewise, the development projects were often user managed. Some 62 percent of the projects were controlled by the business departments. And in several cases in which the system was a large-scale strategic system, a new business unit was formed to control development. It was staffed with line and systems people. Logically, the information systems department managed the more technically complex projects, whereas the business units managed the knowledge complex ones.

This framework provides systems management with guidelines for planning a development strategy, depending on the characteristics of the system, say Meyer and Curley. For instance, technically complex systems will benefit from early involvement by systems people while knowledge-intensive systems need at least close linkage with the business staff, if not control by them. The framework also can be used to evaluate the evolution of existing expert systems, whether they are becoming more technically or knowledge complex, and the implications of this evolution on project requirements.

Take a Balanced Approach

Taking a balanced approach means building both large and small projects. Tom Schwartz [17], a consultant in the field, told us that companies should be able to develop one large expert system and many small ones in three years' time. He believes companies should aim to achieve such a mix.

Encourage Many Small Systems. Many experts recommend using PC-based shells to develop small rule-based systems. The definition of "small" is not clear but probably means a system with 50 to 100 rules. But that does not mean it is trivial. Schwartz gave us his guidelines for determining which applications are appropriate for a fifty-rule system. He calls it his "telephone test."

1. It has fewer than twenty outcomes.
2. The procedure can be taught to someone in three hours to three days' time.
3. A full discussion of the problem between the programmer and the user can occur over the telephone, using no diagrams, in less than one-half hour.

A fifty-rule system can still be complex and important. Robert Anderson of the Rand Corporation [18], described a fifty-rule system that he wrote to determine which missile to fire at a target from a jet fighter plane—based on the distance to the target, the number of targets approaching, their location, their speed, and so on. The possible outcomes are to fire one of three kinds of missiles, or fire nothing at all, based on about one dozen characteristics of the target and the quality of the radar signals. In all, forty attributes needed to be considered. This is appropriate for a fifty-rule system, he said. Although this is a stand-alone system, it is not a trivial one. A fifty-rule system that accesses an external database can be a much more powerful system.

Some applications are "growable" in that they can be divided into chunks that can then be linked together. These chunks can be different functions or the same functions performed on subsets of data. By starting small, the investments are less risky, says Schwartz, and the company can experiment with different ways of measuring economic impact. If the initial prototype does not cost-justify itself, and if it is expandable, it could be the basis for a system that does provide economic payback, says Schwartz. Encourage lots of small applications, he suggests, but be cautious on building large ones.

Develop Large Systems Cautiously. Edward Feigenbaum, an AI pioneer at Stanford University, provided his guidelines for developing large expert systems at one of the Texas Instruments Satellite Symposiums [11]. He suggested choosing only problems that will earn or save several million dollars a year, because large expert systems are expensive to build and can take from one to ten work-years. The crucial phase is formulation, said Feigenbaum. Determining the scope of the project is crucial. It is equivalent to a Ph.D. student choosing a thesis theme. One-half the work is picking the right scope of the project. Therefore, spend money on getting help in guiding the selection process. Next, calculate the value of the system in advance, while you are determining its scope, he suggested. Whether that value represents earnings or savings, keep that number in mind. Be specific about the system's inputs and outputs, and do not change the scope of the system in midstream.

Other speakers at the symposium advised picking projects where the knowledge is so well defined that the output is clear. This implies that the knowledge is known by practitioners, that experts on the subject can agree on the knowledge needed to solve the problem, and that the knowledge base can be made relatively stable.

Finally, other speakers recommended building a prototype in a few weeks' time to determine whether the problem is solvable. One airline estimated that they could increase their revenues by $12 million a year by obtaining just one more passenger on each of their flights. But to achieve that goal, they needed to see quickly their rate structure per flight. They built a prototype and demonstrated that this was possible, so they continued the project. All the speakers recommended proceeding cautiously when developing large expert systems.

Draw on End User Computing Lessons

Companies that are encouraging the use of PC-based expert system shells are reusing lessons learned in the 1980s on managing end-user computing. Here are three such lessons.

Establish a Support Organization. An important lesson from end-user computing is the need to establish a support organization to guide the use of a new technology. This group establishes the strategy, chooses the products, coordinates the training, provides consulting help, and markets the technology within the company.

Standardize on a Few Tools. It is wiser to offer users a few tools than to give them the freedom to choose whatever they want; otherwise, support becomes a nightmare. At Du Pont, they chose four tools that ran on many of their installed machines.

Ed Mahler, the program manager of the Du Pont group, told us that the ideal expert-system tool for end users has five characteristics. First, it *supplies a structure*. All the user needs to do is enter the knowledge. If the resulting answer is wrong, it is due to wrong knowledge, not a problem with the tool. Spreadsheets provide this capability; they supply the wherewithal to process what is put into the cells.

Second, the tool has *type-over menus*. That is, the tool presents a menu with predefined default values, but the user can enter new values. In essence, the system provides a skeleton from which to work, just as graphics packages do. Users can use the default values to see a graph quickly, or they can change the defaults to customize the graph.

Third, the tool has *image capture and display capabilities*, because it is often important to include a picture or diagram—such as a diagram of the position of switches on a machine. It is especially nice if the user can change the images, said Mahler.

Fourth, the system would provide *automatic database interaction* to popular PC packages, because users often download mainframe data to their PCs.

Fifth, an ideal tool has *powerful behind-the-screen facilities*, providing, say, the ability to customize screens or create specialized links to other applications.

Stress User Self-Sufficiency. One of the goals of end-user computing was to make users self-sufficient "programmers." Du Pont is taking the same approach with expert systems. They help users get started using a tool, but users are expected to complete and maintain their own work. Knowledge systems are never finished; they can always be expanded, we were told. So user self-sufficiency is important to avoid creating an expert system backlog in the information systems department.

These three end-user computing lessons can help companies encourage users to build their own expert systems.

CASE EXAMPLE: E. I. du Pont de Nemours

E. I. du Pont de Nemours is a large diversified chemical, energy, and specialty products company with headquarters in Wilmington, Delaware. It has some sixty business units involved in energy, manufacturing textile fibers, polymer products, and agricultural and biomedical chemicals.

Although Du Pont is a large organization, the program manager for artificial intelligence sees it as many small businesses. Thus he believes the company will get greater benefits from artificial intelligence technology by creating many small expert systems rather than a few large ones. An artificial intelligence group was formed and has become the catalyst for widespread expert system development within Du Pont.

Management believed that getting users to use expert systems would be a bigger issue than building the systems. Since users are more likely to use a system they create themselves, the company decided to take an end-user computing approach to building expert systems.

They Help Users Develop Their Own Systems. The artificial intelligence group encourages employees to create their own expert systems. The group's goal is to make expert system development just another computing tool—like word processing, spreadsheets, desktop publishing, and electronic mail. The group selects the tools, provides the training, offers consulting help, serves at the help desk, and sometimes does initial development with users to get them started. In addition to the core group, the company has site coordinators who know about specific expert system tools. The core group trains these site coordinators to handle users' questions. So the company has a two-tier support structure to help users develop expert systems.

Due to this approach, users have developed hundreds of expert systems; the average size is 150 to 300 rules each. Most of the systems provide a seven-to-one to eight-to-one payoff on the full investment—equipment, software, training, and work-hours to develop the system.

Some systems assist the sales people, such as recommending the best Du Pont film to replace a competitor's product. Some assist mechanics in diagnosing problems in process control computers. Others provide engineering expertise around the clock to equipment operators. Still others are value-added services, such as advising volunteer firemen how to handle chemical spills at the scene of an emergency.

They Have Educated Managers as Well as Users. The AI group created three training courses on expert systems within Du Pont. A two-hour management awareness seminar explained expert systems, where they are most useful, how they are developed, and why they are important. A four-hour introductory course for users and supervisors discussed both managerial and technical issues. One management issue is deciding when a system is complete. Users often want to add "just one more function." Management needs to decide when enough is enough.

A third course provides two-day training on how to select the proper tool and then develop a system. During these two days, attendees learn to use three tools. Following this course, users can get consulting help from the staff. In some cases, consultants do help create the first prototype. But they never finish it—they want the user to do that.

They Are Sensitive to "Ownership" and Payback Issues. The success of any systems project depends on getting users to "own" the system—to feel that it belongs to them. When a knowledge engineer develops a system for employees, the users are less likely to feel that they "own" it than if they developed it themselves. To foster experimentation by the end users, the core group used both the formal and informal company structures. Initially, they depended on the informal network of people they knew to attain early successes. Then the formal structure provided the impetus to get systems developed.

Although payback is important, Du Pont does not spend much time analyzing it for the small expert systems. Any task that takes an expert more than a few minutes or less than a few hours to complete is worth prototyping. So the company is aiming for the small applications, because there are lots of them, and they tend to grow and become very useful.

FUTURE DIRECTIONS

In one of his recent columns in *AI Expert* magazine, Lance Eliot [19] reviewed the events at the Ninth National Conference on Artificial Intelligence. His review presents a nice overview of future directions in the field.

He notes that the wild AI claims of the 1980s are gone, and this ninth conference was quiet. Most important, it melded theory with practice. The proceedings of the conference divided the papers into ten categories. Here is his review of each.

1. *Case-based reasoning* was the hottest commercial AI topic, with much of the research now being put into products.

2. *Communication and cooperation* papers discussed distributed AI, that is, intelligent agents interacting and cooperating to solve problems. It also deals with use of AI in education and in user interfaces. Eliot believes this research will move closer to commercial use in the later 1990s.

3. *Constraint reasoning* deals with truth maintenance system verification. The ability of AI systems to track the correctness of their knowledge and actions was a key area of interest at the conference; however, the commercial world has not

yet realized the importance of constraint reasoning. Interest will increase when some expert systems fail, surmises Eliot.

4. *Knowledge representation* papers discussed the trade-offs among the different forms of logic and ways of incorporating probabilities and uncertainty. Today's commercial products use the simplest forms of logic and handle only straight-forward techniques of knowledge representation.

5. *Automated reasoning* dealt with search methods and belief systems. Although commercial products have drawn on this research, they do a poor job of explaining what they have done. Eliot sees the need for further adoption of explanation techniques.

6. *Learning* is still an emerging area; most AI systems still do not learn and must be updated by hand. Learning will not be forthcoming in the commercial world until AI researchers discover how to do learning sensibly and safely, says Eliot. The neural network approach is a viable learning technique now being explored.

7. *Planning and robotics* share a natural bond, writes Eliot. A robot must plan its actions, carry them out, and then revise its plans. Unfortunately, few commercial expert systems handle planning; instead, they try to accomplish their goals without planning. As they become more sophisticated, this act-first-plan-later approach will no longer be applicable, says Eliot.

8. *Physical systems reasoning* focuses on diagnosing faults in physical systems by matching a system's expected behavior with its actual behavior. This work is being done primarily in research labs.

9. *Tractable inference* is a catch-all category dealing with judgments, and the most interesting paper discussed why some judgments seem obvious to people, whereas others do not.

10. *Invited talks* were by Pieto Bonissone of General Electric's AI Lab, who discussed approximate reasoning research, and Drew McDermott of Yale's Computer Science Department, who discussed the need for theory and practice in robotic planning.

Many of the papers were coauthored by industry research and development personnel, and thus indicates that researchers are becoming more pragmatic, said Eliot. The conference demonstrated that the commercial side and the research theorists are attempting to link up with each other.

CONCLUSION

The field of expert systems is no longer limited to laboratories and experiments. Many expert systems have been put in production, either through major expert system projects or by encouraging end users to write smaller knowledge systems. Since both types yield significant payoffs, we believe information systems management should follow a balanced approach to building these systems—encourage many small systems and carefully develop large systems. Expert systems, once viewed as an arcane use of information technology, have become a mainstream tool of systems developers.

QUESTIONS AND EXERCISES

REVIEW QUESTIONS

1. What is an expert system?
2. What are the three components of an expert system?
3. Explain the different ways of representing knowledge.
4. What are three types of expert systems?
5. Explain three uses of expert systems.
6. What five things did the Northern Telecom programmers create with ADS?
7. Describe the four categories of expert systems uncovered by Meyer and Curley.
8. What is a balanced approach to developing expert systems?
9. What are three lessons learned from end-user computing?
10. What are the main components of Du Pont's approach to managing expert system development?

DISCUSSION QUESTIONS

1. Expert system technology is too complex for end users to use. It should be left for information systems developers to create real expert systems. Argue for and against this claim.
2. Expert systems are dangerous. People are likely to depend on them rather than think for themselves. And if the system contains some bad logic, bad decisions will be made, and law suits will result. Argue for and against this claim.
3. The Tulare County and Merced County systems use very different approaches to essentially do the same job—qualify welfare recipients. Which approach is better? Why?

EXERCISES

1. Visit a company in your area that has developed some expert systems. What are the systems used for? Are they support, adviser, or true expert systems? Who has developed these systems and how?
2. Read five articles about expert systems. What new facts did you learn that were not in this chapter? Share these ideas with the class.
3. If you know of an expert system, explain what it does, how it is used, how it was developed, who it meant to help, and what its shortcomings are.

REFERENCES

1. NEWQUIST, H., "Nearly Everything You Want to Know About AI," *Computerworld*, July 29, 1991, p. 64.

2. HOLSAPPLE, C. W. and A. B. WHINSTON, *Business Expert Systems* (Richard D. Irwin, Homewood, IL), 1987.

3. SCHWARTZ, E., and J. TREECE, "Smart Programs Go to Work," *Business Week*, March 2, 1992, pp. 97-105.

4. DYSON, E., "Case-Based Reasoning: A Familiar Story," *Release 1.0*, January 31, 1992, pp. 1-15.

5. SELF, K., "Designing with Fuzzy Logic," *IEEE Spectrum*, November 1990, pp. 42-44, 105.

6. ARMSTRONG, L., "Software that Can Dethrone 'Computer Tyranny,' " *Business-Week*, April 6, 1992, pp. 90-91.

7. COOK, E., and M. GOETZ, "Fuzzy Logic Clarified," *Computerworld*, March 11, 1991, pp. 69-71.

8. O'REILLY, B., "Computers That Think Like People," *Fortune*, February 27, 1989, pp. 90-93.

9. "THE EMERGING WORLD OF MULTIMEDIA," *I/S Analyzer*, March, 1991.

10. PAUL HARMON is editor of *Intelligent Software Strategies*, a monthly newsletter published by Cutter Information Systems, 37 Broadway, Arlington, MA 02174.

11. LUCONI, F. L., T. W. MALONE, and M. S. SCOTT MORTON, "Expert Systems: The Next Challenge for Managers," *Sloan Management Review*, Summer 1986, pp. 3-14.

12. The Artificial Intelligence Satellite Symposiums were sponsored by the Data Systems Group, Texas Instruments, P. O. Box 181153, DSG-100, Austin, TX 78718.

13. Close-Up: Human Services Agency Merced County, California, and Trends In Information Technology, Andersen Consulting, 69 W. Washington, Room 1534, Chicago, IL 60602.

14. ADS is from Aion Corporation, 101 University Ave., Palo Alto, CA 94301.

15. MIKKELSON, M., "Mixing AI and Conventional Techniques," *A Review of Products, Services, and Research*, July 1987, pp. 58–59.

16. MEYER, M., and K. CURLEY, "An Applied Framework for Classifying the Complexity of Knowledge-Based Systems," *MIS Quarterly*, December 1991, pp. 454-472.

17. TOM SCHWARTZ, 801 W. El Camino Real, Suite 150, Mountain View, CA 94040.

18. ROBERT ANDERSON, The Rand Corporation, 1300 Main St., Santa Monica, CA, 90403.

19. ELIOT, L., "Where Theory Meets Practice," *AI Expert* (500 Howard St., San Francisco, CA 94105), October 1991, pp. 9-11.

SIXTEEN

Electronic Document Management

INTRODUCTION

In this final chapter of Part 5 on support systems, we focus on a set of systems and technologies for handling documents. Documents have almost always been the primary mechanism for communication and information storage in organizations. That is not going to change anytime soon, but the form that documents take is changing.

In Chapter 14 we introduced the time/place matrix as a framework for supporting the communication and interaction among people in organizations, with emphasis on goal-based information-handling activities. In this chapter, we deal with the documents required for that communication, and we add support for procedure-based activities. These "workflow" systems are the paperwork systems for performing basic business processes that have not been susceptible to computerization until recently.

This chapter takes the place of the office automation chapter in previous editions of this book, because we believe that electronic document management will encompass most of the computer-based work done in offices. As we will see, documents are the nearly universal unit of information for communication and for executing business processes.

The content of this book illustrates that the past three decades have brought significant advances in the use of information systems. Particularly important have been been database systems that organize data in flexible ways and provide access and analysis to a multitude of uses. These systems, however, have mostly handled facts organized into data records. Far more valuable and important to organizations are the concepts and ideas generally contained in documents. Until recently, IT applications for document processing have been limited to better and faster ways to generate, print, and transport text documents. But that is now changing.

Several trends and developments suggest that we are on the verge of yet another revolution in computer-based information management—managing concepts and ideas represented in a wide variety of forms. Technology developments enabling these advances include digital image processing, large capacity storage, hypertext, multimedia documents, high bandwidth communication channels, electronic printing, electronic mail, facsimile, and improved techniques for retrieval of information and text. Many of these technologies are proving valuable for replacing paper, managing workflow, training and education, records management, and internal reporting.

DEFINITION AND SCOPE

Electronic document management (EDM) can be interpreted narrowly or broadly. The narrow interpretation emphasizes *document management* and concentrates on the use of IT to handle paper documents or their electronic equivalent. A recent technology applied here is digital image processing, which replaces a page of a paper document with a digital image of that page. The digital image can be stored, retrieved, and transmitted more easily than a paper page. Other older technologies for document handling include micrographics, computer output microfilm (COM), and automated records center applications.

The broader interpretation of EDM emphasizes *electronic documents* and their management. An electronic document uses a variety of symbols and media to represent the ideas and concepts in the document. In addition to traditional letters and numbers (written language), an electronic document may contain graphical symbols, photographs, and other images, voice, and video clips. This clustered set of symbols, often called a compound document, can be stored, retrieved, transmitted, and presented electronically.

It is clear that such a clustered set of symbols exceeds the usual connotations of the word "document." We are familiar with documents such as contracts and agreements, reports, manuals and handbooks, business forms, letters, and memos. In the future, an internal report on a product improvement may present, on a computer screen, the text explaining the feature, a photograph, and engineering diagram, a voice notation form the product designer, and a video clip of the product in use. This document is richer than the traditional one. Perhaps it could be dubbed an "infobundle."

The Roles that Documents Play

It is difficult to think of anything more pervasive and fundamental to an organization than documents. The roles documents play in organizations include

- To record and store, or to "document," contracts and agreements. This role is so basic we use a verb form of the noun.
- To record and store policies, standards, and procedures.
- To represent a view of reality at a point in time (reports and plans).
- To create an image or impression.
- To act as a mechanism for communication and interaction among people and groups.
- To act as a vehicle for business processes.
- To provide a discipline to capture and articulate concepts and ideas

Taken together, these roles lead to the conclusion that documents are the stored memory for the organization, its groups and its individuals, as well as being the primary mechanism for conducting business.

The overall impact of applying a set of emerging technologies to document management is potentially significant. Since documents contain concepts and ideas, EDM promises to advance the management of conceptual information in organizations. Because most of the work of information workers at managerial and professional levels deals with concepts and ideas, EDM promises improved levels of support and productivity. And because documents are the primary vehicle for business processes, EDM promises to make a major contribution to business process redesign and quality improvement efforts.

What is Required?

The promise of EDM is significant and seductive. But what will be required to take advantage of these opportunities? What should managers do now to enable the orderly assimilation of these technologies in the future?

One major issue will be structuring the roles and responsibilities of the departments and functions for which documents are strategic. Here are some of the organizational groups and departments that must play a major role in EDM.

- *The I/S department.* The technology is now advanced enough and pervasive enough that the I/S function will be responsible for evolving the technical infrastructure. However, the fundamental structure and processing of the conceptual information in documents is quite different from the facts in data records. Moreover, the principles and techniques of document storage, classification, indexing, retrieval, and retention are foreign to most I/S professions.

- *Records management.* With its traditional role of managing the corporate "records," and with its foundations in library science, the records management department has valuable experience in document management practices. But it tends to view technology in terms of its ability to meet specific short-term needs. The records management tradition also emphasizes paper documents and their electronic equivalent—the narrower view of EDM.
- *Office management.* Much office work has been computerized to some extent, but internal and external correspondence and reports still generate large amounts of redundant and hard-to-access paper files. In the future, these files will need to be cross referenced among departments and linked with I/S databases.
- *Library.* External sources of information are increasingly available in electronic form, with search and retrieval capability from large document collections.
- *Print shop.* Computer-based technology is becoming dominant. The new Docutech line of high-speed printers and copiers from Xerox are digital (not light-lens) and contain more computer power than many mainframes.
- *Training and education.* Increasingly based on multimedia technology and computer-based courseware, education and training can be delivered through EDM technologies and approaches.

. Coordinating the role and responsibilities of these and other departments is important because the applications and the technologies required to realize the promise of EDM are evolving rapidly.

Categories of EDM Applications

We found the world of electronic document management incredibly diverse. It not only means different things to different people, but the breadth of applications is vast. We organize the applications into three categories.

- Administrative document processing
- Transaction document processing
- Publishing

Administrative document processing deals with creating letters, lists, notes, spreadsheets, and so on. Personal computers and traditional office systems have dealt with this portion of office work. Both are being extended to handle more kinds of document processing—hand-written notes, voice messages, images, and graphics.

Transaction document processing includes applications where documents need to be routed around an organization. These applications have characteristics similar to transaction information systems, but they have depended on documents that, until recently, could not be computerized. These applications include invoicing, order processing, service requests, budget planning, and status reporting. Document workflow systems are beginning to be used for these applications. The most common term we have heard for this type of document processing is "document image processing," generally because imaging technologies—specifically optical scanners and optical disks—are integral parts of these systems. Because this type of application is so prevalent in business, and because the benefits of imaging technology are substantial, this has been a rapidly growing industry, as noted by the Association for Information and Image Management [1].

Publishing means "to make public." Published documents include reference manuals, company newsletters, bulletins, service manuals, reports, advertising brochures, and so on. Corporate publishing involves word processing, desktop publishing, corporate electronic publishing, and electronic printing. Desktop publishing is fine for small, individual documents, but mainframe-based publishing systems are needed for tracking revisions, passing revisable documents among workstations, and piecing together large documents.

These three categories of applications show the breadth of electronic document management. They encompass most office and industrial work—wherever work or processing depends heavily on document-based information flows. This definition also points out the current categories of electronic document management products—office systems, document image systems, and electronic publishing systems.

Significant benefits can evolve from better electronic systems to handle document-based applications. Here is an example of a company with document systems that include all three of the preceding categories. Through better forms management and electronic printing, they made major improvements in these applications, while enhancing the corporate image at the same time.

CASE EXAMPLE: Tapiola Insurance Group

Tapiola is a group of three insurance companies with headquarters in Espoo, Finland, a suburb of Helsinki. By Finnish law, an insurance company can sell only one type of insurance; therefore, each of the three companies in Tapiola sells either life, nonlife, or pension insurance. They call themselves "an insurance department store."

Some 90 percent of insurance in Finland is sold by five insurance "groups"; Tapiola is the fourth largest group. They have 14 percent of the market, with 1.5 million customers and 3 million policies. Each year their mail room sends out 4 million letters, so printing is an important and expensive part of their operation. We talked to the people in Tapiola Data—the wholly owned information systems subsidiary of Tapiola—about their electronic document and printing activities.

In the mid-1980s, the Tapiola group offered 150 kinds of insurance policies, and they had 300 different insurance policy forms—half in Swedish and half in Finnish, because both are official languages in Finland. The policy forms were all preprinted by an outside print shop, generally on sprocket-fed computer paper. Then the forms were filled in by printers connected to their IBM mainframes.

This mode of operation presented several problems. If a change was made to a form, the inventory of old forms had to be discarded. Reprinting new forms often took weeks. That time represented possible lost revenue. Also, the computer printers could print on only one side of each sheet of paper. Finally, for more complex policies, they had to use large-size computer paper that was often unwieldy to handle and mail.

Document Processing Goals. The production manager and the insurance applications development manager looked around for an alternative way to print policies and statements. They had several goals. One was, of course, to reduce costs. A second goal was to stop using preprinted forms. Their third goal was to give Tapiola marketing people new ways to advertise insurance products, by making computer-generated letters to customers more flexible. The fourth, and most important, goal was to make Tapiola "the most personal insurance company in Finland." Thus, these two systems managers wanted their computer-generated correspondence to prospective and current policy holders to appear more "human"—as if a Tapiola employee had used a typewriter to write a personal reply to an inquiry or request for information.

Centralized Solution. To overcome the computer-generated appearance of their output, they switched to plain paper printers from Rank Xerox, the European subsidiary of Xerox Corporation. Xerox is best known for their photocopiers, but they are increasingly creating products for electronic document processing—where a document can include text, data, image, and graphics. Conversion of the output equipment at Tapiola took fifteen months, during which time they reduced their three hundred preprinted forms to four.

Four New "Forms." Their four "forms" are actually four types of standard European A4 cut paper. (In the United States, the equivalent would be the 8 1/2 x 11 sheet of paper.) The first form is a plain white A4 sheet of paper. It is used for internal communications within Tapiola.

The second form is the same blank white paper with four holes punched along the left-hand side, to fit in the standard European four-ring binder. (In the United States, the standard is generally a three-ring binder.) This form is also mainly for internal use.

The third form has the Tapiola logo preprinted in green in the upper left-hand corner, and both sides of the paper have the word "Tapiola" printed in *tiny*, faint green letters over most of the page. This form is their standard company stationery, and it has become one of their standard computer printout forms for communicating with the outside world.

The fourth form is the same as the third except that it has a 4- x 6-inch (10- x 15-cm) perforated area in the lower right-hand corner. This form is used for all their insurance policy bills. The tear-off portion can be paid at any bank; the money and information about the payment go directly from the bank to Tapiola.

Programming and Conversion. Reprogramming the IBM applications was extremely easy, we were told, because only the output routines needed to be changed. That programming took two work years of application programmer time. In addition, one systems programmer spent six months working with Xerox on the IBM-to-Xerox system software interfaces. One forms designer spent fifteen months redesigning all 300 preprinted forms into 240 printing formats for the application programmers. About 60 forms disappeared altogether, because they were found to be unnecessary; the remaining 240 forms are not all different, because one-half of them are in Swedish and the other half are in Finnish.

The forms designer used the Xerox forms description language for IBM mainframes, HFDL, after spending ten days learning HFDL. It is a character-based language, not a graphics-based language, so the forms designs were done on an installed IBM character-based terminal. The only new equipment purchased was a Xerox 8700 printer—one of the first installed in Europe—and a Xerox 9700 printer. Tapiola upgraded both to the higher speed Xerox 9790 and bought a third Xerox 9790 printer at the same time.

The conversion was done in two stages. First, customer policy statements were printed in a formlike manner, on two sides of the new size paper. These looked somewhat like the old forms so that policy holders could understand the changeover. Then, the terse, tablelike data was replaced with text to make the statements look more like personal letters.

Envelope Stuffing. Interestingly, these redesigns of customer "documents" were the easy part of the conversion. The more difficult—and sensitive—part was making sure that each envelope contained the correct pieces of paper. Since Tapiola was now using smaller sheets of paper, they often needed to include several sheets in each envelope, and, of course, they did not want to put a cover letter for one policy holder into the same envelope as a statement for another policy holder.

To solve this problem, they found an envelope insertion machine made by PMB Vector, in Stockholm, Sweden. This machine contains a microprocessor that can read an 8-dot code printed at the top of each sheet of paper. Thus, the Xerox printer not only prints the correspondence but, at the same time, it prints a code at the top of each sheet of paper—one code for all pages to go in one envelope. The Vector inserter machine makes sure that each envelope only contains pages with the same code.

Decentralized Expansion. This document processing conversion was just one part of their effort to improve and humanize their customer correspondence. In the midst of the document redesign, Tapiola also decided to move some printing of customer correspondence to their sixty-two branch offices. Thus, they became the first European user of the smaller Xerox 4045 printers. Tapiola now has some one hundred such printers around Finland to print customer letters. These printers are connected to the computers and databases at the Espoo data center, via leased lines and the Finnish public data network.

To illustrate how a remote printer is used, consider the case of a female policy holder who has received medical care. She can mail the medical bills to Tapiola or visit her local office in person. If she visits them and presents her bills to a Tapiola employee, that employee uses an IBM terminal to access the policy holder's data from the central database. If she has brought all the proper documents needed for reimbursement, the employee can initiate a *direct electronic payment* from a Tapiola bank account to the policy holder's personal bank account—no matter which bank they both use.

Once a day, Tapiola transmits all such electronic transactions to their bank, and those transactions are cleared that same day. (The five major Finnish banks have collaborated and created a sophisticated and fast banking system. Many individuals and companies in Finland use debit cards and other forms of electronic banking rather than checks or cash.) The employee then gives the policy holder a letter verifying the transaction. That letter is generated by the central IBM computer but is printed on the local Xerox printer. If the policy holder is missing some information, the employee can create a personalized letter explaining what is missing by assembling phrases stored in the central database and then printing the letter on-site.

The people at Tapiola Data recommend that other information system departments become involved in electronic document management by first looking at the output their computers are generating. It is easy to mix traditional mainframe technology with document processing technology, they told us.

A recent poll of Finnish citizens showed that Tapiola is seen as a dynamic company, and they have the best reputation among young people of all the insurance groups. The people at Tapiola Data believe their use of document processing technology is helping to build and reinforce this image.

THE IMPORTANCE OF EDM

As the Tapiola case example illustrates, there are major savings and benefits available from installing EDM technology. But are these opportunities common and frequent enough to justify the considerable effort involved in developing the organizational expertise and the technical infrastructure for EDM? We see four major reasons for I/S managers to get heavily involved in EDM.

1. It provides substantial benefits.
2. It automates the paper part of systems.
3. Documents are the center of many applications.
4. Publishing is pervasive.

Substantial Business Benefits

A report from the Index Foundation [2] offers evidence that EDM promises substantial business benefits. The report states that like personal computers, document processing provides both a promise and a threat. The promise is that corporate information systems will automate paper files— helping businesses operate more efficiently. The threat is that information systems professionals will be caught unprepared.

The Index Foundation paper defines "document image processing" as the capture and storage of information as images, rather than as text or data, with identifying information associated with each stored image. These systems will bring about a revolution, the report says. But it will be a quiet and gradual revolution, much as office automation was.

Document image processing systems address the largest portion of information kept by companies, says the paper, the 66 percent (1) that could not be computerized because of the legal necessity to keep paper or a microform image, or (2) for which manual rekeying is uneconomical, or (3) that contain signatures, drawings, or pictures that previously could not be captured electronically.

In their research, the Index Foundation found that pioneering users of electronic document management systems concentrated on two types of applications. Both types involve the management of "live" information rather than archival information.

One type is transaction-based systems, such as those prevalent in insurance companies. The benefits in these systems arise from improving efficiency and customer service. The second type is reference systems—for high-value information with a long "shelf-life," such as research information. The benefits in these systems arise from faster delivery of the information product to market and competitive advantage.

Typical offices can achieve a three- to four-year payback on document system investments, says the Foundation, whereas engineering departments generally receive a two-year payback. More important, these systems make data more accessible and can give a competitive advantage to firms that rely on speed and quality in replying to customers.

For example, one document system allowed a financial services firm to double the number of customer queries it could handle. And an international bank reduced the "float" associated with documents that needed to be sent to correspondent banks around the world. The Index Foundation report concludes that these systems can provide substantial business benefits.

Automating Paper Systems

EDM provides a way to automate the paper portion of applications—the portion that has not been susceptible to computerization, says John Connell [3]. He believes that image processing is today's major breakthrough in advanced office technology. It is beginning to have significant impacts on office operations and office-based personnel. By image processing, Connell means systems based on optical disk storage technology, where the electronic equivalent of a photograph is stored. Like their predecessor—microform systems—the images cannot be manipulated. And, in most cases, the images cannot be erased. These two properties are important for truly replacing paper with automation, says Connell, because only nonrevisable documents can become legal replacements for paper. Courts have allowed microform records to be admissible evidence in place of paper. Connell believes nonerasable optical disk records will be given the same status.

All current information systems have two parts, says Connell, one part computerized by traditional methods and the other that could not be automated; this part remains on paper in file folders. The automated part uses the latest technology. The unautomated part uses 1890s office technology. Image processing technology allows firms to address these paper portions of applications—and there are many of them.

The first applications to use document image processing have been high volume systems—just as the first I/S applications were the large ones. These large systems provide the fastest payback. These initial applications have also been mainly stand-alone, departmental systems. Where they need access to a central database, simple dial-up database query links have been created.

Over time, however, smaller image processing systems will appear to serve smaller applications. Information systems and office equipment vendors are starting to offer imaging systems for creating *document* processing applications that work in conjunction with existing *data* processing applications. For example, METAVIEW, a product from Metafile Information Systems [4], allows a department to start with a stand-alone PC-based imaging system, and grow to integrate with existing databases and computer platforms.

Document-Centered Applications

Documents are the center of many applications, because they carry intelligence. Documents are packages or bundles of information authored for human comprehension. The most useful documents increase comprehension or cause action. Companies that learn to handle their information—and their documents—will therefore be more successful.

Documents can exist in three domains. One is paper, the traditional form. The second is electronic *image* form, where the content of the image cannot be manipulated. The third domain is electronic *content* form, where the information can be manipulated. Information technology needs to facilitate the movement of information among these three domains—from paper into electronic form (via an optical scanner) and perhaps to become a word processing document (via optical character recognition software) and then back out to paper (via a printer). Paper will be around for quite a while, because it has numerous advantages, such as portability, ease of use, familiarity, and so on. A total document management strategy would provide the architecture not only to move information among all three domains but also to link them electronically to traditional information systems.

As an example of the benefits from using imaging to automate document-based applications, consider the case of Diners Club.

CASE EXAMPLE: Diners Club

Diners Club was the first credit card company. It was started in 1952 as a club for frequent diners by a man who ran out of money at a restaurant. In 1981, Diners Club was acquired by Citicorp, and became part of their credit card group. The bulk of the retail credit card business handled by Citicorp belongs to Visa and Mastercard; Diners Club aims at business travelers.

Diners Club, with headquarters in Chicago, Illinois, serves two markets—the personal card market and the corporate card market. They help their corporate clients better manage travel expenses by keeping track of employees' credit charges. Clients receive tailored reports of expenses monthly.

Image processing was brought into the Diners Club customer service center in Englewood, Colorado, for use by customer service representatives in the personal card group. Cardholders who have a question about a charge on their Diners Club statement can call a toll-free number for assistance. A significant number of these inquiries require Diners Club customer service representatives to investigate the credit charges. They need to obtain information from the establishment where the charge was made and then determine whether the charge was legitimate, posted to the wrong account, or fraudulent.

Before the imaging system was installed, these representatives had to start a file for each cardholder inquiry, keep track of the accumulating paperwork until it had all been received, make a decision, and then contact the cardholder. All the files were kept on paper. The personal card group handles about ten thousand pieces of correspondence a month, so there was a lot of clerical effort maintaining the paper files.

With the image processing system, all correspondence to the personal card group is scanned at the mail room to digitize it. Each digitized image is stored on an optical storage system and given four indices for retrieval purposes—date received, date of credit card charge, account number, and amount. From there, only the electronic images are used, and the paper is discarded.

Diners Club uses a FileNet system, from FileNet in Costa Mesa, California [5]. The group has thirty-six high-resolution, bit-mapped workstations, linked via a 10 mbps LAN to an optical disk storage unit, called a jukebox. The jukebox—which is somewhat like a record jukebox—holds sixty-four optical disks; each disk can hold approximately fifty thousand page images.

Most departments can write their own FileNet "scripts" (or programs) to direct documents from workstation to workstation using the FileNet WorkFlo language. However, Diners Club hired a systems analyst to create their scripts, because their processing logic is complex. The software tracks each representative's workload and assigns work accordingly. It also (1) maintains the status of each cardholder query, (2) logs each piece of correspondence as it arrives in the system, (3) establishes follow-up dates for action, (4) notifies the representative when a file contains all the paperwork necessary to make a decision, and (5) creates reports for management.

Since the system tracks and routes the work, the representatives now spend their time studying cases and making decisions rather than looking for paper files. Thus, they can handle 30 to 40 percent more files, and 20 percent fewer clerical people are needed to handle the files and create management reports. More important, the system has improved customer service. It ensures that representatives follow consistent procedures and do not miss processing steps. The system also moves work around more efficiently and representatives can respond to cardholder inquiries faster. The personal card representatives like the system, because they no longer have to deal with paper.

Publishing Is Pervasive

Publishing is an important issue because it is ubiquitous—it is done in many departments in firms. Publishing is also important because of its magnitude. If companies tallied up how much money they spend on publishing reports, printing sales literature, creating manuals, reprographics, and so on, they would discover that their corporate-wide publishing bill is third highest—behind personnel and production costs.

Documents vary in complexity. The least complex are office documents used for internal communications. The next most complex are documents sent outside the firm, such as those created by proposal departments or marketing communications departments. The most complex level is technical publishing—documents for external distribution that contain technical data—because they contain so many different forms of data. Complex technical documents can cost $300 a page to create and maintain. In some firms, publication of technical documents involves hundreds of people, and these people need to keep their documents up-to-date for a long time.

Most publishing is still manual, so it is ripe for automation. This strong demand for better electronic publishing is evidenced by the rapid growth of desktop publishing. Large-scale corporate electronic publishing is giving way to smaller desktop publishing systems, with more publishing being done by more people. Although this change is desirable, it also can have some undesirable side effects if desktop publishing is not guided by corporate-wide publication policies. Information systems departments can help their firms' publication departments in at least four ways:

- Keep the publications department up-to-date on new information publishing technologies, and explain what the new systems will do or not do.
- Foster publishing standards, for example, by promoting standard templates that the publications department develops for different corporate documents.
- Handle users' technical questions about how to use the desktop publishing systems.
- Maintain the systems.

Later in the chapter, we offer some guidelines to consider when creating a corporate-wide publishing strategy.

As an example of a company that is focusing on the pervasiveness of publishing, consider the Bose Corporation.

CASE EXAMPLE: Bose Corporation

Bose Corporation, in Framingham, Massachusetts, is a privately owned manufacturer of high-quality sound systems for automobiles, home use, and professional musicians. Warren Harkness, director of information systems at Bose, told us what his department is doing about electronic publishing.

The Bose information systems operation is mostly distributed. The worldwide sales group uses NCR equipment in Europe and Hewlett-Packard (H-P) systems in Canada. Manufacturing also uses H-P. Engineering uses DEC and Prime equipment. And the corporate business functions are centralized in Framingham on H-P equipment. In addition, the company has 250 Apple Macintoshes and 120 other PCs. Harkness is also in charge of administrative services—the mail room, word processing, telecommunications, and reprographics. He has some sixty people in his department.

In the document processing and publishing area, the systems department has a seven-part strategy.

One, they are standardizing on predominantly one workstation—the Apple Macintosh—for desktop and corporate publishing. It is powerful enough to handle their needs, up to the point where a diskette can be sent to a photo-typesetting machine, if that level of print quality is needed.

Two, they are standardizing on one text composition system—WordPerfect—for both their Apple and IBM PCs. They are in the process of selecting standards for all official communications going outside the company. These standard page layouts will be approved by the president of Bose. Harkness believes these standards will make their correspondence, advertisements, and customer publications more consistent and maintain their high quality. For internal communications, minimum standards will be created. "We want people to be creative in how they present information to others in the company," said Harkness.

Three, they are providing connectivity for moving textual and graphical data around the company. They installed Ethernet LANs to connect workstations, publishing systems, and information systems. They want to be able to print documents created on workstations or corporate computers on several kinds of printers—low-speed printers for proofing documents or printing small quantities, their 600 dot-per-inch laser printer for high quality, or high-speed printers in the data center.

Four, the systems department is becoming the firm's center of competence in electronic publishing. Six people are developing applications, such as templates for company documents, and they are helping end users learn how to use the publishing software. Since Macintoshes are easy to use, said Harkness, only four people have been needed to support 250 users.

Five, they are helping other departments to test new publishing applications. Their first work was in advertising. Bose believes that by moving some advertising work in-house, they can gain a competitive edge. They are able to tailor advertising more easily to different marketplaces, prepare ads faster, produce more consistent and higher-quality work, and reduce creation and distribution costs. The savings on taxi fares alone—for running proofs back and forth between their advertising agency and Bose headquarters—will be substantial, Harkness quipped.

Six, with help from Xerox Corporation [6], Bose studied the document flows in their advertising and manufacturing departments. They looked at how they were producing owner's guides, warranty manuals, product-support literature, parts lists, service maintenance manuals, training materials, engineering change orders, and marketing materials.

They uncovered bottlenecks in various areas. For example, they discovered that although JIT manufacturing practices could help them move audio components to auto manufacturers faster, their documentation practices often delayed shipments for one or two days. They therefore moved to in-house desktop publishing to speed up the process.

And seven, they are moving document processing capabilities out to the end users, not centralizing them. End users will be creating their own original documents; the central group in the information systems department will assist users in formatting, finishing, and some other publishing aspects.

"Last year I visited Xerox PARC with the Dooley Group [7], and that experience opened my eyes to the world of documents," said Harkness. "I used to think documents were only on paper, and their main purpose was to archive information. At PARC I realized that documents are for initiating action, and they can include video and audio portions, all now available at a workstation. That realization changed my view of documents. That is why we are looking at documents within Bose. We intend to focus on them in a similar way we address data processing."

To summarize this section, I/S departments have several reasons to focus on EDM—because it promises substantial benefits, it attacks the paperwork problem, documents are central to many applications, and publishing is pervasive.

EDM GUIDELINES FOR INFORMATION SYSTEMS MANAGERS

We have been watching EDM for several years because we think it will be significant. From our conversations with many companies, including those reported in this chapter, and discussions with vendors and consultants, we have created several guidelines for information systems executive to build toward EDM.

1. Treat EDM as an end-user technology.
2. Develop an infrastructure to support EDM.
3. Look for high payoff areas.
4. Develop publishing standards.
5. Develop a strategic plan.
    We discuss each of these in turn.

Treat EDM as an End-User Technology

The impression we get is that electronic document management is not an area that information systems management will either be able to centralize or will want to centralize. It is already springing up in different forms in many companies.

Therefore, we believe the best approach is to treat it as an end-user technology. All the lessons companies have learned about end-user computing apply here. For example, encourage self-sufficiency. Although these systems are more likely to be designed for departments or groups, rather than for individuals, they are still end-user systems. And even the large document systems can be run by functional managers, as is the case at Diners Club.

The newer image systems are also end-user systems, like PCs, and as with PCs, functional departments are installing these systems without going through their information systems department. Thus, at this time some systems executives must first discover what systems have been installed, or are being installed, and then get involved with them.

Information systems executives should take the lead in promoting use of image systems, because these systems are part of overall corporate information management. One systems department is encouraging use of imaging systems by creating a slide show describing these systems, which it presents around the company. Users that show interest are invited to a workshop that helps them evaluate their application to see if it is appropriate.

Like other end user systems, image systems are not stand-alone systems, however. They need links to other systems. In the future, integrated information systems are likely to include scanned images, correspondence created on word processors, electronic-mail messages, voice messages, and traditional data records.

Start with pilot projects that are not too large—less than one-half million images. Choose applications where users want to experiment. And look for applications where different people need to see the documents, or where the document file comes from numerous sources.

For example, consider mortgage loan applications, where the file folder—whether in paper or electronic form—is likely to contain an appraiser's report on the property, a mortgage loan summary, the loan application, a financial history of the borrower, a legal agreement, a promissory note, and more. Over the lifetime of the loan, many people will need to access that file, for many different reasons. They will only need to see the information, not manipulate it. Look for applications that require such shared access.

Develop an EDM Infrastructure

Although line organizations will be able to operate the systems on their own, they need an infrastructure from the information systems department. Generally, electronic document processing requires a higher-capacity IT infrastructure than do traditional information systems.

The infrastructure includes (1) network links with enough capacity to carry images, (2) workstations capable of displaying high-resolution graphics, (3) storage devices that can handle huge image and voice files, and (4) standards for each form of data.

To illustrate these differences, a single, uncompressed one-page image requires 500k bytes of storage. With compression, it drops to 75k bytes. Yet that is about *thirty times* the amount of space required to store the same page in character mode, if it contains only text and no graphics. Thus, image systems require far larger storage systems. This volume also affects workstations and communication links.

A document image processing application generally requires a workstation screen that displays 2 million pixels (i.e., dots) for clear viewing. Yet most PC screens display less than that. Even today's "high-resolution" PCs display only about 500,000 pixels (800 by 600 points). Also, an image workstation needs four to eight megabytes of memory just to display large image files, not including the memory to process them.

Communication requirements are also higher. Not too long ago, leading edge companies were expecting to send one hundred images a day over a local area network. Today, some huge applications are looking at forty thousand images a day. Some companies are even scanning twenty-five pages a minute into their image system, to keep up with their incoming mail.

A 10 mbps LAN is needed, at the least, to send this volume of images around a building. To send images outside the local area, companies will need 56 kbps lines or even T-1 lines—which have speeds of 1.5 mbps. To see why, consider a twenty-page loan file. If each page contains 75k bytes in image form, then the entire file requires 1.5 million bytes. To transmit this file from a branch to headquarters over a 9,600 bps dial-up line would take more than fifteen minutes! That is not tolerable.

Handling the volumes involved in imaging applications also requires putting computer power everywhere: (1) at document entry stations to compress images, (2) at workstations to decompress images, (3) at printers to decompress images, and (4) at file servers to shorten access time. Traditional I/S applications have not needed this much distributed computing power.

Developing the infrastructure is not just a technical issue either; the following case example illustrates the organizational aspects of an EDM infrastructure.

CASE EXAMPLE: Saab-Scania Group

The Saab-Scania Group, with headquarters in Linkoping, Sweden, near Stockholm, manufactures automotive vehicles. The Saab division builds Saab cars; the Scania division builds trucks, buses, and components for Saab cars. Saab also has an aircraft division and Scania does research in military electronics and robotics. Saab-Scania employs some fifty thousand employees; about one-half of them are in Sweden.

Saab-Scania designs their vehicles for easy customization. For example, a customer for a fleet of trucks can choose from a selection of engines, gears, axles, driver cabs, and so on, from which Saab-Scania can create customized vehicles using standard parts.

In the 1980s, an office automation group was formed to manage any piece of office equipment that is electronically linked to other equipment. In addition, they coordinate the use of all unstructured information throughout Saab-Scania, such as text, graphics, images, and video. This ten-person group also creates interfaces for information retrieval from public databases. They handle all products used on PCs, and they coordinate all teleconferencing facilities, message handling systems, and electronic document management systems—including electronic printing and publishing.

They see their role as providing employees with easy access to various PC tools that deal with unstructured data. Their electronic document management work has three components.

1. A document system infrastructure
2. A system architecture strategy
3. Experimenting with willing user groups

Document Systems Infrastructure

The information systems department uses computers from several manufacturers. For administrative information systems and computer-aided design they use IBM. For manufacturing and engineering they use DEC. Their PBX is from Northern Telecom. Their terminals and PCs linked to their mainframes are from Ericsson. And their document workstations and publishing systems are from Rank Xerox.

These various systems are located in a six-building complex with 10-mbps fiber optic links between the buildings. Within the buildings, Saab-Scania has five Ethernet LANs that also operate at 10 mbps. One Ethernet has become the "hub" network for document processing. Through it, users can access laser printers or high-volume Xerox document printers.

Systems Architecture Strategy

Their long-term interconnection goal is to use OSI—the open systems interconnection standards from the International Standards Organization. But because OSI standards are not yet fully available in products, Saab-Scania's interim solution is to rely on three widely used vendor standards—SNA from IBM, DNA from DEC, and XNS from Rank Xerox.

As OSI standards become available, they will migrate to them. For example, X.400 is the OSI electronic-mail standard that handles messages in a store-and-forward mode. Saab-Scania has adopted x.400 as the means for allowing their three electronic-mail systems to "talk" to each other. A message created and sent on their IBM, Digital, or Xerox mail system is translated into the x.400 protocol. Then it is routed to its destination and retranslated into the recipient's mail system protocol. Using standards to perform this translation is much easier than writing specific vendor-to-vendor interfaces, they told us.

They are also working on extending the x.400 capability to electronic mail systems offered by the Swedish PTT and to U.S. and U.K. systems.

Experimenting with User Groups

In document processing, end users generally want much more than is currently technically economical or feasible, we were told. For example, users would like to use their Xerox 6085 graphical workstation to, say, create service manuals that contain text, line drawings, photographs, and color. And they want to print those manuals in high volumes.

Currently, in-house high-volume electronic printing of such complex documents is not feasible, because (1) the company does not have many document scanners for digitizing images, (2) their scanners only record at 300 dots per inch resolution, and (3) color separation is not economical. But the goal of the office automation group is to allow such multimedia documents to be fully composed and printed electronically in-house—in high volume, if need be. These high-volume documents would include their vehicle service manuals, parts catalogs, some advertising brochures, and so on.

The office automation manager has some ambitious goals in the document management and printing area. For example, he believes the company should be able to print a vehicle owner's manual that exactly matches the vehicle that the purchaser buys. Therefore, each owner's manual would be unique. This is not only desirable but achievable, he believes. The cost of producing such tailored manuals is becoming almost as low as the cost of mass producing standardized manuals.

The office automation group is starting with the most economical and feasible uses of new document processing technologies. For example, currently, electronic storage of images is not economically feasible, because each image requires so much storage space. Therefore, the automation group is starting by electronically storing only those images that are needed for a short time, such as images of visual aids for speeches. As optical storage becomes more economical, they will increasingly store longer-term images.

Interestingly, although storage of images presents an economic problem, transmission of images within Saab-Scania does not. The 10-mbps Ethernet LANs have enough bandwidth to last for a long time. The company currently uses only 20 percent of its capacity. And because images are most likely to be transmitted from a file server in a store-and-forward mode—and then manipulated interactively at the workstation—the networks will not become overburdened as more and more images are sent over the network. Putting the processing-intensive manipulation part of the image processing job at the workstation reduces the bandwidth required on the networks.

Thus, Saab-Scania is experimenting with new document processing products with willing departments. Once a system is running in a production mode, the office automation group turns over full operational responsibility to the user group. And they are promoting standards to create a company-wide document processing infrastructure. They want their people to be able to use whatever equipment is best suited for their job, without worrying whether the technology is old or new, or whether the machines will work together.

Look for High-Payoff Applications

Electronic document management adds another dimension to a firm's "IT toolkit." That is, these systems, like traditional information systems, can be used to (1) increase operating efficiency, for example, by moving images rather than paper around the firm; or (2) improve organizational effectiveness, for example, by giving customer service representatives more information so they can make better decisions; or (3) as a competitive tool, for example, by sending customers the images of sales receipts along with their monthly statements. High-payoff applications exist in all three areas. So we think an important element of a strategy is to seek them out rather than wait for users or competitors to uncover them. To choose a high-leverage application, look for operations with lots of paper and lots of people. Look for high volumes, in number of pages processed per day and number of pages in storage. Or look for frequent access to information, such as in customer service.

Also, look for ways to add images without disrupting the current computerized systems. The solution many firms are taking is to create separate image databases, using a client/server architecture where a server or the user's workstation merges the image and nonimage data as needed. Some are adding pointers to the image data in each appropriate mainframe record.

This guideline is no different from those for other types of systems and technology, of course. We have urged using high business value as the prime determinant of systems development throughout this book. It bears restating here because we think that EDM will offer a new set of opportunities for high-leverage systems as companies turn their attention to document-centered applications.

Develop Publishing Standards

We noted earlier that publishing is a significant opportunity for EDM because it is so pervasive. For the same reason, it is important for a corporation to maintain the right amount of standardization in publishing, even though it has become decentralized as an end-user application in the form of desktop publishing. The I/S department can take the lead in establishing guidelines, policies, and standards for electronic publishing. Here are some of the policies and standards we suggest for publishing.

Be Concerned with Corporate Image. A main concern with the proliferation of desktop systems has been protecting the corporation's image. Any documents that go outside the corporation should present a consistent, high-quality image. Desktop publishing allows people to create what appear to be official company publications all by themselves, without following company publishing guidelines. The authors make up their own formats, and the results may not be very professional looking. Corporate publishing guidelines are intended to prevent that problem.

Standardize on Publishing Systems. Besides publishing standards for official documents, companies also need to standardize on the types of publishing systems they use. The wide variety of people doing publishing activities should have to become proficient with only a few products. Formatted documents should be able to flow freely among various workstations and systems, with little or no conversion required. Moving text among dissimilar systems is possible, although not always straightforward. However, moving images, tables, and equations from one desktop package to another rarely works. With the arrival of high-resolution imaging systems and desktop systems that permit colors to be separated for printing purposes, moving data among dissimilar systems may become even more difficult. Corporate guidelines are needed so that inexperienced users with high-powered systems use them to the firm's benefit.

Redefine Responsibilities. Desktop publishing is blurring the traditional responsibilities between authors and publishing professionals. Management needs to redefine the new roles. Spreadsheet packages did not make accounting departments obsolete; likewise, desktop publishing systems are not making publications departments obsolete. However, these systems are changing how some functions are performed. One job that publications departments probably should retain is archiving. Some people believe that it is sufficient to keep files in Postscript format—the primary format used in desktop publishing systems. But Postscript saves documents in page format, and that may not be the wisest storage format. Publishing professionals are standardizing on Standard Generalized Markup Language (SGML) because it allows them to exchange and understand the formatting commands, and it is more flexible than a paginated format. Companies need consistent archiving practices in the electronic world.

Emphasize JIT Publishing. On-demand publishing is the wave of the future, says Connie Greaser, manager of service communications at American Honda Motor Company, because the cost of printing many copies of a document and storing them is becoming increasingly uneconomical. Firms want to print smaller batches, and only when they need them—that is, JIT. But retention of the original document is still important. And guaranteeing integrity among versions is also important. Both jobs are done by many publications departments.

View Documents as the Hub of Applications. Many applications have a document as their focus. For example, in an automobile repair system, the maintenance manual can become the center of the system. If it is kept up to date on a central computer, mechanics can download just the portions they need as they study a repair job. Then they can electronically select from the manual the parts they need for the repair and order those parts electronically—if they also have access to the firm's order entry system. Or the parts manual could be stored on CD-ROM at repair shops, with only the most recent changes accessed via telecommunications. In either case, the maintenance manual is the hub of the application.

Develop Three Levels of Publishing. Distributed publishing will involve publishing automation at three levels—at desktops, in departments, and at the corporate level. Desktop publishing is everywhere. Some departments even have their own workstation-based publishing system. And there may be a corporate publishing group as well. Within five years, companies should aim to have about one-third of their publishing work automated, with some automation at all these organizational levels. This will require (1) an underlying architecture to connect these systems, (2) data standards so that work can be passed among the systems, and (3) electronic publishing guidelines that specify how official publications should look.

Use Emerging Standards. The Computer-Aided Acquisition and Logistics Support (CALS) initiative is an initiative from the U.S. Department of Defense. The goal is interorganizational electronic interchange of technical documentation among government and industry. All U.S. government defense contractors are required to submit technical documents electronically using CALS formats, instead of paper.

This initiative has a direct effect on companies that deal with the U.S. Department of Defense but, it is also having a widespread second-tier effect. Since government contractors are keeping their technical information in CALS, they want to exchange technical information with their suppliers—for both government and commercial work—using those same formats.

For example, one commercial airline company has already been informed by its major airplane supplier that it will supply technical documents only in CALS format. The airline foresees a substantial increase in its information systems spending so that it can accept data from this supplier. The ripple effect of the CALS data formats could become quite widespread.

Since CALS is so important, we present additional detail in this excerpt from the *I/S Analyzer* [8]. It was written by Ivan Blum, now of A. T. Kearney [9].

CASE EXAMPLE: A U.S. Government Initiative Worthy of Attention

An important event affecting the future of technical document management is the CALS initiative; however, its importance in industry is not yet widely recognized. CALS is a program initiated by industry and the U.S. Department of Defense (DOD) to facilitate electronic interchange of *technical data*. The program is being coordinated with other government agencies, such as NASA and the U.S. Departments of Energy, Transportation, and Commerce.

Although government information processing standards often have had little direct impact on the business world as a whole, the CALS initiative is strongly influencing the technologies and business practices of all American manufacturing.

First, it directly affects all major U.S. defense contractors. The DOD now requires all technical documentation related to major weapons systems to be submitted in electronic form using the CALS standards. These deliverables include engineering drawings, product definition data, technical manuals, definitions of support equipment, and logistics support analyses. Subcontractors are also feeling the effects of CALS. And most vendors who supply the industry with hardware and software recognize the importance of CALS. If they do not offer CALS-compliant products, their market share could erode.

Ultimately, CALS will affect the entire discrete manufacturing industry—those in heavy machinery and equipment, aerospace, electronics, automotive, machine tools, and medical and precision equipment. They face problems similar to those in the defense industry—increasingly complex products and growing use of trading partnerships with suppliers and buyers. The CALS initiative is equally relevant to their problems.

CALS currently has two defined phases. Phase One was the digital data exchange phase, where contractors and government agencies exchanged technical data electronically. The intent of this phase was to eliminate paper.

Phase 2—from 1991 through 2000—is the integrated database access phase. The focus is on creating databases within private industry that are accessible by all trading partners and the government. The goal is to create source data once, and reuse it and transfer it many times rather than replicate it.

There are numerous standards adopted in CALS; more are being considered. For the interchange of raster-based images—such as those created by office scanners—CALS has specified the use of the CCITT Group 4 compression standard. For telecommunications, they specify GOSIP, which is a U.S. government implementation of the OSI network protocol.

For the interchange of vector-based graphics—such as engineering drawings—they have adopted Initial Graphics Exchange Specification (IGES). This is the major existing standard in this area. It is not the best one, because it is not truly neutral; however, it is the only one available right now. It is used as an intermediary translator of graphical data between dissimilar CAD systems.

For technical illustrations—such as those found in maintenance and operating manuals—CALS has adopted (CGM) Computer Graphics Metafile. CGM is the preferred exchange standard for two- or three-dimensional graphics and illustrations. It is also used for printing and displaying these graphics.

For text, CALS has specified SGML. SGML is used by publishers to designate the parts of a document and how the text is to be formatted. It consists of codes and declarations that are added to text to designate subject matter and position of text. When SGML codes have been added to text, an entire document can be sent as an ASCII file. Once in SGML format, the text can be output to a printer, magnetic tape, typesetting machine, or even CD-ROM. Tools have emerge that provide SGML capabilities for word processing packages.

These existing standards emphasize the exchange of data *between* systems. But the real goal of CALS is the common development and sharing of databases. These databases are expected to be logically integrated but physically distributed and heterogeneous. In phase 2, when management of the large common databases will be necessary, SQL is targeted as the standard database access language.

One of the key components of the shared databases is common product definitions. The goal is to make these definitions contain sufficient information to be directly interpreted by advanced CAD/CAM application programs. This is the aim of Project Data Exchange Specification (PDES)—to be able to communicate complete and unambiguous product models between organizations. Thus, PDES will handle geometrical data including representations of solid shapes. In addition, PDES will support a wide range of other kinds of product-related data and relationships, such as manufacturing processes, material properties, surface finishes, and support requirements.

> In summary, the emphasis of the CALS initiative is on motivating industry to adopt existing standards for databases and electronic interchange. Its use will spread beyond U.S. government contractors, because it is being heavily pushed by industry, to help them reduce documentation costs. For further discussion of the CALS initiative, see the special government report [10].

Develop a Strategic Plan

The final guideline in our list encompasses the others, and serves as a fitting end to this section. EDM is evolving because of the development of technologies that allow automation and support for handling documents in new and better ways.

It is important to capture the benefits of these technologies as they emerge. Some of the cost savings and productivity improvements from imaging, for instance, are impressive. These savings can be used to fund future advances and improvements. The danger is that these specific applications—in records management, the corporate library, in the training department, in offices—will become "islands" of noncompatible systems reminiscent of the early days of information systems. The solution is a strategic plan with the following three perspectives:

- *Organization*. Defines the roles and responsibilities of all the departments and functions for which EDM will be strategic. Also projects possible changes in business practices and communication flows that EDM will enable.
- *Application*. Develops a staged plan for implementing applications over time so that they are integrated in the future.
- *Technology*. Identifies an architecture for the technology that will enable the assimilation of the emerging EDM technologies into the organization's I/S infrastructure.

The full promise of EDM suggested in this chapter will not be fully realized for several years. It is not too early, however, for information systems management to begin the planning processes that will harness this new set of technologies to improve the handling of documents.

CONCLUSION

Electronic document management is becoming prevalent because of the new technologies that make it possible to computerize information in documents. These technologies include digital imaging processing, large capacity storage devices, high bandwidth communication channels, multimedia devices for handling image, voice, video, and animation, hypertext/hypermedia, and improved methods for retrieval of information and text.

The impact of these developments is significant. Generally, EDM will allow the electronic handling of concepts and ideas in documents, as well as facts in data records. Since managers and executives deal heavily with concepts and ideas, EDM will improve the performance of these high-level employees. Finally, because many important business processes depend on document-based information flows, EDM will support the improvement of these processes.

The challenge for I/S executives is to manage this evolution during the next decade. New technologies should be adopted and used as they emerge, because the benefits are substantial. But over time, they must be integrated to avoid separate, incompatible systems. This will require a strategic plan for EDM that identifies what applications should be developed (and in what order), what roles the many interested parties should play, and what technologies are required. It is clear that EDM will be a significant area of applications in the 1990s.

QUESTIONS AND EXERCISES

REVIEW QUESTIONS

1. Distinguish between the narrow and broad definition of electronic document management. What is an electronic document?
2. What are the roles that documents play in organizations?
3. List the departments in an organization that would be involved in EDM.
4. What are the three categories of EDM applications? Give an example of each.
5. Give two of the major benefits realized by Tapiola Insurance from their EDM project.
6. In general, what does digital imaging do? Why is it valuable?
7. Distinguish among the three forms in which a document can exist. How does the form affect what can be done with a document?
8. Give one major benefit Diners Club derived from their imaging system.
9. Why is publishing so important?
10. Why should EDM be treated as a type of end-user technology?
11. What are the components of a technical infrastructure for EDM?
12. What is the importance of CALS?
13. What is the importance of a strategic plan for EDM? What are the three perspectives that need to be addressed in the plan?

DISCUSSION QUESTIONS

1. Do you agree that the I/S department should take the lead in developing EDM? Why or why not?
2. If your answer to question 1 was yes, how will I/S motivate all the other departments? If no, who will coordinate the development of the systems and how?

EXERCISES

1. Consult the current literature to compile a list of technologies that are important for EDM. For each technology, describe it briefly, and indicate its role in EDM.

2. Visit a local organization that is developing applications in at least two of the areas in EDM—perhaps image processing and desktop publishing. Who is leading the development effort? What benefits are being realized? What are their plans for the future?

REFERENCES

1. *INFORMATION AND IMAGE MANAGEMENT: THE STATE OF THE INDUSTRY*, white paper from the Association for Information and Image Management, 1100 Wayne Ave., Suite 1100, Silver Spring, MD 20910.

2. GUNTON, T., "Document Image Processing: The Next Revolution?" Index Foundation, September 1987.

3. JOHN CONNELL, P. O. Box 65, Pasadena, CA 91102.

4. "METAVIEW: THE DOCUMENT IMAGING SOLUTION," Metafile Information Systems, 421 First Ave. S.W., Rochester, MN 55902.

5. FILENET, 3565 Harbor Blvd., Costa Mesa, CA 92626.

6. FRANK STEENBURGH, Vice-President, Systems Reprographics Division, Xerox Corporation, Xerox Square, Rochester, NY.

7. THE DOOLEY GROUP, 1380 Kenilwood Lane, Riverwoods, IL 60015.

8. ELECTRONIC DOCUMENT MANAGEMENT: PART II, *I/S Analyzer*, June 1989.

9. IVAN BLUM, A.T. Kearney, 500 S. Grand, Suite 1900, Los Angeles, Calif. 90071.

10. CALS REPORT TO THE COMMITTEE ON APPROPRIATIONS OF THE U.S. HOUSE OF REPRESENTATIVES, July 31, 1988. Available from the National Institute of Standards and Technology, CALS Office, Sound/B106, Gaithersburg, MD 20899.

SEVENTEEN

Helping People Become Comfortable with Information Technology

INTRODUCTION

With management's increasing reliance on mission-critical systems and the operational data they supply, information systems management faces a gigantic training and education task. Corporate executives who are reviewing organization-wide plans for computer and communication systems need to know enough about new and emerging technologies to put them to competitive use. Line managers need to learn how to manage in a computer-abundant world, because they are starting to have much of the responsibility for ensuring successful use of systems. End users need to be encouraged to use and experiment with computers. Finally, information systems staff needs to be kept technologically current. In essence, all four groups—top executives, line managers, end users, and systems staff—need to be comfortable with IT. That is the subject of this chapter.

This subject is particularly important to information systems management because of the importance of computers in corporate health and competitive survival. Chuck Gibson of CSC Index [1] points out that information sys-

494

tems management is now being held accountable for system success, not just for their role in the firm. Therefore, they have to be prepared to answer top management's question; Why aren't we up to speed? Being accountable for the successful use of a system these days has as much to do with the human side as the technical side.

Furthermore, the shift of responsibilities for system development and use to end users and line executives requires more technology-literate personnel. As this happens, the systems department plays a coordinating, supportive, and standards-setting role. Part of its responsibility is to build and maintain the organization's technology infrastructure. A coordinated program of computer training and education is an important part of this responsibility, because without the technological maturity to use these resources, the huge infrastructure investments will not be as successfully used.

Increasing Technological Maturity

We define a technologically mature organization as one that realizes the business value of information and systems, and manages the assimilation of it into its business. Its people are comfortable managing, using, and experimenting with new information technology. A mature organization that continually experiments with new uses of computers and telecommunications can more quickly use them in its business. This ability to move quickly is especially important when computers are used for competitive purposes. To maintain a competitive edge, a business must continually enhance its services and products, and understand how new technologies enable such enhancements.

Drawing on the stages of growth work of Gibson and Nolan [2], McFarlan and McKenney [3] describe how information technology diffuses in an organization in four phases: (1) identification and investment, (2) experimentation, learning, and adaption; (3) control; and (4) widespread use. At any point in time, organizations will be at different phases with different technologies. Information systems departments play an important role in moving their organizations through these phases in the following four ways:

- Educating executives on information technology
- Helping line managers manage information technology
- Training end users on the technology
- Training for the future systems organization

EDUCATING EXECUTIVES ON INFORMATION TECHNOLOGY

Top-level policy-setting executives must understand the nature and ramifications of information technology to make the proper decisions for their organizations. This understanding is particularly important because information systems are having a significant impact on the way organizations are structured and the way people work. Although organizations will want to introduce new technologies as smoothly as possible, business reengineering—which often significantly changes how people work—causes organizational upheaval. Such turmoil deserves top management's attention. It rarely received that attention in the past.

Few top executives were concerned about office automation in the late 1970s. Most did not care about the word processing centers that sprang up in their companies, or the computer messaging communities that appeared. But top management *should* be concerned with such developments, because new technology often *upsets established work habits*. A good understanding of computer-based technology, derived from a coordinated education program, gives executives the ability to make the informed decisions necessary to guide their companies in this technology-driven world.

Top corporate executives must also handle the organizational issue of where IT should be managed, says Chuck Gibson. The age-old question of centralization versus decentralization of the information systems function has not been resolved. It is still around, and it is a far more complex issue than most executives realize, says Gibson. Division management wants ownership, but centralized control is necessary to build an organization-wide infrastructure. Since competitiveness often hinges on IT, these organizational issues need to be resolved. That requires executives understanding the issues and ramifications of the various alternatives.

Why Educate Executives?

Executives who understand computer and communication technologies are able to make wiser decisions about

- *Aligning IT with business objectives*. The most important issue on CSC Index's most recent annual survey of CIOs was how to align the information systems function with the company's business direction, Chuck Gibson told us. This alignment issue should be high on top management's agenda; unfortunately, it often is not.

- *Assessing costs and benefits*. Top executives are being asked to make increasingly larger IT investments. They must be able to intelligently assess cost/benefit decisions, says Gibson, concerning both the technology and the information systems function itself. Rules of thumb such as "1 percent of sales" are no longer adequate as companies develop competitive strategies and products based on IT. Furthermore, outsourcing presents management with a whole new range of options for managing the systems function.

- *Envisioning IT as an input to business strategy*. Top management must foresee how key business functions can be made more valuable through information technology, says Gibson, such as by enhancing speed or customer service. Technically astute executives are more likely to see the need for high-level guidance of the company's information resources to coordinate the diverse efforts of information systems, telecommunications, business alliances, corporate restructuring, and so on.

- *Using systems with comfort.* Executives need education so that they are comfortable accessing systems themselves or through a subordinate, says Gibson. Now that data valuable to top executives is available, they should make use of IT. Executive information systems have been revived recently, because the meaningful data is now on-line.

- *Setting the tone of the organization toward technology.* Top executives who assign high-level resources to IT set the tone of the organization toward the use of technology. Executives knowledgeable in new technologies are also more likely to foster experimentation.

- *Enhancing their role in business reengineering.* Only top executives can drive business reengineering. With IT knowledge, they can enhance their role in the implementation of business change, says Gibson, because much of this change is made possible by information technology.

- *Being supportive during a technology's introduction.* Top management can play an important role in introducing large information systems by being sympathetic and supportive during roll-out. Educated executives realize that there will be problems during these times, no matter how much planning has been done. Also, they will be more likely to temper their demands. Without supportive management, experimentation may well come to a halt before it really gets started.

- *Being concerned with government intervention.* Executives who are more familiar with new technologies are also more likely to be aware of the legislative climate in the industries that are developing these technologies. They are also more likely to understand restrictive legislative proposals and then possibly work with governments toward finding solutions that still allow them to conduct their business effectively.

These are some reasons why information systems executives need to be concerned about corporate management becoming knowledgeable about computer and telecommunication technologies. This list makes it clear that a well-designed executive education program will benefit the organization and make the job of information systems executives easier.

Types of Executive Education Programs

There is quite a range of executive education programs in companies. We see three general types that have proven successful. They are categorized by degree of formality.

- Informal programs
- Semiformal programs
- Formal programs

Some companies with an established information system training function have more formal programs; executive education is a part of their function. In other companies, executive education is done informally, because the executives keep themselves well informed. The issue is fitting the program into executive management's needs and preferences.

To choose the appropriate approach, says Gibson, it is important to first assess the executives' current understanding of IT as well as their receptivity to education. This assessment will uncover the appropriate mix of approaches to use.

Informal Programs. These are programs where education is done by the executives themselves as a part of generally staying up to date. They most often use three methods.

- Reading publications
- Through subordinates
- Individual demonstrations

Reading publications. Publications aimed at executives are carrying more and more articles on information technology. For years, *Business Week* has had a section on information processing." *Fortune, Forbes,* and *Newsweek* regularly have special advertising sections on various IT topics, with commentaries by leading consulting firms. The *Wall Street Journal* and the *New York Times* also have a growing number of articles on IT.

Through Subordinates. Another informal program is to educate executives through their subordinates. One highly progressive company regularly introduces its secretaries to new equipment and products, knowing that they will spread the word to their bosses (and in some cases will try to sell them on acquiring the new products). In another company, where management is more conservative, the subordinates do not try to sell their bosses on a new system; they simply use it themselves to demonstrate the benefits.

Individual demonstrations. In a third informal approach, the information systems director keeps top executives up-to-date by inviting them to see demonstrations of new equipment and discussing possible uses and implications.

These informal approaches seem to work best in two types of companies: (1) very progressive companies where the executives keep themselves abreast of new developments, and (2) companies where the executives are not yet ready for highly visible organization-wide information systems. These executives more readily accept implicit means of education than outright educational programs.

Semiformal Programs. These programs are organized education courses usually requested by users; attendance is generally voluntary. These courses can be used for introducing new subjects or for updating current knowledge. Again, we have found three methods in practice.

- Executive briefings
- Brown bag theaters
- Short seminars

Executive briefings. Short briefings, coordinated with management meetings, are a widely used executive education technique. In some cases, information systems teams brief a high-level committee on a technology, such as imaging or groupware, before requesting project funding.

Brown bag theaters. A brown bag theater is where the training department presents a series of video tapes at lunch time. Attendance is voluntary, and the tapes generally have a wide audience appeal—not too technical, people-oriented, and entertaining. Following the video tape showing, a company expert may answer questions.

Short seminars. More formal than the brown bag theater is the short seminar, which lasts one to three hours. Attendance is also voluntary. The seminar topic is chosen for a narrower audience. One successful approach is to include a variety of viewpoints. Such a seminar opens with a formal presentation by an outside expert, either in person or on video tape. This is followed by a company expert who discusses how the technology affects the company. The seminar concludes with a question-and-answer period.

Formal Programs. These courses are designed to introduce executives to new technology and the state of the art quickly. These programs are therefore intensive, generally lasting one to three days, depending on the number of subjects covered. Attendance may also be mandatory for executives at certain levels. Two variations of a formal program are

- A single one- to three-day session
- A series of short sessions

A single session. For many companies, the first concern in executive education is *getting top management's attention.* Executives often need to be away from their office work for a day before they can concentrate on the material being presented. Thus, the best approach is to hold the seminar offsite. This approach can work well, but it requires top management's conviction that the subject is important and deserves their time.

A series of shorter sessions. A second approach is to spread the presentation over several short sessions. Several years ago, an IT training resource company used this approach in an interesting way. It created a three-part program. The first part was a one-day seminar led by an authority in the field who talked about future computer systems. The purpose of this portion was to expose the top executives to a knowledgeable professional who spoke their language. Following his formal talk, the consultant answered questions. The following day the consultant gave a similar seminar for the information system executives of the same companies.

The second part of the program consisted of video tapes that presented an executive overview. Some of these tapes showed the consultant discussing future systems. The training company believed that once the executives had spent a day listening to the consultant, they would be willing to hear more on the subject. Video tapes allowed them to do this at their own convenience.

The third part of the program was a video teleconference between the participants and the consultant. The purpose of this third portion was to give the executives a chance to hear some of consultant's newer ideas and to ask him more in-depth questions.

As an example of a company with a successful company-wide executive education program—a program that became the turning point for getting executives involved in IT decision making—consider Du Pont.

CASE EXAMPLE: E.I. du Pont de Nemours

E. I. du Pont de Nemours is a large diversified chemical, energy, and specialty products company with headquarters in Wilmington, Delaware. Du Pont consists of some sixty major business units, grouped into eight industrial groups, called departments. Five departments are textile fibers, agricultural products, polymer products, automotive products, and fabricated products. In addition, the company has several corporate staff departments—finance, legal, engineering, research and development, and information systems—that provide services to the business units.

In the 1980s, the information systems department reported to the vice-president of engineering; now it reports to the senior vice president for technology, as do the engineering and research and development departments. The information systems department had little credibility with management, because projects were rarely completed on time or within budget, systems did not meet business needs, and costs were out of control. To rectify this situation, management began

- Pushing IT decisions out to line managers
- Educating employees about IT
- Getting their own operation in shape

Until they had proved that they could manage themselves effectively, they felt they did not have a basis for promoting the competitive use of information systems.

Pushing Out the Decision Making. To push IT decisions out to line managers, information systems management divided the computer systems environment in the company into four types: business data processing, process automation and control, office systems, and technical and scientific computing. They told the line managers, "You are responsible for managing all four types within your function, just as you manage other technologies."

Based on these categories, they began supplying management with an annual report on the company's information systems strategy. It described where resources were being deployed, projected growth for the next three years, the direction computer use was taking, and the major issues involved.

The report also categorized systems from a competitive standpoint: Necessity systems, systems to maintain competitive parity, and systems to gain competitive advantage. (Necessity systems now comprise only about 10 percent of the development workload.) The report categorized future systems by functional department and by competitive type. Thus, this annual report presented management with "the supply side" of Du Pont's IT picture.

To uncover "the demand side," several advisory committees were created. The highest level committee is the computer technology advisory committee. It is composed of a director from each of the major functional areas—marketing, manufacturing, research and development, and finance. One objective of this committee is to expedite the use of IT throughout the corporation. They also review the "infrastructure" that the information systems department is putting in place.

Each director on the committee has a staff person advising them on information systems matters. These directors also pass information from the committee to peers on a functional committee. For instance, the manufacturing committee consists of the top manufacturing executives from each of the eight industrial departments.

These committees were formed to promote discussions by higher levels of management about information systems issues—to get "the demand side" of the picture.

The information systems department also promoted the idea that computer and systems planning is an integral part of each manager's planning job. "Only a line manager can tell you whether a system is strategic or not. That is why we want them making the decisions," the vice-president of information systems told us.

Educating Line Management. To foster more knowledgeable IT discussions, the information systems department started a management education program. The three-day, off-site course, taken by all top executives, was taught jointly by Du Pont people and consultants from CSC Index [1]. Each class had twenty attendees, who learned about the issues pertinent to Du Pont, what other companies were doing, and major programs at Du Pont. They even spent one-half day using a PC. The company then started a second education course aimed at the next tier of twelve hundred managers.

These two educational programs have had a major impact on how company management views IT. Before taking a class, most executives and managers viewed the computer as a cost center. Now many of them ask: "How can I use computers in my business?" This change in attitude did not occur overnight. But through education and encouragement from the information systems department, it is happening.

The department is also educating some of the company's future managers in IT, in an innovative way. Promising new information systems employees are put through a six-year training program, consisting of two-year job assignments at three sites. One of the jobs is in the information systems department; the other two are in functional departments. A side benefits of this program has been that technically competent computer people work in all departments. At the end of the six years, the employees are given a choice of several jobs, both inside and outside information systems. Between 20 and 25 percent of these employees choose jobs outside of the systems department.

Through this innovative training program, the corporate information systems department is educating current management in computer technology and future management in various aspects of the business. For years their chemical engineers have taken positions in different areas of the business. Now, their information systems people are doing the same.

Changes in Management Education

Management training in computer technology is not really new, but it has changed over the years. Here's how we view those changes. Back in the 1960s, the courses and seminars were offered to management generally concentrated on how computers worked, and even included some simple programming. Some of the courses described the steps taken in developing application systems, in part to explain to executives "why it takes so long." This generation of courses, therefore, was technology oriented.

The next generation of management training courses did discuss how computers could be used in the business from the standpoint of making existing operations more efficient. The courses stressed how computers could help cut operating costs and accelerate processing.

In the 1980s, with the arrival of the PC, a new era in management training in information technology dawned. Chuck Gibson, of CSC Index [1] talked to us recently about executive education in the 1990s.

Gibson believes the need for executive IT education is increasing. Executives need to know more about the technology and how it can be used to advantage—but most of them still do not realize this fact. Their perception of how involved they must become in information systems decision making has not appreciably changed; however, their requests for "education" have changed.

In the early 1980s, information systems managers typically called CSC Index saying that the company president wanted a seminar on personal computers. The president had just heard about another company president who had a PC, so he wanted to know if he should have one, too. Or the president had just read an article about executives and their PCs.

In the mid-1980s, the requests changed, said Gibson; however, the understanding about computers did not. Corporate officers wanted to know about competitive uses of information systems. They had just heard about a new system of one of their competitors, or they have read about a strategic system in another industry. They asked: "Should we be doing that?" They thought they wanted a three-hour lecture that would teach them a few criteria they could use to decide whether or not to build a strategic system.

In both cases, the requesting officers did not realize they are asking for the wrong thing, says Gibson. They should not be asking whether they need a PC. They should be asking: "What information do I need? And what advantage would it be to me to have that information on-line?"

Likewise, in asking about strategic systems, they did not realize that the true strategic uses of information systems were likely to change the way the company operated, and perhaps even what it did. They should have been asking: "What businesses are we in? How can those businesses be changed to our advantage, perhaps through new uses of computers?" And this, of course, would require them to really understand their businesses—which (perhaps surprisingly) often is not the case.

In the 1990s, we see a widespread appreciation for the impact of IT, Gibson told us. All astute senior executives are conversant in this area. However, despite this growing awareness, there are still unresolved issues in the management and control of the systems function. Senior executives are not paying attention to the important organizational issues of having to balance standardization versus access.

Achieving a Successful Program. To be successful, executive education must have three ingredients, Gibson says.

- It must educate a critical mass of executives.
- It must be accepted psychologically by the executives.
- It must be relevant to their jobs and to current events.

Companies that decide to train all of their executives are more likely to succeed than those who decide to educate just a few. Unless companies attain a critical mass of executives who speak the language, they will not change attitudes about the usefulness of information systems, says Gibson.

Most executives think they need a little training, when they actually need education—to adopt a new attitude about the role of IT. They must become committed to incorporating IT into their work. To obtain such commitment, the education cannot be just lecturing. It must be intensive—such as three days offsite. It must also include homework, debate, hands-on use, and discussion about ways to solve the problems these managers are actually facing. If the participants do not conjure up ideas for putting IT to work, the education has not succeeded, says Gibson, because they do not truly believe in its importance.

The education must also be relevant to the executives' needs. They must be ready to hear what is taught. Executives who are most receptive are those who want (or must) change. They may be downsizing or restructuring. IT holds out the promise of helping them operate on either a larger or a smaller scale. Or the executives may be facing radical changes in their industries, such as deregulation, new competitors, or new bases for competition. Managers in these situations realize they cannot operate as they have in the past. They realize they must change, so they are ready to adopt new attitudes about IT. Education is relevant in these cases.

What if the timing is not right, and the need to change is not so obvious? In these cases, Gibson suggests two strategies. The first is to incorporate education into training they do request. If they want to hear about reengineering, add a section on the IT issues they should be addressing. Indicate the prerequisites they need to know before they can use information systems in this endeavor.

An even more effective strategy is to increase their curiosity before the education session. CSC Index uses this technique under the guise of interviewing the prospective attendees about what they would like to hear in the class. Instead of holding an interview, however, CSC Index turns the meeting into a tutorial, explaining what appears to be happening in the industry and the types of changes that might be needed. "Many times, the interviewed executives end up taking just as many notes as we do," says Gibson. "That is a good sign, because it indicates that we have stimulated their thinking about uses of information systems."

In short, says Gibson, the most effective executive education in the 1990s will be "issues based education," where the educators identify to executives' current needs and design the education to address those needs.

HELPING LINE MANAGERS MANAGE INFORMATION TECHNOLOGY

Information systems executives now realize that line managers play a pivotal role in the successful implementation of IT because they can nurture or kill a new system, consciously or unconsciously, by their support or resistance. As the use of distributed systems spreads, the responsibility for the correct use of IT will shift to line managers. So they will need to become familiar with the risks and problems of new systems in their organization. They will also need to assure that the job, health, and safety needs of their subordinates are being met by a new system. Finally, they will need to understand the differences between a traditional work environment and one where computers play an intimate part, and be able to manage the transition from old to new.

Two areas that have become important to middle management are (1) the ability to manage technological change and (2) championing IT projects. We deal with these two subjects here.

Managing Technological Change

Change management is the process of assisting people in making major changes in their working environment. In this case, the change is caused by the introduction of a new computer system, and line managers are the ones who need to manage this change. The management of change has often not been handled methodically, so choosing a change management methodology and training managers to use IT is a step toward successfully introducing new computer systems.

Change disrupts peoples' frame of reference if it presents a future where past experiences do not hold true, says ODR, a change management firm in Atlanta, Georgia [4]. People resist change, especially technological change, when they view it as a crisis. They cope by trying to maintain control. In the case of an impending new computer system, which they do not understand fully or are not prepared to handle, employees may react in several ways. They may deny the change, they may distort information they hear about it, or they may try to convince themselves, and others, that the new system really will not change the status quo. These are forms of resistance.

ODR offers a methodology to help companies manage technological change. They use three terms from the field of organizational development to describe the types of people involved in a change project. The *sponsor* is the person or group that legitimizes the change. In most cases, this group must contain someone in top management who is highly respected by the targeted user group. The *change agent* is the person or group who causes the change to happen. The *target* is the person or group who is being expected to change, and at whom the change is aimed. ODR recommends a four-step approach for describing and assessing the change.

- Describe the change.
- Assess the sponsors' commitment to the project.
- Evaluate the support or resistance of the targets.
- Assess the change agents' skills.

The purpose of these initial evaluations is to determine whether the change can be made successfully with the current scope, sponsors, change agents, and targets. By evaluating each area, the change agent can see where more education or a new approach is needed to make the project more likely to succeed. One organization that is training its managers to use this approach is the First National Bank of Atlanta.

CASE EXAMPLE: First National Bank of Atlanta

First National Bank of Atlanta, a regional bank with headquarters in Atlanta, Georgia, is a full-service bank with some one hundred branches throughout the state and a large computer-communication network connecting these branches. The bank's executives are taking a market-driven approach to offering products. Therefore, in the deregulated financial services field, managing change has become an increasingly important talent they want to nurture in their middle managers. In particular, implementing new computer systems is one type of change that the bank's people need to learn to manage.

To teach the bank's managers to manage change better, the executive vice president of operations brought in a course entitled "Managing Organizational Change," developed by ODR. Initially taught by ODR, this three-day course is now taught by the bank's organizational development staff.

The executive vice president sees this course creating the bank's framework for evaluating the impact of new computer systems on bank personnel and on bank operations. The course sensitizes attendees to change and how change can be managed by describing the stages in the change process, presenting the uses and misuses of power and influence, and pointing out the various ways people resist change, accept change, and commit to change, both consciously and unconsciously. Also, attendees learn about the three roles people play in a change process—sponsor, change agent, and target.

The attendees leave the workshop with an organizational change implementation planning kit that they can use on their own whenever they plan a major change project. The manager of organizational development told us that she is impressed with how many managers use the questionnaires in their planning work. After completing them, they often ask her to assess the objectivity of their answers.

The executive vice president's belief in the importance of managing change is also affecting how information systems projects are managed. The bank includes this change management methodology in its system development procedures. Once a manager has assessed the readiness for change, project teams work on managing the resistance they have uncovered. They involve users as much as possible in system development to ensure that when the system is installed, the users will feel that they are its owners.

"Championing" Information Technology Projects

As the rate of change in the information system field has increased, we have heard system executives say that they can no longer be "close followers" of competitors, because they are likely to be left behind. They used to be able to catch up with an innovative competitor; today, that luxury is not always available.

How does a firm *smartly* stay at the forefront of technology? One answer is to encourage IT experimentation, especially by people in the operating units. Here are the ideas of two researchers and one user company on how to do that—by supporting IT "champions." These champions they support are likely to be line managers.

Cynthia Beath and Blake Ives, of Southern Methodist University, in Dallas, Texas [5], note that the literature on strategic uses of information technology points out the crucial importance of a "champion"—someone who has a vision and gets it implemented by obtaining the funding, pushing the project over hurdles, putting his or her reputation on the line, and taking on the risk of the project. Beath and Ives ask: "How does an information system executive seek out and encourage such champions of information technology?"

The first step in encouraging champions, say Beath and Ives, is to be able to recognize these people. They are likely to be people you already know about, say the authors, and they may be doing things that make you uncomfortable. For instance, they are probably already circumventing established project approval processes, they are creating isolated information systems, and they may be using nonstandard equipment. They may already be pursuing a vision of how IT can help their business, whether systems people help them or not.

These people are opinion leaders, and they have a reputation for creative ideas or being involved with innovations. They also have developed strong ties to others in their organization, and they command respect within the firm. They have the organizational power to get strategic innovations implemented.

Information systems champions need three things from information systems management, say the authors: information, resources, and support.

They Need Information. "Championing" an IT innovation is an information-intensive activity, note Beath and Ives. Therefore, champions need information—facts and expertise for persuading others that the technology will work. Information systems people can help champions gather and assess information about a technology's capabilities, its costs, risks of operation, and how it might be used in an experiment. Information systems staff also can help by sharing their expertise and by putting champions in contact with other experts, such as vendors or users of a new technology.

Information systems staff can assist champions in understanding current applications and data relevant to their project. Finally, they can help champions understand how the company manages change, because systems people are continually involved in implementing system changes throughout the enterprise.

They Need Resources. The authors cite Rosabeth Kanter, author of *ChangeMasters* [6], who says the thing champions need most is staff time. Giving champions "free" staff time is especially helpful during the evaluation and persuasion portions of a project, say Beath and Ives. But systems management can go even further, by assigning, say, information center consultants to help champions. In addition to staff time, champions are likely to need material resources, such as hardware and software. These can be loaned to them free of charge or provided in some other way.

They Need Support. Finally, champions need supporters—people who approve of what they are doing and give legitimacy to their project. It is important that information systems management corroborate statements made about the technology by the champion, say Beath and Ives. The champion does not need to know how the technology works, only how it might be used. The systems department should handle the technical aspects. Beath and Ives urge demonstrating the champion's claims about the technology, and promoting the technology to build enthusiasm for it and to win support from others.

Finally, information systems management can help a champion win endorsement of upper management, say Beath and Ives, by helping to create the plans for introducing the new technology. The systems department can assist by contacting vendors and assisting in choosing an appropriate implementation approach. All these will improve the quality of the proposal and strengthen it in the eyes of management.

So, Beath and Ives encourage information systems management to make it easier for IT champions to arise and succeed. One company that has successfully supported champions is Aetna Life and Casualty. Here is what they are doing.

CASE EXAMPLE: Aetna Life and Casualty

Aetna Life and Casualty, a financial services company with headquarters in Hartford, Connecticut, sells employee benefit and pension programs to large companies, commercial insurance, and personal insurance—health, life, automobile, and home.

Much of the information systems work has been decentralized; therefore, the corporate administration department focuses on three functions, which they call "plan, build, and run." The operations group runs data center and telecommunication operations. The corporate technology services group assists divisions in selecting, building, and implementing computer systems. The people and technology group also helps divisions build and implement successful systems; they emphasize the human perspective.

The "plan" function is the responsibility of the corporate technology planning group, which is meant to be a catalyst for introducing new technology. Its charter is to help Aetna understand and use "breakthrough" technologies throughout the company. By "breakthrough" they mean technologies that will increase performance by at least 100 percent. "We constantly seek to make the future credible by encouraging innovation, experimentation, and evaluation," a member of this group told us. They see their job as encouraging end users to talk about new technologies and test them out in "real life" situations. The corporate technology planning group fosters discussions and experimentation in three ways.

They Seek Out Business Champions. The group tests technologies by cosponsoring end user projects, acting as a "magnet" to attract people who wanted to experiment with a technology. They hold workshops on specific technologies, publish one-page issue papers describing certain technologies, and talk to people in a wide number of functions.

Their goal was to find end user "champions" who thought a technology could solve their business problem. These people also needed to be willing to share the funding and direction of a pilot project using that technology. The users agree to let the planning group study their use and write about it. So, for a project to be funded, it must have a business champion and be aimed at solving a business problem.

In several cases, they have found champions who recognize the need to test several technologies—some with expected results and others that might change future work life dramatically. These are "smart champions," because they see the value of investing in a portfolio of new technologies.

They Study Pilot Projects. An example of a pilot project they cosponsored was a large voice messaging pilot project with five hundred users in nine areas. The planning group did systematic research during this pilot, using before-and-after questionnaires to measure how attitudes changed. They counted message slips to see if "telephone tag" increased or decreased. They held focus group discussions. And they had some users keep daily diaries of their activities.

Based on this research, they concluded that voice messaging would be beneficial to most Aetna employees. To then promote its use, they created a brochure and video tapes, which they handed off to the corporate operations group for the marketing and management of voice messaging.

They Establish Steering Committees. Steering committees can be surrogate champions to guide and build support for a new technology. When the corporate technology group sees a technology that appears interesting, they may hold a one-day "magnet" session to find champions. Sometimes they find steering committees rather than individual champions, when a topic is really "hot." Several years ago, for example, at their "desktop publishing day," two hundred people volunteered to do pilot projects. Since that was too large a group, a smaller steering committee was formed. It put on four seminars about desktop publishing, got end users thinking about how they might use the technology, and oversaw some projects.

Challenges They Have Encountered. The technology planning group has encountered the following three challenges.

One is simply getting people's attention. When a technology is not immediately available, people do not want to take any action. But many technologies, such as document and image processing, require a learning curve. Even when a technology is not readily available, people should be experimenting with it, so that the company has in-house knowledge when products do begin to appear. So, making a future technology credible to people today is one hurdle.

Keeping people in an experimental mode is another challenge. Once people are funded for a pilot, they want to do it right. They do not want to create a quick-and-dirty system; they want to create a production-quality system. It is difficult to get people to create only quick, experimental systems.

The third challenge is making sure that use will really pay off. The planning group does not want small productivity improvements, they want orders-of-magnitude improvements—at least two-to-one to three-to-one payoffs. So they must constantly ask users: How do you know you will get this payback?

The group's goals are education and action. They want end users to be comfortable using future technologies and achieve a good payback at the same time. For more ideas on how to stimulate innovation, see *Managing Organizational Innovation* [7].

How does such an approach make a company more technologically mature? This happens by putting them in a position more likely to spot new opportunities, experiment with them, and put them into widespread use before their competitors. In a fast-changing world, nimbleness is a sign of maturity. Becoming comfortable with current technology is not enough; being open to accepting emerging technologies is needed.

TRAINING END USERS ON THE TECHNOLOGY

In this section we shift our attention from education, which deals with concepts and understanding, to training, which emphasizes skills. Most end-user training focuses on skills required for nontechnical users to interact with a computer directly. But to use a computer competently, end users also need to understand some basic information systems concepts. The president of a company that sells computer training courses told us that user companies generally order hands-on training courses for their users first, only to discover that they should have ordered the computing concepts courses first, because the users did not understand the basic concepts about computers. Thus end-user training involves both education and training.

Conventional classroom training is group and batch in nature. The class members are taught a wide range of material that they must remember, selecting the pertinent information to perform a particular task. Of growing interest is the use of computers to perform some of the training. In this section we will discuss the newest form of computer-based training called "integrated performance support systems."

Computer-based training permits a very different training environment from traditional classrooms. The training can be on-demand, interactive, specific to the immediate interests of the student, performed where and when the student desires, and (to a great extent) not requiring a human instructor to be active in the process.

Computer-Based Training

The training field, like all fields, has its own set of terms. The following terms are pertinent to the discussion of computer-based training for end users.

Computer-Assisted Instruction (CAI). In CAI, sometimes called computer-assisted learning (CAI), the computer delivers the material to be learned. CAI programs also test the student with questions and then selects the next section to be presented, depending on the correctness or incorrectness of the answers.

Computer-Managed Instruction (CMI). CMI tests the student on what has been learned, evaluating whether or not the learning has been satisfactory, prescribing corrective action in case the material has not been mastered, and controlling the student's progress. In CMI, the computer does not necessarily deliver the material; often, conventional methods are used—classes, books, workbooks, films, video tapes, audio tapes, and so on.

Computer-Based Training (CBT). CBT includes both presenting the material via the computer and managing the administration of the courses using the computer. However, the administrative portion does not appear to be of great interest in end-user training.

Integrated Performance Support Systems (IPSS). IPSS is the newest advance in computer-assisted training. In fact, few such systems currently exist. An IPSS is a training system embedded in a worker's workstation—in the factory or in the office. It generally combines all the help and training facilities a person needs.

The goal of IPSS is to provide on-demand or JIT training. When the employee needs assistance, it is available at the touch of a button. With jobs becoming broader in scope and more complex, employees need help remembering how to perform certain tasks. IPSS is meant to address that need, for both employees who use the computer as their main tool as well as for employees for whom the computer is supplemental to their work. These systems can serve all the following end-user training needs.

End-User Training Needs

End users need five types of training

1. Information systems concepts
2. Quick start
3. Refresher aids
4. Help in overcoming difficulties in advanced use
5. Explanation of the assumptions behind the models they plan to use

Information Systems Concepts. Although training is skills oriented, some conceptual background is usually needed before the skills can be learned. A major focus of concepts training is literacy—learning how things are done by computers. Examples include creating data files, sending electronic messages, and backing up data; all simple concepts that end users need to know. Another example is efficient use of the computer. As information systems professionals know, there is a right way and a wrong way to sort and select data, for instance. The right way is first to select the records you want, and possibly only the desired fields in those records, and then sort only those selected records. The wrong way is to sort all the records and then select the ones you want. The right way makes efficient use of the computer; the wrong way significantly decreases system response time.

Quick Start. End users need a way of quickly learning how to use a new machine, application, or service. Before the Apple Macintosh arrived, users either had to wade through a fat manual (and learn a lot of unneeded information) or wait for a scheduled training class. The Mac, with its intuitive user interface, allowed people to get started very quickly—by experimenting on their own. Computer-based training courses could permit quick start, but not if they impose a rigid curriculum on students. This approach may be fine for educational purposes, but forcing users to follow a rigid curriculum is not desirable.

Gloria Gery [8], who has been in various aspects of the training field for more than twenty years, talked to us about end-user computer-based training. An ideal quick start facility would first give users a mental picture of the organization of the entire system, says Gery. Then it would present "global" procedures—ones that can be used throughout the system in a consistent manner. Once the size and usefulness of the system are made apparent to users, they can choose what they want to learn. Without this global view, they will not understand the capabilities and limitations of the system.

Refresher Aids. Since many end users will not be doing the same tasks every day, they may forget how to perform some operations. For these circumstances, they need to refresh their memory, quickly and on-line. This facility should be easy to initiate and should allow users to choose the topics they want to review. A common approach has been the review capability in some CBT tutorials, which allow a quick overall scan of the key features or commands of a system. Further detail can be obtained, at the user's discretion, by redoing a section of the tutorial, perhaps with answers automatically supplied by the system.

Help in Overcoming Difficulties. There are times when all users run into a situation for which they cannot find an explanation. If these users are executives, managers, or professionals, this time may come in the evening or on a weekend, when their company does not provide human help. Therefore some type of on-line help is needed, preferably available without aborting one's on-line work. Some facilities provide several levels of help. The first level could be an explanation of how to enter a command correctly, the second level could explain how to use the various options, and the third level could be a tutorial. Another approach is calling up a computerized help bulletin board.

Explanation of Model Assumptions. People who create forecasts and projections using modeling packages have to understand the assumptions underlying the models, or else they may use the packages incorrectly. Most CBT products that deal with models present some basic concepts, but they may not explain under which circumstances the model could produce misleading information. Newer modeling packages often have a "parameter screen" or assumption list that acts as an assumption review, as well as a device for controlling the package.

These then are the kinds of information end users may need when doing their work, information and help that computers can supply. To give an example of a futuristic JIT training system, consider the following factory system being built by a large company that wishes to remain anonymous. The example comes from *Trends in Information Technology*, published by Andersen Consulting [9].

CASE EXAMPLE: A Large American Manufacturer

A large American equipment manufacturer, with headquarters in the Midwest, is building a factory of the future where assembly lines will be replaced by guided vehicles that carry engine mounts between manufacturing cells. The factory workers in each cell will assemble all the types of engines the company manufactures, in random order.

To ensure that these workers properly assemble the hundreds of different kinds of engines, the company is building a JIT, multimedia training system. Each cell will have a color workstation that assists the workers in remembering which part to use on an engine, how to mount the part properly, and how to bolt it down correctly. As a new engine enters a cell, the cell controller will automatically begin to display the sequence of images that illustrate how to assemble the part—with bold graphics. The workers will be able to control the sequence, if necessary.

The images will be annotated, by, say, presenting a caution about a typical problem. They will also highlight, enlarge, or point to a section of the image, along with specific instructions. Since the factory floor is noisy, sound will not be used; and because text is slower to read than images, the company is relying on graphics and color to get the message across. Reading text would slow down the workers, the company discovered during a pilot-test of the system.

The images are downloaded from the central computer to each cell's controller at night, based on the next day's workload. The company is using digital video technology to handle the workload. Each image requires from 20,000 to 100,000 bytes, and each cell will receive some one hundred images each night. Using digital video allows the large amount of data to be transmitted over existing LANs; analog video would not.

To create this futuristic system, the company is drawing on the talents of people with experience in video and graphical interface design rather than computer programming. And because assembly will be only as good as the instructions, the designers must verify the procedures before creating the graphics and the videos.

TRAINING FOR THE FUTURE SYSTEMS ORGANIZATION

As the emphasis within the information systems department changes from developing all applications to building infrastructures and developing mission-critical applications with line departments, the composition of the department staff is changing.

The Broadening Systems Staff

Companies that are attempting to manage the full range of system development are creating a spectrum of systems groups. Here are the developments we have uncovered.

The end-user coordinators that flourished in the 1980s are disappearing. They appear to be specializing. Although there is still a need to train people to use computers, that training now accompanies projects. End user computing coordination jobs will subside even further as computing becomes a normal part of people's worklife.

The growth area in end-user support, however, appears to be in PC and LAN technical support. These people never seem to have a free moment, and they can rarely get to a problem quickly. As more LANs are installed, systems departments will need more of these people-friendly problem solvers in their technical support group.

Interestingly, systems departments themselves also need technical support for their own people. With the increasing use of case and workstation-based system development, they need people who can keep their desktop systems and networks up and running. Furthermore, they need people who know the technical ins and outs of the products they use—such as the CASE tools. We believe the systems support and technical support groups in systems departments is another growth area.

We also see a growing need for research and development groups, much like the corporate technology planning group at Aetna, described earlier. This group investigates such diverse technologies as imaging, object-oriented development, wireless networks, handheld computers, neural networks, case-based reasoning, and so on. The purpose of the group is to stay abreast of new technologies and find groups that could put the technologies to good use. In addition to our observations, here is another view of evolving spectrum of information systems professionals.

One View of Future Systems Professionals

PRISM—which stands for Partnership for Research in Information Systems Management—is a joint venture of two consulting firms, CSC Index [1] and Hammer and Co. It is a research service that investigates subjects suggested by its corporate sponsors. In its study of information systems human resources, PRISM identified three types of information systems professionals who need to be sought or developed in the 1990s. Robert Morison, vice president at CSC Index and director of PRISM, described these three types to us. They are

- High-level business analysts
- Multidisciplinary team leaders
- Super technical people

The high-level business analysts identify ways IT can help their business gain competitive advantage. This professional does not exist today in many companies. A more modest version—someone who probably could be found today and developed into a high-level business analyst—is an account executive. An account executive could be a senior analyst who has both company and general business knowledge.

The multidisciplinary team leaders lead small, highly skilled teams of system developers with diverse backgrounds. The work of multibackground teams differs from the current practice in which system development is done in pieces. These teams perform the entire application development. Current systems people who might fill this team leader role are system analysts or application developers who like to work in small groups and are interested in being involved in an entire project rather than a piece of one.

The super technical people know one technology very well and have some knowledge of several complementary technologies. Currently, top technical people tend to work for vendors, spending at least 10 percent of their time on experimental activities that enhance their technical knowledge. User companies can attract these professionals by providing them with similar researchlike opportunities. Highly technical people are important, says Morison, because technology is getting more complex and more difficult to understand and manage.

These, then, are some of the current and potential jobs in the systems department. How might companies train for the future? The people at Aetna Life and Casualty asked that question. Here is what they uncovered.

CASE EXAMPLE: Aetna Life and Casualty

Aetna Life and Casualty, with headquarters in Hartford, Connecticut, is one of the largest insurance companies in the United States. It has been providing corporate education to employees in all its business units for fifteen years through its Aetna Institute for Corporate Education.

Recognizing how radically information technology was changing their business, the institute undertook a major project to uncover the skills and knowledge their employees were likely to need in the 1990s. They looked at all major job functions, with the intent of developing new curricula to support corporate goals. Teams were established to study various business areas.

One team focused on systems professionals—as they work today and as they need to work in the future. The team found, for example, that their systems professionals needed approximately thirty-four skills to do their job effectively just three years ago; now they need approximately ninety-one skills. These professionals had many of the needed technical skills, but not interpersonal skills, business knowledge, or change management skills. To rectify the situation, the Aetna Institute is planning a systems curriculum that is more business driven than technology driven, as we discuss shortly.

Systems Training Needs. Based on their study, they believe their systems employees will need four types of skills.

- Technical skills
- Human resource skills
- Business knowledge
- Transitional skills

In the *technical skills* area, the institute plans to update its systems professional curriculum to include such topics as increasing programmer productivity, new analysis and design techniques, new program maintenance tools, and new languages. They are also developing new courses in telecommunications and expert system development.

Since they believe that systems professionals should first be trained as generalists, the institute is building a core curriculum that includes concept courses on reasoning and logical thinking, how to use technical materials, workstations, database technology, telecommunications, and distributed systems. Once assigned to specific technical areas, systems, or projects, systems professionals then get in-depth training in the technologies needed for their job.

In the *human resource skills* area, the institute is creating a program to teach such things as negotiating with users and vendors; relating to users, peers, and management; goal setting; managing time and stress; and communicating more effectively through business writing and oral presentations.

All the systems professionals interviewed in the study expressed a need for more *business knowledge*—about the changing financial services industry, products and services offered by their business unit, and significant insurance industry issues. To improve their business knowledge, the institute is expanding its business curriculum in two ways. One, they are teaching systems professionals more about the business, products, and culture of Aetna, and they are discussing specific products and services in their classes. Aetna business units are also creating business courses for their people that include discussions about the impact of IT on their business.

Transitional skills were deemed necessary because systems professionals face drastic changes, brought about by business changes and new technology. Transitional training is emphasizing understanding and effectively dealing with change, migrating to new technologies, learning to work closely with people in other areas of the company, understanding organizational behavior, and broadening technical knowledge. This training is tailored to work groups in each business unit.

Three Career Paths. The Aetna study also identified three career paths for systems people—management, project management, and technical—each with its own special training needs.

On *the management path* are managers with first and second level supervisory responsibility. The second level managers will need to become "change agents"—people who foster change—as systems professionals become consultants, business analysts, and technical specialists. These managers need to be adept in the four skills areas mentioned earlier. First-line managers are often technicians who have been thrust into supervisory positions with little or no preparation for managing. To rectify this situation, the institute is building a curriculum for system development technicians so they gain general management skills *before* they become supervisors. In the "management path" they will learn how to manage people, negotiate with employees, and set realistic goals.

The second career path is *project management*. As the need for faster, more flexible, and more accurate systems increases, project managers will need more formal training. Thus, Aetna is updating both its technical and management training programs for project managers.

The third career path, *the technical path*, stresses in-depth IT training. The institute is using vendors to provide in-depth training on new products and in highly technical areas. It is also offering in-house technical training for basic and advanced levels. For example, as cross-division systems increase in number and complexity, system programmers need to know about database management, networking, and how to analyze complex problems. Much of this advanced training is, and will be, delivered by vendors; the institute coordinates the training.

The institute had developed "learning events"—a term they use instead of "course." A "course" implies a classroom environment and a long duration, whereas a "learning event" can use any education media for any length of time—such as a two-hour satellite broadcast or a week-long seminar. New learning events are developed as technology and Aetna's organizational structure change.

Institute instructors increasingly work in Aetna business units as consultants and trainers, to maintain their credibility with business peers and to stay current in business issues and technology. They periodically work on business unit projects.

The people at the institute believe their study of future jobs gave them valuable insights into how they can change their training programs to better prepare Aetna employees for the future.

CONCLUSION

With the growing importance of IT to business success, the information systems department has the responsibility of helping the firm increase its technological maturity—by helping executives, line managers, end users, and systems staff be more comfortable with the technology. In this chapter we have described how this is being done in practice today.

QUESTIONS AND EXERCISES

REVIEW QUESTIONS

1. What is a technologically mature organization?
2. Why do corporate executives need computer education?
3. Name three types of informal executive education programs. In which circumstances are they most appropriate?
4. When are formal executive education programs appropriate?
5. According to Gibson, what three ingredients do executive education programs need to be successful? Briefly explain each one.
6. What does change management have to do with information technology? Why should middle managers have change management training?
7. If a line manager becomes a champion of an information technology project, what does he or she need?
8. How does Aetna Life and Casualty encourage information technology champions?
9. What are five types of computer training that end users need?
10. According to PRISM, what are three future possible staff positions? What might they do?
11. What three information systems career paths is Aetna Life and Casualty training?

DISCUSSION QUESTIONS

1. The typical approach for using this (or another) textbook is for professors to assign a chapter for students to read and then discuss that chapter in class. Some say this is an effective way to educate students. Do you agree or disagree? What other methods of presenting this material would be more effective for you?

2. Education and training approaches are becoming too technology driven; they leave out the human touch. Do you agree or disagree? Where do you see human interaction needed in the learning process?

EXERCISES

1. If you have ever used a computer-based training course, describe the features you did and did not like about it. How would you improve it?

2. Visit a local company that provides computer education for its executives, managers, and end users. Describe some of the course offerings. What is the company's CBT training strategy? Is it developing integrated performance support systems?

3. Read five articles on information system training or education. What new ideas did you pick up? Briefly describe them to the class.

REFERENCES

1. CSC INDEX, 5 Cambridge Center, Cambridge, MA 02142.

2. NOLAN, R. L., and C. F. GIBSON, "Managing the Four Stages of EDP Growth," *Harvard Business Review*, January-February 1974.

3. MCFARLAN, F. W. and J. L. MCKENNEY, "The Information Archipelago: Maps and Bridges," *Harvard Business Review*, September-October 1982, pp. 109–119, and "The Information Archipelago: Plotting a Course," January-February 1983, pp. 145–156.

4. ODR, 2900 Chamblee-Tucker Road, Building 16, Atlanta, GA 30341.

5. BEATH, C., and B. IVES, "The Information Technology Champion: Aiding and Abetting, Care and Feeding," *Proceedings of the 21st Annual Hawaii International Conference on System Sciences*, Vol. 4, pp. 115–123, IEEE Computer Society (P.O. Box 4699, Terminal Annex, Los Angeles, CA 90080). (Vol. 4 has ten papers, case studies, and abstracts from the conference sessions on strategic and competitive information systems.)

6. KANTER, R., *ChangeMasters*, Simon & Schuster (1230 Avenue of the Americas, New York, NY 10020), 1983, 432 pages.

7. JOHNSON, B., and R. RICE, *Managing Organizational Innovation* (Columbia University Press, New York), 1987.

8. GLORIA GERY, Gery Associates, P.O. Box 851, East Otis, MA 01029.

9. MCNURLIN, B. (Ed.), *Trends in Information Technology,* Andersen Consulting, 69 W. Washington, Room 1534, Chicago, IL 60602.

EIGHTEEN

Managing the Human Side of Systems

INTRODUCTION

In this increasingly competitive, time-driven world, management is becoming more concerned with improving employee productivity. Many of the sales claims for new information technologies promise to raise the productivity of employees significantly. These technologies by themselves, however, cannot provide the productivity gains that are the center of attention. Management should not be led to expect this of technology. Instead, it is the *employees*, perhaps with the help of technology, that can provide the big gains.

The key to increased productivity is *people*. Technology can *help* people do their jobs better *if they are willing to use it*. However, many employees have not been impressed with their computerized systems because they have had to adapt to the computer rather than the reverse. Too often they have had to follow the dictates of a computerized application rather than use the computer as a tool to augment their own work style. Increased productivity depends on employee attitudes about their jobs and the feelings they have about how management is treating them. In this chapter we discuss three types of management policies that are important in managing the human side of information systems.

- Having a concern for employee well-being
- Involving employees in job redesign
- Creating the new work environment

A concern for employee well-being has been exemplified by the Japanese approach to management. Encouraging employee involvement in job redesign is described through two approaches to job redesign and an example of a new type of work group, the self-managed work group. Creating the new work environment is a suggested plan to strengthen the human side of information workers' jobs so that the potential benefits of the technologies will be realized. The chapter ends with a case example describing how one company implemented job redesign as it introduced computer technology.

HAVING A CONCERN FOR EMPLOYEE WELL-BEING

Employee well-being is taking on added dimensions. Employers are being increasingly asked to be concerned with more aspects of their employees' lives. "Quality of work life," beyond compensation and fringe benefits, is a growing concern among employees. In the office, for instance, health issues are being raised more often, job discrimination is a constant concern, and even job retraining is becoming an issue in forward-looking companies. These and other issues are becoming part of the underlying challenge of how to best manage and motivate employees.

The Japanese have successfully managed their employees, increasing output while decreasing costs. To explore this subject further, here are some of the main characteristics of the Japanese style of management.

An Example: The Japanese Management Style

The following brief discussion is based on several sources—a seminar given in Los Angeles under the auspices of the Southern California chapter of the Society for Information Management, a paper by R. C. Beaird [1], plus a variety of other materials. The SIM seminar, entitled "Applying Japanese Management Techniques to Improve Productivity," included two executives of Japanese companies plus an executive of a U.S. company who has studied Japanese methods and uses them in his work. Beaird's paper was published by the emerging issues group of the corporate planning division of the AT&T.

Japanese management methods appear to include the following three major components:

- A "family" spirit
- Concern for quality
- Teamwork, not competition

A "Family" Spirit. Japanese management has been concerned about the total well-being of employees (male) throughout their lives, not just during their working hours. Men have been offered employment for a lifetime (meaning until age fifty-five or fifty-eight) as members of the corporate "family." In the same way that a son would not be discharged from the family, a male employee is not discharged from the firm. In the same way that a parent visits a sick child in a hospital, a supervisor visits a sick employee. And in the same way that parents are proud of the accomplishments of their offspring, Japanese companies show their pride in their employees and the accomplishments of the employees.

In periods of bad times, the main concern is to save everyone's job, not just some jobs. If pay must be cut, the cuts start with (and are greatest at) the top. If it makes no sense to produce products because there is no market for them, the employees are kept busy cleaning up the plant, fixing machines, and so on. In Japan, relatively large bonuses are paid each year and represent a large fraction of an employee's income; in recession times, however, the bonuses can be cut or eliminated while the basic pay continues. Thus "unemployment" pay in Japan is spread over all employees and is not limited to discharged employees, as in the Western world. Furthermore, the employees retain their dignity and sense of family membership in recession periods.

If new machines and systems are brought into the firm, they are brought in to *help* employees do their jobs, not replace them. Typically, employees are not fired but leave only when they retire. Another policy is to move people around the company, from department to department, over a period of years, to expose them to more of the company's operations. Japanese management believes that this policy gives the employees a broader view of what the company is trying to do and helps build an emotional attachment to the company. The net result of creating a family spirit is a sense of great loyalty both *by* the company (to the employees) and *to* the company (by the employees).

Concern for Quality. Japanese firms have developed an overriding concern for the quality of their products, a concern that has led to the widespread use of quality teams and TQM techniques. In quality teams, small groups of employees meet on company time to discuss and identify recurring quality problems that they see or that have been pointed out to them. Beaird says that the idea of quality teams really originated in the United States. It was taken to Japan as a means of improving product quality during the days when Japanese quality was not as highly regarded as it is today. Now the concept is recognized as important in contributing to Japan's success. Likewise, TQM was first espoused in the United States by W. Edwards Deming, but only adopted wholeheartedly by the Japanese until the late 1980s when U.S. firms realized that customers wanted quality products—and the only way to build such products was to implement quality processes.

Once a quality team identifies a quality problem, the members trace it back to its source and then find ways to correct it. They seek to produce a product that everyone in the company can be proud of. The goal in TQM is for every employee to be a member of the company-wide quality team, so that quality discussions are a regular part of every job.

Teamwork, Not Competition. Since employee turnover is low (even in Japanese plants in countries outside of Japan), and expansion must be carefully controlled because of the long-term job commitments, there are few job openings on the managerial ladder. This seems to lead to less competition among managers and more of a teamwork spirit.

Related to this teamwork is the concept of *consensus decision making,* where every person involved with a decision is heard. Participants can take sides and members of the group try to persuade others to their view, so it can take a long time to make a decision. But once made, the decision is set; as one of the seminar speakers said, "A committed date is a sacred thing."

A corollary of this teamwork is *group responsibility.* No single person is acclaimed for an achievement; instead, the whole group is acclaimed. One speaker at the seminar said that if one department at his plant sets a record, the entire plant gets a celebration party.

The Key Points. The overriding point that comes through from these Japanese principles of management is that employees are treated as human beings, not just as "human resources." Each employee is part of the "family" and participates in company decision making—through the quality teams, if not otherwise. This organizational culture apparently has built a great sense of company loyalty in the employees and has increased productivity as a by-product. Quality is a main goal and employee well-being is a main goal, and out of these come productivity increases.

Like Japanese firms, companies in the Western industrialized nations are now seeking ways to gain greater employee loyalty and motivation. Does that mean that U.S. companies, for instance, will begin offering lifetime employment to employees? The answer probably is no. U.S. employees probably do not want this, because it limits their ability to change jobs or to move to a different part of the country. Employees in the United States are accustomed to more job mobility. However, it does mean is that U.S. companies have become more concerned about the well-being of their employees and the quality of work processes.

INVOLVING EMPLOYEES IN JOB REDESIGN

Most people have several basic needs in their daily activities, in addition to eating, sleeping, and so on. They need to be treated as individuals, to move around from time to time, to talk with other people (both face-to-face and on the phone), have some task variety, and have some privacy and absence of interruptions for certain types of work.

Furthermore, at least some of the daily tasks must be "rewarding," in the sense that the person feels that something good has been accomplished. For example, when dealing with customers, if the customer goes away happy, then the employee tends to feel good; if the customer goes away mad or unhappy, the employee tends to be upset. Too many negative tasks can spoil job effectiveness and efficiency. Computer systems do not change these basic human needs. But these needs have not been given much consideration in system design, until the advent of client/server systems with their GUI interface and user-controlled processing.

Some managements view "improved productivity" as a main goal, and design jobs to resemble factory assembly line jobs—people doing the same thing, over and over, all day long. The old keypunch operator job was this type; today's data entry jobs are only marginally better. These jobs have traditionally had high turnover, high error rates, and employees who can hardly wait for the end of the work day and work week.

Thus, task variety, the ability to talk with other people and move around from time to time are needs that should be designed into jobs. Making more and more information available on-line runs counter to some of these needs, so good job design in the information age is challenging. This is one reason why we advocate employee participation in the design of their jobs, so that they can participate in the numerous trade-offs that must be made.

Also, one of the concerns that many employees have, when confronted with the need to use a new data system, is that it will de-skill their jobs. They feel that the interesting parts of their jobs will be taken over by the computer, and that they will become automatons, controlled by the computer. Whether or not those fears are expressed, research has indicated that the fears exist.

Two Interesting Studies

Jon Turner of New York University [2], reported on an interesting study conducted at the U.S. Social Security Administration (SSA). The study concerned the use of two data systems and their effect on users, claims representatives of the SSA. These claims representatives conduct face-to-face and telephone interviews with claimants from the general public to assist the claimants in completing their applications and submitting the necessary evidence for entitlement to social security benefits. In these jobs, the claims representatives must access the SSA claim information system, a centralized computer system.

The older system used a centralized computer system. Requests for claimant information were entered into the computer's message queue, and replies would be received in from ten minutes to eight hours. If the claims representative made an error in the input, the whole process had to be repeated.

The newer system used on-line terminals. The claims representatives using this system set up their messages on the terminal screens, corrected them if necessary, and then transmitted them. Response time was almost immediate. Both systems access the same claims database. The only difference, then, was in the "front end" that the claims representatives used. In most cases, a SSA field office had only one of the two systems. In a few cases, an office had both.

The results of the research were surprising. Mental strain and absenteeism increased, and job satisfaction decreased, *with the on-line system*. The researchers did not find a fully satisfactory explanation for the phenomenon, but Turner speculates that the newer system allowed the claims representatives to deal with more people per day. Since many SSA claimants tend to be unhappy (because they feel they will not get all they should receive from SSA, or are having trouble getting their claims approved), this meant that the claims representatives dealt with more unhappy people per day, and hence their mental strain went up. That factor, speculates Turner, apparently was more detrimental than the frustration of using the older, slower system.

The point is that job design, and the impact of computerized systems on the jobs, is a complex issue. Most attention in the past has been paid to technical and economic issues—such as faster access to data, to increase productivity. But the side effects of a new system can be quite different from what is anticipated.

The American Productivity Center in Houston, Texas, performed a study on white-collar productivity sponsored by Steelcase, Inc. [3]. Questionnaires were sent to managers at more than six hundred U.S. companies that had exhibited an interest in increased productivity. Ninety-nine companies returned completed questionnaires, and detailed case studies were conducted at twenty-five of them. This study was the third in a series; the earlier two, performed by Louis Harris and Associates, surveyed attitudes of office workers.

The earlier studies showed that office workers were willing to be more productive if they were provided with the proper tools, if they were brought into the decision-making processes that affected their working lives, and if their comfort requirements were satisfied. The third study showed that real productivity benefits could be obtained and total savings could be huge, but that little was actually done to reap the benefits. When something was being done, it was done haphazardly. The employees were willing and wanted to be involved, but leadership was lacking. There was commitment at the top of the organizations, but confusion reigned at the middle management levels.

This study addressed three main aspects of productivity improvement: human resource development, automation, and environmental considerations. The biggest gains in productivity would occur when all three of these aspects are addressed and when all are integrated into the solutions. However, the study found that there were very few cases where all three aspects actually were being considered by management. One message that comes through from these Steelcase studies is that *employees want to be involved in the decisions when their working conditions are changed.* They want to participate in designing the new jobs.

The number of successful cases of employee participation in job and workplace design is increasing, and there are several approaches now available. The use of the Job Diagnostic Survey is one approach. It is used to learn employee attitudes about their present jobs as a prelude to their participation in job redesign. Another is the sociotechnical system approach. It involves determining the problems that particular sets of employees face in their jobs and then redesigning their jobs to place resolution of these problems as close to the problem source as possible.

What is new in these methods is that the employees participate in the *design* of their new jobs and workplaces rather than only in the data gathering and requirements definition phase. We now consider these two approaches to participative job redesign in more detail.

The Job Diagnostic Survey

J. Daniel Couger, a professor at the University of Colorado, in Colorado Springs, Colorado, has conducted national and international research in the area of motivating and managing computer personnel. His early work was done in conjunction with Robert Zawacki; their initial studies were published in book form [4]. They conducted a national survey of information systems personnel and their attitudes about the job. Couger replicated the study ten years later, then began similar studies in the international arena [5, 6].

The research was motivated by perceptions of the problems in managing computer personnel. Those problems continue in systems organizations, intensified by implementing off-the-shelf software, developing complex applications for areas not previously computerized, building increased sophistication into existing systems, coping with higher maintenance, and consulting with users.

The instrument selected for the research was the Job Diagnostic Survey (JDS), developed in the mid-1970s by J. R. Hackman (University of Illinois) and G. R. Oldham (Yale University). Hackman and Oldham established the validity and accuracy of their instrument by testing more than six thousand individuals who were performing more than five hundred different jobs at more than fifty organizations. From these tests, Hackman and Oldham developed some normative averages on job attitudes. Figure 18-1 summarizes the key elements of the Hackman/Oldham Job Diagnostic Survey.

As an example, the model says that final positive outcomes will occur if employees actually experience meaningfulness in their work. Real meaningfulness results if the work involves the use of several different skills and talents of the employees (skill variety), if the work requires the completion of a "whole" and identifiable piece of work (task identity), if the work has a substantial impact on the lives or work of other people (task significance), if the employees have freedom in accomplishing the tasks (autonomy), and if the job provides some built-in feedback or reward.

The JDS consists of a series of questions in a questionnaire that the employee answers anonymously. Examples of such questions are

- How much independence and freedom do you have in the way your carry out your work assignments?
- How effective is your manager in providing feedback on how well you are performing your job?
- To what extent does your job require you to use several complex or high-level skills?

Figure 18-1 A Model of Human Motivation used by the Hackman/Oldham JDS

- Five core job dimensions
  1. Skill variety
  2. Task identity
  3. Task significance
  4. Autonomy
  5. Feedback from the job itself
- Three critical psychological states
  1. Experienced meaningfulness of work
  2. Experienced responsibility for outcomes of the work
  3. Knowledge of the actual results of the work activities
- Leading to personal and work outcomes (when the above are "right")
  1. High internal work motivation
  2. High-quality work performance
  3. High satisfaction with the work
  4. Low absenteeism and turnover

Employees answer each question by selecting a number from 1 (low) to 7 (high). Only the average scores of a group of people doing the same work is meaningful; individual scores are not. Furthermore, employees are likely to answer with their true feelings only if they believe that the results will not be used against them personally, which argues for complete anonymity. The JDS should not be used for placement purposes or in diagnosing jobs of individuals. Also, people taking the JDS must be moderately literate. The average values ("scores") on each question are then used for analyzing employer perceptions about the job.

The JDS also includes questions to assess some characteristics of the employee to aid in matching the employee to job types. One of the computed measures is *growth need strength*. A high growth need strength indicates that the people in the group have a high need for personal growth and development. In turn, the people in this group will become internally motivated if their jobs have a high motivating potential. The growth need strength score is determined by averaging employee answers for the questions having to do with personal growth and development.

Another computed measure is *social need strength*. A high group score in this indicates that the people in the group have a strong desire to interact with others; a low score indicates that they prefer to work alone. The social need strength measure is obtained from those questions having to do with interacting with other people.

A third important computed measure is the *motivating potential score* of the job. It is computed from questions that measure the five core job dimensions—skill variety, task identity, and so on. There are other computed measures, but these three are the most important for the purposes of this discussion.

To Motivate Information Systems Staff. The initial survey included some 2,500 persons, from fifty organizations—thirty-four companies and sixteen government agencies. The database now contains information on more than 15,000 Americans and 13,500 people from other countries. The U.S. data shows that programmers and analysts have the highest growth need strength of any job category that had been analyzed using the JDS. In a sense, this result is not surprising; information systems management has long known that systems professionals want to work on the latest technology, both hardware and software. However, their high growth need strength means that managers must continually provide new challenge for these employees to ensure that they are motivated.

Another survey finding for the U.S. computer professionals has serious implications for systems management. Programmers and analysts have the *lowest* social need strength of any of the five hundred occupations that have been measured by the JDS. People with a high social need use meetings as a prime device for fulfilling their social need. "Programmers and analysts don't need meetings," says Couger, "and users don't understand why systems personnel show frustration at lengthy or frequent meetings."

The same point applies to project or department meetings, according to Couger. "Programmers and analysts are not antisocial; they will participate actively in meetings that are meaningful to them. But their high growth need also causes intolerance for group activities that are not well organized and conducted efficiently."

Couger, in a discussion, pointed out another factor that systems management must consider. The position of system analyst usually is being filled by people who did well at programming, where low social interaction might be tolerable. But as system analysts, they are expected to interact extensively with users. If they exhibit this low need for social interaction, this means that they probably have as little interaction with users as possible and tend to rush through whatever interactions they do have. "Might not this help to explain why the study of user requirements has often been so incomplete?" asks Couger.

When he initiated his international studies, Couger hypothesized that the survey responses from people from different cultures would be significantly different. His surveys covered such diverse cultures as Taiwan, Hong Kong, Singapore, Australia, Israel, Finland, South Africa, and Austria. The surprising result was that computer professionals in these countries also exhibit high growth need strength and low social need strength. The computer profession appears to attract people with similar characteristics irrespective of their culture. They are more similar to their peers in computer organizations around the world than to people in their own culture. So the approaches to improving motivation would be similar for all these employees, when there is a mismatch between growth need strength and the job's motivating potential.

In many of the organizations surveyed, both nationally and internationally, there were not major problems reported for most of the organization. There tended to be pockets of problems—for example, the programmers in one unit or the analysts in another. In some organizations, the problems centered around the first-line managers and in other organizations around the middle managers. Corrective action involves isolating the problems, typically one or more of the five core job dimensions—skill variety, task identity, task significance, autonomy, and feedback form the job. In his publications, Couger has identified approaches to improving the factors to achieve a satisfactory match between growth need strength and motivating potential score. The following examples come from a study that concentrated on maintenance programmers, conducted by Couger and Colter [7].

Skill variety is the dimension that most often causes employees to perceive maintenance work as less challenging, say Couger and Colter. This job dimension contains two elements: (1) the variety of skills needed to carry out the tasks and (2) the variety of tasks. When the variety of skills is constrained, such as confinement to maintaining a batch application when the person has the skills to work on on-line systems, task variety should be emphasized. An illustration is assigning two people to jointly maintain two systems instead of requiring each to specialize on one system.

Task variety is thereby enhanced for both employees. Task identity can be enhanced in a different manner. Lack of task identity can occur when an individual is working on a module with little awareness of how it relates to the whole system or to the company's work. Supervisors could place more emphasis on these relationships, thus enhancing task identity.

The other component of task identity is completing a whole and identifiable piece of work. An example is working with the user to define the needed changes, revising the program, testing, and then implementing the changes. If the maintenance programmer can be given an entire job instead of only portions of this sequence, task identity would increase.

In several of the surveyed organizations, maintenance programmers were quite removed from the users of the system, so little interaction occurred between the two groups. In such situations, the importance of the work—*the task significance*—was not conveyed to the programmers. This could be improved by asking users to make presentations to the programmers who are maintaining their systems, stressing the importance of their work, or by moving the maintenance people out to the user area.

Another job core dimension that is often rated low for maintenance jobs is *autonomy*. This is not because the supervisors do not give maintenance programmers freedom to operate, but because the procedures or policies provide little flexibility. The systems they are maintaining often provide the constraints, such as the inability to use structured techniques because the original system is "unstructured," or the changes must be written in assembly language to mesh with the original code. Such constraints lower the programmer's autonomy. One way supervisors can enhance autonomy is by encouraging participative goal setting and then not supervising the programmers too closely in the activities required to attain these goals.

In the study, maintenance personnel saw "compliance with schedule" as the most important evaluation factor for their promotion. This factor also illustrates *feedback from the job*. Companies that provide good project management systems, which emphasize that the information is primarily for the programmers and secondarily for the supervisors, are enhancing feedback from the job. Some companies go a step farther by providing the reports to team members several days before supervisors receive them.

This discussion and these examples illustrate how the Job Diagnostic Survey can reveal the need to better match jobs with the types of people who fill them. By analyzing both the activities and the employee, individuals can be matched with tasks, according to their growth need. A proper matching leads to higher motivation and better productivity.

The Sociotechnical System Approach

Another approach to job design is particularly appropriate for the introduction of technology, such as in office jobs that will change with a new information system. The sociotechnical system (STS) approach deals with social and human aspects, as well as the technical aspects of the job. The intent of STS is to design work systems to accomplish the work effectively and, at the same time, provide jobs where the employees have more say about how they perform their work. Sociotechnical analysis is most applicable where there is concern over specific problems in a work group and where the jobs within the group need to be redefined. It is not aimed at redesigning an individual job.

To illustrate this approach to redesigning jobs, consider the work of Dr. James Taylor, while he was at the Center for the Quality of Working Life at the University of California, Los Angeles [8]. Work in this area is going on at numerous universities and companies around the world. Taylor distinguishes between a computer-automated system and a computer-assisted system. In the former, the computer sets the work pace by feeding work to the employees. In the computer-assisted setting, the employees set the work pace and use the computer as they need it. Through the STS approach, Taylor attempts to achieve a computer-assisted system.

In Taylor's work, the STS design work is generally performed by a team of employees from the work group, under the guidance of an STS consultant. The approach has been successfully implemented in both blue-collar and white-collar environments; also, some of the employees used computers, whereas others did not. Here is how Taylor recommends approaching job design.

Step 1: Scanning the work group. The STS approach begins with an examination of the purpose of the work group: What exactly does the group produce? This evaluation defines the boundaries of the group (at what points they relate to other work groups), the inputs they receive, the product(s) they produce, the staff within the group, and their reporting relationships.

Step 2: Technical analysis. In the first portion of this step, the group's work process is dissected into the changes that take place in the product as it moves from "raw material" (say, a customer order received) to "finished product" (say, the shipping orders produced). One "change" in this particular example is receipt of a completed customer order, another change is storage of that order in its proper file, still another is approval (or disapproval) of the customer's request for credit, and so on. In the second part of this step, the design team identifies the technical requirements of the process and the major deviations (key variances) that occur during the process. Key variances are very important because they are the aspects of the process that must be controlled, in one way or another, to ensure favorable levels of product quality, quantity, and cost. For example, if the customer order has been only partially filled out, then some of the necessary data is missing. That is a key variance that someone must handle. Results of breakdowns in the technical process are not considered variances.

Step 3: Variance control. In this step, for each variance the design team determines how that variance is currently being controlled. For example, who finds the missing data for the incomplete customer order? The team should also identify alternative means for handling these variances for future use during the job redesign phase. During this step, the team often finds that variances are not controlled where they originate, and that supervisors are often responsible for controlling them—either by directing a subordinate to handle the problem or by coordinating with other supervisors. One goal of the STS approach is to eliminate the need for supervisors to intervene in the work group's handling of key variances.

Step 4: Social system analysis. The social system refers to work-related interactions among people; it is not the friendship system within a company. It is the coordination needed within a process that makes the technical process actually work under constantly changing situations. The first portion of this step is the examination of each employee's role within the work process under study. The process's boundaries, which were identified in the first step, are important here, because often variances occur in one work group but are handled in another. How these two groups coordinate with each other is an important social relationship that needs to be identified. The second portion of this step is the examination of the relationship of this work group to other work groups—for receiving needed information and supplying information to others. The group's "end product," say, the approval for payment of a supplier's invoice, may be the input to another department, such as the accounting department, where the invoice payments are actually made. The third portion of this step seeks to discover from the employees themselves how they feel about their current jobs. A process that looks fine on paper may actually be stressful, because of physical separation of people who need to communicate often, unnecessary fragmentation or duplication of work, and so on.

Step 5: The sociotechnical design. Once the elements of the technical and social aspects of the work process have been separated, they can be recombined in a new way to keep control of variances within a group. The objective is to allow the employees within the group to determine how they will handle variance control themselves. For example, one possible key variance is an uneven workload—one day a person is swamped with work and the next day has little to do. If the employees are given the authority to schedule their own work within the group, workload can be balanced by them, not assigned by the supervisor. The goal is to place variance control at the earliest possible point in the process and with the fewest number of people involved. Variance control should not involve passing the work from one person to the supervisor, then to another supervisor, and then to a subordinate in another group, unless absolutely necessary.

STS studies often result in pushing decision making down to lower levels within an organization. Typically, the group members, not the supervisor, now schedule the work among themselves. They decide how to handle a problem, not pass the problem along to the supervisor. The supervisor's job is thus changed to involve more training, more coordination with other supervisors, and less resolution of problems within the group's work process. Supervisors who do not have confidence in their subordinates will find this change hard to make.

The benefits of the redesigned jobs are that employees have more control over their work pace and the work they perform. First and foremost, quality and costs of products and services are usually directly improved because the key variances are controlled more effectively. Second, the employees within a group learn to perform several of the jobs within the group, which opens up new career opportunities to them. Also, the realignment seeks to increase the interaction among people, which is what most workers want. In so doing, companies that have redesigned jobs in this manner report that turnover decreases, absenteeism decreases, quality of employee effort increases, and therefore productivity increases.

Tips for Success. Taylor has several hints for improving the likelihood of a successful job redesign effort. First of all, top management must actively support the STS analysis and understand the possibility of changes in organizational reporting relationships, levels of authority, and decision making. This support must be communicated to other employees in the organization, says Taylor, especially middle and first-line managers.

Second, employees must be assured in advance that the STS project will not cause any of them to lose their jobs. The STS approach has been used most successfully when employees at all levels participate in the project; employees will not participate in a project that may cost some their jobs.

Third, management must plan for the consequences of a successful STS project. The methodology has been in use for the past twenty years, and it has improved productivity and the quality of working life where successful.

Failures are generally the result of management reluctance to make the recommended changes. Therefore management needs to plan beyond the first successful project by placing it in the context of a larger organizational change. If management does not plan beyond the first project, that project often appears as a threat to other employees rather than a successful model for change, says Taylor.

To illustrate the use of STS, consider the case of a British chemical company. The principles at work in this case can be applied to the introduction of numerous kinds on information technology, not just word processing.

CASE EXAMPLE: Five Secretaries

In *Designing Secretaries* [9a] Enid Mumford, professor of organizational behavior at Manchester Business School in Manchester, England, describes how five secretaries at a British chemical company redesigned their jobs after two word processors were introduced into the group. Mumford, who has created a participative job design methodology called ETHICS [9b], used it at this chemical company. She acted as the group facilitator by taking minutes of the meetings and helping the secretaries analyze their problems and arrive at a solution that pleased all.

This six-month project occurred when word processing was new and companies did not know what organizational structure would work best. By following the ETHICS method, visiting a few existing word processing centers, and surveying several employees, the secretaries arrived at one of the most unusual word processing arrangements we have encountered.

They decided they would share the word processors—no one secretary would become a full-time word processing operator. Three secretaries would spend two half-days each week at the machine. The other two secretaries would spend four half-days and would become the word processing specialists. Each secretary would do only her own work on the machine, although time could be juggled around if a big job arrived. The two specialists would do urgent work for the others. And each secretary was responsible for asking another one to serve her manager when she was at the word processor.

The changes were accepted by management and were successfully implemented. The secretaries felt they had designed the best structure for them.

In *Designing Secretaries*, Mumford notes that participative job design does have its problems. One is that after she left the group, they seemed to lose momentum. Some of the secretaries moved into other work groups, but their experiences did not spread throughout the organization. However, Mumford did assist one group of buyers in the plastics division to design their own stock ordering and control system.

Mumford notes that it is not unusual for participative design efforts to stall, due to lack of management interest and corporate job design practices. When a manager who encourages participative design moves on, no one may continue to push such a new concept. Like many new ideas, this one needs top management approval and leadership to keep moving.

One of the most important benefits of participative system design is that people learn how to manage their own change. Since change is continual, this benefit alone should encourage companies to experiment with such approaches, says Mumford.

Self-Managed Work Groups

Within the past few years, a growing number of companies have introduced self-managed work groups to replace the typical, supervisor-worker relationships. Often, these changes accompany redesign of the workflow; work is performed in "work cells" rather than assembly lines. Rather than split a series of work steps among the group so that each person specializes in one step, the entire job process (or much of it) is performed by each person for a segment of the workload. Cells appeared first in manufacturing; they have now spread to the service industry. We have heard of work cells for handling mortgage loans, processing insurance claims, and even caring for patients in hospitals. The newest trend in health care is hospitals within a hospital, where each one specializes in specific diagnoses and clusters staff, services, and resources close to the patients. The goal is to both increase health care quality—by providing more continuous personal care—and reduce costs—by eliminating non-value-added work, such as moving patients around a large hospital. In this age of business reengineering, work teams and self-managed work groups hold out the promise for improving both efficiency and effectiveness—and improving quality of work life as well.

Henry Sims and Charles Manz [10] studied several self-managed work groups at a small southern U.S. manufacturing plant of 320 employees, organized into three levels of teams. Notice how significantly their processes differ from from those in a traditional organizational hierarchy.

At the top level are the managers. Their role is to "support" the people actually doing the work. The middle managers in the second level (who would traditionally be supervisors and technicians) act as coordinators and advisers to the operating groups. At the operating third level are thirty-three teams of "natural work units." The assembly line groups are responsible for many duties that are traditionally performed by supervisors and managers. Sims and Manz observed how these functions were carried out, based on the groups' formal and informal conversations. Here are some of their observations.

Groups Hand Out Rewards and Reprimands. Team members often compliment each other on their work or thank them for specific jobs they have done. But team members also reprimand each other for actions that have adversely affected the group. In one instance, Sims and Manz observed a group resolving the poor attendance record of one of its members. The group leader recounted the record to the offending employee and stated that it was unacceptable. The employee agreed to change his behavior or face formal disciplinary action.

Groups Assign Tasks and Schedule Work. Sometimes, say Sims and Manz, the work assignments are essentially permanent. Other times they rotate, on an hourly, daily, or weekly basis. Task assignment is important to some group members, so they "negotiate" with others on work allocation.

In addition, the groups are responsible for production scheduling. At the time Sims and Manz were studying them, there was a decreased demand for the plant's products. Rather than reduce the labor force, the groups decided to reduce production, reduce unnecessary labor hours, and divert time to needed repair and construction. This led to less flexibility in scheduling, but the groups' hour-by-hour and day-to-day decisions saved the company a significant amount of money.

Teams Perform Production Goal Setting and Performance Feedback. Plant production is determined at the corporate level; however, the local groups determine how these goals are to be met. They have the authority to shift product mixes, within certain time limits. The authors also found that the groups discussed quality control goal setting and how they would meet their goals. The teams also received much quantitative feedback— daily, weekly, monthly, and quarterly. These reports were on production quantity, quality, and safety. In fact, the authors noted that "there were charts everywhere"; feedback to employees was important at this plant.

Teams Handle Announcements and Problem Resolution. Routine announcements were frequently heard in the groups' everyday conversations. But problem-solving conversations and meetings were also common. In one incident, a coordinator presented members of two teams with a quality control problem. Some members from the two teams met to discuss the problem. The coordinator, who would be a supervisor in a traditional setting, sat in on the meeting and encouraged people to talk. In the end, several problems were identified as the likely causes of the quality control problem, and the members of the groups took it on themselves to solve those problems.

Teams Handle Communications Problems. When there are difficulties between teams, the teams themselves generally handle the problem. Sometimes, they exchange team members for a short time to increase the understanding of all concerned.

Groups Evaluate Themselves and Choose Their Membership.
Sims and Manz did not observe conversations about compensation evaluations; however, they did hear employees ask other team members to evaluate them on a task performance demonstration. At the plant, wages are based on a "pay by knowledge" scale. Employees are paid for what they are capable of doing rather than what they are doing at the moment. An employee must demonstrate competence on all tasks on two different teams to qualify for a pay advancement; this is where the task performance demonstrations are important. Advancement typically takes two years. This method of pay promotes flexibility among employees, say the authors, and it fosters unusual appreciation for "the other fellow's problems."

Teams also determine their membership. When production was reduced, as mentioned earlier, the teams had to decide which of their members would be assigned to the "temporary construction team" to perform repair and cleanup work. In one group, the members first suggested that the person with least seniority go. But that person objected, so another person, who wanted to work outside and do craft work, volunteered.

Sims and Manz were impressed with how well the teams handled the more difficult problems they faced—reprimanding a team member, reducing team size, and resolving problems with other teams. All was not tranquil and harmonious on the teams, they stressed, but overall they found the employees' motivation and commitment to be higher than they had observed elsewhere.

Comparable benefits from job redesign are occurring in offices, with new information systems supporting and even permitting the new work processes. More meaningful and complete jobs do not automatically "fall out" of new information systems, but good job redesign and more attention to the human aspects of the work can make a positive difference.

CREATING THE NEW WORK ENVIRONMENT

The previous sections have discussed several ideas, policies, and attitudes that are important in managing the human side of systems. Individually, however, their impact will be limited unless a company implements an ongoing program to create a new work environment. The following suggested program is aimed at creating a new work environment in which technology is used. Note that this is an ongoing program that aims at *significant* improvements, not just fine-tuning.

Measure Current Employee Attitudes. The JDS, or something like it, can be used to measure current employee attitudes toward their jobs. This attitude study would use today's work environment as the norm and could point out any areas where attitudes are not up to this norm. Even more important, the study would provide a baseline from which future progress would be measured.

Identify Options for Using Technology. Whoever is in charge of the program for introducing new technology into the organization should develop a list of optional ways for using it. The options should be described in a way that allows the employees to relate such uses to their jobs easily. These options, of course, should include corporate standards, such as standard communications protocols, standard data definitions, and documentation standards, to avoid the proliferation of incompatible systems.

Stress Quality of Products. The Japanese have demonstrated the value of stressing quality of products. The same attitude should be fostered in connection with information systems. The concept of TQM for attacking quality problems has become mandatory in several industries. Unfortunately, the recognition of the applicability of TQM principles in information systems departments generally trails corporate-wide efforts. And, as we noted in the example of Federal Express in Chapter 3, information systems can play a crucial role in providing crucial feedback to employees for maintaining quality.

Train Employees. The employees should receive training both in the need for quality of products and what new technologies can do for them in the performance of their jobs. As noted in Chapter 17, one of the new trends in training is integrated performance support systems, which provide on-demand assistance via computer whenever an employee needs it. With the increasing sophistication of systems, and the growing diversity in people's jobs, JIT training is an important way to help them cope with their more complex business world.

Align Objectives. It is important that the goals and objectives of the organization be brought into harmony with the goals and objectives of the employees. In today's work environment, too often management sets the objectives for the organization, and employees are expected to adjust their personal goals to fit the organization's goals. We believe that in the new work environment, this goal setting will become more of a true dialog.

Redesign Jobs. In the 1990s, we believe companies will emphasize redesigning jobs, to more fully take advantage of the power of information technology and to give people more humane work environments. We also believe that job redesign should be conducted by the employees themselves working in small peer groups. Outside help probably is needed to facilitate the process, offer options, and prevent the discussions from turning into gripe sessions. Most important, this job reengineering should be performed before the computer systems are designed, because automating old ways of working is not fruitful.

Measure Progress (or Lack of It). Again, using the JDS or something like it, progress toward the goal of significantly improved employee attitudes can be measured. Management cannot rely on its intuition to tell whether or not progress is being made, because almost of necessity managers see the world differently from the employees. The JDS provides a way to get a quantitative measurement of how employees feel about their jobs. If the JDS is administered correctly, employee attitudes can be measured accurately and validly.

Repeat the Process. One iteration of the above steps should result in an incremental improvement in employee morale and performance with improved use of technology. Movement toward a significant new work environment, however, will take repeated cycles with improvements from each cycle. Neither employers nor employees know what the ideal situation should be, so it probably will be necessary to have a progressive refinement of the work environment.

We recently observed this iterative process in a business reengineering project in a bank. Since the bank's credit card processing employees could only partially visualize their work life with the new image processing system that replaced paper with electronic images, they could only partially reengineer their work processes to take advantage of the technology. Once the system was in, however, they began to see better alternatives. As Shoshana Zuboff predicted (in Chapter 3), the managers and staff were able to use the data generated by the newly automated process to understand its details—something that had not previously been possible. From that data, they even more significantly redesigned the work in the second iteration. Measuring employee attitudes and process data after a new system is installed, and using that data for the next iteration, is crucial in designing good jobs.

Following is an example of how one firm has put these ideas to work.

CASE EXAMPLE: Monsanto Corporation

Monsanto Corporation, with headquarters in St. Louis, Missouri, is a leading manufacturer of textiles, chemicals, plastics, resins, and agricultural products.

Monsanto took a rather unusual path to implementing office system technology at corporate headquarters. The program did not get off to a particularly auspicious start. The information systems department performed a typical systems study of the tasks performed by a group of office workers. After several months of intense effort, management abandoned the project, because the analysis was not grasping the true office work.

The company switched to a participative program, in which individuals and groups of office workers considered how new information technology might be used to improve their jobs. For this project, they used the organizational units that showed the most interest in improving their work methods and environment. Also, in each section they identified "lead implementers"—the enthusiasts who, while doing their regular jobs, were strong supporters of the new systems. These people received more extensive training than the others. This participative program consisted of three main phases.

- *Office design phase* to review and enhance the physical environment of the office
- *Work effectiveness phase* to evaluate job structure and content leading to job redesign
- *Technology introduction phase* to add technology support for jobs

Here are the detailed steps in each phase and some of Monsanto's experiences in conducting them.

Office Redesign. The first phase of the program was to redesign office and work area layouts, with the goal of improving the work environment and assuring flexibility for future changes. An outside consulting firm aided in this phase. All members of the staff participated in designing their own work areas. The managers then participated in designing the overall layouts for their sections.

Management chose to use an open office layout, with movable space dividers. A set of standard modules—for office furniture, filing cabinets, storage cabinets, and so on—was also developed. Employees can assemble their work areas from these modules to meet their specific needs. Monsanto has made an effort to promote an open management style for many years; this emphasis goes well with the open office layout. The company uses management by objectives concepts, which encourages employees to harmonize their goals with those of their organizational units.

In performing this office and work area design, sufficient cost savings had to be apparent to pay back the costs of changeover in a reasonable time. In reviewing the results in improved productivity and reduced turnover, the company believes that this first phase has paid for itself.

Work Effectiveness Program. The second phase concentrated on work effectiveness. To guide this process, Monsanto used the consulting firm of Roy W. Walters and Associates, Inc., of Mahwah, New Jersey [11]. Walters used the JDS to measure employee perceptions of the design of specific jobs. As a first step, a group of managers from headquarters received three days' training in the use of the JDS, how to spot trouble areas in job designs, and how to develop and implement solutions. Then one of the sections of office workers was selected for a pilot study. Everyone in that section filled out a JDS questionnaire, responding to such questions as, "On a scale of 1 to 7 how would you evaluate the smoothness and efficiency of the work flow in your job?". Supplementary questions ask for comments to explain this quantitative answer.

A team was then formed, with some five people—four representing different activities within the function, plus one person from outside the department. The team, with the help of the consultant, reviewed the JDS scores and compared them with some "norm" scores derived by the developers of the JDS. These comparisons pointed up some possible problem areas. The next step was to review these findings with the section as a whole. This discussion brought out difficulties and workflow problems that the JDS had not uncovered.

Next, the team sent questionnaires to the departments that interacted with this section—either in supplying or receiving information. The questions were designed to get reactions on the work flow in general and the suspected weak points in particular. At the same time, the team member who came from outside the department conducted personal interviews with some of the section members. Finally, the work flows with suspected difficulties were flowcharted to determine just what was actually going on.

By this time, the problem areas were coming into clear focus. So another meeting was held with all of the section employees to go over the findings and to begin a discussion of possible solutions. With the problems well identified and priorities assigned, the next step was for small groups of two to three team members to consider solutions to the problems. As solutions emerged, they were discussed with affected section employees. Finally, recommendations for changes were made to management. On approval, the section began implementing the changes.

The project required a significant number of work hours. Typically, a team held two to three meetings a week, of two to three hours each, for more than three months. The results of all this work were impressive. In several years' time, the office groups had an increase in workload of 20 percent, but the work force decreased by 22 percent. Job redesign typically changed jobs from being "specialized" to being "complete"— handling all types of transactions for a group of customers, for example, instead of handling just one or two types of transactions for all customers. This job redesign, coupled with the redesign of work areas, led a supervisor to comment about one section: "It is hard to believe what they did with their space; it looks like they now have twice the space that they used to have."

Introducing New Technology. The third phase of the program was to encourage employees to make use of new technology in their redesigned jobs. It is up to them to decide how they want to use computers as a part of their jobs. One group of managers received a one-day seminar on new technologies and resulted in their installing a small groupware product.

So Monsanto is approaching the use of information technology in the office through *employee participation* in redesigning jobs to best use the new technology.

One Group's Experience. The function of Monsanto's balance and control group is to audit and verify accounts payable transactions received from the accounting departments in the company's numerous divisions. The group consists of clerks, specialists, a group leader, and a group manager. Before the work effectiveness program, accounts payable invoices were delivered to the group in batches from the various company divisions. The group leader then parceled out the invoices to the audit clerks in random fashion. Furthermore, the clerks had fragmented and specialized jobs; none performed the entire audit job.

The clerks in the group were unhappy about several aspects of their jobs. They thought they did not know enough about the group's entire function, because they only did part of the job. They also believed the group leader had the challenging and interesting parts of the audit process.

Through the work effectiveness program, all the jobs within the group were redesigned to be more meaningful. The JDS was used to identify problem areas in the jobs before job redesign was tackled. In the newly redesigned jobs, the audit clerks were elevated to the position of audit and control clerks, a higher position that only one person had held previously. In this new position the clerks have become fully responsible for the entire audit process for a specific set of vendors. Equally important, each has become the main contact person for the accounting departments of several divisions.

Now when the batches of work arrive from the divisions, the audit and control clerks select their own work; the group leader no longer parcels it out. When people in the divisions have questions, they call their contact person, not the group manager. The clerks have been given more authority; they are responsible for correcting all errors and for releasing the audited transactions for payment. Furthermore, each has several once-a-month jobs that the group leader previously performed.

Technology support was also added to the newly redesigned jobs; the clerks are responsible for using the departmental system for several parts of their work. For example, if a vendor makes an incomplete shipment of an order, two actions are needed: a letter to the vendor and an update to the vendor's file. Using the departmental system, a clerk pulls the file from the IBM mainframe, updates the file on the departmental computer, and then sends the file back to the mainframe. The clerk also composes the letter to the vendor on the departmental system. Previously, only one person was allowed to perform these functions; now everyone does them for their own vendors.

Since the audit and control clerks have more authority, the group leader's job has changed. She handles fewer of the group's problems, so she has taken on some of the group manager's work. She creates the monthly statistical reports and she interfaces with the computer operations people. All of this, in turn, has changed the group manager's job. For example, she now concentrates on expanding the use of payables services, visiting plants and training their vouchering sections, and enhancing her group's procedures.

How has the new structure affected the employees? The manager says that the clerks are much happier with their jobs. Since they have more authority, they have a higher opinion of themselves and their group. At first, they were hesitant to make decisions formerly made by their group leader, but, with some gentle prodding, they have become more confident. They now try to solve problems themselves first before approaching the group leader. Since they helped redesign their own jobs, they are also willing to experiment with new ways to perform their work. They either find a more pleasing way to perform a task or they accept the solution found, knowing that it is the best one for the time being.

In addition, communication within the group has improved. There is less talking about who does what, but there are more group meetings to keep everyone informed. There is more communication with employees in other divisions, and there is much more problem solving within the group. The clerks help each other when they run into problems, a change in attitude that was important in easing their move to a new accounts payable system. The members of the group worked together to solve the problems they encountered using the new system rather than automatically passing the problems on to their group leader and manager. Because of this cooperative effort, the transition was smooth.

The redesigned jobs have provided another benefit. Since the clerks handle all aspects of their jobs, they do not sit at terminals all day long. Their work also involves making telephone calls to division people. This variety has made the introduction of new technology more acceptable. As new technology is introduced, the group members worked together to add it more easily to their work life. In all, the quality of work life for the entire group has improved, and it has been able to adapt more easily to a changing work environment.

A POSSIBLE FUTURE: THE LEARNING ORGANIZATION

To conclude this chapter, we take a look at a possible future by describing the attributes one astute observer believes organizations must adopt to be successful in the 1990s. Peter Senge, director of the Systems Thinking and Organizational Learning Program at MIT's Sloan School of Management, has written *The Fifth Discipline: The Art and Practice of the Learning Organization* [12]. Senge begins his book by noting that most organizations live only forty years—that is, one-half the life of a person. The reason, he says, is because they have learning disabilities. In children, learning disabilities are tragic, he says. In organizations, they are fatal. Therefore, he believes organizations will have to become learning organizations to survive.

Organizational learning disabilities are obvious, notes Senge. Here are just three. One, enterprises move forward by looking backward in that they rely on learning from experience. This approach means that companies end up solving the same problems over and over. Second, organizations fixate on events—budget cuts, monthly sales, competitors' new announcements. Yet the real threats come from gradual processes that move so slowly that no one notices them. Third, teamwork is not optimal, which is contrary to current belief. Team-based organizations operate below the lowest IQ on the team, leading to skilled incompetence.

In the 1990s, organizations that can learn faster than their competitors will survive, notes Senge. In fact, this is the only sustainable advantage. To become a learning organization, an enterprise must create new learning and thinking behaviors in its people. That is, the organization and its people must master the following five basic learning disciplines:

- Systems thinking
- Personal mastery
- Mental models
- Shared vision
- Team learning

Systems Thinking. We live in a world of systems. To understand systems, people need to understand the underlying patterns. For example, people can only understand the "system" of a corporation by contemplating its whole, not its parts. Today's complex corporations are best viewed by looking for the patterns and understanding the whole. Systems thinking is a conceptual framework for making complete patterns clearer. Using and understanding systems thinking can help people see how to change the patterns effectively.

Personal Mastery. There is a special level of proficiency that people can reach where they live creatively, striving for the results that matter the most to them. In essence, their life turns into lifelong learning, in which they continually clarify and deepen their personal vision, focus their energies, and see reality objectively. This is personal mastery and it forms the spiritual foundation for the learning organization. Unfortunately few enterprises foster such aspirations; they are not committed to the full development of their people. Therefore, they foster burnout rather than creativity.

Mental Models. Peoples' mental models are the deeply ingrained assumptions, generalizations, and images that influence how they see the world and what actions they take. Senge notes that Royal Dutch/Shell was one of the first organizations to understand the importance of mental models— that is, how its managers viewed the world and the oil industry. Shell learned how to surface its managers' assumptions and challenge their inaccurate mental models. In so doing, Shell was able to accelerate its organizational learning process and spur the managers to investigate alternative futures—by using scenarios. Then, when the 1974 oil crisis hit, its managers were able to react more appropriately than competitors, because they had already explored the possibility of such a crisis and the best steps to take if one did occur.

To change mental models, people must look inwardly—something few organizations encourage. But those that do realize that they have a powerful tool for fostering institutional learning.

Shared Vision. A shared vision is an organization's view of its purpose; it is its calling. It provides the common identity by which its employees and others view it. Senge notes that Apple's shared vision has been to build computers for the rest of us. IBM's shared vision was exemplary service. A shared vision is vital to a learning organization, says Senge, because it provides the overarching goal as well as the rudder for the learning process. It becomes the force in people's hearts. It is the answer to: What do we want to create? Organizations with shared visions are powerful organizations.

Team Learning. When teams learn, they produce extraordinary results, notes Senge. One of the major tools for team learning is "dialog," where people essentially think together. Senge distinguishes discussions from dialogs by saying that discussions occur when people try to convince others of their point of view. Dialogs, on the other hand, occur when people explore their own and others' ideas—without being defensive—to arrive at the best solution. Few teams dialog; most discuss, so they do not learn.

Team learning, rather than individual learning, is essential in the learning organization, says Senge, because teams are the fundamental unit of the modern organization. If teams do not learn, neither does the organization.

Of these five disciplines, Senge believes that systems thinking is the cornerstone. It is the fifth discipline. Until organizations look inwardly at the basic kinds of thinking and interacting they foster, they will not be able to learn faster than their competitors. Senge's book is both fascinating and thought provoking. We recommend it.

CONCLUSION

Information systems professionals have always been enamored with the technical portions of computer systems; the human side has been of less interest. But it is people who make or break a system through their use or disuse of it. In this chapter we have dealt with the human side of systems by suggesting that increasing employee productivity hinges on being concerned with employee well-being, involving employees in job redesign, and creating an ongoing program to create a new work environment.

However, all such programs for improving employee morale and productivity are likely to have limited effect without a plan for an ongoing program to create a new work environment. As the Monsanto case illustrates, once jobs have been redesigned to encourage experimentation, employees will continue to improve their jobs on their own. Such improvements are likely to result from their making use of new technology.

To conclude this chapter, and this book, we presented Peter Senge's ideas on the five disciplines he believes organizations must foster to survive in the 1990s and beyond. We believe that development of the "learning organization" through practices such as these will be the most significant challenge facing organizations this decade.

QUESTIONS AND EXERCISES

REVIEW QUESTIONS

1. Why are people so important to the successful implementation of new technology?
2. What three management policies are important to managing the human side of systems?
3. In the Japanese management style, why are men given a lifetime job?
4. How do the Japanese deal with employment cutbacks during bad economic times?
5. What are quality teams? What do they do?
6. How is a consensus decision reached in the Japanese management style?
7. What are the five core job dimensions in the job diagnostic survey? How are these determined in a group of employees?
8. What conclusions did Couger reach in his studies of information systems staff?
9. What recommendations do Couger and Colter have for improving the job of the maintenance programmer?
10. What are the goals of the sociotechnical system approach to job redesign? Briefly describe the steps in this approach.
11. What type of work structure often results from an STS redesign of jobs?
12. What kinds of supervisory and managerial tasks do self-managed work groups perform themselves?
13. How can a new work environment be created?
14. At Monsanto, how did the tasks of the audit and control clerks change because of job redesign?
15. According to Peter Senge, what are the five attributes of a learning organization?

DISCUSSION QUESTIONS

1. Giving employees and small work groups the authority to make most of their own decisions seems to be of obvious benefit to companies. Why do you think this type of on-the-job self-management is not more prevalent?
2. Although we have talked about the benefits of job redesign from the employees' point of view, we have not discussed it from management's point of view. Give some reasons why you think management would be for or against such job redesign. What types of managers do you think would be more likely (or less likely) to accept a new environment where they do less supervising and more training and coordinating?
3. Peter Senge's ideas are too revolutionary to be practical. Organizations cannot make such radical changes in the way their people think and interact. Do you agree or disagree? Describe your reasoning.

EXERCISES

1. Read several articles or scan several books on job redesign. What management issues do these present with respect to job redesign? What potential roadblocks do they discuss?

2. Visit a local company and talk to an information systems executive about the company's employment policies. (a) Does the company regularly survey employees' attitudes about their jobs? (b) Are jobs redesigned when new technology is introduced? If so, ask for one or two examples of redesigned jobs. If not, ask what would be required to redesign the job. (c) If a job redesign methodology has been used, briefly describe it and its use through an example.

3. Describe your personal vision for your life. If you work, write the shared vision you believe your organization presents to the outside world. Present both to the class.

REFERENCES

1. BEAIRD, R. C., "Industrial Democracy and Participative Management," in *Labor Issues of the '80s*, Corporate Planning Division, AT&T (295 N. Maple Ave., Basking Ridge, NJ 07920).

2. TURNER, J. A., "Computer Mediated Work: The Interplay between Technology and Structured Jobs," *Communications of the ACM*, December 1984.

3. AMERICAN PRODUCTIVITY CENTER, "White Collar Productivity: The National Challenge," commissioned by Steelcase, Inc., Grand Rapids, MI 49501.

4. COUGER, J. D., and R. A. ZAWACKI, *Motivating and Managing Computer Personnel* (John Wiley & Sons, New York), 1980.

5. COUGER, J. D., H. ADELSBURGER, I. BOROVITS, M. ZVIRAN, and J. MOTIWALLA, "Commonalities in Motivating Environments for Programmer/Analysts in Austria, Israel, Singapore, and the U.S.A.," *Information and Management,* 1990, pp. 41-46.

6. COUGER, J. D., "Comparisons of Motivation Norms for Programmer/ Analysts in the Pacific Rim and the U.S.," *International Information Systems,* July 1992, pp. 16–30.

7. COUGER, J. D., and M. A. Colter, *Maintenance Programming: Improved Productivity* (Prentice Hall, Englewood Cliffs, NJ), 1985.

8. JAMES TAYLOR, All Types Publications, P.O. Box 998, El Segundo, CA 90245.

9. Manchester Business School, Booth Street West, Manchester M15 6PB England.

    a. Mumford, E., *Designing Secretaries*, 1983, 114 pages.

    b. Mumford, E., *Designing Human Systems: The ETHICS Method*, 1983, 108 pages.

10. SIMS, H. P., JR., and C. C. MANZ, "Conversations within Self-Managed Work Groups," *National Productivity Review*, Summer 1982, pp. 261–269.

11. ROY W. WALTERS and ASSOCIATES, INC., Whitney Industrial Park, Whitney Rd., Mahwah, NJ 07430.

12. SENGE, P., *The Fifth Discipline: The Art and Practice of the Learning Organization* (Doubleday, New York), 1990.

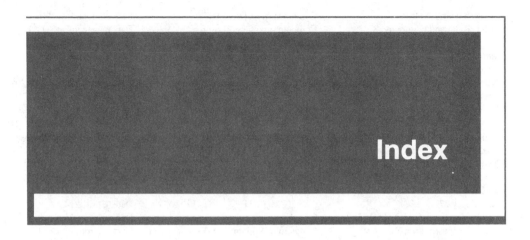

Index